THE BLACKWELL
DICTIONARY
of POLITICAL SCIENCE

By the same author

Labour and Politics, 1900–1906 (with Henry Pelling), 1958;
2nd edn, 1982

Constituency Politics (with J. Blondel and W.P. McCann),
1965

The Social and Political Thought of the British Labour Party,
1970

The Post Office Engineering Union, 1976

The Politics of Independence (with John Sewel), 1981

Democracy in the Contemporary State, 1988

Elements in Political Science (with Richard A. Chapman and
Michael Sheehan), 1999

THE BLACKWELL
DICTIONARY
of POLITICAL SCIENCE

A User's Guide to its Terms

Frank Bealey

BLACKWELL
Publishers

First published 1999
Reprinted 2000

Blackwell Publishers Ltd
108 Cowley Road
Oxford OX4 1JF
UK

Blackwell Publishers Inc.
350 Main Street
Malden, Massachusetts 02148
USA

British Library Cataloguing in Publication Data

A CIP catalogue record for this book is available from the British Library.

Library of Congress Cataloging-in-Publication Data

Bealey, Frank.
    The Blackwell dictionary of political science / Frank Bealey.
    p.   cm.
"Companion volume to the Blackwell dictionary of sociology by
Allan Johnson" —Pref.
Includes bibliographical references and index.
ISBN 0–631–20694–9 (hc : alk. paper)
ISBN 0–631–20695–7 (pbk. : alk. paper)
1. Political science—Dictionaries. I. Johnson, Allan G.
Blackwell dictionary of sociology. II. Title.
JA61.B43   1999   98–33143
320'.03—dc21   CIP

Typeset in 9½ / 11 Plantin by
Grahame & Grahame Editorial, Brighton.
Printed in Great Britain by TJ International, Padstow, Cornwall.

This book is printed on acid-free paper

Contents

Preface

This book is a companion volume to the *Blackwell Dictionary of Sociology* by Allan Johnson. It is hoped that it will be of value to students and teachers of political science alike. It should be noted that it is concerned with the terminology of the subject. The names of specific politicians and political parties cannot be found here. On the other hand, where a policy or a movement has a general significance – for example, privatization, nationalization, socialism or christian democracy – it is included.

As an aid to readers, at the bottom of many entries are other relevant terms. Furthermore, entries mentioned elsewhere are in block capitals. Hence a reader interested in a particular sub-discipline can gain some conception of it through linked entries. In addition, short reading lists are appended to many entries. (The Cambridge, Harvard, Oxford and Yale University Presses are referred to as: CUP, HUP, OUP, and YUP respectively.)

I would like to thank Andrew Campbell, who was of vital assistance to me with his expert knowledge and experience of computer problems. Both he and William Bealey were a great help with computer printouts.

Frank Bealey
May 1998

For Rachel, Rosalind and William

A

absentee voting This procedure is used in many countries when a voter is unable to go to the poll because of age, business obligations, or other reasons. Postal voting is the most common; but proxy voting is also used. Special facilities may be granted to allow people to vote in a different place from the polling booth. Often these provisions allow voters to vote earlier than the date of the general election.
See also ELECTORAL SYSTEMS.

absolutism A term used to describe monarchic rule which has no limitations. It can be regarded as the ancient form of AUTHORITARIANISM. Hence in Europe it is largely a pre-eighteenth century phenomenon though it lingered in Russia until the early nineteenth. The chief philosophers of absolutism were MACHIAVELLI (1469–1527), Bodin (1530–96) and HOBBES (1588–1679). They were all influenced by their experiences of indecision and civil strife and argued that it was necessary to have a strong monarch who imposed his will on his subjects. Another source of absolutist attitudes was the doctrine of 'legitimacy' which held that the king's right to rule was a consequence of the law of God. Hence some absolutist rulers claimed to have a religious sanction, giving their regime a flavour of theocracy. Some

behaved in an arbitrary fashion. Typical absolutist monarchs were Ivan the Terrible (1530–84) of Russia, Ferdinand of Naples (1810–59), known as 'Bomba', and the Turkish Sultans. They were opposed to change. When European monarchies became affected by the ENLIGHTENMENT they converted to Enlightened Despotism, a system maintaining monarchic rule, but diluting the authoritarianism with some respect for the law and not only encouraging economic development (which some absolutists like Czar Peter the Great 1672–1725 had done), but also promoting the improvement of rights of their subjects. Typical of them was Emperor Joseph II of Austro-Hungary (1780–90). Catherine II of Russia (1762–96) flirted with the ideas of the Enlightenment (among other more carnal attachments), but remained an absolutist in action.
See also AUTHORITARIANISM.

Reading
Behrens, C.B.A. 1967. *The Ancien Regime.* London: Thames & Hudson; Hobbes, T. [1651] 1996. *Leviathan.* Oxford: OUP; Shennan, J.H. 1974. *The Origins of the Modern European State 1450–1725.* London: Hutchinson.

abstention Strictly speaking this means a deliberate decision not to vote; but it has come to be applied to all non-voters. Purposeful abstainers are probably quite a small proportion of non-voters who, in most countries, average between 20 and 30 per cent at general elections. At local elections the figure is often a good deal higher. Apathy and a lack of interest in matters outside the immediate family characterize many non-voters. Deliberate abstention is either by those who are alienated from their country's life in a general way, or by those who belong to parties not on the ballot. Anarchist groups often issue instructions about spoiling ballot papers: the Socialist Party of Great Britain, a small left-wing party with few candidates, advised its members to write 'Election invalid' where there was no SPGB contestant.

accountability   A common synonym for this term is RESPONSIBILITY. A government or elected person is account-able in two ways. First, to be accountable is to be in a position of stewardship and thus to be called to order or expected to answer questions about one's activities and administration and those of one's subordinates. This may make for prob-lems in highly complex organizations where it is impossible to monitor every-thing that lower-level administrators do. Hence it may seem unjust, in a highly accountable system, where one is sup-posed to resign when an underling makes a mistake.

Second, accountable means 'cen-surable' or 'dismissable'. A government is accountable when it can be voted out either by the electors or by members of the legislature. Of course, in practice the two meanings are closely related. If ministers fail to account properly for their actions they may incur a vote of censure. An unpopular government may be defeated at the polls. Accountability is usually regarded as a necessary ingredient of DEMOCRACY. In the modern world it may be difficult to ensure its effective-ness. The technicalities of economic

policy often defeat politicians, let alone voters. Lack of information may make it difficult to discover who should be blamed. Sound economic policies intro-duced by one government may not bear fruit until its rivals are in office and gaining all the electoral benefit from them. Conversely, governments in office may suffer from the sins of their predecessors.

See also RESPONSIBILITY.

Reading
Birch, A.H. 1964. *Representative and Responsible Government*. London: Allen and Unwin; Marshall, G. and G C. Moodie. 1971. *Some Problems of the Constitution*. London: Hutchinson.

act   *See* BILLS.

activists   An activist is a person who is much more active in politics than the average citizen. Sometimes the French word 'militant' is used. The term first described people active in political parties, but it has become common to apply it also to PRESSURE GROUPS such as TRADE UNIONS. 'Activism' is defined by the amount of time and commitment a person makes to political activity. Most democratic citizens only participate in politics at election time when they mark their ballot papers. A much smaller proportion – 5 per cent probably ex-aggerates it – are members of political parties. Only a few of these will be activists: most members pay a subscrip-tion to the party and, normally, do little else for it. The activists run the local parties, spending much of their spare time doing it. Only full-time participants, representatives and party bureaucrats, are more active.

This pyramid of participation has been called the model of 'POLITICAL STRATI-FICATION'. It is a helpful concept, but must be qualified in several ways. For example, political activity is seasonal. When elections approach much more party work is required for canvassing, organizing meetings and writing letters. Where there are annual local elections local party organizations need more regular assistance from the most interested party members. At national elections the most effort is required. Activists are likely to be scarcer and to have more problems in rural areas. The urban activist tends to be the classical figure. Finally, the picture is somewhat different in the USA where party organization and party membership, as democratic Europe knows it, scarcely exist. American activism is linked to personality rather party because of the method of candidate selection by PRIMARIES. Candidates therefore construct their own personal organization of election helpers. Some of these will be paid. All will be enlisted for the period of the primary contest and, if their person is then nominated by the party voters as candidate, for the election that follows.

In contrast it is very unusual for European activists to receive monetary reward. Their payments are self-satisfaction in supporting the party of their choice and performing certain functions which give them power, such as choosing candidates (at least where CONSTITUENCIES are small) and taking part in deciding party policy. Hence to be an activist one either needs much spare time or to be prepared to concede what time one has to the party and its cause. Retired people, women whose children are at school or who are able to afford domestic help and teachers belong to the first of these categories. The ideologically inclined belong to the second. Activists tend to be more committed than anyone else to basic party principles. They are often ideological purists.

See also MASS PARTIES.

Reading
Bealey, F.W., J. Blondel and W.P. McCann. 1965. *Constituency Politics*. London: Faber; Berry, D. 1970. *The Sociology of Grass Roots Politics*. London: Macmillan.

additional member system An ELECTORAL SYSTEM used in Germany for the Bundestag. Half the members are elected in single-member constituencies by FIRST-PAST-THE-POST and half by Proportional Representation. In this way it seeks to avoid the disadvantages of both. It does not result in the election of a parliament which grossly distorts the verdict of the voters, nor does it return a lot of small parties from which a majority government cannot be formed. (In Germany this is prevented by the rule that no party achieving less than 5 per cent of the total poll can be represented). Moreover, it is claimed that it maintains the closeness of half the representatives to the constituencies while ensuring that the final outcome is approximately proportionate to the wishes of the electorate. The German voter thus casts two votes for the Bundestag. It might be objected that this will produce two different types of representative, but this does not appear to have happened in Germany. A similar system will be used to elect the Scottish Parliament.

See also ELECTORAL SYSTEMS.

Reading
Paterson W.E. and D. Southern. 1991. *Governing Germany*. Oxford: Blackwell.

administration The act of administering something to someone, perhaps medicine, involves doing them a service. Administrators who serve the public are often decribed as 'public servants'. Earlier uses of the term, before the public service became very large, often indicated people with considerable power. In the nineteenth century, with the growth of the state's functions, administrators were often public servants at a low level who disseminated information and generally dealt with paper-work. For example, those who worked in tax offices were engaged in administration. Administration then came to be seen as concerned with the routine implementation of decisions made by politicians. Woodrow WILSON, when he was a Professor of Political Science, 25 years before he became President, made the classical distinction between administration and politics when he wrote that the former was 'outside the sphere of politics'. It was in 'the field of business' and 'removed from the hurly-burly and strife of politics'. Hence administrators, if they made decisions, only made managerial ones. They implemented the decisions arising from the conflictual arguments of politicians. Wilson was by implication contesting the American practice of appointing administrators by patronage.

In recent times this strict division between the decision-making politicians and the decision-implementing administrators has been somewhat discredited. Partly this is because it was never very realistic. Top administrators, who have much firmer tenure of office than politicians, have often been in a position to make sounder judgements about policies. Furthermore, in the last half century, as policies have become more technical largely owing to the wish to manage economies, administrators have often found themselves policy-making.

See also BUREAUCRACY; PUBLIC ADMINISTRATION.

Reading
Appleby, P.H. 1949. *Policy and Administration.* Montgomery: University of Alabama; Hood, C.C. 1976. *The Limits of Administration.* Chichester: Wiley; Schaffer, B.B. 1973. *The Administrative Factor.* London: Cass; Simon, H.A. 1947. *Administrative Behaviour.* New York: Macmillan; Wilson, W. 1887. 'The Study of Administration', *Political Science Quarterly* 2, 197–222.

administrative board A committee which takes joint responsibility for administration. In British government this has not resulted in ministers avoiding responsibility. For example, the Board of Trade has a President as its minister who is responsible to Parliament. Public utilities and QUANGOs, however, are often headed by boards. Boards also became popular in the USA in state and local government. The Progressive movement favoured them as being non-political and free from corrupt 'BOSS rule'. Yet as the members of administrative boards are usually appointed they can become another form of patronage.

See also QUANGO.

Reading
Wheare, K.C. 1955. *Government by Committee.* Oxford: Clarendon; Wilson, F.M.G., 1955. 'Ministries and boards: some aspects of administrative development since 1832'. *Public Administration,* 43–58.

administrative elites Modern states will have extensive public services. Consequently they will have large numbers of public servants. Many of these will be concerned with manual and routine tasks and only a very small proportion of them will have great responsibility. These will consist of an administrative elite of a few thousand people. Their power and status will vary greatly between countries. In Britain and France they have high status because they are selected through examinations from among some of the best graduates. Their employment is secure and they are detached from politics. Hence the top jobs in the BUREAUCRACY are regarded as highly desirable. In the USA where such appointments are political and change as Presidents change there is little security of tenure. In consequence a professional administrative elite scarcely exists in the USA. In other countries the reputation of the administrative elite will be low because of their corruption. This is often the case in Middle Eastern states.

See also BUREAUCRACY; CIVIL SERVICE; TECHNOCRACY.

Reading
Olsen, J.P. 1983. *Organised Democracy.* Bergen: Universitetsforlaget; Page, E.C. 1985. *Political Authority and Bureaucratic*

Power. Brighton: Wheatsheaf; Yates, D. 1982. *Bureaucratic Democracy: the Search for Democracy and Efficiency in American Government*. New Haven: YUP.

administrative law Administrative law is largely concerned with the exercise of power by the organs of the state. This distinguishes it from constitutional law which is concerned with the relations between different state institutions and the civil liberties of citizens.

The proliferation of state functions and administrative activities and the great volume of legislation has made the control of the executive an increasing preoccupation in the twentieth century. There are two different approaches in democracies to the problem of controlling administrative power. The first tradition, recognizing no distinction between public and private law, is found in common law systems. The extensive use in Britain of DELEGATED LEGISLATION by which broad discretionary powers are given to ministers has in this century led to the development of ADMINISTRATIVE TRIBUNALS and to the civil courts developing principles in order to allow them to declare executive acts illegal if they are unreasonable or a violation of natural justice. Hence although the great British constitutional authority A.V. DICEY (1835–1922) declared that administrative law does not exist in Britain, it has grown in importance in the last thirty years. This had coincided with an increase in the power of the JUDICIARY. But there are no separate administrative law courts in any countries within this tradition.

In the other tradition, largely a feature of many European countries, public and private law are separated and administrative courts operate, applying distinct rules and procedures. The French system of administrative law is always regarded as the classic one. At the top the Conseil d'État presides over a hierarchy of administrative courts. The French model has been widely adopted elsewhere, sometimes in countries with cultures that do not help it to be successful. In France, in spite of complaints about its delays, it has been acknowledged that it has done much to control a powerful bureaucracy.

The familiar picture of maladministration is where a private citizen is the object of it. This may well arise in cases where either national or local administrators infringe property rights: the proposed construction of a motorway or the laying of a new footpath. Discretionary powers may allow the administrators to take such action and, inevitably, they may not always exercise them wisely or fairly. Administrative law, in dealing with specific cases, has tended to define administrators' discretion more and more precisely. Other problems arise, which may affect individuals but are more likely to affect organizations and businesses, because they involve several departments of government each with discretionary powers. Or the administrative act may have been committed by a local government, QUANGO or public corporation, bodies acting under the supervision of a government department. Administrative law should lay down the basic framework of principles for relations between these bodies. If these are clear the citizen is less likely to be the victim of the misuse of discretionary power. Similarly the procedures should be defined. The citizen should be able to discover through what channels a complaint should be made and whether compensation can be awarded.

See also ADMINISTRATIVE TRIBUNALS; DELEGATED LEGISLATION; JUDICIARY.

Reading
Brown, L.N. and J.A. Garner. 1983. *French Administrative Law*. London: Butterworth; Craig, P. 1983. *Administrative Law*. London: Sweet and Maxwell; Davis, K.C. 1958. *Administrative Law Treatise*. 4 vols. St. Paul: West.

administrative tribunals These bodies have become an important part of the British system of administrative justice. It is possible to divide them into two categories. The more important and better known kind are those that settle disputes between aggrieved citizens and some institution or association. Probably Industrial Tribunals, considering claims against employers like wrongful dismissal, have had most publicity. Yet there are tribunals for national insurance, pensions, student grants, housing and the National Health Service. They operate like courts though their procedure may be somewhat more investigatory. It is also less formal so that citizens find the tribunals more accessible, speedier in handing down their verdicts and cheaper than ordinary courts. A tribunal usually consists of a chairman with legal qualifications and two other members who are experts in the specialized field involved. They are required to give reasons for their decisions if this is requested.

The other type of tribunal makes decisions in disputes about details of policy rather than specific citizen complaints. For example, should a certain sort of service be discontinued, or a local hospital be closed. This is a regulatory rather than an administrative function. The decisions of most tribunals can be appealed against, though this does not apply to those for the National Health Service, social security and disputes about immigrants. All, however, are subject to judicial review. Since the Franks Committee on Administrative Tribunals in 1957, the Tribunals and Inquiries Act of 1959 and the foundation of the Council on Tribunals, there has been a tendency to make their proceedings more uniform.

Reading
Farmer, J.A. 1974. *Tribunals and Government.* London: Weidenfeld and Nicolson; Wraith, R.E. and P.G. Hutchesson. 1973. *Administrative Tribunals.* London: Hutchinson.

adversary politics The term was first used by the late S.E. FINER to describe the British situation where two major parties confront one another in hostile stances. An undoubted major factor accounting for this position is the FIRST-PAST-THE-POST electoral system with single-member constituencies, making it very difficult for third parties to emerge in any strength in the House of Commons. Consequently supporters of minor parties are anxious to 'break the mould' by changing the electoral system. A minor factor is the design of the House of Commons which is not in a semi-circle, like most legislatures. Government and OPPOSITION sit facing each other a few metres apart with their leaders on the respective front benches. At Parliamentary question time there is a clash, at least once a week, between the Prime Minister and the Leader of the Opposition. The confrontation elucidates little information; but is the occasion for 'points scoring' of a childish kind. The televising of proceedings seems to have accentuated the need to win the contest which is accompanied by loud cries of agreement or derision from both sets of backbenchers. This 'Yah-boo politics' does little to improve the already low prestige of the House of Commons.

It has been argued that the cause lies in the ideological rift between the parties; but in fact outside the chamber Members of Parliament can behave in an adult way and are often on Christian name terms with people on the opposite benches. There are ideologues on both sides of the legislature, but they seldom achieve leading positions. Moreover, the electorate is doggedly in the centre. The confrontation in the Commons is game-playing, but it has serious consequences for the operation of British policy-making. Rational consideration of policy needs an absence of confrontational rhetoric and partisan posturing. It is now common for political scientists to believe that this is best achieved in a parliament without a majority party and, therefore, with a coalition government in which the achievement of consensus is necessary to survive. The 'mould' can only be 'broken' by adopting Proportional Representation.

Furthermore, adversarial politics is especially dysfunctional for economic policy making, the most compelling concern of contemporary governments. As the electoral system leads to 'winner takes all' the parties are disinclined at election time to advocate tax rises though they may well promise increased expenditure. Indeed, they are more likely to say they will lower taxes or, at least, will not increase them. Then after the election as likely as not economic circumstances will force them to put up taxes. Moreover, in Britain the Labour Party is more inclined to reflate the economy while the Conservatives often emphasize fiscal stringency. Both tend to 'do U-turns' in mid-term to lose the unpopularity which these attitudes engender as the next election approaches. This may play havoc with the economy and partly explains the 'boom-bust cycle' which has characterized British economic history since the 1950s.

See also ELECTORAL SYSTEMS.

Reading
Finer, S.E. ed. 1975. *Adversary Politics and Electoral Reform*. London: Wigram; Finer, S.E. 1980. *The Changing British Party System 1945–79*. Washington, D.C.: American Enterprise Institute; Gamble, A.M. and S.A. Walkland. 1984. *The British Political System and Economic Policy 1945–83: Studies in Adversary Politics*. Oxford: OUP.

advice and consent This phrase is taken from the United States Constitution Article II, section 2, clause 2, which refers to two situations in which the executive must take 'the advice and consent of the Senate'. The President can make treaties 'provided two thirds of the senators present concur'; and his nomi-nations of ambassadors, ministers, Supreme Court judges 'and all other officers of the United States' must be endorsed by the Senate. 'Inferior officers' may be appointed by the President, courts of law, or heads of departments if these latter are vested by Congress with the power to do so. The consent of the Senate has not always been given to either treaties or Presidential nominations, so that the clause has always been an important check to Presidential power.

Reading
Harris, J. 1953. *The Advice and Consent of the Senate*. Berkeley: University of California Press.

affirmative action A term used first in the USA to describe the policy of compensating groups disadvantaged either by public authorities or by private employers. Originally it was the outcome of the Civil Rights movement and related to the black minority. First initiated by President Kennedy in 1961, it was continued in Johnson's Head Start programme, part of his 'war on poverty', beginning in 1965. This not only promoted equal employment opportunity, but also equal opportunity in education. A system of quotas was introduced forcing universities, for example, to allocate a certain proportion of their admissions to ethnic minority students.

The success and advisability of affirmative action is still being debated. Inevitably it was taken up by other groups such as the women's movement and homosexuals. Moreover, it spread to other countries where minorities felt under-privileged. In Europe discrimination of all kinds, as a result of appeals to the European Court of Justice, is facing restriction. Opponents of the trend especially point to the way it can discriminate against members of majorities. This was illustrated in the case of *Bakke* v. *Regents of the University of California*, 1978. Bakke was a white student who was refused entry to the university's medical school which had a 16 per cent quota for ethnic minorities. His rejection, he argued, was unjust because he had higher grades than some of those admitted under the quota. Eventually the case reached the US Supreme Court which directed Bakke should be admitted because quotas infringed the Fourteenth Amendment which says: 'No state shall make or enforce any law which shall abridge the privileges or immunities of citizens of the United States'. Yet the judgement said there was nothing unconstitutional in taking race into account when drawing up admission regulations.

Reading
Affirmative Action Symposium. July 1980. *Wayne Law Review*; Goldman, A.H. 1979. *Justice and Reverse Discrimination*. Princeton: Princeton University Press.

ageism A prejudice based on age difference. It may affect everyone at some time. The young may be discriminated against, but usually it is the old who complain that they are at a disadvantage, especially in the labour market. As people are living longer the oldest age cohorts are becoming proportionally larger in most populations in the developed world. Yet in a recession older people are more likely to be made redundant. Notices such as 'No one over 50 need apply' are regarded as very offensive. Hence ageism is becoming a political issue and AFFIRMATIVE ACTION is being demanded.

Reading
Foner, N. 1984. *Ages in Conflict: A Cross-cultural Perspective on Inequalities between Young and Old*. Glencoe: Free Press.

agenda setting An agenda is a numbered and ordered list of items which is prepared for expediting decision-making. The term 'political agenda', increasingly used, is not so easily defined. This is because in all states, however

freely information is disseminated, there is both a natural tendency for governments to keep details of policies secret and some arguments about the sources of the policies. Thus the questions that arise are: 'Who sets the political agenda? Where is it? What are the sources of the items upon it? How are such agendas drawn up?'

Answers to these questions vary, revealing the complexities of the political process. Policies in democracies are often thought to come from the people through their representatives to parliaments. But legislatures are too large to select and to prioritize proposed measures and so the task passes to the cabinet, a small committee of the party or parties comprising the majority. In fact, a piece of legislation will often be given to the appropriate department to draft. Probably a small committee of the cabinet, or even the Prime Minister alone, may then decide on the legislative timetable, putting different proposals in order.

This above account is a highly simplified version. Items for the political agenda may arise from resolutions passed at PARTY CONFERENCES where party ACTIVISTS have introduced them; or they may result from behind-the-scenes lobbying of powerful PRESSURE GROUPS; or they may stem from the government's perception of contemporary ISSUES and the public's reaction to them which may really reflect the MASS MEDIA's preoccupations. As these latter are often ephemeral it is not easy to discern the political agenda at any specific time. *See also* HIDDEN AGENDA.

Reading
Qualter, T.H. 1985. *Opinion Control in the Democracies*. London: Macmillan.

aggregative parties These are sometimes called 'catch-all' parties and can be contrasted with articulative parties. The latter are parties strongly affirming ideals, ideologies, or group policies which afford little room for compromise. Ideological parties are somewhat like churches in that if they forsake their doctrines they lose their raison d'être. This may much limit their chances of power, the position of many European socialist parties in the first half of the twentieth century. When the German Social Democratic Party at its Godesberg Conference in 1959 got rid of its ideological burden it greatly facilitated its rise to power. Socialist parties have also weakened their electoral appeal by asserting class attitudes. Even when manual workers were two-thirds of electorates the Socialists found it difficult to achieve majorities. Parties representing minority ethnic groups will never do so and, consequently, they may articulate preferential language policies, home rule, or outright separation.

The rise of aggregative parties in Europe may be explained by the decline of IDEOLOGY and class in the latter part of the twentieth century. Such parties are more interested in power than in articulating issues. When they choose issues to pursue they will select those that are likely to win elections and as winning is their main concern they put great emphasis on presentation, public relations and electoral techniques. At elections aggregative parties claim that they are better managers than other parties. So they highlight their leaders' skills, achievements, and personalities. Commentators may argue this is 'presidential style politics'. The Gaullist Party in France is an archetype of the genre, but American parties have always been examples of the IDEAL TYPE. This can be explained by the relative weakness of ideology and class feeling in the USA, by the federal system and by the emphasis on individual, rather than collective, executives. This latter puts a premium on the personality of leaders and their ability to broker between groups and to seize issues which are likely to be electorally profitable.

Reading
Charlot, J. 1971. *The Gaullist Phenomenon.* London: Allen and Unwin; Kirchheimer, O. 1969. *Politics, Law and Social Change.* New York: Columbia University Press; La Palombara, J. and M. Weiner. eds. 1972. *Political Parties and Political Development.* Princeton: Princeton University Press.

aggression Aggression was a keyword in the debate on the League of Nations Covenant. The League, created as a result of the Versailles Treaty, was set up to prevent another war. The Articles of the Covenant, in addition to providing for peaceful resolution of disputes and reduction of arms, allowed for guarantees to members against external aggression. In effect, when a state was declared an aggressor all states belonging to the League should take action to forestall it. It was a system of COLLECTIVE SECURITY. But it implied that member states had to use SANCTIONS, either economic or military, to coerce the aggressor into withdrawing. Military sanctions involved going to war.

Similarly Article 51 of the United Nations Charter 1945 provided for sanctions and permitted the United Nations Security Council to take action, including the use of force. Any member of the Security Council, however, can veto action. There may well be wrangling over who has aggressed. When North Korea invaded South Korea in 1950 the Soviet Union was absent and the resolution for collective action was carried. In other disputes, especially where conflict may grow out of civil war, both sides may claim to have been attacked first. This was the situation in Vietnam. The war between the Vietcong and the government of South Vietnam and the USA was one in which no side declared war. The United Nations did not attempt to intervene. Somewhat similar problems arose when Yugoslavia disintegrated after 1989 and the constituent parts were at war at different times with one another.

See also COLLECTIVE SECURITY; SANCTIONS.

Reading
Art, R.J. and K.N. Waltz. eds. 1983. *The Use of Force: Military Power and International Politics.* New York: University Press of America; Stone, J. 1958. *Aggression and World Order: a Critique of United Nations Theories of Aggression.* Berkeley: University of California Press; Walters, F.P. 1952. *A History of the League of Nations.* Oxford: OUP; Waltz, K.N. 1959. *Man, the State and War.* New York: Columbia University Press.

agrarian parties Parties representing agricultural or rural interests are naturally to be found in countries which are not highly industrialized and where rural populations, therefore, are a high proportion of the electorate. Their main areas of successful activity have been in Scandinavia and eastern Europe. In Britain and France where farms have become larger and farming has become a minority activity, the farmers have had more success in pressure group activity. In Britain they have lobbied governments: in France direct action such as blocking roads and destroying imported agricultural produce have been ways in which French farmers have demonstrated their power.

In eastern Europe agrarian parties have flourished where representative democracy has allowed them to. For example, in the Russian election of 1918 the Social Revolutionary Party, the party of the peasants, emerged as the largest party. It was considerably larger than the Bolsheviks who promptly closed the newly elected parliament down. In Poland before 1939 the Peasant Party represented the interests of the country's largest social group. They were such a strong force that under Communism they resisted collectivization. Although Solidarity arose in 1980 in the Gdansk dockyard, it had great support from local Solidarity groups among the peasants. Since 1989 the Polish farmers have emerged as a political force, but the industrialization of Poland since 1945 has reduced their proportionate strength among the electorate.

In Scandinavia, where farming is a more prosperous activity, the farmers have formed parties which in many ways resemble pressure groups. Their objectives are quite specific and relate to government policies towards agriculture. Subsidies and price supports are their main demands: in fact it has been said that their only concern was the price of milk. This pragmatism has resulted in a willingness to ally themselves with any other parties that will support their aims. Post-1945 a 'Red–Green' coalition was mooted in Finland; but because of the Communists' ideological commitment to collectivization it was unlikely that the Farmers' Party could ever accept them as their only party in government. In Sweden the farmers have quite often coalesced with the Social Democrats though more recently they have looked more to the right. In the 1960s the Finnish, Norwegian and Swedish farmers' parties changed their names to Centre Parties, signifying their ideological neutrality and attempting to be rather less articulative and a little more aggregative.

Reading
Linz, J.J. 1976. 'Patterns of land tenure, division of labor, and voting behavior in Europe'. *Comparative Politics* 8, 365–430; Urwin, D.W. 1980. *From Ploughshare to Ballot-box: the Politics of Agrarian Defence in Europe.* Oslo: Universitetsforlaget.

alienation A term that has become loosely used to indicate strong dislike. In its proper usage it means a feeling of being foreign to a context in which one finds oneself. Thus 'inalienable rights', a concept of John LOCKE (1632–1704) that was incorporated into the American Declaration of Independence, are rights that if relinquished or taken away will deprive a citizen of things that are natural and essential to existence.

HEGEL (1770–1831), who developed the modern usage of the term, believed that individuals were alienated because of their failure to realize universal consciousness. Alienation can therefore be overcome by the attainment of absolute self-consciousness which has been the goal to which humanity has progressed through various stages of history.

MARX (1818–83) adopted Hegel's ideas of consciousness and its gradual realization by a historical process, but he discarded its metaphysical basis and its origin in the individual's psyche. Marx believed people were alienated because of their social and economic environments. The goal for humanity to attain was freedom from the shackles of their material conditions which were all a reflection of the prevailing conditions of production. In the most recent phase of history production is organized on a capitalist basis and human alienation from existence is manifest in several ways. In the factory system workers are alienated from tools and product. They are making with someone else's machines a part of something which they will never see as a whole and which will be sold by employers at a profit which they will not properly share. The status of craftsman and the full value of their labour has been forfeited. Moreover, workers are alienated from one another by the harshness of competition and their failure, at the beginning, to realize their common interests against those of the employer. Alienation can be overcome by the workers developing firstly a collective consciousness, CLASS CONSCIOUSNESS, and finally a consciousness of how by revolutionary action SOCIALISM will succeed CAPITALISM. Under a socialist system of production no one will be alienated.

The concept of alienation was developed more recently by writers of the NEW LEFT who attempted a synthesis of Marx, Freud and the existentialists. Prominent in this school was Herbert MARCUSE (1898–1979) whose analysis was based more on the alienating influences of technology, mass consumerism and the culture engendered by the mass media. Through control of these the capitalist state enslaves humanity.

See also CAPITALISM; CLASS CONSCIOUSNESS; NEW LEFT.

Reading
Blauner, R. 1964. *Alienation and Freedom.* Chicago: University of Chicago Press; Marcuse, H. 1964. *One Dimensional Man.* London: Sphere; Marx, K. [1927] 1964. *Economic and Philosophical Manuscripts of 1884.* New York: International Publishers.

alliance An agreement between two groups to co-operate. It may apply to pressure groups or political parties. Alliances can be formal or informal. In British politics two examples of the latter are the agreement between the Labour Party and the Liberals between 1903 and 1914 that they would not oppose one another with candidates at general elections; and a similar arrangement between the Liberals and the Social Democratic Party between 1983 and 1990. COALITION GOVERNMENTS, common in Europe, involve alliances between parties in order to govern. In some cases these involve a written agreement.

Usually the term applies to agreements between states to co-operate in defence or attack against another state or states. Frequently such alliances will be based on a treaty signed by all participants; although even in international alliances this may be informal. In such cases they may be called ententes (for instance, the Entente Cordiale between Britain and France before 1914), or 'understandings'. Such informal arrangements may sometimes have more force than formal treaties. It depends on the degree of commitment which may vary with time and situation. When commitment is great, as with the North Atlantic Treaty Organization and the Warsaw Pact, war is not unlikely if any AGGRESSION takes place. Other looser agreements were the Holy Alliance, called by A.J.P. Taylor 'the Cominform of Kings', which was an alliance of the despots of Europe after 1815 to oppose any country espousing French Revolutionary ideals; and the Alliance for Progress, an understanding between the USA and Latin American states, designed to offer economic support to the latter and so prevent them from falling to Communist subversion. *See also* AGGRESSION; TREATIES.

Reading
Frankel, J. 1969. *International Relations.* Oxford: OUP; Liska, G. 1962. *Nations in Alliance: the Limits of Inter-dependence.* Baltimore: Johns Hopkins University Press; Walt, S.M. 1987. *The Origins of Alliances.* Ithaca: Cornell University Press; Wight, M. 1986. *Power Politics.* Harmondsworth: Penguin.

all-party groups   These are the parliamentary detachments of pressure groups. The term is used in the British Parliament though similar organizations will be found in most democratic legislatures. It describes a group whose objectives, it believes, are so uncontroversial that they can best be attained by lobbying all parties. In Britain the term was re-defined in 1985. A Select Committee of the House of Commons had become worried that some PRESSURE GROUPS were using the House of Commons for non-parliamentary purposes. It recommended a splitting of 'all-party groups' into two categories. In future 'Parliamentary Groups' or 'Registered Groups' could admit people to its meetings who were not members of either the Lords or the Commons. 'All-Party Groups' could admit no one, except guest speakers, who were not members of either house.

Reading
Bealey, F. 1986. 'The All-Party Group on Social Science and Policy'. *Public Policy and Administration* 1.3, Winter, 48–51; House of Commons. June 1985. *Fact Sheet* No. 7; Second Report of the Select Committee on House of Commons (Services) 1983–4.

alternative vote   A system of ordering preferences for candidates in constituencies where only one can be elected. The voter is required to put the number '1' for the candidate most desired as member, '2' for the second, and so on. No candidate can be returned at the first counting of the votes unless she/he obtains more than 50 per cent of all first preferences. When this is not the case it is usual for the next available preferences of the candidate at the bottom of the poll to be redistributed. If this does not produce a candidate with more than 50 per cent of preferences, the process is repeated, and so on. The method ensures that no candidate can be returned who has received less than a majority of the votes, as happens with FIRST-PAST-THE-POST.

Like the SECOND BALLOT, the alternative vote encourages smaller parties to put up candidates because, even if the latter stand no chance of election, the votes of their supporters carry weight when preferences are redistributed. But it is not a very proportionate system and is most popular with parties likely to be third in favour among the voters. In Britain, however, the Liberal Party recommends Single Transferable Vote in multi-member constituencies. *See also* ELECTORAL SYSTEMS.

Reading
Bogdanor, V. and D. Butler. eds. 1983. *Democracy and Elections: Electoral Systems and Their Consequences.* Cambridge: CUP; Harrop, M. and W. Miller. 1987. *Elections and Voters: a Comparative Introduction.* London: Macmillan; Hogan, J. 1945. *Elections and Representation.* Cork: Cork University Press.

ambassadors   *See* DIPLOMACY.

amendment   There are two main types of political amendment, legislative amendment and constitutional amendment. With regard to the former the ease with which bills can be amended depends on the parliamentary procedures and political complexion of the legislature in question. Where there is no single party in the majority, law-making may involve many compromises and bills may undergo much amendment. Yet because of procedural differences, legislation in the French Parliament is much less likely to be amended in passage than in the British. Legislative amendments can be divided into detailed and substantive amendments. The former can refer to improved drafting and it is not uncommon to entrust them to upper chambers. Amendments of substance are more difficult to pass and may occur when governments give way to pressure from inside or outside the chamber.

Amendments to CONSTITUTIONS will be by a process specified in the document. The procedures will either be complex, producing a rigid constitution, or simple and easy, resulting in a flexible constitution. For example, the US constitution can only be amended after the proposal is passed by legislatures or conventions in three-quarters of states plus the votes of two-thirds of both houses of Congress. This rigidity can be contrasted with the flexibility of the New Zealand constitution, amended by a vote of the one-chamber legislature. Once passed, amendments become part of a constitution. The first ten amendments of the US constitution, passed in 1791 and known as the Bill of Rights, are of great importance. For instance, the First Amendment guarantees freedoms of expression and the Fifth protection of the citizen against deprivation of 'life, liberty, or property, without due process of law'. *See also* CONSTITUTIONS.

amenity   This is a concept related to what is commonly called the 'quality of life'. Amenities are the public services available plus a convenient and pollution-free environment. The costs of unclean air are difficult to calculate and likely to be neglected by commercial interests who plan industrial location. Hence amenities are the source of social benefits. In Britain an Act of 1968 required all public bodies to respect amenities in the countryside, though this duty has been allocated to regulatory bodies since privatization. PRESSURE GROUPS have sprung up in most democracies to defend amenities and they have been seen collectively as the 'amenity movement'.

amnesty   A pardon granted to a group of people, usually for political offences. The pressure group, Amnesty International, publicizes the situation of political offenders everywhere.

anarchism   The term stems from 'anarchy' with a Greek derivation meaning 'no rule' and, therefore, perceived as chaos. Yet anarchists only protest against the rule of the State. They believe society would be better ordered by people controlling themselves. Hence they tend to advocate the superiority of the small community or group. Kropotkin (1842–1921), a Russian anarchist, saw the medieval city as the ideal. Many anarchists are anti-urban and anti-industrial. The commune movement in Europe and America belongs to this tradition. People who 'drop out of the rat race', artists, vegetarians and certain religious groups, for instance, come together to organize a common existence under rules devised by themselves. The Israeli kibbutz could be another example.

Other anarchists have been concerned to reorganize productive industry in small units. Proudhon (1809–65) was of this belief. Bakunin (1814–76) was much influenced by Proudhon and his quarrel with MARX over what he saw as the latter's authoritarian tendencies broke up the First International. This type of anarchism found roots in Spain, Italy and France where industrial enterprises remained small and trade unions were organized as local, general bodies.

Anarchists have been divided by different approaches to the overthrow of the state, though this has sometimes (not always) been affected by the nature of the state they have confronted. The image of the anarchist as a terrorist with a bomb began in Russia, where an anarchist assassinated Tsar Alexander II in 1881. French anarchists assassinated President Carnot in 1894; and American anarchists killed President McKinley in 1901. On the other hand, many anarchists are pacifists who have contributed to all the peace movements in the twentieth century.

See also ALIENATION; ANOMIE.

Reading
Joll, J. 1979. *The Anarchists.* 2nd edn. London: Methuen; Kropotkin, P. 1898. *Fields, Factories and Workshops.* London: Nelson; Miller, D. 1984. *Anarchism.* London: Dent; Woodcock, G. 1963. *Anarchism.* Harmondsworth: Penguin.

anarcho-syndicalism   *See*   SYNDICALISM.

ancien regime   This French term has come to be used to describe the type of rule prevalent in Europe before the French Revolution and its ideas swept the ancien regime away. It depended on the alliance between 'throne and altar'. The Church legitimized the monarchs and supported their law enforcement with its proclamation of moral standards and the necessity of obedience to temporal authority. Its practices and influence are memorably depicted by DE TOCQUEVILLE.

See also ABSOLUTISM; DIVINE RIGHT; ENLIGHTENMENT.

Reading
Behrens, C.B.A. 1967. *The Ancien Regime.* London: Thames and Hudson; De Tocqueville, A. [1856] 1955. *The Old Regime and the Revolution.* New York: Doubleday.

anomie   A term originating from the sociologist, Emile Durkheim (1858–1917) who used it to describe a situation where values and norms become disoriented. This arose from his study of suicide. He discovered that Protestants were more prone to it than Catholics and attributed the difference to the emphasis Protestantism places upon the individual. A person who is less bound up with a community and who, therefore, has less support from it in times of stress will be more likely to commit suicide. Thus in the first place Durkheim's analysis was psychological, but when he turned to causes of increase in individual stress he found the main social factor was industrialization which had destroyed traditional society and weakened the norms and values supporting it. Another obvious factor was war. Hence in the twentieth century anomie, rather like alienation, has become a concept political scientists have found useful.

See also ANARCHISM; ALIENATION.

Reading
Durkheim, E. [1897] 1951. *Suicide.* New York: Free Press; Merton, R. 1938. 'Social structure and anomie'. *American Sociological Review* 3, 672–82.

anti-clericalism   *See* CLERICALISM/ANTI-CLERICALISM.

anti-Semitism   Originally a nineteenth-century term, prejudice and discrimination against Jews has become an important issue in the twentieth century. The feeling and practice, however, can be traced back to the first century. Anti-Semitism has two main roots: Christian and xenophobic nationalist. Where national identity is associated with religion it may be especially strong.

The Jewish Diaspora after the Romans sacked Jerusalem in AD 70 took place while Christianity was also spreading. To early Christians the Jews were 'killers of Christ'. Catholics in medieval Europe believed they were capable of sorcery and sacrificing Christian children. Laws prevented them from entering most occupations, made them wear yellow badges and confined them to ghettos. Separation from others increased their distinctiveness in dress and behaviour. Where these differences were great, as in eastern Europe, pogroms (massacres and mass deportations) of Jews were still occurring in the early twentieth century.

Political anti-Semitism, however, dates from the ENLIGHTENMENT and the French Revolution, from which time Jews in western Europe began to share in the freedoms of other citizens. It was then that they began to excel in finance and intellectual occupations and were seen, especially by nationalist extremists, as an international conspiracy. As Jews began to circulate more in ordinary life and, inevitably, to inter-marry with Gentiles, the suspicious became more paranoid. The *Ligue antisémitique* in France was stimulated by *l'affaire Dreyfus* in which a Jewish staff officer was wrongly accused of treasonable espionage. In Germany the composer, Wagner (1813–83) was anti-Semitic and his daughter married Houston Stewart Chamberlain (1855–1927) a Briton who, in a book titled *Foundations of the Nineteenth Century* (1911), expounded racial theory.

The publication in 1905 of the *Protocols of the Elders of Zion*, a forgery, was taken as evidence of the existence of a Jewish wish to dominate the world. Adolf Hitler (1889–1945) in Vienna in the years before 1914, became convinced of the gradual subversion of the German race by Jewish penetration. When he returned from the trenches to Munich after 1918 he soon joined the National Socialist German Workers Party, a small anti-immigrant grouping which expanded as a result of post-war economic collapse. After he came to power in 1933 the persecution of Jews became a national policy, ending in six million being gassed to death in World War II.

World-wide shame about the Holocaust did not entirely dispel anti-Semitic sentiments which lingered, especially in eastern Europe, and emerged after the disintegration of the Soviet bloc in 1989. In western Europe the National Fronts of Britain and France and parties in Austria and Germany still propagate xenophobic views in which anti-Semitism is one ingredient.

See also NATIONAL SOCIALISM; RACISM.

Reading
Cohn, N. 1967. *Warrant for Genocide: the Myth of the Jewish World Conspiracy.* London: Eyre & Spottiswoode; Poliakov, L. 1974–5. *The History of Anti-Semitism.* Vols 1, 2 & 3. London: Routledge. 1985. Vol. 4. Oxford: OUP; Pulzer, P. 1988. *The Rise of Political Anti-Semitism in Germany and Austria.* 2nd edn. New York: Halban.

anti-system parties A term referring to parties which oppose the democratic system. Hence Communist and Fascist parties have been frequently described in this way. It is argued that ELECTORAL SYSTEMS which allow very small parties to put up candidates and secure their election are responsible for the emergence of such parties. In mind is the very proportional system of the Weimar Republic which is associated with the meteoric rise of the Nazi Party between 1928 and 1932. One method of preventing the recurrence of this phenomenon is an 'electoral threshold', a condition that no party can be allowed representation if it does not obtain a certain proportion of the total vote (say 5 per cent): another is a judiciary which can ban candidatures from anti-democratic parties.

Reading
Sartori, G. 1976. *Parties and Party Systems: a Framework for Analysis.* Cambridge: CUP.

apartheid An Afrikaans term meaning 'separateness'. From 1948 to 1990 this was a policy with theological and philosophic undertones, underpinning the Nationalist Party's rule in South Africa. It involved a separation between the areas in which whites and blacks lived. The latter were either confined to homes in black townships, far from the centre of big cities, or to their tribal 'homelands'. Consequently there was much compulsory movement of blacks to designated areas.

The policy was connected with another concept, *baaskap*, meaning white supremacy. Together these notions led to segregation in schools, bathing beaches, places of entertainment, post offices and transport. Blacks were also controlled by internal passports and forbidden to enter certain occupations. They had no votes and no representatives in the South African parliament. Condemned by international opinion the system was swept away after the release of Nelson Mandela from prison in 1990.
See also RACISM.

Reading
Moodie, D. 1975. *The Rise of Afrikanerdom: Power, Apartheid, and the Afrikaner Civil Religion.* Berkeley: University of California Press; Omond, P. 1986. *The Apartheid Handbook.* 2nd edn. Harmondsworth: Penguin; Uhlig, M.A. ed. 1986. *Apartheid in Crisis.* Harmondsworth: Penguin.

apparatchik A Russian word meaning an employee of the *apparat*, the Communist party apparatus. Because of its derivation the word has passed into pejorative use in the English language and has come to mean a faceless, impersonal, time-serving party official who obeys all orders unthinkingly in return for privileges that the ordinary citizen is not entitled to.
See also CELL; COMMUNISM.

Reading
Armstrong, J.A. 1962. *Ideology, Politics and Government in the Soviet Union.* New York: Praeger; Djilas, M. 1957. *The New Class.* London: Thames and Hudson.

apparentement A device of the 1951 French electoral law to allow alliances between parties at the elections, then held under a system of Proportional Representation with lists in multi-member constituencies. It was introduced by the majority coalition of centre parties who wished to weaken the threat of Communists and Gaullists from the left and right respectively. By declaring an alliance in any constituency the votes of the allying parties were counted in aggregate for the purposes of allocating seats. (The Communists and Gaullists had difficulties in finding allies.) The system allowed the voters to vote for those parties who wished to maintain the Fourth Republic and against those parties who wanted to overthrow it. It helped to keep the centre parties in power but it did not bring them any closer together in their policies. Furthermore, there were variations between the parties allying in different constituencies and so deputies elected for the centre majority were by no means always in agreement.

Reading
Campbell, P. 1958. *French Electoral Systems and Elections Since 1789.* London: Faber; Williams, P. 1954. *Politics in Post-war France.* London: Longman.

appeasement This term, long known to international diplomats, became common currency as result of the effort in the late 1930s of the British Prime Minister, Neville Chamberlain (1868–1940), to prevent war by placating the German and Italian Fascist dictators. 'Appeasement' in consequence acquired a pejorative sense, and has come to imply an illjudged and doomed policy of attempting to make concessions to an aggressive opponent at the cost of principle. In fact, after World War I appeasement was seen as an honourable and sensible policy. There was much friction between both great and small powers and any attempt to reduce it appeared both wise and good.

The League of Nations, set up as part of the Versailles Treaty, embodied in its Covenant what were believed to be complementary peace-keeping ideas of DISARMAMENT, the peaceful settlement of disputes and COLLECTIVE SECURITY. But, in practice, it was not easy to reconcile them. Collective security ultimately involved giving up attempts at appeasement and taking a stand against AGGRESSION. This meant, if necessary, going to war and after the recent bloodshed European states were loath to face up to it.

In consequence nations and peoples who had supported the League as a guarantee against war increasingly were prepared to appease the unappeasable Fascist dictators, first trying to balance Italy against Germany and then conceding to both of them. Appeasement became dishonourable when they were prepared to avoid war by agreeing to concessions at the expense of small nations. Thus 'Munich', where the partition of Czechoslovakia was tacitly agreed to, became an expression of infamy. It also signifies the failure of traditional diplomacy. The British and French negotiators misjudged their own strength and the nature of the Nazis – unforgiveably because the latter's intentions were clear to anyone who had studied their speeches and writings.

One should not deduce from the experience of Munich, however, that it is always wrong and unwise to make concessions to opponents. Appeasement can be sensible in some circumstances. It is a matter of judgement.

Reading
Namier, L.B. 1948. *Diplomatic Prelude 1938–1939*. London: Macmillan; Wheeler-Bennett, J.W. 1948. *Munich: Prologue to Tragedy*. London: Macmillan; Wight, M. 1986. *Power Politics*. Harmondsworth: Penguin.

apportionment The US Constitution in Art. 1, Section 2, clause 3 stipulates that representatives for each state in the House of Representatives shall be apportioned according to population; and that to take account of changes in population they will be re-apportioned every ten years. Once the re-apportionment has taken place the allocation within the state is usually completed by the state legislature. In this way re-districting, the drawing of the boundaries of the Congressional districts, was at the mercy of the majority party or faction in state politics. Especially in the South the practice of gerrymandering, drawing the boundaries irrespective of population or community feeling, flourished until the 1960s. Then the Supreme Court judgement, *Baker* v. *Carr*, 1962, ruled that disputes about re-districting within states could be settled in federal courts. The effect of such rulings has been to lessen state autonomy and to initiate reform in state politics.
See also REDISTRIBUTION.

Reading
Cain, B.E. 1984. *The Reapportionment Puzzle*. Berkeley: University of California Press; *UCLA Law Review*. October 1985. Symposium on 'Gerrymandering and the Courts'.

appropriations An appropriation is a legislative vote to pay a sum of money for some defined purpose. In Britain only a Minister of the Crown can move such a proposal. Other legislators can move to annul or reduce such expenditure; but they cannot initiate it. In contrast, in the USA any member of the House of Representatives can propose expenditure for any purpose.
See also BUDGET.

approval voting A system of election used in some American state legislatures and also in many private organizations. It is suited to a situation where there are several candidates for several seats. The voter can only cast one vote per candidate, but can vote for as many candidates as there are standing. Hence they can 'plump' for only one, if they so wish, though some voters may vote for as many candidates as there are seats and, consequently, will be indicating the candidates they least favour. Thus there can be tactical considerations. To what degree they exist will depend on the intensity of the allegiance voters feel for candidates. A voter who feels strongly for only two candidates and does not know the others, will not vote for the latter, as voting for a non-preferred candidate may damage the chances of the two preferred.

See also ELECTORAL SYSTEMS.

Reading
Brams, S.J. 1983. *Approval Voting.* Cambridge, Mass.: Birkhauser Boston.

arbitration   This is a method of reaching a settlement between two disputing parties. A feature of arbitration is that it does not rely on formal procedures and principles: it is likely to be used where no body of law exists though, over time, where arbitration becomes common, a set of conventions and precedents may be established. Arbitration can only proceed where both parties to the dispute agree to it and agree to be bound by the judgement. They will also agree on a single arbiter, or perhaps a small panel of arbiters. Verdicts tend to be compromises. It is said that arbitration is more likely to produce peace than justice.

There are two areas in which arbitration has had a political relevance: industrial and international relations. The first important instance in Britain of industrial arbitration was an Act of 1872 by which both workers and employers were bound by the terms of an agreement enforceable by the courts. But the parties tended to settle things themselves and the Act was not successful. Consequently in 1896 a Conciliation Act was passed by which the Board of Trade could intervene in industrial disputes on its own initiative or after one of the parties approached it. Either a conciliator or an arbitrator could then be appointed. This Act has some success as have other such bodies in Britain in the twentieth century. It remains the case that arbitration and conciliation have been the last resort, or not resorted to at all. In fact, Australia has been the country in which industrial arbitration has been most used.

With international arbitration the voluntary nature is bound to be even more pronounced. It is very difficult to persuade sovereign nations to undertake a procedure whose results they cannot anticipate. Hence it is likely to be undertaken when relations between the two parties are very good and they both have a common political culture which includes respect for the rule of law. For example, the fishery dispute between Britain and Norway. Or the cause of dispute is very trivial as with the successful resolution by arbitration of the disagreement between Israel and Egypt about a tiny strip of territory in Sinai. Both the League of Nations and the United Nations constitutions encouraged the arbitration process.

Reading
De Visscher, C. July 1956. 'Reflections on the Present Prospects of International Adjudication'. *American Journal of International Law* 50.3, 467–74; Sharp, I.G. 1950. *Industrial Conciliation and Arbitration in Great Britain.* London: Allen & Unwin; Simpson, J.L. and Fox, H. 1959. *International Arbitration: Law and Practice.* London: Stevens.

aristocracy   The Greek derivation of this term is the rule of the best people. Plato in his Republic discusses how such men (not women) can be chosen and trained. He called them the 'guardians' and the virtues he required for them – lack of corruption, a devotion to the service of the public and integrity – are those which might be called 'aristocratic' in the best sense. With ARISTOTLE the term becomes a category of government by the same sort of people, but he gives it a social connotation when he describes the aristocrats as hereditary land-owners. To govern one needs 'a stake in the community'. For Aristotle wealth acquired by commerce is no criteria for responsibility: oligarchy, government by the rich, for him is the corrupt form of aristocracy.

In political writings the Aristotelian usage of the term persisted in some cases until the nineteenth century. Historians and social scientists, however, have used the word to describe a powerful, landed SOCIAL CLASS. In the feudal period a hereditary aristocracy with large estates protected lives and livelihoods of their tenants and serfs with military force and, in return, expected allegiance, labour and, if necessary, service in a private army. The aristocracy received title to their lands from the monarch and were expected to reciprocate with similar favours. Monarchs received their titles from God. Thus revolt could be condemned as heretical. Yet most feudal rebellions were of nobles against kings.

The ENLIGHTENMENT questioned the right of kings and aristocrats to these privileges and, in France, the Revolution swept them away in 1789. In the two centuries since, aristocrats everywhere have seen their political influence decline. Today the term describes a class with hereditary titles and nothing else, though it may be claimed that aristocrats are distinguished by 'breeding' and a sense of 'noblesse oblige'. Quite often, as in Britain, the families of many peers of the realm were only ennobled in the nineteenth century, often for success in commerce or for donating money to the ruling party. To survive, some aristocracies have allied themselves with the military and/or financial and industrial wealth. Often, where they have not done this, aristocrats have become impoverished by taxation imposed by redistributive democratic governments.

DEMOCRACY has not been favourably disposed to aristocracy.

See also DEMOCRACY; ENLIGHTENMENT; SOCIAL CLASS.

Reading
Aristotle [c.330BC]. 1959. *Aristotle's Politics and the Athenian Constitution*. trans. J. Warrington. London: Dent; Giddens, A. 1973. *The Class Structure of the Advanced Societies*. London: Hutchinson; Ponsonby, A.W.H. 1912. *The Decline of Aristocracy*. London: Allen & Unwin.

armies Armies were the first large-scale organization of men. By definition they are armed for the purpose of asserting coercively the will of the authority to which they owe allegiance. Because they are armed and organized to kill they can easily become a power in the land. Thus the Roman legions sometimes determined who should be emperor. Cromwell kept his New Model army on Putney Heath, a day's intimidating march from Parliament. Other revolutionary armies such as the French army under Napoleon, the Red Army under Trotsky and the Chinese Communist Army have been especially powerful. In some countries historical experience results in a political culture according power to the senior officer class. Spain, because its territory was recovered from the Moors by long campaigns, put its provinces under military governors in garrison cities. This practice was later passed on to Latin America and is expressed there in the common resort to military DICTATORSHIP. This is also the experience in the developing world where it is difficult to assert any authority and the soldiers are the only organized formation.

Indeed, it may well be asked why armies do not hold power everywhere. They control the means of destruction. Yet in the democratic world they submit to the civil power for various reasons. They are part of a culture which does not put a premium on brute force and decisions taken in 'chains of command'.

Modern industrialized society is highly differentiated and specialized. Senior soldiers know they are only expert in their own profession: unlike their counterparts in the developing world they are aware that running the government requires technical skills of a high order. The efficiency of the armed forces depends upon funds voted by democratic parliaments. Written CONSTITUTIONS often make their position clear. For instance, the US constitution states that the President is Commander-in-Chief of the armed forces. Furthermore large armies have become unfashionable because they are expensive. Militias and citizen armies, like the Swiss Army, are considered more favourably.

See also CIVIL WAR; GUERRILLA WARFARE; WAR; WARLORDS.

Reading
Craig, G.A. 1955. *The Politics of the Prussian Army*. New York: OUP; Finer, S.E. 1976. *Man on Horseback*. 2nd edn. Harmondsworth: Penguin; Finer, S.E. 1980. *Freedom in the World: Political Rights and Civil Liberties*. New York: Freedom House; Horne, A. 1984. *The French Army and Politics 1870–1970*. London: Macmillan.

arms control   This is a recent form of restriction of armaments following the failure between 1918 and 1939 to eradicate national arms completely. Arms control is a much more pragmatic and gradual approach than DISARMAMENT. The first treaties to restrict armaments were the London Naval Treaties from 1930 to 1936 between Britain and Germany relating to restrictions on the building of warships.

Arms control in international relations can be implemented in three ways, two of which relate to arms production. First, weapons that are especially dreadful, such as germ warfare, might be outlawed by agreement. The 1932 Disarmament Conference tried to outlaw submarines and bomber aeroplanes without success.

In 1987 by the Intermediate Nuclear Forces Treaty, the signatory powers agreed to ban all nuclear missiles launched from Europe with a range of more than 500 kilometres. Secondly, there may be agreements to maintain a fixed ratio of opposing forces. Third is the method adopted in the late 1950s to ensure that wars do not break out by accident. 'Arms control' then came to mean agreements to prevent highly armed opposing powers misunderstanding one another's movements. It involved notifying putative enemies of troop movements and exercises.

In the COLD WAR two power blocs confronted each other with ideological dislike and fears of aggressive expansion. Nuclear missiles greatly augmented the nervousness so that potential crises were always imminent. This emphasized the need for arms control and such agreements as the Anti-Ballistic Missile Treaty in 1972 and the Strategic Arms Reduction Talks Treaty in 1991 demonstrated that world-wide alliances and heavily armed superpowers were capable of limiting their military capacity. The problem still remains of how smaller powers such as Iraq, capable of manufacturing nuclear arms and unwilling to be swayed by international public opinion, can be restrained. Most arms control treaties contain provisions for verification and inspection and satellites have recently helped in this respect; but small installations could still escape detection.

Not only the production of arms needs control, but also their distribution. Two factors have accentuated this necessity. Increasingly the export of arms has been used by the major powers as a way of improving their trade balance. Furthermore, during the COLD WAR arms were supplied by both sides to contending factions in the developing world's civil and anti-colonial wars. Some of this found its way to private arms dealers

who supplied guerrilla armies. The most flagrant example has been the supply of land mines, often undiscriminatingly laid, blowing off children's limbs in parts of Africa and Asia. While it is possible to control the arms trade of large national suppliers, the control of private traders is much more difficult.
See also COLD WAR; DISARMAMENT.

Reading
Dougherty, J.E. 1973. *How to Think About Arms Control and Disarmament.* New York: Crane, Russak & Co; Dupuy, T.N. and Hammerman, G. eds. 1973. *A Documentary History of Arms Control and Disarmament.* New York: Bowker; Institute of War and Peace Studies. 1958. *Inspection for Disarmament.* New York: Columbia University Press.

arms races The term arose from the naval competition between Britain and Germany between 1900 and 1914, regarded by some as one cause of World War I. The metaphor is appropriate because an advance on the part of one competitor will be matched by an overtaking spurt on the part of the other. In seeking to maintain the BALANCE OF POWER the equilibrium is upset and war ensues. The COLD WAR witnessed a similar situation with each side trying to attain technical superiority in weaponry. ARMS CONTROL and limitation is much more easily applied to quantities of armaments, whereas new discoveries will probably not be accounted for in agreements. Thus President Reagan's 'Star Wars' was pronounced as an advance that the Russians could never overtake.
See also ARMS CONTROL; DISARMAMENT.

Reading
Bialer, U. 1995. *The Shadow of the Bomber.* London: Boydell and Brewer; Noel-Baker, P. 1958. *The Arms Race.* London: Stevens; Sheehan, M. 1983. *The Arms Race.* Oxford: Martin Robertson.

articulative parties *See* AGGREGATIVE PARTIES.

association A grouping of people who have come together for some common identity or purpose. It is a very general term though more specific than 'group' which can include objective categories as well as associations. Associations usually have rules and some organized form. The right of people freely to associate is one of the democratic freedoms.
See also GROUP THEORY; PLURALISM; VOLUNTARY ASSOCIATIONS.

autarky A regime which tries to be economically independent by cutting off trade to the rest of the world. Two examples from the inter-war period are the Soviet Union and its policy of 'Socialism in one country' and Nazi Germany and its policy of trade by large-scale barter. Neither regime was completely autarkic. The Soviet Union, for example, needed foreign technology; and Germany needed oil. An autarkic policy does have political significance in that states that restrict trading relations with the outside world are likely to restrict other forms of contact.

authoritarianism Any form of organization or attitude which claims to have the right to impose its values and decisions on recipients who do not have the right or means of responding or reacting freely. With governmental systems it is applied to those that deny democratic freedoms: freedom of expression, freedom of assembly and organization, freedom to oppose the government. Old-fashioned forms of authoritarianism are often described as ABSOLUTISM or DESPOTISM while modern forms may come under the umbrella of TOTALITARIANISM. Another common authoritarian type of government is the MILITARY REGIME.
See also ABSOLUTISM; AUTHORITARIAN PERSONALITY; MILITARY REGIMES; TOTALITARIANISM.

Reading

Acton, J.E.E.D. 1948. *Essays on Freedom and Power*. Ed. G. Himmelfarb. Glencoe: Free Press.

authoritarian personality

This term first arose from the psychological studies of the Frankfurt school, driven into exile in the USA, where a team led by Adorno (1903–69) studied attitudes accounting for ANTI-SEMITISM. As a result of interviewing individuals with a battery of questions, they invented the 'F-scale', intended to be a device for predicting Fascist attitudes; but later alleged to be one to predict a predisposition to Communism. Hence it is now known as the 'authoritarianism scale'. The components of this scale were: adherence to conventional values; aggression towards those who violate them; submissiveness to authority; dislike of tender and imaginative people; a disposition to think in rigid terms; exaggerated concern with the sexual activities of others; preoccupation with the leader-follower relationship; cynicism about human nature; and an inclination to believe in conspiracy theories.

Eysenck, using two factors of personality that Ferguson called Humanitarianism and Religionism, produced two axes of distribution of attitudes. One was from Radicalism to Conservatism and the other from Tender-Mindedness to Tough-Mindedness. This produced four quadrants. The Fascist personality was in the Conservative and Tough-Minded quadrant and the Communist in the Radical and Tough-Minded quadrant. From his studies Eysenck tried to sketch out a theory of political action based on personality.

Reading

Adorno, R.W., E. Frenkel-Brunswik, D.J. Levinson and R.N. Sanford. 1950. *The Authoritarian Personality*. New York: Harper and Row; Eysenck, H.J. 1954. *The Psychology of Politics*. London: Routledge; Ferguson, L.W. 1952. *Personality Measurement*. New York: McGraw-Hill.

authority

This concept is of the greatest importance in political science. It is often said 'politics is about power' and authority is a form of power. A ruler can have power without authority, but not authority without power. An occupying army has power over an occupied people because, fearing severe sanctions for disobedience, the latter will do what the occupying force wants. But the occupied do not accept the authority of their conquerors: they do not accept the LEGITIMACY of their rule, that is, they do not accept it as right and proper. On the other hand, the rule of a government that cannot organize the defence of their country's borders, and/or cannot maintain the implementation of their country's laws, ultimately by force, will not be able to sustain its SOVEREIGNTY intact. It will not be able to exert its power and, consequently, its authority will be lost.

The development of the concept is associated with the writings of Max WEBER (1864–1920) who distinguished between three forms of authority in society. One form of authority is traditional. This is generally accepted by the people governed as legitimate, although its rules remain unpromulgated, because it is long-standing and believed, as with hereditary kingship based on the divine right of kings, to have some mystic or magico-religious sanction. Charismatic authority is based on the extraordinary characteristics which people perceive in the leader. Situations where the ruled accord legitimacy to rulers they see possessing unusual personal qualities are rare and are likely to be where there is a breakdown in norms and values. Revolutionary situations, for example, are likely to be the occasions for charismatic authority to be appropriate.

Legal/rational authority, Weber's third type, is the most familiar and contemporary form. Authority is legitimized by recognized rules, probably codified laws and constitutional procedures. Hence it is the basis of Weber's theory of BUREAUCRACY. But it also congruent with DEMOCRACY in a way that the other forms of authority are not, because democracy lays special stress on the observance of the RULE OF LAW. Laws need to be promulgated and this is not the case with traditional and charismatic authority. In a democratic state legitimacy becomes synonymous with legality.

These three kinds of authority are what Weber called 'IDEAL TYPES'. In any actual situation there will be manifestations of two or more of them. A fourth type of authority, it has been pointed out, arises from the legitimacy accorded to the expert. This it is argued is a feature of the modern world because so many of its situations demand specialist, technical knowledge that lay people cannot understand.

See also BUREAUCRACY; DEMOCRACY; LEGITIMACY; SOVEREIGNTY.

Reading
Eckstein, H. and T.R. Gurr. 1975. *Patterns of Authority: a Structural Basis for Political Inquiry.* London: Wiley; Friedrich, C.J. 1972. *Tradition and Authority.* London: Pall Mall; Haskell, T.L. ed. 1984. *The Authority of Experts.* Bloomington: Indiana University Press; Raz, J. ed. 1989. *Authority.* Oxford: OUP; Weber, M. 1968. *Economy and Society.* 3 vols. New York: Bedminster.

autochthony   A term used in relation to the constitutional position of parts of the Commonwealth. Although their foundation was the result of an Act of the Westminster Parliament, such countries as India and the original Irish Free State regard their constitutions as native to them and their people. Being auto-chthonous is thus a stronger situation than being autonomous.

See also DOMINION STATUS.

Reading
Hogg, P.W. 1983. 'Patriation of the Canadian Constitution: has it been achieved?' *Queen's University Law Journal* 8, 123; Wheare, K.C. 1960. *The Constitutional Structure of the Commonwealth.* Oxford: OUP.

autocracy   Originally this term described an authoritarian regime in which one person ruled without reference to any other source of authority and in an arbitrary fashion. The autocrat does not need to deal with people consistently or fairly. Hence autocracy is typical of primitive societies. Autocratic behaviour can be found in modern societies, but it will not be the distinguishing characteristic. Totalitarian regimes will give plenty of scope for autocrats, but they will have to pay some attention to the framework of regulations. Some democratic politicians will be autocratic in style – one thinks of Charles de Gaulle and Margaret Thatcher – but they will have to operate within the limits of much stricter constitutional restraints.

Reading
Wittfogel, K. 1957. *Oriental Despotism: a Comparative Study of Total Power.* New Haven: YUP.

autonomy   A term meaning self-government. It can apply to individuals and political communities. The 'autonomous individual' is in control of her/his life, free to act independently of external circumstances and unfettered by what William Blake called the 'mind-forged manacles'. The notion thus lies at the base of much liberal thinking. Among political scientists autonomy has been seen as a sort of half-way stage to full independence for regions and provinces. Often control by an elected assembly, with tax-raising powers and authority over schooling and other aspects of governmental services, has been granted in Europe to regions with minority languages. The German-speaking part of the Italian Tyrol and the Basque country and Catalonia in Spain are examples. In both countries these autonomous regions may be, to some extent, harbingers of regionalized states.

Reading

Hannum, H. 1990. *Autonomy, Sovereignty and Self-Determination*. Philadelphia: Philadelphia University Press; Patterson, L. 1994. *The Autonomy of Modern Scotland*. Edinburgh: Edinburgh University Press.

B

backbencher A legislator who is not among the leaders of any of the parties in the legislature. The term springs from the British House of Commons where only members of the Government and of the Opposition leadership sit on the two opposing front benches.

backlash A sudden and strong reaction to an innovatory policy. It originated in the USA where the 'white backlash' against measures to alleviate the position of blacks was sometimes pronounced.

balances *See* CHECKS AND BALANCES.

balance of power A concept going back to Thucydides and consciously used in the eighteenth century, especially to describe British foreign policy. Relations between states are perceived as reverting to Hobbes's state of nature when every state will be fearful of every other and disposed to pre-empt AGGRESSION by striking first. International anarchy will prevail. Hence peace can best be preserved by ALLIANCES, particularly against the most powerful state. After 1815 on the Continent of Europe four great powers, France, Prussia, Russian and Austro-Hungary confronted each other in shifting alliances and it was widely assumed that Britain would throw its weight on whichever side was needed to maintain an equilibrium.

Before 1914 the Central Powers, Germany, Austro-Hungary and Italy confronted Russia and the Entente Cordiale of Britain and France. This balance of power did not prevent World War I and after 1918 the concept lost favour as a method of peace-preservation. Exponents of the notion of the democratic control of foreign policy argued that war was caused by international diplomats and chancelleries who were unable to escape from the influence of arms manufacturers and military hierarchies. World War II could also be attributed to the failure of international statesmen, like Neville Chamberlain, carrying on in the old fashion and failing to understand the new strength of IDEOLOGY in the world.

Yet the onset of the COLD WAR after 1945 led to the resurrection of the balance of power. The two superpowers, the USA and the USSR, with their two alliances, the North Atlantic Treaty and the Warsaw Pact, confronted one another with their nuclear weaponry across the 'Iron Curtain'. What was described as a 'balance of terror' sustained successfully a 'cold peace'.

Reading

Gulik, E.V. 1955. *Europe's Classical Balance of Power*. Ithaca: Cornell University Press; Niou, E.M.S., P.C. Ordeshook and G.F. Rose. 1989. *The Balance of Power*. Cambridge: CUP; Sheehan, M. 1996. *The Balance of Power: History and Theory*. London: Routledge.

balkanization A division of territory into small states so that it looks rather like the Balkans. It is said that those who support the idea of a 'Europe of the regions' want a balkanized Europe. The growth of separatism in many European states lends strength to the concept.

ballot A term used to describe secret voting in elections. Early voting in British elections was in public. There were only a few voters in each constituency and they voted by show of hands at what were called 'the hustings'. This method was open to bribery, intimidation and corruption. Secret voting was used in ancient Greece when pebbles were dropped in urns. With the advent of mass DEMOCRACY extensive organization of elections, polling stations and electoral registers of voters became necessary. The first secret ballot was in South Australia in 1856 and consequently it became known as the 'Australian ballot'. Voters marked the candidate they preferred with a cross on a piece of paper issued by a polling clerk, folded it and dropped it in a ballot box. The method was introduced in Britain in 1872.

In some countries ballot papers are given to each voter by all CANDIDATES. The voter puts the one of his choice into the ballot box in the polling booth. In the USA in some states voting machines are used to prevent the practice of 'stuffing' ballot boxes with fraudulent votes. It is common for the ballot paper to be very long because numerous elections are held on the same day including, in some American states, REFERENDUMS.

See also ELECTIONS; ELECTORAL SYSTEMS.

Reading

Moores, R. 1987. *Conducting Ballots*. London: Industrial Society.

ballot-rigging Any method of improperly conducting an election. For example, 'personation', voting for several other people before they arrive at the poll, making false registrations, which may be done by taking names from tombstones and putting them on the register, and interfering with voting machines. These practices are familiarly associated with the American 'BOSSES' who in large cities controlled electoral organizations, known as 'machines'. The two most famous were Tammany Hall in New York and the Cook County machine which covered Chicago.

Reading

Cooper, W. H. 1962. *Rigging Voting Machines and Voting Machine Laws*. Baton Rouge: W.H. Cooper.

bargaining A political activity which has received some attention from political scientists. It might occur in a situation where a finite resource needed to be divided. Suppose two families, one of four persons and one of five, needed to divide a field between them and physical combat and lottery have been ruled out and it is agreed to proceed to voting. Then the family of four would be outvoted if family ties remained strong. If greed overcame family loyalties, however, one of the larger family might be bought off by the family of four offering the defector a bigger portion of the field. For example, if the family of five had already decided to divide the field up into five portions of 20 per cent each, the family of four might offer the defector a portion of 24 per cent and take 19 per cent each themselves. But then his own family might offer him 25 per cent to retain his vote. Such a process might continue for some time producing what are called 'bargaining cycles'.

See also COALITION THEORY; GAME THEORY.

Reading
Bacharach S.B. and E.J. Lawler. 1981. *Bargaining: Power, Tactics and Outcomes*. San Francisco: Jossey-Bass; Barry, B. 1965. *Political Argument*. London: Routledge; Mueller, D.C. 1979. *Public Choice*. Cambridge: CUP.

behaviouralism *See* POLITICAL BEHAVIOUR.

bicameralism The belief that legislatures should be composed of two chambers or houses. It is usual to call them Upper and Lower or Second and First chambers; and for the Lower chamber to have most power. Various arguments are advanced in favour of two-chambered parliaments. One is that two opinions are better than one. This may beg the question, 'Are not three opinions better still?' Another argument is that first thoughts on a policy result in rash decisions, while second are made on reflection. Thirdly, another chamber allows for people to be represented in a different way, so adding variety to public life. Thus the Irish Republic's Second chamber is chosen by FUNCTIONAL REPRESENTATION. More commonly in federal states the Second chamber represents equally each sub-unit of government while the First is elected on a population basis. This is so in Australia, Switzerland and the USA. In Germany the Second chamber, the Bundesrat, does not have equal representation for each Länder, though the smaller ones like Hamburg, are very over-represented in population terms.

Defenders of UNICAMERALISM are all supporters of the First or Lower chamber. They argue that it is the one with the true popular mandate. Even in the USA where the Senate, the Second chamber, is popularly elected, one third of it was elected four years ago, and another third two years ago. The Lower chamber, the House of Representatives is elected in entirety every two years. The Canadian Second chamber is entirely nominated. In France the Senate is chosen by an electoral college largely composed of local government councillors. In Britain about three-quarters of the members of the House of Lords are there by hereditary succession: the other quarter are nominated for life. Hence Second chambers usually distort the expression of the popular will. Unicameralists, therefore, favour their abolition.

Unicameralists point out that some countries manage quite well with only one chamber. The Scandinavian states are all uni-chambered and New Zealand became so in 1951. Bi-cameralists retort that they are all small countries. Large ones with a greater volume of business would find legislating in one chamber difficult. Moreover, all the unicameral countries appoint a large committee of the single chamber to re-consider draft legislation, so they do not avoid the delay of revision.

The best argument for a Second chamber is probably its useful function of revising BILLS hastily passed by the First chamber. Also uncontroversial legislation may be introduced in the upper house, thus saving parliamentary time; and sometimes debate may be more stimulating there, especially if procedures there are less restricting on speakers. The contention that the delaying and amending functions are necessary and better employed by the Second chamber because it is composed of people who are older, more responsible, with better breeding or educational qualifications, and generally with 'more bottom', is based on a mistrust of DEMOCRACY.

Reading
Bryce, Viscount. 1918. *Conference on Reform of the Second Chamber*. Cmd. 9038. London: HMSO; Marriott, J.A.R. 1927. *Second Chambers*. Oxford: OUP.

bills A bill is a proposal for a law in draft. Once passed by a legislature it becomes a statute or act. Procedures for the passage of legislation vary between one political system and another. For example, in Scandinavia the 'remiss' procedure operates. Government departments set up consultative committees with appropriate interest group representation to prepare reports for draft proposals for legislation. Britain is unusual in that about 90 per cent of legislation stems from the executive. This reflects the domination of the House of Commons by one party from which the government is usually formed and by the standing order that only a minister can propose spending money. The House of Lords has only delaying power and after passing in both Houses Royal assent is automatically given. In the USA, where procedures were originally derived from Britain, the legislative process is quite different. Proposals for legislation have three sources: the President and his programme, interest groups and members of Congress who may be motivated by the needs of their constituents or by interest group pressures. A draft bill can only be introduced, however, by a member of Congress and if it is a financial proposal only by a member of the House of Representatives. Once it passes both chambers the President may sign it into law. Or he can veto it, after which Congress can only pass it over his veto by a two-thirds vote of both houses.

Reading
Anckar, D. and V. Helander. 1985. 'Corporatism and Representative Government in the Nordic Countries' in Alapuro, R. et al. eds. *Small States in Comparative Perspective*, 124–37. Oslo: Norwegian University Press; Bradshaw, K. and D. Pring. 1981. *Parliament and Congress*. London: Quartet; Englefield, D. 1985. *Westminster and Whitehall*. London: Longman.

bill of attainder A device used in the English Parliament, especially in the reign of Henry VIII (1491–1547), by which people were 'attainted' – declared treasonable. It did not involve any judicial process. The last important use of it was in 1696.

Reading
Maitland, F.W. 1961. *The Constitutional History of England*. Cambridge: CUP.

bill of rights A term first used in the English post-revolutionary settlement of 1690. Parliament passed a Bill of Rights which was largely a restriction of arbitrary monarchic power as practised by the Stuarts. In future no public money could be raised or spent without the consent of Parliament; the suspending or dispensing of laws was forbidden; a standing army could not be maintained in times of peace; judges no longer held office only under the monarch's 'good pleasure'; and no Member of Parliament could be arraigned for anything said there.

Declarations of rights are to be distinguished from bills of rights because the latter have some legislative or constitutional legitimacy; but the French Declaration of the Rights of Man, 1789, drawn up by some members of the estates parliaments, is incorporated in the constitution of the Fifth French Republic. The American Bill of Rights, 1791, is the first ten amendments to the Constitution. All are the inspiration of Thomas Jefferson (1743–1826), leader of the faction which thought the federal government had been given too much power. The First Amendment said Congress could make no law 'respecting an establishment of religion' or 'abridging freedom of speech or of the press; or the right of the people peacefully to assemble'. The Second guaranteed the right of the people 'to keep and bear arms'. The Fifth contained the famous 'due process of law' clause.

The US Bill of Rights has been the common inspiration of such constitutional provisions since. The Japanese Constitution of 1946 has 31 of its clauses concerned with fundamental rights. The Indian Constitution also includes guarantees of civil liberties. In Europe the German Basic Law begins with 19 Articles asserting Basic Rights. The 'Socialist' constitutions, such as that of the USSR in 1977 and the People's Republic of China in 1978, also asserted collective rights associated with social and economic welfare.

The effect of Bills of Rights, laying down fundamental freedoms for citizens that should not be infringed, is to separate constitutional law from other law. (Written constitutions do this anyway.) Thus Supreme or Constitutional Courts rule on cases involving basic rights. Hence absolute rights may become qualified in practice. For example, under pressure of public opinion during World War I, the US Supreme Court evolved the 'clear-and-present-danger' doctrine. Justice Holmes stated that when a nation was 'at war many things that might be said in time of peace are such a hindrance to its effort that their utterance will not be endured' and 'no court could regard them as protected by any constitutional right'.

Consequently it is argued by some that Bills of Rights may fail to protect civil liberties when they are most under pressure and most needed. Others argue that though such statements of absolute freedoms are not foolproof and may be qualified by supreme courts, some liberties are so fundamental as to require promulgation in a written document. Thus the British Charter 88 movement supports both a written constitution and a Bill of Rights for Britain.

See also CIVIL LIBERTIES; FUNDAMENTAL RIGHTS; NATURAL RIGHTS.

Reading
Friedrich, C.J. 1967. The Impact of American Constitutionalism Abroad. Boston, Mass.: Boston University Press; Hand, L. 1958. The Bill of Rights. Cambridge, Mass.: HUP; Jennings, W.I. 1933. The Law and the Constitution. London: London University Press; Swisher, C.B. 1946. The Growth of Constitutional Power in the United States. Chicago: Chicago University Press; Zander, M. 1985. A Bill of Rights. London: Sweet and Maxwell.

bipolar   A system in which the entities tend to congregate around two opposing centres. Hence the adjective is sometimes used to describe British ADVERSARY POLITICS. It is also used in international relations to describe a BALANCE OF POWER such as the two alliances in the COLD WAR.
See also POLARIZATION.

blackleg   A term used to describe a worker who goes to work when workmates are on strike. 'Scab' is a synonym. Sometimes employers transport blacklegs in buses to workplaces. As strikers are not paid and under risk of losing their jobs, blacklegging understandably arouses hatred and contempt.

black power   Both a concept and a movement in the USA which began in the 1940s with the imprisonment for burglary of Malcolm Little, known as 'Malcolm X'. In prison he met Elijah Muhammad, leader of the Black Muslims, who believed whites would be destroyed by God and that he would set up a separate black state. After release in 1952 Malcolm X became the Black Muslims' most eloquent speaker and agitator. Denouncing those black groups, such as the National Association for the Advancement of Coloured People, or Martin Luther King and the civil rights movement, who employed constitutional means and sought racial integration, he argued for the legitimacy of violence by blacks in self-defence. In 1965 he founded the Organization of Afro-American Unity, but was assassinated shortly after. Stokely Carmichael and Charles Hamilton gloried in black culture and pigmentation and proclaimed black solidarity must confront white power and not become a wing of the Democratic Party for which most blacks voted. They did not wish to subvert the democratic system, but to develop black socio-political talents and resources in order to participate in it to greater advantage.

Reading
Carmichael, S. and C. Hamilton. 1967. *Black Power*. New York: Random House; Haley, A. and Malcolm X. 1968. *The Autobiography of Malcolm X*. Harmondsworth: Penguin.

block grant   One method by which central governments make payments to local governments. It was first introduced into Britain by the 1929 Local Government Act and into the USA, at the federal level, by the Nixon Administration (1969–74), though the American procedure was called 'general revenue sharing'. With block grants a large part of the payments made to sub-units of government is handed over in one package. It will be calculated in terms of a formula based on such factors as population, poverty and other social needs. The advantages of block grants are the discretion it allows local governments to determine how they allocate their funding and the convenience for central government budgeting.

The other method of disbursing central funds to local governments is through 'specific' or 'categoric' grants. Each need is paid separately by the appropriate central department. Thus there may be separate grants for education, health, unemployment relief, care of the aged and highways. Central government policies determine how each of these is distributed and local governments have no discretion. The latter deal with each central government department separately and consequently confusion may arise. There is thus always a tendency for the national treasury to favour block grants as more efficient and less open to manipulation. Moreover, right-wing governments tend to prefer block grants

and left-wing governments specific grants.

Reading
Break, G.F. 1980. *Financing Government in a Federal System*. Washington, D.C.: Brookings. Newton, K.J. and T.J. Karran. 1985. *The Politics of Local Expenditure*. London: Macmillan.

block vote   A method by which members of a constituency or group of electors agree to cast a vote as a whole. For example, if 100 voters discuss how their vote should be placed and by 51 to 49 decide that it should be cast in a certain way, then their 100 votes will be disposed in that way.

The procedure is likely to be adopted by groups that feel the necessity to maintain solidarity. For instance, the constitution of the USA, in describing the method of choosing a President by an ELECTORAL COLLEGE, does not stipulate that all the electors in each state should vote in a block for one particular candidate. Yet they nearly always do so because they are the nominees of a political party and pledged to support their party's Presidential candidate.

Similarly the need for SOLIDARITY is strong in TRADE UNIONS who must maintain a united front when bargaining with employers. When the Trades Union Congress was set up in Britain it adopted the rule that unions voted in blocks when making decisions and this practice was passed on to the Labour Party when it was set up, largely by the trade unions, in 1900. A new constitution in 1918 allowed constituency labour parties to be affiliated for the first time, but followed the procedure by giving them block votes. Yet the trade unions controlled fourfifths of the vote at annual conferences, leading to constant complaints from the constituency parties where the local party workers operated at election times and selected parliamentary and local government candidates. This situation has recently been changed.

Reading

Harrison, M. 1960. *Trade Unions and the Labour Party Since 1945*. London: Allen and Unwin; Wilmerding, L. 1958. *The Electoral College*. New Brunswick, NJ: Rutgers University Press.

blue collar   A synonym for manual, used to describe manual workers in the USA where 'working class' (or any class designation) is anathematized. It is used as a category distinct from white collar or non-manual workers. Political scientists use these terms especially in voting studies where a clear statistical relationship can be found between manual occupation and voting for left-wing parties. There were always problems about border-line cases such as shop assistants, typists and laboratory assistants. In recent years the categorization has become more blurred as the distinction between manual and non-manual work has become even less clear. There has been a decline in dirty manual labour due to the contraction of the coal/steel industries and an equivalent expansion of jobs in electronics and computer operations. It is thus difficult to determine whether many people are blue or white collar.

See also SOCIAL CLASS; WORKING CLASS.

Reading

Howe, I. ed. 1972. *The World of the Blue-Collar Worker*. New York: Quadruple; Levitan, S.A. ed. 1971. *Blue-collar Workers: a Symposium on Middle America*. New York: McGraw-Hill; Shoslak, A.B. 1969. *Blue Collar Life*. New York: Random House.

bolshevik   The term is derived from the Russian word meaning majority. The Bolsheviks were the faction of the Russian Social Democratic and Labour Party which won the main debate at the party's second congress in 1903. The minority group were called the Mensheviks. Both groups generally accepted Marxist analyses and the main purpose of overthrowing Tsardom and inaugurating a socialist regime. The conflict was about the nature of the party. The Mensheviks wanted a mass party on the lines of Social Democratic parties in western Europe. This was contrary to Lenin's Bolshevik view that the party should remain a smaller network of committed professional revolutionaries working more or less underground. The Mensheviks tended to think the revolution would come through conventional democratic means. The Bolsheviks were essentially a subversive, insurrectionary grouping whose victory in 1903 was significant for Russian, and perhaps world, history for the rest of the century. Although the Russian Revolution of February 1917 owed little to the Bolsheviks, they came to power in the following October by a COUP D'ÉTAT. In January 1918 they suppressed by armed force the newly elected democratic parliament because they did not have a majority of deputies in it. Henceforward Russia, or the Union of Socialist Soviet Republics as it became, was ruled by the Communist Party with its Leninist principle of DEMOCRATIC CENTRALISM. As Marxist theories and Leninist ideas of party organization were adopted in much of the world, Bolshevism can be regarded as a world-wide creed. Bolshevik remained part of the title of the Communist Party of the Soviet Union until 1952.

The slang expression 'Bolshie' is often used to describe someone who shows no deference to authority and is always challenging it.

Reading

Carr, E.H. 1950. *The Bolshevik Revolution 1917–1923*. 3 vols. London: Macmillan; Haimson, L.H. 1955. *The Russian Marxists and the Origins of Bolshevism*. Cambridge, Mass.: HUP; Suny, R. and A. Adams, eds. 1990. *The Russian Revolution and Bolshevik Victory: Visions and Revisions*. Lexington, Mass.: D.C. Heath.

bonapartism A term describing a sort of autocratic political leadership with charismatic features and certain notions about style and structure of government. Because it derives from the reigns of Napoleon Bonaparte (1769–1821) and his nephew Napoleon III (1808–73) it reflects their legacies but, though it is always associated with France, one can detect features of it elsewhere. In some ways it resembles caesarism in that one of its characteristics is a populistic imperialism. It is a rejection of ancient monarchic traditions in favour of strong personal rule with an emphasis on MERITOCRACY and the technical solution of national problems. Thus bonapartism is not democratic. The two Napoleons controlled France through a centralized 'administrative state' in which the PREFECT system was very important as it relayed central government policies to the localities. The 'glory' of the nation, as exemplified by its culture and power, is upheld in both domestic and foreign policy. GAULLISM has clear similarities with it, though this should not be over-emphasized because De Gaulle and his successors have not attempted to suppress democracy.

Reading
Duverger, M. 1961. *De la Dictature*. Paris: Julliard; Fisher, H.A.L. 1908. *Bonapartism*. Oxford: OUP.

bosses A term commonly used in the English-speaking world to describe a certain type of politician who is much more concerned with electoral organization and the garnering of votes than with enunciating policies. It has especial significance in the USA where it was associated with 'machine politics', the dominance of large industrial towns and cities by bosses, able to ensure the return of candidates, usually of the Democratic Party, by their ability to mobilize certain sections of the electorate with the help of their own 'spoilsmen'. The system was inevitably corrupt.

Boss rule was the outcome of several factors operating at the same time. The spoils system existed from the beginning of the American republic at both national, state and municipal levels. It rested on the belief that administration did not need specialized expertise and, therefore that administrators did not need to have tenure. Consequently the practice developed of changing whole administrations after the succession to power of a new government. A PATRONAGE system developed: 'the spoils to the victor' was asserted. When large urban conglomerations appeared as a result of industrialization, municipal government became complicated and there were many more spoilsmen to be appointed. The city bosses, who were sometimes mayors, sometimes other officials, sometimes even unelected people, frequently appointed the police and firemen from among their own supporters. In each polling district they had their own men who knew the voters and their problems.

A most important factor that explains the hold that the boss system attained on American politics is the nature of the American urban voter, particularly in the decades between 1880 and 1940. A flood of immigrants from Europe became US citizens. Most of them could not speak or read English and were resistant to the white, Anglo-Saxon, Protestant ('Wasp') culture on which America was founded. (This explains why most of the early bosses were Irish: they could speak and read English but did not belong to the dominant culture.) The immigrants knew nothing of US politics and only wanted to survive and make their way in a foreign society. The boss machine befriended these different ethnic groups, helped them through the naturalization process and thus made them voters. There was no social security system and often they were found jobs and provided with the seasonal turkey by the bosses. Consequently it was easy to persuade them to vote for the bosses' candidates at election time.

The great year of the bosses was 1932 when, in the midst of depression and urban poverty, they stacked up huge piles of ethnic votes for Franklin D. Roosevelt (1882–1945), the Democratic candidate who promised them relief. Since World War II the power and extent of the boss system has declined because of the increasing replacement of the spoils system by tenured officials, the end of large-scale immigration, the integration of most 'ethnics' (except blacks and Hispanics) and the stabilization of federal and state welfare. There are, however, still machines in the industrial cities of the north-east though they have somewhat fragmented as with the Tammany Hall organization in New York.

See also MACHINE.

Reading
Banfield, E.C. and J.Q. Wilson. 1963. *City Politics*. Cambridge, Mass.: HUP; Key, V.O. 1964. *Politics, Parties and Pressure Groups*. New York: Crowell; Riordan, W.L. 1948. *Plunkitt of Tammany Hall*. New York: McClure, Phillips.

bourgeoisie A term that has changed its meaning more than once. Originally it was a French word describing the merchant class. Karl MARX (1818–83) and Friedrich Engels (1820–95) in their 1848 Communist Manifesto re-defined it as 'the class of modern capitalists, owners of the means of social production and employers of wage labour'. They saw the bourgeoisie, or capitalist entrepreneurs as the most revolutionary agent in world history; by revolutionizing the means of production and bringing industrialization about they had changed the nature of society. Eventually the bourgeoisie would clash with the wage-labourers, the proletariat, the most revolutionary agent of all. Hence with Marx the bourgeoisie are a well-defined specific class with a well-defined role in history.

In recent years 'bourgeois' has again undergone a transformation. It has become used to describe a certain lifestyle and may refer to anyone with what are seen as middle-class aspirations or pretensions. The origins of this probably lie with student neo-Marxists who adopted certain standards of dress and deportment which they felt were revolutionary. Hence one might be described as 'bourgeois' after having a hair-cut.

Reading
Marx, K. [1850] 1959. *The Class Struggle in France*. In *Marx and Engels: Basic Writings on Politics and Philosophy*. Ed. L.S. Feuer. London: Collins.

boycott Derived from the campaign organized by the Irish Land League in 1880 against Captain Boycott (1832–97), a retired British army officer and unpopular agent of landed estates in Ireland, who was ostracized both economically and socially. The term is now used to describe any collective attempt to exclude anyone or any entity from benefits and relationships. A recent example was the international boycott of trade with South Africa.

See also SANCTIONS.

brinkmanship A bargaining tactic employed by one or more parties in a negotiation where concessions are desperately sought to the brink of breakdown. The 'brinkmen' are gambling on the other side giving way. In industrial bargaining the risk taken is the likelihood of failure resulting in a damaging strike or lock-out. In international bargaining, as with the Cuban missile crisis of 1962, it may be nuclear war.

See also BARGAINING.

budget A budget is a statement of expected revenues and expenditures over a specified future period, usually one year. Most sizeable organizations have budgets. Budgets of states have become increasingly complicated as states have taken on wider and wider functions, of which the two most important are national defence and social welfare. Higher taxation and burgeoning expenditure has expanded the duties of national treasuries: indeed, the politics of budgeting has become the focus of the allocation of values.

The first systematic attempt at an annual budget was in France in 1815. In Britain it was Gladstone who, in the 1850s, first used budget-day speeches to give an account of national finances and his ideas about their future management; though presenting to Parliament the annual statement of expected future expenditure together with the budget had to wait until 1993. The USA did not incur heavy defence costs and welfare expenditure until the twentieth century. The constitutional separation of the executive and legislative powers then made the politics of budgeting both disorderly and Byzantine. Moreover, the American government was especially vulnerable to the pressures of interest groups who tried to get their hands into the 'PORK-BARREL'. But all democratic governments facing re-election were bound to consider the allocation of funds to such large categories as pensioners, house-owners, house-renters, parents of school children and industrial workers. To what degree the demands of these groups were satisfied was a matter of moral, economic and political judgement. Prioritization varied as between circumstances, countries and party orientations.

In the 1920s governments discovered that financial rectitude was not enough to manage their national affairs. The inter-war depression and the ideas of Keynes focused attention on the management of economies and this affected budgets which inevitably became part of economic policy-making. Keynesian doctrine allowed deficit financing, and budgeting became an exercise in forecasting and manipulating aggregate demand. Thus taxes were reduced, revenues consequently lowered and deficits produced when unemployment was expected to increase.

Conversely when employment increased and inflation threatened, taxes were raised and a budget surplus engineered. Inevitably politicians could not resist the temptation to increase taxes in the two or three years after an election and lower them a year or two before they were due to appeal to the electorate, thus creating a 'POLITICAL BUSINESS CYCLE'.

Until the early 1970s the general approach to budgeting was one of incrementalism: it was expected that every year would see an increase in expenditure caused by contractual obligations undertaken by governments such as indexed pensions for public servants. Programmes to eradicate poverty and raise educational standards also proliferated. These commitments could be provided for by economic growth. Inflation after the oil-price rise in 1973 put an end to this assumption. It became clear that no longer could unemployment be balanced against inflation: they could both increase together. This situation was called 'stagflation' and gave rise to anti-Keynesian theories such as MONETARISM and to demands to control budgets, leading to the initiation of programming, planning, budgeting systems (PPBS) which attempted, often unsuccessfully, to measure performance and to introduce COST-BENEFIT ANALYSIS.

Contemporary budgeting may therefore be perceived as an arena in which the economy, the polity and technocratic management clash. Values contend with values, politicians with politicians, PRESSURE GROUPS with pressure groups and departments with departments.

Reading

Caiden, N., and A.Wildavsky. 1974. *Planning and Budgeting in Poor Countries*. New York: Wiley; Heald, D. 1983. *Public Expenditure*. Oxford: Martin Robertson; Jordan, A.G. and J.J. Richardson. 1987. *British Politics and the Policy Process*. London: Allen and Unwin; Wildavsky, A. 1986. *Budgeting: a Comparative Theory of Budgetary Processes*. New Brunswick, NJ: Transaction Books.

bureaucracy Bureaucracy is used in two senses: either to describe a particular set of administrators; or as a concept connoting the values, attitudes, beliefs and behaviour that normally characterize administrative apparatuses. It dates from the eighteenth century and is French in origin. Sometimes the term is used pejoratively to refer to officials and their idiosyncrasies; but it was perceived in a favourable light and developed as an idea by Max WEBER (1865–1920). From his time it has been accepted into the vocabulary of all the social sciences.

It is significant that Weber was German because the German state, and earlier the Prussian state, had been renowned for its well-organized and efficient administration. HEGEL had regarded it as the highest form of rationality (see IDEALISM). So did Weber who perceived bureaucracy as the instrument of the rational/legal form of authority that he believed to be superior to any other. His high regard for it was based on its predictability: it would eradicate, as far as possible, uncertainty from the affairs of state. Weber's 'IDEAL TYPE' bureaucracy could guarantee unarbitrary administration because it was underpinned by rules. There should be rules about how to deal with clients, rules defining relations between different levels of officials, rules regulating their recruitment, promotions and pensions, and rules, or laws, regulating the whole framework. Thus, for Weber, the rationality of administration depended on a code of conduct similar to a legal code. Precedents were important and for the sake of consistency the maintenance of a filing system was essential. The character of the bureaucrat was determined by these constraints. He must be impersonal, anonymous, detached, non-political, incorruptible and loyal to his political masters. Bureaucrats merely implemented the decisions of politicians.

As a form of rational organization Weber expected bureaucracy to triumph in all areas of society, especially in business enterprise, though in his last days, the early months of the Weimar Republic, he did express some forebodings about its extension. While Weberian bureaucracy, or 'classical bureaucracy' as it is sometimes called, has come to be accepted as the basis of scholarly discusssion on the subject, there have been some criticisms or revisions of his theory. These have generally contended that modern bureaucratic organization is neither so formalistic nor so efficient and rational as Weber believed. Michel Crozier stressed the difficulty bureaucratic superiors have in enforcing their aims and values on lower levels, especially where the latter are specialized technicians. Anthony Downs portrayed bureaucracies as incapable of collective rationality because of the individual rationality of officials seeking to maximize their status, wealth and power as against those of their colleagues. Yet he perceived benefit from this competition. Innovation might emerge from it. W.A. Niskanen argued similarly in his account of US government agencies who are concerned to inflate their budgets as high as possible at the expense of the national exchequer. Other authors have drawn attention to the modern tendency for bureaucrats to become increasingly involved in the management of national economies, thus deserting their strictly implementary role. In this way bureaucracy has become TECHNOCRACY.

See also TECHNOCRACY.

Reading

Aberbach, J.D., R.D. Putnam and B.A. Rockin. 1981. *Bureaucrats and Politicians in Western Democracies*. Harvard: HUP; Albrow, M. 1970. *Bureaucracy*. London: Macmillan; Crozier, M. 1964. *The Bureaucratic Phenomenon*. Chicago: University of Chicago Press; Downs, A. 1966. *Inside Bureaucracy*. Boston: Little, Brown; Gerth, H.H. and Mills, C.W. 1948. *From Max Weber: Readings in Sociology*. London: Routledge; Kamenka, E. and Krygier, M. 1979. *Bureaucracy*. London: Arnold; Olsen, J.P. 1983. *Organized Democracy*. Bergen: Universitetsforlaget; Page, E.C. 1985. *Political Authority and Bureaucratic Power*. Brighton: Harvester.

bureaucratic authoritarianism A type of repressive regime which arises in semi-developed countries with a history of military rule. Unlike personalist military dictatorships which can be found in more primitive countries, this kind of authoritarianism occurs where the military has become more bureaucratized and conscious of the need to nurture economic development. Hence the army allies itself with technocratic individuals who have risen to the top in large organizations including multinational corporations. It has been seen as part of the process of MODERNIZATION. In Europe, Portugal under Salazar (1889–1970), Prime Minister from 1932 until his death, is the best example. Here it had a Catholic and corporatist tinge. But the most noteworthy examples are in Latin America where Argentina, Brazil, Chile and Uruguay all fit this model.

See also MILITARY REGIMES; MODERNIZATION.

Reading

Collier, D. ed. 1979. *The New Authoritarianism in Latin America*. Princeton: Princeton University Press; O'Donnell, G. 1988. *Bureaucratic Authoritarianism: Argentina 1966–1973, in Comparative Perspective*. Berkeley and Los Angeles: University of California Press; Salazar, O. 1956. *Principes d'Action*. Paris: Fayard.

bureaucratic politics This term is regarded as an appropriate description of the situation within contemporary bureaucracies where, far from realizing the Weberian model of detachment from policy-making, administrators attempt to affect the outcomes in their own interests. There will be conflict because heads of agencies try to acquire higher status by expanding their staffs and functions, competing with one another for prestige and promotion, because the results of policies will probably be to their benefit or disadvantage. Moreover, independently of these factors, different departments often hold different views about the intrinsic worth of one policy as against others.

In the USA the concept has been especially applied to the understanding of foreign policy. It has been argued that conflict among bureaucrats about foreign policy decisions was resolved after much bargaining accompanied by manipulation and arm-twisting. Each contender took up a position reflecting the interests of their agency. Furthermore, these pressures continued with the implementation of decisions. Consequently the elected representatives of the people were perceived as of minor importance by those who adhered to this model. In general, however, most political scientists, while accepting that bureaucrats intervene in policy-making, would argue that they can only be of influence within the terms set by politicians.

See also TECHNOCRACY.

Reading

Allison, G.T. 1971. *The Essence of Decision*. Boston: Little, Brown; Destler, M. 1972. *President, Bureaucrats, and Foreign Policy*. Princeton: Princeton University Press. Downs, A. 1966. *Inside Bureaucracy*. Boston: Little, Brown.

C

cabinet government   Essentially this is a British concept. A cabinet is a small group of advisers. The practice of the monarch to select a small group of Privy Councillors who were sympathetic to his policies, began with Charles II (1630–85). They were known as the 'Cabal' and the habit of calling them the 'Cabinet' dates from the eighteenth century. Robert Walpole (1676–1745) is usually regarded as the first PRIME MINISTER and his ministry as the first to be called a Cabinet though neither term was formally recognized, and even then incidentally, until the Ministers of the Crown Act, 1937. Since Walpole, Cabinet members have been chosen by the Prime Minister from among those politicians who support him. With the rise of MASS PARTIES and the domination of the House of Commons by one party, Cabinets have usually been composed of members of that party drawn either from the Commons or the Lords. (Again this is a convention and occasionally outsiders have been chosen.) In two world wars, however, coalition cabinets have been formed.

The classic pattern of cabinet government can only be found in the Commonwealth. In Australia and New Zealand Labour Cabinets are chosen by the votes of the parliamentary parties, though Prime Ministers can dispose of the departments as they see fit. The Canadian Cabinet is much larger than the others: it numbers about forty (because all the provinces have to be conciliated with positions), compared with about twenty to twenty-five elsewhere. Classic cabinet government has the following features: first, the Cabinet is accountable to and dismissible by the lower house. Once defeated it must either give way to another majority government, or seek re-election. Second, the Cabinet has COLLECTIVE RESPONSIBILITY: its members have no public disagreements about policy because decisions have been reached collectively in private. A minister who does not accept a Cabinet decision must resign before opposing it publicly. Thus they stand and fall together: when any cabinet policy is defeated in parliament they all resign. Third, Cabinet proceedings are secret because if the outside world knows which ministers are identified as for or against certain policies they will be open to political pressures from the supporters of those policies.

These archetypal principles have in recent decades undergone two modifications, both the result of the increasing volume and technicality of policy. Cabinets have ceased to be the main arena for national decision-making which has moved both upward and downward in the political hierarchy. All cabinet systems now have an elaborate apparatus of committees and sub-committees, nominated by the Prime Minister and each responsible for some aspect of policy. The appropriate ministers will be members, together with the Prime Minister and usually a Treasury minister. Many decisions are made in this network and the Cabinet's only part is to endorse them, frequently without discussion. The other change is that Prime Ministers' powers have inevitably increased. They always chaired the meetings; but Morley's phrase that a Prime Minister was 'first among equals' (qualified by his other statement that the office was 'the keystone of the Cabinet arch'), is hardly consistent with the power to 'hire and fire' colleagues. In the twentieth century the introduction of business-like methods into Cabinet deliberations, with a secretary to take minutes and draw up agendas, put much more power in Prime Ministerial hands.

These developments caused CROSSMAN and Mackintosh to argue that Britain now had PRIME MINISTERIAL GOVERNMENT, a contention strengthened during the eleven years (1979–90) in which Margaret Thatcher was in power. Critics of Cabinet government generally have argued that it does not allow for either strategic planning of objectives or for decision-making of more technical virtuosity as practised by business corporations. Memoirs of politicians tend to give the impression that cabinet decision-making is dominated by clashes between the main spending departments over the allocation of funding, with the Chancellor of the Exchequer and the Prime Minister making the ultimate and authoritative judgement. In fact, Cabinets have all these functions and many others, including dealing with national emergencies.

Most Cabinets will anyway not belong to the *genus Britannicus*. Most European democracies have COALITION GOVERNMENT. It is difficult for their Cabinets to preserve COLLECTIVE RESPONSIBILITY because the members may belong to several parties. In some cases each may come under great pressure from their party rank-and-file to support policies specific to their party but not acceptable to the coalition partners. Sometimes a sort of treaty embodying compromises between the ministers representing the different parties is beaten out at the formation of the Cabinet. The intention is to provide the kind of stability enjoyed by the classic British model. Yet in the latter a not dissimilar situation arises where the majority party is much divided over important issues and the Cabinet is split between ministers from the factions in conflict. Then collective reponsibility is more difficult to maintain because ministers want to signal to their supporters in Parliament that they are asserting the faction's point of view. They do this through the tactic known as 'leaking' unattributable information passed on to a friendly journalist. In this way they are escaping from some of the responsibility; but collective responsibility is becoming diluted.

The American Presidential Cabinet is not a committee of politicians. It is appointed by the President and usually includes some departmental heads who have been administrators and businessmen. Often there is a member who has not voted for the President's party. When departmental heads first meet they may have had no previous acquaintance with each other. They are not collectively responsible and, although they are individually responsible to the President, they also owe responsibility to Congress which endorses their nomination. To obtain funds they will have to establish friendly relations with the House of Representatives. Cabinet meetings are thus gatherings at which heads of department report occasionally: they are not even decision-endorsing bodies.

Finally a *cabinet* in the French sense is the personal team of a French minister who appoints experts, consultants and people of like mind, including civil servants. They enable a minister to present vigorously and with expertise his/her own ideas for policy against the powerful and entrenched French BUREAUCRACY and the projects of other ministers. Ministerial cabinets are common in other countries and have been suggested for Britain where the practise of appointing advisers from outside the civil service has also grown.

Reading
Crossman, R.H.S. 1975, 1976, 1977. *The Diaries of a Cabinet Minister.* 3 vols. London: Hamilton, Jonathan Cape; Fenno, R.F. 1966. *The President's Cabinet.* Cambridge, Mass.: HUP; French, R. 1980. *How Ottawa Decides.* Toronto: Lorimer; Hennessy, P. 1986. *Cabinet.* Oxford: Blackwell; Jennings, W.I. 1959. *Cabinet Government.* Revised edn. Cambridge: CUP; Mackintosh, J.P. 1977. *The British Cabinet.* 3rd edn. London: Stevens; Weller, P. 1985. *First Among Equals: Prime Ministers in Westminster Systems.* Sydney: Allen and Unwin.

cadre party This term belongs to DUVERGER's typology of political parties. A cadre party is one that depends on groups of local notables to select candidates by informal methods and to prepare for the ensuing election. Thus its basic unit is the CAUCUS. At other times it may be moribund at the local level. Unlike the MASS PARTY it does not recruit members. Thus the cadre party is typical of a situation of the limited franchise and the French Radical Party was its prototype. *See also* MASS PARTIES; POLITICAL PARTIES.

Reading
Duverger, M. 1954. *Political Parties.* London: Methuen; Epstein, L. D. 1980. *Political Parties in Western Democracies.* New Brunswick, NJ: Transaction Books.

caesarism *See* BONAPARTISM.

campaigning The use of this military term to describe the activities preceding ELECTIONS is quite felicitous. The best electoral campaigns are planned and have an army of helpers, usually volunteers. The campaign proceeds at the national level through the party leaders having access to the media. At the local level it is largely conducted by ACTIVISTS and those they recruit for the duration of the exercise. In legislative elections this may be four or five weeks; but American Presidential campaigns continue for nearly the whole of each leap year, admittedly with many breaks.

The size and nature of the CONSTITUENCY clearly affects the type of campaigning. Where Presidents are elected after a popular vote, as in France and the USA, and the whole country is the constituency, CANDIDATES feel they have to tour throughout the provinces. These days they usually fly, though in the past US Presidential candidates made 'whistle-stops' on trains. Constituency campaigning involves identifying supporters through CANVASSING and then on polling day mobilizing them to go to vote. In general elections, when there is usually a high turn-out, this is not too difficult; but in local elections apathy often reigns, especially in those cases where the candidates do not belong to a political party. In rural areas the whole process of vote mobilization is obviously more difficult than in urban.

Campaigning in the last thirty years has been very much affected by television, possessed by almost every voter. It has put an emphasis on campaigns directed from the centre and so on the views and characteristics of the party leaders. They hold press conferences on national television and are questioned by well-known national political commentators. This has detracted from the local campaigns where such features as noisy meetings with 'hecklers' have virtually disappeared.

Reading

Bealey, F.W., J. Blondel, and W.P. McCann. 1965. *Constituency Politics*. London: Faber; Butler, D., H. Penniman and A. Ranney. eds. 1981. *Democracy at the Polls*. Washington, D.C.: American Enterprise Institute; Kavanagh, D. 1995. *Election Campaigning: the New Marketing of Politics*. Oxford: Blackwell.

candidates A candidate is someone who stands in a competitive election. The final presentation of a candidature will be a legal one through the process of NOMINATION. Otherwise it is unusual for the law to stipulate how candidates are selected, though in Germany electoral law makes the parties vehicles for this purpose. Candidates for the Bundestag must be chosen by party members through secret ballots or nominating conferences.

Whether parties are involved or not the first stage of selection is bound to be self-selection: people only stand if they want to and most do not want to. For the very small minority aspiring to represent their fellow citizens independent candidatures are possible in most countries; but especially in national elections it has become almost impossible to be elected on an independent ticket. One requires to be a party member and to have party backing with the support of party organization and party funding.

How parties select candidates varies widely between countries and parties. It largely depends on the ELECTORAL SYSTEM and the size of constituencies. Where there is Proportional Representation and large constituencies it is common for central party organizations to control the party lists and particularly the order of the list which determines the likelihood of a candidate being successful. The most centralized parties in this respect are in Israel where the CONSTITUENCY is the whole country and each party has to compile and order a list equivalent to the total number of deputies in the Knesset. Where there are single-member constituencies, as in Britain, the parties are highly decentralized as regards candidate selection and the local parties are usually quite capable of withstanding pressure from the central party organizations.

In this, as in so many other ways, the USA is exceptional. Every one of the fifty states has its own method; but almost all require the selection of candidates through PRIMARIES. Candidates for each party are chosen by party supporters in these polls. Hence to be returned to any important office in the USA one has to undergo at least two elections.

See also ELECTIONS; ELECTORAL SYSTEMS; PRIMARIES.

Reading

Ranney, A. 1965. *Pathways to Parliament*. London: Macmillan; Rush, M. 1969. *The Selection of Parliamentary Candidates*. London: Nelson.

canvassing Approaching people to ask for their support. In politics it may be done to ask legislators to support a projected bill or to vote for a certain candidate in a party leadership contest. Most commonly, however, the activity is associated with house-to-house enquiries at election times. The purpose of canvassing is to find where the party's supporters can be found and, conversely, who are the voters opposed to the party's candidate. A good canvass will cover the whole of a constituency and is clearly easier to do in urban areas. Canvassers, who are usually volunteers and often ACTIVISTS, are equipped with canvas cards consisting of sections of the electoral register pasted on to cardboard. Efficient canvassers will approach each voter and make the simple enquiry about voting intention. Then each voter should be categorized by marking on the card 'For', 'Against', or 'Doubtful'. If this is done accurately and neatly a picture can be obtained of the locations of likely supporters and on polling day they can be encouraged to go, or sometimes conveyed, to the polling stations. Unfortunately because canvassers are often activists and, therefore, the most extreme enthusiasts, they may spend too much time attempting hopeless door-step conversions and also be too inclined to mark hostile voters as 'doubtful'.

See also ACTIVISTS; CAMPAIGNING; PARTY ORGANIZATION.

Reading
Liberal Party. 1983. 'Knocking on Doors: Why do we do it?' Guide No. 3. Hebden Bridge: Association of Liberal Councillors.

capitalism First used in the mid-nineteenth century this term may describe variously a historical era, a method of industrial production and a form of political economy with social implications. In fact, it is impossible to consider it properly without dealing with all three perceptions.

Capitalism has been seen both as a market and also as a form of institutional organization. The earliest version was that of the classical economists, the model of 'perfect competition' by which in an entirely free market the cheapest possible price would be obtained by allowing entrepreneurs to compete in selling their products. The state should not intervene in the process except to ensure the safety of property and the sanctity of contracts. Freedom to be an entrepreneur and consumer sovereignty are the principles on which this conception of capitalism is based. Adam Smith, who expounded this ideal system, had little sympathy with many businessmen because they preferred setting up price rings to competition. He was attacking the prevailing mercantilist system and arguing for international free trade.

The classical economists had little to say about the implications of entrepreneurship, but they assumed that industrialization would proceed by the growth of small enterprise untramelled by the state. Developments in the mid-nineteenth century gradually changed this situation and 'early capitalism' gave way to 'corporate capitalism'. The rise of the joint stock company and the growth of large nation-wide banks slowly led to the amalgamation of enterprises and tendencies to an oligopolistic economy. Thus 'private enterprise' which had been regarded as synonymous with the free market was no longer so. Capitalism had become a form of organization in which ownership was said to be in the hands of numerous shareholders while control was in the hands of management. Corporations, most conspicuous in America and Germany, were complex institutions which the sociologist Max WEBER argued would become increasingly bureaucratic. He associated bureaucracy with rational organization and believed enterprises would become more efficient as technology and techniques of calculation inevitably advanced. Eventually, with increasing rationality, private enterprise would be as bureaucratic as public enterprise, though this was not necessarily a criticism and Weber did not see capitalism collapsing. Joseph SCHUMPETER, writing twenty years later, believed that the growth of large-scale enterprise would subvert free competition and that capitalism would evolve into SOCIALISM. (A view similar to the Fabian socialists who believed in 'the inevitability of gradualism'.)

Karl MARX asserted that capitalism was the penultimate historical era between FEUDALISM and SOCIALISM. At each stage in human development the crucial factor was the mode of production and the relationships involved with it. The dominating class was the one that owned the important factor of production. Thus in feudal times the land-owners dominated a society based on serfdom. Under the capitalist mode of production capital would be the major factor and the factory owners, the BOURGEOISIE, would dominate their wage labourers, exploiting them and, if necessary, coercing them through their control of the state. Therefore Marx perceived that capitalism was also a structure of power dependent on privately owned enterprise motivated by the profit motive. He prophesied the rise of corporate capitalism whose oppression of the proletariat would become more and more severe. Eventually the workers would revolt and install a socialist society in which the means of production would be publicly owned. This has happened in no industrialized country, but there has been much speculation about how capitalism has changed and how it will develop in the future.

See also BOURGEOISIE; CONVERGENCE THEORY; FEUDALISM; INDUSTRIAL SOCIETY; LABOUR THEORY OF VALUE; MULTI-NATIONALS.

Reading
Bealey, F. W. 1993. 'Capitalism and Democracy'. *European Journal of Political Research*. January, 203–23; Galbraith, J.K. 1967. *The New Industrial State*. Harmondsworth: Penguin; Giddens, A. 1971. *Capitalism and Modern Social Theory*. Cambridge: CUP; Marx, K. [1867] 1975. *Capital: a Critique of Political Economy*. New York: International Publishers; Miliband, R. 1984. *Capitalist Democracy in Britain*. Oxford: OUP; Schumpeter, J.A. [1931] 1976. *Capitalism, Socialism and Democracy*. 5th edn. London: Allen and Unwin; Schonfield, A. 1965. *Modern Capitalism*. Oxford: OUP; Tawney, R.H. 1926. *Religion and the Rise of Capitalism*. London: John Murray; Weber, M. [1920] 1976. *The Protestant Ethic and the Spirit of Capitalism*. 11th edn. London: Allen and Unwin.

carpet-bagger　The origin of this term is in the period after the American Civil War. The victorious North sent people to act as representatives in the Southern states where they were elected largely by black votes. They carried their few effects in large bags. From this experience the expression has come to mean anyone who is not a local candidate who arrives suddenly expecting to be elected. Because most states now have a 'locality rule', restricting candidatures to local people, carpet-bagging in the USA is no longer easy.

caste　A very strict status grouping with boundaries sanctified by custom and, in most cases, religion. Traces of it can be found in Japan; but it is in India that it is most important, sanctioned by the Hindu religion. There are five basic strata with the Brahmins at the top and the 'untouchables' at the bottom. The latter are now known as the Scheduled Castes because of the provisions of the ninth schedule of the Indian constitution which guarantees 22.5 per cent of all government posts, elected places and educational positions to the 'untouchables'. There are numerous sub-castes. They were all organized in a party, the Scheduled Castes Federation. Although, in accordance with the teaching of Mohandas Gandhi, the caste system was officially banned in 1949, it remains a force especially in rural areas.

Reading
Frankel, F. and M.S.A. Rao. 1989, 1990. *Dominance and State Power in Modern India: Decline of a Social Order*. 2 vols. Delhi: Chanakya; Gould, H.A. 1987. *The Hindu Caste System: the Sacralization of a Social Order*. Delhi: Chanakya.

catastrophe theory　A theory borrowed from physics and mathematics relating to sudden, catastrophic change. On the world scene it could apply to the collapse of an EMPIRE. Attempts to use it as an explanatory tool over the last quarter of a century have not yielded significant results.

See also CHAOS THEORY; GAME THEORY.

'catch-all' parties　See AGGREGATIVE PARTIES.

catholic parties   *See*   CHRISTIAN DEMOCRACY.

caucus   A private meeting of a factional or party group. It is American in origin. First used in the eighteenth century it became common during the Jeffersonian Presidencies (1801–9). It has had both a local and a legislative application. Under Jefferson the caucus was the group of Congressmen the President organized to support his policies. Except for a period during the WILSON Administration (1913–21) the legislative caucus has seldom possessed such a permanence or disciplined cohesion. Both Democratic and Republican caucuses, consisting of all the members of each party, meet at the beginning of the session in each chamber in order to nominate candidates for the chairmanships of both houses and of legislative committees. The majority party will naturally win in these contests. Sometimes caucuses may try to reach agreement on party policies; but party discipline is so weak that they are seldom able to do this. Otherwise caucuses may form around various PRESSURE GROUPS. The best known is the Black Caucus consisting of the Afro-American legislators across both parties.

Locally the caucuses are private meetings of small groups of party supporters who choose delegates to their party conventions, or to county conventions who choose the delegates. This is not common because most American states use PRIMARIES for this purpose. Iowa is best known for its local caucuses because they are held at the beginning of the Presidential election year. In Britain the term had a local connotation, describing party organization in the Liberal Party when it became important after the 1867 Reform Act. It was first used to describe the local parties controlled by Joseph Chamberlain (1836–1914) in Birmingham. Hence his organization was known as the 'Birmingham caucus'. As Chamberlain was influential in founding in 1877 the National Liberal Federation, a body to which all the Liberal constituency parties (usually called 'hundreds' at this time) were affiliated, the term was transferred to that body, though it was coined by Tory opponents. Undoubtedly the term was pejorative in the British context where traditionally-minded people perceived it as conveying both the notion of corrupt, back-room dealing and that of vulgar, populistic politics.
See also PRIMARIES.

Reading
Burns, J.M. 1963. *The Deadlock of Democracy.* New York: Prentice Hall; Ostrogorski, M. [1912] 1964. *Democracy and the Organisation of Political Parties.* 2 vols. Chicago: Quadrangle Books; Pelling, H.M. 1956. *America and the British Left.* London: A & C Black.

cell   The basic unit of Communist Parties. First used by Lenin this biological metaphor was supposed to convey the idea of a small, self-enclosed entity capable of infecting the whole body politic. Thus it was ideal for a dedicated body of professional revolutionaries. Later, the cells were rechristened as primary party organizations. There were about 450,000 in the Soviet Union in 1986 containing approximately 19 million party members. Wherever three or more members found themselves for any length of time they were supposed to set up a primary party organization. The bulk of these were in factories because working-class mobilization was the chief concern of the Communist Party of the Soviet Union; but there were others on collective farms and in cultural and recreational associations. In the democracies Communist Parties also have constituency and ward cells because of the need to compete electorally. In Communist countries the cells are supposed to support the APPARATCHIKS, the full-time paid party workers, in their functions of recruitment, exhortation, education, surveillance and arousing consciousness. They must obey the party rules which implies inner-party democracy with criticism and self-criticism and reporting upwards to the strata above them.

See also APPARATCHIK; COMMUNISM.

Reading
Barghoorn, F.C. 1966. *Politics in the USSR*. Boston: Little, Brown; Hill, R.J. and P. Frank. 1987. *The Soviet Communist Party*. 3rd edn. London: Allen and Unwin; Schapiro, L. 1965. *The Government and Politics of the Soviet Union*. London: Hutchinson.

censorship   The control of free expression by suppressing the flow of information and opinion. Reasons for censorship are the need to uphold religion and morals, or the wish to prevent the organization of opposition to political authority. The effect is to strengthen conformity in thought and behaviour.

The term is derived from the Roman censor, a magistrate entrusted with the control of morals. The Roman Catholic church saw itself as the custodian of European morals and this became a more difficult problem after the invention of the printing press. In 1559 it issued the Index of Prohibited Books which by the nineteenth century was quite extensive. Following the Reformation both Protestant and Catholic states adopted some form of censorship against which such figures as Spinoza (1632–77), Milton (1608–74) and Voltaire (1694–1778) inveighed. After the French Revolution there was fear of subversive literature throughout the despotic monarchies and after 1815 the restored reactionary rulers remained terrified of the liberal ideas of the ENLIGHTENMENT which were increasingly disseminated in intellectual circles. Metternich (1773–1859), the Chancellor of the Austro-Hungarian Empire, and the diplomatic leader of the Holy Alliance of reactionary powers, achieved the enactment in 1819 of the Carlsbad Decrees by which, in addition to many oppressive measures, the press came under strict censorship. He persuaded the Russian Czar, the Prussian king and numerous other German princelings to follow suit. In the same year there was a faint echo of this in Britain when among the notorious 'Gag Acts' was a provision putting a heavy tax on radical newspapers.

In the twentieth century the means of communication became much easier with the invention first of broadcasting after 1918 and second of television after 1945. These electronic devices, soon in almost every home, allowed totalitarian regimes to broadcast their doctrines and purposes on a nation-wide scale. On the other hand, radio and television had no respect for borders so that a monopoly of information and opinion-forming could only be maintained by these regimes if they blocked their citizens' access to outside information. So not only were their people subject to punishment if they listened to foreign broadcasts, the broadcasts themselves were jammed. Moreover, all outside literature was banned and travel abroad became very difficult. In spite of these measures, control of information could never be absolute and television was less easy to jam. In the case of Communist East Berlin the reception of West German television was unimpeded.

Not only authoritarian governments censor: nearly all democracies have laws which ban pornography and many condemn blasphemy, though usually only when it is committed against the prevailing religion. Then there is censorship in national emergencies. It is common to censor some news reports during wars. The British D-notice system prevailed during and after World War II. In the last two or three decades there have been campaigns against these restrictions resulting, for example, in the end of the licensing of drama in Britain in 1968, though films and television are still subject to controls. The latest controversy is about restriction of pornography on the Internet.

Reading
Ernst, M.L. and A.U. Schwartz. 1964. *Censorship*. New York: Macmillan; O'Higgins, P. 1972. *Censorship in Britain*. London: Nelson.

central banks Central banks have the vital functions of issuing the national currency and stabilizing it, as far as possible, both domestically and internationally. In order to do this effectively they must help to control INFLATION by controlling the money supply and/or the overall rate of interest. Because the stability of all the national currencies of the developed nations is important for world trade and general prosperity, their central banks tend to co-operate to maintain one another's currencies. Thus if the franc falls on the international exchanges, other developed countries' central banks will buy francs with their own money.

The relationship between governments and their central banks varies considerably and is the subject of much controversy. The German central bank, the Bundesbank, has great autonomy; but it comes under pressure from the government about its policies, especially on interest rates. The US Federal Reserve System has a board of seven governors appointed by the President and endorsed by the Senate. It is, therefore, not as independent as the Bundesbank. Its British counterpart, the Bank of England, was brought under government control in 1946, largely as a result of the unhappy experience of 1925 when it was independent. The Governor, Sir Montague Norman, after Britain returned to the Gold Standard, on his own initiative fixed the pound at too high a level with the dollar, damaging exports, deepening the depression and so being responsible for the 1926 General Strike.

In years of depression arguments in favour of governments controlling central banks may have force. Inflation produces contrary reactions. Much inflation is caused, it is argued, by governments over funding social services and giving benefits to voters, especially in the year before a general election. Moreover, they fail to make necessary unpopular decisions, like raising interest rates, in the same situation for the same reason. This is inevitable in a democracy, but it is not good for economic stability. Consequently decisions of that kind can only be taken by an independent central bank. This argument doubtless convinced the British Labour Government in 1997, when it returned to an independent Bank of England. One might argue, however, that many other types of decision could be considered too technical and too vital to be in the hands of politicians; but the fact that elected representatives make mistakes is not a good reason for taking decisions away from them. Furthermore, bankers and economists also make mistakes.

See also DEFLATION; INFLATION; POLITICAL BUSINESS CYCLE.

Reading
Deane, M. and R. Pringle. 1994. *The Central Banks*. London: Hamish Hamilton; Goodhart, C.A.E. 1989. *Are Central Banks Necessary?* London: LSE Financial Market Group.

centralization As an abstraction this term can refer to structure or to process. With structure one is concerned with the distribution of power between a centre and the outlying parts. This might be a formal or informal distribution. In the modern state formal distribution will be by constitution or statute or, most likely, by both. Such written documents are likely to define what powers central governments and sub-unit governments possess. With centralization as a process one is concerned with the study of the factors which have contributed to the growth of comprehensive and co-ordinated organization. Thus examination of the developments of BUREAUCRACY, administrative and organizational theory and communications would be relevant.

Centralized structure is often associated with unitary states like Britain and France, whereas federal states like the USA are held to be decentralized. Formal structures, however, are not necessarily always a useful indicator of the actual situation. The capacity of the centre to control the constituent parts may depend on the tautness or otherwise of the chain of command. Where transmission of instructions is weak the sub-units may have much AUTONOMY. Or it may depend on finance. Very poor sub-units with great formal AUTONOMY may in reality have little power in relation to a rich centre from which loans are desperately needed.

Centralizing trends since the late nineteenth century have their origins in vastly improved communications, industrialization and urbanization which have produced many social problems, and egalitarian collectivism which believed central governments were most capable of solving the problems. Total war also contributed greatly to the centralizing tendencies.

See also AUTONOMY; CENTRAL-LOCAL RELATIONS; CENTRE-PERIPHERY RELATIONS; DECENTRALIZATION; FEDERAL GOVERNMENT.

Reading
Fesler, J.W. 1949. *Area and Administration.* Alabama: University of Alabama Press; Griffith, J.A.G. 1966. *Central Departments and Local Authorities.* London: Allen and Unwin; Tarrow, S., P.J. Katzenstein and L. Graziano. eds. 1978. *Territorial Politics in Industrial Nations.* London: Praeger.

central–local relations Much of recent discussion of this subject has explored aspects of the relationship between central and local government which go far beyond the formal and institutional dimension. Consequently it is necessary to state at the outset that in unitary countries local governments can usually only have the competence and authority that are allowed them by the central government. For example, in Britain where Parliament is sovereign a majority in Parliament can, if it so wishes, change the whole configuration of local government. It has done this three times in the twentieth century. In federal countries, constitutions and Supreme Courts may prevent the depletion of the defined powers of the sub-units; but the latter – called variously provinces, cantons, Länder, states – will have relationships with their local governments. And it has been ruled by the courts in the USA (Dillon's Rule, 1868) that municipal authorities are 'mere tenants of the legislature' of each state. They may have Home Rule charters but these are no defence against a paramount state legislature that wishes to amend them. Centralization may thus occur at this level.

Central governments have four main concerns. The welfare function of the modern state is very expensive. Consequently they want local government to be as financially efficient as possible. Second, they need local government to be competent in order to deliver public services that cannot be delivered nationally. This especially applies to personal services. Third, there is the problem of how to organize local government structure. Large area authorities may be better for planning transport and industrial location: small areas may be better for running recreational facilities. Fourth, central governments have to decide how much decision-making autonomy they are going to allow to local governments.

Traditionally the last question was the important one. Local democracy was defended in familiar terms by theorists like John Stuart MILL who argued that local politics was the arena in which the ordinary citizen could best participate because the issues were apparent and intelligible. It was a nursery of DEMOCRACY and it was also obviously more practicable for local people to decide on local problems. But Mill wrote before the era of the collectivist state. Many factors made this ideal picture of what British Liberals called 'parish-pump' democracy something of a fantasy. The sprawl of conurbations and internal mobility, increasing the distance between work and home, weakened the feeling of community and also made it difficult to determine who should pay for what services. The emergence of the state as a universal provider, insurance agent, and general manager led to local government losing many of its functions and becoming a delivery agent for central government. In many countries central government action eroded the tax base of local authorities, leaving them with little scope for local initiatives.

Yet there are countries in which the tradition of municipal autonomy is so strong that the central government has allowed local governments to retain their powers to take important initiatives and to tax their citizens to pay for them. This is so in Germany and Switzerland: in the New England states the townships are allowed considerable scope for municipal self-expression. But it is not only the case in federal systems: in the Netherlands a proportion of the national revenues (decided by parliament) is allocated among the local authorities by a committee dominated by them. In such countries there has never been a Treasury, like the British, which claims a right to dispose of all the revenues as it pleases. They have the 'partnership' model of central–local relations.

Elsewhere what is called the 'agency' model predominates. These countries perceive local government as an agent for distributing services. Local government does not have anything important to give to the ethos of regime. It is given few taxing powers. (Even those they have are now restricted in Britain.) Indeed, many important services will be provided, not by the local authorities, but by FIELD SERVICE ADMINISTRATION. It is common for trunk roads or national highways to be dealt with in this way. Strong bureaucracies at the centre bully and nag local officials.

This model has been strengthened by the intrusion of party politics into local politics. The arguments at the local level tend to be the same as at the national level. Where local authorities are controlled by parties different from those in power nationally they could conceivably be a countervailing force; but in practice they may be a target. For example, it is difficult not to believe that the abolition of the Greater London Council by the Thatcher government in 1986 was because it was a Labour stronghold. Another central government tactic is to cut severely the funding to local governments of a different political complexion. They then have to face the unpopularity of restricting services while the central government hopes to escape blame. Democratic accountability clearly suffers from this politicking.

See also DECENTRALIZATION; FIELD SERVICE ADMINSTRATION; INTERGOVERNMENTAL RELATIONS; LOCAL GOVERNMENT REORGANIZATION.

Reading

Allen, H.J.B. 1987. 'Central/Local Relations'. In *Blackwell Encyclopaedia of Political Institutions*. Ed. V. Bogdanor. Oxford: Blackwell; Jones, G.W. ed. 1980. *New Approaches to the Study of Central–Local Government Relations*. Farnborough: Gower/SSRC; Rhodes, R.A.W. 1981. *Control and Power in Central–Local Government Relations*. Farnborough: Gower/SSRC; Zimmermann, J.F. 1983. *State–Local Relations: a Partnership Approach*. New York: Praeger.

centre party   In simple terms a party that has other parties to each side of it. This assumes, however, a one-dimensional spectrum such as left to right. In this instance a centre party would have an ideological stance that accepted parts of both ends of the spectrum: perhaps a party that supported the welfare state, but was opposed to public ownership. Another one-dimensional spectrum would be working-class to upper/upper middle class with the centre party representing the lower-middle class. In fact, few democratic political systems can be analysed as though their parties are extended on one dimension. Most countries are divided by more than one CLEAVAGE.

It is therefore not always possible to divine a party's politics from the fact that it is described as a 'centre party'. Even when parties call themselves 'centre' their position is not apparent from the name. The Zentrum party in imperial Germany was a Catholic party, conservative but not as nationalist as the parties to the right. The Centerpartiet in Sweden was founded in 1910 as the Farmers' Union, principally to protect farmers' interests. Its new name in 1957 was adopted because of the decline of the rural population and therefore the party's need to appeal to a wider section of the electorate. Between 1932 and 1976 when the Social Democrats were always in power the Swedish Centre party sometimes coalesced with them. Since 1976 it has sometimes formed part of right-wing coalitions, but has defected on the issue of nuclear power stations.

Various factors affect the fortunes of centre parties. The German Free Democrats have been out of government for only eight years since 1949, moving easily from coalition with the Social Democrats to coalition with the Christian Democrats. They are needed usually by both left and right because neither can get a majority of seats to allow them to govern.

Conversely, the British FIRST-PAST-THE-POST electoral system nearly always gives one party an overall majority and so the Liberals, the centre party, are not often courted by either Labour or the Conservatives. As the Liberal Democrats (as they are now called) have little hope of governing, the voters are disinclined to vote for them: their support is 'squeezed'. This is the likely fate of centre parties, if Anthony Downs's theory is to be believed. His argument is based on the economic model of duopoly by which two large major firms in a market will move towards one another's positions squeezing out smaller competitors in the middle. This makes many assumptions, the basic one being the doubtful analogy between economic and 'political markets'.

See also LEFT AND RIGHT.

Reading

Downs, A. 1957. *An Economic Theory of Democracy.* New York: Harper Row; Lipset, S.M. and S. Rokkan. eds. 1967. *Party Systems and Voter Alignments: Cross-National Perspectives.* New York: Free Press; Sartori, G. 1976. *Parties and Party Systems: a Framework for Analysis.* Cambridge: CUP.

centre–periphery relations   This perception of a country's politics resembles central–local relations, but the latter is concerned more with institutional and structural elements. The main factors in the study of relations between the centre and the periphery are geographic, economic, cultural, social and psychological. Peripheral attitudes can be a state of mind, a feeling of remoteness from where the decisions are made, where cultural activity is flourishing, where 'all the money has gone' or 'is made' and where national standards and values are sanctioned and authoritatively allocated. Thus the poor deprived areas of a large city may reflect some of these sentiments. Hence the first question for the analyst to ask is 'what and where is a periphery?'

Various answers can be given. In some

countries the peripheral areas may be deserts, in others tundra, in many they are offshore islands or under-populated regions with poor farming. Comparative poverty is likely to be a feature of them all. They are usually far from the national capital which the peripheral people will inevitably hate. If the peripheral areas are inhabited by an ethnic minority these sentiments will be accentuated. Thus typical peripheral areas in Europe are Brittany, the Basque country and what is called the 'Celtic fringe' in Britain. Others without this cultural differentiation are northern Norway, north-west Jutland and Sicily. The elasticity of the concept, however, becomes apparent when one realizes that in each of these areas there is a sort of metropolis incurring resentment. In Scotland the inhabitants of Orkney and Shetland see Edinburgh as the prosperous and remote centre. Nor is peripheral ethnicity always associated with poverty. The Catalans are the most affluent people in Spain.

As a method of analysis centre–periphery relations is helpful in studying the historical development of the NATION-STATE, known as nation-building. Monarchs, courts, judges and skeletal bureaucracies were usually located in metropolises. Authority was stricter and more regular there, whereas in the peripheries of the territory there might have to be occasional forays to collect taxes. Ambitious monarchs sought both to extend their territories and to make their rule less arbitrary. Thus both annexation, brought about by both war and dynastic marriage, and better administration became their aims. France was constructed slowly by movement outward from Paris and Spain similarly from Madrid. In the latter case it involved long wars to drive out the Moors.

Once the borders of territories were defined there remained the task of socializing the people of the new state into a nation, a task that took some centuries and has, in many instances, never been completed. Several instruments were used by the centre in order to integrate the peripheries. The permanent presence of administrators from the centre was one device, used by both the Bourbon kings in France and later by Napoleon with his PREFECT system. A common educational system could be especially helpful in teaching ethnic minorities to speak the centre's language. Finally communications, first transport and then electronic media, completed the integrative process. Yet cultural traditions remained and from the late nineteenth century onwards produced the ethnic reaction. This may be stronger where language is an issue; but even where it is not disintegrative forces may arise in peripheries. Britain and Italy are examples.

See also CENTRAL–LOCAL RELATIONS.

Reading
Bendix, R. 1977. *Nation-Building and Citizenship*. Berkeley: University of California Press; Mény, Y. and V. Wright. eds. 1986. *Centre/Periphery Relations in Western Europe*. London: Allen and Unwin; Rokkan, S. and D.W. Urwin. 1983. *Economy, Territory, Identity: Politics of West European Peripheries*. London: Sage; Tarrow, S. 1977. *Between Center and Periphery: Grassroots Politicians in Italy and France*. New Haven: YUP; Tilly, C. ed. 1975. *The Formation of National States in Western Europe*. Princeton: Princeton University Press.

chaos theory The theory that very slight changes may cause the collapse of very stable equilibriums. Like most theories borrowed from the natural sciences, its applicability to the social sciences is dubious and undemonstrated. It is difficult to think of any illustration from the study of political systems.

See also CATASTROPHE THEORY.

charisma Derived from the Greek word for 'grace', this term has become part of social science vocabulary through the work of Max WEBER. He wrote that employing charisma was one of three ways of legitimating authority – the other two were by traditional methods and by legal/rational procedures. Charisma referred to the extraordinary qualities of an individual ruler which gave him authority at times of stress. Leaders of revolutionary movements, lacking the authority of institutional legitimacy, needed charisma. By its very nature, then, charismatic authority tended to be transitional. After a time charismatic rule would become 'routinized' and lapse into hereditary succession or procedural change of leadership through elections.

Unfortunately the strength of this concept has been sadly depleted since the media appropriated it and used it to mean the attributes of a strong and attractive personality. It is sometimes used to describe film stars.

Reading
Weber, M. [1921] 1968. *Economy and Society.* 3 vols. New York: Bedminster; Willner, A.R. 1984. *The Spellbinders: Charismatic Political Leadership.* London: Collins.

charter A document, issued by some authority, granting rights and privileges. On occasions it may be also a claim for rights and privileges made by those who are deprived of them. In the English-speaking world it has frequently referred to formal instruments giving corporate powers to the governments of municipalities and certain trading bodies. In Britain the universities and the BBC were set up by charter. Other charters have had a wider application. The Magna Carta, 1215, was a statement of baronial rights wrested from the king. Later it was quoted by most opponents of royal rule. The People's Charter was a set of demands made by the disfranchised in a petition to Parliament in the 1840s. The Atlantic Charter, drawn up by Churchill and Roosevelt in 1941, stated eight points on which they based their 'hopes for a better world'. These included 'freedom from fear and want' and international co-operation for prosperity, peace and disarmament. Charter 77 was a signed statement by about 250 Czechoslovak dissidents complaining in 1977 about their deprivation of human rights under Communist rule. Many of them were later the nucleus of the Civic Forum, the body which led the overthrow of Communism.

checks and balances The phrase is especially used in reference to the American Constitution. The two words are always linked, though a balance is presumably where one power is 'checked' by another. It is confusing to try to separate them. The origins of the notion lie in ARISTOTLE's belief that a 'mixed' constitution is best. Montesquieu re-affirmed this with his view that the British constitution was superior because it rested on the SEPARATION OF POWERS.

In the US Constitution the principle was taken to its logical conclusion. The President is Commander-in-Chief, but Congress declares war. The President can check Congress with his veto over legislation: Congress can 'super-check' him by two-thirds of them passing the measure over his veto. The Supreme Court demonstrates the power of the judiciary by sometimes ruling both Presidential actions and Congressional legislation unconstitutional. The President appoints Supreme Court judges for life; but the appointments must be ratified by the Senate. Moreover, the Separation of Powers extends beyond the balancing of executive, legislature and judiciary. The Senate and House of Representatives balance each other. The former has foreign policy powers while the latter has the power of financial initiative.

There is also a territorial division of power in the USA. The federal system ensures that the 50 states in certain fields have powers which are not subordinate to the central government. This thus provides another balance between the power of the centre and the autonomous powers of the states.

See also FEDERAL GOVERNMENT; SEPARATION OF POWERS.

Reading
Hamilton A., J. Madison and J. Jay. [1788] 1964. *The Federalist Papers.* New York: Mentor.

christian democracy   A general current of thought with political implications, eventually manifested in political parties in two continents. It marked the reconciliation between the Roman Catholic hierarchy and DEMOCRACY. The Vatican had been horrified by the French Revolutionaries who confiscated church lands and favoured secular education. The threat of the Italian Risorgimento to the Papal States and the Europe-wide revolution of 1848, in which Garibaldi (1807–82) and Mazzini (1805–72) set up a Roman Republic, terrified Pope Pius IX (1792–1878) who, at one time quite liberal, became extremely reactionary. In 1864 he issued the Syllabus of Current Errors, repudiating freedom of the Press and universal suffrage. In 1870 he proclaimed the doctrine of Papal Infallibility.

Christian Democracy was a movement within the Church reacting to these tendencies. Its first official manifestation was *De Rerum Novarum,* an encyclical issued by Pope Leo XIII (1810–1903) in 1891 which showed favour to Catholics joining various associations including trade unions. The Church condemned the excesses of capitalism, as well as the class conflict recommended by Marxists; but its stance towards democracy remained ambivalent. Italians who voted still faced the threat of excommunication. Moreover, in France most of the Catholic hierarchy were among the anti-Dreyfusards who applauded the unjust

imprisonment of Captain Dreyfus, the first Jew to serve on the French General Staff. Yet among his supporters were Catholics grouped around *Le Sillon,* a journal arguing that the French Catholic church must accept the Republic and relinquish its hope of restoring the monarchy.

After 1918 the Popular Democrats in Italy under Luigi Sturzo (1891–1979), perhaps entitled to be called the 'father' of Christian Democracy, had some electoral success, as did the German Centre Party in the Weimar Republic. But FASCISM in both countries swept them both away. The Vatican, terrified by the threat of atheistic Bolshevism, did not condemn Fascism but Catholics everywhere in Europe became involved in the Resistance to it. From this grew the Christian Democratic parties which governed in Germany and Italy and which shared in government in France, Austria, Belgium and Holland in the post-war period. They also had some following in Latin America and were in power in Chile between 1964 and 1970. It is difficult to place them ideologically. Supported by Christian trade unions they were to the left in their social policies and opposed to free market capitalism. They could be seen as right-wing in their defence of private property and their opposition to anti-clerical secularization. But they bit much more into the voting support of the conservative parties than of the left and eventually became quite conservative. In Italy, plagued by corruption, they disintegrated in 1993.

See also CLERICALISM/ANTI-CLERICALISM.

Reading
Fogarty, M.P. 1957. *Christian Democracy in Western Europe, 1820–1953.* London: Routledge; Irving, R.E.M. 1973. *Christian Democracy in France.* London: Allen and Unwin; Sturzo, L. 1946. *Nationalism and Internationalism.* Chapter 4, 'Christian Democracy'. New York: Roy; Vaussard, M. 1969. *Storia della Democrazia Christiana.* Bologna: Capelli; Yocelevzky, R. 1987. *La*

Democracia cristiana chilena y el gobierno de Eduardo Frei 1964–1970. Mexico City: Universidad Autonoma Metropolitana.

christian socialism   A term which now may be loosely used to describe any socialist who is a Christian: the British Labour Party may be thus characterized because its present leader, Tony Blair, is a Christian. Yet with a capital 'c' and 's' it quite specifically refers to a small but influential movement which existed in Britain in the last quarter of the nineteenth century. The earliest proponents were Charles Kingsley (1819–75), the novelist and Frederick Denison Maurice (1805–72), a theologian. Both were concerned about the condition of the working classes and tried to win their co-operation. The movement was allied to the High Church wing of the Church of England. Stewart Headlam, who in 1877 founded the Guild of St. Matthew, was a socialist who attached importance to the sacraments and to the revolutionary nature of Christ's teaching. He said the Magnificat was 'the Marseillaise of Humanity'. Canon Scott Holland, who in 1889 founded the Christian Social Union to spread reformist ideas within the Church of England, was also active in inaugurating church settlements in the poor areas of large cities. Clement Attlee (1883–1967), later Prime Minister of the post-war Labour Government, was at one time secretary of Toynbee Hall, one of the settlements.

Manifestations of similar trends elsewhere have tended to be Protestant as the Roman Catholic church has not laid stress on grass-roots action or on anti-hierarchical attitudes. But the 'worker-priest' movement and the clerical radicalism of Liberation Theology, particularly evident in Latin America, could be regarded as equivalents.

Reading
Inglis, K.S. 1964. *Churches and the Working Classes in Victorian England.* London: Routledge; Pelling, H.M. 1965. *The Origins of the Labour Party.* 2nd edn. Oxford: Clarendon.

church and state   For the churches this relationship is a religious issue. For states it is a political, even a constitutional, issue. During the Middle Ages the Popes claimed paramountcy over the Holy Roman Emperors – the spiritual power was superior to the temporal. Outside Catholic Europe in the Orthodox countries to the east the Byzantine principle of state power was exemplified by the dominance of the Russian Czar over the hierarchy of the church. By the seventeenth century in Catholic western Europe the alliance between 'the altar and the throne', the ANCIEN REGIME, reflected the Church's practical acceptance of temporal power as a shield of religion. This had been cemented by the Reformation. The Treaty of Westphalia, 1648, at the end of thirty years of religious war, laid down that the religion of any country should be that of its king. In Protestant lands it was common for one of the churches to be the established religion, giving it a certain superior status and socio-political influence that other churches did not possess. Often the adherents of the latter could be found in opposition to this establishment.

On the political plane in modern times the churches have been most concerned with the issue of the schools. The churches have used pressure to secure a place for religious teaching on school curricula. The Roman Catholics in Europe especially have fought political battles for public funding for Catholic schools and this has been the mainstay of the confessional parties. They have never forgiven the French Revolutionaries for installing a completely secular state education system. On the other hand minority religions have often supported secular education, preferring to give their own instruction in Sunday Schools and at home. In general, as society has become more secularized, it has become common

to exclude religion from political discussion. A conventional view is that politicians should not interfere with the churches and the churches should not intervene in politics. There is suspicion of politicians with religious leanings and of clerics who are openly political. In the USA the separation of church and state as well as the principle of religious tolerance is formalized in the First Amendment to the Constitution 1791 beginning, 'Congress shall make no law respecting an establishment of religion, or of prohibiting the free exercise thereof'.
See also ESTABLISHMENT.

Reading
Merkl, P, and N. Smart. eds. 1983. *Religion and Politics in the Modern World*. New York: University of New York Press; Nicholls, D. 1967. *Church and State in Britain since 1820*. London: Routledge; Silvert, K.H. ed. 1967. *Churches and States*. New York: American Universities Field Staff; Sturzo, L. 1939. *Church and State*. New York: Longman; Whyte, J.H., 1980. *Church and State in Modern Ireland, 1923–1979*. 2nd edn. Dublin: Gill and Macmillan.

citizenship   This concept has gradually developed over two hundred years. The debate on it was initiated by ROUSSEAU (1712–78) whose SOCIAL CONTRACT introduced the idea of a citizen who is an autonomous individual who can consent or withhold consent to rulers. This was promulgated in the French Revolutionaries' Declaration of the Rights of Man and Citizen.

Today Marshall's classic typology of the development of citizenship is widely accepted. In the first place there was the recognition that everyone had equality before the law. This was civil citizenship and was protected by the law courts. With it came freedom of the person from arbitrary arrest, free expression of opinion and the right to own property. Secondly came political citizenship reflected in representative institutions. Universal suffrage and the right of every citizen to be a candidate in elections was only accorded in the twentieth century. By that time the third stage, the granting of social citizenship, was under way. This guaranteed enough social and economic welfare for a decent existence and provided the education for a person to have the means of understanding the issues of the day. Schools and social services were the institutions underpinning social citizenship. Full citizenship was therefore possession of certain defined rights.

The obverse of rights are duties which, it is argued, are the responsibilities of citizens in a democracy. There is the duty to obey the law, to pay one's taxes and, perhaps, to participate. If you are given a share in the making of the laws you should also obey them. But people expected to fulfill such duties without rights are not citizens but 'subjects'. Immigrants may well be in this position. Turkish workers in Germany, for example, find it very difficult to obtain German citizenship, even after many years' residence, but they have the same obligation to obey the laws as German citizens.
See also CIVIC CULTURE; CIVIL LIBERTIES.

Reading
Bendix, R. 1977. *Nation-Building and Citizenship*. Berkeley: University of California Press; Marshall, T.H. 1950. *Citizenship, Social Class and Other Essays*. Cambridge: CUP.

city government   The definition of 'city' is problematic. In the USA very small towns may be called cities and the CITY STATE of the ancient Greeks was also relatively tiny. In Europe today the term would usually connote an urban settlement of at least a quarter of a million inhabitants; but this cannot be definitive because many conurbations sprawl far beyond city boundaries. It is not uncommon in such cases for cities to attempt to annex suburbs and satellite towns outside their borders. One might regard capital cities as archetypes; but even this would be misleading. Washington, D.C. is governed by a Congressional committee, though it is now allowed a mayor and London possessed no city government after it was abolished as a local authority by the Thatcher government.

Large city government is, anyway, unavoidably complex. The provision of many services within a limited space is bound to need much specialized administration. In addition most large cities have the problem of the 'inner city' where frequently the most deprived inhabitants live. Ethnic and immigrant populations and many homeless people will also most often be found there. The problems of the inner city and the 'outer city' are linked. Central decay drives the more prosperous inhabitants out of the city and they become commuters, no longer contributing to the city's revenues but using its services and, probably, clogging up its roads twice a day with their cars on their way to and from work.

National economic decline and world recession have in the last two or three decades accentuated these problems. The situation has been called the FISCAL CRISIS of the cities. Central governments have been both prone to erode the tax base of city governments and to restrict resources paid to them from the central exchequer. In Britain the central government has also put a ceiling on the taxing power of all local authorities. Initiatives by the central government to improve the inner cities have weakened city autonomy. The fiscal crisis has left many cities near bankruptcy and their councillors and officials in near despair.

See also LOCAL GOVERNMENT; TAXATION.

Reading
Banfield, E.C. 1965. *Big City Politics*. New York: Random House; Newton, K. 1976. *Second City Politics: Democratic Processes and Decision-Making in Birmingham*. Oxford: OUP; Robson, W.A. and D.E. Regan. eds. 1972. *Great Cities of the World*. London: Allen and Unwin; Sharpe, L.J. ed. 1981. *The Local Fiscal Crisis in Western Europe*. London: Sage; Yates, D. 1978. *The Ungovernable City*. Cambridge, Mass.: MIT Press.

city manager Many American cities are administered by a city manager in consultation with a small council. The intention is to provide a business-like type of government directed by something like the board of a corporation. The city manager takes a pragmatic attitude to urban problems: he is ideology free, divorced from partisan political attitudes. His functions are to recruit staff, co-ordinate activities, handle the accounting and act within guidelines laid down by the elected council.

The city manager, together with non-partisan elections, was a product of the Progressive movement. This was a re-action against the corruption and ethnic conflict of the city and the domination of the BOSSES. The reformers intended to replace the council elected by WARDS with one elected from the whole area of the city; and to replace the boss with a managerial figure who would be honest and community-oriented instead of party-oriented. It would rationalize municipal government. The policy reduced the power of the ethnic groups and, simultaneously, that of the labour movement in American politics. It was essentially 'middle-class' and illustrated that business had a higher status than politics in the USA.

From that it has been argued that city managers are conservative and naturally favour business as against other forms of association in their urban policy-making. Such research as there is has tended to show that while they are conservative, they perceive themselves as administrators. They have a public service ethos and do not see their activities as similar to those of business executives.

See also CITY GOVERNMENT; COUNCIL-MANAGER PLAN; LOCAL GOVERNMENT.

Reading
Adrian, C. 1961. *Governing Urban America*. New York: McGraw-Hill; Hofstadter, R. 1955. *The Age of Reform*. New York: Knopf; Wells, L.M. 1971. 'Social Values and Political Orientations of City Managers: a Survey Report'. In *Community Politics*. Ed. C.M. Bonjean, T.N. Clark and R.L. Lineberry. New York: Free Press.

city state This term is usually associated with the ancient Greek polis which was more of a centre with a surrounding rural area than a city in today's terms. Aristotle collected all their constitutions, all lost later except for that of Athens, though we have brief descriptions of them in his *Politics*. His own polis, Athens, he describes as a DEMOCRACY, though for him this was a degraded form of government in which the poor, ruling in their own interest, threatened property rights. Although before the American and French Revolutions Athens was regarded as the classic democracy, its arrangements hardly conformed to democracy as modern political scientists understand it. Women, slaves and male inhabitants who were not natives or freemen were not enfranchised.

There were European city states in medieval times. The most important was the Venetian Republic. Only Monaco, 200 hectares on the Riviera, with about 7500 citizens, survives today.

Reading
Jones, A.H.M. 1977. *Athenian Democracy*. Oxford: Blackwell; Waley, D.P. 1978. *The Italian City-Republics*. London: Longman.

civic culture A term devised by Gabriel Almond and Sidney Verba to describe a particular kind of POLITICAL CULTURE. It is one of the best, they imply, because individuals are both citizens and subjects. In the former role they believe in participation and are prepared to be active in political life. They have feelings of competence and confidence in their ability to make themselves heard and accomplish change. In the latter they fulfill their obligations to the community and obey the laws emanating from the state. They have habits of trust and belief in the integrity of authority. In their five-nation study the two authors discovered the civic culture had deepest roots in Britain and the USA, while in Germany they were somewhat shallower. Italy had little of the civic culture and Mexico scarcely any.

See also POLITICAL CULTURE.

Reading
Almond, G.A. and S. Verba. 1963. *The Civic Culture*. Princeton: Princeton University Press; Almond, G.A. and S. Verba. 1980. *The Civic Culture Revisited*. Boston: Little, Brown.

civil defence A form of defence that became necessary when war weapons were invented which facilitated attacks on civilian installations and populations. The two weapons feared most were the bombing aeroplane and gas. In the 1930s it became widely accepted that they would be used in the event of a war and lurid scenarios were painted. The British Prime Minister, Stanley Baldwin (1867–1947) said 'the bomber will always get through'. In this apprehensive mood most of the European nations began recruiting a part-time force of volunteers, known in Britain as 'air-raid wardens', to instruct people in their vicinity about precautions to take in the event of air-raids and to assist them if their house was bombed. By late 1938 Britons were being advised about building air-raid shelters and by the autumn of 1939 they had been issued gas masks.

Civil defence against nuclear attack presented a more difficult problem. At first tentative attempts were made to organize civil defence forces, but these were given up in the 1960s as it became clear that there was no real protection against nuclear warheads carried on rockets at enormous speed from enemy territory thousands of miles distant. In addition radiation would become so pervasive that civilian populations could be eventually destroyed by the explosion of their own side's rockets. Many therefore argued that civil defence could even be an encouragement to a 'strike first' policy because it fostered an unjustified feeling of safety. By the 1970s governments began to regard civil defence as necessary only for high government and military personnel who would be accommodated in very deep bunkers. With the end of the COLD WAR in 1990 nuclear attack was much less likely; but if conventional warfare ensues, civil defence may again be appropriate.

Reading
Wigner, E.P. ed. 1969. *Survival and the Bomb: Methods of Civil Defense.* Bloomington: Indiana University Press.

civil disobedience   A policy associated with Mahatma Gandhi (1869–1948) who used it to mobilize Indian people and world opinion against British colonialism. It consists of refusing to obey a certain law while otherwise acting in a non-violent fashion. Gandhi first used it in South Africa to protest against the condition of Asians there; and afterwards in India in the 1930s and 1940s to publicize the iniquity of the tax on salt and, later, the British presence in the subcontinent. The Indian word for non-violent civil disobedience, *satygraha*, passed into general use. It has usually taken the form of obstruction by sitting down in the highway, or outside government offices, the so-called 'sit-ins'. When arrested no violence must be offered to the police. Hence it appeals to pacifists. Demonstrators 'turn the other cheek' by going to gaol if necessary. The tactics have been used by nuclear disarmers, student rebels and civil rights campaigners. In the USA it was familiarized in years of protest against the Vietnam war.

Demonstrators, of course, are not always non-violent; nor are organized breaches of the law always conducted by demonstrations. Since the 1920s in Britain at times 'rent strikes', refusing to pay the rent, have been organized by council-house tenants complaining about rent rises. Although practitioners of civil disobedience claim the high moral ground, it is difficult to argue that in a democracy one has a right to disobey any law that has been made by the elected representatives of the people. Significantly, there is little record of civil disobedience in authoritarian regimes. On the other hand, democratic publics are more likely to be influenced by non-violent than violent campaigns.

Reading
Bedau, H.A. ed. 1991. *Civil Disobedience in Focus.* London: Routledge; Brown, J.H. 1977. *Gandhi and Civil Disobedience.* Cambridge: CUP.

civil liberties   Those liberties relating to free self-expression, free movement and freedom from arbitrary arrest. Although there is not complete agreement about what is included in the concept, by common consent free speech and a free press are civil liberties. So is freedom of assembly, incorporating freedom of worship. These freedoms are those usually associated with DEMOCRACY. Freedom of the person and the right to a fair trial are part of the situation known as the RULE OF LAW. The former is guaranteed, in all legal systems derived from English common law, by the existence of HABEAS CORPUS. This prevents people being detained without a charge. The right to a fair trial is part of the notion of 'due process of law', a phrase taken from the famous Fifth Amendment to the US Constitution, 1791.

It is often contended that these liberties are absolutes which should be safeguarded in a BILL OF RIGHTS. Yet freedom of self-expression cannot be an absolute if the Rule of Law is to be paramount. For example, freedom of the press is curtailed by laws of libel which allow citizens to bring civil suits to prevent untruths about themselves being published. Freedom of speech does not include freedom to incite others to break the law. Freedom of worship allows prayers to the Devil, but not child sacrifice to him. People cannot assemble freely in the middle of the public highway, thus transgressing the traffic laws.

Threats to civil liberties come from two different directions. One is supreme coercive authority – the state in modern times. Governments in general do not favour freedoms of self-expression and assembly which allow opposition to organize against them. In most countries civil liberties are restricted in some way. Even in democracies, a clear minority of states, there is a temptation for governments to use their powers to suppress these freedoms and citizens often have to use the courts and political pressure to protect them. The other source of danger is what John Stuart MILL called the 'tyranny of the majority'. Freedom of speech allows egregious and unpopular minorities to voice their views. Sometimes the majority may become so incensed with what they hear that they try to prevent its expression. Then the forces of LAW AND ORDER should intervene in order to allow it to be said.

See also BILL OF RIGHTS; DEMOCRACY; HABEAS CORPUS.

Reading
Commager, H.S. 1950. *Majority Rule and Minority Rights*. New York: Smith; O'Higgins, P. 1980. *Cases and Materials on Civil Liberties*. London: Sweet and Maxwell; Peele, G. 1986. 'The State and Civil Liberties' in Drucker, H., P. Dunleavy, A. Gamble and G. Peele. *Developments in British Politics 2*. London: Macmillan; Wallington, P. 1984. *Civil Liberties*. Oxford: Martin Robertson.

civil–military relations The term could relate to the mutual relationship between civilians and the ordinary soldiery; but to political scientists it always refers to that between the government and the military hierarchy. (Navies and air forces are special cases.) Relations take various forms dependent on the state of a country's development, POLITICAL CULTURE and institutional structures. Yet whatever the nature of the polity, there are bound to be difficulties because of the contrast between civilian and military situations and modes of thought. Military life is somewhat isolated from the rest of society, giving it considerable *esprit de corps*. It has its own distinctive rituals and a brisk chain-of-command decision-making system. The army's role as defender of the realm against both internal and external threat involves it inevitably in foreign and defence policy making.

The lack of empathy between senior soldiers and civilian politicians may well lead to the former becoming impatient with what they see as the indecision and lack of leadership of the latter. After a COUP D'ÉTAT they may take over and set up a MILITARY REGIME, one of the most common types of political regime. In other types of regime they may find it less easy to assert themselves. In totalitarian states the official IDEOLOGY and PARTY ORGANIZATION maintain the army's obedience to civilian control. In the Red Army, formed after the 1917 Revolution, no one could be an officer without being a member of the Communist Party and each unit had a political commissar attached to ensure party directives were obeyed and ideological purity adhered to. In the Third Reich (1933–45) the German General Staff, inheriting a proud military tradition, was never entirely permeated by the Nazis. The Nazi Party had its own private army, the notorious SS. When the generals became aware that the war was lost they began to conspire against Adolf Hitler (1889–1945) and the Nazi regime.

The classic pattern of civil–military relations is in democracies where the army is ideologically neutral and faithfully serves whatever government is in power. It thus conforms to WEBER's ideal-type civil servant. This does not prevent the military hierarchy influencing the government. Acceptance of civil paramountcy by army officers can only happen when they have internalized democratic values and when they feel that their role is appreciated and their status maintained as it should be. This is only likely to be the case in long-standing democracies and developed political cultures where roles are highly differentiated.

Reading

Bond, G. 1984. *War and Society in Europe, 1870–1970.* London: Fontana; Craig, G.A. 1964. *The Politics of the Prussian Army, 1640–1945.* Oxford: OUP; Finer, S.E. 1976. *Man on Horseback.* 2nd edn. Harmondsworth: Penguin; Huntington, S.P. 1957. *The Soldier and the State.* Cambridge, Mass.: HUP; Janowitz, M. 1964. *The Military in the Political Development of New Nations.* Chicago: University of Chicago Press; Nordlinger, E.A. 1977. *Soldiers in Politics.* Englewood Cliffs: Prentice Hall.

civil rights   *See* CITIZENSHIP.

civil service   The term is derived from British experience and refers to public servants working in departments of central government. Australia, Canada and New Zealand have similar systems. Its features closely approximate to the model of Weberian BUREAUCRACY. People enter the service to undertake a professional career and to serve whatever government is in power. Recruitment of the higher levels is by examination and interview. There are no patronage appointments. After retirement they are entitled to a pension. Senior civil servants are supposed to offer their best advice on policy to ministers, irrespective of their own or the minister's political leanings; but faithfully to carry out the minister's decisions once they have been made. Ministers take the blame for civil servants' actions. Hence civil servants are anonymous, impersonal, detached and loyal. Their reputation is one of honesty, industry, self-effacement and the wisdom acquired from serving different governments for decades. Their employment, however, has recently become more insecure and their names are frequently mentioned in British SELECT COMMITTEES.

Not all bureaucracies are of this kind. For example, the French administrators and those in other European countries, while they possess many of the above features, are more involved with policy, more specialized in specific aspects of it and more openly political. Many American administrators are still appointed by a system of PATRONAGE: as one Presidential administration gives way to another many of the highest and lowest posts are vacated to be filled by nominees of the new President. This practice may produce more forceful policy-making: on the other hand it is obviously open to corruption because many of the appointments are awarded as prizes for political support. The Progressive movement, which made most impact between about 1896 and 1918, campaigned for the replacement of patronage jobs at both state and federal level by a 'civil service system', an obvious reference to the incorruptibility of British administration.

See also BUREAUCRACY; TECHNOCRACY.

Reading

Campbell, C. 1983. *Governments Under Stress: Political Executives and Key Bureaucrats in Washington, London and Ottawa.* Toronto: University of Toronto Press; Chapman, B. 1959. *The Profession of Government.* London: Allen and Unwin; Chapman, R.A. 1984. *Leadership in the British Civil Service.* London: Croom Helm; Dogan, M. ed. 1975. *The Mandarins of Western Europe.* London: Halstead.

civil society A term used to describe associations and other organized bodies which are intermediate between the state and the family. In recent years it has become fashionable, perhaps partly because of some revival of interest in the German philosopher HEGEL (1770–1831) who wrote much about its desirability; but perceived it as a stage of development towards a mature state. A more likely explanation for its recent popularity is that commentators on post-Communist Europe deplored the lack of any freedom from party control there. TOTALITARIANISM cannot allow FREEDOM OF ASSOCIATION. Hence 'civil society' is used more or less as a synonym for PLURALISM. Although it may be an area of organized activity independent of the state, civil society is bound to be liable to state intervention even in democracies. *See also* DEMOCRACY; PLURALISM.

Reading
Hegel, G.W. [1821] 1942. trans. T.M. Knox. *Philosophy of Right*. Oxford: Clarendon.

civil war A period of sustained armed fighting in a country between two groups contending for supreme coercive power. In all the classic examples the matter for dispute was the nature and/or boundaries of the state. Ideological undertones are common. This applies to the English Civil War when the issue was royal or parliamentary dominance, one side espousing Puritanism and the other a monarchy sliding towards Catholicism. The victory of the North in the American Civil War ensured the country did not split into two states, with the South maintaining the 'peculiar institution' of slavery which the North regarded as inhuman and immoral. The Irish Civil War was fought over the Treaty of Westminster, 1921, by which the six counties of Northern Ireland remained part of the United Kingdom, and a new British Dominion, originally known as the Irish Free State, was set up. Because Michael Collins and Arthur Griffith, the Irish negotiators of the treaty, had not achieved a republic and had agreed to swear an oath to the crown, De Valera and his followers would not accept it. The two sides for some months fought a bitter civil war during which Collins was killed. The Spanish Civil War, 1936–9, broke out when the army revolted against all the policies of the Popular Front republican government elected in 1934. Led by General Franco, the soldiers objected to its secular leanings and to its granting of autonomy to Catalonia and the Basque country. Franco stood for a return to rule by the altar and the throne, but he was supported by the Falange, a Spanish version of FASCISM and later German and Italian arms and troops. The Republic stood for modernization and liberal democratic government, but it was supported by the Communist Party and later the Soviet Union.

Civil wars must be distinguished from rebellions which may take place without sustained fighting and from periods of GUERRILLA WARFARE which may often be waged against hostile occupying armies. Yet the distinction can never be sharply drawn. The war against the guerrillas of the Miskito Indians of Guatamala, pursued by the government since the late 1970s, could be called a civil war. Only slightly less appropriate to the category is the armed incursion in the late 1980s of the American-backed Contras in Nicaragua against the democratically elected Sandinista government. Finally, civil war is only known to international law when both sides are recognized by other states.

Reading
Eckstein, H. ed. 1964. *Internal War: Problems and Approaches*. New York: Collier–Macmillan; Ellis, J. 1973. *Armies in Revolution*. London: Croom Helm; Thomas, H. 1961. *The Spanish Civil War*. Harmondsworth: Penguin; Wiiliams, T.D. ed. 1966. *The Irish Struggle 1916–1926*. London: Routledge.

class *See* SOCIAL CLASS.

class conflict Conflict between social classes has been a resonant theme in the late nineteenth and twentieth centuries. It has been more often stressed by social scientists than class co-operation. Much of the concentration on it stems from the ideas of MARX who argued that social change emerged from the class struggle. Thus CAPITALISM developed as the entrepreneurial class overthrew the land-holding ARISTOCRACY, changing feudal society to industrial society. As a result a working-class emerged who in turn would overthrow the entrepreneurial BOURGEOISIE and introduce socialist society. Class conflict would then end: there would be a classless society.

Hence Marx foresaw a gradual simplification of society. Yet what has transpired has been a society of much greater complexity. Class conflicts are no longer struggles between two classes; but between numerous classes or sub-classes. The professional classes resent the wealth of the business managerial class who resent the intellectual preten-sions of the professions. Skilled workers are an object of envy for the unskilled. The long-term unemployed are an 'underclass'. Images of class are often the basis for hostility, though these images may be based as much on status and life-style as on wealth. Again, resentments may be directed against other groups such as immigrants. Working-class soli-darity has been especially weakened by the decline of the iron-steel and mining industries and the rise of modern technology.

Reading
Dahrendorf, R. 1959. *Class and Class Conflict in Industrial Society.* London: Routledge; Korpi, W. 1983. *The Democratic Class Struggle.* London: Routledge; Marx, K. [1850] 1959. 'The Class Struggle in France, 1848–1850'. In *Marx and Engels: Basic Writings on Politics and Philosophy.* Ed. L.S. Feuer. London: Collins.

class consciousness Consciousness of one's class had been noted by earlier writers, including HEGEL; but it was MARX who imputed collective conscious-ness to class. Class, he argued, was based on consciousness of a common relation-ship to the means of production. The peasantry could not possibly have this collective consciousness as their circum-stances made them individualists who were unable to organize. (He could not have been more wrong.) The industrial workers were brought together in facto-ries and so were aware of their common exploitation by the employers. They organized at first for wage bargaining, but later for political action. In Marx's terms they would become a 'class for them-selves'. Ultimately this involved the working class becoming conscious of its role in history. National, and later inter-national, action would be undertaken by the workers who would overthrow capitalism as they discarded their national consciousness and realized their world-wide common interest.

Consciousness of class can exist, however, without having Marxist impli-cations. Answers to survey questions have often revealed a ready acceptance of class membership. This normally coincides with occupational category, though by no means always. In societies with acceler-ating social mobility, owing to increasing educational opportunity, consciousness of class is likely to weaken.

See also COMMUNISM; FALSE CONSCIOUS-NESS; MARXISM; SOCIAL CLASS.

Reading
Gorz, A. ed. 1976. *The Division of Labour.* Harvester: Brighton; Mann, M. 1973. *Consciousness and Action in the Western Working Class.* London: Macmillan.

class parties A political party may call itself a class party when: (1) it claims to represent one social class; (2) it speaks in the language of class ideology; (3) its elec-toral strength is predominantly located in one class; (4) its legislative representation is predominantly located in one class; (5) it wins the votes of the great majority of one class. No democratic political party fulfills all these criteria and few of them have the temerity to claim they do. When Communist Parties were in power they claimed to be the parties of the PROLE-TARIAT; but they did not allow other parties to exist and the composition of their legislative representation was only proletarian when 'workers by brain' were included in the working class. Where large Communist Parties have operated in democracies, principally in France and Italy, they could not fulfil (5) and only partially fulfilled (4). This was because they both had to compete with another party claiming to represent the working class, the Socialist Party.

Socialist parties in democracies have tended to moderate their ideological and class vocabulary because of the need to win power. Thus they have increasingly become AGGREGATIVE rather than articulative PARTIES. For example, even in the period after World War II, when class voting was most common, the British Labour Party had to rely on the fifth of its vote coming from non-manual workers in order to secure a majority. Hence one might say that if there are class parties they are parties with their electoral centre of gravity in one social class. Complete identification of a whole class with a party does not seem credible.

See also COMMUNISM; DEALIGNMENT; SOCIAL CLASS; SOCIALIST PARTIES.

Reading
Abrams, M. 1967. 'Social Class and Politics'. In *Class*. Ed. R. Mabey. London: Anthony Blond; Bonham, J. 1954. *The Middle Class Vote*. London: Faber; Eulau, H. 1962. *Class and Party in the Eisenhower Years*. New York: Free Press; Franklin, M. 1985. *The Decline of Class Voting in Britain*. Oxford: OUP; Robertson, D. 1984. *Class and the British Electorate*. Oxford: Blackwell.

cleavages This concept is important for describing those divisions in society which are wide (or deep) enough to find political expression. They may then be reflected in two ways: in the number of political parties and in the relationships between them. Ultimately the latter is more important for the stability and endurability of a political system. In fact, probably the least stable political system is one with only one cleavage in which the division between the two parties is irreconcilable. Another factor is their relative size. If they are about equal, conflict about the nature and goals of the polity will break it up.

Social cleavages can exist along dimensions of class, race, religion, and language. (Gender also some might add.) The relative significance of these is much debated by social scientists. Marxists would argue that class is the most universal and pervasive: ultimately CAPITALISM will lead to CLASS CONFLICT from which will emerge a victorious working-class, putting an end to conflict of all kinds. Consciousness of other cleavages is FALSE CONSCIOUSNESS; only CLASS CONSCIOUSNESS is the true consciousness. Events in the twentieth century have not given much support to MARX. Ethnic divisions nearly always corresponding to language divisions have often proved deeper cleavages than that of class. But religion may prove to be the worst of all where history and culture are deeply involved. It is the Catholic/Protestant divide that troubles the island of Ireland: both sides speak English. In Bosnia the three sides, Catholic Croats, Orthodox Serbs and Moslems, all speak Serbo-Croat.

The stability of democracies will depend on how much different groups are characterized by SOLIDARITY. Where it is strong instability will be greater and political life more conflictual. Then the way the cleavages are handled by the leaders and ELITES will be important. Its strength may be gauged by the ability of political parties to capture voters who are different from the majority of supporters of the party. Thus in the 1950s British parties were often described as 'class parties'; but one-fifth of the vote of the 'working-class party' came from non-manual workers and and two-fifths of the vote of the 'middle class party' came from manual workers. Since then DE-ALIGNMENT between class and party has increased, signifying that the class cleavage has become shallower. This may partly explain the rise of nationalist parties seeking independence in Scotland and Wales. Contrary to MARX's view ethnic consciousness may have greater depth and resonance than class consciousness.

One theory explaining the stability of many democracies is that of 'cross-cutting cleavages'. The parties in their struggle for power have to appeal to other categories of voters than those comprising their main source of support. They become AGGREGATIVE PARTIES and, as a result, less clearly reflect the aspirations of any particular socio-demographic group. Yet this outcome is likely to be dependent on the ELECTORAL SYSTEM. With Proportional Representation there will be more parties and no party strong enough to form a government on its own. Parties will tend to hold on to their basic support and remain articulative parties. Cleavages are then more likely to be maintained. But where democratic procedures are internalized in cultural values, as in the Netherlands, a religious cleavage for instance may become less divisive as time goes on. See also LEFT AND RIGHT.

Reading

Dahl, R. 1971. *Polyarchy*. New Haven: YUP. Lijphart, A. 1968. *The Politics of Accommodation*. Berkeley: University of California Press; Lorwin, V.R. 1974. 'Segmented Pluralism: Ideological Cleavages and Cohesion in Smaller European Democracies'. In *Consociational Democracy: Political Accommodation in Segmented Societies*. Ed. K. McRae. Toronto: Toronto University Press; Rae, D. W. and M. Taylor. 1970. *The Analysis of Political Cleavages*. New Haven: YUP; Rokkan, S. and E. Allardt. eds. 1970. *Cleavages, Parties and Mass Politics*. New York: Glencoe Free Press.

clericalism/anti-clericalism In general anti-clericalism covers any feeling of protest against established religion, its privileges, its priesthood and its power. In particular, on the continent of Europe it describes the intellectual revolt against the Roman Catholic church, receiving its main initial political impetus from the French Revolution. The revolutionaries took away the church's lands and its privileges, and instituted secular education and a worship of Reason. They also executed the King and inaugurated a Republic based on Liberty, EQUALITY and FRATERNITY. From this time the chief cultural and political division until 1945 in France, and to a lesser extent in the rest of Europe, was between anti-clericals and clericals, the parties supported by the Roman Catholic Church. Among the former grouping could be found Protestants, atheists, Jews (especially after the wrongful imprisonment and persecution of Alfred Dreyfus), freemasons (freemasonry was condemned as a heresy), liberals (often called Radicals), and Marxist socialists who thought religion was 'the opiate of the people'.

The opposition of liberal nationalists to hereditary monarchical rule did not recommend them to the Papacy. Fleeing from Rome in 1848 when Mazzini and Garibaldi set up the Roman Republic, Pope Pius IX (1846–78), formerly a liberal, became a conservative when he returned. In 1864 he issued the Syllabus of Current Errors, repudiating freedom of the press and popular sovereignty. The Pope was temporal ruler of Rome and the Papal States until they were incorporated in the new kingdom of united Italy in 1870. Pius IX then excommunicated the new dynasty, the

House of Savoy, and forbade Catholics from all political activity including voting. In 1872 Bismarck (1815–98) the first Chancellor of the new German Empire and a Protestant, began a struggle with the Catholic Church in Germany, centred in religious instruction in schools, known as the Kulturkampf. It ended in a stalemate. In France the Third Republic, inaugurated in 1870, witnessed a renewal of the struggle culminating in 1905 in the introduction of the lay state. Catholic schools continued but without much state support. The Vichy regime, 1940–4, was the final effort of the clerical/monarchist forces.

The situation changed with the rise of the pagan Nazis and the atheistic Communists. After 1945 the Papacy, realizing that democracy was not an enemy, and wishing to counter the threat of Soviet Communism, supported the Christian Democratic movement. Henceforward only voting Communist was prohibited for Catholics. In the last half of the twentieth century the division between clericalism and anti-clericalism was no longer an important issue in western Europe.

See also CHRISTIAN DEMOCRACY.

Reading
Chadwick, O. 1976. *The Secularisation of the European Mind in the Nineteenth Century.* Cambridge: CUP; Schapiro, J.S. 1967. *Anticlericalism: Conflict between Church and State in France, Italy and Spain.* Princeton: Princeton University Press.

clientelism   A relationship between a bestower of PATRONAGE and a series of supplicants with benefits for both. For the patron the reward will be access to political power. For the 'clients' jobs, government contracts, licences for bars or construction purposes etc. will be the profits. The patron may often be an elected person or a party organizer. Clientelism may be practised at all levels, but it is most common at the local level. In Latin America the patrons are frequently rural notables called *caciques* in Mexico and *patrones* elsewhere. In urban environments, like the large northeast American cities, they are described as BOSSES. Poverty, the absence of a professional bureaucracy and political illiteracy are the main causes of this sort of politics. Affluence is likely to be its destruction.

See also BOSSES; PATRONAGE.

Reading
Clapham, C. ed. 1982. *Private Patronage and Public Power: Political Clientelism in the Modern State.* London: Pinter; Eisenstadt, S.N. and R. Lemarchand. eds. 1981. *Political Clientelism, Patronage and Development.* Beverly Hills: Sage; Schmidt, S.W., J.C. Scott, C.H. Lande and L. Guasti. eds. *Friends, Followers and Factions: a Reader on Political Clientelism.* Berkeley: University of California; Smith, P. 1979. *Political Recruitment in Twentieth Century Mexico.* Princeton: Princeton University Press.

closed shop   An agreement between TRADE UNIONS and an employer by which the latter will only employ members of unions. Often it is linked to an arrangement whereby the employer deducts union subscriptions from wage packets and then hands them over to the unions, thus acting as an agent for them. When there is only one union involved the variant is called a 'union shop'. Some large employers do not object to this practice as negotiating with only one union, speaking for all employees, simplifies bargaining. Small employers and ideological right-wing politicians feel that all closed shops give the unions too much status and power. The closed shop was banned in the USA in 1947 and in Britain in 1988. It has not existed on the continent of Europe.

See also TRADE UNIONS.

Reading
McCarthy, W. E. 1964. *The Closed Shop in Britain.* Oxford: Blackwell; Von Beyme, K. 1980. *Challenge to Power.* London: Sage.

closure A procedure to end debate in a legislature. One way is to move 'next business', another is to move that a vote be taken. In all parliaments restriction on speeches is necessary to permit business to be concluded. Even in the US Senate, the least restricted of chambers, closures have been necessary. In the House of Commons 'guillotines' allow specific timetables for measures; while 'kangaroos' allow the Speaker to select and combine amendments and to reject delaying motions.

Reading
Bradshaw, K. and D. Pring. 1981. *Parliament and Congress*. London: Quartet; Wheare, K.C. 1963. *Legislatures*. Oxford: OUP.

coalition government A government formed from ministers drawn from more than one party. The conventional wisdom is that coalition governments are less stable than one-party governments. Because ministers support different policies disagreement will be much more common: there will be pressures from the BACKBENCHERS and ACTIVISTS of the parties composing the coalition and it will find it difficult to get its legislation passed in the legislature. In these circumstances collective responsibility of the government will not be easy to maintain. All policies will be the result of horse-trading and compromises. Government posts tend to be allocated between the different parties on a proportionate basis. Some coalition governments actually draw up and publish a sort of treaty at the time of their formation. The result may be discontent among the coalition parties' voters who find promises made in the election discarded.

ELECTORAL SYSTEMS often determine PARTY SYSTEMS and are, therefore, the main factor in determining whether a country has a coalition or MAJORITY PARTY GOVERNMENT. Where FIRST-PAST-THE-POST is the method of election, as in Britain and Canada, the system disproportionately allocates the seats to the advantage of the two larger parties, giving one of them an overall majority. Coalitions are only common in wartime and then, known as 'grand coalitions', they are formed from all the parties. With Proportional Representation multi-party governments are extremely likely, though sometimes in Scandinavia Social Democratic governments have ruled on their own with legislative support from another party. Switzerland always has grand coalitions and West Germany had one between 1966 and 1969; but neither of the two large German parties, the Christian Democrats and the Social Democrats, ever acquired a large majority and alternately they coalesced with the small Free Democrats. This was an example of a small centre party possessing pivotal power and reflects the likely situation of the Liberal Democrats if Britain adopted any form of Proportional Representation. After the 1998 election the Social Democrats formed a coalition with the Greens.

It cannot necessarily be assumed that coalitions are inherently unstable. German and Scandinavian coalitions have often lasted for the duration of the legislature. But they are naturally less stable than one-party majorities. The latter, however, are less accountable to the electorate and to Parliament. Conflict is within the government and much less within the legislature which is much less powerful because it is unlikely to overthrow the government. It is much easier to discipline one party than several and backbenchers in one-party dominated parliaments have a great deal less power. *See also* COALITION THEORY; ELECTORAL SYSTEMS; HUNG PARLIAMENT; MAJORITY PARTY GOVERNMENT.

Reading
Bogdanor, V. ed. 1983. *Coalition Government in Western Europe*. London: Heinemann; Browne, E.C. and J. Dreijmanis. eds. 1982. *Government Coalitions in Western Democracies*. New York: Longman; Dodd, L.C. 1976.

Coalitions in Parliamentary Government. Princeton: Princeton University Press.

Theories and Cabinet Formations. Amsterdam: Elsevier.

coalition theory   This is an attempt to predict what sort of coalition will form in which circumstances. It is intended to apply not only to government coalitions but to any form of grouping of different people in an ALLIANCE. Hence it can be applicable to international relations or to human sub-groups. In national politics it can also apply to 'legislative coalitions', alliances formed in parliaments possibly on an ad hoc basis; or to 'electoral coalitions', alliances between parties at election time in SECOND BALLOT or Proportional Representation systems. According to devotees of GAME THEORY, rational actors when making strategic decisions will ally with whichever partner, or partners, gives them the maximum return for least cost. In political terms this might imply the fewer partners one has to attain a 'minimum winning coalition', the fewer bargains and the fewer hostages to fortune. But clearly arithmetical calculations are of no use in politics. Parties are most happy when coalescing with parties nearest to them on the ideological spectrum whose policies are nearest to theirs. Always assuming that a majority coalition will result, left-wing parties will be happier allying themselves with parties immediately to the left or right of them; and right-wing parties similarly. In practice coalition partners of both left and right tend to be nearer the centre, possibly because democratic electorates are invariably nearer the centre.

See also COALITION GOVERNMENT; ELEC-TORAL SYSTEMS; GAME THEORY; SECOND BALLOT.

Reading
Browne, E.C., J. Frendreis and D. Gleiber. 1986. 'The Process of Cabinet Dissolution: an Exponential Model of Duration and Stability in Western Democracies'. *American Journal of Political Science* 30, 628–50; Riker, W.H. 1962. *The Theory of Political Coalitions.* New Haven: YUP; Swaan, A. de. 1973. *Coalition*

coat-tails of President   When American Presidential elections are held, every Leap Year on the first Tuesday after the first Monday in November, the whole of the House of Representatives and one-third of the Senate are also elected. In addition, state and local elections are sometimes held on the same day. Thus voters have many ballots to cast. The US Constitution declares in Art. 1, sect. 4 that the 'manner of holding elections' is a matter for the state concerned. Many states use voting machines which often allow the voter to 'vote the ticket', that is, vote simultaneously for the candidates of one party for every position at once. Even where this is not so they may be on one ballot paper and the Presidency will be at the top. Hence a popular candidate for the Presidency will carry other party candidates for other elective positions with him. 'Getting in on the President's coat-tails' explains why incumbent and aspiring candidates for Congress take an interest in the choice of Presidential candidate for their party.

codetermination   An institutional relationship between employees and employers. It is common in Scandinavia, and is especially famous in Germany where it is known as *mitbestimmung*. The principle is one of workers and/or trade-union representatives serving on executive boards of industrial enterprises with voting rights and in equal numbers with employer representatives. First used in the British occupation zone, in 1951 it was extended to the coal, iron and steel industries and in the following year to all heavy industry. An attempt to broaden the procedure in 1976, to all firms employing more than 2000 workers, occasioned employer opposition. This first resulted in the weakening of the legislation and then in a reference to the Constitutional Court which ruled that workers' representatives could never again be granted equal representation as this was an infringement of the rights of private property. There are, however, works councils with consultative rights for all enterprises employing more than five people.

Recently the principle of codetermination has been incorporated into the Social Chapter of the Treaty on European Union 1991, commonly known as the Maastricht Treaty. The then British government objected most strongly to the principle. In spite of this some British employers have since accepted it for their enterprises.

See also INDUSTRIAL RELATIONS; TRADE UNIONS.

Reading
Markovits, A.S. 1986. *The Politics of the West German Trade Unions*. Cambridge: CUP; Paterson, W.E. and Southern, D. 1991. *Governing Germany*. Oxford: Blackwell.

cohabitation A slang term used to describe the French situation where the President and the majority in Parliament, and consequently the President and Prime Minister and Cabinet, have different political allegiances. When the Fifth Republic was inaugurated in 1958 it was often described as 'De Gaulle's Republic' because the constitution gave the President considerable executive powers, while the legislature was weak. The Prime Minister was to be appointed by the President, though it was difficult to see how anyone without the support of a majority in the legislature could hold the office. While De Gaulle, a dominating personality and national father-figure, remained President and his party received the confidence of the electorate in the legislative elections, no problem arose. Yet the contingency arising from a two-headed executive was always present and could arise because the term of office for the President was seven years, but for the legislature it was only five. In 1986 a right-wing majority was returned and

Mitterrand, the Socialist President, was forced to select Chirac, a Gaullist, for Prime Minister. It happened again in 1993 in similar circumstances. Described as 'cohabitation', the situation was not disastrous for France, though it called for political skill on the part of both offices. *See also* DUAL EXECUTIVE.

cold war The term coined by Walter Lippmann to describe the confrontation between the Soviet and western blocs. Fortunately it never became a 'hot' war; but between 1947 and 1989 much of the world was divided between two armed camps and Europe was divided by what was called an 'Iron Curtain' few travellers were allowed to cross. The cold war can be divided roughly into four periods. From the Berlin crisis in 1948–9 until the early 1970s was what some call the 'First Cold War' in which the worst event was the Cuban Missile crisis of 1962. The second period is that of DÉTENTE beginning in the early 1970s, with its two high peaks of conciliation in the Strategic Arms Limitation Talks (SALT) in 1972 and the Helsinki Accords of 1975. The third phase, what is often called the 'Second Cold War', began with the Russian invasion of Afghanistan in 1979, included the early years of the Reagan and Thatcher administrations, and ended with the accession of Gorbachev in 1985. Finally in the late 1980s Gorbachev implied he would not use the tanks to prevent eastern Europe from going its own way, resulting in the fall of the Berlin Wall and the end of the Cold War.

Halliday describes four sets of interpretations of the Cold War. One perceives it as a continuation of great power rivalry for domination and strategic advantage. Another sees it as a result of tragic misperceptions of motives, leading to the breakdown of the alliance which had won the war against FASCISM and a failure of the powers concerned to extricate themselves from the arms race. A third believes that it was largely promoted by those who stood most to benefit from it, namely generals and arms manufacturers. Finally there are those who believe the souce of the conflict was ideology: the rivalry between CAPITALISM and COMMUNISM, or between DEMOCRACY and TOTALITARIANISM, or both combined. To many people all four factors seem likely to have contributed.

Reading

Halliday, F. 1986. *The Making of the Second Cold War*. London: Verso; LaFeber, W. 1980. *America, Russia and the Cold War*. New York: Wiley.

collective action

Literally any form of action that is not individual action is collective action. Thus the spontaneous behaviour of crowds in a revolutionary situation is indisputably collective. Much of the literature about collective action, however, refers to organized activity in pursuit of a common interest, especially where that interest is the acquisition of a share of a PUBLIC GOOD.

All PRESSURE GROUPS undertake collective action. Shopkeepers' organizations lobby local and national governments to reduce taxes; environmental groups demonstrate to persuade politicians and fellow-citizens of the need for unpolluted water and air; cartels will organize to restrict prices and maintain profits; vigilantes on housing estates are formed to ensure law and order. Yet in all such groups there are likely to be people who are content to allow other members to do the work. They are thus maximizing their benefits by avoiding the cost of time and effort spent in the common activity. Such a person is called a FREE RIDER.

The success of political activity, inevitably a form of collective action, is thus dependent on the number of people willing to forego time and effort, and probably money. Democratic electorates are huge so it is not surprising that some voters insist: 'What difference can one vote make?' If everyone took this position

elections would be aborted and democracy would founder. Yet this has not happened because most voters feel enough about it to expend what is usually the small price in terms of time and trouble incurred by going to the poll.
See also FREE RIDER; PUBLIC GOOD.

Reading

Barry, B. and R. Hardin. eds. 1982. *Rational Man and Irrational Society?* Beverly Hills: Sage. Hardin, R. 1982. *Collective Action*. Baltimore: Johns Hopkins University Press; Olson, M. 1971. *The Logic of Collective Action: Public Goods and the Theory of Groups*. Cambridge, Mass.: HUP.

collective leadership

The term might apply to any form of leadership that was not individually exerted. But the phrase is associated with discussion within the Communist Party of the Soviet Union (CPSU), especially in regard to succession crises. Formally according to the rules of the CPSU collective leadership was the 'supreme principle'. In practice the General Secretary was the dominating figure, beginning after the death of Lenin in 1924 when Stalin, who succeeded him as General Secretary, established an autocratic supremacy, bolstered by a CULT OF PERSONALITY until his death in 1953. There followed three or four years of disputed succession before Khrushchev secured his position as leader in 1957. He was deposed in 1964 when it was agreed that the General Secretary and the Prime Minister should never again be the same person. After a short period in which collective leadership was again proclaimed, Brezhnev became clear leader until his death in 1982. This saga of Soviet leadership over sixty years is often cited as an illustration that a totalitarian regime, whatever rules it adopts, is bound to revert to one-man hegemony.
See also COMMUNISM; TOTALITARIANISM.

Reading

Hough, J.F. 1980. *Soviet Leadership in Transition*. Washington, D.C.: Brookings;

Rush, M. 1965. *Political Succession in the USSR*. New York: Columbia University Press; Schapiro, L. 1970. *The Communist Party of the Soviet Union*. London: Methuen.

collective responsibility This doctrine relates to the decision-making procedures of the British cabinet system. It is separate from the ACCOUNTABILITY or responsibility of the Cabinet to Parliament. Collective responsibility ensures that all members of the Cabinet, as Lord Melbourne when Prime Minister memorably put it, 'tell the same story'. No public statement of any minister should contradict government policy; and every public statement of a minister should express government policy. Since the Attlee Governments (1945–51) the doctrine has been taken to include all members of the government including Parliamentary Private Secretaries, about 100 people all told. The inevitable disagreements about policy, even in one-party government, may be expressed privately; but once the Cabinet has made a decision all members of the government must either abide by it or resign. If they express public disagreement and do not resign they will be dismissed by the PRIME MINISTER.

Problems naturally arise about the exact nature and timing of future government policy. Joynson-Hicks when Home Secretary in the Baldwin Government (1924–9), announced that it had decided to extend the franchise to women under 30. Although the decision had not been made, it was in agreement with general policy and Baldwin decided to accept it as a statement of such and not call on the minister to resign. Ministers often become 'departmentalized': so concerned with their own departments that they neglect decisions relating to others. The proliferation of Cabinet committees and sub-committees whose important decisions, it has been ruled, are binding on government members, make it even more difficult to determine what is happening. As Cabinet meetings frequently do not discuss many committee decisions, a minister whose civil servants are not vigilant enough may find himself faced with an unwelcome *fait accompli*. In such circumstances Heseltine resigned from the Thatcher Government in 1986. Sometimes a minister may declare and proceed to carry out agreed cabinet policy, as Hoare did in 1935 when he negotiated the annexation of part of Ethiopia to the invading Italians. He was then 'thrown to the wolves' and forced to resign when the APPEASEMENT was found to be unpopular in Parliament and the country.

On two occasions in the twentieth century the doctrine has been breached when decisions of vital importance have to be made which split the Cabinet. COALITION GOVERNMENTS find collective responsibility more difficult to observe and in 1932 the MacDonald National Coalition (1931–5) 'agreed to disagree' on the introduction of a tariff. Ministers who objected to the desertion of the principle of Free Trade spoke out publicly. Again in 1975 the Wilson Government (1974–6), deeply divided though not a coalition, agreed that members could publicly take different sides in the campaign on the referendum to decide whether Britain stayed in the European Common Market. These are extreme examples of the pressure on the doctrine which has in recent years become manifest in 'leaks': a device by which ministers in disagreement with Cabinet policy, with the help of journalists, spread the rumour of their position and so hope to avoid responsibility.

See also CABINET GOVERNMENT.

Reading
Birch, A.H. 1986. *The British System of Government*. 7th edn. London: Allen and Unwin; Jennings, W.I. 1951. *Cabinet Government*. Cambridge: CUP; Punnett,

R.M. 1971. *British Government and Politics.* 2nd edn. London: Heinemann.

collective security A system for maintaining peace by an agreement between several nations to resist collectively any AGGRESSION against a single member. The term became familiar in the 1920s because it was embodied in Article X of the Covenant of the League of Nations, under which member states agreed to defend each other's borders against aggression. It was argued that this was a contravention of the idea of neutrality in disputes with which one was not involved and also an inroad into the principle of the sovereignty of states. League enthusiasts contended that any war anywhere involved all states and that all treaties of alliance weakened a state's independence of action. Unfortunately the principle failed the first major test when Japan invaded the Chinese province of Manchuria in 1931. Britain and France, the two most powerful members (Germany, the Soviet Union and the USA were not members), having suffered grievous losses in a long war a little more than a decade earlier, were reluctant to send their armed forces in an intervention on the other side of the world. This was a signal for Italy, Germany and the Soviet Union to commit aggression without fear of restraint between 1931 and 1939.

For a collective security pact to be successful several ingredients are necessary. It must be militarily viable with armed forces at the ready to repel an aggressor. All its members must be prepared to stand by their guarantees of support. A definition of what constitutes aggression must be clear and accepted. These conditions are likely to be found where the threat of war is apparent and the direction from which aggression is likely to come is easily identified. Such circumstances attended the setting up of the North Atlantic Treaty Organization in 1949. By a policy of CONTAINMENT it was able successfully to resist the Warsaw Pact powers and, eventually, to see it disintegrate.

See also AGGRESSION; CONTAINMENT; SANCTIONS.

Reading
Brown, S. 1994. *The Causes and Prevention of War.* 2nd edn. New York: St. Martin's Press. Carey, R. and T. Salmon. 1992. *International Society in the Modern World.* London: St. Martin's Press; Walters, F.P. 1952. *History of the League of Nations.* 2 vols. Oxford: OUP; Zimmern, A. 1936. *The League of Nations and the Rule of Law.* London: Macmillan.

collectivization The Communist policy of virtually abolishing private ownership of farms and amalgamating them in much larger collectively owned enterprises. It is justified by Marx's view that the same productive relations should exist in the countryside as in industry. As he anticipated that the future of the world lay in industrialization, it was logical to 'industrialize', as it were, agriculture by taking advantage of the economies of scale and introducing more technology.

The policy was first applied by Stalin in 1929 by expropriating the peasantry's land, goods and livestock. Large-scale deportations to Siberia cowed considerable resistance exacerbated by the fact that the Revolution only ten years earlier had for the first time given the peasants land. Lenin's New Economic Policy to encourage food production had also resulted in a class of rich peasants known as KULAKS. Collectivization produced a demoralized set of farmworkers, few of whom were members of the Communist Party, who were paid no wages but were forced to subsist on the income from their sales of produce. Many were driven into the towns to become part of a vastly expanded industrial work force. Those left in the countryside faced famine in the early 1930s. A concession to allow them small private plots resulted in the collective farms being more neglected. In 1955 Khrushchev admitted that Russian agricultural production was lower than it had been in 1914. Notwithstanding Russian experiences all the Communist regimes adopted the policy except Poland and Yugoslavia.

See also COMMUNISM.

Reading
Korbonski, A. 1965. *Politics of Socialist Agriculture in Poland 1945–1960*. New York: Columbia University Press; Nolan, P. 1988. *The Political Economy of Collective Farms: an Analysis of China's Post-Mao Rural Reforms*. Boulder: University of Colorado Press; Nove, A. 1969. *An Economic History of the USSR*. Harmondsworth: Penguin.

collectivism This term has been rendered vague as a result of its usage changing over time. With Bakunin a collective was a sort of COMMUNE. In late nineteenth century Britain it referred to measures passed by both Liberal and Conservative governments which afforded protection and conferred benefits on the more under-privileged groups in the population. In the early twentieth century it began to be employed in describing types of public enterprise in such utilities as gas, electricity and water. Hence collectivist policies were interventionist, broadly egalitarian and smacking of CORPORATISM. BEER conceives of a 'collectivist theory of representation' which explains the way in which different strata of British society have their interests satisfied in differing government policies. Some critics such as HAYEK perceive collectivism slipping into SOCIALISM and thence into serfdom.

See also SOCIALISM; WELFARE STATE.

Reading
Beer, S.H. 1965. *Modern British Politics*. London: Faber; Dicey, A.V. [1905] 1962. *Law and Public Opinion in England During the Nineteenth Century*. 2nd edn. London: Macmillan; Hayek, F. 1944. *The Road to Serfdom*. London: Routledge.

colonialism The term is used to describe those situations where one people holds another one in some subject and subordinate position. In this meaning it is more or less synonymous with IMPERIALISM. It can also be employed to indicate a set of values and attitudes which are typical of colonizers. Hechter has argued that the English have colonized the Celtic areas of the British Isles and, indeed, in medieval times in Wales and the fifteenth and sixteenth centuries in Ireland, English small farmers were settled to act as a buffer against the indigenous inhabitants. Before NATIONALISM became a powerful world-wide force after the French Revolution, it was not regarded as strange or wrong that one people should rule another. Under the dynastic ANCIEN REGIME it was common for monarchs not to speak the tongue of their subjects. Once POPULAR SOVEREIGNTY and liberal values were accepted, colonial policies became less respectable. In the twentieth century most of the empires collapsed and with them much of the vocabulary. Thus the term 'colonials', used in Britain to describe Canadians, Australians and New Zealanders, was no longer accepted.

See also COLONY; EMPIRES; IMPERIALISM; NEO-COLONIALISM.

Reading
Hechter, M. 1975. *Internal Colonialism*. London: Routledge.

colony The word is derived from the Latin and described the estates established in external territories by settlers from the Roman Empire. Yet before that the Greek CITY STATES had such settlements, though they were outside the jurisdiction of the homeland. Probably the origin of these early colonies lay in expanding populations and consequent land hunger.

The origins of later colonies included the need to find land to be cultivated. For example, this was one of the reasons for the Italian drive for colonies. In some cases such as Portugal, Holland and Britain the earliest impulses were commercial. The British colonies began with licensed trading companies in India and North America. Great power rivalries in the eighteenth and nineteenth centuries then led to the seizures of much more overseas territory. Other motives were Christian proselytizing, greed and military adventurism. It has been said that the Spanish American Empire was founded for 'gold, God and glory'.

Justifications for colonizing followed later and helped to develop attitudes of COLONIALISM.

Reading
Furnivall, J.S. 1948. *Colonial Policy and Practice*. Cambridge: CUP.

command economy   An economy in which the state attains a very high degree of control over all economic activity. Land and labour are publicly owned and labour strictly controlled. Prices, including the price of labour, are fixed by the state and investment of all kinds, including industrial location, is state-directed. Consumption cannot be so easily controlled: it is not easy to make people buy things, but they can be restricted in their purchases by rationing by quota and price. The rationale for such an economy is usually a Plan.

The classic command economy was that of the Soviet Union where the central planning committee (GOSPLAN) drew up output targets for the Plan. They were allocated to different industrial ministries who passed them on to separate enterprises with instructions about distribution. As the initial drive was that of a dominantly agricultural country attempting rapid industrialization, and investment, by socialist definition, could not be financed by money markets, it could only be obtained from saving on consumption. Hence the work-force was obliged to labour on a low standard of living for a generation to secure the socialist society of the future. Workers were exhorted to work harder, subject to inspection and surveillance, and prevented from forming trade unions and indulging in collective bargaining with the employer-state.

Command economies are bound to be politically organized because so much coercion is involved in their inception. In practice only Communist states have had command economies. Hypothetically a democracy could decide it wanted a command economy, but to date no democratic electorate has voted for anything remotely resembling one. Conversely where a Communist Party has relaxed its control and allowed even a modicum of citizen choice the command economy has begun to show signs of strain. They are bound to suffer from bureaucratic restriction, making innovation and technological advance difficult. The pursuit of production targets leads to inefficiency because managers neglect costs. Fraud also is not uncommon, especially as bad performances can lead to harsh sanctions.

See also CAPITALISM; COMMUNISM; MARKET FORCES; PLANNING.

Reading
Beckwith, B.P. 1949. *The Economic Theory of a Socialist Economy*. Stanford: Stanford University Press; Prybyla, J.S. 1987. *Market and Plan Under Socialism: the Bird in the Cage*. Stanford: Stanford University Press.

commission   A group of people appointed for some special purpose. They may be temporary and ad hoc: they may be permanent and entrusted with some special function. In the former category are the famous British Royal Commissions, bodies of experts selected by the government to look at some problem likely to require legislation. Famous examples have been commissions to investigate the employment of children in factories and the workings of the Poor Law. None were appointed under the Thatcher government because the Prime Minister disliked expertise which could run counter to her own prejudices. Another specific purpose may be where local government has failed and a commission of government administrators is sent to take over. This has been common in the USA where it was first used in Texas when Galveston was partly destroyed in a hurricane. Commission government then became popular though the members, about five or six usually, were elected.

Many permanent commissions have regulatory functions such as, in Britain, the Monopolies and Mergers Commission; and they are more numerous in the USA where two of the most important are the Interstate Commerce Commission, created in 1887, and the Federal Communications Commission. Sometimes they comprise a public enterprise like the British Forestry Commission.
See also COMMITTEES; REGULATION.

Reading
Chapman, R.A. 1973. *The Role of Commissions in Policy Making*. London: Allen and Unwin; Rice, B. R. 1977. *Progressive Cities: the Commission Government Movement in America*. Austin: University of Texas Press.

committees Small groups of people to whom larger groups have delegated powers to make recommendations. Sometimes they may be very powerful, especially where the delegating body, for example a legislature, is very large. In every type of organization committees are important and the government of the modern state could not exist without them. Executives have committees: for instance, British cabinet committees. Legislatures have several types of LEGISLATIVE COMMITTEES. The strategic position of committees may give them power. Thus committees that draw up rules and fix agendas are particularly powerful.
See also CABINET GOVERNMENT; LEGISLATIVE COMMITTEES.

Reading
Wheare, K.C. 1955. *Government by Committee*. Oxford: OUP.

common law Normally used to distinguish the system of law in the English-speaking world from 'civil law' systems which operate in the rest of the world. Unlike the latter, common law systems are uninfluenced by Roman law. They are uncodified and adversarial rather than inquisitorial. English law grew gradually from custom and developed cumulatively by precedent on precedent. Consequently much of it is judge-made and the judges, when unable to find precedents, took into account the principle of equity which has been administered with common law in the ordinary courts since 1875. It is distinct from STATUTE LAW, the laws passed by the legislature. The whole laws of the European Union now have to be considered by the English courts. This will inevitably change the operation of common law in England.
See also STATUTE LAW.

Reading
Milsom, S.F.C. 1981. *Historical Foundations of the Common Law*. London: Butterworth; Stein, P. 1984. *Legal Institutions*. London: Butterworth.

common market The term means more than a CUSTOMS UNION. A group of countries form a common market when they agree to adopt certain similar fiscal policies and to allow the free movement of capital and labour within their borders. It is difficult for them to do this without expecting political implications. This has been the case with the European Union, founded in 1957 as the European Economic Community, the most successful example to date.

Reading
George, S. 1991. *Politics and Policy in the European Union*. Oxford: OUP.

commonwealth A term first used to describe the ideal state in which the PUBLIC GOOD was realized. The Cromwellian state, 1649–60, described itself as the Commonwealth. Thomas HOBBES (1588–1679), the political theorist, wrote of the 'common weal', a situation of stable government and agreed values which citizens would accept and defend. The first journal of the Socialist League, founded by William Morris (1834–96) in 1884, was *Commonweal*. Four of the earliest British American colonies called themselves commonwealths when they became American states. In the case of Massachusetts and Pennsylvania this reflected their Puritan origins.

The term today refers to associations of states. The former British Empire became the Commonwealth after the Statute of Westminster in 1931 declared that the self-governing dominions – Australia, Canada, New Zealand and South Africa – were sovereign under the British Crown. As such, they declared war separately on Germany in 1939. Later members, from India in 1947 onwards, have usually declared themselves REPUBLICS with PRESIDENTS; but they have accepted the British sovereign as 'Head of the Commonwealth'. Hence the Commonwealth is a looser association than it was. Another Commonwealth is that of Independent States, founded in 1991 and including all the former Soviet republics except the Baltic states. It remains to be seen how dominated by Russia the CIS will be.

Reading
Doxey. M.P. 1989. *The Commonwealth Secretariat and the Contemporary Commonwealth*. London: Macmillan; Mandelbaum, M. ed. 1991. *The Rise of Nations in the Soviet Union*. New York: Council on Foreign Relations Press.

communalism This describes the type of society which exists when CLEAVAGES of ethnicity, language and religion divide so deeply that the sub-cultures are institutionalized socially, economically and politically. People undertake their everyday activities without leaving their sub-culture. There will be separate schools for each, and associations such as TRADE UNIONS and POLITICAL PARTIES will reflect the diverse pattern. In western Europe, Northern Ireland, Belgium and Holland have this type of society; but the classic case is India where different sub-cultures live in different quarters of cities. Conflict may sometimes be expressed in communal riots. Parties will form around the different sub-cultures so that Proportional Representation may be the best political solution to the problem; but where the different groups are not territorially separate the New Zealand practice of allowing voters to register on either the Maori or non-Maori voters' roll may be helpful. Where sub-groups are not too disparate in size CONSOCIATIONAL DEMOCRACY may be the answer. *See also* CLEAVAGES; CONSOCIATIONAL DEMOCRACY; PLURAL SOCIETY.

Reading
Levine, S. ed. 1978. *Politics in New Zealand*. Sydney: Allen and Unwin; Lewis, W.A. 1965. *Politics in West Africa*. London: Allen and Unwin; Vorys, K. von. 1975. *Democracy without Consensus: Communalism and Political Stability in Malaysia*. Princeton: Princeton University Press.

commune A term originally used to describe a small group of people of like minds who chose to live together and to share their worldly goods. Some early Christians formed communes. Early anarchists formed communes and the Israeli KIBBUTZ was inspired by such ideas. In recent years in industrialized societies people of radical disposition 'dropped out' to live in communes. ROUSSEAU's unit of PARTICIPATORY DEMOCRACY was that of the small community. The French Revolutionaries, in consequence, called their smallest unit of local government a *commune*. (They number today about 36,000.) Each was intended to mirror the revolutionary purpose of the central republican state. The Paris commune with its revolutionary leaders between 1792 and 1794 intimidated the elected assembly which sat there. A later Paris Commune became a revolutionary body after the Franco-Prussian War ended in French defeat in 1871. With the help of the Prussian troops it was put down by the French government and its leaders executed. Although its most revolutionary achievement was to municipalize the laundries, it was hailed by MARX as the portent of a proletarian revolt that would inaugurate SOCIALISM. The French word for the soldiers of the Commune was *communard*, and this was Anglicized as 'communist'.

See also ANARCHISM; COMMUNISM.

communications All groups have a pattern of interaction that can be described as a communication system. Even in families this is so; but as societies have become very much larger the structure of communications has become more and more important and inevitably more complex. The advance of technology has vastly increased mobility of both people and information and, in effect, made the world a much smaller place.

There have been two periods of great advance in communication technology. Both have had profound social, economic and political effects. The first in the mid-nineteenth century was the construction of the railways and the coincident invention of the telegraph. These facilitated the organization of nation-wide associations such as business CORPORATIONS, PRESSURE GROUPS and POLITICAL PARTIES. They greatly assisted the mobilization of large citizen armies for total war. They encouraged the expansion of markets and the CENTRALIZATION of state administration, leading to a much more complicated society and polity.

The second period of advance in communication technology was in the later twentieth century, when the computer, the microchip and satellite broadcasting enhanced all the effects of the first period. It has accelerated the trend towards the GLOBALIZATION of the market and towards the phenomenon of businesses operating on an international level, the so-called 'transnationals'. It has increased the mobility of finance capital and, to a lesser degree, of labour. Furthermore some would argue that its main outcome has been the extended transmission of a world culture and the advent of an 'information society'. This has changed the pattern of POLITICAL COMMUNICATION. The simple process by which, through a political meeting, a candidate for office presented his proposals and received feedback from the audience, has given way to one in which the mass media and information technology are predominant.

Television became the important channel of communication between political source and political recipient. Yet it is a medium used largely for entertainment. Many adults spend as long watching it as they spend at work and children longer hours than they spend at school. Politicians have to compete with these attractions and have come to employ the methods of the commercial world to convey their messages. The opportunities for presenting detailed proposals are limited. Hence political information is slight in the 'information society'.

See also GLOBALIZATION; MASS MEDIA; POLITICAL COMMUNICATION.

Reading
Deutsch, K. 1963. *The Nerves of Government: Models of Political Communication and Control.* Cambridge, Mass.: MIT Press; Entman, R.M. 1989. *Democracy without Citizens: Media and the Decay of American Politics.* New York: OUP.

communism The term has two meanings. It refers to a theory and also to the political movement, or movements, founded on that theory. More frequently today the theory would be referred to as MARXISM because its tenets are derived from Karl MARX. In the Soviet bloc the theory became Marxism-Leninism because of Lenin's role in the Russian Revolution and his doctrine of the way the Russian Social Democratic Party (as it was then called) should organize and operate. Marx began to describe his ideal post-revolutionary society as Communist after the 1871 Paris Commune, which he admired; but Lenin did not re-name the Russian party the Communist Party of the Soviet Union until 1919.

At the same time it was felt that the post-revolutionary situation did not merit calling the economy a 'communist' one. Under the periods known respectively as 'war communism' and the 'New Economic Policy' much private ownership remained. Hence, at the time of the death of Lenin in 1924, it was described as 'socialism', a stage on the way to communism which had not then been reached. Later under Stalin and his successors both terms were used. It was common after 1945 for Moscow to refer to the 'Socialist countries', meaning the Soviet bloc, North Korea, China (after 1949) and Cuba (after 1959). On the other hand, in the rest of the world they were referred to as the 'Communist countries' and SOCIALISM usually meant SOCIAL DEMOCRACY. The Social Democratic parties were bound to differ greatly from Communist parties. The former had to respond to the democratic political environment in which they appealed for support. Communist parties were organized on Leninist lines with their basic unit the CELL and their principle of DEMOCRATIC CENTRALISM which, in practice, involved strict control from the centre.

See also BOLSHEVIK; MARXISM; SOCIAL DEMOCRACY; SOCIALISM.

Reading
Holmes, L. 1986. *Politics in the Communist World*. Oxford: Clarendon; Morris, L.P. 1972. *Eastern Europe since 1945*. London: Heinemann; Plamenatz, J. 1947. *What is Communism?* London: National News Letter.

communitarianism A belief in and support for the values and procedures of community. Its advocates would perceive smaller groupings as superior to larger. The different dimensions of the term 'community' make it dificult to define. It can mean a locality where relationships are face-to-face. Wider economic and political implications would not enter into this simple, primitive notion of community. Another perception would be of a situation in which all people were of similar culture and genetic stock. Here the idea of community might embrace the NATION-STATE. Sometimes communitarianism is close to COMMUNALISM as with terms like 'the Indian community'. Academics are guilty of using it to decribe a clutch of specialist scholars as with 'the Strategic Studies community'. Those political scientists who espouse the concept believe in AUTONOMY for the small political unit, though Easton uses the term 'political community' to describe what in practice amounts to the electorate.

The differing conceptions of community are reflected in the diverse values claimed for it. The most common ingredient attributed to communitarianism is fraternity, a sense of identity with one's neighbours or fellow-citizens linked with a willingness to share burdens with them. Tönnies in *GEMEINSCHAFT UND GESELLSCHAFT* thought inter-dependence and shared experience characterized communities. Like many other theorists he argued that urban, metropolitan values and experiences were hostile to communitarianism. Others have seen the local community as stifling in its traditionalism and prejudiced against people and ideas from elsewhere. Wright MILLS expressed the feelings of many aspiring rural and small-town young, when he said: 'to stay local is to fail'.

Among practising politicians communitarianism has taken practical form with such examples as those British Liberal Democrats who advocate 'community politics', attention to local politics at the most detailed level such as the state of the pavements and council-block lifts; and the enthusiasts for the War on Poverty of President Johnson (1908–73) and their support for the 'maximum feasible participation' of the poor in operating the community action programme. More recently the European Community's adoption of the principle of SUBSIDIARITY has prompted campaigns for local autonomy.

See also AUTONOMY; COMMUNALISM; SUBSIDIARITY.

Reading
Etzioni, A. 1994. *The Spirit of the Community*. London: Simon and Schuster; Frankenburg, R. 1966. *Communities in Britain*. Harmondsworth: Penguin; Moynihan, D.P. 1969. *Maximum Feasible Misunderstanding*. New York: Free Press; Sandel, M. 1982. *Liberalism and the Limits of Justice*. Cambridge: CUP; Yates, D. 1973. *Neighbourhood Democracy*. Lexington: D.C. Heath.

community politics *See* COMMUNITARIANISM.

community power The study of communities began as a sociological enterprise and was somewhat in the tradition of anthropological research. It was usual to study small towns and those close to universities were especially likely to be targets. In the USA early works were about Morriston, Illinois (Middletown) and Muncie, Indiana (Jonesville). In Britain Banbury in Oxfordshire was the location of a pioneer study. Inevitably the authors could not avoid discussion of the local politics and political scientists were not slow to follow. Again their earliest efforts were in the USA: two of the first studies were of Atlanta, Georgia and New Haven, Connecticut, both large cities. In the former Floyd Hunter dis-

covered a ruling elite and from that assumed that all power in the USA was similarly oriented; while in the latter Robert DAHL found that PLURALISM was the guiding principle.

All community power studies are necessarily case studies and it was absurd to attempt to construct a general theory of power in the state from a few examples which naturally demonstrated differing historical, cultural and institutional contexts. Yet this is what happened, inexcusably because Dahl had examined the changing power structure of New Haven from its beginnings. Moreover, the small area of study involved in each case should have permitted exhaustive treatment. Community studies are *par excellence* inter-disciplinary studies and if undertaken in this manner can illuminate many aspects of political life, such as attitudes to active political participation, the links between religion and politics, and political change caused by extensions of the voting right or industrialization. Many of the assumptions about local politics have had to be discarded as a result of them.

See also URBAN POLITICS.

Reading
Bealey, F.W. and J. Sewel. 1981. *The Politics of Independence: the Study of a Scottish Town*. Aberdeen: Aberdeen University Press; Dahl, R.A. 1964. *Who Governs?* New Haven: YUP; Hunter, F. 1953. *Community Power Structure*. Chapel Hill: University of North Carolina Press; Lynd, R.S. and H.M. Lynd. 1929. *Middletown*. New York: Harcourt Brace.; Stacey, M. 1960. *Tradition and Change: a Study of Banbury*. Oxford: OUP; Warner, W.L. 1949. *Democracy in Jonesville*. New York: Harper.

comparative politics Sometimes the term used is 'comparative government' or 'comparative political systems'. They all indicate that comparative method is a common way of learning and teaching political science. One learns by comparing entities that have some similarities and then examining the reasons for the observed differences.

The earliest practitioner was ARISTOTLE who used his students to collect details of the institutions and procedures of 158 Greek CITY STATES (unfortunately now lost). From this data he drew up his famous typology of political systems. Later exponents included DE TOCQUEVILLE, who, sometimes explicitly and at other times implicitly, in writing about the USA was comparing it with his native France. Much of his brilliant generalization was based on travel and observation. BRYCE and LOWELL early in the twentieth century pursued similar methods, though examining in depth several countries and going beyond their constitutional frameworks to study their parties.

'Comparative political institutions' is frequently a component of undergraduate Political Science syllabuses and consists, at the most formal level, of comparing between different states the trinity of 'powers' – executive, legislative and judicial – which constitutional lawyers take to be the dimensions of a country's political system. While understanding cannot be complete without undertaking this exercise, it does not always produce a realistic assessment of either the functioning or the power structure of a modern state. To cite only one instance; judges can make laws and executives often draft them and secure their passage with only the most perfunctory reference to the legislature.

More ambitious political scientists have extended comparative treatment to political parties, PRESSURE GROUPS, CENTRE–PERIPHERY RELATIONS and PO-LITICAL DEVELOPMENT. The success attending such analyses is often dependent on the possibility for reliable quantification. Thus comparative studies of ELECTORAL SYSTEMS may produce fairly reliable predictive models. On the other hand, attempts to draw up 'demo-cratic indices' in order to predict which developing countries are likely to evolve into sustainable democracies may fall back on trying to devise indices of tolerance or trust. Values are not easily quantifiable. These difficulties, however, do not detract from the great enlightenment for political scientists that has been derived by comparative method.

Reading
Bryce, J. 1921. *Modern Democracies*. 2 vols. London: Macmillan; Hague, R. and M. Harrop. 1982. *Comparative Government: an Introduction*. London: Macmillan; Heckscher, G. 1957. *A Study of Comparative Government and Politics*. London: Allen and Unwin; Lichbach, M.I. and A.S. Zuckerman. 1997. *Comparative Politics*. Cambridge: CUP; Mayer, L.C. 1972. *Comparative Political Inquiry*. Homewood, Ill.: Dorsey; Russett, B. 1964. *World Handbook of Political and Social Indicators*. New Haven: YUP.

competitive party systems

All democratic PARTY SYSTEMS are competitive. Yet some are more competitive than others. Two criteria of competitiveness might be advanced. One relates to the number of parties: the other to the degree of alternation of incumbency. Where there were only two parties of any size and one of them was nearly always in office it would be fair to say the system was not very competitive. This situation would characterize Britain between 1970 and 1997. Where there were many parties and no party, or coalition of parties, was in power for long it might be described as a very competitive political system. Finland and Israel are, perhaps, the nearest to this position.

See also PARTY SYSTEMS.

Reading
Beyme, K. von. 1985. *Political Parties in Western Democracies*. New York: St. Martin's Press.

compulsory voting

For some time the law in Australia and Belgium has made it compulsory to vote in elections. People who abstain pay a small fine if they have no good excuse. In spite of this, turnouts are only about 90 per cent, though this is approximately 15 per cent higher than the average turnout in other democracies. It is thought the effects of compulsory voting are: first, ignorant and apathetic voters tend to put their crosses at the top of the ballot paper, increasing the advantage of candidates whose names begin with initials early in the alphabet; second, parties of the left whose supporters are rather less keen may gain slightly; and third, party organizations can be more relaxed about getting their voters to the poll. Its effects can be measured by experience in the Netherlands where average turnout was 94.7 per cent before compulsory voting ended in 1971. Since then it has been 83.7 per cent.

See also ABSTENTION; TURNOUT.

Reading
Crewe, I. 1981. 'Electoral Participation'. In *Democracy at the Polls*. Ed. D. Butler, H.R. Penniman and A. Ranney. Washington, D.C.: American Enterprise Institute; Finer, H. 1950. 'Compulsory Voting' in *The Theory and Practice of Modern Government*. London: Methuen. 568ff.

concentration camps A term first used during the latter part of the Boer War (1899–1902) to describe camps in which rural Afrikaner civilians were concentrated. This was to prevent them giving assistance to the Boer commandos, the guerrilla groups which were so effective in prolonging the war. When epidemics caused some deaths in the camps there was an outcry amongst British 'pro-Boers'. Later totalitarian regimes have used such camps to imprison their opponents. Often they have been a source of slave or very cheap labour. From 1922 onwards they existed in the Soviet Union and under Stalin their numbers swelled to many millions as peasants who opposed collectivization, Baptists, intellectuals, and the victims of the 1930s purges were incarcerated in

them. Many prisoners died. Communist China has similar camps. The Nazi concentration camps were set up early in the Third Reich to imprison political opponents. Later camps – Auschwitz, Majdanek, Sobibor, Treblinka, to name a few – specialized in extermination and in the later stages of World War II (1939–45) did little else. Political opponents, Jehovah's Witnesses, homosexuals, gypsies and Jews were the bulk of the inmates and from 1943 onwards there was a systematic policy of gassing them. Six million Jews were exterminated in the Holocaust.

See also ANTI-SEMITISM; NATIONAL SOCIALISM; TOTALITARIANISM.

Reading
Gilbert, M.J. 1986. *The Holocaust*. London: Collins; Hoess, R. 1959. *Commandant of Auschwitz*. London: Weidenfeld; Levi, P. 1987. *This is a Man*. London: Abacus; Solzhenitsyn, A. 3 vols. 1974, 1976, 1978. *The Gulag Archipelago*. London: Fontana.

concurrent majority A procedure by which all interests involved in a decision must agree with it. It is always associated with John C. Calhoun (1782–1850), the chief defender of the Southern states in the controversy over slavery during the years before the American Civil War. He feared the South would be out-voted and proposed a scheme for, in effect, dividing the USA into two regions in each of which there would be a President. Each President would be able to veto the decisions of the other. It was really a recipe for stalemate and eventual separation.

The term is not used today, though the principle applies in certain CONFEDERATIONS. For example, in the European Community's decision-making, in some instances unanimity is required. Other formulas for overcoming the difficulties of making decisions in societies divided by sectional CLEAVAGES include CONSOCIATIONAL DEMOCRACY.

See also CONFEDERATIONS.

Reading
Calhoun, J.C. [1851] 1968. *A Discourse on the Constitutional Government of the United States.* New York: Russell.

condominium A system of joint rule. It is very uncommon; but Andorra, a tiny state in the Pyrenees, has two rulers, the French President and the Spanish bishop of Urgel. The New Hebrides in the Pacific, now the independent state of Vanuatu, were administered jointly by Britain and France between 1906 and 1980.

confederations Sometimes called confederacies, these are groups of states with common purposes, usually defensive or economic, allied by a treaty. In time they may transform themselves into 'federations', one state with FEDERAL GOVERNMENT. Two prominent examples of this are the United States and Switzerland. The former began as the Continental Congress, a confederation of revolting British colonies which had declared independence from the home country in 1776. They issued their own currency and raised an army; but after defeating the British with the help of France in 1780 found agreeing on policy difficult. In 1787, therefore, they became a federation, the United States of America.

In ordinary parlance, though not in political science terminology, confederations and federations are often confused. One reason may be that Switzerland, a federation since the fourteenth century, is formally titled the *Confédération Suisse.* There may be tendency for a confederation to adopt FEDERAL GOVERNMENT. At present the European Union is a confederation; but there is much discussion about whether it should become a federation. On the other hand, the North Atlantic Treaty Organization (NATO) is a confederation that is never likely to be a federation.

See also FEDERAL GOVERNMENT; SUPRANATIONAL GOVERNMENT.

Reading
Action Committee for the United States of Europe. 1969. *Statements and Declarations, 1955–67.* London: PEP; Forsyth, M. 1981. *Unions of States: the Theory and Practice of Confederation.* New York: Holmes and Meier; Spaak, P-H. 1959. *Why NATO?* Harmondsworth: Penguin.

conferences A rather elastic term which may be used for meetings of fairly short duration and moderate size. Some so-called conferences may be little more than committees. Usually, however, it applies to rather structured meetings to which REPRESENTATIVES or DELEGATES are appointed, with detailed agendas and clear purposes. They may last some days. POLITICAL PARTIES commonly hold annual conferences at which party policy is discussed by representatives drawn from across the country. In the USA, where they are often called 'conventions', they are frequently concerned with nominating candidates for elections. Such gatherings are often televised.

Reading
Crotty, W. and J. Jackson III. 1985. *Presidential Primaries and Nominations.* Washington, D.C.: CQ Press; Minkin, L. 1978. *The Labour Party Conference.* Manchester: Manchester University Press.

confessional parties *See* CLERICALISM/ANTI-CLERICALISM.

conflict Political science is much concerned with conflict: indeed, without conflict it would not exist because politics would not be necessary. Conflict not only relates to physical interaction; but also to any form of disagreement about ends to be pursued. Traditionally conflict was viewed as an aberration because it was believed that the natural state of man was harmony with other men. This was the belief of ARISTOTLE and it was consecrated by the Catholic Church as the true Christian position. Until the eighteenth century this remained the generally accepted position, challenged by only a few mavericks suspected of atheism, such as MACHIAVELLI and HOBBES.

The modern perspective sees conflict in personal and social relations as natural. The role of DIPLOMACY, at all levels, is to limit the damage it can cause. MARX believed that the whole of history had been a story of CLASS CONFLICT. Before it ended there would be revolutions and wars. Other writers have seen the family as a battleground. It is now agreed by most social scientists that society consists of groups competing for wealth, status and power. Politicians have offered different ways of resolving conflict. Authoritarians favour the strong autocratic leader who bangs people's heads together. Democrats advocate discussion, conciliation and compromise. As Winston Churchill (1874–1965) said: 'Jaw-jaw is better than war-war'.
See also CLASS CONFLICT; CONSENSUS.

Reading
Dahrendorf, R. 1959. *Class and Class Conflict in Industrial Society*. London: Routledge.

congress   It has a very similar meaning to CONFERENCE, although the implication is of a somewhat more grand gathering. For example, the Congress of Vienna, 1815, which settled the boundaries and terms of post-Napoleonic Europe, met for some weeks and was memorable for its display of finery. Following it, the 'Congress system' was an arrangement for periodic meetings of the Chancelleries of Europe to ensure the settlement was maintained. The Continental Congress was a gathering of representatives of the revolting British colonies in North America. When the US Constitution was drawn up in 1787 the bicameral legislature was called Congress. The Indian National Congress, founded in 1885, was a political party pressing for Indian independence. Achieving this in 1947, it became the largest party in the Indian Parliament. Hence the word has a rather broad usage.

Reading
Jones, C.O. 1982. *The United States Congress*. Homewood: Dorsey Press.

consensus   An agreement about basics which can take two forms: agreement about objectives to be pursued and agreement about procedures to be used. Consensus about procedures, such as how one government succeeds another, is held to be basic to DEMOCRACY. Consensus about objectives is not. Sometimes there is general agreement about what is practical and desirable: at other times political life is a scene of CONFLICT. For example, it is often observed that in many countries between 1945 and approximately 1970 there was a consensus about the need to maintain Keynesian economic management, the WELFARE STATE and full employment. This disintegrated in 1973 and until the 1990s dissensus reigned. Then there were signs of a re-establishment of another consensus.
See also CLASS CONFLICT; CONFLICT.

Reading
Christoph, J.B. 1965. 'Consensus and Cleavage in British Political Ideology'. *American Political Science Review* 59. September, 629–47; Lane, R.E. 1965. 'The Politics of Consensus in an Age of Affluence'. *American Political Science Review* 59. December, 874–95; McClosky, H.S. 1964. 'Consensus and Ideology in American Politics'. *American Political Science Review* 58, 361–82; Partridge, P.H. 1971. *Consent and Consensus*. London: Pall Mall Press.

consent   In political philosophers' writings this term is associated with the theory of POLITICAL OBLIGATION which attempted to answer the question 'Why should the government be obeyed?' This became more pressing after the belief in the Divine Right of Kings – they should be obeyed because they were appointed by God – began to collapse in the seventeenth century. John LOCKE, regarded as the philosopher of the English Revolution of 1688, advanced the theory that there was a contract between the authorities and the citizens which laid down obligations for both. The citizens should obey as long as the ruler fulfilled his side of the bargain; but they had the right to revolt if he did not. Locke seemed to be aware of the lack of historical evidence to support the contract theory and also of the difficulty of interpreting the exact nature of consent. Most of us do not consent to belong to our particular state. We do not consent to it when we come of age. We have not consented to our political system. Therefore he devised the notion of 'tacit consent': we agree to it by not dissenting from it or, at least, not revolting against it. Later democratic theorists have pointed out that even when we dissent from policies – as many of us will have done by not voting for the government in power – we have consented to the procedures by which the government was chosen which includes the right to express dissent.

See also CONFLICT; CONSENSUS; DEMOCRACY; SOCIAL CONTRACT.

Reading
Dahl, R.A. 1956. *A Preface to Democratic Theory*. Chicago: University of Chicago Press.
Locke, J. [1689] 1970. ed. P. Laslett. *Two Treatises on Civil Government*. Cambridge: CUP.

conservation This term can be applied to any attempt to conserve environments; but in political vocabularies it has usually been reserved for endangered flora and fauna, rural resources and the countryside generally. It dates from the Presidency of Theodore Roosevelt (1901–9) who, in 1908, appointed a Conservation Commission which was especially active in re-afforestation in north-western USA. Hence conservation has come to mean adaptation and not merely the retention of the status quo. In all the industrialized states it has become one of the key-words of the environmental movement. Urban conservation has stood for the protection of civic amenities against pollution, private and public developers and the motor car.

See also ECOLOGICAL POLITICS.

conservatism Like LIBERALISM and SOCIALISM, conservatism is a 'family of concepts'. Some would describe it as an IDEOLOGY, but in reality it is a denial of ideology. Conservatives are pragmatic. It is not a doctrine but a 'disposition' says OAKESHOTT.

Conservative values include a desire for STABILITY and a predisposition against change because its implications can never be predicted. When change is inevitable, or has already taken place, conservatives will attempt to moderate it and to adjust to the changes with minimum disturbance. REVOLUTIONS are anathema. Conservatives value AUTHORITY and LAW AND ORDER: they put a premium on the security of property and the maintenance of the forces safeguarding it. Authority should be respected. Good leadership is vital.

PATRIOTISM is another conservative value. It is bound up with love of what is familiar, including family and locality. This has nothing to do with reason. Love of country is similar to love of family and we should feel a similar sense of responsibility towards both. This involves paying taxes and taking up arms. We should defend our country because we value its culture and traditions transmitted from generation to generation. They are bound up with what Oakeshott calls 'the voice of poetry in the conversation of mankind'. Conservatives do not value rationalism in the way that liberals and socialists do.

Conservatives may be divided into three categories – reactionary, moderate and radical – depending on their attitudes to change. It could be said that re-actionary conservatives have never recovered from the French Revolution and its political consequences. The philosopher of the restored monarchs' counter-revolution after 1815 was De Maistre (1753–1851) who believed that a nation 'should be surrounded by dogmas from the cradle' and that the executioner was the symbolic defender of Church and State. The European Revolutions of 1848 resuscitated alarm in reactionary circles. The Catholic European countries were much affected by this attitude, especially France and Italy where the secularizing policies of the anti-clerical republican, left-wing parties were perceived as heretical and imperilling the fabric of society. In France the rift led to the Vichy regime (1940–4) and in Italy helped to fuel Fascist sentiments.

Most conservatives are moderate conservatives. Their most important spokesman is still Edmund BURKE (1729–1807) who believed that Britons were free because the law guaranteed their traditional rights. Consequently he defended the revolting American colonists, declaring that they were only claiming to be treated 'according to English ideas and on English principles'. He supported their Declaration of Independence. Yet he condemned the French revolutionaries for their abstract assertions of reason and EQUALITY and he was horrified by their contempt for tra-dition, taken to extremes by their execution of aristocrats and the royal family. Views not very different from Burke's were expressed by the Founding Fathers of the American Revolution. In the Federalist papers written in 1787–8 Alexander Hamilton condemned 'the tyranny of Jacobinism' which 'confounds and levels everything'. The American constitution of 1787 owed little to the concept of POPULAR SOVEREIGNTY. It was, and has remained, an essentially Burkean achievement. Significantly,

moderate conservatism has been typical of the English-speaking world and Scandinavia, all Protestant countries. Conservative acceptance of democracy in Catholic countries had to wait until the rise of FASCISM and COMMUNISM in the mid-nineteenth century and the realiza-tion of the Papacy that alliance with liberals was necessary.

Radical or neo-conservatism, or the conservatism of the New Right, is largely a phenomenon of the decades since the 1960s. It is a reaction against the con-servatism of the period 1930–70 because it was too interventionist, accepting the welfare state and consequent high taxes, public ownership of utilities and Keynesian management of the economy with policy negotiated between business, labour and government. Probably the two most formative influences on the radical conservatives were both economists. Frederick HAYEK argued that economic decision-making was too complex for governments. Interference with the deli-cate mechanism of the market would result in inefficiency and higher prices for consumers. Milton Friedman, famous for his phrase that there was 'no such thing as a free lunch', made an attack on Keynesian economics which he held chiefly to blame for high inflation. A return to orthodox economics was required with control of the money supply as the only form of intervention. A moral dimension to radical conservatism was added by Michael Novak who argued that economic choice and initiative followed directly from Christian teach-ing. A moral crisis had overtaken the democracies and authority could only be asserted by challenging the 'adversary culture' of the new class of professional experts.

There is little in common between the three strands of conservatism. Moderate conservatives such as Oakeshott condemned the infection of rationalism expressed, for example, in the 'ideology' of Hayek.

Reading
Bealey, F.W. 1999. 'Conservatism'. In Bealey, F.W., R.A. Chapman and M. Sheehan. *Elements in Political Science.* Edinburgh: Edinburgh University Press; Hayek, F. 1988. *Fatal Conceit.* London: Routledge; Novak, M. 1982. *The Spirit of Democratic Capitalism.* New York: American Enterprise Institute; Oakeshott, M. 1962. *Rationalism in Politics and Other Essays.* London: Methuen; Rossiter, C. 1955. *Conservatism in America.* London: Heinemann; Scruton, R. 1980. *The Meaning of Conservatism.* Harmondsworth: Penguin; Weiss, J. 1977. *Conservatism in Europe 1770–1945.* London: Thames and Hudson.

consociational democracy A form of democracy for segmented plural societies. The CLEAVAGES are accepted and power is shared in government by all the important ethnic/religious/linguistic groups. Where possible, power is also decentralized territorially: otherwise, where there is no concentration of any group regionally, segmental autonomy takes the form of PILLARIZATION, as in Holland. Proportionality not only characterizes the voting system, but also the apportionment of posts in public service. Each group has a veto over important decisions. This type of political system operates successfully in the Low Countries, Switzerland and Austria.
See also DEVOLUTION; REGIONALISM; PILLARIZATION.

Reading
Barry, B. 1975. 'The Consociational Model and its Dangers'. *European Journal of Political Research* 3.4, 396–412; Dunn, J.A. 1972. 'Consociational Democracy and Language Conflict'. *Comparative Political Studies* 5, 3–40; Lijphart, A. 1977. *Democracy in Plural Societies.* New Haven: YUP; McRae, K.D. ed. 1974. *Consociational Democracy: Political Accommodation in Segmented Societies.* Toronto: McClelland and Stewart.

constituency This term has two usages. The less familiar is employed to describe the support a politician seeks, or depends on. The more common use is as a description of the unit of representation in a national parliament; but in Canada these are called 'ridings' and in the USA 'congressional districts'. The important features of constituencies are how many representatives are allocated to them, how many voters they represent, how big they are and how their boundaries are drawn.

Multi-member constituencies are usually associated with Proportional Representation while single-member constituencies are regarded as characteristic of FIRST-PAST-THE-POST and the SECOND BALLOT. But two Members of Parliament were returned from British constituencies before 1885. The 'halfway house' of the two-membered constituency exists under the ADDITIONAL MEMBER SYSTEM of the German Federal Republic. The number of voters represented varies greatly, with the US Congressional District at one extreme containing about half a million and, at the other, the British constituency of about 60,000 voters on average. This clearly affects representatives' comparative work-loads.

The drawing of the boundaries is bound to arouse controversy. Only in Israel is this avoided because the whole country is one constituency. In the USA, where the number of congressional districts per state is re-allocated on a population basis after each census, each state is left to re-draw the boundaries. When they are given one more district they may decide not to re-draw, but to make the extra Representative a 'Congressman-at-large'. Changing boundaries gives scope for gerrymandering. Shifting populations necessitate re-drawing and in the United Kingdom, Australia and New Zealand it is done by neutral boundary commissioners. In multi-member constituencies adjustment may be made by adding to, or subtracting from, the number of members. Even where there is no intention of skullduggery, precise equality is scarcely attainable and often regarded as undesirable. The British boundary commission has a remit to allow uniquely distinct conmmunities like islands to be constituencies in spite of populations a good deal lower than the average. This is also the case in Norway. In general, rural areas tend to be over-represented in legislatures.

Reading
Steed, M. 1985. 'The Constituency'. In *Representatives of the People?* Ed. V. Bogdanor. Aldershot: Gower.

constitutional courts They interpret CONSTITUTIONS, enforce constitutional law and exercise supreme appellate jurisdiction. Hence their political functions are of the utmost importance. In their judgements they will define the relationships of the constituent parts of the political system as laid down in the constitution. In so doing they may define the position of the JUDICIARY in relation to the EXECUTIVE and LEGISLATURE. Moreover, as most constitutions have a BILL OF RIGHTS stating the rights of citizens, they will interpret and define the relationship between the individual and the state.

They are especially important in federal states because the important relationship between the central authority and the autonomous sub-governments needs to be defined. Inevitably conflicts of laws and disagreements about relative powers will arise. The United States Supreme Court, the most famous of constitutional courts, has been called on to pass judgement on all these issues. Its first important verdict in *Marbury* v. *Madison*, 1803, established the principle of judicial review, that is that the Supreme Court has the right to rule an act of Congress unconstitutional. Constitutional courts can also be important in

unitary states. The French Conseil Constitutionnel has to be consulted before the President can take emergency powers and acts as a referee for the constitution of the Fifth Republic. Before 1974 reference to it could only be made by the President, Prime Minister, or Presidents of both houses of the legislature, but since then, by sixty members of either house. It can rule on whether a bill is a constitutional measure. If it is, the Council can rule on the bill's constitutionality. In this way it has established a degree of judicial review.

Reading
Luchaire, F. 1980. *Le Conseil Constitutionnel*. Paris: Economica; Murphy, W.F. and J. Tanenhaus. 1977. *Comparative Constitutional Law*. London: Macmillan; Swisher, C.B. 1946. *The Growth of Constitutional Power in the United States*. Chicago: University of Chicago Press.

constitutional law *See* CONSTITUTIONAL COURTS.

constitutional monarchy A situation in which the HEAD OF STATE is the successor to a royal dynasty. There are about 40 constitutional monarchies in the world; but seventeen of them, countries of the Commonwealth, share the same HEAD OF STATE, at the moment Queen Elizabeth II. Most of the others are in western Europe: Belgium, Holland, Luxemburg, Denmark, Norway, Sweden and Spain have constitutional monarchs. Their duties are largely honorific, such as hosting garden parties, presenting honours and opening Parliaments, but they may exert influence. BAGEHOT classically described the rights of the British monarch as 'the right to be consulted, the right to encourage and the right to warn'. In national emergencies constitutional monarchs may have an important role. In cases of political deadlock, where there is no clear majority in a legislature, they may be helpful in pointing the way to the formation of a new government. They may by prompt action avert a military coup as did King Juan Carlos of Spain in 1981. Above all, in times of war they may embody the national spirit, as did King Haakon of Norway when he refused to abdicate after the German invasion in 1940 and took refuge in Britain where he broadcast daily to his oppressed people. It has been argued that constitutional monarchs ensure social and political stability, but it is more likely that where a country has stability its royal house will survive. Greece has been unstable both as a monarchy and a republic.

See also HEADS OF STATE; KINGSHIP.

Reading
Bagehot, W. [1867] 1922. *The English Constitution*. 3rd edn. London: Kegan Paul; Bogdanor, V. 1995. *The Monarchy and the Constitution*. Oxford: OUP; Hardie, F. 1970. *The Political Influence of the British Monarchy*. London: Batsford.

constitutionalism   This term is sometimes used to describe a position of respect for constitutions, constitutional procedures, constitutional conventions and the RULE OF LAW. Clearly it is essential for the stability of DEMOCRACY that the attitude prevails among the bulk of the citizenry and especially among the politicians. If the leader of government in power failed to obey the convention that it resigns when it is defeated at the polls the whole fabric of trust on which the system depends would be destroyed.

See also CONSTITUTIONS; CONVENTIONS OF THE CONSTITUTION; DEMOCRACY; RULE OF LAW.

Reading
Franklin, D.P. ed. 1995. *Political Culture and Constitutionalism*. New York: Sharpe.

constitutions   Constitutions are sets of formal written rules governing states and organizations. The term was first used in relation to the Revolution of 1688 in Britain. Eighteenth-century French writers like Montesquieu referred favourably to the 'British constitution' which

either does not exist, or is an 'unwritten constitution', a contradiction in terms. The first written constitution was the American one drawn up by the Philadelphia Convention in 1787. It has provided a model for many others.

Constitutions may be categorized in several ways. They may be monarchic or republican depending on whether their HEAD OF STATE is a monarch or a president. They may be unitary or federal, a federation being a state where great autonomy is accorded to the sub-governments which will have their own constitutions. They may be parliamentary, where the EXECUTIVE sits in the LEGISLATURE, or presidential where the SEPARATION OF POWERS forbids such dual membership. Finally, they may be flexible and easily amended, or rigid and amended with difficulty.

A written constitution will have to be interpreted and, inevitably, this implies CONSTITUTIONAL COURTS and constitutional law. Hence a system of law different from COMMON LAW or STATUTE LAW will develop. Only in countries without written constitutions, like Britain, will this not be so. In Britain the constitution can be amended by a vote in Parliament like any other ordinary measure.

See also HEADS OF STATE; CONSTITUTIONAL COURTS; SEPARATION OF POWERS.

Reading
Duchacek, I.D. 1973. *Power Maps: Comparative Politics of Constitutions*. Santa Barbara: ABC-Clio; Duverger, M. 1957. *Constitutions et Documents Politiques*. Paris: Presses Universitaires de France; Wheare, K.C. 1966. *Modern Constitutions*. Oxford: OUP.

containment   The term originated in 1947 with George Kennan, an American diplomat, who advocated a strategy to restrain the threat of Russian expansion. This was part of the climate of thought in which President Truman enunciated his Doctrine, committing the USA to a global policy of containment of Communist aggression. For the next four decades much of the argument about strategy was about the scope and nature of the Soviet threat and how best to counter it. For example: Did it extend to the Asian and South American continents and were indigenous Marxist insurgencies there directed from Moscow? The general strategy, however, could be claimed as successful. Soviet Communism collapsed without a major war having to be fought to restrain it.

See also COLD WAR; COMMUNISM; MARXISM.

Reading
Gaddis, J.L. 1982. *Strategies of Containment.* New York: OUP; 'X' (George Kennan). July 1947. 'The Sources of Soviet Conduct'. *Foreign Affairs* 25, 566–82.

continuous revolution A policy of Mao Zedong set out by him in 1958. It involved a serious criticism of Soviet society which Mao condemned as stagnant, hierarchic and bureaucratic. Stalin's policies of industrialization and COLLECTIVIZATION of agriculture, Mao argued, had not achieved SOCIALISM. Soviet society had many CONTRADICTIONS and DIALECTICAL MATERIALISM had still to proceed through other stages. Mao's programmes of the 'Great Leap Forward' and 'Cultural Revolution' were intended to ensure Communist China did not remain at the same stage of development. Continuous revolution must end with popular participation in the march towards true SOCIALISM.

See also PERMANENT REVOLUTION.

contract A bargain between two parties with legal sanction. In political theory the term is usually redolent of the SOCIAL CONTRACT. Yet Sir Henry Maine (1822–88) saw contract as the outcome of a historical development from STATUS. The latter was the situation of the individual under tribal, patriarchal control where social position and economic function was unbargainable.

Evolution to a progressive society would allow contracts to be made between independent agents. Herbert Spencer had also been concerned to defend the basis of contract because business and trade was impossible without its maintenance. It was the only proper function for the state, beyond the maintenance of law and order.

See also SOCIAL CONTRACT.

Reading
Maine, H. 1861. *Ancient Law.* London: Murray; Spencer, H. 1851. *Social Statics.* London: Chapman.

contradictions A technical term used in Marxist writings on DIALECTICAL MATERIALISM to refer to conflicts in feudalism and capitalism. It presented the Bolsheviks with problems once SOCIALISM had been achieved. Mao's answer was that there were still contradictions in Soviet society because SOCIALISM had not been achieved. Soviet ideologists decided that the conflicts in Soviet society, engendered for example by planning and COLLECTIVIZATION, were not contradictions in terms of dialectical materialism.

See also COMMUNISM; CONTINUOUS REVOLUTION; DIALECTICAL MATERIALISM; SOCIALISM.

Reading
Mao Tse Tung. 1964. 'Khrushchev's Phoney Communism and its Historical Lessons for the World'. In *Thoughts of Chairman Mao.* 1966. Peking: Foreign Languages Press.

conventions of the constitution
Accepted rules derived from customs, past practices or agreements, and precedents. They will not be laws, though they may be documented in authoritative textbooks. Constitutional conventions are found in all systems of government; but they are inevitably more important in Britain because there is no written constitution. It could be said that all the British constitution is a convention. Formally the CROWN has extensive prerogatives, but

the convention is that the monarch only exercises them on the advice of ministers. Formally the sovereign could refuse assent to an act passed by both Houses of Parliament, but by convention no monarch has refused assent since Queen Anne (1702–14). Other conventions relate to collective Cabinet and ministerial responsibility.

With usage some conventions may be weakened. For example, the doctrine of the COLLECTIVE RESPONSIBILITY of the British Cabinet has been weakened by ministerial behaviour in the last three decades. Sometimes the response to the breaking of constitutional conventions has been to make them formal laws. For example, it was a convention the House of Lords did not interfere with financial legislation. When they threw out Lloyd George's budget in 1909 the government eventually forced through the Parliament Act, 1911, which restricted House of Lords power over legislation to a two-year suspensive veto. (This became one-year in 1949.) In the USA there was a convention that no President would serve for more than two terms. When broken by the Democrat, Franklin Roosevelt (1933–45) who was elected four times, the Republicans waited until they had a Congressional majority and then secured the passage, later confirmed by three-quarters of the states, of a resolution which became the 22nd amendment to the Constitution, stating: 'No person shall be elected to the office of the President more than twice'.

See also COLLECTIVE RESPONSIBILITY; CROWN.

Reading
Dicey, A.V. [1885] 1915. *Introduction to the Study of the Law of the Constitution*. 8th edn. London: Macmillan; Marshall, G. 1984. *Constitutional Conventions*. Oxford: OUP.

convergence theory This was a thesis which emerged during the period of DÉTENTE between the western powers and the Soviet bloc. Broadly the theorists argued that there was an inevitable convergence between the two societies which would inevitably make conflict less likely. There were several strands in this school of thought. The most resilient went back to Weber's view that CAPITALISM and SOCIALISM would both finally be dominated by BUREAUCRACY. Another important ingredient arose from the concept of MODERNIZATION which was present in both types of society. Thus ARON coined the phrase 'modern industrial society' and Galbraith argued, in similar vein, that advancing industrialization and urbanization would produce societies with similar concerns and problems. Among economists Rostow asserted that economic growth in the Soviet Union and increased economic planning in the managed economies of the capitalist world demonstrated their eventual convergence. Scientific rationalism would characterize both societies as technological advance continued and values would become more homogeneous. In the Soviet Union it would be impossible to deny individual liberties. In the 'second Cold War' interest in this theory receded. Events since 1989 might, or might not, confirm its validity.

See also COLD WAR; DÉTENTE; MODERNIZATION.

Reading
Aron, R. 1968. *Progress and Disillusion*. London: Pall Mall; Galbraith, J.K. 1967. *The New Industrial State*. Harmondsworth: Penguin; Rostow, W.W. 1960. *The Stages of Economic Growth*. Cambridge, Mass.: HUP.

co-operatives Co-operatives are groups of people who have agreed to work together on fairly equal terms. By their nature they are likely to be small, though national networks of co-operatives often develop. There are two basic types of co-operative: the consumers' co-operative and the producers' co-operative. Probably the most famous consumers' co-operative began in Britain with the Rochdale Equitable Pioneers who set up their first store in Toad Lane, Rochdale in 1844. The enterprise's motive was to evade the notorious truck system by which employers sold goods at inflated prices in company stores. The Pioneers were working-men who bought their own goods and sold them at low profits. After running costs were deducted some of the profits were returned to customers through dividends. The experiment spread and a Co-operative Wholesale Society was established in 1864. An example of working-class self-help, the co-operative movement had socialist undertones and in 1917 founded its own party which became affiliated to the Labour Party and sponsored Labour candidates for Parliament. In recent years the co-operative movement has declined, finding it dificult to compete with the supermarkets.

Producers' co-operatives have been most successful in agriculture. French farmers' co-operatives, for example, began about nine decades ago. In the second half of the twentieth century they have greatly expanded, moving from marketing and distribution to ventures in food-processing. French governments have tended to support their activities. Producers' co-operatives can also be found amongst fishermen who jointly own their boats and share the profits. A few producers' co-operatives have existed in industry, though they have not usually been successful.

Reading
Keeler, J.T.S. 1987. *The Politics of Neo-Corporatism in France.* Oxford: OUP; Ostergaard, G.N. and A.H. Halsey. 1965. *Power in Co-operatives.* Oxford: Blackwell; Redfern, P. 1938. *A New History of the CWS.* London: Dent.

corporate management   A term used in Britain to describe a new system of management in local government. It was obviously borrowed from the management of the CORPORATIONS; but corporate management could, as many pointed out, easily be a replica of CABINET GOVERNMENT. The belief in the 1960s that a new decision-making process was needed for local government led to the inauguration of two committees, Bains for England and Wales and Paterson for Scotland. Reporting in 1972 and 1973 respectively, they both recommended three innovations for all local authorities. First, a policy committee, drawn from among the elected councillors, concerned with setting priorities and allocating resources. Second, a management team of the professional officers of the council, specialized bureaucrats responsible for administering different services. Third, the appointment of a chief executive to head the management team and to be the principal adviser to the elected council. In the past the town clerks, invariably lawyers, had been the chief advisers, but concentrated more on the legal validity of policies to be pursued than on their practical and financial implications. While the new structure provided more technically efficient local government, it tilted the balance of power in local government decision-making towards administrators and away from elected representatives.

See also CORPORATIONS.

Reading
Greenwood, R. and J.D. Stewart. 1974. *Corporate Planning in English Local Government.* London: Charles Knight; Hampton, W. 1987. *Local Government and Urban Politics.* London: Longman.

corporations   Originally large business enterprises, usually formed from the amalgamation of smaller firms. Holding companies, sometimes called 'trusts', were formed to facilitate this procedure. The USA provides the first example, Standard Oil, created in 1881 by Rockefeller and controlling 90 per cent of the US capacity for oil-refining. By the early twentieth century it had been joined by United States Steel, General Electric and the chemicals giant, Du Pont. In

Germany IG Farben and Siemens and later in Japan, Mitsubishi, were similar structures. Britain had ICI and Lever Brothers, later to amalgamate with other firms and become Unilever. After World War I the motor manufacturers similarly became corporations. In consequence, many markets were competed in by few firms, what economists call 'oligopoly'. Profits tended to be relatively easily acquired, though corporations might suffer from government attention as in the USA where the Sherman Anti-Trust Act was passed in 1890 and the Clayton Act in 1913, allowing the federal government to bring suit to prevent restraint of trade. A consequence of becoming a political issue was that corporations began to lobby governments for favours. Monopoly power was supplemented by political influence.

By the late nineteenth century left-wing critics of CAPITALISM began to attack the corporations. For Marxists such concentration of industry was validation of MARX's prophecies and portended a fiercer onslaught on labour. Other socialists, especially the Fabians, believed the corporations would provide an easy target for a socialist government committed to nationalize much of industry. They coined the phrase the 'inevitability of gradualism' to convey the idea of the peaceful and irresistible progress to SOCIALISM. Less theoretical left-wing politicians, principally British trade-union leaders, produced the working model of the public corporation after the Labour victory of 1945. Examples were British Rail, British Steel and the National Coal Board. Their day-to-day commercial activities were not accountable to Parliament which could only debate their general policies. The PRIVATIZATION policies of the Thatcher governments (1979–90) destroyed most of the British public corporations, though similar organizations survive elsewhere, usually in the area of public utilities.

It should be said that there is an earlier meaning of the term. 'Corporation' in the English-speaking world described the governing body of a town and its municipal application still lingers on in such phrases as 'corporation transport'.

See also MONOPOLY CAPITALISM; MULTI-NATIONALS.

Reading
Berle, A.A. and G.C. Means. 1932. *The Modern Corporation and Private Property*. New York: Macmillan; Friedman, W. ed. 1954. *The Public Corporation: a Comparative Symposium of Thirteen Countries*. Toronto: Carswell; Hannah, L. 1976. *The Rise of the Corporate Economy*. London: Methuen.

corporatism A term which has acquired several connotations and, therefore, has become confused in meaning; but it always refers to relations between groups and political authority with restrictionist implications for economic policy. Those in favour of corporatist solutions have wanted to reduce social confrontation and CONFLICT, while those against have believed competition is inevitable and to be desired. In this respect corporatism can be seen as a middle way in the class war. In corporatist society neither labour nor capital has won.

The Catholic Church with its dislike of class war and its predilections towards social harmony never accepted CAPITALISM entirely and in 1891 Pope Leo XIII, worried about the condition of the working classes, issued the encyclical *De Rerum Novarum* in which he argued that capital and labour were inter-dependent and should co-operate under the aegis of, and in terms of the values of, the Catholic Church. The state should sanction the activities of social groups such as TRADE UNIONS and employers' associations, and establish organizations to enable them to work together. A guided capitalism restricted by Catholic principles and a state sympathetic to Catholicism was the ideal. It has remained the goal of Catholic social theory and reflections of it can be found in the contemporary European Union's policies.

The other direction from which support comes for corporatism is that of NATIONALISM. Nationalists want the nation to be united: not divided by class or ideological conflict. Right-wing parties, the British Conservatives with their 'one nation' approach and the French Gaullists with their emphasis on patriotism, exemplify this spirit. More extreme nationalists accepted corporatist structures for the economy for the same reason. It is significant that the Catholic countries which turned to FASCISM in the inter-war years – Italy, Spain, Portugal – all adopted tri-partite committees of representatives of employers, unions and the state in which social and economic policy was supposed to be made. In fact, this corporatism was fraudulent and the Fascist state made the decisions. Doubtless the attraction of the functional representation structure was to avoid the danger of popular elective democracy.

Most recently neo-corporatism has been used to describe the bargaining and negotiations between employers, unions and democratic governments about economic policy. Working relationships between these three parties dated from World War II, but it was the breakdown of Keynesian economic management with the onset of INFLATION in the 1970s which led to more formal attempts to hammer out economic policies by tri-partite negotiation and outside the procedures of representative democracy. These systems were most formally exemplified in Austria where every member of the work-force was obliged to belong to a centralized union and all associations were represented on equal terms by their peak organizations in bargaining over prices, wages and economic policy. Once agreements were reached they became obligatory and each leadership was supposed to maintain control over followers. Rather less formal systems operated in Scandinavia, Switzerland and the Netherlands. In Britain efforts to set up similar procedures foundered on the rocks of strongly entrenched trade-union autonomies.

Neo-corporatism was often confused, sometimes wilfully, with 'corporate pluralism', a term coined by Stein ROKKAN which he used to describe systems of bargaining between groups and groups, and groups and the state. A natural consequence of pluralist democracy, these interrelationships might, or might not, approximate to corporatism. It depends on the circumstances. In the 1980s inflationary pressures and the emergence of anti-Keynesian, radical conservative ideas led to the dismantlement of much of the neo-corporatist structures.

See also CLASS CONFLICT; FASCISM; PLURALISM.

Reading
Cawson, A. 1986. *Corporatism and Political Theory*. Oxford: Blackwell; Lehmbruch, G. and P.C. Schmitter. 1982. *Patterns of Corporatist Policy Making*. London: Sage; Rokkan, S. 1966. 'Numerical Democracy and Corporate Pluralism'. In *Political Oppositions in Western Europe*. ed. R.A. Dahl. New Haven: YUP; Williamson, P.J. 1985. *Varieties of Corporatism*. Cambridge: CUP.

cost benefit analysis A method of calculating the practicality of a project, going beyond simple accounting and attempting to put a monetary value on benefits and costs in the distant future. When applied to government projects it involves calculating the benefits and costs for the whole society, including such items as environmental impacts. The essence of rationality in decision-making to some, to others it is a sort of technical mumbo-jumbo.

council-manager plan Often the term used to describe government by a CITY MANAGER. It might sometimes imply that

there is a joint government in which the city manager is not so dominant.
See also CITY MANAGER; CITY GOVERNMENT; LOCAL GOVERNMENT.

counter-insurgency A governmental strategy to defeat an organized attempt to overthrow it. Measures taken may be military, political and financial: their nature will clearly depend on the type of insurgency. Where insurgencies rely on popular support, especially among rural peasantry, anti-guerrilla campaigns will be brutal, repressive and probably self-defeating. Where subversion and TERRORISM by minority movements have to be countered, espionage and specialized policing will be necessary.

Counter-insurgency became an important strategy during the COLD WAR. Insurgent movements of any kind against the western powers were likely to receive the backing of the Soviet Union. The USA was prominent in devising programmes to support regimes threatened by them. It gave money, arms and armed assistance; but found it difficult to persuade tyrannical regimes, against which most of the revolts took place, to purge themselves of abuses. Consequently it was a failure in Vietnam and in Central America it succeeded in propping up some of the most reactionary regimes in the world.
See also GUERRILLA WARFARE.

Reading
Shafer, D.M. 1988. *Deadly Paradigms: the Failure of US Counter-Insurgency.* Princeton: Princeton University Press.

counties Territorial divisions of a country, frequently corresponding to local government units. The term has a rural connotation, but counties can be urban. The USA has about 3000 counties, though county governments are somewhat less common than they were. For example, Connecticut abolished county government in 1960. In Britain the local government reorganizations of

the 1970s tended to abolish or amalgamate some counties; but those in the 1990s restored many of them.
See also LOCAL GOVERNMENT; LOCAL GOVERNMENT REORGANIZATION.

county-manager plan In the second half of the twentieth century there has been a tendency in the USA for counties which have become increasingly urbanized to appoint county-managers like the cities.
See also CITY MANAGER.

Reading
Adrian, C.R. 1961. *Governing Urban America.* New York: McGraw-Hill; Sofen, E. 1966. *The Miami Metropolitan Experiment.* New York: Anchor.

county-mayor plan The STRONG MAYOR PLAN adapted for counties, especially urbanized counties.
See also STRONG MAYOR PLAN.

coup d'état Literally a blow of the state: of French origin with Bonapartist undertones. Louis Napoleon in 1851 had already been elected President of France and wanted to crown himself the Emperor Napoleon III. He successfully deployed armed force to secure the throne. This type of *coup* in which the architects have strong popular backing seems to be a European phenomenon. A second type is where one lot of soldiers overthrows another faction. This has been common in Africa and South America. A third is the pseudo-Marxist Bolshevik-type *coup* as when the sailors of the Red Fleet suppressed the democratically elected Russian constituent assembly in 1918; or when armed Communist militiamen overthrew Czechoslovak democracy in 1948. The German term is *putsch*.
See also MILITARY REGIMES; *PRONUNCIAMENTO*.

Reading
Finer, S.E. 1976. *Man on Horseback.* 2nd edn. Harmondsworth: Penguin; Luttwak, E. 1979.

Coup d'État: a Practical Handbook. Cambridge, Mass.: HUP.

covenant Sometimes used as a synonym for CONTRACT, frequently an agreement between two parties, the term is more often used to describe an agreement between several parties. HOBBES, who seems to have used the words interchangeably, writes of a covenant among all men by which they agree to set up Leviathan, a ruler to enforce law and order. 'Covenants without swords are but words', he famously remarks. The Covenant of the League of Nations, signed by many states, illustrates this point. COLLECTIVE SECURITY was one of its principles; but there was no world Leviathan to ensure that the member-states implemented it. Experience proved it was merely words.
See also COLLECTIVE SECURITY; CONTRACT; SOCIAL CONTRACT.

crisis A crisis is a period of challenge to the stability and sustainability of a system. The system may be the governance of a country or the fabric of international peace. Government may change or the country may lapse into anarchy. The balance of international power may change, or war may break out. On the other hand, the challenge may fade and anarchy or war averted. If not crises will be prolonged and intensified. Hence scope, length and intensity are the three important features of crises. They may well be interrelated.

Lengthy periods may be judged as crises. Thus E. H. Carr called his account of the troubled inter-war period *The Twenty Years Crisis* (London, 1939). Viewed in terms of the above definition the title had validity. Others might regard the Cuban Missile crisis, which lasted for about a month in 1962, as more of a 'real crisis'. It was an international confrontation of SUPERPOWERS which threatened all human life, thus satisfying the criteria of both great scope and intensity. DIPLOMACY and compromise averted the immediate danger.

The management of crises obviously involves efforts to prevent the extension of their scope and intensity. This may be difficult as decision-makers under pressure to act quickly and decisively may antagonize opponents into taking up more intransigent positions. Extending their scope and intensity will probably extend their length, allowing more opportunities for hostile signals. What begins with a shot fired in Sarajevo may end in world war.
See also BRINKMANSHIP; COLD WAR; DIPLOMACY; SUPERPOWER.

Reading
Brecher, M., J. Wilkenfeld and S. Moser. 1988. *Crises in the Twentieth Century.* 2 vols. Oxford: Pergamon; Williams, P. 1976. *Crisis Management.* London: Martin Robertson; Young, O. 1968. *The Politics of Force: Bargaining During Super-power Crises.* Princeton: Princeton University Press.

critical theory More a body of criticism than a theory. Associated with the Frankfurt School's criticism of MARX, especially his concept of consciousness, two recent critical theorists who are important for political scientists are MARCUSE (1898–1979) and Habermas (1929–). They were both critical of modern technology and the mass media which forged an ideology preventing people from attaining their true consciousness. Mass production of consumer goods and distortion of reality were the ways in which the capitalist class had impeded the path to revolution.

Reading
Habermas, J. 1971. *Towards a Rational Society.* London: Heineman; Marcuse, H. 1964. *One Dimensional Man.* London: Routledge.

crown A constitutional term distinctive to the United Kingdom and those Commonwealth countries which are still

monarchies. At one time it would have referred to the monarch, but since the eighteenth century it has come to mean the institutions in which the former power of the Crown is vested. Thus in the courts criminal prosecutions are pursued by the Crown; and the government of the day exerts Crown power. What is left of the old privileges of the Crown are referred to as the royal prerogative. Most of these are unimportant such as the granting of commissions in the armed forces. There are two with constitutional significance: one is the duty of the monarch to select a Prime Minister. This only arises in the most unusual event of the choice not being obvious because no party has a majority, and only then if the parties cannot sort out the problem by two or more of them coalescing to form a majority. The other is the right to dismiss a Prime Minister which when used by the Governor-General (proxy for the Queen) in Australia in 1975 caused a constitutional crisis.
See also HEADS OF STATE; ROYALTY.

Reading
Marshall, G. 1971. *Constitutional Theory*. Oxford: OUP.

cube rule A statistical pattern by which in FIRST-PAST-THE-POST elections the ratio between the seats the two major parties win is a cube of the ratio of their share of the votes. Thus if the latter ratio is 3:2 the ratio of their representation in the legislature will be 27:8. It helps to illustrate the gross disproportionality of this electoral system. A large third party, or the lack of a uniform swing over the nation, may result in the rule not operating to the same exaggerated degree. Indeed, in Britain it has not operated since 1974.

Reading
Kendall, M.G. and A. Stuart. 1950. 'The law of cubic proportions in election results'. *British Journal of Sociology* 1, 183–97.

cult of personality A term used by Khrushchev to describe the exaggerated idolatry of Joseph Stalin during his time in power (1923–53). In posters, paintings, literature and through the media the Soviet dictator received sickening praise. This adulation of an individual, though common enough in other despotic regimes, was contrary to the collective rule of the party which was part of the Leninist doctrine. It was revived, though not to the same degree, under Brezhnev (1964–82). It has also been a feature of Communist leadership in China and in other totalitarian societies.

Reading
Gardner, J.F. 1974. *Leadership and the Cult of Personality*. London: Dent.

cumulative vote A system by which in a multi-member constituency a voter can cast all of her/his ballots for one candidate. Thus a party with only one candidate stands a good chance of electing one representative. Used in England for the election of school boards between 1870 and 1902 it was intended to ensure that minority religious groups obtained representation on them. This was because the position of denominational schools had become a contentious issue with the introduction of popular education.

customs union An agreement between a group of countries that they adopt a standard level of external tariffs. A well-known one was the *Zollverein*, 1819–70, in which nearly all German states except Austria were included. It did much towards the achievement of German unity.

D

---

dealignment A term which first rose to prominence among British political scientists in the 1970s. Before that analysis of voting motives showed that the main alignment of the British electorate was broadly between SOCIAL CLASS and political allegiance. In the two elections in 1974 more MPs from the minor parties were returned than had been for 45 years. Surveys of voting at the same time showed that a higher proportion of Conservatives were manual workers and a higher proportion of Labour voters were non-manual workers than a decade before. Social class was less of an indicator of voting intention than earlier in the 1950s. One explanation was the decline in the proportion of manual workers among the electorate. An additional theory was the 'bourgeoisification' of the working class. On the other hand, the expansion of the proportion of non-manual workers and their much increased propensity to vote Labour in the 1997 election could not realistically be called the 'proletarianization' of the middle-class. It was certainly, however, a further example of dealignment.

Reading
Crewe, I., B. Sarlvik and J. Alt. 1977. 'Partisan Dealignment in Britain 1964–1974'. *British Journal of Political Science* 7, 129–90; Franklin, M. 1985. *The Decline of Class Voting in Britain*. Oxford: OUP; Inglehart, R. and A. Hochstein.
1972. 'Alignment and Dealignment of the Electorate in France and the United States'. *Comparative Political Studies* 5, 343–72.

decentralization The term describes both a structural situation and a process. Constitutionally the most decentralized states are federal countries, though even with them there are degrees of decentralization. For example, Switzerland is a good deal more decentralized than the USA. The Swiss constitution gives the cantons more formal powers than the US constitution gives the states. The legal allocation of powers, however, may have little to do with the actual situation, which may be conditioned by the local governments' degree of dependence on loans and grants from the central government; and this in turn may be a reflection on how much the tax base of the local governments has been eroded by central government incursions.

There is much controversy about decentralization as a process. Many see the nation-state as too centralized and powerful and argue that its time as a useful instrument has passed. Within the European Union they are the supporters of SUBSIDIARITY and 'Europe of the regions'. Others believe the globalizing tendency and new information technology will ultimately result in a centralized world state. A third group contend that there is no contradiction between these two tendencies. Evidence from recent political experience illustrates the problems of assessing contemporary trends. The Thatcher governments (1979–90) could claim to be very decentralizing because they privatized the utilities and nationalized industries; on the other hand, they emasculated local government powers, replaced many elected positions with their own appointments and attacked the autonomy of the universities.

See also CENTRALIZATION; CENTRAL–LOCAL RELATIONS; CENTRE–PERIPHERY RELATIONS; SUBSIDIARITY.

Reading
Mény, Y. 1974. *Centralisation et Décentralisation dans le Débat Politique Français 1945–1969*. Paris: Librarie générale de droit et de jurisprudence; Sharpe, L.J. ed. 1979. *Decentralist Trends in Western Democracies*. Beverly Hills: Sage; Smith, B.C. 1985. *Decentralization*. London: Allen and Unwin.

decisions Political scientists have given considerable attention to the study of decisions, drawing on aspects of psychology, mathematics and computer theory. A decision might be defined as deciding on a line of action (or inaction) and then carrying it out. Early perspectives conceived of decision-making in rational terms: decisions are made by rational actors in a situation of information about possible options and the outcomes of each option. Hence the abstract ECONOMIC MAN under conditions of perfect competition 'optimized' benefits. (Perfect competition in perfect markets assumes total information is available.) Later, realization that politicians, let alone anyone else, could never be in this situation, led to the notion of the 'satisficer' who makes the best decision possible in situations where all the options and their outcomes can never be available and 'something has to be decided' quickly. Risk and uncertainty are the natural conditions of human decision-making. Moreover, not only the uncertainties of the decision-making context have to be taken into account by politicians. There are also the uncertainties of how people will respond. Social legislation, for that reason, often has different outcomes from what was expected.

See also CRISIS; GAME THEORY; POLICY ANALYSIS.

Reading
Allison, G. T. 1971. *The Essence of Decision: Explaining the Cuban Missile Crisis*. Boston: Little, Brown; Janis, I.L. 1982. *Groupthink: Psychological Studies of Policy Decisions and Fiascos*. Boston: Little, Brown; Quade, E.S. 1975. *Analysis for Public Decisions*. New York: Elsevier.

decolonization The process by which a COLONY becomes an independent state, possessing the attributes of SOVEREIGNTY. As a general term it describes the collapse of IMPERIALISM. Hence the great period of decolonization is in the last half of the twentieth century when the British, French, Belgian, Dutch, Japanese and Russian EMPIRES came to an end. Rule passed from colonizing powers to indigenous peoples. Yet the laws and often the bureaucracies of the imperial powers remained. Sometimes even the languages of the latter survived as a *lingua franca* for a multinational state. Moreover the boundaries of the new states, drawn up by the colonizing powers, often did not correspond to ethnic divisions. Hence the era of decolonization was one of problems which, in some cases, became problems for the international community. Furthermore, the ending of imperialist domination did not coincide with the attainment of independence in all dimensions. Sovereign states were becoming more interdependent and it was hardly surprising that ex-colonies often remained culturally and economically dependent on their former rulers. NEO-COLONIALISM was the term coined to describe this situation.

See also COLONIALISM; COLONY; EMPIRES; IMPERIALISM; NEO-COLONIALISM.

Reading
Kahler, M. 1984. *Decolonization in Britain and France*. Princeton: Princeton University Press. Lapping, B. 1985. *The End of Empire*. London: Granada Television; Smith, T. 1981. *The Pattern of Imperialism: the United States, Great Britain and the Industrializing World since 1815*. Cambridge: CUP.

decrees   Regulations issued by a minister which have the force of laws but which have not passed through a parliament. They are a feature of the democracies of continental Europe, especially France. The constitution of the Fifth French Republic especially relies on decrees. Article 47 says that if Parliament has not decided on a budget bill in 70 days it can be put into operation by decree. Parliament cannot question such decrees though they cannot be revised except by Parliament. (British DEL-EGATED LEGISLATION is thus hardly decree law.) Unsurprisingly, decrees often arouse resentment in democratic countries and are one reason why anti-state sentiments are expressed in continental Europe.
See also DELEGATED LEGISLATION.

deference   An attitude of acceptance of the opinions and judgements of those that one perceives as older, or superior in status, knowledge, birth, wealth or wisdom. Deference in political terms has been used to explain the perpetuation of aristocratic rule long after a large part of the population has been given the vote. BAGEHOT, in his exposition of the British political system, used the term in this way, but it must be remembered that he wrote when the franchise was very limited and educational opportunity scarcely existed. By the late twentieth century social deference of this kind had largely disappeared in the democracies and had little political significance. People's acceptance of their rulers could be attrib-uted variously, to apathy, an inclination once governments are elected to be passive and to 'let them get on with the job of governing', 'brain-washing' by the media, and the knowledge among the non-accepting that 'we can throw the rascals out at the next election'.

Reading
Almond, G.A. and S. Verba. 1963. *The Civic Culture*. Princeton: Princeton University Press; Bagehot, W. [1867] 1922. *The English Constitution*. 3rd edn. London: Kegan Paul; Nordlinger, E.A. 1967. *The Working-class Tories*. London: McGibbon and Kee.

deficits   Countries are likely to have annual deficits on their financial accounts. At one time this was regarded as the correct Keynesian response to a depression. Today a more likely explanation is the unwillingness of democratic governments to become unpopular by cutting expenditure on public services or, alternatively, putting up taxes. Governments that declare their intention to behave with financial stringency, for example President Reagan's administration, often culminate in the biggest deficits. This was in spite of the 1985 Deficit Reduction Act, sponsored in Congress by Gramm, Rudman and Hollings, which was intended to produce a steady reduction in the fiscal deficit. In the USA as elsewhere the end of the COLD WAR was expected to provide an opportunity for great reductions in arms spending and consequent balanced budgets. This expectation has been largely disappointed, reflecting the power of PRESSURE GROUPS and the problems of taking away benefits which voters have come to see as a right rather than a privilege.
See also BUDGET.

deflation   A term used to describe the situation during a recession when prices and wages fall. The value of money therefore rises and consumption decreases leading to unemployment. A fall in the rate of interest and/or a cut in taxes may therefore be needed to stimulate more spending and so increase employment. (This would be called 'reflation' which might end in INFLATION.) Deflation as a policy refers to a government increasing interest rates or squeezing credit in order to reduce consumption and to stop INFLATION.

See also INFLATION.

de-industrialization A term coined in the 1980s to describe what was seen as the contraction of the industrial bases of all the industrialized countries. The perception may have been caused by the decline of the old industrial areas due to the running down of coal-mining and the iron and steel industry. The newer, cleaner trades replacing them were often not seen as 'industries'. The new technological trades employed more part-time and female labour, contributing to the decline of the image of the old working class. Moreover, even in these trades there was competition from the 'tiger' economies of Asia. De-industrialized countries, such as Britain, tried to compensate by developing service industries such as tourism. The Thatcher governments deliberately accelerated the de-industrializing trend, claiming that there was no particular advantage in manufacturing industry. But manufactures had provided the bulk of British exports and, though oil was a substitute, once the oil ran out there might be a permanently unfavourable trade balance.

See also INDUSTRIAL SOCIETY; MODERNIZATION.

Reading
Bluestone, B. and B. Harrison. 1982. *The De-industrialization of America*. New York: Basic Books; Reich, R.B. 1993. *The Work of Nations*. London: Simon and Schuster.

delegate A person mandated to convey the opinions and decisions of a group to a larger body or assemblage. On the strictest interpretation of the term a del-egate should do nothing else and certainly should not make proposals of her/his own or vote on other proposals than those for which a MANDATE has been given. If applied to legislatures this would mean that debates were not necessary. The whole concept was vigorously attacked by Edmund BURKE who considered that a REPRESENTATIVE should speak and vote according to his mature judgement and conscience. Parliament was not 'a congress of ambassadors . . . but a deliberative assembly of one nation'.

See also MANDATE; REPRESENTATIVE.

Reading
Burke, E. 1975. 'Speech to the Electors of Bristol'. In *Edmund Burke on Government, Politics and Society*. Ed. B.W. Hill. London: Fontana.

delegated legislation Legislation issued as a result of discretion given by an act. Hence delegated legislation is sometimes called 'executive legislation'. It is the English-speaking world's nearest equivalent to decree law. The American Congress has been recognized to have the right to delegate powers of law-making: to sub-units of government in respect of powers of local autonomy; and to the federal executive with regard to events that might happen in the future, or with regard to the actual content and application of a law. Similarly in Britain it has been used in emergencies such as wartime and when a new comprehensive structure such as the National Health Service was first set up and all the difficulties of implementation could not be anticipated. It can take the form of STATUTORY INSTRUMENTS, orders in council, or codes of practice. Delegated legislation can be challenged in Parliament, though it is not usual to do so. In both the USA and Britain it can be challenged in the courts on the grounds that it is not based on powers given in the act. Clearly there is always a danger that such rule-making powers, extensively and increasingly used, may be abused. On the other hand it gives flexibility to administration and saves time for a legislature which is sorely pressed for it.

See also DECREES; STATUTORY INSTRUMENTS.

Reading
Allen, C.K. 1950. *Laws and Orders*. London: Stevens; Hart, J. 1925. *The Ordinance Making Powers of the President*. Baltimore: Johns Hopkins University Press.

delegation The term has several meanings. It may mean the act of delegating. Or it may be used to describe a group of delegates, though normally when employed in this sense it refers to a group chosen by a larger group to convey greetings and gifts and with no important MANDATE. Confusingly it is also used to describe a set of unmandated representatives from a particular area. Thus in the US House of Representatives reference may be made for example to the 'Illinois delegation', meaning all the Representatives, both Democrats and Republicans, elected from Illinois.

See also DELEGATE; REPRESENTATIVE.

demagogue A pejorative word used to describe a rabble-rouser. A populist politician might be termed a demagogue by a political opponent. The distinction is that a demagogue is supposed to incite a crowd to illegal behaviour by irrational statements and inflammatory oratory. The crowd becomes a lawless MOB.

See also MOB; POPULISM.

democracy A concept with several dimensions. Its meaning has developed as the problem of government has been transformed. It has also suffered because it is seen as an absolute good and so every state has been anxious to claim that it is democratic. Thus until very recently there were quite repressive states calling themselves 'people's democracies', for example the Democratic Republic of East

Germany. Yet the attribution of 'the PEOPLE' to the image of the regime could be held by some to make it democratic.

This is hardly surprising because the word's Greek derivation means 'rule by the people'. Democracy was one of ARISTOTLE's six types of political system; though it was one of the corrupt forms, a corruption of 'the polis', best translated as 'constitutional Government'. Aristotle feared rule by the people (a very restricted electorate anyway in ancient Athens), because they would not respect property or the law. Democracy to him promised to be a confiscatory regime.

The practical questions for politicians and political scientists have been: Who are the people? and How can a people rule? More theoretical questions for political philosophers and theorists have been concerned with the manner in which the rule takes place and what values should support democracy.

The problem of who the people are has been finally settled in the twentieth century with the generally agreed conclusion that they should be all sane, non-criminal adults. Their decisions, if they are to govern, can hardly be made by unanimous votes because that would result in no decisions being made. Consequently, questions, it is generally agreed, must be settled by simple majorities. This would have just been possible in Athens with a tiny electorate, and the REFERENDUM can be used in microstates; but in the modern nation-state DIRECT DEMOCRACY has largely given way to REPRESENTATIVE DEMOCRACY. Hence, decisions are made by elected representatives in assemblies, small gatherings where policies can be debated and votes taken more easily than in the nation as a whole.

The question of what values are inherent in democracy has been answered by some theorists in terms of intellectual and cultural history. They draw their inspiration from the rational, liberal values of the Enlightenment. Political historians are more inclined to attribute its emergence to the legacies of the English, American and French Revolutions. They may attribute it to the gradual arrival of CONSTITUTIONALISM, or to the winning of the FRANCHISE by the masses. Some philosophers associate it with the 'good society'. Fairness, social justice, EQUALITY, FRATERNITY, and liberty are often seen as democratic values; but there is difficulty in defining democracy in terms of values. The values themselves evoke different responses. What is socially just is what so much of democratic debate is about. FREEDOM for some may mean restriction for others. The ultimate allocation of values may be in the hands of a not very liberal majority.

More recently political scientists have attempted to define 'a democracy' by proposing an IDEAL TYPE. DAHL advances two necessary features of democracy as 'inclusiveness' and 'public contestation'. The former is the right of every adult to participate in political activity, including the right to stand as a candidate at elections. The latter are all those civic freedoms which allow citizens to express preferences, criticize authority, organize opposition against the government and dismiss it if a majority wishes to do so. There are also underlying values in such systems. Tolerance of those with whom one disagrees and a respect for and acceptance of their civic freedoms are necessary for such a system to operate. Furthermore it is necessary for a feeling of trust in political opponents' willingness to follow the constitutional procedures to be inculcated. This is especially important in relations between political leaders.

A major problem of contemporary democracy is the increasing technicality of policies. One result is that even parliamentary representatives may not properly understand them. Increasingly they are drawn up in small committees by members of executives and their techno-cratic advisers. Much therefore depends on the ability of members of governments to explain policies to their followers and, ultimately, to members of the public. Another outcome of increasing complexity of legislation is that the voters find it difficult to attribute blame. ACCOUNTABILITY is therefore likely to suffer. It all presents a challenge to democratic politicians, and to voters, for final responsibility is in their hands.

See also CIVIL LIBERTIES; CONSOCIATIONAL DEMOCRACY; DIRECT DEMOCRACY; REPRESENTATIVE DEMOCRACY.

Reading
Bealey, F.W. 1988. *Democracy in the Contemporary State*. Oxford: OUP; Dahl, R.A. 1971. *Polyarchy*. New Haven: YUP; Dahl, R.A. 1956. *Preface to Democratic Theory*. New Haven: YUP; Held, D. 1987. *Models of Democracy*. London: Polity Press; Lijphart, A. 1984. *Democracies*. New Haven: YUP; Macpherson, C.B. 1973. *Democratic Theory*. Oxford: Clarendon; Resnick, P. 1997. *Twenty-First Century Democracy*. Montreal: McGill-Queens University Press; Sartori, G. 1965. *Democratic Theory*. New York: Praeger.

democratic centralism One of the underlying principles of the internal arrangements of Communist Parties. It was the notion of Lenin who thought it would combine party discipline with intra-party democracy. The theory was that there could be wide-ranging discussion at every level of the party and resolutions could be passed upwards to higher levels; but once the Central Committee's Politburo had decided on party policy it must be strictly adhered to by every member at every level of the party irrespective of what their former views were. In practice, as critics were quick to point out, it was 'more centralized than democratic'.

See also BOLSHEVIK; COMMUNISM.

Reading
Lenin, V.I. [1902] 1988. *What is to be Done?* Revised edn. Harmondsworth: Penguin;

Waller, M. 1981. *Democratic Centralism*. Manchester: Manchester University Press.

democratic elitism A discussion of DEMOCRACY in the context of the existence of ELITES. At one extreme would be the followers of ROUSSEAU who believed democracy consisted of appealing to the people for guidance about what to do and who condemned group activity as subversive. At the other are those who perceive elite groups as essential to democracy because they are autonomous entities who challenge the power of the state: indeed, it is almost irrefutable that the successful claim of certain elite groups to freedom of activity and expression produced an early pluralistic society in which democracy could be established. It does not follow that one can move from this latter intellectual position to arguing that the autonomy of elites is a fundamental principle of democracy. Some ELITES, such as the military elite, have the resources to overthrow democracy and have frequently done it. For democracy to be maintained, the political or 'state elite', the one elected by the people, must discriminate between other elites according to their perceived threat or benefit to the regime. Thus the military elite should be vigilantly supervised while elites concerned with freedom of expression should not be impeded.

See also DEMOCRACY; ELITES; PLURALISM.

Reading
Bachrach, P. 1967. *The Theory of Democratic Elitism*. Boston: Little, Brown; Bealey, F.W. July 1996. 'Democratic Elitism and the Autonomy of Elites'. *International Political Science Review* 17.3, 319–31; Etzioni-Halevy, E. 1993. *The Elite Connection*. Cambridge: Polity Press.

democratic socialism *See* SOCIAL DEMOCRACY.

democratization The process of becoming democratic. It may be self-motivated, as with much European democracy, or it may be imposed from outside as with Japan's experience after World War II. There have been several periods during which progress to democracy has seemed almost inevitable. This was commonly believed by European liberals during the decades after the French Revolution. Again, in the intellectual climate after 1918, with all the new European nations emancipated by President Wilson's doctrine of SELF-DETERMINATION inaugurating democratic constitutions, it was assumed that an era of peace and freedom had begun. Then in the era of DECOLONIZATION after World War II, beginning with Indian independence in 1947 and continuing in Asia and Africa until the 1970s, there was some optimism. Finally, since the collapse of the Soviet bloc and empire and the foundation of many new states in 1989–91 there are new hopes of democratization. Periods of AUTHORITARIANISM are followed by periods of emancipatory enthusiasm.

See also NATIONALISM; POST-COLONIALISM; REVOLUTIONS.

département One of 96 territorial administrative units into which France has been divided since 1789 when the Revolution swept away the ancient provinces. (Except that the collaborationist Vichy regime restored them during the occupation, 1940–4.) Each one, on average, is sub-divided into about 370 *communes*. The départements are the main repository of local power since the *loi Defferre* in 1982 gave their councils more powers and reduced the controlling power of the PREFECTS. This was in spite of the 22 regions, with their local planning powers, becoming elected bodies under the same law.

See also COMMUNE; FIELD SERVICE ADMINISTRATION; PREFECT.

Reading
Bourdon, J. 1993. 'Le Département, Dix Ans Après les Lois de Décentralisation'. In *La*

Décentralisation Dix Ans Après. Eds. G. Gilbert and A. Delcamp. Paris: CRGL.

department A term used generally to describe a specialized section of an administrative organization. It is used in business bureaucracies and in local government. With a capital 'D' it usually refers to a section of central government administration. For example, each part of the US federal administration is an executive department, such as Defense or Education, whose head will be a member of the presidential cabinet. Similarly European cabinets will include ministers in charge of the most important departments.

See also BUREAUCRACY; BUREAUCRATIC POLITICS.

Reading
Pitt, D.C. and B.C. Smith. 1981. *Government Departments*. London: Routledge; Wettenhall, R.L. 1986. *Organising Government: the Uses of Ministries and Departments*. Sydney: Croom Helm.

dependency A territory dependent on a government elsewhere, usually overseas. Most dependencies are colonies, but some were former colonies entrusted by the League of Nations after 1919, or the United Nations after 1945, to colonial powers. In the former case they were called 'mandates' and in the latter 'trusteeships'.

The term also describes a relationship between one country and another in which one of them is dominant. 'Dependency theory' seeks to explain the nature of this relationship and how its unacceptable consequences can be mitigated. It attempts to explain the economic imbalance between the prosperous industrialized world and the developing world and the tendency for the wealth gap between them to increase. While this leads itself to a Marxist interpretation, ultimately most dependency theorists do not advocate revolution but concentrate on various social, cultural and economic solutions to alleviate the relative poverty of the developing world.

Reading
Amin, S. 1976. *Unequal Development: an Essay on the Social Formation of Peripheral Capitalism*. New York: Hassocks; Frank, A.G. 1967. *Capitalism and Underdevelopment in Latin America*. Harmondsworth: Penguin; Prebisch, R. 1977. *Critica al capitalismo perefico*. Montevideo: Centro Latinamericano de Economica Humana.

deputies A term commonly used for the members of lower houses of legislatures.

derivations Pareto's term to describe the desire of people to be rational while at the same time being irrational. This is the tendency popularly called 'rationalization'. Pareto argued that politicians used derivations in order to arouse emotional responses, thus strengthening the masses' support for politicians' irrational objectives. It was an early beginning to a theory of propaganda.
See also FASCISM; RESIDUES.

Reading
Finer, S.E. ed. 1966. *Vilfredo Pareto: Sociological Writings*. London: Pall Mall Press.

despotism *See* ABSOLUTISM.

destabilization A strategy employed by one state to weaken another, usually a smaller one. It comes within the category of 'low-intensity warfare' and has the advantage of avoiding large-scale miltary action such as invasion. Numerous tactics are used. A propaganda campaign can damage the international image of the target country. Financial and trade links may be cut. Dissident groups can be supported with arms supplies. Sabotage against ports, dams and power stations may be carried out. Local leaders and skilled professionals in the target country may be threatened and even assassinated. Crops may be burnt and peasants made homeless. Even torture may become common on the part of the dissident forces and their major backer. These were the policies of the USA in Nicaragua and of South Africa in Mozambique in the 1980s.

See also COUNTER-INSURGENCY; GUERRILLA WARFARE.

Reading
Tjonneland, E.N. 1989. *Pax Pretoriana: the Fall of Apartheid and the Politics of Destabilization*. Uppsala: Scandinavian Institute of African Studies.

détente A diplomatic term used to describe the easing of tension between states. More recently it has become common usage as a description of the reduced tension between the SUPER-POWERS from the Partial Test Ban Treaty in 1963 until the Soviet invasion of Afghanistan in 1979.

Reading
Litwak, R.S. 1984. *Détente and the Nixon Doctrine*. Cambridge: CUP.

deterrence A way of preventing attack by the threat of retaliation. As a conscious policy it must be backed by will and capability. Threats are not credible if it is known bluffs can be called, either because the potential deterrer will 'chicken out' at the crucial moment, or because the resources, largely armaments, to provide the capability for a 'pre-emptive strike' or counter-strike are not present. It can be claimed that the ending of the COLD WAR in 1989 was a proof that the policy of nuclear deterrence had been successful. It may be so; but a proper evaluation is dependent on a consideration of whether the Soviet Union would have collapsed from internal weaknesses regardless of NATO's technical superiority in arms and Reagan's Strategic Defense Initiative (Star Wars).

See also COLD WAR; DÉTENTE.

Reading
Buzan, B. ed. 1987. *The International Politics of Deterrence*. London: Pinter; Russett, B. 1993.

'Deterrence'. In *Oxford Companion to Politics of the World*. Oxford: OUP; Snyder, G.H. 1961. *Deterrence and Defense*. Princeton: Princeton University Press.

development A vague and general term which has acquired a more precise meaning for social scientists in the last half century. Development theory was both axiomatic and prophetic. There were those who assumed that the Third World would become more developed because all countries were moving from the primitive towards more sophistication through economic and technological progress. Prophets like MARX foresaw a movement through industrialization to CAPITALISM and then SOCIALISM. Anthropologists and economists were therefore prominent in this area of thinking about MODERNIZATION and much of it was stimulated by Latin American experience. Political scientists arrived rather later on the scene as the new states of Asia and Africa emerged in the 1960s. Development theory in their case involved studies of comparative political cultures, nation-building and the construction of stable institutions and administrations.

See also DEPENDENCY; MODERNIZATION.

Reading
Ake, C. 1979. *Social Science as Imperialism: the Theory of Political Development*. Ibadan: Ibadan UP; Almond, G. and J.S. Coleman. eds. 1960. *The Politics of Developing Areas*. Princeton: Princeton University Press; Almond, G. and G.B. Powell. 1966. *Comparative Politics: a Developmental Approach*. Boston: Little, Brown; Rostow, W.W. 1971. *The Stages of Economic Growth*. 2nd edn. Cambridge: CUP.

devolution A delegation of power from a central to a regional institution. There is both administrative and legislative devolution. There is at the moment (1997) in Britain administrative devolution from London to Edinburgh and Cardiff. The Scottish and Welsh Offices administer all government functions, for

Scotland and Wales respectively, except for foreign and financial affairs which remain centrally directed in the Foreign Office and the Treasury. Britain will soon have legislative devolution because law-making powers for the Scottish Parliament and Welsh Assembly are contained in recent legislation. Between 1920 and 1973 Northern Ireland had a Parliament, Stormont, in Belfast; but it was closed down by the central government which felt that it must over-rule the policies of the Northern Ireland government and its support in the Protestant majority. By the 1998 'Good Friday' agreement, Stormont was restored. This illustrates the difference between devolution and federalism. In a federal state the constitution would define the powers of the central government and the constituent parts. Constitutional law would probably prevent a provincial parliament being dissolved by a central government.

Devolved parliaments are a feature of modern Europe. Italy, Spain and, more recently, Britain have devolved powers to provincial assemblies; and devolution might be considered a half-way house to a FEDERAL GOVERNMENT if the example of Belgium is to be taken as a precedent. See also CONSOCIATIONAL DEMOCRACY; FEDERAL GOVERNMENT; REGIONALISM.

Reading
Bogdanor, V. 1979. *Devolution*. Oxford: OUP; Fitzmaurice, J. 1996. *The Politics of Belgium*. London: Hurst.

dialectical materialism An adaptation by MARX of HEGEL's theory of the Dialectic, further developed by Engels. The dialectic of Marx and Engels is concerned with the growth of the consciousness of man in society and not with the unfolding consciousness of the 'world spirit'. Hence it is 'economic' or 'material'. Society will pass through changing phases as 'contradictions' at one stage of history are resolved in the passage to another stage. These contradictions are evinced in the clash between those who own the factors of production and those who do not. CAPITALISM, the phase that was emerging from feudalism as they wrote, was already revealing the contradiction between its betterment of man's material condition and the fact that wealth was unfairly distributed. The evidence was in the industrial conflict between employers and workers. The outcome would be a final 'synthesis' which would be SOCIALISM.
See also IDEALISM; MARXISM; SOCIALISM.

Reading
Carew Hunt, R.N. 1954. *Marxism Past and Present*. London: Geoffrey Bles; Engels, F. 1892. *Socialism: Utopian and Scientific*. London: Sonnenschein; Feuer, L.S. 1969. *Marx and Engels: Basic Writings on Politics and Philosophy*. 2nd edn. London: Fontana.

dictatorship Government by one ruler. Usually associated with arbitrary rule, dictators may be constitutionally appointed. Under the ancient Roman Republic a dictator could be appointed by the Senate and the popular assembly in a national emergency; but only for six months. Modern dictatorships are of dubious constitutionality. They could be divided into two kinds: military dictatorships inaugurated when soldiers seize power; and what (for want of a better term) could be called 'popular dictatorships' whose leaders are charismatic and backed by mass support. Cromwell and Bonaparte were early exemplars, both believers in 'a whiff of grapeshot' as a clarifying agent. Both saw themselves, and were recognized by many, as saviours of their country.

In the twentieth century Benito Mussolini (1883–1945) is the acknowledged prototype. He liked to look back to the Roman dictators but his rule from 1925 onwards was unchecked by mandate. He entitled himself 'Il Duce' (the leader) and ruled despotically through his Fascist Party apparatus. Adolf Hitler

(1889–1945), coming to power later, consciously modelled his rule on Mussolini's. Their examples raise the issue of whether totalitarian rule inevitably leads to dictatorship, or whether it is a distinctive feature of FASCISM. The exponents of the former view point to the 30-year domination of Stalin in Communist Russia; while those of the latter see Stalinism as an aberration from the proper Leninist principle of collective leadership.

See also COLLECTIVE LEADERSHIP; COMMUNISM; FASCISM; NATIONAL SOCIALISM.

Reading
Duverger, M. 1961. *De la Dictature*. Paris: Julliard; Friedrich, C.J. and Z.K. Brzezinski. 1967. *Totalitarian Dictatorship and Autocracy*. New York: Praeger; Moore, B. Jnr. 1967. *Social Origins of Dictatorship and Democracy*. Harmondsworth: Penguin.

dictatorship of the proletariat A term which is part of the Marxist canon. It was not greatly used by MARX. In his early work he appears to refer to a transition period between CAPITALISM and the establishment of SOCIALISM in which the 'revolutionary dictatorship of the proletariat' would ensure there was no counter-revolution while taking over the means of production and transforming class relations. When complete, no state would be needed as coercion would become a thing of the past. Yet when the first apparent example of workers' power, the Paris Commune, occurred, Marx seemed to approve of its quick decentralizing activity and its democratic, rather than dictatorial, nature. Lenin discussed both models, but the Bolshevik COUP D'ÉTAT of 1917 and the regime's early authoritarianism led to criticism from Marxists elsewhere. The most prominent was Karl Kautsky (1854–1938) who argued that the dictatorship of the proletariat meant popular democracy in which the working-class dominated. Many Trotskyists have taken this position, while the world Communist

Parties have taken the term to mean the dictatorship of the VANGUARD OF THE PROLETARIAT.

See also COMMUNISM; MARXISM; VANGUARD OF THE PROLETARIAT.

Reading
Kautsky, K. 1924. *The Dictatorship of the Proletariat*. London: National Labour Press. Lenin, V.I. 1917. *The State and Revolution*. London: Lawrence and Wishart; Marx, K. [1871] 1933. *The Civil War in France*. London: M. Lawrence.

difference principle A principle first put forward by John Rawls. Inequalities should only be accepted in a society where equal opportunity reigned and the least prosperous members would benefit from the activities of the wealthier.

Reading
Rawls, J. 1971. *A Theory of Justice*. Oxford: OUP.

diplomacy In ordinary parlance to be diplomatic is to be tactful and to show skills in 'handling' people. These are the personal qualities required by those who deal with their country's interests in a foreign capital, a diplomatic corps headed by an ambassador. Ideally, however, they should also be highly intelligent, sensitive to nuances of expression and gifted linguistically. Diplomacy is a specialized profession. Diplomats have two main interdependent functions: to relay and to explain their government's attitudes and policies to foreign powers and to transmit back home any messages, signals, reactions and impressions from where they are stationed. In the contemporary world embassies display a division of labour between those who specialize in contact with foreign leaders (Chancellery in British terminology), military attachés, cultural attachés, labour attachés and those who are engaged in collecting information, including espionage.

Diplomacy as a profession probably dates from the seventeenth century when in Europe the orientation was French. The Congress of Europe after 1815, which involved regular meetings between representatives of the powers, was the period in which diplomacy became recognized as a necessary international institution. Although it is sometimes suggested that instant electronic communication will ultimately render it an expensive and unnecessary exercise, it is hardly likely to be completely redundant. See also AMBASSADORS.

Reading
Nicolson, H. 1939. *Diplomacy*. Oxford: OUP; Satow, E. 1922. *Guide to Diplomatic Practice*. London: Longman.

direct action   A term whose origins are in pre-1914 SYNDICALISM. It signifies an impatience with conventional means of achieving ends and a belief that authority, of whatever form, cannot be influenced by those methods. It is often spontaneous and irrational, implying that will rather than reason governs people's motivations. It is bound to be a sign of distrust of legislatures and political parties, so direct action will be extra-parliamentary even when it is not extra-legal. Frequently it is undertaken by PRESSURE GROUPS such as environmentalists, and anti-nuclear campaigners whose issues, they feel, are neglected by party politicians. There is thus a possible indication that it will become an even more common form of action. On the other hand, it may well be that for many it is a transition stage ending in incorporation into conventional political action. See also PASSIVE RESISTANCE; SYNDICALISM.

Reading
Benewick, R. and T. Smith. 1972. *Direct Action and Democratic Politics*. London: Allen and Unwin; Carter, A. 1973. *Direct Action and Liberal Democracy*. London: Routledge; Tarrow, S. 1989. *Democracy and Disorder*. Oxford: OUP.

direct democracy   A form of democracy in which decision-making rests with the mass of the people. It is thus in sharp contrast with REPRESENTATIVE DEMOCRACY. It comprises a trio of devices – the REFERENDUM, the INITIATIVE and the RECALL. It was advocated by ROUSSEAU who had experienced it in his native Geneva and who perceived political systems in terms of small communities. Hence direct democracy has been most successful in small, decentralized states. Its classic case is the government of Switzerland; but it is also practised in American states, especially in western USA. Otherwise it is often an appropriate device for decision-making in local government. See also INITIATIVE; RECALL; REFERENDUM; REPRESENTATIVE DEMOCRACY.

Reading
Bealey, F.W. 1988. *Democracy in the Contemporary State*. Oxford: OUP; Lowell, A.L. 1914. *Public Opinion and Popular Government*. New York: American Citizen Series.

directed democracy   See   GUIDED DEMOCRACY.

directives   Instructions issued by a higher authority to a lower, requesting it either to stop doing something it is doing, or to do something it is not doing. They differ from DECREES in that the latter are promulgated. In recent years directives have been associated with the European Union's Commission which issues them to member states on all issues within the scope of its Treaties.

dirigisme   A French term signifying direction of the economy by the state. This will take the form of indicative PLANNING, control over industrial location, subsidies, legal requirements intended as frameworks and general intervention. In France this began with the Bourbons and has continued ever since.

disarmament   A long-sought objective of international idealists is the elimination of national armaments. The hypothesis behind this aspiration is that armaments cause WAR. The high peak of the disarmament campaign was the Disarmament Conference at Geneva in 1933–4. Its collapse was partly a reflection of the distrusts the great powers felt for one another, but it could scarcely have survived anyway after the rise of the aggressive Fascist powers. The United Nations Special Session on Disarmament, 1978, was more realistically concerned with ARMS CONTROL; but that was soon followed by the Soviet invasion of Afghanistan and President Reagan's massive rearmament programme.

Pacifists argue that the presence of armaments makes war likely. It foster an atmosphere of MILITARISM in which military men become important national figures. Their natural interests, and those of the arms manufacturers, are to support increasing armaments and aggressive foreign policies. Even defensive arms make foreign powers suspicious. Hence distrust leads to ARMS RACES, crises of increasing intensity and finally war. Nuclear weapons make disarmament even more necessary.

Those opposed to disarmament argue that conflict between nations is an unfortunate reality and it would therefore be foolish to disarm unilaterally. Nuclear weapons make UNILATERALISM even more unwise. It is more sensible to establish NUCLEAR PARITY between the superpowers. Rational calculation on both sides will then preserve a situation of nuclear deterrence.

See also ARMS CONTROL; ARMS RACES; NUCLEAR PARITY; NUCLEAR PROLIFERATION; UNILATERALISM.

Reading
Barnet, R.J. and R.A. Falk. eds. 1965. *Security in Disarmament.* Princeton: Princeton University Press; Dupuy, T.N. and G. Hammerman. eds. 1973. *A Documentary History of Arms Control and Disarmament.* New York: Barker.

discretion   The amount of latitude allowed to those implementing laws. At the lowest level it may happen when a police officer warns a driver over a parking offence instead of proceeding with prosecution. At the highest, discretion may be exercised under the terms of an Act allowing a minister to issue more detailed supplementary regulations. In the English-speaking world this is known as DELEGATED LEGISLATION. The obvious objection to discretion is that it is arbitrary. In England constitutional lawyers such as A.V. DICEY and judges like Lord Hewart argued that any discretion is a breach of the RULE OF LAW. Others have argued that certain decisions, such as the allocation of welfare benefits or local planning permits cannot be made without the exercise of discretion and as long as appeals are permitted there is no other viable way of proceeding.

See also ADMINISTRATIVE LAW; DECREES; DELEGATED LEGISLATION.

Reading
Dicey, A.V. [1885] 1985. *Introduction to the Study of the Law of the Constitution.* 10th edn. London: Macmillan; Hewart, Lord. 1929. *The New Despotism.* London: Benn; Titmuss, R. 1971. 'Welfare 'rights', law and discretion'. *Political Quarterly* 42, 113–32.

discrimination   The practice of distinguishing between people so that some receive unfavourable treatment. It can take various forms. At its worst it can result in some being regarded as *untermenschen*, sub-humanity eventually destined, as in the case of the Nazi holocaust of the Jews, for the gas chambers. South African APARTHEID deprived blacks of most of the life-chances of whites. The poll tax in the American South was one of the measures to stop blacks voting. English DISSENTERS, Catholics and Jews were discriminated against until the nineteenth century. Discrimination can be in educational opportunity and employment prospects.

At its lowest level discrimination can be merely social: probably something experienced by most people at some time.

Originally thought of in terms of race and religion, discrimination has increasingly also been a complaint of age groups, genders and the physically disabled. Policies of AFFIRMATIVE ACTION first carried out to benefit ethnic groups have since been advocated and sometimes implemented for other discriminated sections of society. They all to a greater or lesser degree provoke a BACKLASH. It is impossible to select all the applicants for one job and naturally the unsuccessful may feel they have been unfairly rejected. Any particular complaint, therefore, has to be treated on its merits.

See also AFFIRMATIVE ACTION; APARTHEID; BACKLASH; RACISM.

Reading
Pettigrew, T.F. 1975. *Racial Discrimination in the United States*. New York: Harper and Row. Schiller, B.R. 1980. *The Economics of Power and Discrimination*. Englewood Cliffs: Prentice Hall; Thompson, D. ed. 1964. *Discrimination*. Harmondsworth: Penguin.

dissenters A dissenter is someone who disagrees with a majority proposal. With a capital 'D', however, the term refers to those people in the seventeenth century who opposed the domination of the Church of England. The two main sects were the Baptists and the Independents (later called Congregationalists). They formed the backbone of the Parliamentary forces which overthrew Charles I and set up the Commonwealth; and were discriminated against after the Restoration of the monarchy in 1660. Later non-conformist sects, such as Methodists, may also be regarded as Dissenters – the term is not entirely definitive. In the nineteenth century the 'non-conformist' vote was an important part of electoral support for the Liberal Party.

dissidents A term that became popular in its application to those opposed to the regime in states of the Soviet bloc and Communist China. They were frequently imprisoned, persecuted, deprived of citizenship and, in the case of Solzhenitzyn, deported.

dissolution of the legislature Most legislatures can be dissolved on the decision of the executive before their term has lapsed. Exceptions where parliaments have fixed terms are the USA, Norway and Switzerland. The disadvantages of fixed-term legislatures are their distance from a changed public opinion towards the end of their life and the existence of a government that may have lost the confidence of the people as well as the legislators. As both the government and their opponents know when the next election will take place it can be argued that fixed terms are fairer: on the other hand the incumbent government may be clever enough to manipulate the economy in order to produce a boom in time for the election. This produces what is called the POLITICAL BUSINESS CYCLE.

Dissolution of legislatures may be hedged around with conditions. Art. 12 of the French constitution means the President can dissolve the legislature after consulting the Prime Minister and chairmen of both houses, but there cannot be another dissolution in the year following. Art. 68 of the German Basic Law allows the Federal Chancellor to move a vote of confidence; but if this is not agreed to by a majority in the Bundestag the President may dissolve it. Art. 67 says the Bundestag can only reject such a vote if it nominates a successor, who must then be appointed by the President. This is known as the 'constructive veto'. In Britain there are only conventions to regulate the dissolution procedure. The Prime Minister decides when to dissolve, usually without consulting the Cabinet. She/he has to ask the permission of the monarch; but it is believed that the only ground for royal refusal is if the last election was very, very recent. In 1974 there were two elections within eight months.

The right to dissolve is likely to favour incumbent governments who can manipulate the economy by stimulating a short boom when they intend to hold an election. Where there is a right of dissolution the Opposition parties cannot know the date, they can only guess. Quite often governments call 'snap' elections, probably hoping to benefit from a rise in their support in the PUBLIC OPINION polls. This may not always transpire. In general, however, the right of dissolution is a powerful weapon in the hands of the executive, allowing it not only to choose the occasion of the election; but also to some extent the issue on which it is fought. It assists party discipline because when an election is threatened fractious elements are under pressure to re-affirm their loyalty.

See also ELECTIONS; POLITICAL BUSINESS CYCLE; PUBLIC OPINION.

Reading
Forsey, E.A. 1968. *The Royal Power of Dissolution of Parliament in the British Commonwealth*. 2nd edn. Toronto: OUP; Lauvaux, P. 1983. *La Dissolution des Assemblées Parlementaires*. Paris: Economica; Markesinis, B. 1972. *The Theory and Practice of Dissolution of Parliament*. Cambridge: CUP.

distributive justice The principles governing what benefits and penalties should be distributed among people. Where material wealth is concerned it is sometimes called 'redistributive justice'. As there is always, in every society, disagreement about what is just and 'fair', so there is disagreement about the principles to be applied. In a democracy, therefore, it is likely that the principles will be mixed.

The basic question is: From whom should we take and to whom should we give? One answer would be that we should take from those who can afford it and give to those who are in need. Another might be that we should take from those who are not entitled to what they have and give it to those who are entitled. Finally, we might decide who merits rewards and who deserves to be penalized. Once these questions are answered the next problem is how we determine the categories. Neediness and affluence are the easiest to calculate though they are by no means free of controversy. Entitlement and merit may be far more open to dispute. Ultimately and inevitably in the democratic process there will be those who claim they need, deserve or are entitled to more (or all three) and there will be those protesting that they cannot afford or do not deserve to be deprived of so much, or arguing that their rights are being infringed by high taxation. Needs, deserts and rights will be determined in the long run by majority votes.

See also DIFFERENCE PRINCIPLE; EGALITARIANISM; WELFARE STATE.

Reading
Runciman, W.G. *Relative Deprivation and Social Justice*. London: Routledge.

divine right The belief that the right to have authority is God-given. Its best known aspect was 'the Divine Right of Kings' which was the legitimizing principle of the dynastic state. In Europe in the Middle Ages it was accepted that hereditary succession was a right that came through the Church and its hierarchy. This claim to ultimate authority by the Pope was challenged by absolute monarchs as they developed temporal power. Protestant monarchs claimed that God handed power to them directly and the politcal philosopher, Filmer, argued that divine right began when God made Adam the first father-figure. This was refuted by LOCKE and more pragmatically by the English and French revolutionaries who showed their disrespect for their monarchs by chopping off their heads.

See also ABSOLUTISM; DESPOTISM; DYNASTIC STATE.

Reading
Filmer, R. [1680] 1949. *Patriarcha*. Oxford: Blackwell; Locke, J. [1690] 1970. ed. P. Laslett. *Two Treatises on Government*. Cambridge: CUP.

division of labour   The term has both a general meaning and a more specific one. In its general connotation it applies to all societies except the most primitive. Different kinds of people will have different functions and this differentiation is beneficial to the social system. Plato recognized this in his depiction of his republic. Modern society is far more complex. Durkheim (1858–1917) perceived that industrialization made us all interdependent on one another and yet at the same time less comprehending of one another's interests. His solution was a new type of structure, the corporation, and a new kind of ethic which would help us to recognize our common interests and which would therefore provide a sort of moral cement for society.

The specific meaning is related to the organization of industry. Adam Smith (1723–90) marvelled at the number of operations necessary to manufacture a pin, each one delegated to a different workman. This division of labour made industrial enterprise more efficient and therefore more prosperous and increased the productive capacity of the economy. The organization of the textile factory spelled the end of the hand-loom weavers. Its logical conclusion was the assembly belt. For MARX, the new system, depriving artisans of their tools and putting them to work on employers' machines, often ignorant of what they were producing, resulted in ALIENATION. It would be the beginning of the development of revolutionary consciousness.

See also ALIENATION; CAPITALISM; CLASS CONSCIOUSNESS; NEW LEFT.

Reading
Durkheim, E. [1893] 1984. *The Division of Labour in Society*. London: Macmillan; Smith, A. [1776] 1904. *The Wealth of Nations*. 2 vols. Oxford: OUP.

dominion status   The self-governing colonies in the British Empire began to be called 'dominions' before 1914 to distinguish them from colonies which were not autonomous. The Balfour Report in 1926 described them as 'autonomous communities within the British Empire equal in status, in no way subordinate one to another in any aspect of their domestic or external affairs, though united by a common allegiance to the Crown and freely associated as members of the British Commonwealth of Nations'. In 1931 the Statute of Westminster, embodying these sentiments, was enacted by the British Parliament. From that time the dominions were virtually sovereign states though their special status is symbolically recognized in various ways. For example, they do not exchange ambassadors but 'High Commissioners'. *See also* AUTOCHTHONY.

Reading
Attlee, C. 1960. *Empire into Commonwealth*. Oxford: OUP; Wheare, K.C. 1953. *The Statute of Westminster and Dominion Status*. 5th edn. Oxford: OUP.

domino theory   First used as a metaphor by President Eisenhower in 1954 in order to explain the strategic significance of Vietnam. If you put up a line of dominoes and knock the first one over they will all go over in succession quite quickly. Hence if Vietnam succumbed to Communism the countries of South-East Asia would all follow and Australia and New Zealand would be finally threatened. The domino theory motivated American foreign policy elsewhere in the world. For example, President Reagan apparently believed that if the Sandinistas won in Nicaragua all of Central America would become Communist and Texas would be in peril. The basis of the theory lay in the history of the 1930s when one small nation after another became a prey to Fascist aggression. From this it was induced that 'freedom is indivisible' and that one must make a stand at the first instance of aggression. If one does not the whole democratic world will be under threat. A lesson might be that analogies are dangerous.

See also DETERRENCE.

Reading
Gaddis, J.L. 1982. *Strategies of Containment.* New York: OUP.

doves   *See* HAWKS AND DOVES.

droop quota   Named after H.R. Droop, a nineteenth-century English lawyer and supporter of Proportional Representation. He said the correct number of votes entitling a party to a seat in a multi-member constituency was the total vote cast divided by the number of seats plus one rounded up to the nearest whole number. Thus if 250,000 votes were cast in an eight-member seat the Droop quota would be 250,000 divided by 9 = 27,778.

See also ELECTORAL SYSTEMS.

Reading
Droop, H.R. 1868. *Methods of Electing Representatives.* London: Macmillan.

dual executive   A term usually applied to France under the Fifth Republic. Presidential government, as in the USA, has a presidential executive. Parliamentary government has an executive cabinet with a Prime Minister at its head. France has both because the constitution was a compromise between those who wanted Presidential government and those who wanted Parliamentary government. The criterion of the latter is usually taken to be a government responsible to the parliament. Art. 20 of the French constitution says that 'it is responsible to parliament'

and also that it 'determines and conducts the policy of the nation'. Art. 21 says 'the Prime Minister directs the Government's action'. Yet Art. 8 says 'the President of the Republic appoints the Prime Minister', and Art. 9 'the President of the Republic presides over the Council of Ministers'. Moreover, Art. 16 gives the President powers to take 'the measures required' in a national emergency. Finally, since 1962 the President is popularly elected. Thus France has a presidency somewhat reminiscent of the American and, like the American President, the French may have to deal with a legislature with a hostile majority; but in the French case that majority will have a natural leader, the Prime Minister. The two experiences of COHABITATION have seen a sort of division of labour between the two executives with the President claiming dominance in foreign policy.

See also COHABITATION.

Reading
Blondel, J. 1984. 'Dual Leadership in the Contemporary World'. In D. Kavanagh and G. Peele. *Comparative Government and Politics.* London: Heinemann; Hayward, J.E.S. 1983. *Governing France.* London: Weidenfeld and Nicolson.

due process of law   A phrase from the Fifth Amendment to the US Constitution, part of the Bill of Rights, 1791. The amendment guarantees that a person must be charged before being tried and that no one must 'be deprived of life, liberty, or property, without due process of law'. This is repeated with respect to state governments in the Fourteenth Amendment, 1868. Supreme Court rulings in the earlier part of the twentieth century tended to interpret it in order to invalidate legislation regulating the economy. Thus the verdict in *Lochner* v. *New York*, 1905, struck down a state law regulating hours of labour; and in *Schechter Poultry Corporation* v. *United States*, 1935, virtually declared the first part of Franklin Roosevelt's New Deal unconstitutional. In the 1950s the Supreme Court based its defence of civil liberties on the due process clause.

Although the term is not used elsewhere the principle is a familiar feature of most legal systems. Chapter 39 of Magna Carta, 1215, declared that no free man could be imprisoned or suffer deprivation of property except after trial by peers or by the law of the land. Legal judgements later broadened these terms to mean trial by jury and due process of law. The phrase is also included in the United Nations declaration on Civil and Political Rights. Art. 5 of the European Convention on Human Rights defined the circumstances in which anyone may be detained and Art. 6 guarantees the right to a fair and public trial.

Reading
Levy, L.W. 1968. *Origins of the Fifth Amendment.* Oxford: OUP; Schwartz, J. and H.W.R. Wade. 1972. *Legal Control of Government.* Oxford: OUP.

dyarchy A term used to describe the structure of British colonial government in some of the Indian provinces between 1919 and 1935. Financial and security matter remained under British control, while other departments of government were under Indian ministers and responsible to the provincial legislature. Conflict soon arose and after 1935 complete ministerial responsibility was established at the provincial level.
See also COLONIALISM.

Reading
Baker, C.J. 1976. *Politics in South India 1920–1937.* Cambridge: CUP.

dynastic state *See* ANCIEN REGIME.

E

ecological politics Politics concerned with the environment and 'green issues'. The agitation against nuclear armaments and nuclear power expanded into a more general movement against technological advance and industrialization in the 1960s. The campaigners sounded alarms about air pollution, 'global warming', the destruction of animal species like the whale, and the spoiling of the countryside by the building of more motorways and airports. Their underlying philosophy was either merely the pragmatic one of making the world a safer and pleasanter place for human life; or, among a minority, a much more intellectualized belief in Nature, leading to an enthusiasm for the primitive and a return to a paganism in which worship of the elements was important.

Ecological politics is the salient example of SINGLE ISSUE POLITICS. By the 1970s there were ecological parties in most European countries, though they always retained some of the features of pressure groups and suffered from factionalism. In Germany where the Greens were strongest they were divided between the 'realos' who were willing to coalesce in government with other parties and the 'fundis' who were not. In Sweden they were in alliance with the Farmers' Party. They were not so successful in France and in Britain their only triumph was when they obtained 15 per cent of the vote at the 1989 European elections. Nearly all voters and politicians appear to be sympathetic to the 'greens', while their eminently newsworthy protests and demonstrations win them a good deal of support; but it is a different matter to persuade either people to give up using their cars or governments to restrict industries which pollute.

See also NEW SOCIAL MOVEMENTS.

Reading
Dalton, R.J. 1994. *The Green Rainbow*. New Haven: YUP; Goodin, R.E. 1992. *Green Political Theory*. Cambridge: Polity Press; Kolinsky, E. 1989. *The Greens in West Germany*. Oxford: Berg; Muller-Rommel. F. ed. 1989. *New Politics in Western Europe: the Rise and Success of Green Parties and Alternative Lists*. Boulder: University of Colorado Press; Smith, R.J. 1998. *Ecologism*. Milton Keynes: Open University Press.

economic man A concept of the early classical economists that sees everyone maximizing their benefits in a free society and competitive market. It assumes that the economic actor is perfectly rational, exercising free choice in a condition of perfect competition. Thus as a consumer, one will buy in the cheapest market and as a producer, sell where one can obtain the highest price. Later economists introduced the idea of a declining rate of benefit which will affect economic man's calculations. For example, the longer one works the less an extra minute adds to one's benefit. One will reach a 'margin' at which there is no profit in continuing. Applicable to all market transactions, this concept is known as 'marginalism'.

There are clear objections to the concept of economic man. In the first place it assumes rational choice is available; but this can only be so where the individual has complete information. Except in the simplest markets, this is well-nigh impossible for most individuals. Few 'perfect markets' exist. Moreover, the concept becomes more difficult when applied to the entrepreneur who has little place in classical economics. An exact calculation of risks even in the short term, let alone the medium or long term, is not easy even with computers. Misinformation can move around the markets as quickly as correct information. Furthermore, social costs and benefits are difficult to fit into the equation. What monetary value can be placed on a clean and noiseless environment? Economic man is a useful concept for understanding how the economy operates; but all the above qualifications must be borne in mind.
See also PUBLIC CHOICE THEORY; RATIONAL CHOICE THEORY.

Reading
Drucker, P.F. 1939. *The End of Economic Man.* London: Heinemann; Galbraith, J.K. 1987. *A History of Economics.* London: Hamish Hamilton; Gray, A. 1948. *The Development of Economic Doctrine.* London: Longman; Marshall, A. [1890] 1920. *Principles of Economics.* 8th edn. London: Macmillan.

economic planning   *See* PLANNING.

egalitarianism   A belief in the value of making people more equal. It can apply to wealth, status and power and will involve identifying inequalities and attempting to remedy them. As regards inequalities of wealth, the WELFARE STATE is the outcome of efforts to mitigate them through DISTRIBUTIVE JUSTICE. It will require political action using the coercive strength of the state to achieve. Inequalities of status may be cultural and be demonstrated in privileges accorded, for example, to ARISTOCRACY, men and the aged. These may be remedied by education, though again political action is likely to be necessary. Inequalities of power can hardly be eradicated without abolishing governmental control completely. DEMOCRACY, however, gives everyone the right to contest for power, though few avail themselves of it; but it does ensure that the holders of power can be dismissed by a majority of the powerless.

Although complete equality may be an unobtainable, and some would say an undesirable objective, developments in the last two centuries would seem to justify the view that inequalities have become less cumulative. In primitive societies the people of highest status tend to be the people with most wealth and power. Indeed, the acquisition of political power is seen as an opportunity for accumulating wealth. Modern trends have seen the people of high status deprived of political power which has often passed to people representing those of low status. People with wealth are at one disadvantage in democracies: they have few votes.
See also DEMOCRACY; DISTRIBUTIVE JUSTICE; EQUALITY; WELFARE STATE.

Reading
Benn, S.I. and R. S. Peters. 1959. *Social Principles and the Democratic State.* London: Allen and Unwin.; Jackman, R.W. 1975. *Politics and Social Equality.* New York: Wiley; Lenski, G. 1966. *Power and Privilege.* New York: McGraw-Hill.

elections   An election is an act of choosing someone as a representative. It is therefore an essential part of representative democracy. Authoritarian states also sometimes hold elections but either there is only one candidate to vote for, as in the former Communist states, or there is corruption and intimidation at the polls as in countries like Indonesia and Mexico. The purpose of the election in such cases is not to select representatives and a government, but to legitimize the regime.

In a free and fair democratic election any citizen will have the right to stand, but independent CANDIDATES are rare these days and most will be the nominees of a political party. It is usual for them to represent a territorial area, though its size will differ according to the electoral system. With Proportional Representation there might be a large CONSTITUENCY with as many as eight members. To prevent bribery voting is now by secret ballot. Where votes cannot be checked there is no advantage to be gained from it. In the secrecy of a booth the voter marks a paper with a cross or, in some American states, uses a voting machine.

The organizational effort needed for elections is considerable. It is necessary to compile an electoral register of voters, a task undertaken normally by local authorities, though in most states in the USA the intitiative is left to the individual voter. Officials have to oversee and verify the nomination of candidates. On polling day electoral officers have to be appointed in each polling booth and a vast army of counters recruited to count the votes after the poll has closed.

Party organization is also conspicuous during the campaign and especially on election day. ACTIVISTS have been busy CANVASSING in order to discover supporters beforehand. They will try to organize proxy or postal votes for those unable to vote in person. On the day itself they man the polling stations as 'tellers', checking on their supporters as they vote. 'Knockers up' contact those who have not voted later in the day and an operation is put into effect to get them to the poll. The elderly, the disabled and the sick who are not registered for proxy or postal votes may need transport to carry them to vote. In rural areas, where polling stations may be some distance away this may be important. The parties will also have observers at the count to watch the counting and prevent any chicanery.

The modern election campaign is very expensive although in most democracies there are elaborate laws about the spending of money by parties and candidates. In the USA, where parties have to buy television time, elections are particularly expensive, but everywhere it is now customary to run poster campaigns and use helicopters to convey leaders around the country. Political parties frequently demand laws to permit state funding for their campaigns where laws do not exist. The extra expense has been brought about by a change in the nature of campaigns since the advent of television. Much of the debate takes place on television in the form of press conferences and the cross-examination of party leaders by television commentators. It puts a premium on party leaders and on the management of news. A new generation of SPIN DOCTORS and pollsters have led to a commercialization and professionalization of party election strategies.

This has led to a questioning of the effect of campaigns and what they decide. The ideal of nineteenth-century liberals like John Stuart MILL was that elections should educate the voters about policy choices. This assumed that the contending parties would seriously debate policies. Instead, it is more common for them to obfuscate about policies, deeming them too technical for the voters to understand, or too controversial and likely to lead to voter panic. The parties prefer to attack their opponents and misinform the electorate about their records and likely intentions. Research evidence appears to show that it is only the most politically interested who learn from the campaigns. Most voters remain sceptical of all politicians' intentions and consider elections as a boring distraction. But they vote, which tends to suggest that they are aware of the implications of policies which affect themselves. Elections also demonstrate the accountability of democratic governments and legitimize the democratic process. They socialize new young voters into the political community.

It is argued by some observers that elections decide little. Even when the incumbents in power change, the issues and problems remain the same and in the end any government would be forced to implement the same policies because they are conditioned by outside circumstances. Yet there are from time to time watershed elections, as in 1932 in the USA and 1945 in Britain, when new governments sweep to power committed to innovatory programmes which they proceed to carry out, changing the nature of society.

See also ACTIVISTS; SPIN DOCTORS; VOTING BEHAVIOUR.

Reading
Butler, D., H. Penniman and A. Ranney. eds. 1981. *Democracy at the Polls*. Washington, D.C.: American Enterprise Institute; Mackenzie, W.J.M. 1958. *Free Elections*. London: Allen and Unwin; Penniman, H. ed. 1975. *At the Polls: a Series of Election Studies*. Washington, D.C.: American Enterprise Institute; Pomper, G. M. and S.S. Lederman. 1980. *Elections in America*. London: Longman; Pulzer, P.G.J. 1975. *Political Representation and Elections in Britain*. London: Allen and Unwin.

electoral college A group of people with the duty of electing someone. A well-known example is the College of Cardinals which elects the Pope. Political instances of electoral colleges involve indirect election. For example, Art. II of the American constitution states that each state must choose electors to be members of a college which, in turn,

elects the President. The number of electors to which each state is entitled is the number of its Senators (always two) plus the number of its Representatives in the House of Representatives which is determined on the basis of population. Thus the Founding Fathers deliberately avoided the direct popular election of the President. They hoped each state would choose 'worthy people' as its collegiate electors. Political parties soon intervened, however, and drew up lists of candidates for the college. Hence, since quite early in the nineteenth century, each state returns a block of electors pledged to support one party's Presidential candidate. The constitution of the French Fifth Republic also had a provision for a Presidential electoral college of over 80,000 members who were mostly local government councillors. But it only operated once, for in 1962 the constitution was amended. Since then French Presidents have been elected by direct popular vote.

Reading
US Congress: Senate. 1977. 'The Electoral College and Direct Election'. In *Hearings* 95th Congress. 1st session. Washington, D.C.: Government Printing Office; Wilmerding, L. 1958. *The Electoral College*. New Brunswick, NJ: Rutgers University Press.

electoral geography A sub-discipline of political science pioneered by André SIEGFRIED during the French Third Republic. Later research was done by KEY in the American South, and by Pelling for late Victorian and Edwardian Britain. While the cartography of elections is interesting there are some obvious problems. Clearly it is more easily done with single-member CONSTITUENCIES. Maps of successive ELECTIONS even in their case will only show seats which change allegiance, unless more elaborate techniques with different sorts of shading are used. More importantly, it can be argued that explanations of geographic political allegiances are not necessarily derived from the cartography. The so-called 'ecological fallacy' tells us that only inferences, not definite socio-demographic findings, can be discovered from electoral geography. This consideration discouraged researchers for some time, but recently interest has revived with the use of new techniques.

See also APPORTIONMENT.

Reading
Johnston, R.J. 1985. *The Geography of English Politics*. London: Croom Helm; Key, V.O. 1949. *Southern Politics*. New York: Random House; Mohan, J. ed. 1989. *The Political Geography of Contemporary Britain*. London: Macmillan; Pelling, H.M. 1967. *Social Geography of British Elections 1885–1910*. London: Macmillan; Siegfried, A. 1913. *Tableau des Partis de la France de l'Ouest*. Paris: Colin.

electoral systems   Methods of electing representatives vary greatly. There are differences between the number returned from each CONSTITUENCY; differences in the method used to calculate the winner or winners; and differences in the degree to which the voter can influence the placing of candidates on the ballot paper.

It is often assumed that single-member constituencies, found in France and most of the English-speaking world, are necessarily bound up with the FIRST-PAST-THE-POST system. Yet for some centuries Britain had only two-member constituencies. Again, it is usually believed that under Proportional Representation, party lists drawn up by the parties cannot be influenced by the voter so that when seats are apportioned those candidates not favoured by party organizers and placed at the bottom of the list will stand no chance of election. Yet in some countries with PR, by what is known as 'preferential voting', voters are allowed to ring candidates they prefer, or even to alter the order on any one of the lists. Under the French Fourth Republic, by the system known as *panachage*,

voters could even extract candidates from all the party lists and write out their own list.

Preferences between types of electoral system will depend on how much weight is attributed to arithmetical fairness, needs of territorial or cultural and socio-demographic representation and effects on the political life of the country. All these factors are matters for discussion among political scientists. Those who argue for quantitative justice see it as an ingredient of DEMOCRACY. If the people are to be represented they must be represented accurately. Even countries who come close to this model, such as the Netherlands, have a 'threshold' of 0.67 per cent. Parties receiving a smaller proportion of the total vote than this are not entitled to participate in the apportionment of seats. Opponents of extreme PR argue that it inevitably produces coalition governments which are inherently unstable because they are at the mercy of small parties. This can be refuted by the example of PR in Sweden, ruled by the Social Democrats for 43 years.

Much of the analysis of political scientists has been concerned with the effect of electoral systems upon the nature and number of political parties. Duverger's seminal work in the 1950s leaned heavily to the view that the electoral system was the major factor in determining the configuration of the parties. Later commentators have tended to argue that electoral systems are often chosen that suit the political culture and/or are appropriate to a country's pattern of CLEAVAGES. Less charitable critics have alleged that parties in power often change electoral systems to improve their electoral chances. The general conclusion must be that no definitive statement can be made about the influence of electoral systems on party systems. The consequences may be slight or they may be quite considerable. The question to ask is: Does the electoral system moderate or intensify the socio-cultural cleavages?

See also ADDITIONAL MEMBER SYSTEM; ALTERNATIVE VOTE; APPROVAL VOTING; CUMULATIVE VOTE; ELECTIONS; FIRST-PAST-THE-POST; FRANCHISE; LIMITED VOTE; PARTY SYSTEMS; SINGLE TRANSFERABLE VOTE; VOTING BEHAVIOUR.

Reading
Bogdanor, V. and D.E. Butler. eds. 1983. *Democracy and Elections: Electoral Systems and their Political Consequences.* Cambridge: CUP; Carstairs, A.M. 1980. *A Short History of Electoral Systems in Western Europe.* London: Allen and Unwin; Duverger, M. 1954. *Political Parties.* London: Methuen; Rae, D. W. 1971. *The Political Consequences of Electoral Laws.* New Haven: YUP.

electoral volatility The propensity to change one's voting allegiance quite often. The concept is bound to be relative as vote-changing has always existed. The term has become familiar as a result of the increased volatility of the voters in western Europe from the 1960s onwards. In the first two decades after World War II it was common to portray political allegiances as fairly loyal and changes of government as brought about by marginal changes of voters' attachments. Increasing electoral volatility has been attributed to social changes over the last thirty years. It has been linked with the 'end of ideology' thesis and the emergence of 'post-materialist' values. The 'new politics' is much more a matter of issues such as crime, drugs, the environment and citizen participation.

See also POST-MATERIALISM; SWING.

Reading
Crewe, I. and D. Denver. eds. 1985. *Electoral Change in Western Democracies: Patterns and Sources of Electoral Volatility.* London: Croom Helm.

elites Groups who in some way are superior to the rest of the community. The superiority may rest upon social status, intellectual brilliance, the posses-sion of great wealth, or a position of superordination. A dominant elite may possess, or be assumed to possess, all four characteristics. Pareto (1848–1923) was first attracted to the study of elites by his discovery that wealth in all societies had been very unevenly distributed, with a few owning a very large proportion of it. From this he derived his theory that there are elites in every walk of life. They are the people who excel. But he was primarily interested in the political elite, the people who excelled in governing. His contemporary, Mosca (1858–1941), held that political power had always rested with an oligarchy that in early times was aristocratic. Later elites might be democratic.

Later writers have been concerned to relate political elites to social and economic dominance. MARX's political elite, the state, is the 'executive committee of the bourgeoisie', the RULING CLASS in society. MILLS, instead, argued that the American elite had a functional basis in the corporation bosses, the military leaders and the top people in Washington, D. C. and, further, that they had common backgrounds, similar values and were interlocked in a 'power elite'. It was not difficult for other writers to claim that there was a similar position in France and Britain, or that it existed everywhere in some form. On the other hand, the pluralists led by DAHL argued that power was held diffusely and claimed to have demonstrated it in the field of COMMUNITY POLITICS. They contended that the demonstration of interlocking cadres was no proof of elite domination: a study of decision-making revealed that leaders adjusted policies to the opinions and reactions of their followers.

See also DEMOCRATIC ELITISM; ELITISM; POLITICAL CLASS; RULING CLASS.

Reading
Aron, R. 1960. 'Classe sociale, classe politique, classe dirigeante'. In *European Journal of Sociology* I–II, 260–81; Dahl, R.A. 1958. 'A

Critique of the Ruling Elite Model'. In *American Political Science Review* 52. June, 463–9; Eldersveld, S.J. 1989. *Political Elites in Modern Societies*. Ann Arbor: University of Michigan Press; Mills, C.W. 1956. *The Power Elite*. New York: OUP.

elitism   The term has been used in two ways. First, it describes a subject studied by the 'elitist' theorists. The classic elitists are Mosca, Pareto and Michels; but there are numerous other writers about elites in recent years, both among political scientists and sociologists.

Second, it has a rather loose usage as a description of attitudes that are ascribed to a higher social class, or to anyone in a superordinate position. Thus people seen as 'snobbish', 'uppity', or with 'pretensions of excellence' were described as 'elitist' by the radicals of the 1960s. Even leaders of revolutionary groups might be accused of elitism. Thus its implications were somewhat anarchistic and in favour of DIRECT DEMOCRACY.

See also DEMOCRATIC ELITISM; ELITES; PARTICIPATORY DEMOCRACY.

Reading
Bottomore, T.B. 1966. *Elites and Society*. Harmondsworth: Penguin; Keller, S. 1963. *Beyond the Ruling Class*. New York: Random House; Michels, R. 1915. *Political Parties*. London: Jarrold; Mosca, G. [1896] 1939. *The Ruling Class*. New York: McGraw-Hill; Pareto, V. [1916] 1935. *Mind and Society*. 4 vols. London: Cape; Parry, G. 1994. *Political Elites*. London: Allen and Unwin.

emergency powers   The use of power which is arbitrary and not concerned with legal niceties is a common feature of all times and places, but in democracies such behaviour by governments is not considered legitimate except in emergencies. Yet provision for emergency powers exists in most democratic constitutions. It is not always easy, however, to decide when there is an emergency and consequently there is always unease at their deployment. The US Constitution does not mention emergencies, but some Presidents have claimed their right to special powers during wars; what Lincoln called the 'war powers' under Art. 2, Section 2, making the President Commander-in-Chief. Roosevelt employed such powers during World War II, but when Truman (1945–53), during the Korean conflict, claimed the right to take over the steel mills when they were on strike, the Supreme Court ruled that he had acted unconstitutionally.

In France the President is granted powers under Art. 16 of the constitution to 'take measures demanded by the circumstances' (after consultation with the Prime Minister, the presidents of both chambers as well as the Constitutional Council) when the 'institutions of the republic, the independence of the nation, the integrity of its territory, or the execution of its international obligations are threatened in a serious and immediate manner'. Parliament must remain in session while the state of emergency remains in force. These broad powers, originally intended to be a safeguard against Communist subversion, have only been used once when the 'revolt of the generals' threatened De Gaulle's government in 1961 during the Algerian war of independence.

In Britain the powers of the CROWN allow the royal prerogative to be exercised in undefined circumstances, but legislation allows a state of emergency, under parliamentary control, to be declared for one month. An Act of 1976 permits the armed forces to be used when workers in vital services are on strike. Since 1973 there have also been special powers for the police and army in Northern Ireland. All such circumstances arouse misgivings in democratic countries. Once states of emergency are imposed there is always a governmental reluctance to end them.

See also MARTIAL LAW.

Reading

Friedrich, C.J. 1957. *Constitutional Reason of State*. Providence: Brown University Press; Rossiter, C. 1948. *Constitutional Dictatorship: Crisis Government in Modern Democracies*. Princeton: Princeton University Press.

eminent domain   An American term connoting the rights of the state over private property which, in the cause of public good, it can appropriate against the wishes of the owner, though, by the terms of the Fifth Amendment, fair compensation must be paid. Similar arrangements exist elsewhere. In Britain compulsory purchase by central or local government is possible, though there is no right to compensation at full market value. Nevertheless, it is nearly always paid.

empires   Empires comprise states which govern territories beyond its borders with subject peoples. There have been two broad types – landward empires and maritime empires – the former connected with national defence and military ambitions, the latter with trade and naval prowess, though both had similar problems.

The Roman Empire was the first example of an *imperium*, an order based on law. It established the principle of citizenship which was later granted to non-Romans (St Paul was a Roman citizen), and with its restless legions spread itself and its civilization through half of Europe. The Holy Roman Empire was conceived as its successor but, in its long life between 800 and 1806, it remained a loose confederation. As Voltaire said, it was 'neither Holy, nor Roman, nor an Empire'. The Russian Empire remains the only other example of a landward empire, constructed by eastward expansion enveloping peoples who, except in the Caucasus, were fairly primitive and pacific. The Soviet Union inherited it and proceeded with modernization and Russification, though these processes may have encouraged the growth of nationalisms which led to its disintegration after 1990.

The maritime empires were the British, the Portuguese, the Dutch and the French. Of these the French was the most distinctive with its concept of cultural assimilation, achieved by the spread of the French language, French civilization, and an elite bureaucracy trained in Paris. It resembled the Roman in that it held out the promise of French citizenship to those subjects who reached the required standard. The British and the Dutch kept native peoples much more at arm's length. The British Empire, in its heyday in the 1930s, covered almost a quarter of the world's land surface. Its territories could be grouped under three headings: there were the self-governing dominions, the colonies ruled directly from Whitehall, and those where INDIRECT RULE applied and imperial control was exerted through a native ruler advised by a British 'Resident'. The Dutch also used this latter method in Indonesia.

Between the 1940s and the 1970s all these maritime empires collapsed, in the Portuguese case because the country and its army was exhausted by a long colonial war. Considerations of financial and psychological exhaustion were present with the other maritime empires, but in their cases empire was perceived to be no longer consistent with liberal and democratic values. Today the only existing empire is the Indonesian, small compared with the others and more repressive.

See also COLONIALISM; DOMINION STATUS; IMPERIALISM; INDIRECT RULE.

Reading

Fieldhouse, D.K. 1982. *The Colonial Empires*. London: Macmillan; Koebner, R. and H.D. Schmidt. 1964. *Imperialism 1840–1960*. Cambridge: CUP.

employers' organizations   Employers combine to defend their common interests. In many ways they compete with one another, but they find combination helpful against threats from labour and from governments. TRADE UNIONS may threaten with industrial action and employers in the same industry will then associate to conduct negotiations especially about pay. Governments may threaten with legislation to restrict employer freedom, or they may introduce policies which increase employer costs.

Employer associations may be at a local level in chambers of commerce. These are important in most European countries and in Austria and Germany enterprises must belong to them. In the USA about 3000 of them are federated in the Chamber of Commerce of the United States. 'Peak associations' of employers at a national level include the National Association of Manufacturers in the USA, the Confederation of British Industry in Britain, the *Bundesvereinigung der Deutschen Arbeitgeberverbande* in Germany and the *Comité National du Patronat Français* in France. They tend to be dominated by the smaller members, and for this reason in the USA the largest enterprises formed the Business Round Table.

Globalization of the economy will ultimately result in international organizations of employers, but at the moment the MULTINATIONALS exert global pressures, not on trade unions but against regulatory pressures from international organization, for example the European Commission. Normally employers have the disadvantage in democracies of only having a few votes; but this does not arise in the global economy because there is no global state, let alone global democracy.

See also GLOBALIZATION; LABOUR; MULTINATIONALS; TRADE UNIONS.

Reading

Bauer, R., I. de Sola Pool and L.D. Dexter. 1972. *American Business and Public Policy*. Chicago: Aldine; Grant, W. and D. Marsh. 1977. *The CBI*. London: Hodder and Stoughton; Wilson, G.K. 1985. *Business and Politics*. London: Macmillan.

enlightenment The name given to a period of intellectual history dating broadly from the mid-eighteenth century to the American and French Revolutions. Although the thinkers associated with the Enlightenment had diverse views they all rejected the institutions and values of the ANCIEN REGIME. Above all, they challenged the authority of the Catholic church and the monopoly of hereditary monarchy and ARISTOCRACY over knowledge. This was a natural consequence of the scientific revolution of Galileo, Lister and Newton and the writings of HOBBES, LOCKE and Descartes. Together they resulted in the development of both deductive and inductive logic. This produced an intellectual climate of scepticism in which questions hitherto stifled began to be asked loudly. 'Is there a God?'; 'What legitimacy does heredity confer?'; 'Why are governments instituted?'; 'Why should some men have more basic rights than others?' (Women were hardly considered at first; but soon they began to assert their rights.) These questions are still being asked.

The Enlightenment was influential in Europe and North America; but its centre was undoubtedly France. Leading figures were Montesquieu who published his criticism of the ANCIEN REGIME, the *Spirit of the Laws* in 1748; Diderot and D'Alembert who produced their first volume of their famous *Encyclopaedia* in 1751; and Voltaire who, in the same year, published his *Age of Louis XIV*, an attack on the corruption of the monarchy. In his *Letters from the English* Voltaire compared the civil liberties they enjoyed to the repressive intolerance of France. ROUSSEAU is often excluded from Enlightenment thought because of his pessimism and romanticism, but in his two *Discourses on The Inequality of Man* (1750 and 1754) he claimed that men's natural rights were to be free and equal.

He thus laid the basis for the doctrine of popular sovereignty.

There was also a Scottish Enlightenment in which Hume and Adam Smith were leading figures. They had links with France and America where Paine and Jefferson were the leading spirits. The latter drafted the Declaration of Independence in 1776 and as American ambassador in Paris influenced Lafayette, who had fought for the American Revolutionaries, in writing the Declaration of the Rights of Man in 1789. Influenced by Condorcet, Jefferson had a firm belief in Progress and adapted a rationalist approach to almost everything he did – politics, architecture, librarianship and even gardening.

It is no exaggeration to say that the modern world dates from the Enlightenment.

See also LIBERALISM; RATIONALISM.

Reading
Cassirer, E. [1932] 1951. *The Philosophy of the Enlightenment*. Princeton: Princeton University Press; Cobban, A. 1960. *In Search of Humanity: the Role of the Enlightenment in Modern History*. London: Cape; Laski, H.J. 1936. *The Rise of European Liberalism*. London: Allen and Unwin; Martin, K. 1962. *French Liberal Thought in the Eighteenth Century*. London: Harper.

entryism The tactic of penetrating other organizations with active people who aim to take it over for their own purposes. For it to be successful the permeating group needs to be procedurally adroit and to be entering a larger organization in which the membership is not so active and not so coherent in its pursuit of its objectives. The technique is not new and is not necessarily covert. It is best illustrated by the example of the British Communists and the Labour Party from the 1920s onwards. Individual Communists joined local Labour Parties and trade unions. Every year the Communist Party applied for affiliation to the Labour Party and every year it was rejected at the annual conference of the Labour Party. There was no secret about it though it was consistent with the conspiratorial tactics advocated by Lenin. In the 1960s, and until the 1980s, a Trotskyist organization, Militant, tried to penetrate the Labour Party in the same way.

Entryism is most attractive to small extremist groups where the electoral system does not favour small parties and, consequently, where political life is dominated by large parties who, by their very nature, are heterogeneous and subject to internal conflicts. Under Proportional Representation small parties may be less inclined to favour penetration. Yet it is always possible they will want to operate in both ways.

environmentalism *See* ECOLOGICAL POLITICS.

equality At first sight this appears to be a simple concept. Equal means equal. Yet humanity is not uniform. One cannot treat grandmothers like babes-in-arms. Moreover, there are several different aspects of equality. Equality can sometimes mean that all must be dealt with in the same even-handed manner. This would be called 'equity' in the courts and 'fairness' in common parlance. It is not a far step from here to civic equality involving citizenship and the franchise for all. Colonel Rainboro in the Putney debates in the Cromwellian army in 1647, demanding universal manhood suffrage, declared 'the poorest he that is in England hath a life to live as the richest he'. He was protesting against the inequality of civic rights in his day.

Equality is frequently taken to mean economic equality, equality of wealth, equality in the distribution of goods. This subject is permanently on the world's agenda. Both within states and between states there is a demand that goods should be allocated so that each person receives an equal amount. Yet it is widely recognized that extreme EGALITARI-ANISM is not practical and in some democracies there has even been a movement towards more inequality. Moreover, market economies do not guarantee equality of the right of access as a producer. Inequality of the chance to be an entrepreneur stems from the other inequalities.

Social equality depends on equality of status within the wider society. This will vary with time and place but in modern industrialized society status is likely to be measured by perceived achievement. This may be determined by luck, hard work, presentation of self-image and access to higher education. EQUALITY OF OPPORTUNITY is one aspect of equality that most people readily accept though there is no guarantee that it will not increase economic inequality.

Equality is grouped with liberty and FRATERNITY in the French Revolutionary slogan. Yet their association is by no means inevitable. Equal competitors may feel little brotherhood for each other. An authoritarian regime may contain more equality of wealth, and consequently more fraternal feeling, than a democratic one.

See also AFFIRMATIVE ACTION; EGALITARI-ANISM; EQUALITY OF OPPORTUNITY; FRATERNITY; FREEDOM.

Reading
Beteille, A. ed. 1969. *Social Inequality.* Harmondsworth: Penguin; Pennock, J.R. and J.W. Chapman. eds. 1967. *Equality.* New York: Atherton; Rae, D. 1981. *Equalities.* Cambridge, Mass.: HUP; Rees, J. 1971. *Equality.* London: Macmillan; Tawney, R.H. 1938. *Equality.* London: Allen and Unwin.

equality of opportunity This is a common slogan among politicians. It has the benefit of apparently being about equality without necessarily producing a more egalitarian society. MERITOCRACY may be an admirable thing in itself but it may only result in a more resentful

society. This is because legally guaranteed equal right of access to the avenues of advancement is not the same as equality of opportunity. It could only be the same if there was no variety of family background. Handicapping children from privileged backgrounds at some point might equalize opportunity. But at what point in the race does handicapping end?

Even so, it is generally acknowledged that equality of opportunity has increased in modern society. The professional and managerial classes have expanded and access to them has become easier. Yet this has not necessarily led to an increase in equality. Even in a society like the USA, where the historical rhetoric is dedicated to equality, much inequality exists.

See also AFFIRMATIVE ACTION; EGALITARI-ANISM; EQUALITY; MERITOCRACY.

Reading
Parkin, F. 1971. *Class, Inequality and Social Order.* London: McGibbon and Kee; Young, M. 1958. *The Rise of the Meritocracy.* Harmondsworth: Penguin.

equal protection An American term derived from the Fourteenth Amendment, Section 1 (1868) which says no state can 'deny any person within its jurisdiction the equal protection of the laws'. At first interpreted by the courts in the sense of safeguarding DUE PROCESS OF LAW, under the chairmanship of Earl Warren the Supreme Court began to use it to outlaw racial discrimination. In the case, *Brown* v. *Board of Education of Topeka*, 1954, the Court decided that the equal protection clause made segregation in public (state) school education unconstitutional.

escalation A military term used to indicate accelerating stages of response to attack or the threat of attack. It has been widely employed by nuclear warfare specialists. The metaphor is either from escalators or ladders and suggests inevitability rather than acceleration. This may explain why it has become unpopular and is often replaced by the notion of flexible response. Instead of relying on an inexorable strategy it is better to leave one's options open and suit the reply to the situation.

See also CRISIS; MASSIVE RETALIATION; MUTUALLY ASSURED DESTRUCTION.

Reading
Bobbitt, P., L. Freedman and G.F. Treverton. eds. 1989. *US Nuclear Strategy: a Reader.* Basingstoke: Macmillan.

establishment   An official relationship between an institution and the state. It usually applies to churches. Thus the Church of England is an established church. Similarly the Lutheran Church is established in Scandinavia. A universal religion like Roman Catholicism does not need establishment, though the Vatican may sometimes have arrangements or even treaties with countries in which it operates, such as the Lateran Treaty with the Italian state in 1929.

'The establishment' is a term coined by journalists in the 1950s to describe people who held power in Britain. It included leading politicians, senior civil servants, top bankers and industrialists, governors of the BBC and even members of the Trades Union Congress General Council. Later usages broadened the group and, consequently, the meaning of the term, which was never very clear. It reflected a vague feeling that there was too much unidentifiable and unaccountable power in Britain.

See also ELITES; ELITISM; RULING CLASS.

estates   Privileged social categories with corporate status, fulfilling the function of political representation in medieval times. Monarchs often allowed them to discuss taxation, present grievances and sometimes legislate. The usual division was that of three estates, clergy, nobles and burghers of important towns. In Central Europe they were often called 'Diets'. The most famous was the French Estates General with three orders – clergy, aristocracy and commoners. Admission was strictly controlled and membership largely inherited. Louis XVI recalled it in the financial crisis of 1789, the first time it had met since 1614. The commoners, the Third Estate, drew up the Declaration of the Rights of Man which spelt the end of the Estates General and the ANCIEN REGIME itself.

Reading
Koenigsberger, H.G. 1971. *Estates and Revolutions.* Ithaca: Cornell University Press; Major, J.R. 1980. *Representative Government in Early Modern France.* New Haven: YUP.

ethnicity   The characteristic of belonging to an ethnic group. Thus it is a matter of identification with people one sees as similar to one's self in the first place and is clearly subjective. Yet common identification could define CLASS CONSCIOUSNESS so the question must be: 'What are the special features of ethnic consciousness?' It is not easy to answer.

The most obvious identifying features are cultural – religion and language. These do not necessarily correspond. For example, the Serbs, Croats and Bosnian Muslims speak a common language and between 1918 and 1989 were all called 'Yugoslavs'. (That was their NATIONALITY.) But they are divided by different religions, the Serbs are Orthodox and the Croats Catholic. A common historical experience is also cited as a feature of ethnic groups. Yet this is more commonly regarded as an attribute of the NATION and nations are often 'multi-ethnic'. The fact is that the terms 'ethnic group' and 'nation' are often used interchangeably. Thus Britain, like many other countries, is multi-ethnic and 'multi-national'. Perhaps the best way of approaching the problem is to say that ethnic groups may either aspire to be nations, in which case they will want 'state-hood', or they will merely want some form of autonomy. Quite often, like the Basques, or the French Canadians, or the Scots, they will be divided on this issue.

There is much academic discussion about the origins of ethnicity. In the 1960s and 1970s there was a resurgence of groups in Europe long since thought dead. The Friesians and the Occitanians, claiming their dialects were buried languages, asserted their claims to consideration. (To some this heralded a BALKANIZATION of Europe.) Explanations might be that it was a BACKLASH against the threat of a global culture; or that it represented the expansion of the highly educated classes with more leisure and a finely developed knowledge of history; or that it was a reaction against the political centralization of the state and the bureaucracy of the European Union, though encouraged by the latter's principle of SUBSIDIARITY. Theorists of the origins of ethnicity are divided between the 'primordialists' who see it almost as a God-given condition; and 'instrumentalists' who perceive it as an outcome of a certain historical situation.

Whatever the case, there is no doubt that ethnic conflict is a most serious threat to world peace and the stability of nations. Often socio-cultural differences are intensified by economic inequalities. For example, hatred of the Ugandan Asians was because they were a prosperous commercial class in an otherwise under-developed society. Dislike of immigrant minorities in Europe as a working-class phenomenon is associated with the fear that they will accept lower wages and thus successfully compete in the labour market. Sometimes a landless ethnic group will feel hostile to another which owns the land. The prewar anti-Semitism of eastern European professional men has been attributed to the very high proportion of Jews among the professional classes.

It is common to say that education and DEMOCRACY will help to resolve the conflict. Yet mass culture and political mobilization may accentuate the divisions. Leaders of different groups may negotiate compromises: on the other hand, they may feel it is in their interests to proclaim their hatred of other groups. There may even be fisticuffs in the legislative chamber. Ultimately partition and separate states may be the solution, though this is not possible where populations are mixed.

See also ETHNOCENTRISM; NATIONALISM; NATION-STATE; RACISM.

Reading

Brass, P. ed. 1985. *Ethnic Groups and the State.* Beckenham: Croom Helm; Glazer, N. and Moynihan, D. eds. 1975. *Ethnicity, Theory and Experience.* Cambridge, Mass.: HUP; Horowitz, D.L. 1985. *Ethnic Groups in Conflict.* Berkeley: University of California Press; Nnoli, O. 1989. *Ethnic Politics in Africa.* Ibadan: Ibadan UP; Smith, A.D. 1986. *The Ethnic Origins of Nations.* Oxford: Blackwell.

ethnocentrism   The tendency to view everything from the perspective of one's own culture. This may lead to erroneous conclusions for the social scientist engaged in cross-cultural research. A familiar example is the statement that Columbus discovered America and not the Red Indians who may have come from Asia a millennium before. Clearly researchers should strive to avoid ethnocentrism. At the other extreme 'xenocentrism' is viewing everything from the perspective of a foreign culture.

Reading

Sumner, W.G. 1906. *Folkways.* Boston: Ginn.

eurocommunism   The name given to the reconstructed Communism which emerged in the Italian and Spanish Communist Parties after 1975. The Italian party, the largest in western Europe, under its leader Enrique Berlinguer hoped to share governmental power for the first time with the ruling Christian Democrats, the so-called 'Historic Compromise'. This was prevented by the assassination of Aldo Moro.

Eurocommunism was partly a reflection of the thirty years of democratic politics during which western European Communist parties had become socialized in democratic ways; and partly an indication of tiredness of control from Moscow which, since the break with China, was not the only centre purveying ideological correctness. Long experience and some success in local government had also inculcated a pragmatism that was at odds with Stalinism. Hence it was a call for transformation.

Reading

Vannicelli, M. 1981. *Eurocommunism: a Casebook*. London: Allen and Unwin.

executives The most visible and most powerful institution in most modern states. The classical role of executives was to implement the laws made by LEGISLATURES, while JUDICIARIES interpreted the laws as cases arose in the courts. This was the scheme of Montesquieu (1689–1755) who believed these three functions should be separate. Of course, today some states still have neither legislatures nor independent judiciaries but they all have executives.

The most simple division of executives is between those in authoritarian and those in democratic states. In the former, executive power may be exerted by one man – still the case in some archaic sheikhdoms and MILITARY REGIMES – or by a JUNTA of generals, or the collective leadership of a totalitarian party. (Mercifully few of these latter now exist outside China and North Korea.)

Within democracies the classical trinity will always be found. Here the main division is between those with the SEPARATION OF POWERS and those without it. This corresponds to the division between PRESIDENTIAL SYSTEMS and PARLIAMENTARY SYSTEMS. In presidential systems LEGISLATURES have more power. Because members of the executive are not privy to their deliberations they have independent control over law-making. Their COMMITTEES are more powerful than those in parliamentary systems and they have greater supervision over executive spending. Even so, in recent decades much more policy has stemmed from the President. In the USA, for example, this trend began in the 1930s and to a greater or lesser extent 'positive government' has continued since, though it naturally depends on a majority in the legislature sympathetic to the executive in order to translate its policy into legislation and to support it until its passage into law.

In parliamentary systems where the executive sits in the legislature its power depends on the configuration of the political parties and, to a lesser extent, on the support it gets from parliamentary procedure. A legislature with no parties, in which every legislator was an independent, would have great control over the executive because the government would have difficulty in anticipating how its policies would be received. The government might be defeated at any moment. In the real world all democratic legislatures have parties. COALITION GOVERNMENT still gives considerable control to the legislature. It is MAJORITY PARTY GOVERNMENT, as in Britain, which allows most power to the executive. British governments can have great confidence that their policies will be passed. In effect, most legislation will be drafted in the Cabinet and its committees.

In the contemporary world executives have become more powerful because of the need to produce increasingly complex and technical policies, to cost them and to prioritize them. It is difficult for an assembly to fulfill these functions. Yet there is general discontent with the growth of executive power. A more active citizenship, a more responsible media and increased monitoring power for LEGISLATIVE COMMITTEES are all suggested as the necessary remedies.

See also DECREES; DELEGATED LEGISLATION; GOVERNMENT; JUDICIARY; LEGISLATURES; PARLIAMENTARY SYSTEMS; POLICY MAKING; PRESIDENTIAL SYSTEMS; SEPARATION OF POWERS.

Reading
Blondel, J. 1982. *The Organization of Governments*. London: Sage; Hague, R. and M. Harrop. 1982. *Comparative Government*. London: Macmillan.

executive privilege   A claim by successive American Presidents that they had a right to withhold information by forbidding federal officials from giving evidence to Congressional committees or to courts of law. The claim was based on the Separation of Powers and the need to protect national security. In *US* v. *Nixon* 1974 the Supreme Court did not rule that there was no such thing as executive privilege (though there is no reference in the constitution to such a doctrine), but they weakened the claim by rejecting President Nixon's assertion that he did not need to hand over the tapes relating to the Watergate burglary and his cover-up of it.

existentialism   There is no doubt that existentialist ideas made a political impact in the twenty years after World War II. The problem is to assess it. Its origins were in the theology of Kierkegaard and the philosophy of Heidegger, but its main exponents were the French philosophers Albert Camus (1913–60) and Jean-Paul Sartre (1905–80). Both men were important on the Parisian literary scene and their novels irradiate their philosophies about the human predicament. Camus, who was a *pied noir* from Algeria, was a radical anti-imperialist. Sartre always remained an uneasy Marxist with a hatred of Stalinism and a pedagogic

dislike of 'lazy Marxists'. He was an individualist who rejected Marxist determinism. He believed that we are totally responsible for ourselves and our actions that we must perform in a world bereft of meaning. Hence Sartre's most characteristic and influential notion is his emphasis on ALIENATION. This appealed to the politicized student generations of the 1950s and early 1960s with their instinctive reaction against authority of any kind.

Reading
Cranston, M. 1975. 'Jean-Paul Sartre: Solitary Man in a Hostile Universe'. In A. de Crespigny and K. Minogue. *Contemporary Political Philosophers*. New York: Dodd, Mead.

exit, loyalty, voice   Hirschman's trio of terms to explain the three positions that members of any organization may take up. If they become dissatisfied they can protest. If this has no effect and they no longer wish to remain loyal they can 'vote with their feet'. This was originally an economist's model applied to the situation of the consumer in the free market. Exit from markets is easy: rarely if ever are we forced to buy what we have rejected. The analogy is not so apt when applied to the citizen in the 'political market' of the state. Voice is not difficult in a democracy but the costs of exit (emigration) may be excessive. If they stay many citizens will have to accept some policies they dislike.

Reading
Hirschman, A.O. 1970. *Exit, Loyalty, Voice*. Cambridge, Mass.: HUP.

exit poll   A poll taken of voters as they leave the polling station after voting. It is believed such polls predict more accurately as they exclude non-voters and they give the voters less chance of forgetting how they voted. Evidence from most elections supports this belief, though in Britain in 1992 exit polls misled people to think Labour had won. Consequently in the 1997 General Election people were very sceptical about an exit poll predicting a Labour landslide.

See also PUBLIC OPINION; RANDOM SAMPLE; SAMPLE SURVEYS.

exploitation   Taking advantage of a person's or group's situation. It is thus a central concept in any examination of injustice and oppression. MARX saw the exploiters as the class that owned the means of production. Under CAPITALISM the BOURGEOISIE expropriated 'surplus value' from the workers. This was the difference between the product's true value, which was based on the amount of labour the worker put into it, and the money value at which the employer sold it.

The concept was extended by MARCUSE to include 'sexual exploitation'. In the modern world social domination results in what he calls 'surplus repression' which suppresses the sexual libido. Humanity must be liberated and sexual relations freed from monogamy and other conventional restrictions.

See also EXPROPRIATION.

Reading
Marcuse, H. 1972. *Eros and Civilisation.* London: Sphere; Marx, K. [1867] 1975. *Capital.* New York: International Publishers.

expropriation   At every stage of history since Man left his primitive state when metals were discovered, MARX said there would always be the exploiters who expropriated from the rest of society. When SOCIALISM was reached, however, at the final stage 'the expropriators would be expropriated'.

See also EXPLOITATION.

extermination camps   *See* CONCENTRATION CAMPS.

externalities   Costs and benefits incurred by people who are not involved in the decisions which caused them. Thus external benefits are enjoyed by people who work in a local government area in which they do not live, or holiday-makers who use beaches similarly. In both cases the incomers will not be paying the local taxes needed to pay for the costs of the upkeep of the roads or the cleansing of the beaches. The local government will find it difficult to tax them. This would not be the case with a small country. For example, Switzerland's geographic position results in an enormous amount of traffic crossing the country from one side to another. It levies a substantial tax on all motorists using its territory, even for short periods.

An example of external costs relates to air pollution caused by factories, or by motor cars. It is very difficult to measure these. In terms of a nation's health or the well-being of the whole world they may be enormous. Externalities demonstrate that markets cannot always provide the greatest happiness for the greatest number.

Reading
Mishan, E.J. 1993. *The Costs of Economic Growth.* London: Weidenfeld; Pearce, D.W. 1989. *Blueprint for a Green Economy.* London: Earthscan Publications.

F

faction A dissident minority group within a larger body. The internal disagreement may be over policy, or it may be about personalities and leadership. Often it is about both. Some political parties are much more faction-ridden than others. Frequently the political system is a cause. For example, in some methods of Proportional Representation candidates of the same party will compete with one another. POLITICAL CULTURE will also affect the degree of faction. In eighteenth-century Britain parliamentary politics was ruled by PATRONAGE. 'Party' and 'faction' were then synonyms, for the groups in conflict were often competing about places. Twentieth-century Japanese politics, in spite of universal suffrage, is full of factions, especially in the Liberal Democratic party which is usually in power. The factions are connected with patronage posts and relations of CLIENTILISM with constituencies.

When parties become highly organized, especially when they have strongly articulated policies, the incidence of faction may not be so high. Nevertheless there may still be contentious factions grouped around different stances on issues which arise. Thus in Britain, the Labour Party was badly divided over nuclear disarmament and both major parties have known internecine strife about policy towards Europe.

See also CLIENTILISM; PATRONAGE; POLITICAL PARTIES.

Reading
Benjamin, R. and K. Ori. 1981. *Tradition and Change in Post-industrial Japan.* New York: Praeger; Schmidt, S.W., J.C. Scott, C.H. Lande and L. Guasti. eds. 1977. *Friends, Followers and Factions.* Berkeley: University of California Press.

factors of production The classic factors of production were land, labour and capital. Land means space, soil and, possibly, minerals. Labour refers to the human effort needed. Capital is both financial, accumulated funds needed for development, and industrial capital which includes buildings and machinery. Each factor had gains from the productive process. Land had rent, labour wages and capital interest. Later economists added a fourth factor – entrepreneurial and managerial skill. The organizers of production were paid profits for success in using these skills and for the risks they took.

false consciousness Although he did not use this term himself, it is consistent with MARX's idea of consciousness. Marxist writers who employ it are referring to feelings of togetherness, leading to collective action, expressed by the WORKING CLASS in favour of non-socialist objectives. For example, workers who are mobilized by Fascist parties, or those who espouse nationalistic movements. Thus both Protestant workers and Catholic workers in Northern Ireland, each largely devoted respectively to British or Irish nationalism, are in error as far as Marxists are concerned. They are not listening to the voice of their true revolutionary CLASS CONSCIOUSNESS. This would tell them to unite against the capitalist class, their real enemy, which is exploiting them both. True consciousness is reminiscent of the Thomist idea of 'right reason'.

See also CLASS CONSCIOUSNESS; COMMUNISM; PROLETARIAT.

fascism Fascism is a totalitarian doctrine and a form of political system that was prevalent between the two world wars. The word was coined from the 'fasces', a bundle of rods that the magistrates of the Roman Empire used to chastise people. The Fascist movements saw themselves as punitive, purifying agents of a new national spirit that must redeem their nations from the decadence and defeatism into which they had sunk. Concerned to rejuvenate their nations, their doctrine presented an analysis of the reasons for national disaster and the principles by which national greatness was to be restored. They anticipated much conflict in this enterprise. Fascism was essentially a militant form of NATIONALISM. War was glorious.

The predicament in which the nation found itself was the result of its attachment to LIBERALISM, EGALITARIANISM and DEMOCRACY. These notions represented a rejection of the nation's true, old values for a false conversion to values which were internationalist. Democracy was a slow and unsatisfactory way of making decisions and it allowed much arguing with rulers. Moreover, its populist possibilities were encouraging socialists and Bolsheviks to take power. Hence it is not surprising that the major locations for the emergence of Fascism were Italy and Germany. Both countries had achieved nationhood in 1870; both had since then experienced a rather unsatisfactory form of parliamentary democracy; both felt shattered by their experiences in World War I (though Italy was on the side of the victors); and both felt threatened by the results of the Russian Revolution in 1917 with workers' and soldiers' councils, strikes and general disorder common in central Europe.

Fascist rule would reverse these tends. For disorder it would substitute Fascist discipline; for democratic delay it would substitute swift decisive action, Will rather than Reason would prevail; instead of division there would be national solidarity; in place of egalitarian values there would be a return to hierarchy and leadership. Fascism promised to resurrect the old values which had been discarded during the flirtation with democracy. But the instrument for this rejuvenation was not the old discredited aristocratic elite, but a new meritocratic elite with modern technological expertise. Consequently, Fascism could appeal to either conservatives or radicals, they could be united under its nationalistic appeal. This spirit would also permeate industrial relations. There could be no conflict and the Fascist state would supervene over worker and employer – the so-called Corporate State.

Much is sometimes made of the differences between the Italian and German regimes. It is interesting to consider these, though they are not very important. For the most part they are either cultural, or concerned with the philosophic roots, such as they were, of the two parties. Italy could scarcely be called an industrialized country. It had an inferior communications system and even in the

1920s national feeling was not strong. Consequently, in spite of all his efforts, Mussolini never succeeded in thoroughly indoctrinating his countrymen, or mobilizing them and militarizing them for battle. Moreover, Italian ELITISM had a pedigree going back to MACHIAVELLI, recently delineated by Mosca and Pareto. There were also Hegelian undertones in the philosophy of Gentile. Yet Mussolini had been influenced in his syndicalist period before 1914 by Sorel and the idea of the importance of the Myth. 'Our myth is the greatness of the nation', he declared.

What is noteworthy is that in spite of considerable differences these two countries produced dictatorial, totalitarian systems which were very similar. It is an example of the importance of historical experience as an explanation of socio-political phenomena.

See also AUTHORITARIANISM; ELITES; NATIONAL SOCIALISM; TOTALITARIANISM.

Reading

Bealey, F.W. 1999. 'Fascism'. In Bealey, F.W., R.A. Chapman and M. Sheehan. *Elements in Political Science*. Edinburgh: Edinburgh University Press; Carsten, F.L. 1967. *The Rise of Fascism*. London: Methuen; Mussolini, B. 1932. *La Dottrina del Fascismo*. Milan/Rome: Tuminelli; Payne, S.G. 1961. *Falange – a History of Spanish Fascism*. Stanford: University of California Press; Rossi, A. 1966. *The Rise of Italian Fascism*. New York: Fertig.

fatwa   A word which has passed into political usage since the *fatwa* issued by the Iranian Shi'ite mufti against Salman Rushdie, author of *The Satanic Verses* which they judge to be a blasphemy. The *fatwa* of a Shi'ite mufti must be obeyed. In Rushdie's case the *fatwa* was an order to kill him, though this is not the necessary consequence of every *fatwa*. The Iranian President declared in 1998 that Rushdie's *fatwa* no longer had force. Other Muslims disagreed.

favourite son   An expression much used in American politics though it can apply anywhere. It refers to the especially strong support which a political candidate can expect to receive from his home territory. In the USA it more specifically applies to the extreme likelihood that a Presidential candidate will carry his home state. This explains why it is an advantage for a favourite son to come from a highly populated state with a large representation in the ELECTORAL COLLEGE.

federal government   A constitutional type which is the opposite of UNITARY GOVERNMENT. Under federal government powers are distributed between the central and regional authorities so that each has SOVEREIGNTY within the area of its responsibilities. Inevitably this involves a written constitution which specifies the powers of both central government and sub-governments and the areas in which each has power. In addition, a constitutional court must act as an arbitrator between the different authorities. (Of course, many unitary states have written constitutions and constitutional courts; but federal states *must* have them.)

Federations should not be confused with CONFEDERATIONS which are essentially alliances between several sovereign states to agree to adopt certain similar procedures and policies. The European Union is at the moment (1997) a confederation. If it set up a central executive with some sovereign powers over member states, it would become a federation. Although this would be a centralizing move the European Union would remain a highly decentralized organization. However decentralized a unitary state becomes as a result of handing powers to local governments, it can never be as decentralized as a federal state. Federalism is a response to central domination and is intended to strengthen local identity, to increase political participation and to encourage experimentation in institutional change.

Evidence that federal constitutions provide for flexibility is to be found in the institutional variety of different federations. The United States is distinguished by the SEPARATION OF POWERS and presidential government, while Australia and Canada both have their executives sitting in their legislatures, the touchstone of PARLIAMENTARY SYSTEMS. Again in the USA and Australia both UPPER HOUSES are based on the principle of equality of representation for each state, while in Canada and Germany the representation of the provinces/Länder is unequal. Germany is probably the most centralized of federations: the Länder act as agents for the central government, administering policies which, except in the fields of education, land use and policing, have been decided centrally. Switzerland is almost certainly the most decentralized. The cantons have retained many powers. Decisions within them, and nationally, are often made by referendums.

Federal government is a system in which political entities with somewhat different interests may agree to disagree. But if the extent of the differences is too great they may fall apart when the situation presents itself. Thus federation, accepted as a model by the British Colonial Office for holding disparate components of ex-colonial states together, failed in the cases of the Central African and West Indies Federations. The component parts, reflecting ethnic antipathies in the former and island rivalries in the latter, did not feel enough common identity to remain together. Only CIVIL WAR has preserved Nigeria as a federation.

See also CONFEDERATIONS; UNITARY GOVERNMENT.

Reading

Elazar, D.J. 1984. *American Federalism*. New York: Harper and Row; Hughes, C.J. 1954. *The Federal Constitution of Switzerland*. Oxford: Clarendon; Sawer, G.F. 1969. *Modern Federalism*. London: Watts; Wheare, K.C. 1963. *Federal Government*. 4th edn. Oxford: OUP.

feminism Feminism began with the ENLIGHTENMENT. If men had rights why should women not have them also? In Britain free-thinking women like Mary Wollstonecraft (1759–97) and Harriet Taylor (1807–59) made demands for feminine equality, supported by the Utilitarians. Always in the vanguard of the struggle have been the women of Scandinavia.

Feminist action and feminist theory have been sometimes complementary and sometimes inter-reactionary. The earliest strategy was to press for the female suffrage with the notion that once it was achieved female equality would be assured. WOMEN'S SUFFRAGE movements sprang up in Europe and America at the end of the nineteenth century. The first successes were in Finland (1906) and Norway (1907). By the mid-twentieth century women were enfranchised in many countries but they had much less success in securing election to legislatures. As yet only in Iceland has a women's party won many seats.

When women discovered that possessing the franchise did not deliver complete parity with men they turned to other activities. The 'women's liberation' movement of the 1960s raised female consciousness by indicating all the forms of sexual inequality. Stimulus had come from greatly expanded higher education for women, and especially from their increasing participation in the labour market. The radical feminists argued that their inability to secure superordinate positions was the result of a collective male attempt to maintain their inequality. Feminine reaction to male dominance took many forms. One was to organize pressure groups and claim an end to 'gender discrimination' just as black groups had attacked racial discrimination. Considerable success was achieved in some countries in securing laws to stop discrimination against women. Other radical feminists in the socialist tradition argued that exploitation of women was part of capitalist exploitation and could only be ended by revolutionary female action. Lesbian feminists alleged that heterosexuality was the root cause of the oppression of women. Some feminists argued that people are socialized by language which emphasizes male dominance. 'Chairman' became 'chairperson' as a result but God was still generally referred to as 'He', though with the abolition of all gender-specific language 'it' would be correct.

As femininity is a characteristic of half of humanity it is scarcely surprising that feminism has assumed global proportions. Women persuaded the UN that their cause was just and from 1976 to 1985 it declared a Decade for Women and organized three women's conferences. Initially there was some disagreement between First and Third World Women: the latter's struggle was still at an early stage of demanding civic rights. But by the time of the third conference at Nairobi in 1985 some sign of unity was emerging. It seems merely a matter of time before women win equal political power with men.

See also GAY POLITICS; POLITICAL CORRECTNESS; REPRODUCTIVE POLITICS; WOMEN'S SUFFRAGE.

Reading
Charvet, J. 1982. *Feminism*. London: Dent; Freeman, J. 1975. *The Politics of Women's Liberation*. London: Longman; Millett, K. 1977. *Sexual Politics*. London: Virago; Stacey, M. and M. Price. 1981. *Women, Power and Politics*. London: Tavistock.

feudalism   A term loosely used in everyday speech to describe any sort of deferential relationship. Yet historians are careful to define it as a system of landholding involving a network of allegiances

and obligations. It grew up as Europe emerged from the Dark Ages after the collapse of the Roman Empire and only disappeared towards the end of the nineteenth century.

Under the feudal system land was granted by lords to their vassals on condition that goods and services were available in return. Usually a portion of a crop and a number of days labour were expected, but on occasion military service might be required. The lord required these payments in order to exist and to fulfil his own obligations to the monarch who had granted him his estate. These bargains were sealed with sworn oaths but they could be contested so that armed force might be necessary to defend one's property to which, as yet, there was no strict legal right. For the landholding peasant the advantage was that his right to his land was likely to be defended by his lord. The whole system was one glorified protection racket.

In the contemporary world the nearest equivalent to feudalism can be found in the *latifundia* of Latin America where absentee landlords appoint agents to oversee their estates on which day-labourers work. But the latter are landless so the analogy is not exact.

See also SERFDOM; SLAVERY.

Reading
Bloch, M. 1962. *Feudal Society*. 2 vols. London: Routledge; Postan, M.M. 1972. *The Medieval Economy and Society*. London: Weidenfeld.

field service administration   The method of delegating administrative guidance, oversight and implementation to agents throughout the country. The classic case is the prefect system set up by Napoleon Bonaparte and surviving, with modifications, in France to this day. A relationship known as *tutellage* existed between the prefects and sub-prefects and the local authorities. But the *tutelle* of the prefect has recently been abolished under the *loi Defferre*, 1981. Field service administration is usually regarded as the mark of a centralized state. It is 'deconcentration' rather than devolution. It can, however, be applied to a specialized service. Many of these, for example employment centres, must operate locally but can hardly be a function for local government.

See also DECENTRALIZATION; DEVOLUTION.

Reading
Fesler, J. 1980. *Public Administration: Theory and Practice*. Englewood Cliffs: Prentice Hall; Lundquist, L. 1972. *Means and Goals of Political Decentralisation*. Malmo: Studentlitteratur.

filibuster A method employed by some legislators to block business by uninterrupted speech-making. Most parliaments have adopted devices such as guillotine motions to limit the possibilities for filibustering. The most favourable location is still the US Senate where Senators are jealous of their right to speak freely and a few determined ones may impede the passage of an important bill they do not like. Because Senators are considered to be speaking for their states the majority are reluctant to intervene. The cloture can only be applied if a petition for it is supported by two-thirds of the Senators present and voting. Passage of such motions is very uncommon.

first chambers The lower houses of legislatures. The term 'lower' is a reminder that at one time the members had lower social status as representing the commoners or Third Estate. Today first chambers are almost invariably more important and powerful than SECOND CHAMBERS. They are more likely to be elected by popular vote and, therefore, to be more responsive to, and more representative of, PUBLIC OPINION. Frequently, as in Britain and the USA, they are the only house with financial initiative. Some countries have only one chamber.

See also ESTATES; SECOND CHAMBERS; UNICAMERALISM.

first-past-the-post A metaphor from horse-racing used to describe electoral systems like the British. The two distinctive features are single-member constituencies and the rule that the candidate with most votes wins the seat. Where several candidates are contesting the outcome may well be the election of one supported by only a small proportion of those voting. In fact, where there are more than two candidates it is quite common for the successful one to have less than 50 per cent of the votes cast, so that the constituency becomes what is called a 'minority seat'. On a nation-wide scale this often results in an over-representation in the legislature of the party with the highest national aggregate vote, a corresponding under-representation of the party with the second highest national total of votes and a grossly unfair underrepresentation of other smaller parties. It is the basis for TWO PARTY SYSTEMS. The electoral injustice of such systems generates demands for Proportional Representation. Yet almost any other system would result in COALITION GOVERNMENT. The system also results on occasions in violent swings, as in 1945 and 1997 in Britain, bringing many new members into the legislature and acting as a generally refreshing stimulus for parliamentary democracy.

See also CUBE RULE; ELECTORAL SYSTEMS; TWO PARTY SYSTEMS.

Reading
Butler, D.E. 1954. *The Electoral System in Britain 1918–1951*. Oxford: Clarendon.

first strike A term in the jargon of nuclear weaponry meaning an unprovoked attack on a potential enemy. Although a highly aggressive act, 'first strikers' claim it is a defensive measure to destroy the enemy's 'second strike' capacity. This is the so-called 'pre-emptive strike'. An example, using conventional aerial weapons, was the Israeli attack on Iraqi nuclear reactors in 1980.

See also COLD WAR; DETERRENCE; ESCALATION.

first world Not such a common term as THIRD WORLD, 'first world' describes the industrialized nations – North America, the Antipodes, western Europe and Japan. 'Second world' referred to the Communist world.

See also THIRD WORLD.

fiscal crisis A crisis resulting from the failure of a government to raise enough revenue from taxation, because if it increases taxation, or decreases social benefits, the electorate will eject it from power. When succeeding governments also fail in this way it will be a crisis of democracy. In the 1970s the Marxist writer, James O'Connor, argued that increased spending on the WELFARE STATE could no longer be sustained by the industrialized democracies. This would endanger the compromise between capital and organized labour engineered by social-democratic or Keynesian centrist governments. Social expenditure financed by taxation reduced employers' potential costs and underpinned industrial peace. When welfare expenditure was not held at the expected level a 'contradiction of capitalism' would be revealed. The fiscal crisis was a crisis of CAPITALISM as well as a crisis of capitalism's protective facade – DEMOCRACY.

O'Connor's thesis achieved some acceptance because it seemed to be borne out by the events of the late 1970s. In 1976 the International Monetary Fund would only grant Britain a loan if the government cut public expenditure. The fiscal crisis spread to local government, often dependent on subventions from central government. In 1977 New York City became bankrupt. Inflationary problems added to the rather apocalyptic mood. The right-wing author, Samuel Brittan, argued that democratic politicians could not resist the temptation to bid for votes by promising not to increase taxation and not to cut social benefits. The Thatcherite policies of the 1980s appeared to dispel these gloomy prognostications. A majority of voters would accept fewer unearned social benefits. Yet the fiscal crisis will always be a key element in democratic policy-making.

See also CONTRADICTIONS.

Reading
Brittan, S. 1977. *The Economic Consequences of Democracy*. London: Temple Smith; Newton, K. and T.J. Karran. 1985. *The Politics of Local Expenditure*. London: Macmillan; O'Connor, J. 1973. *The Fiscal Crisis of the State*. New York: St. Martin's Press.

flexible response *See* ESCALATION.

floating voter A voter without firm allegiance to a political party who 'floats' between them from one election to another. In Britain, where in the post-war years large blocs of voters remained loyal to the major parties, floating voters were seen as a small, disinterested, rational and well-informed group who might decide elections by moving from one side to the other. Voting research then showed that most of them were among the least politically conscious and informed voters. They were as likely to move to not voting as to another party. When they transferred their allegiance their motives were likely to be irrational and with little concern for party policies.

In more recent times the number of floating voters has increased almost everywhere. Loyalty to party has declined and the new type of floating voter is much more like the electorate as a whole. There has been an increase in ELECTORAL VOLATILITY and issue voting leading, some assert, to the politics of POST-MATERIALISM.

See also DEALIGNMENT; ELECTORAL VOLATILITY; VOTING BEHAVIOUR.

Reading
Benewick, R.J. 1969. 'The Floating Voter and the Liberal View of Representation'. *Political Studies* 17, 177–95; Sarlvik, B. and I. Crewe. 1983. *Decade of Dealignment*. Cambridge: CUP.

floor leader A term used in the US Congress. The 'majority floor leader' in the Senate leads the party in a majority, organizing their legislative programme and acting as their spokesman. Much of his time is spent bargaining with his colleagues and pressure group representatives in order to secure the passage of laws. In the House of Representatives the majority floor leader ranks second to the Speaker in these concerns. 'Minority floor leaders' in both houses perform similar functions for their parties as far as their minority situations will allow.

force majeure The recognition that vastly superior force cannot be withstood if an aggressor chooses to use it. A ruler who asserts rule through sheer oppression is employing *force majeure*.

fordism A term believed to have been coined by Gramsci (1891–1937) to describe the new type of CAPITALISM which followed the introduction of mass production. Henry Ford who opened his new plant at Detroit in 1912–13 was regarded as the harbinger of the new era. It was symbolized by the introduction of the assembly belt. With this went the manufacture of interchangeable parts, the disconnection of tasks and processes, the assignment of specific work to specific workers and the elimination of craftsmen from the workforce. It was based on scientific management, the new study of work processes and techniques which was supposed to foreshadow the most efficient organization of industry yet devised.

In the 1980s 'fordism' was used by Marxists to describe an accumulation regime associated with mass consumption as well as mass production; CORPORATISM and the WELFARE STATE; and governments committed to Keynesian management of economies.

See also FISCAL CRISIS; POST-FORDISM; TAYLORISM.

Reading
Hounshell, D. 1984. *From the American System to Mass Production, 1800–1932*. Baltimore: Johns Hopkins University Press; Scott, A.J. and M. Storper. eds. 1992. *Pathways to Industrialization and Regional Development in the 1990s*. London: Routledge.

formal organization An organization comes into existence when procedures are introduced to assist its survival. Formal organization has clear definition of goals and norms and possesses sanctions to enforce them. BUREAUCRACY is the most developed type of formal organization. It is very complex, with elaborate rules governing its structure and functions. Impersonality, rationality and an absence of arbitrariness characterize its behaviour. It has a hierarchical division of labour and all its interrelationships are formal and directed to the accomplishment of its tasks. Within formal organizations, however, people often develop informal relationships which may facilitate business.

See also BUREAUCRACY.

Reading
Kamenka, E. 1989. *Bureaucracy*. Oxford: Blackwell.

franchise A synonym for SUFFRAGE. It means the eligibility to vote. Historically the franchise has been limited everywhere. It was very restricted in ancient Athens and it remained limited throughout the nineteenth-century. Universal suffrage, what DAHL calls the principle of 'inclusiveness', was regarded even by nineteenth-century liberals as a dangerous revolutionary step. Hence a franchise for all adults is a twentieth-century phenomenon. Finland adopted it in 1906, Denmark in 1915 and Britain in

1928. Catholic countries tended to adopt it later: France and Italy achieved universal suffrage after World War II. In federal states some parts may adopt it before it becomes the law for the whole nation. Thus, although Wyoming had universal suffrage in 1890, it did not exist for federal elections in the USA until 1965 when the 24th Amendment and the Voting Rights Act were passed. Switzerland did not enact it until 1971.

Some countries have strong residence qualifications which may cause difficulties for voters who move house. All countries have minor restrictions. For example, in Britain convicted criminals and certified lunatics are disqualified. So are peers because they sit in the House of Lords, although they can vote in European elections. Furthermore, while in the last quarter of a century many democracies have extended the franchise to the 18–21 age group, there is as yet no pressure to give children the vote.

See also CITIZENSHIP; CIVIL LIBERTIES; DEMOCRACY; WOMEN'S SUFFRAGE.

Reading
Bryce, J. 1921. *Modern Democracies*. 2 vols. London: Macmillan.; Lindsay, A.D. 1929. *The Essentials of Democracy*. Oxford: OUP; Ross, A. 1948. *Varfor Demokrati?* Stockholm: Tidens Forlag.

fraternity   The third component of the French Revolutionary slogan. Unlike liberty and EQUALITY it has lacked salience in the modern world. Reasons for this comparative neglect are not hard to find. 'Brotherhood' does not have POLITICAL CORRECTNESS: the 'sisterhood of woman' has a different connotation from the 'brotherhood of man', an old liberal and socialist motto with international resonance. It is difficult to rally people to hold fraternal relations with one another if they do not want to. This type of camaraderie is often associated with totalitarian regimes which want to mobilize people for collective objectives. They desire the whole nation to be a fraternal association in which citizens, or 'comrades', embrace one another. But modern democratic men and women frequently value their privacy and individualistic values emphasize 'keeping oneself to oneself'. Caring for others needs close identification with them, a more likely situation in wartime when a nation has a common collective objective. Communitarian ideas are less commonly inculcated in times of peace.

See also COMMUNITARIANISM; GEMEINSCHAFT UND GESELLSCHAFT.

Reading
Mazzini, G. [1844] 1907. 'Duty to Humanity'. In *The Duties to Man and Other Essays*. 41–51. London: Dent.

freedom   It is generally contended that there are two kinds of freedom or liberty. Negative freedom is the absence of external restriction. One is free as long as no one, or no law or custom, prevents one from doing what one wants, or makes one do what one does not want to do. Positive freedom is at the core of the philosophic tradition of IDEALISM. Freedom here is seen, not as an absence of restriction, but as the freedom to do good. When one makes the wrong choice and does not do good it is because of inner constraints on choice stemming from one's social and intellectual environment. These may be the 'mind-forged manacles' of William Blake, but to neo-Marxists they are the manipulative influences of modern consumerism and particularly the media.

The above is a simple account of a complex subject. For political scientists neither sort of freedom can be absolute. Much of the exercise of government consists in restraining people. Every democratic government restricts some people's freedoms because their assertion restricts the freedoms of other people. Thus law and order constrain some freedoms in order to protect the operation of other freedoms. The problem of every government is to know what to restrict and what not to restrict. With democratic government this is basically decided by counting heads. Unsurprisingly the outcomes from such ballots will vary with time and place. Consequently what is 'freedom' in one era may not be 'freedom' in another.

See also DEMOCRACY; LIBERALISM.

Reading

Berlin, I. 1969. *Four Essays on Liberty*. New York: OUP; Bury, J.B. 1913. *A History of Freedom of Thought*. London: Williams and Norgate; Mill, J.S. [1859] 1985. *On Liberty*. Oxford: OUP; Milne, A.J.M. 1968. *Freedom and Rights*. London: Allen and Unwin; Oppenheim, F. 1961. *Dimensions of Freedom*. New York: St. Martin's Press.

freedom of association   This is always regarded as one of the basic democratic freedoms. It is rather different from the other democratic freedoms which are concerned with FREEDOM OF EXPRESSION. Freedom of association is concerned with freedom of activity on an organized scale. It develops naturally from 'freedom of assembly' which may guarantee the right of spontaneous demonstration but must also guarantee the right of people to assemble regularly. Hence, as with religious congregations, organization or ASSOCIATION develops. Where a state allows free associational activity we have a situation known as PLURALISM.

While freedom of speech and of the press are almost absolute in a democratic regime, freedom of association may be curtailed in numerous ways. The extent of limitation will depend on the nature of an association's activities. Witches' covens may be tolerated, but not if they indulge in child sacrifice. Political parties and pressure groups are part of the necessary democratic process of governing and opposing the government. Their activities can only be restricted if they begin to recruit private armies and to deny the right of other parties and pressure

groups to exist. TRADE UNIONS and employers' associations may find their activities restricted by law. Clearly in a democracy much depends on the wishes of the majority. Where hunting mammals is banned, fox-hunts cannot freely associate.

See also DEMOCRACY; DEMOCRATIC ELITISM; INDUSTRIAL RELATIONS; PLURALISM.

Reading

Bealey, F.W. 1988. *Democracy in the Contemporary State*. Oxford: OUP; Boulding, K.E. 1953. *The Organizational Revolution*. New York: Harper; Held, D. 1987. *Models of Democracy*. Oxford: Polity Press.

freedom of expression   A group of the most important democratic rights. Freedom of speech and freedom of the press allow people to express their opinions and preferences and to communicate these to others. They allow criticism of those in power and are basic to freedom to oppose the government. No authority can be sacred where freedom to criticize exists. It is not uncommon for this freedom to be enshrined in a BILL OF RIGHTS. Thus the First Amendment to the US Constitution reads: 'Congress shall make no law . . . abridging the freedom of speech or of the press'.

In the sixteenth and seventeenth centuries freedom of expression was encouraged by scientific discovery and the invention of printing. Thus by the time of the eighteenth-century ENLIGHTENMENT there was a larger public ready to accept the liberal ideas of writers like Voltaire and Tom Paine. Art. 11 of the Declaration of the Rights of Man (1789) affirmed: 'The unrestrained communication of thoughts and opinions being one of the most precious rights of man, every citizen may speak, write and publish freely . . .'

Art. 11 continued, 'provided he is responsible for the abuse of this liberty, in cases determined by the law'. Thus the French Revolutionaries did not see freedom of expression as an absolute right and democratic regimes since have made exceptions in cases of slander, libel, blasphemy (with less and less conviction), incitement to racial hatred and sedition and to crime generally. The crucial factor is the definition and scope of 'abuse'. It would clearly be an abuse to use freedom of speech to make a rabble-rousing speech at a public meeting encouraging the audience to burn down the houses of political opponents. It is not an abuse to encourage them to vote out the government at the next election; but the exact position at which rancorous criticism and untrue statements become abuse can only be determined by the courts in civil cases. While it has been known for democratic politicians to sue newspapers for libel, it is almost unknown for them to sue other politicians for slander.

See also CIVIL LIBERTIES; DEMOCRACY; ENLIGHTENMENT; LIBERALISM.

Reading
Castberg, F. 1981. *Freedom of Speech in the West*. Oslo: Oslo University Press; Hohenberg, J. 1973. *Free Press, Free People*. New York: Free Press; Street, H. 1982. *Freedom, the Individual and the Law*. Harmondsworth: Penguin.

freedom of information The free access of citizens to public documents. It is argued by its supporters that the 'right to know' is a democratic right. People in possession of this right are in a much better position to participate in democratic debate. Governments with a monopoly of information are at an unfair advantage.

The first country to establish a right of access to government documents was Sweden in 1766. Others have followed much more recently: the USA exactly two centuries later in 1966. British governments have been under some pressure to pass similar legislation; but the culture of secrecy still grips the politicians and the civil servants. In fact, the recent Official Secrets Act, 1989, makes it even more difficult to obtain access to government documents.

See also OPEN GOVERNMENT.

Reading
Cross, H. 1953. *The People's Right to Know*. New York: Columbia University Press; Rowat, D. ed. 1979. *Administrative Secrecy in Developed Countries*. London: Macmillan.

free rider Someone who profits from the activities of others without participating in them. An example is a worker in a unionized industry who does not join the trade union and pay a subscription to it, but who benefits when the union's negotiators win a pay rise. Where there is a common good to be achieved, everyone benefits from its acquisition, even those who did not strive for it. In this situation there is an obvious incentive for the rational, profit-maximizing person to avoid the costs in time and effort and, possibly, money incurred by the union's efforts to achieve the collective good. It will be attained anyway. Such a person is called a 'free rider'. Very large organizations are more likely to be prone to suffer this opting-out and if members become aware of it the effect might be cumulative. Hence organizations tend to develop rules and incentives to prevent free-riding. Trade-unions, for example, try to negotiate CLOSED SHOPS with employers.

See also CLOSED SHOP; PUBLIC GOOD.

Reading
Olson, M. 1965. *The Logic of Collective Action*. New Haven: YUP.

free trade The right of anyone to trade anywhere irrespective of international frontiers. Barriers to international trade include TARIFFS, duties levied on imports, and QUOTAS, restrictions on the quantity of a particular commodity imported. These are examples of PROTECTIONISM, the policy of protecting home industry against competitive imports from abroad. A more extreme case is that of mercantilism, the system operating in most European states until the nineteenth century. Under its precepts countries granted monopolies to trading companies and even prevented imports of certain goods unless they were brought by their own ships.

Free Trade was advocated by Adam Smith and David Ricardo who argued that both parties benefit from trade. Hence the national interest in abolishing restrictions is also in the international interest. Trade between nations is not a zero-sum game as mercantilists believed. Britain took the lead in free trade measures by repealing the Corn Laws in 1846. The principle never gained complete international acceptance and in the USA and Germany, especially, protectionist policies triumphed. By the 1940s trade restrictions were common everywhere.

Consequently in 1947, believing protection to be harmful to living standards throughout the world, the seven major trading nations instituted a partial free-trade regime and agreed to meet periodically for the purpose of widening their agreement, the General Agreement on Tariffs and Trade (GATT). For two decades this succeeded in freeing trade, but the developing nations were excluded and their agricultural exports were limited by the GATT nations, especially by the Common Agricultural Policy of the European Union. Thus in 1990 at Uruguay there was unprecedented conflict ending in 1992 with unsatisfactory compromises.

See also CUSTOMS UNION; QUOTAS; TARIFFS.

Reading
Bhagwati, J. 1991. *The World Trading System at Risk*. Princeton: Princeton University Press. Wilcox, C. 1949. *A Charter for World Trade*. New York: Macmillan.

free vote A vote in a legislature without any party discipline applied. In the House of Commons it is usual to have free votes on such issues as capital punishment, abortion and fox-hunting.

fronts A term first coined by the Third International in the 1920s. The United Front was ostensibly an alliance of all left-wing parties against CAPITALISM, but was actually a device for permeation and eventual absorption. The Popular Fronts of the 1930s were similar combinations against FASCISM. Generally the term indicates a rallying of forces against enemies within. Thus the National Fronts of Britain and France are xenophobic alliances against immigrants and those of foreign extraction.

fudge A slang term for an unsatisfactory compromise formula, often used as a term of abuse to describe agreements reached by political opponents. So it is a case of 'I compromise, you fudge'.

functional representation An alternative to territorial representation. The notion is that collective entities ought to receive representation and that decisions will thus be made by bargaining between corporate groups. The idea for functional representation may have sprung from medieval parliaments with their ESTATES. Early blueprints in Britain were the theories of the Guild Socialists in the 1920s and Churchill's Romanes lecture in 1930. Functional representation became discredited in the 1930s because of its use by Mussolini in Italy. There remains support for it in some quarters and in France the Social and Economic Council has had some success.

See also CORPORATISM; ESTATES; GUILD SOCIALISM.

Reading
Cole, G.D.H. 1920. *Social Theory*. London: Methuen; Hayward, J.E.S. 1966. *Private Interests and Public Policy*. London: Longman; Webb, B. and S. Webb. 1920. *A Constitution for the Socialist Commonwealth of Great Britain*. London: Printed by the authors for the Trade Ministry of the United Kingdom.

functionalism A method of analysis first used by Durkheim who followed Comte in believing that societies can be explained by the relationships that different phenomena within them bear to one another. Malinowski (1884–1942) adopted this methodology to social anthropology and was the first to call it 'functionalism'. Talcott Parsons later introduced values as an additional factor in his explanations of how systems survive. Merton distinguished manifest functions which are intended to produce expected consequences and latent functions which may result in unexpected consequences.

Although functionalism has remained very much a tool for sociologists, it has been adopted by political scientists concerned with comparative method because of its supposed superiority over the traditional study of comparative political institutions. This adoption was necessary in order to include in the schematic analysis new developing nations with primitive political cultures and few formal institutions. Easton, however, the most prominent of the political science functionalists, was influenced by cybernetics and computer theory. The application of his model of the political system certainly allows comparison of quite disparate systems, but its explanations of system survival and system breakdown are too simple to satisfy most of those anxious for detailed knowledge. A more general criticism of functionalism is that its emphasis is on stability and that its implications, therefore, are inherently conservative.

See also STRUCTURAL FUNCTIONALISM; SYSTEMS ANALYSIS.

Reading
Almond, G.A. and B.G. Powell. 1978. *Comparative Politics*. Boston, Mass.: Little, Brown; Easton, D. 1965. *A Systems Analysis of Political Life*. New York: Wiley; Merton, R.K. 1968. *Social Theory and Social Structure*. New York: Free Press; Parsons, T. 1952. *The Social System*. London: Tavistock.

fundamentalism A religious position claiming strict adherence to basic beliefs. This frequently results in intolerance towards other beliefs and believers in one's own creed who do not strictly observe and who do not profess to hold an extreme position. Thus Protestant fundamentalists scorn Protestants who fail to perceive a danger from Catholicism; Jewish fundamentalists attack Jews with secularist leanings; and Muslim fundamentalists believe they have a duty to purge Islam of any concessions to cultural modernization. A political implication is the tendency of fundamentalists to turn to TERRORISM.

See also ISLAMIC FUNDAMENTALISM; TERRORISM.

fundamental rights Fundamental human rights have been variously defined as 'freedom from want and freedom from fear' and rights to 'life, liberty and property'. They are of relatively recent origin, perhaps first identified in the seventeenth century. Their legitimation on the world scene dates from the San Francisco Charter of 1945 in which the embryonic United Nations affirmed its faith in 'fundamental human rights' and declared that discrimination against sex, religion, and race was repugnant. The Universal Declaration of Human Rights in 1948 proclaimed not only the traditional rights and freedoms, but also 'economic, social and cultural rights'. In 1950 the newly-formed Council of Europe produced the European Convention of Human Rights, supported by two new organs, the European Commission on Human Rights and the European Court of Human Rights.

The United Nations Commission on Human Rights acts as a watchdog to see how much these guidelines are observed. In many of the developing countries, in particular, there are clear violations of them and in 1962 the General Assembly of the United Nations declared that breaches of Human Rights took place in all parts of the world. Some states complain that the Commission's activities infringe their sovereignty. Yet any country's claim that the way it treats its subjects is no one else's business has now become a relic of a past age.

See also BILL OF RIGHTS; CIVIL LIBERTIES; NATURAL RIGHTS.

Reading
Ganji, M. 1962. *International Protection of Human Rights*. Geneva: Droz; Gewirth, A. 1982. *Human Rights*. Chicago: University of Chicago Press; Robertson, A.H. and J.G. Merrills. 1993. *Human Rights in Europe*. 3rd edn. Oxford: OUP; Vasak, K. 1964. *La Convention Européenne des Droits de l'Homme*. Paris: Librairie Générale de Droit et de Jurisprudence.

G

game theory An example of political science borrowing from economics. It can refer to several competitive situations in which choice is dependent on the choice of others and where each 'player' can only anticipate what others will do. In political science bargaining has been associated with GAME THEORY, especially with zero-sum games and non-zero-sum games. The former describes a situation where gains and losses of everyone playing add up to zero. If it is 'winner takes all' there is no scope for co-operation between the players. A political situation might be where a finite material resource needed to be divided between two groups. The result will depend on the method of division. If by combat the stronger group may take all of the resource. A similar outcome would arise if a lottery were to decide the result – but this method would hardly be agreed to unless the resource were trivial. If voting were adopted the side with most votes would take everything; but if their votes were equal, to avoid the costs of combat they might bargain about shares by discussion and negotiation. Where there were more than two groups a similar set of circumstances might occur if they formed two alliances. This sort of situation is dealt with in the field of COALITION THEORY.

Non-zero-sum games occur when some outcomes will result in higher aggregates than others. There is therefore scope for strategic thinking and bargaining by the parties involved but no certainty that they will behave in these ways. There are two well-known 'games' – Prisoners' Dilemma and Chicken – in which if the parties in conflict co-operate and bargain they will reach an agreement by compromise. Chicken is appropriate to nuclear confrontation and wage bargaining. In the latter activity, if all trade unions think they will get the maximum benefit by pitching their demands higher than what they think other unions will ask for, all unions may obtain very high increases, though at the price of run-away inflation, in which case they are all worse off. Or the employers may resist their demands and the unions will find themselves in a crippling strike. Consequently their best strategy is to bargain and compromise.

See also BARGAINING; BRINKMANSHIP; COALITION THEORY.

Reading
Brams, S.J. 1990. *Negotiation Games: Applying Game Theory to Bargaining and Arbitration.* London: Routledge; Neumann, J. von. and O. Morgenstern. 1944. *Theory of Games and Economic Behavior.* Princeton: Princeton University Press; Rapoport, A. 1960. *Fights, Games and Debates.* Ann Arbor: Michigan University Press; Shubik, M. 1982. *Game*

Theory in the Social Sciences. Cambridge, Mass.: MIT Press.

garden cities A British movement for garden cities was a reaction to squalid nineteenth-century industrialization. It was associated with the aesthetic SOCIALISM of the William Morris school. Its leader, Ebenezer Howard, advocated small towns with houses interspaced with greenery and everything architecturally designed. It was thus an early example of urban planning and was put into practice with the building of Letchworth and Welwyn. It was also the inspiration of the garden suburbs of the 1930s and the New Town policy of the 1940s and 1950s.

Reading
Howard, E. [1898] 1945. *Garden Cities of Tomorrow.* London: Faber.

gate keeping A metaphor to describe the activity of someone who controls access to life chances, services and benefits. Even when access is determined by rules there is often the possibility of discretion. It may apply to promotion in large organizations, or to the allocation of municipal housing, or to the provision of a special service. Gatekeepers may enjoy just the feel of exercising power, but the position obviously offers opportunities for bribery and the trading of favours.

gauleiter The leader of a Nazi party district organization. With a highly hierarchic party structure, all gauleiters were appointed by Hitler and, following the *führerprinzip* (leader principle), the authority of the Führer and his dictatorial powers were handed down to them. The term is now sometimes used in a vaguely humorous way to describe anyone in authority with a tendency to autocracy. *See also* NATIONAL SOCIALISM.

Reading
Broszat, M. 1981. *The Hitler State.* London: Arnold; Neumann, F. 1942. *Behemoth.* London: Gollancz.

gaullism The ideas of Charles de Gaulle (1890–1970), founder of the Fifth Republic and of the Gaullist party, most often in power since that Republic's foundation in 1958. The term has now acquired something of a general connotation in reference to a NATIONALISM associated with the assertion of cultural and political distinction and 'glory'. In Europe it often involves anti-Americanism. Institutionally it implies a mixture of presidentialism and plebiscitary democracy. Gaullists are suspicious of political parties and factious legislatures dissipating the national will, which is best expressed by strong leadership and a centralized state.

Reading
Touchard, J. 1978. *Le Gaullisme 1940–1969.* Paris: Seuil.

gay politics The politics of the organized movements of homosexual men and women. Sometimes the term used is 'gay and lesbian' politics. Liberal sympathies for homosexuals were probably first aroused by their persecution and liquidation by the Nazis. In the thirty years after World War II there was a general legalization of relations between people of the same gender in western Europe and North America. In 1978 the International Lesbian and Gay Association was founded. Since then the World Health Organization has removed homosexuality from its list of diseases and the Council of Europe has passed a resolution to fight discrimination against homosexuals. Although homosexuals are a small proportion of populations they tend to congregate in communities and this may sometimes give them political clout. For example, it was the existence of a gay suburb in San Francisco, California's marginality as a state and its large proportion of the electoral college vote that led to Clinton promising, if he were elected in the 1992 Presidential election, to end discrimination against homosexuals in the US armed forces.

gemeinschaft und gesellschaft
So distinctive is this concept that it is often not translated. The best translation is 'community and association'. It is the name of a seminal work by Ferdinand Tonnies (1855–1936) who depicted the change from an old society of face-to-face communities with stable universal values in which relationships were quite different from modern society. In the latter, values are shifting and heterogenous and relationships are based on contract.

Also with WEBER, Tonnies believed the transition was marked by an increasing rationality. Durkheim accepted Tonnies's main idea of transition, but rejected his view that the state would be important as a coercive agent in modern society.

Reading
Tonnies, F. [1887] 1955. *Community and Association*. London: Routledge.

gender gap
The gap in political attitudes and behaviour between men and women. It seems to be especially great in the USA where women have much less political representation. The proportion of women in Congress is almost the lowest in the democratic world. In Scandinavia the position is the reverse with the Norwegian parliament having 40 per cent feminine representation.

See also FEMINISM; VOTING BEHAVIOUR; WOMEN'S SUFFRAGE.

Reading
Mueller, C. ed. 1988. *The Politics of the Gender Gap*. Berkeley: University of California Press. Norris, P. 1985. 'The Gender Gap in Britain and America'. In *Parliamentary Affairs* 38.2, 192–201.

gender politics
See FEMINISM.

general strike
A nation-wide stoppage of work by the labour force. Such stoppages are very rare. They are basically of three kinds. There is the syndicalist general strike, ideologically motivated and intended to overthrow CAPITALISM. Second, is the political general strike with the purpose of bringing down the government in power. Third, the economic general strike occurs when all employees stop work in an effort to prevent wage cuts or to secure wage rises. Although right-wing and centrist politicians often believe political strikes to be undemocratic, this is not always clearly the case. The successful general strikes in Belgium in 1893 and Sweden in 1902 were called to secure an extension of the suffrage, that is to improve democracy. The French general strike in 1961 was to forestall the revolt of the generals in Algeria against a democratic government. Most general strikes, however, like the British one in 1926, are wage strikes. Prime Minister Baldwin had declared all workers had to take a wage cut and they struck, unsuccessfully, to prevent it.

See also STRIKES; SYNDICALISM; TRADE UNIONS.

Reading
Symons, J. 1957. *The General Strike*. London: Cresset Press; Von Beyme, K. 1980. *Challenge to Power*. London: Sage.

general will
A concept enunciated by Jean-Jacques ROUSSEAU (1712–78), an eighteenth-century Swiss philosopher. In order to express the general will everyone in the state should participate in its articulation. People should not consider their own interests: that would only ascertain the 'will of all'. Instead, they should voice a preference for the good of the whole community. When they did this they would vote for the General Will. Rousseau made the assumption that such activity would take place in small communities like his native Geneva. Yet his ideas inspired the insurrectionary

nationalism of revolutionary France and its belief in popular sovereignty. He disliked factions and their sectional wills and believed the community should speak as a whole. Thus he is a early supporter of DIRECT DEMOCRACY.

See also DIRECT DEMOCRACY; PUBLIC GOOD; SOVEREIGNTY OF THE PEOPLE.

Reading
Rousseau, J-J. [1772] 1913. *The Social Contract*. London: Everyman.

genocide An organized attempt to exterminate a whole population, tribe, or nation. Ethnic and/or ideological hatred is the main motivation. If one national group regards a different one as an irreconcilable and dangerous enemy, then it seems rational to exterminate them. Genocide has been common throughout history and the twentieth century has been no exception. In 1915 the Turkish Empire systematically murdered a million and a half Armenians. Their crime was to be Christians and to be strategically well placed for encouraging the Russian army's advance in the Caucusus. It was done by old-fashioned methods of throat slitting and drowning. The Nazi Holocaust of six million Jews and gypsies in gas chambers between 1942 and 1945 was a technological innovation, though its motives were paranoid fears of permeation of the 'Aryan race' by a sub-human species. The Khmer Rouge, the Cambodian Communists, between 1975 and 1979 committed genocide against its own people, sending that part of its population it believed to be influenced by foreign contacts or technology into labour camps in the countryside where they were brutally treated. It is estimated that between one and two million died.

See also CONCENTRATION CAMPS; RACISM.

Reading
Horowitz, I.L. 1980. *Taking Lives: Genocide and State Power*. New Brunswick, NJ: Transaction Books; Kuper, L. 1981. *Genocide*. Harmondsworth: Penguin.

geopolitics A study of international relations in terms of the geographical location and characteristics of states. It is an attempt at a total explanation. Kjellen (1846–1922), who invented the term, gave it a Darwinian dimension. The German school of geopolitics was prominent in the first half of the twentieth century and believed that Germany's survival depended on a strong Mitteleuropa and the acquisition of living room (*lebensraum*) to the east of Germany. This notion was enthusiastically seized on by the Nazis. Since then the subject has not had academic respectability. Its chief exponent in Britain, Halford Mackinder (1861–1947), a Liberal MP, argued that the conflict between land and sea power dominated history. The maritime nations were threatened by the Eurasian Heartland. Much map drawing supported this assertion. Clearly strategic location will always be basic to national foreign policies but it is merely one consideration for most countries. The geopolitical factor will vary dependent on size of country and proximity of threats.

Reading
Kjellen, R. 1917. *Der Staat als Lebensform*. Leipzig: Hirzel; Mackinder, H. 1919. *Democratic Ideals and Reality: A Study in the Politics of Reconstruction*. London: Constable; Parker, G. 1985. *Western Geopolitical Thought in the Twentieth Century*. London: Longman.

gerontocracy Rule by the old.

gerrymandering *See* APPORTIONMENT.

glasnost A Russian word meaning 'openness' which passed into the English language with the reforms of Gorbachev in the 1980s. It was an attempt to reform Soviet society, and especially the economy, by laying it open to criticism.

Gorbachev hoped that freeing expression would reveal the truth about the inefficiency of Russian industry and coerce it towards *perestroika*, social and economic reconstruction. In fact, it led to criticism of Gorbachev and demands for democracy.

See also PERESTROIKA.

Reading
Gorbachev, M. 1987. *Perestroika*. London: Collins.

globalization A term indicating a movement to a world society. There are different views about which causes are most important. Most obviously the increasing ease and cheapness of world travel has a shrinking effect on world size. People are increasingly mobile. Foreign countries and cultures become less strange. Linked to the communication factor is that of the spread of a world culture. Three influences can be observed here. First is the development of computers, leading in the 1990s to the growth of an internet allowing the international conveyance of information and the exchange of messages between ordinary people across the world. Second is satellite television which facilitates the spread of culture. Third is the dissemination of 'pop culture', which tends to make the youth of the world feel they have much in common. Finally, many would argue that the most important factor is the globalization of the economy. The General Agreement on Tariffs and Trade (GATT) is a move towards a world economy. Finance capital especially has become highly mobile and multinational enterprise moves between nation and nation, sometimes to the detriment of the work-force. The logical countervailing force is international trade unionism. Global political organization, as always, lags behind.

See also DEPENDENCY; MULTINATIONALS.

Reading
Featherstone, M. ed. 1990. *Global Culture, Nationalism, Globalization and Modernity*. London: Sage.

governability The governability of countries depends on two factors: the nature of the governed and their amenability to the process, and the capacity of the government to deal with its problems.

Clearly the extent of the CLEAVAGES among the population in any society will affect the ease of ruling. The divisions will probably be reflected in the PARTY SYSTEMS. Multi-party systems result in COALITION GOVERNMENT which may lack decisiveness compared with one-party government, though this will not always be detrimental to governmental success. Coalition government is more likely to carry a majority of the voters with it. Constitutional forms will affect the capacity of the government. Where power is constitutionally diffused governments may find the exercise of power difficult. The three main types of power diffusion are the SEPARATION OF POWERS, FEDERALISM and JUDICIAL REVIEW. The USA has them all because the drafters of the Constitution did not want powerful government.

Finally, in recent years it has been argued that the governability of democratic governments has declined because of OVERLOAD. Governments were faced with increasing demands for public spending while at the same time voters were increasingly inclined to revolt against increased taxation. Budgets were swollen and so were bureaucracies, yet governments lacked the will to make economies. Hence there was a crisis in confidence. This was also connected with the notion of 'veto groups'. It was believed that there were certain powerful PRESSURE GROUPS, capital and labour were usually cited, whose opposition would prevent the implementation of any policy they disliked. Much aired in the

1970s, the theory became less popular in the 1980s when governments privatized and cut public expenditure a little.

Reading
Peters, B.G. 1981. 'The Problem of Bureaucratic Government'. *Journal of Politics* 43, 56–82; Rose, R. ed. 1980. *Challenge to Government: Studies in Overloaded Politics.* London: Sage; Taylor, C.E. ed. 1983. *Why Governments Grow.* Beverly Hills: Sage.

government   To govern is to control. The supreme controlling force within society is the STATE. Government (without the definite article) is an abstract term referring to the style, range, scope, purposes and degree of control. Such areas of academic discussion are sometimes also referred to as 'governance'. Broadly, there are two different philosophic approaches to government. One group of thinkers perceives it as a necessary instrument for maintaining order and reconciling conflicts in society. The other sees it as concerned with guiding humanity from lower forms of civilization to higher forms. Government is not just the tool of whoever is in power but a device for maintaining a moral order and/ or advancing to a better order. These two schools have been called the mechanistic and organic theories of government, though more frequently they are regarded as theories of the state.

'The government' usually refers to the rulers, that group of people who are in charge of the state at a particular time. Terminology is not universal even in the English speaking world. In the USA it is usual to call them the 'administration'. (Thus (in 1996) one would write of the Major Government in Britain and the Clinton Administration in America.) The characteristics of the people who rule, their behaviour in office and the methods by which they reach their positions, are paramount in any analysis of POLITICAL SYSTEMS.

The way one set of rulers succeeds another is one of the main distinguishing marks of political systems. In very traditional systems there may be one-man rule. This is usually dynastic rule and succession is by the hereditary principle, but in pre-Communist Tibet monks used esoteric methods to discover the next Dalai Lama. In many countries the method of succession is not prescribed and adventurists may seize power by force of arms. Much of the world is governed by MILITARY REGIMES and power changes hands after successive coups d'état. In countries ruled by single parties succession may be decided in small committees in secret and the procedure is obscure. In democracies succession of governments takes place through ELECTIONS, either directly, or as a result of negotiations by elected representatives.

An old-fashioned definition of government was in terms of a trinity – EXECUTIVES, LEGISLATURES and JUDICIARIES. Legislatures made laws, executives implemented them and judiciaries ruled on them. All these were seen as methods of control and all were part of 'government'. They were also sometimes termed 'powers' and it was widely thought, by Montesquieu among others, that they should be quite separate. Although the tripartite division may still have its uses, it is not common to apply it to comparisons between political systems today. It is too simple to conceive of laws as the only outputs. Many decisions handled by executives are responses to events and are untouched by legislatures. Moreover, increasingly laws are drafted by executives and legislatures merely formalize them. The legislative programmes drawn up by executives have their sources in political parties and PUBLIC OPINION. Indeed, the emergence of mass parties, from among whose representatives ministers may be chosen as members of governing executives, has tended to fuse the executive and legislative power, though this is not universally the case. For the most part, however, the judicial power remains separate from either. A further complication is that reference to 'the government' or 'the executive power' may include both politicians and administrators.

Throughout the developed world, and even in much of the developing world, the scope of government has extended greatly. Today governments employ many more people and spend much more money than they did a century ago. The multi-functional modern state is elaborately complex. This is true without considering the territorial divisions between central and local government with the intermediate form of regional government in some cases. Hence the governability of the contemporary state, especially in democratic systems, has become a concern of politicians and political scientists. The view that governments are 'overloaded' was partly the result of the fiscal crisis following the rise of oil prices in 1973, giving rise to general inflation and demands from voters for lower taxes. In the 1990s this concern has become less intense, probably because pressures on governments have been to some extent relieved by the reduction on taxation at the expense of social benefits, the quality of public services and the number of public officials.

The problem of governing modern industrial society has been accentuated by the acceptance of rulers generally that they should manage, or 'steer', the economy. This arose for various reasons: the realization that the condition of the economy is the most important issue for most of the electorate; the gradual emergence of a world economy (the 'globalization' effect); and the belief (perhaps not altogether justified) that instruments were at hand to facilitate 'steering'. It is significant that even democratic governments, such as those of

Reagan and Thatcher, claiming that in free market economies state intervention was much diminished, still maintained many of the instruments of economic management.

See also BUREAUCRACY; CENTRALIZATION; DECENTRALIZATION; ELECTIONS; EXECUTIVES; FEDERAL GOVERNMENT; JUDICIARIES; LEGISLATURES; MILITARY REGIMES; PARLIAMENTARY GOVERNMENT; POLITICAL SYSTEMS; PRESIDENTIAL SYSTEMS; PUBLIC OPINION; REGIONALISM; TOTALITARIANISM; UNITARY STATES.

Reading
Barker, E. 1942. *Reflections on Government.* Oxford: OUP; Crossman, R.H.S. 1939. *Government and the Governed.* London: Christophers; Dahl, R.A. 1991. *Modern Political Analysis.* 5th edn. Englewood Cliffs: Prentice Hall; Finer, H. 1932. *The Theory and Practice of Modern Government.* London: Longman; Finer, S.E. 1970. *Comparative Government.* Harmondsworth: Penguin; Hamilton, A., Jay, J and Madison J. [1787] 1911. *The Federalist or the New Constitution* London: Everyman; Montesquieu, C.S. [1748] trans T. Nugent. 1949. *The Spirit of the Laws.* New York: Haffner; Spender, J.A. 1938. *The Government of Mankind.* London: Cassell.

governor Someone appointed to govern a region or province. Frequently in the process of state building and territorial acquisition they were soldiers. This was usually the position in Spain and the Spanish Empire. Other colonial empires at first followed this practice. Later bureaucrats might be appointed.

The governors of American states, however, are elected chief executives. Like the President most governors serve four-year terms and also like the President they stand in a similar relationship of SEPARATION OF POWERS. Governors' powers are restricted by state legislatures and state supreme courts. A state governorship is a position of prominence and it is not surprising that eighteen of the forty-two presidents have previously been governors.

See also FEDERAL GOVERNMENT.

Reading
Beyle, T.L. and L. Muchmore. 1983. *Being Governor*. Durham, NC: Duke University Press; Walker, E.A. 1943. *The British Empire*. Oxford: OUP.

governor-general Heads of state in nations of the Commonwealth other than Britain. Formally, they are proxies of the British monarch and stand in exactly the same relationship to the other institutions. But they do not refer to the British Crown, though they are guided by the conventions of constitutional monarchy as exercised in Britain. In recent decades the governors-general have been local people. Like British monarchs their powers are so limited that they have excited little controversy. An exception was when the Australian governor-general, Sir John Kerr, dismissed the Whitlam government in 1975.
See also DOMINION STATUS; HEADS OF STATE; MONARCHY.

Reading
Hasluck, P. 1979. *The Office of Governor-General*. Melbourne: Melbourne University Press.

gradualism An approach to governing. Gradualists put their faith in slow, incremental progress towards a policy objective. The strategy is usually associated with SOCIALISM. Most socialists are not revolutionary and believe it will come about through constitutional, democratic means. The British Fabians argued that industrial organization was inexorably becoming more concentrated and there would be an easy transition to public ownership. Sidney WEBB, a Labour minister and leading Fabian, coined the phrase 'the inevitability of gradualism'. Revolutionary socialists contended that the gradualists were making terms with CAPITALISM.
See also SOCIAL DEMOCRACY; SOCIALISM.

grant-in-aid A payment by a higher government to a LOCAL GOVERNMENT.

When these payments are general, without conditions, they are known as BLOCK GRANTS. Quite often they are specific and are known in the USA as 'categoric grants'. Frequently central or regional governments impose conditions, so that grants-in-aid are often methods of controlling local government expenditure.
See also BLOCK GRANT; FISCAL CRISIS; LOCAL GOVERNMENT.

greens *See* ECOLOGICAL POLITICS.

group theory The term has various connotations dependent on the importance one attaches to the activity of groups in politics. The theoretical level of treatment also varies greatly. BENTLEY, whom some see as the father of group theory, believed all political phenomena could be interpreted in terms of group interaction. At the other end of the spectrum are largely empirical studies of PRESSURE GROUPS. The examination of these latter was much stimulated in the USA by the 1946 Federal Regulation of Lobbying Act which required the registration of all groups with agents operating in the lobbies of Congress. Truman studied the influence of pressure groups on policy-making and presented a theory of their activity. He argued that in a society where PLURALISM prevailed any group asserting an objective was likely to give rise to a countervailing group. In between Bentley and the students of the legislative lobbies are the theorists of what are variously called 'strategic groups', 'functional groups' and 'elitist groups'. They are concerned with such groups, or 'group interests', as armies, the BUREAUCRACY, capital, labour and the media. Finally, there is the work of OLSON who examined the internal dynamics of groups and the motivations of their leaders and members.
See also DEMOCRATIC ELITISM; FREE RIDER; INTEREST GROUPS; PLURALISM; PRESSURE GROUPS.

Reading
Bentley, A.F. [1908] 1949. *The Process of Government*. Evanston: Principia; Truman, D.B. 1951. *The Governmental Process*. New York: Knopf.

guerrilla warfare The word 'guerrilla' entered the English language during the Peninsular War, 1808–14. The French army with long and difficult communications was attacked by Spanish partisans in local ambushes. The French retaliated on the civilian population. This has remained the classic pattern of guerrilla warfare. It is most successful in rural areas where both the terrain and the population are hostile to the occupying army. In World War II Russia and the Balkans were areas in which guerrilla activity was rife. Communist Revolution in Asia depended for its success on an insurrectionary peasantry, its leaders having discovered that urban revolt was not appropriate. Maoist tactics in China brought the Communists to power and in Vietnam led to the defeat of a superpower with highly developed military technology. In Malaya, however, the British army was able to devise a counter-guerrilla strategy. Guerrilla tactics also helped Castro to power in Cuba and caused much turbulence in other poor countries in Latin America.

Urban guerrillas, on the other hand, though responsible for terrorist outrages that spread alarm, have had little success. Unlike their rural counterparts they earn the antipathy, rather than the support, of the local population.

Reading
Guevara, C. 1969. *Guerilla Warfare*. Harmondsworth: Penguin; Lacqueur, W. 1977. *Guerrilla*. London: Weidenfeld; Short, A.G.N. 1975. *The Communist Insurrection in Malaya 1948–1960*. London: Muller; Zedong, M. 1961. *On Guerrilla Warfare*. Peking.

guided democracy A term first used to describe the regime President Sukarno set up in Indonesia in 1959 when he suspended the parliamentary regime instituted at independence ten years earlier. 'Guided democracy', the regime's slogan, was based on the 'three pillars' of Indonesian society – NATIONALISM, religion and COMMUNISM. In effect, it was an uneasy attempt to maintain simultaneously the loyalty of the army and the Communists. It was not DEMOCRACY. The term is sometimes used in the context of similar nationalistic regimes in which leaders are anxious to stifle dissent. General Suharto, who succeeded to power in 1968, set up a 'New Order' preceded by the slaughter of hundred of thousands of Communists. He was forced to stand down in 1998 as the result of popular protests and demonstrations.

guild socialism A Utopian form of SOCIALISM which flourished in the British labour movement in the first two decades of the the twentieth century. It was a revolt against large-scale industrialism and the centralized state. One strand in it looked back to the simple craftsmen of the medieval guilds and wanted a return to small-scale production organized in small units with functional representation. It was thus close to anarcho-syndicalism. Another more modern strand wanted self-government in a re-organized industry. Each industry would be a guild, though there would be local guilds also. The national guilds would be functionally represented in a 'parliament of industry', while local guilds would be functionally represented on trades councils. This strand was a form of SYNDICALISM. Guild socialism was a form of prescriptive PLURALISM.
See also INDUSTRIAL DEMOCRACY; SOCIALISM; SYNDICALISM; WORKERS' CONTROL.

Reading
Cole, G.D.H. 1920. *Guild Socialism Restated*. London: Parsons; Glass, S.T. 1966. *The Responsible Society: the Ideas of the English Guild Socialists*. London: Longman.

guillotine   A device to enforce closure of parliamentary debate. The term is used in both the USA and Britain. In the latter it was first employed against the obstructionist tactics of the Irish nationalists. An 'allocation of time motion' strictly limits debate on a specific bill. When it lapses the guillotine comes down.

gulag   A Russian acronym for Chief Administration of Corrective Labour Camps, the Soviet prison system under Stalin. Solzhenitsyn described it as an 'archipelago' because the territory of the Soviet Union was like a sea dotted with islands of penal settlements.

Reading
Solzhenitsyn, A. 3 vols. 1973, 1974, 1978. *The Gulag Archipelago*. London: Collins.

H

---

habeas corpus   A Latin term meaning 'you should have the body'. It is a writ, found in all legal systems with roots in English common law, requiring a court to rule on the legality of anyone detained. If the court rules the detention is unlawful the person will be released. In the United Kingdom it only applies to England and Wales. It is enshrined in the US Constitution. Art. I. sect. 9 (2) reads: 'The privilege of the writ of *habeas corpus* shall not be suspended, unless when in cases of rebellion or invasion the public safety may require it'. The writ is not the guarantee of absolute rights that is often imagined. There is nothing to stop the British Parliament, for example, authorizing the detention of someone without trial.

Reading
Sharpe, R.J. 1976. *The Law of Habeas Corpus*. Oxford: Clarendon.

hawks and doves   Two terms from the COLD WAR to describe on the one side, those who favoured forceful actions and words, and on the other, those who believed conciliation and pacific language was the correct approach. An outstanding hawk was General Le May who was George Wallace's vice-presidential running mate in 1968. His strategy for dealing with the Soviet Union was 'lobbing one into the men's room in the Kremlin'. Although soldiers are likely to be more hawkish and diplomats more doveish it is by no means an iron law. Some soldiers are peace-loving and some diplomats quite bellicose. While the origin of these terms was American they have become widely used to indicate foreign policy attitudes. Israeli politicians are categorized in this way.
See also COLD WAR; DÉTENTE.

heads of state   The phrase relates to a formal position which is not usually a seat of power. Heads of state perform honorific duties. They confer honours, pin medals on people, open exhibitions and receive foreign ambassadors. The office has two kinds of incumbent – the president and the constitutional monarch, one elected and the other anointed after hereditary succession. Both perform the same functions. There are more presidents than monarchs in the world today. They can be elected either by legislators as in Germany, or by popular election as in Ireland. The former is much more common.

Although heads of state may sometimes seem mere figureheads they tend to exert influence in three circumstances. One is in times of emergency such as wartime when they may embody national spirit. The second role is as behind-the-scenes arbiters when there is civil strife. George V of Britain in 1926 did much to prevent oppressive measures being used against the strikers during the General Strike. Monarchs have less difficulty with this role because, unlike most presidents, they are not identified with any faction or party. The third is when after an election there is no clear majority and a cabinet crisis ensues. Then a respected and discreet head of state, who is not closely identified with any political party may, with skilful diplomacy, succeed in conjuring up a government. Italian presidents have especially needed this skill. Two who were especially successful were Einaudi (1948–55) and Pertini (1978–85).

American Presidents are examples of American 'exceptionalism'. They are both Heads of State and chief executives, fulfilling both honorific and governmental roles. Some Latin American heads of state and, more recently, the President of the Fifth French Republic, approximate to this position.

See also CONSTITUTIONAL MONARCHY; PRESIDENTS; PRIME MINISTERS.

hegemony A dominating nation or group is said to exercise hegemony. The term has been used by neo-Marxists and international relations theorists. With the former it dates from Gramsci (1891–1937) who conceived that the BOURGEOISIE were hegemonic in capitalist society. He departed from classical Marxism in that he attributed their domination to their power to define the 'limits of the possible' so that people could see no alternative to the prevailing social and economic order. The bourgeoisie had imposed their world outlook on everyone else.

Among international relations theorists concern has been largely with superpower confrontation and American hegemony in the world. American writers have anticipated American decline and theories of cyclic power balances have become popular. Thus the depression of the interwar years is associated with the decline of the hegemonic British Empire. The argument is that an international hegemony is needed to ensure a liberal economic world order. This is the theory of hegemonic stability which raises the question of what will follow American decline. Will it be a new hegemony or a period of economic and political disequilibrium?

See also CHAOS THEORY; MARXISM.

Reading
Gill, S. 1990. *American Hegemony and the Trilateral Commission.* Cambridge: CUP.; Gramsci, A. 1971. *Selections from Prison Notebooks.* London: New Left Books; Kennedy, P. 1987. *The Rise and Fall of the Great Powers.* New York: Random House; Keohane, R.O. 1984. *After Hegemony: Cooperation and Discord in the World Political Economy.* Princeton: Princeton University Press.

hermeneutics A method of explaining a work in terms of its context. Originally applied to the Bible it was adapted by Heidegger (1889–1976) for social theory. A simple summary of hermeneutics would be that in order to understand the way people behave, we need to understand their motives for doing what they are doing and what they think they are doing, and also to know their world outlook and how they see their place in the world.

See also IDEOLOGY; POSITIVISM.

Reading
Bauman, Z. 1978. *Hermeneutics and Social Science.* London: Hutchinson; Ricoeur, P. 1981. *Hermeneutics and the Human Sciences.* Cambridge: CUP.

hidden agenda A term whose use reflects a society and polity in which suspicion is rife, although the belief that the government has a set of policies it does not want to reveal is not unjustified. It is often correct. Unsurprisingly, governments, if they can, choose not to publicize policies until they have to because they know any policy will arouse some OPPO-SITION. Citizens are often aware of this. *See also* AGENDA SETTING.

hierarchy A system with well-delineated strata in which power at all levels is clearly defined. The more layers, the more hierarchical it will be. AUTHORITY will be vested in widely acknowledged and recognized roles. The Roman Catholic church is a good example. Hierarchy is a familiar, but important concept. It can be found in the STATE, VOLUNTARY ASSOCIATIONS, armies and educational institutions. *See also* AUTHORITY; ELITES; POLITICAL POWER.

historical materialism *See* DIALECTICAL MATERIALISM.

historicism A concept that history is determined by laws that shape all features of each period. Historicists, such as HEGEL, Comte and MARX, perceived history in successive phases. This sort of history has become known as 'meta-history'. POPPER, who popularized the term, condemned historicists as potential totalitarians. They think, unlike most of us, that they know the secret of historical transition and this gives them the right to drag the rest of mankind in their wake. *See also* DIALECTICAL MATERIALISM; IDEALISM.

Reading
Popper, K.R. 1957. *The Poverty of Historicism*. London: Routledge.

homosexuality *See* GAY POLITICS.

hostages Taking hostages is probably as old as human conflict. In the two World Wars it was a common procedure of invading armies. It has been practiced by terrorists. In the last twenty years hostage-taking has become especially prominent because of its adoption as a tactic by Islamic fundamentalists. The first notorious example was when Iranian revolutionaries held the American embassy staff hostage between November 1979 and January 1981. Numerous other westerners were later kidnapped and held hostage. Some died in captivity. After 1991 the tactic ceased to be profitable. The Gulf War divided Islamic states and the USA was for a time less inclined to back Israel. The collapse of the Communist bloc also weakened resistance to making peace with Israel.

human rights *See* FUNDAMENTAL RIGHTS.

hung parliament A British term to describe a House of Commons without a party with a clear majority and thus unable to form a government. The result will be a coalition, generally regarded in Britain as anathema. *See also* COALITION GOVERNMENT.

Reading
Butler, D. E. 1986. *Governing without a Majority*. 2nd. edn. London: Macmillan.

hypothesis A generalization predicting that a relationship exists between variables. Many generalizations about politics are a sort of folklore. Others proceed from earlier work carried out by social scientists. Within the social sciences most statements about behaviour relate to large groups of people. Hence, testing any hypothesis in the field of political science will involve statistical method. It will be dealing with probabilities.

To test a hypothesis one must pose a null hypothesis. If we wanted to test the validity of the common generalization, 'manual workers tend to vote for the Labour Party' we would begin by assuming the statement was untrue. The investigation would require a SAMPLE SURVEY in which manual workers were identified and questions put to them. It would need to be done in several constituencies in different parts of the country. Having collated the data we would use the evidence to test the null hypothesis, employing statistical techniques to assess the probability of acquiring such data if the null hypothesis were correct. These techniques are known as 'significance tests'. They estimate the probability that the rejection of a null hypothesis is a mistake. If the statistical tests indicates that the odds against it being a mistake are 1000 to one, then this is stated as a '.001 level of significance'.

The fact that the research showed that it was highly likely that manual workers 'tend' to vote for the Labour vote would not satisfy most political scientists. They also want to understand those who did not. Consequently much more work would need to be done to refine the hypothesis and define the tendency with more accuracy. Whatever the case, a hypothesis in the social sciences about a group or socio-demographic category can never tell us about the behaviour of an individual in that group or category.

See also SAMPLE SURVEYS; SURVEY RESEARCH.

Reading
Parten, M.B. 1950. *Surveys, Polls and Samples.* New York: Harper and Row; Popper, K. 1959. *The Logic of Scientific Discovery.* New York: Basic Books.

I

idealism This term has two meanings. Idealism with a small 'i' is applied usually to beliefs based unrealistically on a pursuit of unobtainable ideals. Idealists in this sense are visionaries. A typical example of modern idealism, often quoted, is the attempt after World War I to inaugurate a League of Nations which would guarantee peace in the world through the general acceptance of the doctrine of COLLECTIVE SECURITY.

Idealism with a capital 'I' is a philosophic concept which is contrary to the empiricist notion that knowledge can only be gained by experience. Idealists believe that reality can only be grasped through consciousness. Early intimations of this notion can be found in Plato. Kant (1724–1804) argued that experience could only be understood by understanding concepts derived through consciousness before experience. Hardly a political thinker, Kant may also be regarded as an idealist with a small 'i' because in his tract *Political Peace* (1795) he argued for an international authority to assert an international RULE OF LAW and so ensure peace between nations. Friedrich HEGEL (1770–1831), generally regarded as the quintessential Idealist philosopher, has had a profound influence on subsequent political thinking. The connection he made between his theory of the state and the phasing of historical development had wide-ranging implications.

Hegel regarded the STATE as the embodiment of reason. The state should be the paramount power in society, but should exercise it according to the law. In this way the state would guarantee the stability of 'CIVIL SOCIETY', the nexus of associations and communities which stood outside the formal state organization. He had little time for the individual citizen as a rational entity and consequently he had no regard for popular sovereignty or democratic institutions. For Hegel there was no FREEDOM without LAW but he tended to convert this attitude into the position that freedom was wherever there was law.

Hegel's theory of history perceived reason preceding history. He foresaw a movement always towards a higher plane of rationality. The history of civilization was the consciousness of reason unfolding through time. It was the progress of the World Spirit proceeding by a process he called the Dialectic. This was based on the opposition of forces: a succession of Thesis and Antithesis, a chain of contradiction only finally completed in the final Synthesis when the highest form of reason would be achieved. Hegel applied the Dialectic to his scheme of intellectual and cultural development. Through obedience to a universal principle civilization would pass through three phases. In the first, the Oriental, it was known that 'one was free'; in the second, the Greek and Roman world, people were aware that 'some were free'; but in the third and final Synthesis the world would reach the German phase in which 'all would be free'. The German nation would thus embody the attainment of higher consciousness and rationality.

Hegel's Idealism influenced quite diverse currents of thought. It obviously provided strength to German nationalism and later, Italian (though strangely not German) Fascism. On the other side of the ideological spectrum, MARX was quite consciously influenced. He reversed Hegel's view that reason is prior to history and transformed his dialectical phasing of history into DIALECTICAL MATERIALISM. Finally, Hegel influenced late nineteenth-century British LIBERALISM. T.H. Green (1836–82) conceived of freedom as something beyond a mere negative absence of restriction. He advanced a positive notion of freedom which placed an emphasis on developing the capacities of the population so that they could fulfill their potential to the utmost. Freedom thus became a social conception, not merely the narrow individualism hitherto espoused by British liberals. His ideas were further extended by his student Bernard Bosanquet (1848–1923) and by L.T. HOBHOUSE (1864–1929) who argued strongly in favour of state intervention in order to further the moral and intellectual condition of the population.
See also FASCISM; LIBERALISM; MARXISM; SOCIALISM.

Reading
Bosanquet, B. 1899. *The Philosophical Theory of the State*. London: Macmillan; Green, T.H. 1885. *Lectures in Political Obligation*. London: Longman; Hegel, G.W.F. 1942. trans T.M. Knox. *The Philosophy of Right*. Oxford: OUP; Hegel, G.W.F. 1956. trans J. Sibree. *The Philosophy of History*. New York: Dover; Hobhouse L.T. 1918. *The Metaphysical Theory of the State*. London: Allen & Unwin; Pelcynski, Z.A. ed. 1984. *The State and Civil Society : Studies in Hegel's Political Philosophy*. Cambridge: CUP.

ideal type A concept closely identified with Max WEBER who used it especially for his famous characterization of BUREAUCRACY. An ideal type is an abstraction, an 'identikit' of a concept. It is a model of a social or political structure to which a social scientist expects examples in the real world to approximate. To depict an ideal type does not connote any value judgement. Hence social scientists with quite different personal value-systems should be able to agree on the degree to which an actual case diverges from the ideal type. Thus it is a very useful device for making comparisons.
See also COMPARATIVE POLITICS; POLITICAL SOCIOLOGY.

Reading
Weber, M. 1947. *Theory of Social and Economic Organization*. New York: Free Press.

ideology An Anglicization of *ideologie*, the word is a product of the French Enlightenment, in which Destutt de Tracy published a 4-volume work, *Elements of Ideology*, between 1801 and 1815. De Tracy and his followers claimed it was a new science of ideas concerned with universal explanations. For the most part it has retained this meaning, though in the modern world its usage has become confused. In fact, it seems to have four connotations.

In the most familiar sense it is applied to systems like FASCISM and COMMUNISM. They each possessed the following features: a universal system of thought explaining the human condition; a theory of the historical process in which there was the certainty of a better future; a rejuvenating new order to replace an old order discredited by the dominance of a discredited group (such as Jews or capitalists); an emphasis on revolutionary action to overthrow the old order and put the precepts of their ideology into practice. Ideology in this sense is akin to a secular religion.

Today 'ideology' is sometimes applied to the belief systems of individuals. Nearly all have some conception of the world even if it is a distorted one. A better word to describe these mental constructs would be 'mind-sets'. Robert LANE in *Political Ideology* (1962) studied the mind-sets of fifteen ordinary Americans. His hypotheses were that their beliefs about the political system were based on a brief acquaintance during their school days with the Constitution and the Declaration of Independence. They were largely validated by his research, though the ideas of his respondents were often obscure. They lacked information and the habit of reasoning. Mind-sets are often vague world-outlooks.

The third use of 'ideology' is to be found in the work of the German sociologist, Karl MANNHEIM. He argued that groups, classes and historical eras had characteristic ideas, systematized enough to have a semblance of universality. He borrowed from HEGEL the term *WELTANSCHAUUNG* – world-outlook – which passed into the jargon of social scientists. Mannheim held that people will be biased by their social and cultural environment and by their own interests. Ruling groups can become so absorbed in their own interests that they cease to be able to make a rational judgement on a situation. To do so would be to subvert their own position. 'Ideology' was the term he applied to this illusion of the hierarchs. On the other hand dissident groups will construct their own illusory *weltanschauung* which he entitled 'Utopia'.

The fourth usage is as a bundle of ideas, 'a family of concepts' as Plamenatz described it. This was an acknowledgement of the confusion about it. Academic commentators now call LIBERALISM and CONSERVATISM ideologies. During the COLD WAR it was suggested the West's ideology was DEMOCRACY. The phrase 'our way of life' adumbrated a feeling about culture, society and politics that was akin to an ideology in the sense that it was now loosely used.

From the 1960s onwards, writers like Shils and ARON tried to soften the impact of the debate with the thesis that we had reached the 'end of ideology'. Daniel Bell, the chief prophet of this group, believed a general consensus between right and left had been achieved in the West. This was because of the effects of democracy; the new affluence of the working class; and its understanding of the reality of life under Communism. Yet Bell was aware that new ideologies were being shaped in Asia and Africa. By the 1970s the 'end of ideology' was being discounted.

See also COMMUNISM; FASCISM; TOTALITARIANISM.

Reading

Bell, D. 1960. *The End of Ideology*. Glencoe: Free Press; MacRae, D.G. 1961. *Ideology and Society*. London: Heinemann; Mannheim, K. [1929] 1960. *Ideology and Utopia*. London: Routledge; Plamenatz, J. 1970. *Ideology*. London: Macmillan; Shils, E. 1969. 'Ideology and Civility: on the Politics of the Intellectual'. In *Ideology, Politics and Political Theory*. Ed. R.H. Cox. Belmont: Wadsworth; Thompson, J.B. 1990. *Ideology and Modern Culture*. Cambridge: CUP.

image A term borrowed by political observers from the advertising industry. An 'image' in this context is the perception of a person, institution or association by the mass public. As few people will personally come into contact with public personalities the perception of most of the population will be derived from the MASS MEDIA. Consequently politicians and political parties will be much concerned with ensuring that they project a favourable image. Appearances on television are particularly important for this purpose: the belief that a politician is 'no good on television', if widespread, is enough to eliminate any party leadership ambitions.

It is not surprising, therefore, that a whole industry, that of public relations, has grown up for the purpose of manufacturing reputations and public personae. Where political leadership is particularly important, as where chief executives are popularly elected, there are specialists on dress and deportment, speech therapy, public presentation and opinion analysis involved. It is believed the 'image makers' can promote or destroy a public career.

See also PUBLIC OPINION; SPIN DOCTORS.

Reading
Boorstin, D.J. 1961. *The Image*. Harmondsworth: Penguin; McGinnis, J. 1970. *The Selling of the President*. Harmondsworth: Penguin; Qualter, T.H. 1985. *Opinion Control in the Democracies*. London: Macmillan.

immigration   An immigrant is someone who goes to make a home in another country. Early movements of population were often enforced. Conquering nations drove whole peoples into exile and slavery. Immigration in the seventeenth century was often to escape religious persecution. In the eighteenth began the infamous slave trade. By the nineteenth century there were large-scale movements from Europe to North America and the Antipodes by people escaping war and revolution and looking for a more prosperous life. There was also some deportation of convicts. By the late nineteenth century immigrants, or 'ethnics', were becoming a political issue in the USA, where the values of European Catholics, Jews and Orthodox Christians clashed with the prevailing Protestantism. It was largely an urban phenomenon; to give only one example of its dimension, it was said there were more Czechs in Chicago than in Prague.

In the twentieth century, world immigration has increased. The reasons for it remain the same. Partly it is the result of a serious refugee crisis which has been accentuated by the increase in the number of oppressive regimes throughout the world and partly it is economic. There are over-populated countries with low standards of living and there are other countries with high standards of living and shortages of labour. The heyday of immigration was in the 1950s when the decolonizing empires not only needed labour, but also had values of common citizenship with the inhabitants of their former colonies. The British Empire had become a Commonwealth and the French Empire the French Community. Germany also needed labour and large numbers of Turks went there to work. Australia and New Zealand also greatly expanded their intake and ceased to limit it to people of British origin.

By the late 1950s the economic situation had changed. The demand for immigrant labour had slackened and there was agitation among indigenous people who became increasingly intolerant of those of unfamiliar appearance and culture and also perceived them as a threat to their jobs. The prosperous, industrialized countries began to restrict immigration quite severely and in some cases, the worst being Britain, began even to forbid the entry of persecuted refugees. In France and Germany, however, the immigrant issue provoked fiercer reaction. The USA remained relatively tolerant though there was a good deal of resentment against Hispanic entrants.

Immigration remains an important world issue. Democratic majorities often want to restrict the movement of people although it is contrary to both liberal and free-market principles.

See also CITIZENSHIP; LIBERALISM; SLAVERY.

Reading
Dowty, A. 1987. *Closed Borders: the Contemporary Assault on Freedom of Movement.* New Haven: YUP; Kritz, M.M. ed. 1983. *US Immigration and Refugee Policy: Global and Domestic Issues.* Lexington: Lexington Books; Rex, J. 1973. *Race, Colonialism and the City.* London: Routledge.

immobilisme A concept associated with the inability of the Third and Fourth French Republics to make important decisions that resolved problems that were endangering their stability and survival. This inability was based on deep social and political cleavages and their expression in the legislature, but it was enhanced by constitutions that gave governments little power. The situation of 'government by assembly' tends to produce weak government and political immobility. *Immobilisme* has also been used to describe the Weimar Republic and post-war Italy.

impeachment A legal device for removing people from public office. The last case in Britain was in 1806 but in the USA it always remains a last resort because Art. II, Sect. 4 says: 'The President, Vice-President and all civil officers . . . shall be removed from office on impeachment for and conviction of treason, bribery, or other high crimes and misdemeanours'. Art. I gives the House of Representatives the 'sole power of impeachment' and the Senate 'the sole power to try all impeachments'. Conviction needs the 'concurrence of two-thirds of the members present'. If the President is tried the Chief Justice of the Supreme court must preside. President Andrew Johnson was impeached, in 1868, escaping conviction by one vote. When arraigned in 1974 President Nixon resigned before proceedings could begin. President Clinton was impeached in 1998.

Reading
Berger, R. 1973. *Impeachment: the Constitutional Problems.* Cambridge, Mass.: HUP.

imperialism Sometimes this term denotes an attitude of mind, though this use might be a synonym for JINGOISM. Usually, however, it refers to social and economic forces that have helped to shape world history. EMPIRES go back two millennia. 'Imperialism' probably developed from 'Imperial Federation', a term first employed by Disraeli in 1872.

The term became an important concept with the publication of HOBSON's book in 1902 in the middle of a period of imperialistic rivalries which was a factor contributing to the outbreak of war in 1914. Hobson saw the competition for colonial territory as an extension of the struggle for overseas markets. Finance capitalism was prominent in this contest which did not encourage domestic production. He therefore rejected the notion that colonial possessions brought advantages to home workers. Hilferding in his study of finance capital noted the oppressive nature of colonial regimes. He also believed that imperialistic rivalries would lead to war. As MARX had prophesied, it was the last stage of CAPITALISM. The fight against imperialism was the same as the fight for SOCIALISM.

Lenin, writing during World War I, quotes both Hobson and Hilferding in his development of Marx's theory of capitalism collapsing amid war and revolution. He connected the struggle for colonial emancipation with the struggle against capitalism. Class war and anti-colonial revolt were both facets of the same historic movement. This theory was adopted by Stalin, the Third International and, later, Communist rulers throughout the world. Consequently in the inter-war period liberals and 'progressives' sympathetic to the anti-colonial struggle were often favourably disposed to the Soviet Union and to the Marxist analysis of imperialism.

Later commentators, most notably SCHUMPETER, have argued that imperialism was a manifestation of an aggressive desire for territorial expansion. It was 'expansion for its own sake'. Among nations with imperialistic intent it was the militaristic aristocracy that possessed this attitude and the resources to exploit it. The commercial classes only followed in its wake when it was profitable. Hence the Soviet Union could be regarded as an imperialist power. It was aggressively expansionist, yet threatened by nationalisms within its empire. It would not hesitate to repress them. By the 1970s the Chinese Communists were denouncing the Russians as 'social imperialists'.

More recent observers have argued that imperialism is not a matter of territorial conquest. It is a form of world-wide commercial hegemony by the finance capital of the industrialized states over the poorer peripheral nations. This analysis is linked to the concept of GLOBALIZATION. *See also* COLONIALISM; EMPIRES; GLOBALIZATION; JINGOISM.

Reading
Hilferding, R. [1910] 1981. *Finance Capital: a Study of the Latest Phase in Capitalist Development*. London: Routledge.; Hobson, J.A. 1902. *Imperialism*. London: Allen and Unwin; Lenin, V.I. 1916. *Imperialism: the Highest Stage of Capitalism*. London: Lawrence and Wishart; Schumpeter, J.A. 1955. *Imperialism and Social Classes*. New York: Meridian Books; Wallerstein, I. 1974. *The Modern World System*. New York: Academic Press.

imperial preference A policy advocated in Britain by Joseph Chamberlain and the Tariff Reform League in the 1900s. They argued that in the face of German and American competition, Britain and its colonies should form a single economic unit extending preferential tariffs to one another, but raising duties against the rest of the world. This rejection of the traditional policy of Free Trade probably led to the Liberal victory in the 1906 General Election. In the 1920s imperial preference was again urged by Beaverbrook and his Empire Crusade and partially adopted by the Ottawa conference in 1932. It was gradually abandoned after 1945 and expired when Britain joined the European Union in 1973.
See also FREE TRADE.

implementation The process by which a policy is carried out. It is not as simple a matter as might at first appear. Failures of implementation occur for various reasons. In developing countries too ambitious policies may fail because there is no bureaucracy capable of administering them. In the developed world complex social legislation may founder because parliaments in a hurry have not drafted it properly. Bureaucrats may find it difficult to translate politicians' vague goals into detailed implementation. There may be problems where there are difficult relations between different layers of government.

Political scientists have become increasingly interested in implementation in recent years. It is now accepted, for instance, that the simple division between POLITICS and ADMINISTRATION is no longer valid. They are interrelated activities. There is, as it were, 'politics' in all administrative action.
See also ADMINISTRATION; BUREAUCRACY.

Reading
Dunsire, A. 1978. *Implementation in a Bureaucracy*. Oxford: Martin Robertson; Pressman J.L. and A. Wildavsky. 1973. *Implementation*. Berkeley: University of California Press.

impoundment A refusal by the US President to spend funds legally appropriated. Rarely used, the procedure became controversial when used by President Nixon to prevent the passage of laws he did not like. A compromise in the Congressional Budget and Impoundment Act of 1974 was later ruled unconstitutional. It is therefore not clear whether the President has the power of impoundment or not.

See also LEGISLATIVE VETO.

Reading
Fisher, L. 1975. *Presidential Spending Power*. Princeton: Princeton University Press.

incomes policy An economic strategy developed by many governments in the 1960s for dealing with the problem of INFLATION. Trade unions were securing large wage rises and these were pushing prices up. The process was a spiral of acceleration. Incomes policies were intended to decelerate the ability of trade unions to increase wages. It was thought wages were easier to control than prices or profits. Government employees could be directly influenced when they bargained with the government. Other workers presented a more difficult problem.

There were two main types of income policy – the statutory and the voluntary policies. Britain tried both. Where there was a tradition of industrial law statutory policies stood more chance of success. On the other hand, any breach of the law resulted in the difficult procedure of enforcing sanctions in an area where hundreds of thousands of people might be involved. Voluntary policies could only be successful, as they were for a long time in Sweden and Austria, where trade-union structure was simple and centralized, union leaderships were trusted and capable of obtaining members' agreement for negotiated deals and governments had close relations with labour movements through long Social Democratic rule.

Lack of these characteristics doomed most incomes policies. Expectations that they would fail was one reason for their failure. Bodies set up to monitor the economy, such as the Prices and Incomes Board in Britain, disappeared in the process. By the 1980s most governments had fallen back on monetary policy and increasing unemployment in order to keep down wages.

See also INFLATION; PLANNING; TRADE UNIONS.

Reading
Dorfman, G.A. 1979. *Government Versus Trade Unionism in British Politics since 1968*. London: Macmillan; Goldthorpe, J.H. ed. 1984. *Order and Conflict in Contemporary Capitalism*. Oxford: Clarendon; Moran, M. 1977. *The Politics of Industrial Relations*. London: Macmillan.

incorporation A term used to describe the process by which an individual or a group becomes integrated into a larger structure or a recognized pattern of behaviour. Incomes policies, for example, were denounced by some trade-unionists because the unions and/or their leaders became 'incorporated' in CAPITALISM. Groups involved in extra-parliamentary action and wary about the democratic process may become 'incorporated' in it as a result of their experiences. There is the implication of entrapment in the way radical militants use the term, suggesting that people are not in control of their own volitions. Marxists believe incorporation is a victory for the BOURGEOISIE because the workers have been hoodwinked into accepting settlements against their real interests.

See also CLASS CONSCIOUSNESS; INCOMES POLICY; NEW SOCIAL MOVEMENTS.

Reading
Crouch, C. 1979. *The Politics of Industrial Relations*. Manchester: Manchester University Press; Tarrow, S. 1989. *Democracy and Disorder*. Oxford: OUP.

incrementalism The term given to a pattern of decision making. It implies changes in policy are made by slight increments over a continuous period. It best applies to budgetary policy: it is common for democratic governments not to want to shock the voters by presenting them with a sudden change in their economic expectations. On the other hand its use as a model can be exaggerated. Much policy has to be made in response to unexpected external forces and incremental change in such circumstances is not appropriate.

Reading
Lindblom, C.E. 1959. 'The Science of Muddling Through'. In *Public Administration Review* 19, 79–99; Lindblom, C.E. 1979. 'Still Muddling, Not Yet Through'. In *Public Administration Review* 39, 517–26.

independent politics The politics of a political system where all candidates are independent because organized political parties do not participate in elections. It is usually found in small-town politics where it may be thought the intervention of the parties is not appropriate for the slight functions of local government. In the USA institutional arrangements may make party candidates almost impossible. For example, non-partisan ballots, the prohibition of party titles on candidate application forms or ballot papers, leave most voters unable to identify political affiliations. Elections are often 'at large' – there is no division into wards which normally allow for the representation and mobilization of social cleavage. Hence personalities rule the political process.

Reading
Bealey, F.W. and J. Sewel. 1981. *The Politics of Independence*. Aberdeen: Aberdeen University Press; Lee, E.C. 1960. *The Politics of Non-partisanship*. Berkeley: University of California Press.

indicative planning *See* PLANNING.

indirect democracy *See* REPRESENTATIVE DEMOCRACY.

indirect election A two-stage election in which the first election chooses 'electors' who then vote for the person or assembly they prefer. The best-known example is that of the US President who is chosen by an ELECTORAL COLLEGE of 538 electors, voting two months after the electorate of approximately 150 million people has voted. Sometimes SECOND CHAMBERS are elected indirectly. The German Bundesrat, the second chamber, is composed of representatives of the governments of the 16 Länder.

indirect rule A form of colonial government through traditional local rulers. It had low administrative costs and it allowed for the preservation of local culture, recommending it to some and not to others. It was a feature of British administration in parts of both Africa and India.

industrial democracy This term comprises a wide range of notions. One dimension stretches politically from the left to the right. Is industrial democracy co-existent with CAPITALISM or SOCIALISM? Another relates to the scope and power of employee participation. Is it about marginal or central policy decisions? A third dimension is concerned with the form of decision-making. Are decisions made by REPRESENTATIVE or DIRECT DEMOCRACY and who votes?

One of the early features of the British trade-union movement was that members were participating in elections for their union representatives and executive councils long before they had the franchise in national and local elections. It was this that most excited the Webbs in their study. There seemed quite a short distance from this to arguing like COLE that unions were capable of running their industries after public ownership had been achieved. This was not socialism of the statist kind. Various schemes of WORKERS' CONTROL were suggested in the syndicalist and guild socialist literature. From time to time the ideas have recurred. In recent years workers' 'self-management' in Yugoslavia (whose success has probably been much exaggerated), has given encouragement to some labour movements.

Yet the involvement of employees in the decision-making of industrial and commercial enterprises has also been regarded as a way of preserving a healthy capitalism. A happy workforce is good for productivity. Thus in Germany after World War II councils elected from employees became an obligation for larger enterprises. This policy of *mittbestimmung* has since become the model for the European Union and is incorporated in its Social Chapter. Another strand is the idea of employees being given shares in their company, sometimes known as 'worker capitalism'. Smaller enterprises in the form of workers' co-operatives in some countries receive encouragement from their governments. An interconnected system of these at Mondragon in the Basque country has become famous. In Sweden, a 1983 law obliges employers to allocate shares to investment funds on whose boards employees have a majority. This variant of industrial democracy gives the workforce considerable control over important policies.

Much of the controversy about industrial democracy in labour movements rages around the question as to whether representation should be by trade unions at a national or local level, or whether it should be by representatives elected from among enterprises' workers by enterprises' workers. Thus the 1975 Bullock committee in Britain, set up to recommend a 'radical extension of industrial democracy ... by means of representation on boards of directors', met with little trade-union support. The trade-union leaders wanted direct representation.

Whatever form it takes, there is much liberal backing for industrial democracy. Such political scientists as DAHL and LINDBLOM, scarcely socialists, view the hierarchical decision-making structures of modern corporations with misgiving. The latter writes that the 'large private corporation fits oddly into democratic theory and vision'.

See also GUILD SOCIALISM; SYNDICALISM; WORKERS' CONTROL.

Reading

Cole, G.D.H. 1917. *Self-Government in Industry*. London: Bell; Dahl, R.A. 1985. *A Preface to Economic Democracy*. Berkeley: University of California Press; Lindblom, C.E. 1977. *Politics and Markets*. New York: Basic Books; Schuller, T. 1985. *Democracy at Work*. Oxford: OUP; Webb, S. and B. Webb. 1897. *Industrial Democracy*. London: Longman.

industrial relations Relations between employers and their employees are important for the prosperity of any society. Hence governments are bound to be interested in their health. Work is an outstanding aspect of almost everyone's life and therefore industrial relations will be an important issue and a matter of concern for every democratic government. In democracies where there is FREEDOM OF ASSOCIATION, trade unions organize workers for collective action. Employers are also organized at industry level and negotiations with unions are likely to be conducted on a nation-wide scale.

Industrial relations are conditioned by several factors. Salient among them is the state of the world economy. When there is general prosperity with prices rising as consumption increases employers will be competing for labour and collective bargaining is likely to be successful in earning wage increases. Where employers are uncompliant there may be strikes but strikes are short, though numerous, in times of prosperity. When there is depression, demand for labour falls, resulting in employers demanding lower wages and, if this is unsuccessful, dismissing workers. Unemployment weakens the unions. In depression employers are stronger.

Strikes are few, though those that happen may be long and bitter.

Custom and tradition is another significant factor. Where a country's industrial culture was formed when laissez-faire was the predominant value there has been a tendency for the state not to intervene in industrial relations which, in consequence, develop in a disorderly fashion. Trade-union structure will tend to be untidy and management styles to be brusque and unprofessional. Where industrialization is more recent, and it took place when industrial technology was more advanced and free market values less pronounced, trade unions are likely to be rationally structured and management professionally trained. Industrial relations are likely to be better, though there may be more legal restrictions on collective bargaining and striking. Yet this factor can be exaggerated. Australia industrialized late, has a highly regulated industrial relations system, but is a byword for its industrial militancy.

Finally, the relationship of trade unions to political parties may affect industrial relations. Where one party is identified with the employers and the other with the unions, as in Britain (a gross simplification of the position), industrial conflict may be reflected in party conflict. There is no danger of this in the USA where there is no labour party of any size. In Italy and France ideological cleavages split the unions and weaken them generally. In France most employers did not recognize unions for collective bargaining purposes until after the 'events of 1968'.
See also CORPORATISM; INDUSTRIAL DEMOCRACY; TRADE UNIONS.

Reading
Bean, R. 1985. *Comparative Industrial Relations*. London: Croom Helm; Hyman, R. 1972. *Strikes*. London: Fontana; Knowles, K.G.J.C. 1952. *Strikes*. Oxford: Blackwell; Phelps Brown, E.H. 1965. *The Growth of British Industrial Relations*. London: Macmillan.

industrial society A term associated first with Saint-Simon who saw it as following agrarian society. Industrial society is characterized by new technology and factory production, organized to a strict time schedule and dependent on division of labour. Urbanization with all its social consequences, is closely linked. MARX called it 'capitalist society' and others have described its later stages as Fordist.

ARON coined the term 'modern industrial society', excluding ideological implications because the main features of industrialization could also be found in the Communist states. BUREAUCRACY, as WEBER had prophesied, served both CAPITALISM and SOCIALISM. This was part of the CONVERGENCE THEORY which arose in the late 1960s and early 1970s. Later writers have detected a new phase called POST-INDUSTRIAL SOCIETY. Gershuny has depicted a 'service society' in which distributive and recreational services become a large sector of the economy.
See also CONVERGENCE THEORY; FORDISM; POST-FORDISM; POST-INDUSTRIAL SOCIETY.

Reading
Aron, R. 1967. *Eighteen Lectures on Industrial Society*. London: Weidenfeld; Gershuny, J.L. 1978. *After Industrial Society*. London: Macmillan.

inequality See EGALITARIANISM; EQUALITY.

inflation A continuous and extraordinary increase in the price level. This leads to wage demands and industrial unrest, a decline in saving and an increase in borrowing and spending. It discourages investment and generally makes it difficult to plan ahead. Consumers, anticipating more price rises, start 'panic buying' and this accelerates the cycle of inflation. The world experienced this phenomenon after the sudden rise in oil prices in 1973. It caused political instability. Different attempts to deal with it were INCOMES POLICY and MONETARISM.

See also INCOMES POLICY; MONETARISM.

Reading
Hirsch, F. and J.H. Goldthorpe. eds. 1978. *The Political Economy of Inflation*. London: Martin Robertson.

initiative   A component of DIRECT DEMOCRACY, the initiative, enabling citizens to initiate laws, is used in many of the western states of the USA and Switzerland. In Switzerland if 50,000 citizens sign a petition for an amendment to the constitution it is put to a federal REFERENDUM. It is also used in the Swiss cantons. In California a petition for an initiative needs to be signed by 5 per cent of the TURNOUT in the last election for a governor. Although initiatives encourage citizen participation they are frequently organized by PRESSURE GROUPS who have the resources to collect signatures.

inner city   Generally a problem area in industrialized countries. Drugs, crime and homelessness are its characteristics. The effect is to accelerate the movement of inner-city dwellers to the suburbs, leaving the centres of large cities in decay. Thus inner cities have become a political issue, though politicians have not succeeded in doing much about it.

institutions   Although this term has different meanings in other social sciences, to political scientists an institution is a public body with formally designated structures and functions, intended to regulate certain defined activities which apply to the whole population. Political institutions include governments, parliaments and judiciaries. Their inter-relationships will be defined in CONSTITUTIONS. An institution differs from an ASSOCIATION in that the latter is a voluntary body which does not have universal application; but internal arrangements in associations may take institutional forms.

An understanding of institutions is a necessary possession for an intelligent comprehension of the political life of a country, though it is not sufficient. One also needs to study the interplay of associations like political parties and PRESSURE GROUPS and to examine POLITICAL BEHAVIOUR generally.

See also ASSOCIATION; CONSTITUTIONS; POLITICAL BEHAVIOUR; POLITICAL PARTIES.

Reading
Finer. S.E. 1970. *Comparative Government*. Harmondsworth: Penguin.

intellectuals   An intellectual could be defined as someone who is principally guided by the intellect rather than emotion. Yet as a reference to a group it connotes people with certain values. Intellectuals prize free expression of ideas and artistic forms. They tend to dislike materialism and convention. This often sets them apart in society. They may stand aside from political activity. On the other hand, when they do engage in politics they may become committed. In the twentieth century they have often been under suspicion because of their tendency to accept totalitarian theories.

Reading
Benda, J. 1927. *La Trahison des Clercs*. Paris: B. Grasset; Shils, E. 1958. 'Ideology and Civility: on the Politics of the Intellectual'. In *Sowanee Review*. Reprinted in R.H. Cox. ed. 1969. *Ideology, Politics and Political Theory*. Belmont: Wadsworth.

intelligence   As a political term this refers to information gathered for military and defence purposes. The latter may have a wide scope. For instance, monitoring what are regarded as subversive groups may be part of it. Much intelligence will be obtained from available documentation; but the romantic part of it involves espionage. Well-known intelligence agencies are the British MI5 and

MI6, concerned with home and foreign intelligence respectively; the American CIA; the Israeli Mossad; and before 1989, the Russian KGB.

Reading
Andrew, C. 1985. *Secret Service: the Making of the British Intelligence Community*. London: Heinemann; Ranelagh, J. 1986. *The Agency: the Rise and Decline of the CIA*. London: Weidenfeld; Wright, P. 1987. *Spycatcher*. Richmond, Victoria: Heinemann.

intelligentsia A Slav word sometimes used as a synonym for INTELLECTUALS. Milosz says that it includes everyone with higher education. In nineteenth-century eastern Europe the intelligentsia were highly politicized. In Russia many became Communists: indeed, almost all the members of the original Politburo were of this type, presenting a problem doctrinally as, according to Marxist theory, they should have been proletarians. Hence the BOLSHEVIK formula, 'workers by hand and by brain'.

Reading
Milosz, C. 1980. *The Captive Mind*. Harmondsworth: Penguin.

interdependence A word increasingly used to describe contemporary relations between states. Improved communications – both of people and information – more and freer trade, MULTINATIONALS, and the growth of international organizations have much increased the number of contacts. More relations does not necessarily mean better relations. Good relations depend on various factors such as the sharing of common values and goals and the symmetry of the relationship. Co-operation between democratic states is always easier than between states with different political regimes. The growth of many more industrialized countries in the Pacific Rim has increased symmetry in international economic relations.

Reading
Keohane, R. and J.S. Nye, 1989. *Power and Interdependence*. 2nd edn. Boston: Little, Brown; Stein, A. 1991. *Why Nations Co-operate*. Ithaca: Cornell University Press.

interest groups Sometimes this term includes PRESSURE GROUPS. At other times the two are differentiated and interest groups are less formal interests such as churches and the military, while pressure groups are more concerned with legislation and advertising their causes. Another division is between groups which achieve consultative status – governments make a point of discussing relevant policy with them – and groups which never attain this favoured position.
See also CORPORATISM; DEMOCRATIC ELITISM; GROUP THEORY; PRESSURE GROUPS.

Reading
Ehrmann, H. ed. 1958. *Interest Groups on Four Continents*. Pittsburgh: University of Pittsburgh Press.

interests A vague term which may refer to INTEREST GROUPS. British politicians before proposing legislation often mention the need to 'consult the interests involved'. At other times vagueness may suggest a rather dubious implication. Bentham wrote about 'sinister interests' who would pervert the course of justice or the drafting of legislation.

intergovernmental relations First used in the USA in the 1930s to describe the interactions between different levels of government. Federal systems naturally have more relationships of this kind than unitary systems but the term has come to be used generally. It encompasses constitutional relationships, financial relationships and those between officials at the different levels.

Federal countries, however, are bound to be more complex. The USA has over 80,000 governmental units. Conscious that as government policies proliferated interrelationships had become more elaborate, in 1959 the Eisenhower Administration appointed the Advisory Commission on Intergovernmental Relations with twenty-six members to do research and produce reports and policy recommendations on the problems involved.

See also CENTRAL–LOCAL RELATIONS.

Reading
O'Toole, L.J. ed. 1985. *American Intergovermental Relations*. Washington, D.C.: CQ Press; Wright, D.S. 1982. *Understanding Intergovernmental Relations*. Monterey: Brooks/Cole.

internal colonialism *See* COLONIALISM.

international law International law has two sectors – private international law and public international law. The former relates to the rules and agreements, often contractual, between individuals and associations in different states. Because of the globalization of the economy and especially the increasing number of transactions between MULTINATIONALS, private international law has become a growing institution.

Public international law is concerned with the relations between states. It consists of understood rules regulating the behaviour of states and a great deal of detail from treaties between them. These have been growing since the mid-seventeenth century. In 1625 GROTIUS wrote *De Jure Belli ac Pacis* in which he posited an international community of sovereign states with shared needs, including a law of nations. He recognized the desire of states for self-defence and acknowledged that in certain circumstances they had a right to go to war. In 1648 the Peace of Westphalia concluded the Thirty Years War and accepted the right of Protestant states to exist, thus signalling the waning of the power of the Catholic church and the Holy Roman Empire.

Since then public international law has developed and includes such subjects as the use of gas, germ warfare, the treatment of prisoners of war, international air traffic, GENOCIDE, extradition and the law of the sea bed. It also covers the circumstances in which a state has the right to go to war. These are administered by numerous bodies. The best known is the International Court of Justice at the Hague, the judicial instrument of the United Nations. It has not always been effective. For example, the Court ruled unanimously in favour of the USA in 1980 during the Iran hostage crisis. In 1984 it ruled in favour of Nicaragua who took the USA to court for mining its harbours. In neither case did the verdicts have any effect. The Iranians accused the Court of bias in favour of modernism, the Americans of bias towards the Third World and Marxism. The episodes illustrate the criticism that international law, without a coercive apparatus to enforce international order, is not law.

Despite its only partial acceptance, international law has become increasingly important since World War II. An important factor in this trend has been the universal feeling that nuclear weaponry ought never to be used. Another is the growth of international institutions of all kinds, leading to more continuous, complex and co-operative relations between states. Again, new international problems requiring regulation, such as terrorism and world pollution, affect all states and obviously require co-operation.

See also DIPLOMACY; JUST WAR; REALISM; REALPOLITIK.

Reading
Bull, H., B. Kingsbury and A. Roberts. eds. 1990. *Hugo Grotius and International Relations*. Oxford: OUP; Deutsch, K. and S. Hoffman. eds. 1971. *The Relevance of International Law*. Garden City, NY: Doubleday; Falk, R.A. 1989. *Revitalizing International Law*. Ames, Iowa: Iowa University Press; Lauterpacht, H. 1958. *The Development of International Law by the International Court*. London: Stevens;

Onuf, N.G. ed. 1982. *Law-Making in the International Community*. Durham: North Carolina Academic Press.

international relations An academic discipline that studies the international system. It is sometimes seen as a branch of political science, but generally claims autonomy as a subject. Although reflections on relations between states can be found in Thucydides, International Relations (IR) as a university subject dates only from the years after World War I. In Britain the landmark was the inauguration of the Woodrow Wilson Chair of International Politics in 1919 at the University of Wales College, Aberystwyth.

In the early years an idealist school flourished, stimulated by reaction against the mass killing of the war and the hope that international peace could be maintained by the League of Nations. Idealists believed people were essentially good and stressed the need to bring rationality into relations between states. Some were enthusiasts for world government, others were pacifists. The failure of democratic politicians to appreciate the true nature of totalitarian dictators and to stand up to them, leading to the outbreak of World War II, encouraged the growth of a realist school which interpreted world politics with Hobbesian perspectives. Realists put their faith in national security and regarded the state as the only important international actor.

In the last half century IR has much proliferated. It has developed numerous sub-disciplines such as international political economy, foreign policy analysis, strategic studies, and the study of international organization. It has also burgeoned into other schools. The Liberal-Pluralists dispute with the Realists about the state as the actor, arguing that IR should cover a much wider field, taking in international issues and accepting that non-governmental organizations are ever becoming more important. They do not like the conflictual model of inter-state relations. Globalists argue that the significant point about the international system is that it is driven by world forces. They emphasize the importance of economic factors and many of them are Marxists. Their analysis is conflictual and Realist.

See also DIPLOMACY; GLOBALIZATION; INTERNATIONAL LAW; PEACEKEEPING; WAR.

Reading
Burchill, S. and A. Linklater. 1996. *Theories of International Relations*. London: St. Martin's Press; Rosenau, J.N. and E-O. Czempiel. 1992. *Governance without Government: Order and Change in World Politics*. Cambridge: CUP; Russett, B. and H. Starr. 1981. *World Politics*. San Francisco: Freeman; Sheehan, M. 1999. 'International Relations'. In Bealey, F.W., R.A. Chapman and M. Sheehan, *Elements in Political Science* Edinburgh: Edinburgh University Press; Viotti, P. and M. Kaupi. 1993. *International Relations Theory*. New York: Columbia University Press.

international socialism Socialism has a tradition of FRATERNITY and support for the Brotherhood of Man. In the Communist Manifesto in 1848 MARX and Engels called for workers of all countries to unite. A common socialist slogan was that 'the workers have no fatherland'. So NATIONALISM would not appeal to them. Marx founded the First International in 1864 with this in mind but it was not a success. The Second International founded in 1889 was a confederation of both Marxist and non-Marxist socialist parties. Its main objective was to stop war by all its members declaring an international general strike when war threatened. It never clearly adopted this policy and in 1914 the workers of all countries accepted mobilization. After the war the Second International was resurrected but the newly founded Communist parties joined the Third International based in Moscow in 1919. It changed its name to Cominform in 1943. The Fourth International is a confederation of the breakaway

Trotskyist parties. The Third collapsed with the Soviet Union in 1991; but the Second persists, though it is now known as Comisco.

See also COMMUNISM; GENERAL STRIKE; MARXISM; SOCIALISM; TROTSKYISM.

Reading
Braunthal, J. 1980. *History of the International*. London: Nelson; Joll, J. *History of the Second International, 1889–1914*. London: Routledge.

interpellation A device used in some parliaments by which any member of the legislature can ask any minister about an action or policy. It can initiate debate on a vote of confidence. In the French Third and Fourth Republics this procedure was often used and contributed greatly to the instability of their governments. In Italy interpellations are still in use.

iron curtain A phrase made famous by Churchill in his Fulton speech in March 1946. He was describing the boundary imposed by the Soviet Union between its satellites and western Europe. Very few people and only censored information was allowed to pass westward. It also became very difficult for visitors to cross the line eastward. The Soviet Union constructed a formidable barrier of several lines of barbed wire and watch-towers to prevent it. A dramatic example was the Berlin Wall built in 1961 to separate the Communist East of the city from the West.

iron law of oligarchy A concept of Roberto MICHELS (1876–1936) who is regarded as a 'classical elitist'. He summed it up in the phrase: 'Who says organization says oligarchy'. This is a tautology. It is a basic feature of organization that the few control the many. Michels began his political life as a social democrat but he became disillusioned with the weakness of rank-and-file participation and influence. If there was no 'democracy' in socialist parties then it could not exist in any parties and democracy in the nation as a whole was an impossibility. He ended his life as a member of the Italian Fascist Party.

Although his statement of the iron law is rather trite, Michels's analysis of the reasons for the power of political party leaders is impressive and has probably never been surpassed. There were three reasons. First, were the 'technical and administrative' reasons. Direct government by the 'masses' was a 'mechanical and technical impossibility'. Leaders with expertise were needed and parties, like all organizations, develop a bureaucracy. Party competition necessitates 'strategic promptness' which gives leaders power. Once elections are over, leaders need fear little from rank-and-file control. Second, were 'psychological reasons'. Here Michels concentrated on the feelings of the 'masses'. They had a need for leaders, feeling gratitude and even reverence towards them. Finally, there was the intellectual superiority of the leadership. Compared with them the 'masses' were uneducated and incompetent.

It must be remembered that Michels was writing before 1914 when democracy was limited especially in Germany, his homeland. No socialist party in Europe had ever been in power. Moreover, by the 'masses' whom he clearly despised, he meant party members, a very small and unrepresentative proportion of the electorate. It never seemed to occur to him that ultimately democratic leaders are bound to be more concerned with voter influence than pressures from party organization.

See also ELITES; ELITISM.

Reading
Beetham, D. 1977. 'From Socialism to Fascism: the Relation between Theory and Practice in the Work of Roberto Michels'. In *Political Studies* 25. 3–4, 161–81; Michels, R. [1902] 1914. *Political Parties*. London: Jarrold and Sons.

irredentism   From the Italian *irredenta*, meaning 'unredeemed'. Unredeemed Italy were those parts like the Trentino and Istria which remained in Austrian hands after Italy had largely been unified in 1870. Numerous other examples of this kind can be found throughout the world. Thus irredentism remains a troublesome aspect of the world scene. *See also* NATIONALISM.

islamic fundamentalism   A phrase frequently used by the western media to describe a group of sometimes disparate Islamic movements. Western liberals tend to be unsympathetic to Islam because its values and procedures are inconsistent with those of the Enlightenment. The position of women under Koranic law is especially unacceptable to liberals and democrats. Although Islam is not hierarchically organized the clergy seem to have a domination over the minds of the laity that rational anti-clericals deplore.

Particularly British and American journalists, however, often associate FUNDAMENTALISM with TERRORISM. Yet most Islamic fundamentalists merely want a return to a less secular society: they are opposed to both CAPITALISM and SOCIALISM. They abhor westernized law and want to replace it with the Shari'a, early Islamic law. Under this there are savage punishments, such as amputation for theft and stoning for adulterers, but the terrorists are a minority among fundamentalists. The terrorists desire an assertion of Islam, one of the world's major religions, as a world power.

At one time an obvious vehicle for this objective was Arab nationalism. Arabic is the language of prayer and the Islamic scriptures. The inauguration of the state of Israel in 1948 powerfully strengthened the bond between Arab nations. Unfortunately, not only are most of the world's Muslims not Arabs, but also Arab unity was transient. Egypt and Tunisia were hostile to Libya and most Arab states became hostile to Iraq, many of them lining up with the West against Iraq in the Gulf War (1990–1). Iran, a non-Arab Islamic state, also fought a long war between 1980 and 1988 against Iraq. Iran backed different groups from Pakistan fighting in the guerrilla struggle against the Russian invasion of Afghanistan after 1979. Moreover, there is a religious divide between the Sunnis, the majority sect, and the Shias who believe that Mohammed's son-in-law, Ali, was his rightful successor. *See also* FATWA; FUNDAMENTALISM.

Reading
Ruthven, M. 1984. *Islam in the World*. Harmondsworth: Penguin; Smith, W.C. 1957. *Islam in Modern History*. Princeton: Princeton University Press.

isolationism   A nineteenth-century policy of the British 'Little Englanders'. Goschen, Chancellor of the Exchequer (1886–92), spoke of Britain's 'splendid isolation', though he was quoting Sir George Foster, a Canadian statesman. In the twentieth century the term has referred to an American foreign policy stance, usually towards European entanglement. The USA did not sign the Versailles Treaty or join the League of Nations. In 1935 Congress passed the Neutrality Act which forbade the sale of arms to any belligerent state and, initially, the USA avoided entering World War II. Small countries like Switzerland may remain resolutely isolationist.

issues   A political issue arises when people are aware of disagreement which becomes a public matter. The disagreement will be about either local or national policy with which personalities are likely to be involved. The importance of an issue may depend in the first place on people's perceptions of it but if the media seize on it they may make it appear more important. Then the politicians may feel they should exploit it if they think taking one side or the other will improve their electoral chances. Thus new issues may be incorporated into political party programmes. Conversely, if the politicians choose to leave an issue alone it may lose importance. On the other hand, if it has strong support it will probably persist, supported by media interest. In Britain some salient national issues, such as capital punishment and fox-hunting, may be left to a FREE VOTE of the House of Commons.

issue politics   In recent years it has been contended that more and more issues no longer fit into party policies and are supported by strong PRESSURE GROUPS. People believe they exert more political influence by belonging to a pressure group rather than joining a party. But parties amalgamate, prioritize and rationalize issues. The voters choose between party programmes at elections. In contrast, pressure groups sectionalize public opinion and national politics. It is argued that the rise of groups of this kind, such as the environmental lobby, herald a new kind of politics – issue politics.

Issue politics, it is argued, involves 'issue voting'. Whereas voting in the 1940s and 1950s was often guided by habits formed as a result of long issues of a materialistic, class nature, voting since has been more concerned with the disposition of a candidate to a specific issue. This may in time signal a shift from representative to DIRECT DEMOCRACY.

The DEALIGNMENT of the voters from party and class allegiances portends the beginning of the politics of POST-MATERIALISM. The politicians are being forced to be more flexible as the former stable 'issue networks' of pressure groups no longer exist.

See also CORPORATISM; DEALIGNMENT; GROUP THEORY; INTEREST GROUPS; POST-MATERIALISM; PRESSURE GROUPS.

Reading
Heclo, H. 1978. 'Issue networks and the Executive Establishment'. In *The New American Political System*. Ed. A. King. Washington, D.C.: American Enterprise Institute; Nie, N.H., S. Verba and J.R. Petrocik. 1979. *The Changing American Voter*. Cambridge, Mass.: HUP; Wilson, G. 1981. *Interest Groups in the United States*. Oxford: OUP.

item veto   This procedure, existing in most American states, allows the governors to veto sections of bills appropriating money. It is a potentially powerful device for defeating RIDERS. US Presidents do not have it.

J

jacobinism The Jacobins were a French revolutionary group founded in 1789 under the leadership of Robespierre (1758–94) who was responsible for the Reign of Terror. They were the original 'left' and were strong centralizers and upholders of the view that the SOVEREIGNTY OF THE PEOPLE rested with the elected assembly. In France the term 'jacobin' still implies someone with these political beliefs but in the rest of the world it is more likely to be used to describe a radical, rather ruthless, populist politician.

See also LEFT AND RIGHT.

jingoism A term originating in 1878 from a British music-hall song during the Eastern crisis. It began: 'We don't want to fight; but by jingo if we do/ We've got the ships, we've got the men, we've got the money too'. This boastful NATIONALISM characterized a section of the press and public opinion for the next quarter of a century. It was weakened by the Boer War (1899–1902) and disappeared as an important force in World War I (1914–18).

Reading
See also IMPERIALISM; NATIONALISM.
Hobson, J.A. 1901. *The Psychology of Jingoism*. London: G. Richards.

judicial activism A term of reference to an attitude of the American Supreme Court. In two periods the Court has shown a strong tendency in its verdicts to assert its right effectively to make policy. Justices Black (1937–71) and Douglas (1939–75) were prominent in a majority on the Court which used the Bill of Rights and especially the First Amendment actively in their rulings. From 1953 to 1969 the Court's Chief Justice was Earl Warren. It made a momentous decision in the case *Brown* v. *Board of Education*, 1954, ordering an end to racial segregation in schools.

The opposite tendency is that of 'judicial restraint'. The classic proponent of this principle was Justice Holmes (1882–99; Chief Justice 1899–1902) who held that the correct Court attitude was one of deference as an appointed body towards the elected legislature and the executive. Justice Frankfurter (1939–62) also took up a strong position on 'self-restraint'.

See also BILL OF RIGHTS; JUDICIAL REVIEW.

Reading
Frankfurter, F. 1961. *Mr. Justice Holmes and the Supreme Court*. Cambridge, Mass.: Belknap; Mendelson, W. 1961. *Justices Black and Frankfurter: Conflict in the Court*. Chicago: University of Chicago Press.

judicial function and process   The ability to listen and assess with detachment the outcome of cases between litigants, including cases in which the state is involved. The processes vary between legal systems though the functions should be the same. There are reputedly eight families of law, though the best known are Roman Law and Anglo-American COMMON LAW.

Reading
Ehrmann, H.W. 1976. *Comparative Legal Cultures*. Englewood Cliffs: Prentice Hall.

judicial review   The power of courts to invalidate laws and executive actions. Judicial review of some kind exists in most states, but it originated in the USA. (In Britain 'judicial review' means judicial power to keep administrative bodies and inferior tribunals within their jurisdiction.) It was not mentioned in the Constitution of 1787 and became an accepted part of constitutional practice as a result of the judgement of the Supreme Court in *Marbury* v. *Madison*, 1803, by which part of the Federal Judiciary Act of 1789 was declared unconstitutional. Chief Justice Marshall asserted that the power of the legislature was limited and the Constitution was written to make that clear. What was the purpose of committing these limitations to writing if those limits 'may at any time be passed by those intended to be restrained'? It was therefore 'emphatically the province and duty of the judicial department to say what the law is'.

Since then, judicial review in the USA has never been challenged legally. Political pressures can arise because vacancies on the Court are filled by Presidential appointment and endorsed, or otherwise, by the Senate. The nine Justices have their own legal and political philosophies and over the years these produce different attitudes to what is constitutional. From the Civil War to the early 1930s, conservative majorities were concerned with freedom of contract and struck down much interventionist social legislation. From the late 1930s to the 1960s the Court had a liberal majority and tended to accept Congressional legislation, though it began to restrict Presidential powers.

Judicial review can be seen in three constitutional areas. It has defined Civil Liberties as expressed in the BILL OF RIGHTS; it has defined more precisely the interrelations between the judiciary, the legislature and the executive; and it has similarly defined the relationships between the states and the federal government and between state and state. It is thus especially appropriate for countries with federal government: Australia, Canada and Germany all have similar institutions. Written constitutions with BILLS OF RIGHTS often have a form of judicial review. Britain, without any of these features, only has a weak form of it. *See also* BILL OF RIGHTS; FEDERAL GOVERNMENT; JUDICIAL ACTIVISM.

Reading
Blasi, V. ed. 1983. *The Burger Court: the Counter-Revolution that Wasn't*. New Haven: YUP; Brewer-Carias, A.B. 1989. *Judicial Review in Comparative Law*. Cambridge: CUP; McWhinney, E. 1986. *Supreme Courts and Judicial Law-Making*. Dordrecht: Nijhoff.

judiciary   A country's body of judges: more abstractly a specialized institution concerned with the resolution of legal conflicts and, by implication, possessing a certain political function. Judicial qualities are objectivity and detachment and these can only be guaranteed where the judiciary is independent of the executive and legislature. Guarantees in the US and British political systems are, respectively, through the Constitution and Act of Settlement. On the European continent judicial independence is developed in long legal training and the fact that judges are separate from ordinary lawyers.

Clearly the way judges are recruited

will affect their objectivity. In many countries the politicians will try to interfere. In totalitarian states and many developing countries judges may be little more than agents of the executive. It is often alleged that English judges, who are recruited from amongst barristers, are class-biased. Where reactionary elements dominate the judiciary, ethnic minorities may find it hard to obtain JUSTICE. The Dreyfus case is an example of ANTI-SEMITISM affecting the French judiciary. On the other hand, where judges are elected, as in many American states, they may come under popular pressure. In some states the RECALL may apply. In 1987 the Californian Chief Justice, Rose Bird, was not re-elected because of her liberal verdicts.

The judiciary is especially important where JUDICIAL REVIEW is constitutional procedure. But it may also have wider discretionary powers where ADMINISTRA-TIVE LAW is a significant element in the policy-making process.

See also ADMINISTRATIVE LAW; COMMON LAW; JUDICIAL FUNCTION AND PROCESS; JUDICIAL REVIEW.

Reading
David R. and J.E.C. Brierly. 1978. *Major Legal Systems in the World Today*. London: Stevens; Kirchheimer, O. 1961. *Political Justice*. Princeton: Princeton University Press.

junta Originally local unelected groups of worthies who controlled local government in Spain. Central government sometimes asserted itself with a central junta. The term's familiar use has come to be given to the small cliques of senior armed forces officers who control MILI-TARY REGIMES in Latin America. Similar oligarchies can be found in Africa and Asia and were not unknown until recently in Europe.

See also ARMIES; MILITARY REGIMES.

jurisprudence The study of legal theory and legal systems with the intention of understanding the principles upon which they are based. Jurisprudentialists can use comparative method like political scientists or they can evaluate law in relation to morality. Some have a wide interpretation of 'law' which can include informal codes, positive law and natural law: others do not.

Reading
Lloyd, D. 1979. *Introduction to Jurisprudence*. London: Stevens.

jury A number of adult lay people who receive the summons to attend a trial to decide whether the accused is guilty or not in criminal cases, or, in civil cases, which litigant is in the right. Trial by jury has been established for about eight centuries in England and the American Constitution in Art. III, Sect. 2, clause 3 states: 'The trial of all crimes, except for impeachment, shall be by jury'.

justice A preoccupation of political thinkers from early times, justice is a many-sided concept. There are two main categories in ordinary dialogue – procedural justice and social justice. Procedural justice is about DUE PROCESS OF LAW. This involves fair trials and proper legal procedures. Social justice, or 'substantive justice', is concerned with a just, or fair, or equitable, society. It raises the questions of what criteria are applied to obtain such a society and who decides how to apply the criteria. Plato saw a just society, described in the *Republic*, as one in which things were done properly by the right people, his 'guardians'. At the head was a 'philosopher king'. ARISTOTLE believed a just society was one in which people were rewarded according to their deserts. Their deserts were their expectations of what they were entitled to, and had been entitled to in the past. Thus these ancient philosophers perceived justice as connected with order, a conservative position.

More modern attitudes have related social justice to the reward of merit. But this begs the question of merit for what? Again, merit might be equated with social status. But it might be merit at acquiring wealth. A just society might be one in which there are no obstacles to people acquiring wealth freely, or with more qualifications, acquiring it without limitations except legal ones. The most socially just society is one with a free market. Others will argue that merit relates to what a person does for the community. This might entail a COMMAND ECONOMY in which the government decides what people are entitled to by virtue of their performance.

Another criterion for deciding what is socially just is that of need. This implies 'distributive justice' which, in effect, is usually 'redistributive justice'. It involves taxing some to confer benefits on others. But there may be disagreements about what constitutes need. Some may see the old as more needy than the young, others may not. People's needs may include greed.

The fact is that what social justice comprises is a controversial matter. The utilitarian method of settling the matter of the greatest good for the greatest number is to allow everyone their say and then to take a vote. What is social justice is what people argue about in a democracy. This is unsatisfactory to followers of Rawls who prefer the contractarian to the utilitarian approach to justice. Rawlsians wish to revive natural rights. Liberty is the primary one; but equality is important. To obtain a just or fair society people must make their choice about social policies behind a 'veil of ignorance', that is, discarding all their own prejudices based upon their own backgrounds and perceptions. Rawls's ideas of justice are stimulating but they are difficult to imagine in application in any known society. Many people feel they are the unprejudiced ones and that others are self-interested and prejudiced in their judgements about social policies. How

does one imbue a whole society with Rawlsian values?

See also DEMOCRACY; DIFFERENCE PRINCIPLE; DISTRIBUTIVE JUSTICE; EGALITARIANISM; EQUALITY; SOCIAL CONTRACT; UTILITARIANISM.

Reading

Ackerman, B.A. 1980. *Social Justice in the Liberal State*. New Haven: YUP; Barry, B. 1973. *The Liberal Theory of Justice*. Oxford: OUP; Hobhouse, L.T. 1922. *The Elements of Social Justice*. London: Allen and Unwin; Rawls, J. 1971. *A Theory of Justice*. Cambridge, Mass.: HUP.

justiciability Any matter within the jurisdiction of a court is justiciable there. Courts may sometimes develop precepts about their own justiciability. In many countries they tend to be wary about making actions of the executive justiciable, often ruling that foreign policy and defence activities are not appropriate subjects for them to consider. British courts have tended in recent years to widen their areas of justiciability, not infrequently ruling discretionary acts of ministers illegal.

See also ADMINISTRATIVE TRIBUNALS; DELEGATED LEGISLATION; JUDICIAL REVIEW; PREROGATIVE.

Reading

Marshall, G. 1961. 'Justiciability'. In *Oxford Essays in Jurisprudence*. Ed. A.G. Guest. 1st. ser. Oxford: Clarendon.

just war A war with a just cause that is conducted without committing atrocities. The concept originates with the natural law philosopher, Aquinas (1225–74), who separated just and unjust war. There were two features of a just war that were not to be found in an unjust war. *Ius ad bellum* related to justice of the cause and *ius in bello* to justice in the conduct. Suarez (1548–1617) refined the conditions for a just war, believing that natural law is conditional on circumstances. Even so, there are obvious difficulties in applying these criteria to belligerent situations. Do the rules of war allow for retaliation and would this extend to aerial bombardment of cities and, if so, to what degree? Nuclear attack might be considered unjust. Was nuclear deterrence similarly immoral?

See also CIVIL WAR; LAW; WAR.

Reading
Midgley, E.B.F. 1975. *The Natural Law Tradition and the Theory of International Relations*. London: Elek.

K

keynesianism The mixture of economic theory and social policy that stemmed from the thought of J.M. Keynes (1883–1946). A Cambridge economist, Keynes had criticized the Versailles Treaty, in the *Economic Consequences of the Peace*, 1919, predicting (correctly) that it would impoverish Europe. He gave much thought to the causes of the inter-war depression and came to the conclusion that it was owing to the failure of aggregate demand. In his *General Theory of Employment, Interest and Money*, 1936, he advanced this view, claiming that it was the decline in the spending of the public on consumer goods and of the producers and governments on investment goods that had resulted in so much unemployment. Hence the remedy was to encourage spending. Governments could do this by fiscal policies such as lowering interest rates and decreasing taxation which would temporarily result in budgetary deficits. They could also increase employment and spending on investment by a programmes of public works. Thus more money would be circulating in the economy, the famous 'pump-priming' theory, and aggregate demand would increase.

Keynesian ideas affected both economic theory and political policy. His support for government intervention in the economy and his attack on conventional *laissez-faire* economics and balanced budgets slowly permeated the minds of the policy-makers so that after World War II there was a determination that pre-war depression must be avoided by adopting Keynes's prescriptions. It provided left-wing governments with a fiscal policy for full employment that was an alternative to public ownership. It is often said that Keynes 'saved capitalism'. He was a member of the Liberal Party and certainly not a socialist, but unlike many economists he believed in institutional remedies. Thus he was one of the main architects of the Bretton Woods agreement which stabilized international currencies and led to the creation of the International Monetary Fund and the International Bank for Reconstruction and Development. For thirty post-war years these provided a world economic climate in which international trade and investment could expand.

Keynes's thought led to a revolution in classic economic theory. He virtually founded macro-economics, the study of the aggregate behaviour of consumption, saving and investment as the engines of the world economy. Yet there were earlier, though less elaborate, 'demand side' economists such as J.A. HOBSON

(1858–1940). Further, the Swedish Social Democratic government and the Roosevelt Administration in the 1930s adopted Keynesian measures (unconsciously with the latter) to increase employment. But after the 1950s, economic management became more ambitious with 'fine tuning', the process of manipulating the levers of the economy in order to obtain perfect equilibrium. Gradually Keynesianism became the orthodoxy and most governments accepted it. In 1972 President Nixon declared: 'We are all Keynesians now'.

The economic situation of the late 1970s, in which rising unemployment coincided with rising inflation – so-called 'stagflation' – was one for which Keynesianism had no remedy. Some said the Keynesians were responsible for it. The last quarter of the twentieth century has been characterized by a return to orthodox monetarist policies and balanced budgets. Large-scale unemployment has become accepted by some with regret and by others as a useful way of restraining wage demands.

See also PLANNING.

Reading
Furner, M.O. and B. Supple. eds. 1990. *The State and Economic Knowledge: the American and British Experiences*. Cambridge: CUP; Wattel, H. ed. 1986. *The Policy Consequences of John Maynard Keynes*. London: Macmillan; Worswick, G.D.N. and J. Trevithick. eds. 1983. *Keynes and the Modern World*. Cambridge: CUP.

kibbutz An Israeli rural collective based on the socialist ideas of the Zionists who saw it as the way to create a new Jewish society in Palestine. The first kibbutz was in 1909. They had a high status in early Israel as they were connected with the founders of the state, the army and the Israeli Labour Party. At one time having a great appeal for urban Jews in the West, today they have lost much of their importance and only about 2 per cent of the population live in them.

Reading
Krausz, E. ed. 1983. *The Sociology of the Kibbutz*. London: Transaction Books.

kingship Kingship or monarchy is the rule of one man and one of ARISTOTLE's six categories of government. With ARISTOCRACY and POLITY it is one of the good forms because the monarch rules for the good of the whole society. The corrupted form of kingship is tyranny. Here one man rules for his own good. Under tyranny power is exercised in an arbitrary fashion.

See also ARISTOCRACY; POLITY.

kinship An anthropological concept that has relevance for political science because of kinship's importance in primitive society. It is connected with social obligations, power and inheritance which may confer power. There is kinship by blood and by marriage. Both are relevant to dynastic rule. Wider kinship may be called 'clanship'. Kinship considerations may be important in modern political systems. The inheritance of a name like Churchill or Kennedy or Gandhi may confer electoral advantage.

Reading
Fortes, M. and E.E. Evans-Pritchard. eds. 1940. *African Political Systems*. Oxford: OUP. Mair, L. 1962. *Primitive Government*. Harmondsworth: Penguin.

kitchen cabinet A term used in the USA and Britain to describe a group of informal 'back-room' advisers and their support staff. It is supposed to date from President Jackson's (1829–37) meetings with such a group in the White House kitchen. It was also used to describe a similar, though larger, organization set up by Lloyd George when he was Prime Minister (1916–22). He is supposed to have pursued the typists. Informal advisers may prove a problem for political leaders when formal advisers resent them.

kremlinology The art of interpreting Soviet politics. Political conflict in the Soviet Union only occurred at the very highest level. It was possible for Soviet experts to guess what was happening by reading Russian documents, but it was always a little like crystal gazing.

Reading
Nove, A. 1964. 'The Uses and Abuses of Kremlinology'. In *Was Stalin Really Necessary?* Ed. A. Nove. London: Allen and Unwin.

kulak The Soviet term for a rich peasant. During the collectivization of agriculture in the 1930s the kulaks were liquidated. The term is now used to describe wealthy farmers in a jocular manner.

L

labour   In classical economics labour is one of the factors of production with land and capital. For social scientists generally it differs from the other two factors by being composed of human beings.

labour aristocracy   A concept found in socialist historiography. It is derived from the Marxist theory of the segmentation of labour markets. The aristocracy of labour are the skilled workers with higher pay, more assured employment and stronger trade-union organization than less skilled workers. They will have higher social status and may tend to look down on the other workers. From this it was argued that they had been less inclined to feelings of solidarity and so were less likely to be involved in the general labour movement and with the nascent labour parties which were emerging in the late nineteenth century. There is, however, little historic evidence to support this last point. As far as the foundation of the British Labour Party in 1900 is concerned, the crucial factor in determining union affiliation was the extent to which they felt threatened by certain legal judgements. This bore little relationship to whether they were skilled or unskilled.
See also LABOUR MOVEMENTS; LABOUR PARTIES; TRADE UNIONS.

Reading
Bealey F.W. and H.M. Pelling. 1958. *Labour and Politics 1900–1906*. London: Macmillan; Hobsbawm, E. 1964. *Labouring Men*. London: Weidenfeld.

labour camps   *See* CONCENTRATION CAMPS; GULAG.

labour courts   A court to judge issues concerned with labour. This may involve disputes between employers and workers about conditions of work; complaints about wrongful dismissal; questions about breaches of agreements between both sides in industry; and actions brought by the state against either employers or trade unions relating to breaches of laws. Different political systems have diverse ways of dealing with such cases. Britain has a tradition of informal arbitration and conciliation, or tribunals for dealing with individual grievances. Australia has a fully-fledged system of industrial law and labour courts.
See also ARBITRATION; LAW; TRADE UNIONS.

labour movements   A general term to cover several types of collective organization in the labour force. CO-OPERATIVES, LABOUR PARTIES and TRADE UNIONS are often included under this rubric. It depends on the context. In the USA, where a strong labour party has never existed, the term refers to the trade-union movement. Where constellations of different types of labour organization exist, as frequently in Europe, they almost certainly strengthen the power of the WORKING CLASS. Thus, in a depression when the industrial bargaining strength of the trade unions is weakened by unemployment, workers can turn to political action through labour parties, while in prosperity, collective bargaining may achieve better results.

The term 'movement' suggests an ultimate destination but this may not always be clear. Labour movements grew up as a response to industrial CAPITALISM but their subsequent development in different countries was diverse. It was affected by the course capitalism took; the reaction of other social groups; the stage at which the working class was given the vote; the extent to which the trade unions are able to federate and show unity; political institutions which might or might not favour pressure-group activity; factors affecting the labour market such as IMMIGRATION; the availability of alternative occupation outside industry in countries where there was much free or cheap land; and legal frameworks.

Briefly, labour movements have presented themselves with three options. The first is a class struggle to overthrow capitalism. This could take two forms. SYNDICALISM is a militant trade-union belief in industrial action, distrusting political organization, and with little idea of how society will be ordered when the workers take over. The other form is Marxist SOCIALISM, predicating political action as a necessary final stage of the proletarian revolution. It has been much espoused by non-proletarian intellectuals. Syndicalists have never been in power; but where the Marxist socialists have been in power trade unions have ceased to exist. (This is not a Marxist 'contradiction': theoretically they have

achieved a 'classless society' and so they do not need a labour movement.)

The second option is what has been called the 'democratic class struggle'. The labour movement, having obtained the FRANCHISE and a high level of organization, uses both its political and industrial power to obtain the very best position it can for its members, both by legislation and by using its weight in the labour market. This option is SOCIAL DEMOCRACY and has been relatively successful. It could be seen as an attempt to limit capitalism.

The third option is 'business unionism'. Capitalism is the dominant force and the way society and its values have developed have not encouraged the growth of a labour party. In these circumstances the trade unions are likely to achieve the best results by concentrating on effective collective bargaining. For example, the American labour movement has tried to sharpen its arguments by employing accountants and economists, and to improve its IMAGE by employing public relations men. It is an attempt to come to terms with capitalism.

In most labour movements traces of all these strategies may be found, though in democratic countries there will be little support today for the overthrow of capitalism. During the world recession, which began in 1973, unemployment has inevitably weakened the trade-union membership and its bargaining strength. In the USA less than 20 per cent of the labour force is now unionized. As in all downturns of the trade cycle, an employer offensive has also had some success. As long as there is productive activity, however, labour movements are likely to be on the economic and political scene.

See also LABOUR PARTIES; SYNDICALISM; TRADE UNIONS; WORKING CLASS.

Reading
Bean, R. 1985. *Comparative Industrial Relations*. London: Croom Helm; Dunlop, J.T. and W. Galenson. eds. 1978. *Labour in the*

Twentieth Century. New York: Academic Press; Korpi, W. 1983. *The Democratic Class Struggle*. London: Routledge; Perlman, S. 1928. *A Theory of the Labour Movement*. Evanston, Ill: Harper and Row.

labour parties

In the English-speaking world significant parties calling themselves 'Labour' can be found in Britain, Australia, New Zealand, Ireland and Jamaica. The name tends to indicate that the origins of the party are in the trade-union movement. Outside the English-speaking world the parties describing themselves as 'Workers' rather than 'Socialist' or 'Social Democratic' include (as translated into English) the Dutch, Norwegian and Maltese Labour Parties in Europe and the Israeli Labour Party outside. The distinction between labour parties and socialist parties may not be significant, but labour or workers' parties are more likely to be based on the working class and to be less ideological than socialist parties. If, like the British Labour Party, they have been preceded by and founded by a well organized trade-union movement, their immediate objectives will be the acquisition of social benefits. Even those parties who call themselves 'social democratic' at one time employed Marxist rhetoric. On the other hand the distinction may be no guide to pragmatic tendencies. The British Labour Party became more committed to public ownership than the Swedish and Danish Social Democratic parties and took nearly eighty years to relinquish its commitment to 'the common ownership of the means of production, distribution and exchange' – the famous Clause 4.

See also CLASS PARTIES; LABOUR MOVEMENTS; MARXISM; SOCIALIST PARTIES; TRADE UNIONS.

Reading
Paterson, W.E. and A.H. Thomas. eds. 1977. *Social Democratic Parties in Western Europe*. London: Croom Helm; Paterson, W.E. and A.H. Thomas. eds. 1986. *The Future of Social Democracy*. Oxford: Clarendon; Pelling, H.M. 1954. *The Origins of the Labour Party*. London: Macmillan.

labour theory of value

A concept that exerted great political influence because it implied that workers were exploited. It was first tentatively advanced by John LOCKE (1632–1704) who contended that a man was entitled to anything that 'he hath mixed his labour with'. He was asserting a right to property; but the economist David Ricardo (1772–1823) adapted the idea to manufacturing production. The price of a good, he argued, was determined by the amount of labour involved in its production. This included the labour used in getting the raw materials and making the capital goods. MARX accepted this theory of value and argued that the worker was entitled to receive the full value of the product whereas all the employer gave him in wages was enough to persuade him to work and reproduce children. The capitalist creamed off a 'surplus value' in profits for himself.

The theory neglects the consumers. Without demand, supply is unnecessary however much labour is put into the commodity. With no demand it is pointless to produce.

See also CAPITALISM; COMMUNISM; MARXISM.

Reading
Locke, J. [1681] 1947. *Second Treatise of Government*. In *The Social Contract*. Ed. E. Barker. Oxford: OUP; Marx, K. [1867] 1975. *Capital: a Critique of Political Economy*. New York: International Publishers; Ricardo, D. 1817. *Principles of Political Economy and Taxation*. London: Murry.

labour unions   *See* TRADE UNIONS.

laissez-faire

This could be translated as 'leave alone', a general injunction to avoid interference. Yet it has come to mean the social and political policy of not intervening in the economy. It represents a belief in economic individualism with buyers and sellers transacting exchange in free markets. This was one of the pillars of nineteenth-century liberal thought. It was a reaction against mercantilism, the policy of state monopolies and restriction of foreign trade which prevailed in the eighteenth century.

In practice no governments have ever been committed to complete laissez-faire and it is worth noting that Adam Smith (1723–90), the father of the theory, believed that the state had many functions beyond law and order. As a university teacher he ruled out a free market as the way of providing an educational system. See also CAPITALISM; FREE TRADE.

Reading
Smith, A. [1776] 1904. *The Wealth of Nations*. 2 vols. Oxford: OUP.

lame duck The term to describe a government near the end of its term and with little power. The Major Government in Britain 1992–7 was sometimes called a 'lame duck' by journalists because in its last months in office it was dependent on Ulster Unionist votes. But the origin of the term is American and used to decribe an incumbent President whose term really ends in November, but who must stay in the White House until the following January when his successor takes over. If he has been defeated for re-election he is especially in no position to effect anything.

land reform A very important political issue in the twentieth century. The basic idea is that the state will acquire land from large land-owners and transfer it to poor tenant farmers and landless farm labourers. Over twenty countries have adopted land reform programmes in recent decades. Many of them were Communist states, though in their case land was transferred to collective farmers and individual peasant farming did not result, as it did after revolution in some Latin American states such as Mexico.

There were also land reforms after World War II, carried out with American encouragement and backing, in Japan, Taiwan and South Korea.

In much of Central America, Asia and Africa, however, the problem of the rural landless poor is still strikingly evident. It leads to violence and civil war, making development very difficult. Extensive land reform programmes would remove the reasons for this agrarian unrest, halt the drift from the countryside to urban shanty towns, increase agricultural production and raise the standard of living. See also DEVELOPMENT; MODERNIZATION.

Reading
Herring, R.J. 1983. *Land to the Tiller*. New Haven: YUP; Prosterman, R.L. and J.M. Riedinger. 1987. *Land Reform and Democratic Development*. Baltimore: Johns Hopkins Press.

law Law sets standards of human conduct. The law of the state, with which political scientists are most concerned, will be backed up by a coercive apparatus.

There are two basic traditions of legal thinking. One is the natural law school, prominent in Continental Europe, which believes in a permanent law over and above statutory laws and not dependent on particular law makers. This tradition goes back to Aquinas (1225–74) and was adopted by the Catholic Church as a reconciliation between divine revelation and rationality. Aquinas argued that God has given us reason which, if we use it properly, will tell us what we should do and not do. 'Right reason' will inform humanity about how a proper legal system should operate and what its content should be. The law of the state, therefore, should be based on natural law. A natural law philosopher is thus in a position to judge whether state law is compatible with natural law. For example, a Catholic may condemn a state law which allows free availability for abortion because it conflicts with natural principles of law.

The positive law tradition has predominated in America and England. Laws do not exist before law makers produce them. This was re-affirmed by the Utilitarians and by John Austin (1790–1859) who held that laws were basically the emanations of sovereign power. The law is what the courts judge it to be. Hence positivists may not find it easy to deal with tyrannical acts. How could positivists justify the Nuremburg Trial when the Nazi defendants could claim that they could not be tried because they had broken no law? They were arraigned for crimes against 'peace' and 'humanity'.

In recent years in the West there has been some revival of the natural law tradition by writers such as Dworkin and Finnis. The Positivist school has shifted ground somewhat because of its acceptance of the necessity of judicial discretion.

See also JUDICIAL REVIEW; LAW AND ORDER.

Reading

Finnis, J.M. 1980. *Natural Law and Natural Rights*. Oxford: OUP; Hart, H.L.A. 1961. *The Concept of Law*. Oxford: OUP.

law and order A condition in which the regular processes of law operate without serious breach. 'Order' is maintained by the apparatus of law enforcement, the police. Without law and order ordinary domestic life cannot proceed. People will feel insecure. Consequently law and order safeguards FREEDOM. In contemporary society the increase in crime has become a salient political ISSUE with which politicians of all parties have to take account.

See also RULE OF LAW.

leadership Leadership is necessary for any sort of enterprise or organization. It operates at numerous levels. Primitive societies may be characterized by simple leadership, but in all modern political systems there will be some hierarchy of leadership though at lower levels it may well be a part-time matter.

Leadership is a relationship. There cannot be leaders without followers. Unless they are compelled to follow, which may be the case in an authoritarian state, people will follow because they identify with their leader. The identification may be because they see him as their 'liege-lord', as in a feudal society, or because they see him/her as a person of the same socio-demographic background, or as someone good at obtaining benefits for them. In the modern democratic state leaders of some groups will be the competitors of leaders of other groups.

Political leaders tend to be different from most people. It is an unusual activity because most people do not want to do it. They do not want to exercise power at a high level for several reasons: it is a specialized activity which takes up a great deal of time, it prevents one leading a 'normal' life, it gives one a heavy burden of responsibility and it makes one liable to scathing criticism under the glare of publicity. Many observers think that political leaders are quite different personality-types from the majority of people. Barber argued that emotional deprivation in childhood had led many US Presidents to seek compensation in high political office. Bass divided leaders into three groups: self-oriented ones with strong power-drives who may not be good at helping their followers; task-oriented leaders who are pragmatists, good at attaining specific objectives; and interaction-oriented leaders who have the skills to resolve conflicts among their followers.

All these types can be found among democratic leaders who may exhibit features of all three. This also applies to WEBER's threefold categorization of traditional, charismatic and legal/rational leadership. Yet clearly circumstances are much to do with the sort of leader a country produces. Heroic circumstances such as wartime may produce heroic leaders. Clemenceau, Churchill and Roosevelt were all hailed as 'great leaders'. On the other hand, an important internal cleavage may emphasize the role of the interaction-oriented 'broker-politician'. Canadian leaders must be pragmatists, mediating between the French and British communities.

Modern political leadership requires a variety of skills, especially in a democracy. An obvious one is the ability to think on one's feet and to be good at rejoinders to hostile comment. At the same time, more discreet committee-type skills such as bargaining and negotiating are important. Political campaigning emphasizes theatrical skills which will be inappropriate for dealing with television interviewers, an imperative today. It is usually a mistake for a political leader to show distress at harsh criticism or the untruths of opponents. The public like their leaders to be 'unflappable'. Democratic publics, however, may expect too much of their leaders. Democratic control by vigilant monitoring should be exerted by critical minds. Leaders are essential; but without an electorate as interested in the policies as in the personalities, democracy may eventually be in trouble.

See also AUTHORITY; CHARISMA; LEADERSHIP SELECTION; PRESIDENTS; PRIME MINISTERS.

Reading
Barber, J.D. 1977. *Presidential Character*. Englewood Cliffs: Prentice Hall; Bass, B.M. 1985. *Leadership, Psychology and Organisational Behaviour*. New York: Harper and Row; Blondel, J. 1980. *World Leaders*. London: Sage; Edinger, L.J. ed. 1967. *Political Leadership in Industrialized Societies*. New York: Wiley.

leadership selection A very few leaders, like the Dalai Lama in Tibet, are chosen by esoteric rituals. Others, as in Arab sheikhdoms, may lead as a result of hereditary succession. Otherwise, in most political systems leaders assume power as a result of competition and conflict. Becoming a leader is like running a race with many hurdles. In military dictatorships it is often a matter of seizing the right moment and correctly assessing the troops on which one can depend. Fascist leaders have frequently organized and led the insurrectionary party that takes over power. Communist leaders emerge from secret cabals within the party.

Even in democracies leaders are, initially, self-selected. It is not a common instinct to want to lead. The most common avenue is through membership of a local party. Some ACTIVISTS may become local representatives, which may be the first step to being selected as a candidate for the national legislature. Many may discover, however, during this process that they do not want to go further. In the USA the procedure in most states is different. At state and national levels one becomes a party candidate by first competing for the nomination with other hopefuls in a primary. If selected, one then has to compete with the nominees of other parties. It is a grinding ordeal.

National party leaders are sometimes chosen by the party's representatives in the legislature. More often they are selected by party members. American Presidents are chosen by an ELECTORAL COLLEGE whose electors are popularly elected in each state, while French Presidents are elected by direct popular vote under the SECOND BALLOT system.

See also ACTIVISTS; ELECTORAL COLLEGE; ELECTIONS; LOCAL POLITICS; PARTY ORGANIZATION.

Reading
Pomper, G. 1980. *Elections in America*. 2nd edn. London: Longman; Ranney, A. 1965. *Pathways to Parliament*. London: Macmillan.

league A vague term used to describe a loose temporary ALLIANCE or a weak CONFEDERATION. In the twelfth century there was the Lombard League. The Hanseatic League was a medieval trading agreement between European ports. More recently the League of Nations and the League for Economic Co-operation in Europe, founded in 1947 to support a customs union, are examples of the term being applied to international organizations.

See also ALLIANCE; CONFEDERATIONS.

left and right Denoting a spectrum of political attitudes these two terms derive from the first French revolutionary parliament in 1789. The Jacobins, who sat on the extreme left, were the most revolutionary of the parties. In the centre were moderate people. On the extreme right were clericals and royalists. On the far left there was a strong attachment to popular sovereignty, a belief in the dispossession of aristocratic and church lands, an egalitarian attitude to privilege and wealth and a determination to uphold a lay state and secular education.

These remained familiar CLEAVAGES in Europe until the twentieth century, though becoming less important as the class division emerged with industrialization and the extension of the FRANCHISE. The left then supported a WELFARE STATE, trade-union rights and intervention in the economy. The right became a defender of middle-class interests and free markets.

Yet this is a simple model. The two cleavages became 'cross-cutting'. Moreover, few voters identified themselves strongly with either extreme. They remained in the 'centre'. Furthermore, the Communists on the extreme left and the Fascists on the extreme right were similar in their rejection of DEMOCRACY. Hence although the terms are in regular use they can be misleading.

See also CLEAVAGES; JACOBINISM; POLITICAL PARTIES.

Reading
Laponce, J.A. 1981. *Left and Right*. Toronto: University of Toronto Press; Smith, D. 1970.

Left and Right in Twentieth Century Europe. London: Longman.

leftie A slang term of mild derision used rather indiscriminately by people on the right to describe intellectuals whom they think have left-wing leanings. There is no equivalent term such as 'rightie'.

legalism Sometimes used to indicate a situation where lawyers dominate society and the political process. This may happen for two reasons. Where the legal system encourages people to be litigious, for example by allowing litigants who lose civil suits not to pay lawyers' fees, the courts will be very busy. Again, where there is a federal system and complex relationships between political authorities, lawyers' services are likely to be much in demand. It is often said, 'federalism means legalism'.

See also FEDERAL GOVERNMENT; JUDICIAL REVIEW.

legislative committees It is truly said that the strength of LEGISLATURES is reflected by the strength of their committee systems. Generally legislative committees have three functions. Their primary one is to deal with proposed legislation. This may involve actually shaping and drafting it but more often it implies discussing and revising its details. A second function is the supervision of a sector of public policy, such as health or education. Such committees will be able to call the relevant minister or her/his civil servants to appear before them for questioning. They are called 'specialist committees'. The most important specialist committee will probably be the one that oversees the national finances. Thirdly, legislatures set up committees to regulate their procedures and, if necessary, discipline bad legislative behaviour.

The strongest legislature in the democratic world, the US Congress, has the strongest legislative committees. They are not only 'specialist', but also have investigative and subpoena powers, and are capable of drafting their own legislation. The French legislative committees, by contrast, are weak. Their number is six and each one has 120 members. In consequence it is impossible for them to specialize. Since 1979 Britain has had many more specialist committees, but the executive is so strong it is able largely to ignore their recommendations. Weak committees reflect weak legislatures. In Europe one only finds strong legislative committees in Scandinavia. They are not specialist, but ministers are excluded from their discussions. Frequently they draft legislation.

See also LEGISLATURES; PARLIAMENTARY BUSINESS; PARLIAMENTARY QUESTIONS; SELECT COMMITTEES; STANDING COMMITTEES.

Reading
Horsch, H. and M.D. Hancock. 1979. *Comparative Legislative Systems*. New York: Free Press; Loewenberg, G. and S.C. Patterson. eds. 1979. *Comparing Legislatures: an Analytic Study*. Boston: Little, Brown; Olson, D.M. 1980. *The Legislative Process: a Comparative Approach*. New York: Harper and Row.

legislative veto   An American legislative procedure declared unconstitutional by the Supreme Court in 1983. By this device Congress, in statutes delegating powers to the executive, inserted a clause specifying that during a stated period a certain delegated power would be nullified if Congress voted disapproval of it.

Reading
Martin, D. 1982. 'The Legislative Veto and the Responsible Exercise of Congressional Power'. In *Virginia Law Review* 68, 253–302.

legislatures   'Parliaments' is now a synonym for this term though the etymology of neither word indicates their wider functions. 'Parliament' was derived from the French verb 'to speak'. Legislatures in the classic scheme of

government were the law-making bodies. Today they combine both these functions with several others.

Legislatures represent people in two different ways. First, the representatives can transmit the hopes and fears of the area they represent to the other members of the legislature and to the executive. To what degree they are ruled by the opinions of their constituents is a matter of opinion. The representative who expressly obeys the instructions of the majority of them is a DELEGATE, while one who behaves in the opposite way is a 'trustee'. (These are IDEAL TYPES: in the real world representatives will be somewhere between these extremes.) Second, legislatures can represent a cross-section of the nation. They can be a 'mirror image' of their society. This ideal has never even been approximated to. Most legislatures are dominated by highly educated middle-class males. Women and manual workers are grossly underrepresented.

Legislatures still spend the bulk of their time dealing with proposals for laws. Yet the US Congress is exceptional in that it frequently draws up and passes proposals it has initiated. In most countries the proposals have been drafted by the executive and the parliament is a mere formalizing agent. For example, in Britain it has been calculated that 82 per cent of all bills begin in government committees and 95 per cent of these end up on the statute book. France is close to this position. Consequently one can assume that many democratic legislatures do not have much power. This can be demonstrated by examining their control over their agendas, as well as their opportunities for legislative initiative. In France Art. 48 of the constitution rules that the government has priority in determining parliamentary business. In Britain the House of Commons agenda is drawn up by negotiation between government and opposition WHIPS. Non-ministers can only introduce legislation that does not involve spending money, and then only on Fridays. About 10 per cent of it becomes law. Two factors may explain where legislatures have autonomy. Either a constitutional principle, such as the SEPARATION OF POWERS in the USA, or a multiparty system as in the Italian Parliament will make executive dominance impossible.

Another important legislative function is exercising control over the executive. Most of them can scarcely 'control' but they can exercise some sort of supervision. In the first place as democratic governments usually depend on majority support, a succession of defeats in the legislature will normally result in their dismissal. Second, supervision can be exerted, it is claimed, by parliamentary questions. Except where the INTERPELLATION procedure exists this is a very inadequate method of control because ministers have so much more expertise at their command and, anyway, they are often evasive in their answers. The third method, control by legislative committees of enquiry, is the most effective. Especially where, as in the USA, they can subpoena witnesses, the possibility of facing their investigatory activities may inhibit executives.

Legislatures are also places where most national LEADERSHIP is trained and selected. To many new legislators parliamentary life will be at first disappointing. Members who overcome initial frustration and learn to participate with dissimilar people in order to produce a viable policy are likely to be those who will emerge as political leaders. In PARLIAMENTARY SYSTEMS members of the executive are commonly chosen from among members of the legislature and even in PRESIDENTIAL SYSTEMS, like the USA, Presidents have often earlier been legislators.

Finally parliaments are supposed to be national forums where a continuous debate about national issues takes place. Since the advent of television the whole nation can sometimes get a glimpse of them. Liberals at one time believed they would educate the public about the chief issues of the day. This ideal has not been realized. Democratic publics as a whole have little interest in the discussion, though much in the outcomes. Yet parliaments remain the centre of political life. Decisions are legitimized there and within their proximity much political bargaining and compromise is effected. Although their influence has declined, especially as supervisors of governments, they have become more representative of electorates with the increasing representation of women.

See also PARLIAMENTARY SYSTEMS; PRESIDENTIAL SYSTEMS.

Reading
Hague, R. and Harrop, M. 1982. *Comparative Government and Politics*. London: Macmillan; Loewenberg, G. and S.C. Patterson. 1979. *Comparing Legislatures*. Boston: Little, Brown. Mény, Y. 1990. *Government and Politics in Western Europe*. Oxford: OUP; Norton, P. 1990. *Legislature*. Oxford: OUP; Wheare, K.C. 1968. *Legislatures*. Oxford: OUP.

legitimacy An important concept in the social sciences popularized by Max WEBER. A political regime is legitimate when it is accepted by its citizens as right and proper enough to be obeyed. Obedience in itself is not enough because people will obey the orders of a regime that terrorizes them; but they do not accept it as having legitimate AUTHORITY. Authority is legitimized power.

It is not an easy concept to operationalize because it rests in the minds of the largely inarticulate non-elite. Moreover, it cannot be anything else but an intellectual artefact based on the notion of an 'average citizen'. In every state there will be a few people who do not accept it as legitimate. More appositely, many citizens will accept some aspects of the regime as legitimate and others as illegitimate. A British republican may not accept the monarchy as legitimate; but otherwise accepts British parliamentary democracy. Furthermore, the degree to which a regime is legitimate may fluctuate over time. DAHL has a useful metaphor in seeing legitimacy as a reservoir which a wise regime will keep at a certain level. If the level of legitimacy becomes too low the regime may fall.

Hence the concept of legitimacy is connected with that of STABILITY, and in considering the former it is impossible to avoid the behaviour of ruling ELITES. Governments in power can clearly do much to enhance or to deplete the regime's legitimacy by the way their activities affect the attitude of the non-elite. Some rulers may be concerned and others unconcerned to improve or to maintain their legitimacy. It may depend on what sort of stability they desire. An occupying army will want to crush resistance: they will not expect to be accepted as legitimate. A Fascist or Communist government may use fear to ensue compliancy, but will also be concerned with inculcating ideological precepts. They will want to be accepted. In sum: governments may be conscious of the need to nurture legitimacy. They may do this by trying to manipulate attitudes and to influence values.

Weber produced a trichotomy of regime-types in which authority is legitimated. With traditional authority there is an element of the sacred about legitimization. This was clearly associated with DIVINE RIGHT and the ANCIEN REGIME, though it might also apply to the Dalai Lama. With charismatic authority legitimacy is conferred by the personality of the ruler. Weber regarded this as a transitional form. It applies to one-man revolutionary or Bonapartist rule. It would either revert to traditional authority or it would become 'routinized' by rules and laws. It would become rational/ legal authority in which accepted procedures legitimize. Weber's third type is associated with bureaucracy and constitutional government. Here legality and legitimacy converge.

A regime may strengthen its legitimacy through the processes of POLITICAL SOCIALIZATION. This can be done through intervention in the school: for example, required singing of the national anthem every morning. Marxists argue that the capitalist state has bolstered its legitimacy by permeating the media with its values and conciliating the proletariat with masses of consumer goods. Habermas contends that modern regimes of all kinds depend on an ideology of science and technology that is constricting for democratic discourse and will produce a crisis of legitimation.

See also CITIZENSHIP; CRISIS; POLITICAL SOCIALIZATION; POSTMODERNISM.

Reading
Beetham, D. 1991. *The Legitimation of Power.* London: Macmillan; Connolly, W. ed. 1984. *Legitimacy and the State.* Oxford: Blackwell; Habermas, J. 1975. *Legitimation Crisis.* Boston: Beacon; Weber, M. [1921] 1968. *Economy and Society.* New York: Bedminster.

leisure class   A theory associated with the sociologist, Thorstein Veblen (1857–1929). He argued that at a certain stage of CAPITALISM prosperity reaches a point where there emerges a class who are so affluent that they can devote themselves to leisurely activities. With their rise goes a lifestyle that is concerned with the display of wealth. Status then becomes linked to this capacity to exhibit, and even to waste, worldly goods on a large scale. This tendency is passed down in society which becomes obsessed with the desire for conspicuous consumption. The notion is of interest to political scientists because increasing affluence and devotion to the acquisition of consumer durables, it is argued, has led to the 'bourgeoisification of the WORKING CLASS'. This explains their lack of enthusiasm

for class-war analyses and their growing disinclination to vote for left-wing parties.
See also VOTING BEHAVIOUR.

Reading
Galbraith, J.K. 1958. *The Affluent Society*. Harmondsworth: Penguin; Veblen, T. [1899] 1934. *The Theory of the Leisure Class*. New York: Modern Library.

liberalism Liberalism is a family of concepts. The underlying philosophy begins with a statement of the autonomy of the individual, but the intellectual history is concerned with the idea of emancipation – the emancipation of Man (later Woman as well) and the emancipation of the PEOPLE. It is thus associated with FREEDOM in all its dimensions. This explains the confusion about the term. There are many liberalisms. Freedoms can be contradictory. My freedom may be your chains.

The intellectual origins of liberalism are in the scientific revolution of the sixteenth and seventeenth centuries, the ideas of the ENLIGHTENMENT with its diverse currents of thought and the American and French Revolutions which asserted the doctrine of NATURAL RIGHTS. The Industrial Revolution which vastly changed society also stimulated a questioning attitude to the social and economic status quo. The motors of change could be grouped under the heading of MODERNIZATION: the atmosphere of sceptical enquiry and criticism characterized a trend to RATIONALISM.

The Age of Reason and rationality queried the existence of God. Religion was seen as part of the imprisonment of the human mind by unreason. The French Revolutionaries confiscated church lands and introduced civil marriage. Anti-clericals demanded a separation of church and state as foreshadowed in Article 1 of the US Bill of Rights (1791), 'Congress shall make no law respecting the establishment of religion'. Religious toleration was confirmed as an important liberal principle. Reason also governed the ideas of the Utilitarians who wanted to reform antiquated laws and legal and constitutional procedures. According to them good government should be ordered by the principle of UTILITY. Jeremy Bentham (1748–1832), the father of the school, believed in free markets but declared inalienable Natural Rights were 'nonsense upon stilts'.

Classical economic liberalism was concerned to emancipate trade from the chains of mercantilism. Classical liberals like Ricardo and Adam Smith argued that with the freeing of trade from irrational regulations, everyone's prosperity would be enhanced. Thus there was an incentive to wider international contacts. Liberal internationalism was not only inspired by emotional ideas about the Brotherhood of Man, but also by a belief in rational self-interest. Free markets and FREE TRADE not only stimulated producers, but also benefited consumers.

More revolutionary liberals were concerned to break the shackles of a mannered society and an artistic world ruled by the canons of classicism. ROUSSEAU (1712–78) idealized the 'noble savage' and in *Émile* gave an early exposition of 'progressive education'. The primitive was natural and superior to the sophisticated. Ordinary people were the repositories of truth. Thus the Romantic Movement was born. It had two streams: one with its source in 'the PEOPLE' and the other in 'the NATION'. Wordsworth (1770–1850), who had hailed the French Revolution, in his 1800 Preface to the Lyrical Ballads wrote of 'low and rustic life' where 'the essential passions of man . . . speak a plainer and more emphatic language'. Burns (1759–96) wrote poetry in the Scots dialect. ROMANTICISM discovered the 'common man'. The Romantics were naturally in sympathy with oppressed peoples. The poet Byron (1788–1824) died for Greece and was sanctified by European liberals as their romantic hero.

In the nineteenth century most of the nations in middle and eastern Europe were subjects of three empires – the Austro-Hungarian, the Russian and the Turkish. They were unable to feel free until their nations were emancipated. Thus NATIONALISM was linked with liberalism in the minds of nineteenth-century progressive thinkers. The most typical, Mazzini (1805–72), the philosopher of the movement for united Italy, sincerely believed that when the oppressed nations achieved statehood they would all have democratic institutions and live in peace with each other. In his writings NATIONALISM is associated with internationalism.

Nineteenth-century liberals often espoused egalitarian ideas such as the affirmation that men are 'born free and equal'. Yet they were often rather timid about granting 'power to the people'. Many perceived liberalism in terms of CONSTITUTIONALISM, but did not trust the lower orders enough to believe in extending the FRANCHISE. They feared the latter might be a danger to property, would not be able to understand political issues and would be intolerant to liberal principles like free speech. This was so with the French liberal, Benjamin Constant (1767–1830), and the British Utilitarians. The main early proponent of participatory democracy was Rousseau who had little time for constitutions and who regarded property as an evil. He foresaw decisions made by referendums which would express the General Will of the people. The Utilitarians believed in the greatest happiness for the greatest number. When Jeremy Bentham (1748–1832) considered how this could be achieved, he concluded that it could only be done by allowing everyone to express their preferences and then to vote for them. But he only supported universal

suffrage reluctantly and his two disciples, James Mill (1773–1836) and his son John Stuart MILL (1806–73) were similarly cautious.

To understand the term today it is better to approach it from the angle of social and intellectual history rather than that of philosophy. Liberals in the interwar years were welfarists and supporters of trade-union rights. In the last years of the twentieth century those who claim to be 'liberals' as likely as not want to eliminate most welfare benefits and restrict trade unions. The word, anyway, means different things to philosophers, economists and political scientists.

See also DEMOCRACY; ENLIGHTENMENT; FREEDOM; NATIONALISM; RATIONALISM; ROMANTICISM; SOCIAL DEMOCRACY; UTILITARIANISM.

Reading
Gray, J. 1989. *Liberalisms*. London: Routledge; Hall, J.A. 1988. *Liberalism: Politics, Ideology and the Market*. Chapel Hill: University of N. Carolina Press; Laski, H.J. 1938. *The Rise of European Liberalism*. London: Allen and Unwin; Moore, M. 1993. *Foundations of Liberalism*. Oxford: OUP; Ruggiero, G. 1927. *The History of European Liberalism*. Oxford: OUP.

liberal democracy   *See* DEMOCRACY.

liberation theology   Emerging in the 1960s, mainly in Latin America, this current of Catholic thought argued that Christian belief in Man's liberation could not be satisfied without liberating the poor and oppressed. A major cause of poverty in Latin America, liberation theologians believed, was American CAPITALISM. By 1979 the final statement of the conference of Latin American bishops condemned the free market economy and proclaimed that the duty of the Church was the liberation of the millions of poor. In the same year the left of the movement was supporting the Sandinistas in Nicaragua. Involvement with Marxist revolutionaries was embarrassing because of the atheism of the Marxists and in the 1980s there was criticism in the Church and Vatican warnings about association with rationalist ideas. Even so Pope John Paul II in 1986 wrote to Brazilian bishops describing the movement as 'useful and necessary' as long as it was consistent with Catholic doctrine. In 1990 the election of Father Aristide as President of Haiti was a political victory for liberation theology.

See also DEVELOPMENT; REVOLUTIONS.

Reading
Berryman, P. 1987. *Liberation Theology*. London: Tauris; Gutierrez, G. 1971. *A Theology of Liberation*. Maryknoll: Orbis; Sigmund, P.E. 1990. *Liberation Theology at the Crossroads*. Oxford: OUP.

libertarianism A term with three different implications. Early libertarians believed in free will and were opposed to determinism. Then the word became used to describe a belief in unrestricted human thought and action. In the nineteenth century this was associated with free love and opposition to the state. Libertarianism equalled ANARCHISM. It was espoused by anti-state socialists. In the late twentieth century the word has come to mean a belief in inalienable rights, extreme economic individualism and free markets. It represents a revolt against managed economies and high taxation. These libertarians are in the camp of radical CONSERVATISM. An extreme wing advocates the right to take drugs and marry one's own sister! Neither left- nor right-wing libertarianism has anything but a tiny political support.

See also ANARCHISM; COMMUNE; PACIFICISM.

Reading
Barry, N.P. 1986. *On Classical Liberalism and Libertarianism*. London: Macmillan; Nozick, R. 1975. *Anarchy, State and Utopia*. Oxford: Blackwell.

liberty *See* FREEDOM.

life chances Part of WEBER's theory of SOCIAL CLASS. He ascribed differences of class to differences in one's 'life chances in the market'. Thus a student with a lower income than an unskilled labourer could not be categorized as proletarian. Access to higher education was an important class difference. Opportunities to rise, including educational opportunity, greatly improved life chances. Other factors were possession of capital, family background and skilled training. Characteristics such as gender and ethnicity might in some contexts worsen life chances.

See also SOCIAL CLASS; STATUS.

Reading
Weber, M. [1921] 1968. *Economy and Society*. New York: Bedminster.

lifestyle A way of living that indicates the goods which people like to consume; their preferences in recreational and cultural activities; and the type of education they choose for their children. The values connoted by these choices may well reflect political attitudes.

See also LEISURE CLASS.

limited vote A method of election in which each voter in a multi-member constituency has fewer votes than the number of candidates to be elected. It is used to elect the Japanese lower house.

limited war A term used in the COLD WAR to describe any war in which both SUPERPOWERS were not involved and, consequently, the employment of nuclear weapons was unlikely.

linguistic politics As language is the main vehicle of culture it is an important part of a group's identity. It will often be the only distinguishing mark between one group and another that speaks a different language. There are few states in which only one language is spoken. Consequently language is one of the important political CLEAVAGES – as important as class and religion with which it may be intertwined.

Two obvious factors are important in determining the depth and reducability of the linguistic cleavage. One is the history of conflict between the language groups and the other is their number and configuration. Where the history has been one of a dominant ethnic group or groups from which other language groups achieved national emancipation, as with the disintegration of the Austro-Hungarian Empire in 1918, the former dominant groups, the Germans and the Magyars, are likely to be at a disadvantage. Even today (1997) the Hungarian minorities in Slovakia and Rumania are not accepted as first-class citizens. An analagous situation is that of the ethnic Turks in Bulgaria.

Where there is approximate equality between the groups equilibrium may be maintained. In Belgium the Francophones were at one time the dominant group in culture and trade, though about the same population size as the Flemish-speakers. Since World War II the latter have asserted themselves with the result that Belgium has become a virtually federal state with a boundary line between the two autonomous groups. Only their roughly equal strength preserved the STABILITY and integrity of Belgium, though another important factor was that both groups accepted democratic procedures.

Yet another pattern exists in India where a state with many languages uses English, the tongue of the former imperial power, as a lingua franca and official language. In Sri Lanka, on the other hand, the majority Sinhala-speaking group rejected English and introduced legislation that the minority Tamil-speakers disliked. The result of this majority assertion was an intractable CIVIL WAR and a society and economy with difficult problems.

Although with the extension of the Internet the English language may become an important vehicle of the international exchange of information, a counter-balance to this instance of GLOBALIZATION may be the emergence of language differences as political cleavages in Africa and Asia. With the spread of public education and the increasing use of the law courts many of the new multi-lingual states may find their stability shaken. There are signs of this trend in India.

See also CIVIL WAR; CLEAVAGES; CONFLICT; ETHNICITY; NATIONALISM.

Reading

Laponce, J.A. 1984. *Langue et Territoire*. Quebec: Les Presses de l'Université Laval; McRae, K.D. 1983. *Conflict and Compromise in Multi-lingual Societies*. Vol. 1. Switzerland, 1986. Vol. 2. Belgium. Waterloo, Ontario: Wilfrid Laurier University Press; Rabushka, A. and K.A. Shepsle. 1972. *Politics in Plural Societies*. Columbus, Ohio: Merrill.

lobbying   The term is derived from the corridors and foyers of legislative chambers which, in the English-speaking world, are known as 'lobbies'. It has become the practice for the agents of PRESSURE GROUPS, usually paid, to gather there in order to persuade legislators to support legislation favourable to them. Sometimes the whole parliamentary pressure group constellation is called the 'lobby'. Lobbying is also occasionally used to mean any sort of approach in order to elicit support.

See also CANVASSING; INTEREST GROUPS; PRESSURE GROUPS.

Reading

Finer, S.E. 1958. *Anonymous Empire : a Study of the Lobby in Great Britain*. London: Pall Mall; Tomkins, D.C. 1956. *Congressional Investigation of Lobbying*. Berkeley: University of California Bureau of Public Administration.

local government   In unitary states without regional government local government will be the tier below central government. Where federalism or regional government obtains, local government will be the third-tier. Whatever the case, the governments of municipalities and rural areas will derive their powers from the centre. Central government can alter the boundaries, structures and functions of government with less or greater ease depending on the political and legal position.

Some of the reasons for supporting a local government system are obvious. Except in micro-states central government cannot possibly make some local decisions where only local people will have knowledge of or understanding of the background. Nor could central government possibly deal with so many decisions. Indeed, in all the large democracies, and many smaller ones, they have long delegated much of their administration to local governments. This is especially so with personal services like health and education. Even where, as in France until the 1980s, a system of FIELD SERVICE ADMINISTRATION existed with the prefect exercising a *tutelle*, the local mayor and councillors still had a role.

Other reasons for local government relate to its importance for the democratic process. Representative institutions have been a feature of most mature democracies since the nineteenth century. Local authorities are often centres where a party different from government is in power. They provide opportunities for participation in government for those who do not have the time or inclination to be representatives at the centre. For those who do, local representative democracy is an important training and recruiting ground.

Most local governments are legally responsible for a range of services. They are usually multi-purpose authorities. It is common for them to provide education, water, sewerage, public transport, roads, land-use planning, some kinds of welfare, and cultural and recreational facilities. In fulfilling all these roles they employ large numbers of people and spend much public money. In recent years, especially in Britain, it has become common to reduce elected local control over many functions by two procedures. One is for the central government to set up appointed bodies, QUANGOS, to carry out some of these services. Secondly, local authorities have been encouraged to contract out locally such functions as refuse collection.

Local executives have two basic forms which very generally correspond to the parliamentary and presidential. Outside the USA, local authorities in the English-speaking world are governed by elected councils and their committees. In the USA and France the Mayor is the executive – sometimes elected popularly and sometimes by the council. This practice has recently been advocated for British cities. It may provide much needed leadership and it may result in a kind of 'personality politics', ending in celebrities being chosen.

The problems of local government relate to its ACCOUNTABILITY, AUTONOMY and sustainability. Like all governments it needs money, yet it has difficulty in acquiring revenue. As a representative institution it must be accountable to its voters and yet many of its actions are determined by central government instructions and restrictions. It needs expertise although it cannot always afford it. Moreover, because of its small size many of its services are used by people who do not pay its taxes.

See also CENTRALIZATION; CENTRAL–LOCAL RELATIONS; DECENTRALIZATION; LOCAL GOVERNMENT FINANCE; LOCAL GOVERNMENT REORGANIZATION; LOCAL POLITICS.

Reading
Bowman, M. and W. Hampton. eds. 1983. *Local Democracies*. Melbourne: Longman Cheshire; Dye, T.R. 1981. *Politics in States and Communities*. 4th edn. Englewood Cliffs: Prentice Hall; Humes, J. and E. Martin. 1969.

The Structure of Local Government: a Comparative Survey of Eighty-one Countries. 2nd edn. The Hague: IULA; Robson, W.A. and D.E. Regan. eds. 1972. *Great Cities of the World.* 3rd edn. London: Allen and Unwin; Stewart, J.D. 1983. *Local Government: the Conditions of Local Choice.* London: Allen and Unwin.

local government finance

The problems of the funding of local government are bound up with its relations with the centre. Without exception, in modern industrialized democracies local governments receive part of their revenue from government grants. The rest they can raise themselves from charging for the use of services, from borrowing (which tends to need central government permission) and from local taxation. These components vary proportionately between country and country, though in all central government contributes a great deal. France and Italy are noteworthy for dependence on heavy grants from the centre. In Scandinavia there is much reliance on local income tax – the best system for strengthening local autonomy. In Britain and the USA local governments tax property, a progressive tax as the amount to be paid increases with the value of the property. There is great variety between states in the USA. In some, local governments receive larger BLOCK GRANTS from the state than from the central government. British governments allocate a 'rate support grant' which has been as much as 40 per cent of the gross domestic product. This helps to finance national services administered by local governments. As the tax bases of local governments vary greatly, the more prosperous areas will need less support. Thus the grants vary accordingly, with poorer areas receiving more per capita.

The FISCAL CRISIS of the 1970s was a crisis for local government. Inflation and the electoral penalties for increasing taxation made it difficult for central governments to maintain their level of local spending. Solutions included encouraging local authorities to borrow from private sources, introducing measures like corporate management to save money and to improve decision-making and LOCAL GOVERNMENT REORGANIZATION. The last implied changing structures, functions and areas. One disastrous solution was Mrs. Thatcher's abolition of the 'rates', a property tax, replacing it with the community charge. Each local authority was required to set a standard charge, a 'poll tax', applicable to every individual voter.

See also CENTRAL–LOCAL RELATIONS; FISCAL CRISIS; LOCAL GOVERNMENT; LOCAL GOVERNMENT REORGANIZATION.

Reading
Newton, K. 1980. *Balancing the Books: Financial Problems of Local Government in Europe.* London: Sage; Rose, R. and E. Page. eds. 1982. *Fiscal Stress in Cities.* Cambridge: CUP; Travers, T. 1986. *The Politics of Local Government Finance.* London: Allen and Unwin; Yates, D. 1977. *The Ungovernable City.* Cambridge, Mass.: MIT Press.

local government reorganization
Most local government was organized in the nineteenth century. In France the triumph of rationalism led to the abolition of the Royalist provinces by Napoleon and their replacement by smaller DÉPARTEMENTS with boundaries and names appropriate to geographical features. British local government was gradually constructed between the 1830s and the 1890s. As it emerged, London had special status and the rest of the country was divided between county government for rural areas and small towns, and single-tier, multi-purpose county boroughs for larger towns. The USA had largely inherited a similar system from Britain but between local government and Washington, D.C. was the layer of autonomous states.

Western local government systems made only slight adjustments to these structures and functions until the second half of the twentieth century when several factors brought about reorganization. Perhaps the chief one was technological – the rapid increase of ownership of the motor car, enabling people to live considerable distances from their work. This combined with the spread of suburbia and the growth of large conurbations to produce a situation where residence and workplace were apart. Some local authorities were providing services for those who did not pay for them, while others were escaping lightly. At the same time popular intellectual fashions for urban and transport planning and organizational theory resulted in demands for much larger multi-purpose authorities. It was argued that they would have the advantages of greater specialization of expertise among professional staffs.

In Italy, Spain, France and Scotland these were called 'regions'. In the two former countries they had some relationship to ethnic communities, but in the two latter their origins were technocratic. The 22 French regions only had the function of regional planning and the *départements* probably remained the most important units. In Britain Conservative governments attacked large units. London's government and those of the six English metropolitan counties, conurbation governments, was abolished in 1986 and the Scottish regions followed nearly a decade later. By 1996 there was a return almost to the status quo before 1975. Yet regional government is likely to remain on the political agenda of countries of the European Union because of the regional orientation of policies from Brussels.

See also CENTRAL–LOCAL RELATIONS; FISCAL CRISIS; REGIONALISM.

Reading
Butcher, H., I.G. Law, R. Leach and M. Mullard. 1990. *Local Government and Thatcherism*. London: Routledge; Rowat, D.C. ed. 1980. *International Handbook on Local Government Reorganisation*. London: Aldwych; Schmidt, V. 1990. *Democratizing France*. Cambridge: CUP.

local politics   A term that is used in several ways. The most obvious meaning is about the electoral politics of local councils, their meetings and decision-making, their contacts with local interests and PRESSURE GROUPS and the councillors' relations with their bureaucracies. Studies of this area would be within the ambit of community politics. A variation on this theme might be the study of local party organization, its selection of parliamentary candidates and local parties' relations with the headquarters of their parties. Or a more sociological approach might be the investigation of local elites and their exercise of power. This might be especially appropriate in developing countries such as Latin American states.

Another area of the study of local politics is concerned with the efforts of local authorities to obtain benefits for their locality by approaching central authorities. Much will depend here on ease of access to parliament. In the USA where access is easy Congressmen are used to gaining grants from the national budget for their state or district. In France the practise known as *cumul des mandats* by which the mayors of the largest towns often held several other elective offices including that of local deputy for the National Assembly was, until recently, the normal avenue of local access to the centre. Since the law of 1982 only two mandates can be held and it has become more common for the chairpersons of the departmental councils to make the approach (though still they are often deputies). In Britain approaches to Parliament are often made by the federations of local authorities such as the Association of Municipal Authorities in England and Wales and the Convention of Scottish Local Authorities in Scotland.

Neo-Marxist theorists have argued that while central government is concerned with production, local government is concerned with consumption. Thus the move to bigger units and more technocratic management reflects the power of capital, whose delivery of social benefits through the local government system is concerned with mollifying the working class and ensuring the reproduction of the labour force. Other neo-Marxists argue that local government might become, as in Bologna, the appropriate arena in which working-class power can be exerted. In general local government, unless there are legal/constitutional limitations, has only the power that central government allows it.

See also COMMUNITARIANISM; LOCAL GOVERNMENT; REGIONALISM.

Reading
Ashford, D.L. 1982. *British Dogmatism and French Pragmatism*. London: Allen and Unwin; Becquart-Leclerc, J. 1976. *Paradoxes du Pouvoir Local*. Paris: Fondation Nationale des Sciences Politiques; Cockburn, C. 1977. *The Local State*. London: Pluto; Hill, D.M. 1974. *Democratic Theory and Local Government*. London: Allen and Unwin.

localism The sort of LOCAL POLITICS which focuses on local issues. (A good deal of local politics is concerned with national issues.) Frequently this style of politics is INDEPENDENT POLITICS. It is probably associated with a certain type of POLITICAL CULTURE and is likely to flourish in a territorially vast federal state like the USA. Again, 'local politics' may be used to describe those issues of national politics which have a local orientation. Those who adhere to localism in politics will be traditionalists, while those who hate it will be modernizers.

See also CENTRALIZATION; CENTRAL–LOCAL RELATIONS; CENTRE–PERIPHERY RELATIONS; DECENTRALIZATION; INDEPENDENT POLITICS.

Reading
Bulpitt, J. 1983. *Territory and Power in the United Kingdom*. Manchester: Manchester University Press; Fenton, J.H. 1957. *Politics in the Border States*. New Orleans: Hauser; Key, V.O. 1949. *Southern Politics*. New York: Alfred A. Knopf; Key, V.O. 1956. *American State Politics*. New York: Alfred A. Knopf.

logrolling The procedure by which legislators or PRESSURE GROUPS representing different and specific interests agree to support each other's policy objectives.
See also PRESSURE GROUPS.

lower class A term that may be used as a synonym for UNDERCLASS. On the other hand, it is suggested that the latter denotes permanent poverty and deprivation while those in the lower class, mostly long-term unemployed, may be able to rise above it to the unskilled WORKING CLASS. 'Lower classes' is an antiquated term, probably used by old members of the ARISTOCRACY to describe anyone beneath them socially.
See also SOCIAL CLASS; UNDERCLASS; WORKING CLASS.

lower houses *See* FIRST CHAMBERS.

loyalty *See* EXIT, LOYALTY, VOICE.

lumpenproletariat *See* UNDERCLASS; WORKING CLASS.

M

machine A term sometimes used to describe PARTY ORGANIZATION. Thus it would include the professional bureaucratic organization of the party at the centre and, possibly, in the regions, and also the ACTIVISTS, the unpaid party workers at the local level. The latter are especially important at election time when they are needed to get party supporters to the poll. All successful democratic parties have this kind of organization.

In the USA, where the metaphor with its implications of smooth efficiency was probably first used, the term has a pejorative ring. It describes party organization, usually in the big cities of the North-East and mid-West. The party workers and the boss are motivated by the promise of patronage. The activists are paid by being appointed to municipal jobs which enable them to keep in constant touch with the voters. It is common for policemen or firemen to fill these roles. In the best organized machines there will be one in every voting precinct: hence their title of 'precinct captains' or, in some cities, 'ward heelers'. They are often expected to contribute a proportion of their pay to electoral funds and to help to nominate the BOSSES' candidates. The possibilities for corrupt dealing are apparent and many machines have been involved with corruption.

As the twentieth century has progressed the power of the machines has declined, but some observers argue that their decline has been exaggerated. *See also* BOSSES.

Reading
Gosnell, H.F. 1926. *Machine Politics: Chicago Model*. Chicago: Chicago University Press; Mayhew, D.R. 1986. *Placing Parties in American Politics*. Princeton: Princeton University Press; Wolfinger, R.E. 1974. *The Politics of Progress*. Englewood Cliffs: Prentice Hall.

macroanalysis *See* MICROANALYSIS.

magistrate A person who exercises judicial powers, though in the English-speaking world the term may be used only for such people in lower courts. In England Stipendiary Magistrates are trained lawyers who are appointed for large cities. Justices of the Peace are normally not legally trained and sit on 'benches' of two to seven magistrates. Criminal cases begin in Magistrates' Courts; but grave offences, if evidence justifies, are committed to Crown Courts.

majoritarianism The belief that DEMOCRACY consists of nothing but voting, and then implementing the decision of 50 per cent + 1 of the electorate.

majority leader The leaders of the majority party in the US Senate and House of Representatives, selected by its members in order to facilitate the passage of legislation. The Majority Leader in the House is subordinate to the Speaker in expediting party business. 'Minority Leaders' have similar roles in respect of the minority parties.

majority party government A government formed from a party with an overall majority in a legislature. This is likely to be the case in a TWO PARTY SYSTEM with a FIRST-PAST-THE-POST electoral system: one majority party government, as in Britain, will follow another, producing the situation of ADVERSARY POLITICS. 'Majority government' might well describe a coalition majority in power.

See also ADVERSARY POLITICS; COALITION GOVERNMENT; TWO PARTY SYSTEMS.

Reading
Lijphart, A. 1984. *Contemporary Democracies: Patterns of Majoritarian and Consensus Government in Twenty-one Countries.* New Haven: YUP.

majority rule This apparently simple term posits several problems. It may sometimes refer to the decision-making procedure by which 50 per cent +1 of those voting impose their will upon the minority of those voting. Yet if one takes the word 'rule' seriously it becomes clear that a very large number of people cannot govern or exercise coercive control. Modern administration and policy-making are too complex and technical for that. Moreover, MAJORITARIANISM is not the same as DEMOCRACY, though majority rule might imply it. The TYRANNY OF THE MAJORITY occurs when certain minority rights are over-ridden. These are rights of CITIZENSHIP such as the rights to use the courts, to have a fair trial and to vote, and CIVIL LIBERTIES including free speech, a free press and the right to organize opposition. Institutional devices to give minorities added protection include systems of Proportional Representation and, instead of a 50 per cent +1 majority, substituting (say) a 60 per cent +1 majority.

See also DEMOCRACY; MAJORITY VOTING; TYRANNY OF THE MAJORITY; UTILITARIANISM.

Reading
Arrow, K.J. 1951. *Social Choice and Individual Values.* New York: Wiley; Heath, A. 1976. *Rational Choice and Social Exchange.* Cambridge: CUP; Pennock, J.R. 1979. *Democratic Political Theory.* Princeton: Princeton University Press.

majority voting It may appear on first thought that taking a vote and then accepting the majority decision is common sense. (If minority voting were to be the rule people would vote against the outcome they preferred.) It is not usually so simple because often there are more than two options to choose from. Moreover, it does not follow that every voter will place a number of options in the same order of preference. Suppose there are three options – A, B and C. There may be no 50 per cent +1 majority for any of them. When asked to rank them possible orders may be A,B,C; A,C,B; B,A,C; B,C,A; C,A,B; C,B,A and a clear ranking majority may not emerge. Obviously it would be even more difficult with four options to obtain a clear majority for an option. Consequently rules other than 50 per cent +1 may be devised.

Reading
Berg, E. 1965. *Democracy and the Majority Principle.* Stockholm: Scandinavian University Books.; McLean, I. 1982. *Dealing in Votes.* Oxford: Martin Robertson; Spitz, E. 1984. *Majority Rule.* Chatham, NJ: Chatham House.

maladministration Failure to adhere to the proper standards of administration.

Incompetence may not be considered maladministration unless the complainant has suffered loss of some kind; but the precise meaning will vary according to the jurisdiction. In many European countries a system of ADMINISTRATIVE LAW will deal with complaints. In Scandinavia and Britain appeal to the OMBUDSMAN, or an action in the ordinary courts, may be the method of claiming restitution or stopping the kind of administrative behaviour that is objected to.

See also ADMINISTRATION; ADMINISTRATIVE LAW; OMBUDSMAN.

Reading
Gellhorn, W. 1967. *Ombudsmen and Others: Citizens' Protectors in Nine Countries.* Cambridge, Mass.: HUP; Wheare, K.C. 1973. *Maladministration and its Remedies.* London: Stevens.

managerialism A set of beliefs, attitudes and values which support the view that management is the most essential and desirable element of good administration and government. Consequently in all enterprises and services, whether private or public, expertise in management must be inculcated by training and incentives to excel. In the political world it may take the form of asserting that much conflict and argument are unnecessary for solving problems. All that is needed is a rational assessment of the problem and this involves gathering and collating information, listing the options, calculating costs of each, evaluating consequences and choosing the best course of action. Recent managerialism has included such devices as 'performance indicators', purporting to measure the relative efficiencies of different managers and 'market testing' which compares public sector managers' responsibilities and tasks with those of managers in the private sector in order to assess their pay. It is criticized for weakening the public service ethos.

See also CORPORATE MANAGEMENT; MANAGERIAL REVOLUTION; THATCHERISM.

Reading
Pollitt, C. 1993. *Managerialism and the Public Services.* Oxford: Blackwell; Ranson, S. and J. Stewart. 1994. *Management for the Public Domain.* New York: St. Martin's Press; Zifcak. S.P. 1994. *New Managerialism.* Buckingham: Open University Press.

managerial revolution The origin of this term is a famous book of this name by Burnham. In it he developed the theme of the separation between ownership and control, brought about by the rise of the corporation. The result, he argued, is that power is passing into the hands of the managers. 'Corporate capitalism' is also 'managerial capitalism'. Optimists believed this would result in the profit motive being less emphasized and industry becoming more socially responsible. Recent assessments have seen Burnham's thesis as somewhat exaggerated. Many managers have a part share in ownership and are profit conscious. Family firms, though fewer among large enterprises, have by no means disappeared. Profit still overshadows social responsibility.

Reading
Burch, P.H. 1972. *The Managerial Revolution Reassessed.* Lexington: D.C. Heath; Burnham, J. 1941. *The Managerial Revolution.* New York: Day; Galbraith, J.K. 1967. *The New Industrial State.* London: Hamish Hamilton.

mandate In ordinary parlance the term means an authoritative command from a superior. A DELEGATE is mandated in order to carry out the wishes of those who have chosen her/him. In political terminology it has several connotations. To 'possess a mandate' may mean to have the authorization of a certain set of voters to carry out a specific policy: BURKE argued that MPs could not be mandated. Sometimes it is only used to apply to the elected majority who will claim a mandate to implement the promises in their manifesto. Again, League of Nations mandates were provided for the former colonies of the defeated powers after World War I. Their government was entrusted to the victorious powers with the condition that they were to be guided towards self-government.

See also DELEGATE; MANDATE THEORY; TRUSTEESHIP.

Reading
Jennings, I. 1959 edn. *Cabinet Government.* Cambridge: CUP; Marshall, G. and G. Moodie. 1971. *Some Problems of the Constitution.* London: Hutchinson.

mandate theory The 'doctrine of the mandate' is taken to mean that an elected government must not do anything that it did not put to the electorate at the last election, but must strive to carry out all the policies listed in its manifesto, the printed programme it publishes on the eve of the election. Such a doctrine is clearly easier to follow in a TWO-PARTY SYSTEM. In COALITION GOVERNMENT there may be difficulties between conflicting party promises. Moreover, it is obvious that matters will arise, especially in the field of foreign policy, that governments must deal with in spite of having no MANDATE.

The mandate theory dates from the period in which the FRANCHISE was being extended and it was particularly espoused in Britain by the Liberal and Labour parties. It is interesting to note, however, that it was first used by the House of Lords to justify their opposition to Liberal measures such as the 1886 Irish Home Rule Bill. The theory first developed when parties became so disciplined in the House of Commons that governments could depend on their policies being accepted. Parties began to draw up programmes to put to the electorate, the first instance being the Newcastle Programme, accepted by the Liberal Party conference in 1891, and containing several radical measures. On occasions governments have dissolved Parliament to secure a mandate for a measure they did not raise at the last election. Thus Prime Minister Baldwin dissolved Parliament and fought the 1923 election to obtain a mandate for TARIFF reform. The National Government claimed a 'doctor's mandate' at the 1931 election, partly because they were a coalition and did not wish to proclaim policies on which they might be divided and partly to allow them freedom to prescribe remedies once they had diagnosed what was wrong with Britain.

The mandate theory cannot be ignored by governments in power because of the strength of the belief in popular consent. The argument that the government has used its majority to implement policies on which the electorate has not been consulted is a powerful one. Oppositions are quick to use it as a stick to beat governments. Yet it is not possible for contemporary British governments to carry out all their manifesto commitments because the parties promise so much though, frequently, in rather vague terms. Few voters are likely to read the manifestos or remember what is in them. Increasingly, however, governments are proposing REFERENDUMS for issues which are important and more frequently oppositions are calling for them in order to embarrass governments.

See also MANDATE; MANIFESTOISM.

Reading
Bealey, F.W. 1988. *Democracy in the Contemporary State.* Oxford: OUP; Emden, C.S. 1956. *The People and the Constitution.* Oxford: OUP; Punnett, R.M. 1968. *British Government and Politics.* London: Heinemann.

manifesto *See* MANDATE THEORY; MANIFESTOISM.

manifestoism The term was coined by Henry Drucker to describe the Labour Party's attachment to the belief that a Labour government must carry out nothing more nor less than what is set out in the party's manifesto at the previous election. Wilson describes how when coming to power he kept a copy of the manifesto in his desk and ticked off each item as they were implemented. The Conservative Party has also moved in this direction, its leaders drawing attention to their fidelity to their promises. Margaret Thatcher was so grieved that she had not redeemed her 1983 pledge to abolish the rates that she insisted on it at the 1987 election and so committed herself to the disastrous poll tax.

See also MANDATE; MANDATE THEORY.

Reading
Drucker, H. 1979. *Doctrine and Ethos in the Labour Party*. London: Allen and Unwin; Hoffman, J.D. 1966. *The Conservative Party in Opposition 1945–51*. London: MacGibbon; Wilson, H. 1977. *The Labour Government 1964–70*. London: Weidenfeld.

marginal seat A seat in a legislature which seems likely to change hands at the next election because the incumbent candidate has a small majority. The concept of marginality is only relevant in ELECTORAL SYSTEMS with single-member constituencies. In FIRST-PAST-THE-POST systems the CUBE RULE results in a disproportionate allocation of seats to the two main parties and a national SWING brings a disproportionate movement of seats. Hence the extent of marginality and its effects varies. 'Safe' seats, not marginal at one election, may become marginal after another. At the 1997 British General Election, Tatton, the fifth safest Conservative seat fell to an Independent candidate, the outcome of a huge national swing and other reasons connected with allegations of the involvement in corruption of the incumbent Conservative.

See also ELECTIONS; ELECTORAL SYSTEMS; SWING.

Reading
Curtice, J. and M. Steed. 1986. 'Proportionality and Exaggeration in the British Electoral System'. In *Electoral Studies*

5, 209–28; Milne, R.S. and H.C. Mackenzie. 1958. *Marginal Seat, 1955*. London: Hansard Society.

market forces The political catchphrase of the 1980s and early 1990s. Especially since the 1989 revolution destroyed the Soviet bloc, DEMOCRACY succeeded Communism and market forces were released by the abolition of the COMMAND ECONOMY, the notion has had a strongly evocative appeal. It strengthened the idea that CAPITALISM and democracy were interdependent. Yet the analogy between the consumer sovereignty of the market economy and the voter sovereignty of the 'political market' can be very misleading. The voter has a choice but, unlike the consumer who does not buy what is not wanted, she/he may have to accept the option she/he did not want when their elected representatives are in a minority. The SOVEREIGNTY OF THE PEOPLE can be an illusionary concept.

See also CAPITALISM; COMMAND ECONOMY; DEMOCRACY; FORDISM; SOVEREIGNTY OF THE PEOPLE.

Reading
Bealey, F.W. 1993. 'Capitalism and Democracy'. In *European Journal of Political Research* 23, 203–23; Levitas, R. 1986. 'Competition and Compliance: the Utopias of the New Right'. In *The Ideology of the New Right*. Ed. R. Levitas. Cambridge: Polity; Nozick, R. 1974. *Anarchy State and Utopia*. Oxford: Blackwell.

market socialism A combination of the market economy and public ownership of enterprise. Production is a matter for public enterprise but distribution is a matter for the market. Most social democratic countries have approximated to this model, though public ownership has often been limited to public utilities and some distribution, such as that of health care, has not been subject to MARKET FORCES. Even in the Communist bloc, Hungary had introduced a measure of distributive freedom. Hence recent use of the term can only indicate a relative move towards the market. It has usually been applied to those left-wing governments who deplore too much bureaucracy and who are less egalitarian in social policy than others.

See also MARKET FORCES; NATIONALIZATION; SOCIAL DEMOCRACY; SOCIALISM.

Reading
Miller, D. 1989. *Market, State and Community.* Oxford: OUP.

martial law   The imposition of military rule on part or the whole of a country. It involves control by soldiers and drastic penalties for law and order offences such as rioting and looting. There has been no case of it in any democracy since World War II. Where there is legislation for a state of martial law, it usually requires a proclamation. In English law it is not clear whether it exists. Such co-operation of soldiers with police as can be seen in Northern Ireland is regarded as a pragmatic response necessitated by the law and order situation.

See also CIVIL LIBERTIES; LAW AND ORDER; RULE OF LAW.

Reading
Heuston, R.F.V. 1964. *Essays in Constitutional Law.* London: Stevens.

marxism   The term has become increasingly complicated since it first referred to the ideas of Karl MARX (1818–83) and Friedrich Engels (1820–95). Later Marxism-Leninism incorporated the doctrines of Vladimir Lenin (1870–1924) whose two additions to the canon were an analysis of IMPERIALISM and a theoretical basis for the rules, duties, procedures and structures of Communist parties.

The writings of Marx and Engels are voluminous but much of what they believed is contained in the Communist Manifesto they issued in 1848. They claimed to transcend 'Utopian' SOCIAL-

ISM and to replace it with 'scientific' socialism. Marx's theories can perhaps be best discussed under four headings. First, the LABOUR THEORY OF VALUE, adapted from the classical economists, contended that the value of a product is determined by the amount of labour put into it. The worker sells his labour to the employer for a wage, but it does not reflect the value of what he produces because his employer has taken from it a share for himself, an unmerited surplus. This is EXPLOITATION and the worker has become a 'wage slave', without his craftsman's tools. Because of the division of labour he may not know what he is producing. The worker is 'alienated' and, therefore, a potential revolutionary.

Second, a theory of historical development influenced by the German philosopher HEGEL (1770–1831) from whom Marx took four features: history was divided into epochs; each was distinguished by a different type of consciousness; changes resulted from a basic motivating force, a 'World Spirit', and took place through the 'dialectic', a process of conflicting forces, Thesis and Antithesis contradicting each other; the world force would triumph in the final phase, the Synthesis, when contradictions were resolved and the destiny of humanity would be realized.

Third, Marx distilled a body of prophecy from his analysis of CAPITALISM and his theory of historical development. He rejected a metaphysical dynamic and asserted that the motive force in history was material and economic. Each phase of history was characterized by different class relationships. 'All history was the history of the class struggle'. The class that owned the main factors of production exerted coercive power through its control of the STATE. With industrialization the main factor of production was capital and the capitalists, or entrepreneurs – Marx calls them the BOURGEOISIE – would control the state. It was 'the executive committee of the bourgeoisie' and it would be used to repress the workers or proletariat. As capitalism developed it would become more concentrated and fiercely competitive and workers' wages would be cut, unemployment increase and the proletariat become more embittered. Intermediate classes would be ground down leaving a class struggle between the bourgeoisie and the proletariat. During the course of this, working-class consciousness would emerge. Initially, consciousness of their common interests across national boundaries, and then consciousness of the workers' historic role which was the overthrow of capitalism and the installation of socialism. In the transition to socialism the workers would set up a DICTATORSHIP OF THE PROLETARIAT while the capitalists were being expropriated. Finally a classless society in which everyone had a share of ownership of the means of production would ensue. There would be no need for repression and so there would be no state. It would wither away.

Fourth, though it is often said that Marx was vague about socialist policies, the Communist Manifesto lists measures which workers' governments might be expected to implement. Among these are: abolition of landed property; a progressive income tax; centralization of credit in a national bank; nationalization of communications and all instruments of production; free state education; abolition of child labour; industrial armies to be established, especially for agriculture; and the gradual ending of the distinction between town and country. Many of these measures were later carried out by left-wing governments. The vagueness of Marx lay in the absence of how a socialist society would be administered without the coercive apparatus of the state and how a socialist economy would be run. He said nothing about 'planning'.

Since Marx's death Marxism has passed through several phases. In the years before 1914 most European socialist parties (none of whom were in power) spoke the language of Marxist rhetoric. Their main collective endeavour was to stop war and in 1889 they joined together in the Second International. (Marx had founded the abortive First in 1864.) In 1914 the workers in all the belligerent countries obeyed the call to mobilize. Between the two wars world depression led to Marxist theoreticians concentrating on the labour theory of value, while the Communist parties admired Soviet planning, though the growth of TROTSKYISM and the foundation of the Fourth International caused misgivings.

After 1945 the development of Marxism was influenced by two main factors: increasing knowledge of the nature of the Stalinist regime in the Soviet Union and the growing affluence of the western industrial proletariat which showed little sign of revolting against capitalism. In the 1950s Marx's earlier, more philosophic, writings were translated into English for the first time and younger academic Marxists (called the New Left in Britain) became interested in the concept of 'ALIENATION'. (It was the intellectuals who were alienated not the workers.) By the 1960s most Marxist theoreticians had decided that the Soviet Union would have not been regarded by Marx as a socialist society. They began to incorporate certain social science concepts into their conspectus. For example, POLITICAL CULTURE was accepted even by Communist sociologists as a useful notion in the study of consciousness. LEGITIMACY was important in answering the question, Why has the capitalist state endured? The neo-Marxist response was that the workers had been either bamboozled by propaganda through the mass media, or bought out by social benefits and the delusions of 'consumerism'.

See also ALIENATION; BOLSHEVIK; CLASS CONFLICT; COMMUNISM; CONTRADICTIONS; DICTATORSHIP OF THE PROLETARIAT; LABOUR THEORY OF VALUE; NEW LEFT; POLITICAL CULTURE; TROTSKYISM.

Reading

Berlin, I. 1939. *Karl Marx*. Oxford: OUP; Carr, E.H. 1966. *The Bolshevik Revolution*. 3 vols. London: Macmillan; Graham, K. 1986. *The Battle for Democracy*. Brighton: Wheatsheaf; Habermas, J. 1975. *Legitimation Crisis*. London: Heinemann; Hay, C. 1996. *Re-stating Social and Political Change*. Buckingham: Open University; Hook, S. 1961. *From Hegel to Marx*. Detroit: University of Michigan Press; Hunt, R.N.C. 1954. *Marxism Past and Present*. London: Geoffrey Bles; Jessop, B. 1985. *Nicos Poulantzas: Marxist Theory and Political Strategy*. London: Macmillan; McLellan, D. 1973. *Karl Marx: His Life and Thought*. London: Macmillan; Offe, C. 1984. *The Contradictions of the Welfare State*. London: Hutchinson.

mass man   See MASS SOCIETY.

mass media   The mass media of communications include newspapers and magazines, the cinema, radio and television. Modern technology has increased their range and extended their markets. The latest development, satellite television, enables world-wide coverage and is yet another aspect of GLOBALIZATION.

The importance of the mass media is both social and political and their influence on society has a political implication. Although much information is purveyed by the media the prime function of most of their outlets is to entertain. Especially television has this effect and some surveys have shown many people spend four hours in every day watching it. In general the result is a public that has less time for politics. Trivialization of issues has become common. Being serious is not popular.

Yet the media has become indispensable to the political parties. They need it to convey their intentions to the public and they hope to mobilize support in this way. So television, in particular, has become very important at election time. It makes the choice of personable and articulate leaders crucial for the political parties. It is said that a widely-held view that a politician is 'no good on television' will destroy her/his chances of ever becoming party leader. Television is therefore prominent in the 'image building' which all parties now indulge in. Moreover, party managers are aware of how unpopular too much political broadcasting can be and they attempt to keep the 'messages' short. The ultimate in brevity is the 'sound bite', a brief snappy statement, often one abusing political opponents.

A very important question relates to the ownership of the media and their relationships to political parties and governments. Most television and broadcasting channels and newspapers in the democratic world are privately owned, though in some countries there is a tradition of public service broadcasting. Owners may exert pressure over the expression of political opinion, though their main concern will be to sell the product, while journalists and commentators may also influence their audiences. Even when they are objective in their handling of politicians their skill in questioning them sometimes greatly exceeds that of members of legislatures. Hence some may object that television is subverting the power of parliaments while others may feel that it enriches democracy.

See also COMMUNICATIONS; MASS SOCIETY; POLITICAL COMMUNICATION; PROPAGANDA.

Reading

Blumler, J.G. and M. Gurevitch. 1982. 'The political effects of mass communication'. In *Culture, Society and the Media*. Ed. M. Gurevitch, M. Bennett, M. Curran and J. Woollacott. London: Methuen; McQuail, D. 1983. *Mass Communication Theory*. London: Sage; Postman, N. 1985. *Amusing Ourselves to Death*. London: Methuen; Qualter, T. 1985.

Opinion Control in the Democracies. London: Macmillan.

mass parties One of DUVERGER's categories of party. A mass party has a formal nation-wide structure based on individual membership, in contrast with a CADRE PARTY. The typical mass party developed in the last years of the nineteenth century as the FRANCHISE was extended to the WORKING CLASS. So mass parties were usually socialist parties, though there is one exception which Duverger does not note. The British Liberal Party developed a mass organization in the 1880s with local parties in every CONSTITUENCY and a programmatic approach to ELECTIONS. In the twentieth century centre and right-wing parties were forced by electoral competition to adopt similar organizations.

Mass parties are vehicles for mobilizing large groups of voters at election time. The result is that the people who carry out this exercise, the ACTIVISTS, become important and are rewarded by the right to participate in making party policy. Normally they also select CANDIDATES and sometimes de-select sitting legislators. Since the advent of television the monopoly of the local party organizations over mobilization has declined and the IMAGE of the national party leader has become more important. Strong allegiance to party has weakened and party memberships have declined.
See also ACTIVISTS; CADRE PARTY; PARTY ORGANIZATION.

Reading
Duverger, M. 1954. *Political Parties.* London: Methuen; Epstein, L. 1980. *Political Parties in Western Democracies.* New Brunswick, NJ: Transaction Books; LaPalombara, J. and M. Weiner. eds. 1966. *Political Parties and Political Development.* Princeton: Princeton University Press.

mass politics The concept of mass politics was forged by the association of MASS SOCIETY with the MASS MEDIA.

Wright MILLS in the *Power Elite* (1956) commented that the USA was not 'altogether a mass society', nor had it ever been 'a community of publics'. These were two extreme ideal types. There were four dimensions in which the difference between them was apparent. In the mass society a few people communicated to the many; a monopoly of communication prevented people answering back; people had limited opportunities 'to act out their opinions collectively' and institutional authority infiltrated every aspect of public life.

Kornhauser developed these ideas, constructing a typology of 'mass man' who was self-oriented and self-alienated as opposed to 'autonomous man' who was self-oriented and self-related. If and when mass man ceased to be self-oriented and became group-oriented he would be transformed into 'totalitarian man'. In his typology Kornhauser speculated about how mass society could become totalitarian society. A 'pluralist society' was one in which it was easy for non-elites to gain access to ELITES, but the latter did not find the non-elites available for MOBILIZATION and manipulation because of the existence of intermediate groups. When elites began to find non-elites available, because of the decay of PLURALISM/ CIVIL SOCIETY, 'mass society' was on the way. 'Totalitarian society' would come about when the elites also ceased to be accessible. Manipulable non-elites would then be at the mercy of elites. Hence there was an implication that the USA was a mass society and could possibly become a totalitarian society. This has not happened because pluralism was stronger than implied. Totalitarian society has collapsed.
See also MASS SOCIETY; PLURALISM; TOTALITARIANISM.

Reading
Bell, D. 1956. 'The Theory of Mass Society, a Critique'. In *Commentary* 33. July, 75–83. Kornhauser, W. 1960. *The Politics of Mass Society.* London: Routledge; Riesman, D.

1953. *The Lonely Crowd.* Garden City, NY: Doubleday.

mass society   A concept which became popular in the 1930s with the work of Ortega y Gasset. He argued that because of the expansion of population, and greater prosperity owing to mass production and DEMOCRACY, 'mass man', a new type of individual had emerged. In spite of much greater freedom people were dissatisfied without being clear why. Mass man was nihilistic and mass society lacked a morality. The theme was taken up by Chakotin some years later. He explained the rise of FASCISM in terms of the inability of the masses to cope with totalitarian PROPAGANDA. The concept is of particular interest to social psychologists, especially those who study crowd behaviour. Therefore it is bound to attract the attention of political scientists.
See also MASS MEDIA; MASS POLITICS; PROPAGANDA.

Reading
Chakotin, S. 1940. *The Rape of the Masses.* London: Routledge.; Giner, S. 1976. *Mass Society.* London: Macmillan; Le Bon, G. [1895] 1960. *The Crowd.* New York: Viking; Y Gasset, O. 1932. *The Revolt of the Masses.* London: Allen and Unwin.

massive retaliation   The policy of the Eisenhower administration after 1954. The USA would use nuclear weapons at any time, anywhere, to forestall Soviet expansion. The reason for this strategy was the unfavourable balance in conventional weapons the West suffered while the USSR's nuclear capacity was weak. By the late 1950s, as the disparity lessened, flexible response became the doctrine, then MUTUALLY ASSURED DESTRUCTION.
See also ESCALATION.

Reading
Bobbitt, P., L. Freedman and G.F. Treverton. eds. 1987. *US Nuclear Strategy: a Reader.* Basingstoke: Macmillan.

materialism   A set of ideas associated with the view that only the material world explains all manner of mental phenomena. Man's attempt to cope with it is basic and human feelings and beliefs are secondary. The Marxist theory that economics ultimately determines historical development is the form known as DIALECTICAL MATERIALISM, though it was Engels who elaborated the 'materialist conception of history'. Idealist philosophers and religious believers are bound to challenge these ideas.
See also DIALECTICAL MATERIALISM.

matriarchy   The term generally means rule by women, but more specifically it refers to a system of hereditary rule by matriarchal descent. It is not uncommon in Africa and Asia.
See also QUEENS.

mayor   The head of town or city government in much of the English-speaking world, though in Scotland the equivalent officer is called the provost. Mayors can be chosen by the elected councillors or by the voters, though in Holland the *burgemeester*, while possessed of considerable independence of action, is appointed by the central government. Direct election by citizens is common in North America. In France, Sweden and Britain the councils elect the mayors. In some countries mayors are merely chairmen of councils, but in others they have strong executive powers. The French mayors are spokesmen and bargainers at the centre for their town. In many American cities they may have managerial and entrepreneurial roles, with the obligation to find private investment. Some American mayors, especially in the industrial cities of the north-east, have wielded great power because of their control of the party (usually Democratic) MACHINE.
See also CENTRAL–LOCAL RELATIONS; CITY GOVERNMENT; CITY MANAGER; LOCAL POLITICS; MACHINE.

Reading
Becquart-Leclerc, J. 1976. *Paradoxes du Pouvoir Local*. Paris: Fondation Nationale des Sciences Politiques; Jones, G.W. and A.L. Norton. eds. 1978. *Political Leaders in Local Government*. Birmingham: Institute of Local Government Studies; Lowi, T.J. 1964. *At the Pleasure of the Mayor: Patronage and Power in New York City 1895-1958*. Glencoe: Free Press.

mayor-administrator A practice in some US cities is for the MAYOR to appoint an administrator who, in some cases, he may dismiss. The device is to allow the mayor to deal with future policy, lobbying state and national legislatures and fund-raising, while the administrator is concerned with routine implementation.
See also CITY GOVERNMENT; CITY MANAGER; LOCAL POLITICS.

Reading
Banfield, E.C. ed. 1961. *Urban Government*. New York: Free Press.

mayor-council An American situation where both the MAYOR and the council are popularly elected. There may be either a STRONG MAYOR PLAN or a WEAK MAYOR PLAN.

mercantilism *See* FREE TRADE.

meritocracy A society in which people's success is based on their merits rather than the hereditary principle, prejudice, class bias and gender or racial discrimination. Its earliest statement was the new French Revolutionary and Napoleonic criterion of 'the career open to talents'. It presupposes early promotion as a result of examinations and thus places emphasis on the educational system. Although it may seem egalitarian it may produce a more hard-hearted and smugger elite than an aristocratic one. Lower social strata may be neglected because they are seen as less intelligent and/or more lazy.

See also ELITES; ELITISM; POSITIVE DISCRIMINATION; UNDERCLASS.

Reading
Young, M. 1958. *The Rise of the Meritocracy*. London: Thames and Hudson.

methodology The logic underlying social science research. This is frequently based on a combination of various approaches – empirical, deductive and inductive. In political science research empirical method is often based on a range of methods and techniques. Documentation, the searching of archives and published works, is actually a technique used by historians. Two other common techniques are the stock-in-trade of anthropologists and sociologists. These are observation (for example, of elections) and interrogation which can involve interviewing politicians, or may frequently be done through SURVEY RESEARCH. Interrogative techniques often require statistical method to interpret the data.
See also PUBLIC OPINION; SAMPLE SURVEYS; SURVEY RESEARCH.

Reading
Duverger, M. 1964. *Introduction to the Social Sciences*. London: Allen and Unwin; Morrow, R.A. and D.D. Brown. 1994. *Critical Theory and Methodology*. London: Sage; Singleton, R.A., B.C. Straits and M.M. Straits. 1993. *Approaches to Social Research*. Oxford: OUP.

microanalysis The type of analysis which deals with individual people, or single actions or situations. 'Macroanalysis' is the opposite, dealing with aggregations.

middle class A general term in common use meaning people who neither belong to the ARISTOCRACY or gentry, nor to the WORKING CLASS, those who work with their hands. They are often divided into the 'lower middle class', clerks and small shopkeepers, and the 'upper middle class', managerial and professional people and wealthier businessmen. Boundaries between these categories may be blurred and the increase in social mobility makes them even less well-defined. Marxist interpretation is unrealistic because MARX saw them as a residual group which would eventually be ground down into the proletariat. Instead, in most industrialized countries opinion polls today find much more than half the population claiming to be 'middle class'. The term has come to signify a 'status group' defined by dress and deportment, consumption habits and LIFESTYLE. These have also changed as a result of higher standards of living, the increase of foreign travel and more congenial and cleaner work situations so that the BLUE COLLAR part of the population is much smaller and less evident. People on very poor pay may be university graduates working as waiters and chambermaids.

See also ARISTOCRACY; BOURGEOISIE; LOWER CLASS; WORKING CLASS.

Reading
Butler, T. and M. Savage. eds. 1995. *Social Change and the Middle Classes*. London: UCL Press; Lewis, R. and A. Maude. 1949. *The English Middle Classes*. London: Phoenix House; Westergaard, J. and H. Resler. 1976. *Class in a Capitalist Society*. London: Penguin.

migration   The movement of peoples from one country to another is a source of international tension. Even migration within the same country can be a political problem. Immigrants are usually in search of either personal safety or economic prosperity – sometimes both. They have few possessions and may need financial support from the host country. They will often be resented by the native population because of ethnic and religious differences, their willingness to accept low wage rates and their multi-occupation of houses, lowering the house prices of adjacent indigenous owner-occupiers. The largest migration in modern history was the immigration into the USA between 1880 and 1910, giving

rise to all these reactions, but internal hostility was mitigated by American capacity for geographical and economic expansion. The effect on Europe, from where most had emigrated, was to relieve tensions on land and living space and to reduce competition for jobs. In the contemporary world great inequalities of living standards between 'North and South' (as it is now put), and much greater ease of travel, are factors encouraging migration. Yet the unwillingness of many prosperous countries to allow mass immigration is a potentially explosive international issue.

See also ETHNICITY; MULTI-ETHNIC POLITICS; RACISM; REFUGEES; XENOPHOBIA.

Reading
Dowry, A. 1987. *Closed Borders: the Contemporary Assault on Freedom of Movement*. New Haven: YUP; Hammar, T. 1985. *European Immigration Policy: a Comparative Study*. Cambridge: CUP; Kritz, M.M. ed. 1983. *US Immigration and Refugee Policy: Global and Domestic Issues*. Lexington: D.C. Heath.

militants   See ACTIVISTS.

militarism   A state of mind or set of attitudes which accord high prestige to the military, to their pursuits and to their values of patriotism, discipline and hierarchy. Where militarism prevails the military are likely to have great power. This may be the consequence of fears of aggression from outside; or the result of national integration by the use of military force. Even where civil power is dominant, as it is in democracies, such situations are likely to make the armed forces more assertive.

See   also   CIVIL–MILITARY   RELATIONS; MILITARY REGIMES.

Reading
Eide, A. and M. Thee. eds. 1980. *Problems of Contemporary Militarism*. London: Croom Helm; Gillis, J.R. ed. 1989. *The Militarization of the Western World*. New Brunswick, NJ: Transaction Books; Vagts, A. 1960. *A History*

of *Militarism*. Revised edn. London: Meridian Books.

military-industrial complex

A term used by President Eisenhower in his Farewell Address in 1961. He was warning about the danger to civilian rule from pressures exerted by the tacit alliance between the military and the large armament manufacturers who were needed by the government to provide the weapons for the rearmament programme, made necessary by the COLD WAR. Contracts were vetted and budgets drawn up by a committee of Congressmen, all anxious to obtain investment and employment for their own congressional districts. Corruption was always a possibility. Evidence suggests that in the Soviet Union, where about 20 per cent of GNP was spent on arms, the problem was much greater and greatly contributed to economic decline. Other democracies besides the USA had similar troubles and scandals about defence contracts were common.

See also CIVIL–MILITARY RELATIONS.

Reading
McNaugher, T.L. 1989. *Old Politics: America's Procurement Muddle*. Washington, D.C.: Brookings.

military regimes

A term relating to states where rule is by the armed forces (which may include the navy and air force). FINER asks the pertinent question, 'Why are they not in power everywhere: they have all the guns?'; and, indeed, there are over 30 regimes in the world which might be described as 'military'. Some of them, because of the dominance of one charismatic senior officer, could be called 'military dictatorships'. Others are governed by JUNTAS. It is common for military rule to be the outcome of a COUP D'ÉTAT. Frequently one set of soldiers overthrows another.

The most marked feature of military regimes is that they dislike DEMOCRACY.

AUTHORITARIANISM characterizes their style. They suppress civic feedoms. Otherwise they vary with the state of economic and political development. For example, in Brazil the military ruled with the consent of the business and financial interests who feared the threat to stability of working-class activism. In less developed countries the army may be the only institution where technical skills are common and which has a nation-wide organization. Even junior officers may take over. In Liberia Doe, who overthrew civilian rule in 1980, was a sergeant. (Institutionally, Liberia was so backward that his coup plunged the country into almost permanent CIVIL WAR.) In Burma the military not only dominate the economy, they also participate in administration. But one cannot generalize too much about military rule. The Turkish constitution stipulates that the army is the guardian of secular and civilian government. In 1980 General Evren took power and guided his country back to civilian rule three years later.

See also CIVIL–MILITARY RELATIONS; CIVIL WAR; COUP D'ÉTAT; GUERRILLA WARFARE; JUNTA.

Reading
Finer, S.E. 1976. *The Man on Horseback*. Harmondsworth: Penguin; Nordlinger, E.A. 1977. *Soldiers in Politics*. Englewood Cliffs: Prentice Hall; Perlmutter, A. 1977. *The Military in Politics in Modern Times*. New Haven: YUP.

militias

Citizen soldiers who train occasionally and who can be called on in time of emergency. In the English-speaking world the term was used in the nineteenth century. In Britain the militia could be called out to quell riots. In the USA colonial militias dated from before independence and were the nucleus of US forces in the War of Independence and later in the Civil War. In Britain they became the Territorial Army before 1914 and in the USA they became the National Guard in 1916, though still organized on a state basis. Countries with a tradition of conscription do not have militias or, to put it differently, all males who have completed their military service are part of the reserves and can be used in the same way as militias. For example, in Switzerland they report for training annually until they are 50 and are organized to defend local targets in case of invasion.

millenarianism A set of beliefs in some miraculous future event that will deliver us from present oppression and misfortune. Millenarial or 'chiliastic' movements are likely to arise in times of great upheaval such as WAR and industrialization. They may thus be associated with political radicalism and the overthrow of the regime in power. Christian millenarianism, professed by the Anabaptists in the sixteenth century or Jehovah's Witnesses today, asserted that, after the rise of anti-Christ, Christ would come again and rule for a thousand years. The Pacific islanders' cargo cults believed boat- or plane-loads of riches would arrive if they built models of the transport. Much millenarianism is a rejection of politics: salvation will arrive when the time comes and the present world is not worth dealing with.
See also MYTH; REVOLUTIONS.

Reading
Sandress, E.R. 1970. *The Roots of Fundamentalism: British and American Millenarians, 1800–1930.* Chicago: Chicago University Press.

mind-sets *See* IDEOLOGY.

minister The political head of a government department. In some systems there are senior and junior ministers with only the former being allowed in the inner circle of higher decision-making, or cabinet. In the USA heads of departments, more administrators than politicians, are called 'secretaries'. Because government functions have

everywhere expanded there has been in recent years a considerable increase in the number of ministers, thus adding to the problem of GOVERNABILITY.

Reading
Blondel, J. 1985. *Government Ministers in the Contemporary World.* London: Sage.

ministry The term has two meanings, the most common being a description of a government DEPARTMENT. A more old-fashioned usage is a synonym for 'government' as in, for example, 'the Thatcher ministries 1979–90'.

minorities The connotation of this term is more socio-political than numerical. Women, for example, are in a majority yet not infrequently they are referred to with other minorities, such as recent immigrants, blacks and 'gays'. This is because a minority has come to mean a socially disadvantaged group. Ethnic minorities may need legislative protection from racial attacks or given privileges by policies of POSITIVE DISCRIMINATION. Some minority groups are well organized and campaign vociferously, so raising their public profile. This activity and responses to it give rise to 'minority politics'.
See also CIVIL LIBERTIES; ETHNICITY; FEMINISM; GAY POLITICS; ISSUE POLITICS.

Reading
Horowitz, D.L. 1985. *Ethnic Groups in Conflict.* Berkeley: University of California Press; Laponce, J.A. 1984. *Langue et Territoire.* Quebec: Presses de l'Université Laval; Van Dyke, V. 1985. *Human Rights, Ethnicity and Discrimination.* London: Greenwood.

minority government A government supported by less than half the legislature under parliamentary government. Unsurprisingly such governments tend to be unstable and less effective than majority governments. If they are also COALITION GOVERNMENTS they are even more unstable. Minority governments were a

feature of the Weimar Republic (1919–33) and the French Fourth Republic (1946–58), both classical examples of governmental instability. Minority governments have also occurred in Denmark, Italy, Canada and Ireland among others. They are very uncommon in Britain because of the FIRST-PAST-THE-POST electoral sytem.
See also COALITION GOVERNMENT.

Reading
Lijphart, A. 1984. *Democracies: Patterns of Majoritarian and Consensus Government in Twenty-One Countries*. New Haven: YUP.

minority leader *See* MAJORITY LEADER.

mixed government The earliest proponent of this concept was Aristotle who based it on his love of moderation, most often found among the MIDDLE CLASS. He concluded that 'the middle type of constitution is clearly best'. Polybius (205–125BC) transformed Aristotle's balance of classes into a theory of power, stabilized by CHECKS AND BALANCES. This was continued by Montesquieu (1689–1755) in his interpretation of British stability as based on the SEPARATION OF POWERS. After the Glorious Revolution of 1688–9 in Britain the idea that the constitution was a happy balance of monarchy, ARISTOCRACY and DEMOCRACY came under attack from the doctrine of popular sovereignty. Yet the view that power should be balanced by power so that no one and no group or institution should be too powerful remains an important part of political thinking.

Reading
Fritz, K. von. 1954. *The Theory of the Mixed Constitution in Antiquity*. New York: Columbia University Press.

mob Fear of 'the mob' became a preoccupation of the middle classes after the French Revolution. The theory of mob psychology was put forward first by the French sociologist, LE BON. He believed that a crowd was a collection of people. They became a mob when stimulated to collective action. Then they lost their individual capacity to think and make moral judgements and obeyed the will of emotional DEMAGOGUES. Although a mob is different from a mass – a more extensive societal category – there are connections between the idea of the mob and that of MASS SOCIETY. Both have little regard for the will and rational capacity of the individual citizen.
See also MASS SOCIETY; REVOLUTIONS.

Reading
Le Bon, G. [1895] 1960. *The Crowd: a Study of the Popular Mind*. New York: Viking; Rudé, G. 1967. *The Crowd in the French Revolution*. Oxford: OUP.

mobility Geographical and social movement are common features of modern society. They both have an impact on political life. Migration from one part of a country to another will affect the demographic pattern of the electorate as well as raising political issues such as housing policy. IMMIGRATION into a country has everywhere led to social problems – immigrants often (though by no means always) become deprived groups – and to the rise of political parties and PRESSURE GROUPS opposed to the spread of MULTICULTURALISM. Social mobility can be both upward and downward. It can happen within an individual's lifetime but social science research has usually concentrated on comparing people's social and economic position with that of their parents. In the late twentieth century social mobility has been largely upward owing to the improvement of living standards and the decline in the proportion of blue-collar occupations. These trends are often adduced as the major reason for the decline of left-wing thinking among voters in most of the democracies. 'Political mobility' also has occurred.

See also DEALIGNMENT; LIFESTYLE; MULTI-CULTURALISM; SOCIAL CLASS.

Reading
Mach, B. and W. Wesolowski. 1986. *Social Mobility and Social Structure*. London: Routledge.

mobilization Political mobilization is the activity of rousing masses of people, both to express themselves politically and also to undertake political action. In a totalitarian system it will be the duty of the party to exhort the MASSES, for example, to vote at elections for the party candidate, the single contestant. Coercion may well be applied. In democratic regimes leaders compete in rousing both the electorate and volunteers in local party organizations in order to get supporters, known to them as a result of CANVASSING, to go to the polls on election day. The campaign generally will have a mobilizing effect because of extensive coverage in the press and on the television screens.

See also CAMPAIGNING; CANVASSING; MASS POLITICS.

model A model in the social sciences is a general sketch of the main features of some social phenomenon. It tries to explain these features and the pattern of their relationships with one another. WEBER'S IDEAL TYPE is of this genre. It is a model, simplifying reality, against which actual examples can be placed for comparative purposes. Much more ambitious are predictive models. They are particularly used in economics because the different variables can be quantified.

In political science non-mathematical models can be used to verify hypotheses about the relations between different phenomena. Structural-functional analysis, the attempt to understand a political system by relating its structures and functions, presupposes an interdependence between these entities.

Easton's model of the political system is the best-known example of this type of analysis. As with many of these models, it assumes that the major motive of the system is survival. Inputs and outputs of the system represent supports for it and demands upon it. If its supports cannot cope with its demands the system may fail. Outside the boundaries of the political system is its environment – social, economic and international. Several objections can be raised to this and other similar models. For example, they are so general that all examples in the real world have some elements of deviation for which the model has no answer. It is useful for studying system survival but political scientists have more interesting questions about most political systems than 'How does it manage to survive?'

See also GAME THEORY.

Reading
Blalock, H.M. ed. 1985. *Causal Models in Experimental and Panel Designs*. Chicago: Aldine; Easton, D. 1965. *A Framework for Political Analysis*. Englewood Cliffs: Prentice Hall; Jones, R.E. 1967. *The Functional Analysis of Politics*. London: Routledge.

mode of production The way a society is organized to produce goods and services. Marxist theory perceives the factors of production – land, labour and capital – allied to the means of production – tools, machinery and organization. The relations of production, however, between people and the means of production and especially between employers and the workers, are the important distinctive characteristic of any mode of production. This will vary at different stages of history.

See also CAPITALISM; CLASS CONFLICT; CLASS CONSCIOUSNESS; FEUDALISM; FORDISM; MARXISM; POST-FORDISM; SOCIALISM.

Reading
Marx, K. [1867] 1960. *Capital: a Critique of Political Economy*. New York: International Publishers.

modernization   A term borrowed from sociology describing the process by which primitive societies evolve into modern industrialized societies, becoming more differentiated and complex in their social structure. When applied to political life the process is one of chieftain rule, evolving through a transitional stage of upheaval into one in which bureaucracies are formed, institutions developed and nation-states built. There is much academic controversy about the thesis which is grounded in western social and political theorists such as MARX and WEBER. Critics ask, 'Is there any reason why the non-industrialized world should develop in this way and is there much evidence to suggest that it is?' It has been argued that it is a form of western 'intellectual imperialism' in alliance with global CAPITALISM.
See also DEPENDENCY; DEVELOPMENT; POST-MODERNISM.

Reading
Ake, C. 1979. *Social Science as Imperialism: the Theory of Political Development.* Ibadan: Ibadan University Press; Almond, G.A. and G.B. Powell. 1982. *Comparative Politics: a Developmental Approach.* Boston, Mass.: Little, Brown; Apter, D. E. 1965. *The Politics of Modernization.* Chicago: University of Chicago Press; Huntington, S.P. 1968. *Political Order in Changing Societies.* New Haven: YUP.

monarchism   The belief that monarchy is a necessary and desirable part of a country's life, supplying a 'dignified element' (as BAGEHOT put it) that an elected president cannot emulate. A hereditary ruler, monarchists argue, embodies the tradition of the nation. In the twentieth century monarchism has become much weaker as the supporters of restoring the dynasties have declined in numbers, in France, Italy and Greece for instance, though they have had a success with the restoration of the Spanish monarchy in 1975 after a lapse of over 40 years. In some countries in post-Communist Europe there are also small but clamorous groups urging restoration. Where CONSTITUTIONAL MONARCHY has survived, the argument for maintaining the institution is usually functional. Monarchs are non-political and succeed automatically, whereas presidents might well be interfering politicians and their elections divide the nation.
See also CONSTITUTIONAL MONARCHY.

monarchy   *See* HEADS OF STATE; KINGSHIP.

monetarism   The economic doctrine that the quantity of money determines the price level. First posited by the classical economists, it was revived in the 1950s by Milton Friedman and the Chicago school. Their central point was that in order to stem inflationary tendencies the money supply must be controlled. The 'monetarists', conscious opponents of the prevailing Keynesianism which perceived government intervention as necessary to stimulate the private sector, argued that if private enterprise was left alone the economy would be healthy, while government intervention was destabilizing and inflationary. Thus monetarism was seen as much more than controlling the money supply. Politically the term came to imply free market economics and all those policies associated with the Reagan and Thatcher administrations such as privatization, lower taxation and legislation directed against trade unions. Ironically, it was Denis Healey, a Labour Chancellor of the Exchequer, who first began to control the money supply in 1976 while in the 1980s the Thatcher government relaxed the policy because it found it impossible to implement in practice. Other policies were then adopted to control inflation.
See also INFLATION; KEYNESIANISM; SUPPLY-SIDE ECONOMICS.

Reading

Cuthbertson, K. 1979. *Macroeconomic Policy: the New Cambridge, Keynesian and Monetarist Controversies.* London: Macmillan; Smith, D. 1987. *The Rise and Fall of Monetarism.* Harmondsworth: Penguin; Woolley, J.T. 1984. *Monetary Politics: the Federal Reserve and the Politics of Monetary Policy.* Cambridge: CUP.

monopoly capitalism   The latest stage of CAPITALISM in which, as prophesied by MARX, smaller enterprises would be forced to amalgamate. In the twentieth century this prediction was supplemented by the theory of oligopoly. This depicted large enterprises controlling the prices and quantities of their production and so dominating large sections of markets. They did this by colluding with their rivals and so subverting competition. Neo-Marxists argued governments were forced to deal with the monopolists and probably preferred to do so. Thus monopoly capitalism became involved with CORPORATISM. Economic and political power were linked in alliance in the repressive capitalist state.

See also CAPITALISM; CORPORATIONS; CORPORATISM; MULTINATIONALS.

Reading

Baran, P.A. and P.M. Sweezy. 1966. *Monopoly Capital.* Harmondsworth: Penguin.

moral majority   A term coined in the USA in the 1970s to describe right-wing fundamentalist religious groups who were hostile to various tendencies and wanted them made illegal. The issues of abortion and homosexuality were prominent on their agendas. They also wanted school prayer made compulsory and divorce made more difficult. The main thrust for these changes came from the strong puritan element, mainly Baptist, in the South, though revivalist Christianity had spread throughout the nation, especially to the west. On many 'family' issues they joined forces with the Roman Catholic church and the whole movement was tinged with hostility to the 'evil empire', President Reagan's phrase for Communism. The emergence of popular evangelical speakers on radio and television, with a political as well as religious message, helped to weld the forces together. In 1979 they formed a pressure group which they called Moral Majority. Although it changed its name in 1986 to Liberty Federation this section of the NEW RIGHT was still often called by its old name.

See also NEW RIGHT.

multiculturalism   The term reflects the effort in many countries to reconcile the differences between the majority culture and the cultures of various disparate minority groups. In the USA, where the problem first arose on a large scale, the political parties and some pressure groups have attempted to float the idea that one type of 'hyphenated American' is as good as another. They are all Americans and, the argument goes, the nation should glory in its diversity, not perceive it as a cause for conflict. Similar sentiments have been advanced in Britain and France, two countries with many diverse groups. At the 1997 conference of the British Conservative Party multiculturalism was attacked by Lord Tebbit, a senior member of the party. William Hague, the party leader, rejected the criticism by asserting that the Conservative Party intended to appeal to people of all cultures.

multi-ethnic politics   The main cultural differences are usually the result of ethnic differences, although language and religion may be contributory factors. The response of politicians of the majority group has been twofold. In order to placate their constituencies they have legislated to restrict entry of further members of minority groups. At the same time they have introduced measures to protect minorities from discrimination and prejudice.

multilateralism Originally coined as the opposite of UNILATERALISM, the term first meant a belief that disarmament, especially nuclear DISARMAMENT, could only become reality when all the countries involved were prepared to negotiate it. More recently the term has been applied to all international issues needing negotiations on a world scale. The General Agreement on Tariffs and Trade (GATT) is a noteworthy example of multi-lateral bargaining and compromise. Global warming and the sea bed are other topics receiving the same treatment. Often multilateral agreements are preceded by preliminary agreement between the major powers.

See also DISARMAMENT; UNILATERALISM.

Reading
Gilpin. R. 1988. *The Political Economy of International Relations*. Princeton: Princeton University Press.

multi-nation state An expression denoting a state whose borders contain several nations. When understood, it helps to distinguish between the NATION and the STATE. It is not necessarily the same as a multilingual state. Switzerland has four official languages, but none of the language groups to any marked degree claims to be a nation. On the other hand Britain has four nations (though there is some dispute about whether the English are a nation) but all predominantly use one language, English. This raises the question of whether the British are a 'super-nation'.

See also NATION; NATIONALITY; NATION-STATE; STATE.

multinationals The shorthand for 'multinational corporations' (MNCs), large enterprises operating simultaneously in several countries. They are also known as 'transnationals'. At one time known as 'international trusts', they date from the 1890s but from the 1970s onwards MNCs expanded in size and numbers and became much more active,

the result of the freeing of trade barriers and the growth of the global economy. Nationalists often condemn them because they are subversive of national cultures and, more importantly, subversive of national SOVEREIGNTY. TRADE UNIONS have been especially critical of them because of their flexibility, enabling them to move quickly to low-wage economies in pursuit of lower costs, so avoiding minimum wage legislation. This provides an argument for those favouring international organization. In 1990 the European Union in its Company Statute has tried to control their activities but it cannot easily prevent them moving elsewhere. Socialists perceive them as instruments of global capitalism.

See also CAPITALISM; CORPORATIONS; GLOBALIZATION; MONOPOLY CAPITALISM.

Reading
Gilpin, R. 1976. *US Power and the Multinational Corporation*. London: Macmillan; Mytelka, L. ed. 1991. *Strategic Partnerships: States, Firms and International Competition*. London: Pinter; Sampson, A. 1975. *The Seven Sisters*. London: Hodder and Stoughton.

multiparty systems The term can be misleading because it is not used to mean a situation where there are several political parties, the normality in any democracy. It refers to the position where there are more than two parties in the legislature and none of them has enough representation to form a single-party government. In multiparty systems CO-ALITION GOVERNMENT is almost inevitable. Bargaining between parties to form a majority government may take a long time. In Holland there have been cases of five months elapsing between an election and the formation of a new government. One result is that voters cannot feel that they are choosing a government at election time. There is a close connection between multiparty systems and Proportional Representation which gives more seats proportionately to

smaller parties. But the relationship is not entirely dependent on ELECTORAL SYSTEMS. Sweden, with PR, has sometimes had MAJORITY PARTY GOVERNMENT, while Canada with FIRST-PAST-THE-POST has sometimes had coalition government. The nature and number of CLEAVAGES, both ideological and socio-cultural, within a country is an important factor in determining the number of parties and will also affect their propensity to coalesce with one another.
See also COALITION GOVERNMENT; ELEC-TORAL SYSTEMS; TWO-PARTY SYSTEMS.

Reading
Duverger, M. 1954. *Political Parties*. London: Methuen; Sartori, G. 1976. *Parties and Party Systems*. Cambridge: CUP.

mutually assured destruction   The name given to the US nuclear defence policy, introduced by Robert Mac-namara, Defence Secretary to President Kennedy (1961–3). It refers to a situation where both contending powers are so well armed that any damage, however great, that one expects to inflict on the other can never be vast enough for the other not to have preserved enough nuclear capability to strike back. The concept, known as MAD, was a consequence of the USSR beginning to achieve nuclear parity with the USA. The essence of this theory of DETERRENCE was that each country should have the nuclear capacity for a 'second strike' with enough destructive power to prevent a FIRST STRIKE.
See also DETERRENCE; FIRST STRIKE.

Reading
Rotberg, R.I. and T.K. Rabb. eds. 1989. *The Origin and Prevention of Major Wars*. Cambridge: CUP.

myth   A popular misleading belief given uncritical acceptance. Religions may be based on sacred myths. In politics myths have been used to support a feeling of identity in movements, parties and nations. Heroic figures and heroic epi-sodes such as wars may provide a mythological basis of legitimation. In a more trivial way a tabloid newspaper with a snappy headline may give an erro-neous impression about a politician or political action which comes to be accepted as reality. For example, in Britain during the long strikes of 1978–9, some remarks of Prime Minister Callaghan intended to reduce the alarm, were headlined by the *Sun* as 'CRISIS! WOT CRISIS?' He never said this, but it is widely believed he did.

N

nation   A body of people who possess the consciousness of a common identity, giving them a distinctiveness from other peoples. Hence 'togetherness' and 'separateness' are important parts of national consciousness. This consciousness will be based upon common historical experiences (which may be partly based on MYTH), and other shared features such as geographical propinquity and a common culture including a literature and a language. As with all feelings, that of belonging to a nation is bound to be relative. Different nations may be encompassed within the boundaries of states. For a century and a quarter there was no Poland – it had been partitioned – but the Polish nation remained. Some Jews did not identify with ZIONISM but in 1948 the state of Israel came into being. Sometimes the expression of nationhood may lead to statehood and, conversely, the foundation of a state based on nation is likely to strengthen national feeling.

See also ETHNICITY; NATIONALISM; NATION-STATE; ZIONISM.

Reading

Armstrong, J.A. 1982. *Nations Before Nationalism*. Chapel Hill: University of North Carolina Press; Hobsbawm, E. 1990. *Nations and Nationalism Since* 1988. Cambridge: CUP; Smith, A. 1986. *The Ethnic Origins of Nations*. Oxford: OUP.

nationalism   A conscious assertion of the NATION in terms differing from patriotism – mere love of country. Nationalists have aims and programmes going beyond a belief that one should pay one's taxes or rally to the colours when the motherland is attacked. Yet nationalism takes different forms. Its intensity basically depends on the distance or separateness felt towards other national groupings. How much are they liked, tolerated or hated? (Extreme nationalism is often called 'chauvinism'.) Its form of expression depends on the historical, political and territorial context.

Historically nationalism scarcely existed among rural, pre-industrial societies. GELLNER argues convincingly that nationalism arose with public education, literacy, national conscription, bureaucracy, centralization and industrialism. It is a feature of 'modern times', though with improved communication it may be taken up by non-industrial ethnic groups. Hence the rise of nationalism in subject nations; first in nineteenth-century Europe and then in twentieth-century colonial empires. Colonial nationalism was a desire for emancipation from the imperial power and so post-colonial states often maintained the same borders as former

colonial territories. Thus Indian nationalism (even after the former colonial territory was split into two to make way for Pakistan), was composed of numerous ethnic groups with different cultures, religions and languages. Unsurprisingly, nationalist movements have since arisen among Sikhs, Assamese hill peoples and others. Irredentist nationalism arises where an ethnic group that has achieved statehood wishes to incorporate other members of the group left outside its borders. Nations not given to nationalist expression may be capable of it when they feel threatened. Danish and British nationalists campaign against incorporation in a 'European superstate'. Internationalism stresses the common humanity of peoples and nationalism emphasizes their differences.
See also COLONIALISM; IRREDENTISM; MULTI-NATION STATE; NATION; NATION-STATE; STATE.

Reading
Breuilly, J. 1982. *Nationalism and the State*. Manchester: Manchester University Press; Gellner, E. 1983. *Nations and Nationalism*. Oxford: Blackwell; Kedourie, E. 1966. *Nationalism*. London: Hutchinson; Seton-Watson, H. 1977. *Nations and States*. London: Methuen; Smith, A. 1983. *Theories of Nationalism*. London: Duckworth.

nationality A legal concept usually determined by one's country of birth. Sometimes nationality may be conferred by marriage. Dual nationality, the possession of two passports, is becoming more common. Only two countries, Germany and Israel, confer nationality or refuse it on the basis of ethnicity.

nation-building *See* CENTRE-PERIPHERY RELATIONS.

nation-state The combination of two concepts. The NATION is historical and cultural, the STATE is defined by territory and coercive power. Specialists in international relations see the nation-state as their unit of study. To international lawyers the 'international system' is a world of equal sovereign entities. Yet very few nation-states satisfy the ideal-type of one nation within one set of borders. Members of the United Nations are *states*, some of them striving unsuccessfully to be nation-states. Some states like Belgium and Canada have deep ethnic cleavages. This may be even more marked with ex-colonial states where ruling elites, in their efforts to forge nations from multi-ethnic communities, may have badly destabilized their countries. Even in the earliest nation-states such as Britain and Spain there are distinct nations. Some observers claim the nation-state is in decline and will be replaced by international confederations.
See also NATION; NATIONALISM; STATE.

Reading
Akzim, B. 1964. *State and Nation*. London: Hutchinson; Mayall, J.B. ed. 1982. *The Community of States*. London: Allen and Unwin; Tivey, L. ed. 1980. *The Nation-State*. Oxford: Martin Robertson.

national interest *See* PUBLIC INTEREST.

national socialism Often abbreviated as Nazism, the term is derived from the ideas of the *Nationalsozialistische Deutsche Arbeiterpartei*, a tiny party discovered by Adolf Hitler (1889–1945) when, before demobilization in 1919, he was employed in investigating subversive groups in Munich. He was attracted to its vague policies – a mixture of SOCIALISM, immigration control and saving Germany from party politics and Bolshevism – and joined it as 'No. 7'. He soon became chairman and, as a result of a series of rallies and speeches, increased its membership to 3000 by 1921. Impressed by the success of Mussolini's March on Rome, Hitler tried to seize power in Munich with a PUTSCH in November 1923. Sixteen Nazis were shot dead and

Hitler was arrested, spending the next nine months in prison.

In prison he wrote *Mein Kampf* which, though a turgid 'stream of consciousness', contains the conspectus of Nazi policies. Much was reminiscent of Italian FASCISM. What was different was the form of Nazi ELITISM, based on RACISM, which was pursued with much enthusiasm in Italy. Although Hitler had not read Nietzsche (1844–1900), the idea of the Superman was widely known. Hitler advanced the theory of the 'master race', the Aryan people destined to rule the world. Underneath them was a descending hierarchy of races with the Jews at the bottom. In his years before 1914, in cosmopolitan Vienna, Hitler had developed a hatred of the multi-ethnic Habsburg Empire. His first sight of a Jew led him to buy anti-Semitic works from which he learnt of Jewish control of crime, culture, socialism and CAPITALISM and their stated aim in the *Protocols of the Elders of Zion* (a forgery dating from 1905) of dominating the world. Other peoples deserving contempt were Africans, gypsies and Slavs. They were incapable of higher thought and ought to be enslaved. Nazi racism was developed by Alfred Rosenberg, its arch-priest of doctrine, in his *Myth of the Twentieth Century* (1930). He contended that only races had 'souls'. God had created races and miscegenation, which destroyed racial personality, was a sin. Physical features were the outward sign of race. The Aryan race, to which Germans belonged, was blonde and blue-eyed. Hence German domination of the world would produce a New Order, a higher form of life.

See also FASCISM; TOTALITARIANISM; XENO-PHOBIA.

Reading

Hitler, A. 1939. *Mein Kampf* (unexpurgated translation). London: Hurst and Blackett; Mosse, G. 1966. *The Crisis of German Ideology: Intellectual Origins of the Third Reich.* London: Weidenfeld; Noakes, J. and G. Pridham.

1986. *Nazism 1919–1945.* 3 vols. Exeter: Exeter University Press; Viereck, P. 1965. *Metapolitics: the Roots of the Nazi Mind.* New York: Capricorn.

nationalization The key policy of many socialist parties, consisting of the transfer of privately owned enterprise to the public sector. Its origins are Marxist, 'the expropriation of the expropriators', and only in Communist countries has most private ownership been abolished. Elsewhere public ownership to a much lesser degree has been common.

Several arguments are advanced in its favour. For example, there are some industries which are natural monopolies because of the heavy social costs of competition. This applies to public utilities like gas, water and electricity where units can be metred and the installations of competing firms would be difficult to inspect and dangerous to society. A similar reason persuaded the US government to nationalize part of its railway network – Amtrak. It feared all the railways might disappear: they were uncompetitive with the road network, but there were environmental arguments against expanding the road programme as well as social benefits from preserving passenger transport. Again there were industries, like British coal-mining, in which industrial relations were so bad that it was felt that a national asset, as coal was in 1947, was best exploited by a monopoly public enterprise. Finally there were those who feared the political power of large-scale industry and finance and believed it was inimical to left-wing governments. Therefore the latter must seize 'the commanding heights of the economy'. This attitude characterized much post-war nationalization, especially in Italy and France, where part of the car industry was nationalized, and in Britain where it led to the disastrous nationalization of the iron and steel industry.

Argument also raged around the organization and administration of nationalized enterprise. Early British socialists proceeded on the model of the Post Office, a highly successful operation. Thus each industry would be a government department, subject to questions in Parliament about its detailed running. When the London Passenger Transport Board adopted the structure of the public corporation in 1933, however, it became a model for further nationalization. Nationalized enterprise after 1945 was only accountable to Parliament for general policy and the day-to-day administration was left to professional management. Since the 1970s nationalization has fallen out of favour and PRIVATIZATION has become conventional wisdom's choice for industrial policy pundits.

See also CORPORATIONS; MONOPOLY CAPITALISM; PRIVATIZATION; PUBLIC CORPORATION; SOCIALISM.

Reading
Chester, N. 1975. *The Nationalization of British Industry 1949–1951*. London: HMSO; Hanson, A.H. ed. 1963. *Nationalization*. London: Allen and Unwin; Morrison, H. 1933. *Socialism and Transport*. London: Constable.

natural law   *See* LAW.

natural rights   Rights attributable to people by natural law, or by nature. They are possessed by everyone irrespective of location or period. They are not the same as rights attributable by 'natural justice', a lawyer's concept, though they are often spoken of in the same absolute sense. These are procedural rights in a legal system: what in the USA is called DUE PROCESS OF LAW. Bentham (1748–1832) said inalienable natural rights were 'nonsense upon stilts', by which he meant that one could not envisage rights without corresponding duties. Moreover, rights could only be guaranteed by courts, judicial processes and force to back them up. Hence the only rights worth having were legal rights or 'positive rights'. Numerous declarations of FUNDAMENTAL RIGHTS or human rights in the past and present show that Bentham's view has not always been accepted.

See also BILL OF RIGHTS; CIVIL LIBERTIES; DUE PROCESS OF LAW; FUNDAMENTAL RIGHTS; LAW; LIBERALISM.

nazism   *See*   FASCISM;   NATIONAL SOCIALISM.

neo-colonialism   A term used to describe the post-colonial situation in which, it is argued, the former colonial powers still dominate their former colonies. They do this economically because of their control of the markets in which the ex-colonies need to sell their goods and in which the latter (new states with a much lower standard of living) need to buy the technological products only made by the former colonial powers. Political control also takes place as a result of constant interference by the former colonial powers in the affairs of the THIRD WORLD. It is not difficult to point to many instances of American intervention, both open and secret, in the Third World in order to prop up discredited right-wing rulers who are compliant with the aims of American government diplomacy and – either incidentally or deliberately – the needs of the big corporations. The basis of this theory was first spelt out by Kwame Nkrumah, first president of independent Ghana.

See also COLONIALISM; DEPENDENCY; IMPERIALISM.

Reading
Nkrumah, K. 1965. *Neo-Colonialism: the Last Stage of Capitalism*. London: Nelson.

neo-corporatism   *See* CORPORATISM.

networks   The linkages between people in communities and organizations. 'Networking' is a skill in developing a pattern of human relationships. Political scientists have found the study of networks useful in identifying

structures of power within local communities. Within society at large and within the nation the significant factor may be the linkages between different organization though, again, these will be conducted by individuals. The approach is helpful in understanding the nature of power. For example, networks provide channels of information, both in small and large communities, without which people may be powerless. People in networks are thus strategically placed to exert power and people at the centre of networks may be said to have 'pivotal power' or 'strategic power'. This assumes that where one is and what one knows are the factors determining power possession. It places no emphasis on the uniqueness of power-holders.
See also COMMUNICATIONS; POLITICAL POWER.

Reading
Marsden P.V. and N. Lin. eds. 1982. *Social Structure and Network Analysis*. Beverly Hills: Sage.

neutralism A policy of non-involvement in power struggles between states, especially large states. It is almost a state of mind. Many THIRD WORLD countries took up a neutralist position during the COLD WAR. Its end in 1990 made the policy less relevant.
See also COLD WAR; NEUTRALITY; NON-ALIGNMENT.

neutrality This differs from NEUTRALISM in that it is a legal position in a situation of 'hot war'. Neutral states can under INTERNATIONAL LAW claim rights which warring states should respect.
See also INTERNATIONAL LAW; NEUTRALISM.

new class The title of a book by Yugoslav dissident, Milovan Djilas. His argument was that a distinct class system existed in Communist society based on the hierarchical structure of the Communist Party. The 'new class' were the APPARATCHIKS at the top who were in a

position to manipulate everyone else's social position and to award themselves and their families special privileges. Hence, in spite of the abolition of CAPITALISM and large aggregations of private property, there was no EGALITARIANISM under COMMUNISM. Djilas's analysis refuted the Marxist theory of social classes based on relations to the means of production. Instead it suggested that class was based on political power.
See also CLASS; POLITICAL CLASS; SOCIAL CLASS.

Reading
Djilas, M. 1957. *The New Class*. London: Thames and Hudson.

new left A general term applied to a political tendency rather than an organization. It dates from the late 1950s when the monolithic Soviet state and international Communism were shaken by the revelations of Khrushchev about Stalin's dictatorship. The Civil Rights movement in America, the suppression of the Hungarian Revolution by Russian troops, the campaign for nuclear disarmament and the Cuban Revolution all contributed to the new left tendency in both Europe and America.

The first use of the term seems to have been the foundation of the *New Left Review* by former Communist intellectuals, such as Edward Thompson and Raymond Williams, who had resigned from the party after Hungary in 1956. They joined with a younger generation who had discovered the early philosophic, more humanitarian, writings of MARX (only recently translated) and the Prison Notebooks of Antonio Gramsci (1891–1937), a dissident Communist who died in one of Mussolini's gaols. Their attack on CAPITALISM stressed the ALIENATION of modern man and his failure to develop revolutionary consciousness because of the demoralizing effect of consumerism, advertising and the triviality of the media, particularly television. They did not see salvation coming from the Labour Party.

The American new left also drew inspiration from literary figures like Ginsberg and Kerouac. Some of them were impressed by the life and writings of romantic revolutionaries such as Che Guevara, others believed revolution would come from the UNDERCLASS, BLACK POWER, GAY POLITICS and radical students. American groups gathered in a convention in 1962 at Port Huron, sponsored by Students for a Democratic Society (SDS), and issued the Port Huron Statement recommending nuclear disarmament, university reform, the end of racial discrimination and the abolition of poverty.

By the late 1960s the movement had everywhere been fuelled by the lingering Vietnam War. The concept of participation was taken seriously as a way of transforming society and efforts were made to take it into the workplace, but their only partial success was in occasionally disrupting the life of the most liberal part of western society, the universities. The 'events of May 1968' in Paris, resulting in electoral victory for De Gaulle and the ending of the 'Prague Spring' by Russian invasion in August 1968 turned many to thoughts of violent revolution rather than demonstrations and 'sit-ins' but the lack of an organized party in any country rendered them ineffective. By the 1970s one result of their activities became apparent – a right BACKLASH.

See also ALIENATION; MARXISM; SOCIALISM.

Reading

Cranston, M. W. 1970. *The New Left*. London: Bodley Head; Gitlin, T. 1987. *The Sixties: Years of Hope, Days of Rage*. London: Bantam Books.

new right   Sometimes called 'neo-conservatives' and sometimes 'radical conservatives' the new right is a heterogeneous set of groups opposed to 'old' or 'moderate' CONSERVATISM. On one side,

fundamental conservativism is often associated with it: on the other, it takes its ideas from liberal classical economists and even flirts with LIBERTARIANISM. Historians may see its peak in the rules of Reagan (1981–9) and Thatcher (1979–90). Their rhetoric was radical though their actions were less ideological and more affected by electoral expediency.

Neo-conservatism was both a reaction against the post-war consensus about the relationship between the state and the economy and against the 'trendiness' of the permissive ideas of the 1960s. Some neo-conservatives argued that right-wing governments in the period 1930–70 had come to terms with the left in accepting the welfare state, a high rate of taxation to pay for it, public ownership of utilities which was stifling to entrepreneurial initiative, and too much economic policy made by bargaining between business, labour and public servants imbued with KEYNESIANISM. Other neo-conservatives argued that the problem was moral. SOCIALISM and CORPORATISM, leading to slackness and inflation, had sapped the will to deal with a crisis of authority so that stability of government, and even civilization, was threatened. An 'adversary culture' must be confronted and its representatives – scientists, teachers, journalists and social workers – put in their place. Punitive, rather than permissive, values should be asserted.

Theorists became unusually important to conservatives in their reaction against post-war consensus and the NEW LEFT. HAYEK (1898–1992) was the arch-priest of non-interference in economies by governments. His student Milton Friedman (1912–) became famous for his adage 'there is no such thing as a free lunch'. His main attack was on Keynesianism which he blamed for inflation. The free market and democracy were mutually dependent, he argued, as did Michael Novak (1933–) who added a moral dimension, asserting that individual economic choice was part of Christ's teaching. In the USA the religious right was a powerful element in the new right and the evangelical preacher, Jerry Falwell with his Moral Majority, were an important crusading force for Reagan. In 1992 another evangelist, Patrick Buchanan, strongly challenged the incumbent President, George Bush, for the Republican nomination. Finally, Robert Nozick (1938–), advocating a 'minimal state' which should do nothing but keep order and safeguard property, became guru of the 'libertarian conservatives'.

See also CONSERVATISM; CORPORATISM; INFLATION; KEYNESIANISM; WELFARE STATE.

Reading
Levitas, R. ed. 1986. *The Ideology of the New Right*. Oxford: Polity; Peele, G. 1984. *Revival and Reaction: the Right in Contemporary America*. Oxford: OUP.

new social movements A vague term which, nevertheless, has become generally accepted as an umbrella to cover a constellation of organizations operating in democratic states. The consequential style of politics has been called SINGLE ISSUE POLITICS: the ethos has been described as POST-MATERIALISM. In all democracies there are instances of ECOLOGICAL POLITICS, FEMINISM, GAY POLITICS, HUMAN RIGHTS organizations like Amnesty International and anti-nuclear movements. They are especially strong in Europe and North America and have all developed international organizations which, when they lobby the gatherings of representatives of states, are known as non-governmental organizations (NGOs). In Africa, Asia and Latin America (and in eastern Europe before 1989) they sometimes emerge as the only opponents of non-democratic rulers. They have also operated at the local level in the form of squatters' associations, peasant groups, human rights activists, protesters against new roads and airports or the bussing of school-children, and animal rights associations.

Whatever the issue or level of activity the new social movements represent a new type of politics. Occasionally they may, like European Green parties, seek legislative representation, but usually they operate through demonstrations, often of an unusually dramatic kind, and a skilful exploitation of television. For example, multinational groups such as Greenpeace are quite prepared to risk the sinking of their ships and other environmental protesters live in tunnels or trees to resist new development. They form alliances with local people of every social class, but their nucleus is one of young graduates who are imbued with 'post-material' values. Concern for humanity and the quality of life, *on an international scale*, is their common belief.

See also ECOLOGICAL POLITICS; FEMINISM; GAY POLITICS; POST-MATERIALISM; SINGLE ISSUE POLITICS.

Reading
Dalton, R. and M. Kuechler. eds. 1990. *Challenging the Political Order*. Cambridge: CUP; Mueller-Rommel, F. ed. 1989. *New Politics in Western Europe*. Boulder: University of Colorado Press.

nihilism A belief that society is so bad that only the destruction of all existing institutions can lead to anything better. Some nihilists reject all values and beliefs as meaningless. The term's origin was in a group of nineteenth-century Russian anarchists who believed TERRORISM and assassination were justified to achieve revolution.

nimby An acronym for 'not in my backyard'. A nimby believes in development as a general policy, but objects if it goes ahead near to his own property.

nomenklatura The system of filling posts in the Communist Party of the Soviet Union. There were about two million positions and appointments were

made by officials at higher levels from a list of candidates thought suitable because of their efficiency, reliability, and likely compliancy with the wishes and ambitions of some senior member of the party. It seems 'croneyism' was rife and bureaucratic networks of influence were common. The Central Committee's power over promotion extended to about 50,000 posts and the term is sometimes applied just to this ruling oligarchy.
See also APPARATCHIK; COMMUNISM.

Reading
Harasymiw, B. 1984. *Political Elite Recruitment in the Soviet Union.* London: Macmillan; Voslensky, M. 1984. *Nomenklatura: Anatomy of the Soviet Ruling Class.* London: Bodley Head.

nomination   The act of putting forward a CANDIDATE. In small groups it is usual to do this by someone proposing, and someone else seconding, the name of a person. For local and national ELECTIONS it is usual in the area for which the election is to be held for a number of voters, specified by law, to sign what in Britain are called 'nomination papers'. These are then scrutinized by an election official. Most candidates, however, are nominees of political parties and procedures differ as to how they are chosen. Usually a committee of the local party will select from a short list. In some countries and parties much larger gatherings, consisting of delegates from different parts of the constituency and affiliated bodies, may make the choice. In American PRIMARIES, party members decide who their candidate will be. An American party's Presidential candidates are chosen at a national nominating convention of the party. Most nominating processes are gruelling ordeals for the aspirants.

non-alignment   The position of those who remained allied to neither side in the COLD WAR. They were mostly African and Asian states who commanded a majority in the United Nations. In 1955 many of them met at Bandung and led by Nehru, the Indian Prime Minister, adopted policies of NEUTRALISM and working for DECOLONIZATION. At their first summit in Belgrade in 1961 they called themselves the Non-Aligned Movement. By 1989 they had about 100 members. The collapse of Communism, the end of the Cold War and regional conflicts to some extent resulting from it, have thrown non-alignment as a strategy into some disarray.
See also NEUTRALISM; NEUTRALITY; NON-INTERVENTION.

Reading
Singham, A.W. and S. Hune. 1986. *Non-alignment in an Age of Alignments.* Westport, Conn.: Lawrence Hill.

non-governmental organizations
See NEW SOCIAL MOVEMENTS.

non-intervention   A term used to describe a policy of not intervening in two fields. It may be used when not interfering in the running of the economy is advocated. It is also used when a state or group of states decides to avoid any entanglement in a war. For example, 'non-intervention' was the official attitude of Britain and France in the Spanish Civil War (1936–9).

non-proliferation   A policy of preventing the spread of nuclear weapons. It was hoped that the Non-Proliferation Treaty signed by Britain, the USA and the USSR in 1968 would have that effect although two powers known to be possessors, France and China, said they would not sign until 1992. They have both signed since. Israel, India and Pakistan have had nuclear capability for some time, and it is believed Iraq, Iran and North Korea may also have it. Hence non-proliferation may not be a viable international policy, especially as it becomes progressively easier to acquire nuclear capacity.

See also ARMS CONTROL; MULTILATERALISM; NUCLEAR PROLIFERATION; UNILATERALISM.

Reading
Spector, L.S. 1991. *Nuclear Threshold: the Spread of Nuclear Weapons*. Boulder: University of Colorado Press.

non-voters   *See* ABSTENTION.

norms   A confusing term used in several senses. The popular usage refers to normal practice. For example, it is the norm for people to get up in the morning and go to bed at night. A statistical norm refers to that which happens most often. To sociologists norms are a cultural phenomenon. They connect social behaviour with its consequences. Hence they have a regulatory effect. Different societies may have different norms and different patterns of non-conforming with norms. Finally KELSEN's legal theory envisaged law as a structure of norms: it contained assertions about proper and improper standards of behaviour. In political science normative judgements about political life are assessed by political theorists.

See also DISSENTERS; DISSIDENTS.

Reading
Gibbs, J.P. 1965. 'Norms: the problem of definition and classification'. *American Journal of Sociology* 70, 586–94.

nuclear parity   Something like equality between the nuclear capacities of the SUPERPOWERS was probably reached in the early 1980s as a result of Soviet nuclear expansion during the previous decade. The USA had more warheads, but the USSR had more launchers and missiles. In the terminology of the day the Russians had achieved 'nuclear parity'. This led to the re-thinking of NATO's overall strategy which had depended on American nuclear superiority balancing Soviet superiority in conventional weapons. In consequence negotiations began for a mutual reduction of non-nuclear arms, ending in 1990 in the signing of the Conventional Forces in Europe Treaty.

nuclear proliferation   The spread of nuclear technology and nuclear weapons. At one time when there was a nuclear ARMS RACE between the SUPERPOWERS vertical proliferation was the fear. Since the 1980s and agreement about limitation between the USA and the USSR, and especially since the end of the COLD WAR, horizontal proliferation – the acquisition of nuclear potential by states who were not formerly possessors – has been the major worry. It is feared those states most often involved in conventional war, who possess nuclear technology, may resort to nuclear aggression. It is likely to occur in such areas as the Middle East and the Indian sub-continent.

See also ARMS CONTROL; DETERRENCE; NON-PROLIFERATION.

Reading
Bobbitt, P., L. Freedman and G.F. Treverton. eds. 1989. *US Nuclear Strategy*. Basingstoke: Macmillan.

O

obligation Some would regard this term as synonymous with 'duties'. A duty is what we must do, or should feel we ought to do. But applied to the political context this raises more questions than it provides answers. The point about incurring an obligation is that it is made voluntarily and involves making a promise in a contract or treaty which includes a commitment. Hence political theorists have had problems in dealing with many political situations. Most of us are citizens of a state to which we have made no promise: we have been born in it. Thus philosophers such as LOCKE (1632–1704) devised a contract theory of tacit consent: he was concerned to defend the Glorious Revolution of 1688, which implied arguing that the pre-1688 government had broken its contract to its citizens. As the state had not kept its side of the obligation the citizens had no obligation to keep theirs. Later writers such as Hume (1711–76) thought a theory of obligation was not needed. Habit and expediency lead us to tolerate a reasonable and stable state.
See also CONTRACT; TOLERATION.

Reading
Hume, D. [1777] 1985. ed. E. Miller. *Essays Moral, Literary and Political.* Indianopolis: Liberty Classics; Locke, J. [1689] 1970. ed. P. Laslett. *Two Treatises on Government.* Cambridge: CUP.

oligarchy *See* ELITES.

oligopoly *See* MONOPOLY CAPITALISM.

ombudsman An office, first instituted in Sweden in 1809, set up to investigate citizen grievances. Most other countries who adopted it did so after 1945, including Denmark in 1954, Britain in 1967 and Australia in 1976. The institution enables a citizen who feels a victim of MALADMINISTRATION to make an official complaint and to have it investigated. Federal countries may have them at several levels and Britain has a local government ombudsman as well as banking and insurance ombudsmen. Their powers vary greatly. The Scandinavian ombudsmen are the most powerful, while the New Zealand ombudsman may investigate complaints of unreasonable actions by administrators. Germany has an ombudsman for the armed forces. Complaints to the British parliamentary ombudsman must be submitted in writing through a Member of Parliament. Ombudsmen's reports, usually transmitted through legislatures, do not have the force of law in any country. Hence they are not part of the judiciary. It is thus possible to exaggerate their powers.

See also ADMINISTRATION; ADMINISTRATIVE LAW; JUDICIARY.

Reading
Gregory, R. and P. Hutchesson. 1978. *The Parliamentary Ombudsman*. London: Allen and Unwin; Stacey, F. 1978. *Ombudsmen Compared*. London: Allen and Unwin.

one-party states Usually associated with some form of AUTHORITARIANISM, one-party rule may occur for long periods in democracies: for example, the Congress Party's dominance in India for years after independence. But a one-party state exists where only one party is politically tolerated and/or legally permitted.

All one-party states are characterized by a ruling elite which is determined to maintain national unity while pursuing controversial goals. The elite is convinced of the rightness of its policies and the wrongness of any opposition, especially organized opposition. In consequence the rulers of one-party states are people convinced of possessing knowledge making them superior to the masses. They are either ideologues, or members of an educated elite in a developing country: frequently they are both. The party is an instrument of their hegemony as well as of their revolutionary intentions. It has a variety of functions: mobilization for work, surveillance for security purposes, endoctrination to secure understanding of party purposes, and exhortation to revitalize.

Broadly there are two varieties of the one-party state. The classic form is the ideological party of the totalitarian state, either Fascist or Communist. Lenin (1870–1924) was the creator of both the concept and the organizational structure and Mussolini (1883–1945), the founder of the Italian Fascist Party, was aware he was imitating the Bolshevik original. Through the Communist International one-party domination was passed on to much of eastern Europe. Although this structure collapsed in 1989 it remains in Communist China and North Korea. The second type of one-party state can be found in newly independent countries of Africa and Asia, usually where a western-educated elite in a former colony is attempting to weld together a nation from among disparate peoples and mobilize them for modernization. Sometimes they are tinged with Marxism and sometimes they reflect the ideas of the leader as with 'Nkrumahism' in Ghana.

Conceivably one-party states are at an early stage of modernization and, in time, a more pluralistic society may evolve. The case of Mexico, dominated by the Institutionalized Party of the Revolution (PRI) since 1927 with its mixture of force, corruption and electoral fraud, may give some hope. In the 1980s it began to face pressures for change and opposition parties began to win elections. In Africa the example of South Africa, though hardly typical, may also encourage oppressed oppositions.

See also AUTHORITARIANISM; MARXISM; MILITARY REGIMES.

Reading
Clapham, C. 1986. *Third World Politics: an Introduction*. London: Croom Helm; Sartori, G. 1970. 'The Typology of Party Systems'. In *Mass Politics: Studies in Political Sociology*. Eds. Allardt, E. and S. Rokkan. New York: Free Press; Zolberg, A. 1966. *Creating Political Order: the Party States of West Africa*. Chicago: Rand McNally.

open government Government whose policy-making and decisions are open to inspection at any time. Access by citizens to government documents is total and not restricted by espionage laws, rules about confidentiality and the obstructions of officialdom. FREEDOM OF INFORMATION is merely part, though an important part, of this concept. Scandinavian countries and the USA are very 'open' systems, while Britain remains 'closed'.

See also FREEDOM OF INFORMATION.

Reading

Galnoor, I. 1977. *Government Secrecy in Democracies*. New York: Harper and Row.

open primaries   See PRIMARIES.

operationalize   An ugly term to describe the process by which a research hypothesis or project is actually carried out. When METHODOLOGY gives way to method.

opinion polls   Opinion polls are usually thought of as political opinion polls, yet they have been used to measure all aspects of opinion. Indeed, one of the ancestors of the political poll was the market research survey, dating from 1912 when advertising firms realized its potential. The other parent was the 'straw poll', an attempt by newspapers to predict election results by balloting their readers. In 1936 a straw poll by the *Literary Digest* before the US presidential election predicted a victory by Landon over Roosevelt, while the recently established Gallup and Roper Polls got the correct result. Since that time the 'polling industry' has grown throughout the democratic world and its claims, to be able to correctly predict the outcome of elections within + or −3 per cent, have been validated since 1945. In only two General Elections, 1970 and 1992, have the British polls failed. In each case the result was close.

Because it is alleged that opinion polls affect voters' choice – there is a 'bandwagon effect' favouring the predicted winners – many countries ban the publication of their results during election campaigns. The argument is that bandwagons are bad for democracy: voters should not be influenced by what other voters intend to do. On the other hand, it can be argued that all possible political information should be available at election time. Certainly where there are FIRST-PAST-THE-POST elections, as in Britain, constituency pre-election polls encourage TACTICAL VOTING.

See also SAMPLE SURVEYS; TACTICAL VOTING.

Reading

Worcester, R. ed. 1983. *Political Opinion Polling*. London: Macmillan.

opposition   Opposition is a normal condition of democratic politics. It takes several forms. First, there is the difference between individual opposition and collective organized opposition. Where there is FREEDOM OF EXPRESSION individuals may criticize the government in the press, at public meetings and over the air waves. Second, are opposition organizations which are likely to worry governments much more because they represent large numbers of voters. Organized opposition may come from inside or outside the legislature. From outside it is likely to be centred around PRESSURE GROUPS, each one concerned with a separate issue, but there may also be the organizing of demonstrations by opposition parties.

Within democratic legislatures the nature of opposition will depend on the political system and the configuration of the parties. Presidential government will differ from parliamentary government. In PRESIDENTIAL SYSTEMS like the USA the SEPARATION OF POWERS results in a popularly elected President with executive power and a popularly elected legislature in which anyone with an executive post is constitutionally prohibited from sitting. In no sense can Congress contain an alternative government and, consequently, the position of Leader of the Opposition does not exist in the USA. In PARLIAMENTARY SYSTEMS the opposition parties' representatives will be challenging the government in the legislature. In MULTIPARTY SYSTEMS COALITION GOVERNMENT is likely to succeed a defeated government which loses its majority. The oppositions will find it difficult to draw up coherent policies and a potential leader of a coalition may not always be clear. In TWO-PARTY SYSTEMS where a majority government is nearly always a single party, the second largest party contains the nucleus of an alternative government, in Britain known as the 'shadow cabinet'. Its leader since 1937 is in receipt of an official salary and is known as 'Leader of Her Majesty's Opposition'. As DAHL said, opposition in Britain is 'opposition with a capital O'.

See also COALITION GOVERNMENT; PARLIA-MENTARY SYSTEMS; PRESIDENTIAL SYSTEMS; TWO-PARTY SYSTEMS.

Reading
Dahl, R.A. ed. 1966. *Political Oppositions in Western Democracies*. New Haven: YUP; Ionescu, G. and I. de Madariaga. 1968. *Opposition: Past and Present of a Political Institution*. London: Watts; Kolinsky, E. ed. 1987. *Opposition in Western Europe*. London: Croom Helm.

organization theory The theory of formal organization which developed with the growth of large-scale enterprise and the need for study of the problems involved. The impetus at first was clearly the profit motive. The need for the best possible administrative and decision-making frameworks led to the study of management. Later Business and Management Studies became a discipline taught in universities. It has obvious links with the social sciences including political science. For example, decision-making in industry can be very similar to political decision-making. There are problems of communication, group behaviour and bureaucracy in all organizations and crisis management may offer help.

See also BUREAUCRACY; PUBLIC ADMINIS-TRATION.

Reading
Beer, S. 1966. *Decision and Control*. London: Wiley; Handy, C.B. 1987. *Understanding Organizations*. 3rd edn. Harmondsworth: Penguin; Perrow. C. 1979. *Complex Organisations*. 2nd edn. Glenview, Ill.: Scott, Foreman; Pugh, D.S. 1984. *Organization Theory*. 2nd edn. Harmondsworth: Penguin.

oriental despotism A concept mentioned by Montesquieu in his 'climatic typology'. MARX wrote of the Asiatic mode of production and this was taken up by Wittfogel who believed that oriental despotisms depended on planned irrigation projects. He called them 'hydraulic societies'. His book was banned in the USSR.

See also ABSOLUTISM.

Reading
Wittfogel, K. 1967. *Oriental Despotism*. New Haven: YUP.

overkill The threat of, or use of, more than necessary force. It is a term in the jargon of nuclear weaponry, applying to powers with enough capacity to destroy all enemies and, possibly, blow up the world.

overload *See* GOVERNABILITY.

P

pacificism   A position not so absolute as PACIFISM in that it allows the taking up of arms in certain circumstances. For example, pacificist Marxist war resisters believe it will be acceptable to fight in the international working-class revolution against CAPITALISM. Pacificists hate MILITARISM and national military training but accept that citizen militias and peasant guerrilla armies may be formed to combat evil regimes. Most pacificists in World War II joined up to fight FASCISM.

See also MILITARISM; PACIFISM.

pacifism   The belief that all wars are unacceptable. Pacifists refuse to participate in them though they may try to mitigate their consequences: for example by driving ambulances. Christian pacifists base their attitude on Christ's instruction to 'turn the other cheek'. Christian sects who entirely abstain from politics are pacifist and others, like the Quakers, believe the example of refusing to respond to attack will finally be accepted by all aggressors. Rational pacifists argue that no rational person can possibly descend to physical retaliation. In modern times Gandhi's philosophy of non-violence or 'passive resistance' has been adopted by many as an alternative to armed struggle.

Pacifism was greatly stimulated by the onset of 'total war' in which men were conscripted to fight. The horrors of World War I in which millions lost their lives gave rise to several pacifist movements like the Peace Pledge Union. The Marxist interpretation of war as a clash between imperialist capitalist powers also became quite popular. Many put their faith in the League of Nations as a force to prevent another war. After World War II the possibility of nuclear war reinvigorated the pacifist cause. The pacifist position was accepted by most democracies in terms of the right of conscientious objection to military service. Objectors were expected to undertake some form of public service in lieu of it.

See also JUST WAR; PASSIVE RESISTANCE; WAR.

Reading
Dungen, P. van. den. ed. 1985. *West European Pacifism and the Strategy for Peace*. London: Macmillan; Sharp, G. 1979. *Gandhi as a Political Strategist*. Boston, Mass.: Porter Sargent.

panachage   *See* ELECTORAL SYSTEMS.

panel   A sample of a population periodically questioned about its opinions. They may be either random or quota samples, or they may be volunteers, though this last type is much less reliable as a representative of what the population thinks. Panels are used especially by tele-

vision channels to test viewer reactions to programmes.
See also SAMPLE SURVEYS; SURVEY RESEARCH.

pantouflage From the French word meaning 'slippered' and therefore retired, this term refers to the practice of pensioned public servants moving into lucrative private-sector jobs on retirement. It is criticized because it is clearly open to corruption.

papal encyclicals Letters relating to doctrinal or moral matters issued by the Pope. They may contain exhortations, admonitions or commendations. The term was not in common use until the eighteenth century.
See also CLERICALISM/ANTI-CLERICALISM.

Reading
Fremantle, A. 1956. *The Papal Encyclicals.* New York: Mentor.

paradigm A set of assumptions about the field in which we are interested (for instance, political science), which implies certain questions and their answers. Political scientists are likely to ask questions about the workings of institutions and the nature of power and conflict.

paramilitaries Uniformed and armed forces who are not soldiers and not police, but somewhere in between. They may be full-time or part-time. Their functions go beyond normal police duties and are concerned with serious threats to law and order, such as unruly demonstrations and riots. In France the gendarmerie is a nation-wide paramilitary force. It could be argued the National Guard in the USA is a similar body, but it is used less frequently and is a part-time state militia, though subject to call-out by the President as well as the state governor. Britain raised the notorious Black and Tans, an auxiliary force which operated in Ireland between 1919 and Irish independence in 1922. Similar were the

B Specials in Northern Ireland, disbanded in 1972. Liberals everywhere dislike paramilitaries. Yet police and the public generally think ordinary police forces should not be involved in the sort of duties paramilitaries perform.

parastatals Publicly-owned enterprises formed to enhance the economic performance and quality of life of a nation. They are most common in the THIRD WORLD, especially in former colonial countries where governments after independence took over the assets of the former colonial power. This was likely to happen where governments held ideological objections to domestic enterprise being subject to foreign control and foreign investment decisions. The difficulty was that there was often an absence of the entrepreneurial skills necessary to make the parastatals profitable.
See also COLONIALISM; DEPENDENCY; MULTINATIONALS; NATIONALIZATION.

Reading
Nayar, B.R. 1991. 'Property Rights Theory and Government Efficiency: the Evidence from India's Public Sector'. *Development Policy Review* 9. 2, 131–50.

parish The smallest unit of local government. Historically in England they were ecclesiastic sub-divisions of bishoprics. Each parish had a priest. In the sixteenth century they became administrative units responsible for roads and the poor law. In 1894 elected Parish Councils, able to raise a tiny tax, were established. Parishes also exist in Ontario and Quebec.
See also COMMUNE.

parliamentary business What a parliament is doing and what it is scheduled to do. The latter can be obtained from its agenda. In the British House of Commons the business for the following week is communicated to the House every Thursday by the Leader of the House, a front-bench member of the Government.

parliamentary privilege In many LEGISLATURES members have immunities from the legal consequences of speeches made and acts committed while in the chamber. In the UK and Commonwealth countries legislators enjoy freedom from criminal or civil action for what is said or done in the course of debate or legislative proceedings. They cannot be subject to civil action for slander so that absolute freedom of speech exists. More controversial is the right to punish people for contempt of the legislature in speech or writing, or by defying its orders or those of its committees. This is rarely exercised today and is probably becoming obsolete.

parliamentary procedure The rules of a legislature which govern the conduct of PARLIAMENTARY BUSINESS, the proceedings of debate in the chamber and its committees, the details of PARLIAMENTARY PRIVILEGE, the length of sessions and hours of sitting, the apportionment of time between government business and other business and, especially, the passage of legislation.
See also LEGISLATURES.

Reading
Inter-Parliamentary Union. 1986. *Parliaments of the World*. 2 vols. Aldershot: Gower; Jennings, I. 1969. *Parliament*. 3rd edn. Cambridge: CUP.

parliamentary questions Put by a member of the legislature to a member of the executive in PARLIAMENTARY SYSTEMS, parliamentary questions are widely regarded as a way of making governments accountable. Much admired in conventional texts about the British constitution, question time became formalized in 1849. Since 1902 there can be written answers. It is now televised. Yet there are serious doubts about the usefulness of British parliamentary questions, either as a tool of ACCOUNTABILITY or even as a method of elucidating information. Many questions asked by government frontbenchers are designed to give ministers chances to praise their own activities. Prime Minister's questions, in particular, are a diverting gladiatorial joust between him and the Leader of the Opposition; but practised politicians usually have no difficulty in thinking of clever retorts which give little away.
See also ACCOUNTABILITY; INTERPELLATION.

Reading
Chester, N. 1981. 'Questions in the House'. In *The House of Commons in the Twentieth Century*. Ed. S.A. Walkland. Oxford: OUP.

parliamentary sovereignty A doctrine first developed by Blackstone in his *Commentaries on the Laws of England* (1770) and expounded by DICEY at the end of the nineteenth century. It states that parliament has unlimited authority: it cannot be overruled or have its laws set aside by the courts. It can make, or amend, any law. Clearly the doctrine cannot apply in federal systems where sub-governments have legislative rights. Nor can it apply to Britain because the law of the European Union since 1972 supersedes laws passed by the British Parliament. Hence it now only applies to New Zealand.

Reading
Dicey, A.V. [1885] 1959. *Introduction to the Study of the Law of the Constitution*. London: Macmillan; Jennings, W.I. 1933. *The Law and the Constitution*. London: University of London Press; Marshall, G. 1957. *Parliamentary Sovereignty and the Commonwealth*. Oxford: Clarendon.

parliamentary systems The opposite of PRESIDENTIAL SYSTEMS. In parliamentary systems there is responsible government which is not present in presidential systems. The touchstone is that in a parliamentary system the government, whose members are also members of the legislature, must resign or dissolve if it is defeated on a motion of confidence. There is thus no separation of executive and legislative powers as there is in presidential systems. Instead the executive and legislative powers are somewhat fused. This makes for strong government, though the strength of governments under parliamentary systems is largely dependent on PARTY SYSTEMS and ELECTORAL SYSTEMS. Britain with its FIRST-PAST-THE-POST electoral system, resulting usually in one party having a majority and, therefore, able to form a one-party government, has thus an especially strong executive.

See also PRESIDENTIAL SYSTEMS; RESPONSIBILITY.

Reading
Birch, A.H. 1964. *Representative and Responsible Government*. London: Allen and Unwin.

parliaments *See* LEGISLATURES.

participant observation A research method in which the observer of politics also participates in it. There are at least two objections to it. In the first place the researcher may find it difficult not to be influenced by the attitudes and opinions of those associated with. Secondly, however objective the researcher remains, others will identify her/him with the group observed. Hence research findings will be suspect even when they are a model of scholarly detachment. Consequently participant observation is only advisable when no other way of observing is possible.

participatory democracy The main criticism of DEMOCRACY as it operates today is that not enough citizens participate in it. In fact, the average citizen is content only to cast a vote at national elections. There are some observers who argue that it is the non-participation of the vast majority that keeps democracy stable. If everyone joined in the decision-making process either nothing would ever be decided or, when the decisions were

eventually taken they would be bad because few people have the necessary technical grasp of the complex issues in the present world.

On the other hand, there has been since John Stuart MILL (1806–73), a tradition that participation in politics is necessary because it educates the electorate about the procedures, personalities and issues. In this way democracy will be strengthened. Various prescriptions have been recommended to secure much wider participation. One is to substitute DIRECT DEMOCRACY for REPRESENTATIVE DEMOCRACY, a notion stemming from ROUSSEAU (1712–78). Another is to devote much more school time to educating children in democratic institutions. A large number of commentators, beginning with Mill, have perceived local government as the place for people to cut their democratic teeth. The argument is that they are much more likely to be interested in local matters, though a corollary is that to induce greater participation at local levels there should be much more devolution to sub-units of government. One finds a variant of this approach among supporters of INDUSTRIAL DEMOCRACY. Except for COMPULSORY VOTING, used only in a few places, there have been no attempts in democracies to compel people to participate. Presumably it would be highly unpopular with the great majority of citizens.

See also DIRECT DEMOCRACY; INDUSTRIAL DEMOCRACY; POLITICAL PARTICIPATION; REPRESENTATIVE DEMOCRACY.

Reading
Mill, J.S. [1861] 1960. *On Representative Government*. London: Dent; Pateman, C. 1970. *Participation and Democratic Theory*. Cambridge: CUP.

party conferences The term 'conference' is mainly used outside the USA to describe annual gatherings, lasting for a few days, of representatives from local organizations and, often, in socialist parties from bodies like trade unions and co-operatives. These assemblies of ACTI-VISTS vary in their functions for the national party. Generally in left-wing parties the conferences play some part in policy formation, especially when the party is in opposition. They give dissident groups the opportunity to 'let off steam', often elect party committees which may be involved with candidate selection and policy-making, and allow the leadership to rally the party with old war cries. In centre and right-wing parties conferences may also perform these functions; but the tendency is for their meetings to be less critical of the leadership and more an occasion to close ranks behind the leader.

See also POLITICAL PARTIES.

party conventions The term 'convention' may be a synonym for conference, but the functions of American party national conventions are fewer than those of European party CONFERENCES. The only two of any importance, the Democratic and Republican conventions, meet only every fourth year, three to four months before Presidential ELECTIONS, in order to nominate Presidential and Vice-Presidential CANDIDATES for their parties. Although they also draw up 'platforms', or policy statements, this function is robbed of importance because Presidential candidates insist on their own policy pronouncements. In recent years the conventions have lost much of their excitement because of foregone conclusions about the candidates that will be chosen. The 2–3000 delegates are selected state by state, usually in PRIMARIES, in numbers roughly proportionate to the party's vote in each state at the last presidential election. They are pledged to support a particular candidate. Consequently these pledged delegates can be added up and forecasts made about the likely winner of each nomination.

party identification A term used by American pollsters in order to describe a respondent's underlying political allegiance. It was intended to take account of temporary desertion on the hypothesis that people had permanent political attachments to which they would return. It is not used so much today, probably because firm political loyalties, such as were common in the 1950s, seem no longer so evident in the democratic world.

See also DEALIGNMENT; ISSUES; VOTING.

party labels The indication of a candidate's party, used everywhere except where, as in some American local elections, there are 'non-partisan' rules. Elsewhere non-party candidates usually label themselves 'Independents'. It has increasingly become common for party labels to appear on ballot papers. Where literacy is not high symbols are sometimes allowed.

party lists Some systems of Proportional Representation require voters to choose from among party lists without expressing any preference for candidates. When seats are apportioned proportional to votes cast the order of the list determines who is elected. Hence the party list system gives great power to PARTY ORGANIZATION.

See also ELECTORAL SYSTEMS.

party organization Political parties may have formal or informal organization. The classic case of the latter type, the CADRE PARTY, was the French Radical Party. MASS PARTIES have formal organization; often to such a degree that they are almost miniature political systems, with constitutions, bureaucracies, disputing factions and executives and legislatures. (Attlee described the British Labour Party conference as 'the parliament of the movement'.) The mass party is based on individual membership and is motivated by the small minority of members who become ACTIVISTS. They tend to see the party as theirs and, in consequence, clash inevitably with the party in the legislature and its leadership which must ultimately be more concerned with the needs of the voters rather than those of the activists.

Both constitutional and ideological differences affect party organization. For example, in the USA FEDERAL GOVERNMENT and the SEPARATION OF POWERS explain much about American party organization. A large continent in which power is diffused both territorially and between the legislature and the executive results in a very large number of elections. Co-ordination of policies is very difficult as the issues vary from one state to another. An individual executive popularly elected puts a premium on personality for presidential candidates. Party membership and central party organization do not exist in the European sense. There is no leader of the opposition. In contrast European parties have been influenced by operating in parliamentary systems. Issues tend to be nation-wide, more ideological and more conducive to the development of mass parties.

See also AGGREGATIVE PARTIES; CADRE PARTY; IRON LAW OF OLIGARCHY; MASS PARTIES.

Reading
Duverger, M. 1964. *Political Parties: their Organization and Activity in the Modern State.* London: Methuen; Le Blanc, H. 1982. *American Political Parties.* New York: St. Martin's Press; Michels, R. 1915. *Political Parties.* London: Jarrold; Ostrogroski, M. 1902. *Democracy and the Organization of Political Parties.* London: Macmillan.

party systems Party systems are a distinguishing feature among different democracies. The configuration of the parties – their number, objectives, relationship to each other and disposition to govern or share in government – is clearly significant for any assessment of a POLITICAL SYSTEM. Much political science literature is concerned with explaining and categorizing party systems.

DUVERGER was the first systematic pioneer of the phenomenon. He laid great stress on the type of electoral law in determining whether a country had a 'two-party' system or a 'multiparty' system. By the former he implied the British situation where two major parties compete for office and the 'winner takes all', that is, monopolizes government. In the latter Proportional Representation resulted in coalition government. Duverger was also aware that social cleavages were responsible for party formations and that in much of Europe these dated back to two revolutions, the French which had produced the clerical/anti-clerical split and the Industrial which had left a middle/working class division.

Lipset and ROKKAN laid stress on this latter factor, contending that at the time of mass enfranchisement the social cleavage in particular had become transfixed. This argument explained much of the past, but at about the time they were writing, class divisions in Europe began to weaken in intensity and the WORKING CLASS began to diminish in numbers. SINGLE ISSUE POLITICS, with its emphasis on PRESSURE GROUPS rather than parties, portended the decline of explanations of modern parties in terms of deep-seated cleavages. The parties in this political climate tended to be AGGREGATIVE rather than articulative.

There has also been much discussion about the merits of the various party systems for good democratic government. The conventional wisdom was that TWO-PARTY SYSTEMS were the best because they gave the voters a clear choice between two policies and made the majority feel responsible for the changes. It alternated governments and so fostered moderation. Two-party politics was pragmatic and compromising.

Later assessment has challenged all these assertions. In Britain one party remained in power from 1979 to 1997. Elections do not provide clear choice because the issues are technical and the politicians obfuscate them. Therefore ACCOUNTABILITY is very much impaired. Further, competition in the legislature is detrimental to a cool, rational appraisal of policies: in fact, the two parties in the House of Commons indulge in ritual abuse of each other like two gangs of school boys. Above all, the two-party system is particularly bad for management of the economy. Holland provides a contrast with its succession of coalition governments. Their formation may take weeks but otherwise, once bargaining has ceased, widely-based governments can rationally discuss policy.

See also ADVERSARY POLITICS; COALITION GOVERNMENT; MULTIPARTY SYSTEMS; ONE-PARTY STATES; TWO-PARTY SYSTEMS.

Reading
Lijphart, A. 1968. 'Typologies of Democratic Systems'. *Comparative Political Studies* 1.1. 3–44; Lipset, S.M. and Rokkan, S. 1967. *Party Systems and Voter Alignments*. New York: Free Press; Sartori, G. 1976. *Parties and Party Systems: a Framework for Analysis*. Cambridge: CUP.

passive resistance Known otherwise as 'non-violent resistance', this method of political action is seen as useful by those who believe conventional methods through parliaments, often involving access to parties, is slow and uncertain. In democracies, where freedom of demonstration is permitted, direct action of this kind, especially if one can attract the television cameras, is a good way of mobilizing opinion. BOYCOTTS and strikes are also examples of non-violence of which there are various degrees. One is concerned not to break the law thus ruling out damaging property and obstructing the highway. At the opposite extreme are people who, by provoking the police to violence, wish to develop a revolutionary consciousness in the passive population. In between are several positions including pacifists who are prepared to go to prison in order to promote their determination to win and to provide a martyr for their cause. Passive resistance has been popular in the last half-century because of the success of Gandhi's campaign for Indian independence. Martin Luther King later adopted it in the American struggle for Civil Rights. It should be noted that in both cases the fight was won against democratic governments.

See also BOYCOTT; INDUSTRIAL RELATIONS; PACIFICISM; PACIFISM.

Reading
Carter, A. 1973. *The Politics of Non-Violent Action*. London: Routledge.

paternalism A paternalistic regime treats its citizens in the way a father treats his children. It is assumed that because of lack of knowledge or experience they are not able to make their own choices. Hence the state must make their choices for them, promote their welfare and protect them from harmful pressures. A paternalistic culture is likely to be one with an aristocracy which respects the code of *noblesse oblige*.

patriarchalism A form of simple dynastic rule. According to WEBER, it is an early form of traditional authority, beginning when the head of one particular family exercises authority from one generation to another.

patrimonialism This occurs when patriarchal rule begins to develop an administrative apparatus. It was typical in medieval Europe emerging from feudalism.

See also AUTHORITY; FEUDALISM; LEADERSHIP; LEGITIMACY.

Reading
Gerth, H.H. and C.W. Mills. eds. 1948. *From Max Weber*. London: Routledge.

patriotism 'The last refuge of a scoundrel', according to Dr. Johnson. Before her execution by a German firing squad, Nurse Edith Cavell said it was 'not enough'. It means love of country without any nationalistic implications. A patriot can understand without resentment the love of people of other countries for their motherlands. There is also local patriotism which may be little more than parochialism.
See also NATIONALISM.

patronage Appointments made by an authority, based on its own interests rather than on the skill or merit of the appointees, are patronage positions. In eighteenth- and early nineteenth-century Britain the whole of the public service, including commissions in the armed forces, was appointed on this basis. In the USA many federal postmasterships and even some ambassadorships are still patronage posts. Although not always illegal, patronage appointments are often seen as corrupt.
See also CLIENTELISM; PORK BARREL; QUANGO.

peacekeeping A term that can be applied to all efforts to prevent WAR, though more recently it has been used more specifically to describe the United Nations policy of sending international forces, the famous 'blue berets', to police troubled areas such as Bosnia and the border between Lebanon and Israel.
See also CIVIL WAR; GUERRILLA WARFARE; WAR.

Reading
James, A. 1990. *Peacekeeping in International Politics*. New York: St. Martin's Press.

peasants A peasant is a subsistence farmer who farms a small amount of land, (say less than 50 acres), which he may or may not own. The peasantry has often been an agent of revolution, yet at the same time has a conservative image. Peasants concentrate on family survival which may at times be precarious. In western Europe and North America the constraints of the market economy have made small farm holdings uneconomic and the peasant has given way to the businessman-farmer.

Peasant society is intensely local and peasant politics not easy to discern. Lenin saw the peasantry as incapable of political organization – it could never be a class 'for itself'. Urban observers find the localism of rural society hard to penetrate. Peasants fear outsiders, suspecting them of being agents of the landlord or the tax-gatherer. Consequently their political image tends to be superficial tranquillity punctuated by sudden explosions, as in the Mexican revolution. Peasant organization on a national scale only appears when they are prosperous enough to own motor cars to take them to mass demonstrations and to block roads. By then they have often ceased to be peasants.
See also MARXISM; REVOLUTIONS.

Reading
Banfield, E.C. 1963. *The Moral Basis of a Backward Society*. Glencoe: Free Press; Magagna, V.V. 1991. *Communities of Green: Rural Rebellion in Comparative Perspective*. Ithaca, NY: Cornell UP; Scott, J.C. 1985. *Weapons of the Weak: Everyday Forms of Peasant Resistance*. New Haven: YUP; Shanin, T. ed. 1988. *Peasants and Peasant Societies*. Harmondsworth: Penguin; Solokoff, S. 1985. 'Socialism and the Farmers'. In *Socialism, the State and Public Policy in France*, 245–64. Ed. P.G. Cerny and M.A. Schain. London: Pinter.

people 'The people', a phrase beloved by populist politicians, is also part of revolutionary imagery. Thus the title of Delacroix's famous painting of the 1830 Revolution in Paris, is 'Liberty Leading the People at the Barricades'. 'Avanti Populo!' (Forward the People) begins the song of the Italian Communists. Popular revolutions overthrew dynastic despotism in Europe. Consequently the people were seen as the natural supporters of democracy: indeed, in nineteenth-century writings the term 'the democracy' is often used. It suggests a collective will among all ordinary folk which does not exist. Politicians and political scientists know that people are divided in their views and will remain so. This is even true of the proletariat, the Marxist substitute for 'the people'.

See also POPULISM; SOVEREIGNTY OF THE PEOPLE.

people's democracy   A term invented by the Soviet Union to describe the Communist states. It featured in the debate in the United Nations, immediately after World War II, about the 'two concepts of democracy'. Briefly, to Marxist minds 'capitalist' or 'bourgeois' democracy was a procedural form. The Soviet Union and its satellite states were true democracies because 'the people', that is the working class, was in power.

See also DEMOCRACY; MARXISM; POPULISM; SOVEREIGNTY OF THE PEOPLE.

perestroika   A Russian word meaning 'reconstruction' which has passed into common usage through its origin in the call of Mikhail Gorbachev, last secretary of the Communist Party of the Soviet Union, for radical reform in all Soviet policies. His ideas were not spelt out in convincing specifications.

See also GLASNOST.

Reading
Gorbachev, M. 1987. *Perestroika*. London: Collins.

periphery politics   *See*   CENTRE-PERIPHERY RELATIONS.

permanent revolution   A concept Trotsky (1879–1940) developed in order to reconcile the Russian revolution in a rural, backward semi-feudal society with the Marxist prophecy of the overthrow of capitalism by a large WORKING CLASS. Trotsky declared that the duty of the small Russian proletariat was to keep the

revolution unfolding while inspiring revolutions in those countries further west in Europe in which CAPITALISM and the bourgeois revolution had been achieved and which were more ready for a socialist takeover in a proletarian revolution. Unfortunately for Trotsky he never succeeded in arousing the west European working class and the idea of continuing and permanent revolution was rejected by Stalin who advocated 'Socialism in one country'. He drove Trotsky into exile. Yet the Trotskyist version of Marx has received more support in societies where rebellious, land-hungry PEASANTS vastly outnumber industrial workers.

See also MARXISM; TROTSKYISM.

Reading
Knei-Paz, B. 1978. *The Social and Political Thought of Leon Trotsky*. Oxford: OUP; Trotsky, L. 1962. *The Permanent Revolution*. London: New Park.

petite bourgeoisie   The small bourgeoisie are the class between the BOURGEOISIE, the capitalists, and the workers. MARX included in this class small tradesmen, shopkeepers and small farmers. Many were self-employed workers who used their own tools and were not involved in exploitation. Like all classes intermediate between the entrepreneurs and their employees, the *petite bourgeoisie* would eventually be ground between them and would have to choose which side to take. Marx believed some of them would agitate with the workers for democratic rights, but would then desert them and side with the bourgeoisie because they feared the proletarian revolution and its threat to private property. Only a few who were intellectuals would remain loyal to the socialist aim of the proletariat.

Marx's prediction of the way class systems would be simplified as time went on could hardly have been more wrong. Class structures have become more complex and the *petite bourgeoisie* is as strong as ever and has remained quite right-wing. Sections of it have been attracted to FASCISM and POUJADISM.

See also BOURGEOISIE; MIDDLE CLASS; POUJADISM; SOCIAL CLASS; WORKING CLASS.

pillarization a translation of the Dutch word *verzuiling*. It refers to the division of Dutch society into four different segments with different religious, cultural and ideological backgrounds. These are the Catholics, Protestants, secular Socialists and Liberals. Each 'pillar' has its own interest groups, media and political party. A system of Proportional Representation and COALITION GOVERNMENT ensures a certain balance is maintained between them.

See also CONSOCIATIONAL DEMOCRACY.

Reading
Lijphart, A. 1975. *The Politics of Accommodation: Pluralism and Democracy in the Netherlands*. Berkeley: University of California Press.

planning Most human beings believe it is prudent, where it is possible, to plan for the future. Parents plan for their children and householders plan for their property. Heads of business enterprises would be irresponsible if they did not take into account the likely expansion or contraction of their markets, the expected pressure for higher wages from their employees and any movement in the future in the prices of their raw materials or national interest rates. In some industries such as aircraft construction, almost a decade may lapse between blueprints of new models and their appearance in the market. Some form of planning is, therefore, a rational requirement.

The modern technology of knowledge – computers and the Internet, for example – reinforce the view that problems of POLICY MAKING can be solved by rational means. Define the nature of the difficulty, set out in detail all the factual background and then, with 100 per cent information, the correct solution to

choose should be clearly apparent. Perfect rationality in decision-making is then possible.

In the twentieth century this perception first gained great strength from Soviet planning. Beyond a reference in the *Communist Manifesto* to organizing production 'in accordance a common plan' there was nothing in the Marxist scriptures to help Lenin and the Bolsheviks in setting up a socialist economy. After brief periods of 'war communism', followed by resort to the electrification of industry plus scientific management in the New Economic Policy, it was left to Stalin to introduce the first Five Year Plan in 1928. This set for the period detailed production targets reflecting the drive for rapid industrialization. Labour was obtained from peasants driven from the countryside by the COLLECTIVIZATION of agriculture. Prices and wages were controlled by the highly centralized Plan administration. Trade unions were prohibited. A coercive regime ensured there was no organized opposition by 'Trotskyist wreckers and saboteurs'.

Meanwhile, in the industrialized countries the post-war recession deepened in the late 1920s and faith in CAPITALISM and private enterprise was badly shaken. The contrast between the democratic world where unemployment was high and the Soviet Union where it was (officially anyway) nil was conspicuous and from this time the term 'Planning' became common in the discourse of centrist and left-wing politicians and intellectuals. It received strong stimulus from the ideas of the economist John Maynard Keynes (1883–1946), who argued that a good deal of government intervention in the economy was not inconsistent with democracy. Keynes's way out of the world depression was through governments instituting public works programmes which would lower unemployment, thus increasing spending power. Higher consumption would then stimulate more investment. It was an ascending spiral assisted by low rates of interest.

KEYNESIANISM became the basis for democratic economic planning to a greater or lesser extent accepted by all the democracies after World War II. It has been likened to planning in competitive markets by large corporations and called 'strategic planning'. Governments were committed to maintaining full employment by monetary and fiscal policies which expanded or contracted demand. The prevailing metaphor was taken from early television sets with their numerous levers. Government economic management could produce an optimum equilibrium by 'fine tuning'. When government sought other economic goals such as national growth, involving much more than controlling consumption, more complex schemes of economic management were needed, though without centralized control. 'Indicative planning', originally a French concept, was motivated by the desire to set national economic goals without causing wage demands and inflation. It consisted of drafting a probabilistic model allowing for freedom of choice but guiding economic actors towards government objectives. This involved much consultation between government, business and the trade unions in order to clarify goals and establish an order of priorities. It was hoped the rationality of the government planners would be communicated to the others as a result of bargaining and consultation.

In the 1980s planning became unpopular. Inflation was a problem that Keynesian prescriptions could not cure. A world economy with more free trade made it difficult for states to control their economies. Hence democratic planning was hardly practicable, though government intervention in economies was still practised. It is doubtful if planning had ever threatened DEMOCRACY: although it undoubtedly increased the power of bureaucrats and technocrats and weakened that of elected representatives, it had been accepted by majorities of electorates as an insurance against a return of pre-war unemployment. Comprehensive planning of the Soviet kind, however, would have been impossible in a democracy because voters are not prepared to make sacrifices in the present for future generations. Only in a mobilized, coercive political system can comprehensive planning be enforced.

See also BUREAUCRACY; COMMAND ECONOMY; COMMUNISM; DEFLATION; KEYNESIANISM; SOCIAL DEMOCRACY; TECHNOCRACY; TROTSKYISM.

Reading

Branch, M.C. 1990. *Planning: Universal Process*. New York: Wiley; Budd, A. 1978. *The Politics of Economic Planning*. London: Fontana; Coombes, D. and S.A. Walkland. 1980. *Parliaments and Economic Affairs*. London: Heinemann; Faludi, A. 1973. *Planning Theory*. Oxford: OUP; Lindblom, C.E. 1977. *Politics and Markets*. New York: Basic Books; Nelkin, D. 1977. *Technological Decisions and Democracy*. Beverly Hills: Sage; Wootton, B. 1945. *Freedom Under Planning*. London: Allen and Unwin.

platform A set of proposals put forward by an individual or party seeking election. Each specific proposal is often described as a 'plank'. Party platforms are usually constructed at party CONFERENCES or conventions. Where the planks come from very diverse PRESSURE GROUPS or sectors of public opinion, as with American parties, the resulting platform might be embarrassing for candidates if they paid too much attention to it. Usually this is not the case. Where policy-drafting procedures vary greatly, as in Europe, platforms, or manifestos as they are called in Britain, have varying significance for parties. In some instances MANDATE THEORY is important.

See also MANDATE; MANIFESTOISM.

Reading

Craig, F.W.S. 1975. *British General Election Manifestos, 1918–1966*. London: Parliamentary References Publications; Porter, K.H. and D.B. Johnson. 1961. *National Party Platforms, 1840–1956*. Urbana: University of Illinois Press.

plebiscitary democracy   *See*   DIRECT DEMOCRACY.

plebiscite   Often used as a synonym for REFERENDUM. Yet it may apply to a special type of referendum: one where the inhabitants of a whole territory are asked to which country they wish to belong. In 1935 and 1955 the people of the Saarland voted by a large majority to be part of Germany. In 1956 British Togoland, a former League of Nations mandate, voted to become part of Ghana instead of joining with French Togoland.
See also DIRECT DEMOCRACY; INITIATIVE; REFERENDUM.

plural society   A term first used by J.S. Furnivall, with South-East Asia particularly in mind, to describe societies where groups with different ethnic backgrounds, religions and cultures live within the same borders. They were, therefore, places with great tensions. Political solutions offered are separation where it is possible geographically to divide the groups territorially. Often it is not and other suggestions are communal representation, CONSOCIATIONAL DEMOCRACY and Proportional Representation.
See also CLEAVAGES; COMMUNALISM; CONSOCIATIONAL DEMOCRACY.

Reading

Furnivall, J.S. 1939. *Netherlands India*. Cambridge: CUP.

pluralism   A situation in which numerous groups exist. This might describe any society in which there is specialization of function. Specialized or strategic groups such as the armed forces, the police, or the bureaucracy, existed from the beginnings of the modern STATE. Consequently in the writings of political scientists pluralism is often defined in terms of more than one centre of power. In a pluralist society neither the state nor any one group holds supreme power. Power is shared.

Furthermore, DEMOCRACY guarantees pluralism. FREEDOM OF ASSOCIATION is a democratic right and where the right to form VOLUNTARY ASSOCIATIONS exists organized political activity is possible. Hence democracy cannot exist without pluralism, though pluralism exists in many societies where democracy has not yet developed. Once voluntary associations with no functional utility for state authority begin to appear in hitherto authoritarian states, democracy may well be in the offing. Thus the emergence in 1980 of Solidarity, a trade union prepared to confront the Polish Communist state, not only sounded the death knell of Communism in Poland, but also heralded its end throughout eastern Europe. Following the revolutions of 1989, in which so many different freedoms were regained, the term 'pluralism' was often confused with democracy or even the right of free self-expression.

With political scientists the study of pluralism has progressed through several phases. The earliest manifestation was before 1914 when the French legal theorist, Leon Duguit (1859–1928), contested the idea of SOVEREIGNTY solely resting with the state. LASKI (1893–1950) and many on the intellectual left were associated with the belief that the state was merely one association among many, a notion that had received inspiration from the wave of SYNDICALISM before World War I. The weakness of labour during the post-war depression and the rise of the totalitarian states with their denial of freedom of association enfeebled the notion of legal pluralism.

Pluralism appeared again in the

discourse of political scientists during the 1950s. It was stimulated by the work on pressure groups, itself a by-product of the new Register of Congressional Lobbyists necessitated by the Federal Registration of Lobbying Act, 1946. David Truman, who had excavated the work of A.F. BENTLEY (1870–1957), emphasized in an empirical study the importance of groups in democratic politics. It was natural that the impetus for this new insight should come from the USA where DE TOCQUEVILLE long before had extolled the virtues of associational activity and where federalism and the SEPARATION OF POWERS much weakened the power of central government. Robert DAHL (1915–) in his study of New Haven concluded that absolute power existed nowhere in the city: power was exerted by different people in different decision-making sectors.

The later pluralists naturally were criticized by Marxists, and by elitists who might be described as 'political monists'. Much of the argument since about the nature of the interrelationship between society and the state has been between these three groups. Polsby's view that 'nothing categorical' can be assumed about power in any community was a signal for researchers to examine power structures in numerous places with diverse results. The elitists and Marxists contended that power had left the communities in industrialized countries and was exercised from the centre where an elite, either aristocratic or meritocratic, dominated. The pluralists admitted that not all groups exerted power. Dahl and LINDBLOM recognized that diffusion of power did not mean equality of power among groups and stressed the power of business corporations. Others such as Bachrach and Baratz and Lukes argued, respectively, that power over agendas and power to manipulate people's minds reflected hegemony by an elite or RULING CLASS.
See also DEMOCRACY; ELITISM; GUILD SOCIALISM; MARXISM; POLITICAL POWER; PRESSURE GROUPS; SOVEREIGNTY; STATE; SYNDICALISM; VOLUNTARY ASSOCIATIONS.

Reading
Bachrach, P. and M. Baratz. 1970. *Power and Poverty*. Oxford: OUP; Dahl, R.A. 1961. *Who Governs?* New Haven: YUP; Dahl, R.A. and C.E. Lindblom. 1976. *Politics, Economics and Welfare*. New York: Harper and Row; Dahl, R.A. 1982. *Dilemmas of Pluralist Democracy*. New Haven: YUP; Duguit, L. [1911] 1921. *Law in the Modern State*. trans. H.J. Laski. London: Allen and Unwin; Dunleavy, P. and B. O'Leary. 1987. *Theories of the State*. London: Macmillan; Laski, H.J. 1917. *Problems of Sovereignty*. New Haven: YUP; Polsby, N. 1963. *Community Power and Political Theory*. New Haven: YUP; Truman, D. 1951. *The Governmental Process*. New York: Knopf.

plurality In an election the largest total of votes for one candidate is a plurality, enough to win in FIRST-PAST-THE-POST electoral systems. In other systems a 'majority', obtained by a vote of 50 per cent +1, is necessary.
See also ELECTORAL SYSTEMS; MAJORITY RULE.

pocket veto An American President normally signs a Congressional bill before it becomes law; but if he declines to sign it then it becomes law within ten days, provided Congress is still sitting. If he vetoes a bill it is returned to the chamber where it originated with his objections. The bill can then be passed over his veto by two-thirds of members present. When Congress adjourns before ten days has lapsed a bill does not become law if he does not sign it. The President vetoes it by putting it 'in his pocket'.

polarization A metaphor used by political scientists when they want to describe a system in which two extremes are the predominant feature. Hence it might be appropriate when a TWO-PARTY SYSTEM was characterized by confrontation between an extreme left and an extreme right party. The metaphor is extended in a bizarre fashion by Sartori in his concept of 'polarized pluralism'. He conceives of a multiparty system of more than five parties in which there are *three* poles, including a *centre pole*!

See also MULTIPARTY SYSTEMS; PARTY SYSTEMS; POLITICAL PARTIES; TWO-PARTY SYSTEMS.

Reading
Sartori, G. 1976. *Parties and Party Systems*. Cambridge: CUP.

police An organization of people, usually uniformed, employed to maintain civil order, to prevent and investigate crime and to bring criminals to book. Police forces are often quite specialized. For example, in France there are the national police, the *gendarmerie* or civil guard and a contingent of riot police. Police forces use doctors, lawyers, photographers and specialists in fingerprinting, DNA tracing and financial fraud. Their structures of accountability may be complex. For example, in Britain the Metropolitan Police are responsible to the Home Secretary, but outside London police forces are the responsibility of local authorities. In federal states police forces are naturally decentralized. In the USA the 50 states have their own forces and so do the local authorities within them, but pursuing interstate and highly specialized crime is the duty of the Federal Bureau of Investigation (FBI). European police forces are often centralized which may, or may not, make for greater efficiency and makes ACCOUNTABILITY both simpler and more distant.

Accountability is an important issue with regard to the police because of their involvement with CIVIL LIBERTIES. They are concerned both with enforcing the law and capable, at times, of breaching it. Two main factors influence their conduct in this context. One is the degree of force accompanying their constraint. In all the United Kingdom, except Northern Ireland, the police are not armed. In many countries they are and the police can be used in a paramilitary capacity. This may not produce a good climate of public relations. Second is the recruitment of the police from areas in which they patrol which helps them to understand the local people. On the other hand it results in their sharing the prejudices of the inhabitants and may encourage corruption, especially in big cities. Hence the problem of policing the police and dealing with complaints against them. This may be best done by some regulatory body, or legislative committee.

See also CIVIL LIBERTIES; MILITIAS; PARAMILITARIES; SECRET POLICE.

Reading
Goldstein, H. 1977. *Policing a Free Society*. Cambridge, Mass.: Ballinger; Reiner, R. 1985. *The Politics of the Police*. Brighton: Wheatsheaf.

police state A term coined in the 1930s and a translation of the German *polizeistaat*. The police state is an essential part of any totalitarian system because it is only in such contexts that political crime exists. As the suppression of OPPOSITION is their chief function and as opposition will have gone underground the police will be involved in internal espionage: indeed, they are often described as the SECRET POLICE. Their arrests may be arbitrary and on a mass scale. Consequently they are the main instrument of state terror and as such a power within the land.

See also CONCENTRATION CAMPS; GULAG; TERROR; TOTALITARIANISM.

Reading
Conquest, R. 1968. *The Soviet Police System*. London: Bodley Head; Delarue, J. 1966. *The History of the Gestapo*. London: Corgi.

policy analysis The analysis of policy is of two kinds, carried out by two different sorts of people for two different purposes. Analysis 'for policy' is practised by people in the governmental apparatus whose motivation is the development of better policy. It may well be stimulated by policy failure. Analysis 'of policy' is the approach of academics whose motivation is relatively detached. Their interests include all stages of policy formation, including IMPLEMENTATION. Analysis concentrates on programmes, is often interdisciplinary and takes a comparative approach, either between different countries or between different policy areas. The study of POLICY MAKING has become a major interest of political scientists, especially those involved in the area of PUBLIC ADMINISTRATION.

See also ADMINISTRATION; BUREAUCRACY; IMPLEMENTATION; POLICY OUTPUTS.

Reading
Hood, C. 1987. 'Policy Analysis'. In *Blackwell Encyclopaedia of Political Institutions*, 432–3. Ed. V. Bogdanor. Oxford: Blackwell; Wildavsky, A. 1980. *The Art and Craft of Policy Analysis*. London: Macmillan.

policy making   It is difficult to distinguish policy from politics: in fact, the French word *politique* can be translated as either. Policy formation is the core of the political process, both from the side of government policy and from the opposition side which may seek to amend, emasculate and deflect rather than to condemn and vote against. Policy making can cover all that goes on in relation to one issue or set of issues before reaching the desks of the legislative draftsmen. Numerous inputs will have come from the voters at election time, or between elections, from party ACTIVISTS and party CONFERENCES, from PRESSURE GROUPS and BUREAUCRACIES. Different political systems will attribute differently weighted proportions to these elements.

At the early stage of policy making policy objectives may be stated in a very general way. To provide the details needed for a legislative proposal much will depend on the specialized knowledge required. The expertise might be highly technical, as with financial policy, or it might be that of practitioners, as with

legislation about safety regulations in deep mines. Policy development may continue through several committees. When they are committees of the executive several departments may be involved and they have different views of the proposal. Hence compromise may be necessary. In addition, administrators may comment favourably or otherwise about the problems of implementing a policy once it becomes law. They may want revision. Finally there is the relating of a specific policy to other policies. Coordination is needed to produce a PROGRAMME.

See also POLICY ANALYSIS; POLICY OUTPUTS; PROGRAMME.

Reading
Jordan, A.G. and J.J. Richardson. 1987. *British Politics and the Policy Process*. London: Allen and Unwin; Richardson J.J. ed. 1982. *Policy Styles in Western Europe*. London: Allen and Unwin.

policy outputs   The term 'outputs' was introduced into political science through Easton's book, *A Systems Analysis of Political Life* (1965). Until that time there had not been much study of political outputs; the discipline had concentrated on 'inputs', all those elements which had gone into POLICY MAKING. Research was largely of a statistical nature and based upon public expenditure tables. In the USA it was discovered that variations depended upon social and economic factors and that the party that happened to be in power made little difference; but studies in Europe demonstrated that changes of governments with differing ideological leanings were significant to some degree. Later work on policy outputs has turned to public expenditure cuts. PUBLIC CHOICE THEORY and RATIONAL CHOICE THEORY have been incorporated into recent studies.

See also SYSTEMS ANALYSIS.

Reading
Dye, T. 1972. *Understanding Public Policy*. Englewood Cliffs: Prentice Hall; Sharpe, L.J.

and K. Newton. 1984. *Does Politics Matter? The Determinants of Public Policy*. Oxford: OUP.

polis   *See* POLITY.

political action committees   American committees formed to finance and support a candidate for office. They are particularly important at PRIMARIES where party funds can be of no use; but they are also important once NOMINATION is achieved because American parties are not well funded locally. Political action committees (PACs) were first used on a considerable scale by the Congress of Industrial Organizations (CIO) in the 1930s to obtain nominations in Democratic primaries for trade-union activists. Their numbers have grown greatly, however, since the Federal Election Campaign Act in 1971 and its 1974 amendments strictly limiting campaign contributions. Since 1974 groups contributing money to a candidate must do it through a PAC and give not more than $5000 per primary election and $5000 per general election. Over 4000 PACs now exist and they contribute about 30 per cent of all campaign expenses. They have even further weakened the political parties as fund raisers. *See also* POLITICAL FINANCE.

Reading
Sabato, L.J. 1984. *PAC Power: Inside the World of Political Action Committees*. New York: Norton.

political anthropology   Anthropology is the study of the culture of human society; but with the development of sociology it has come to mean the study of the cultures of primitive societies. Within this framework there is scope for studying the politics of primitive societies. Although these societies may have little organized government they frequently display some conflict and also attempts to resolve it. They often have no written records and research has to be confined to obser-

vation and interrogation. The latter may be resented.
See also CONFLICT; POLITICAL CULTURE; POLITICS.

Reading
Fortes, M. and E.E. Evans-Pritchard. eds. 1940. *African Political Systems*. Oxford: OUP. Mair, L. 1962. *Primitive Government*. Harmondsworth: Penguin.

political attitudes   An attitude is a predisposition or orientation towards the world. It thus may be congenital or engendered by culture; probably by both. It may give rise to statements and to actions or non-actions. Political attitudes will be based on social attitudes and on experiences in political life. Hence the study of political attitudes will be an area in which social psychology, sociology and political science meet. It has been concerned with research into both the attitudes of political leaders and of the masses. In the last three decades the concept of POLITICAL CULTURE has been used in the examination of people's attitudes to their own POLITICAL SYSTEM.
See also POLITICAL CULTURE; POLITICAL PSYCHOLOGY.

Reading
Allport, G.W. 1954. *The Nature of Prejudice*. Cambridge, Mass.: Addison Wesley; Katz, E. and P.F. Lazarsfeld. 1955. *Personal Influence: the Part Played by People in the Flow of Mass Communications*. Glencoe: Free Press; Lasswell, H. 1930. *The Psychopathology of Politics*. New York: Viking.

political behaviour   Emphasis on the study of political behaviour arose in the 1950s as a reaction to what was seen as the domination of political science by political theorists and others studying institutions. The 'behaviourists' turned to the study of VOTING, ACTIVISTS, POLITICAL PARTIES and PRESSURE GROUPS. Many aspects of these areas could be quantified and so statistics became a familiar feature of behavioural studies. The research was much facilitated by the discovery of sample survey methods in the 1930s. If the earlier examples of behaviourism in political science related to election studies, later work extended into attempting to answer questions about the political development of individuals – the processes by which they acquired political information and attitudes, the reasons why so many were almost non-political, and the nature of the untypical minority who became politically active and even political leaders. Political scientists began to study the internal workings of parties and VOLUNTARY ASSOCIATIONS. Comparative method was used in all these research areas.

Some enthusiasts among the behaviourists made exaggerated claims about the 'scientific' nature of their research and its findings. These were encouraged by the advent of the computer which greatly extended people's research horizons. Compile a vast amount of quantitative data, put it in the computer for statistical testing and the resultant tables will explain everything, it seemed they were suggesting. But what such an exercise provides is much more detailed description: explanation is still needed. Hence correct prediction is by no means assured. Quantitative analysis is likely to eliminate some suggested outcomes of a political situation; but it can never, except by luck, indicate the actual outcome. Of course, this does not invalidate its indispensability as a tool for political scientists.

Another objection to behavioural methods is their concentration on ELECTIONS and electorates. It is argued that they neglect elite behaviour which is the real basis of political life. The mass public's opinions, as elicited by the polls, have little effect on what political leaders do between elections, it is alleged. There is some truth in this criticism: on the other hand, they often affect what political leaders *do not do*, something the critics

overlook because it is not so easy to discern non-actions and non-decisions. Again, it is said that the findings of quantitative studies assume a bias towards the status quo; but this is a more common and more valid objection to SYSTEMS ANALYSIS.

See also ELECTIONS; ELECTORAL GEOGRAPHY; METHODOLOGY; POLITICAL SCIENCE; SAMPLE SURVEYS; SYSTEMS ANALYSIS; VOTING BEHAVIOUR.

Reading
Allardt, E. and S. Rokkan. eds. 1970. *Mass Politics*. New York: Free Press; Jaros, D. and L.V. Grant. 1974. *Political Behaviour*. Oxford: Blackwell.

political business cycle The business cycle refers to the succession of economic recession and recovery, or in extreme cases, booms and slumps, which are characteristic of the capitalist economy. The policies of governments naturally affect this cycle. Changes in interest rates, or in the exchange value of the currency, are known to influence the performance of the economy and Keynesian theory encourages such intervention. It is not a long step from this sort of interference to manipulating the economy in order to win elections. An element of reflation of the economy in the budget before the election will stimulate a 'feel good' quasi-prosperity, it is hoped, and after the election is won a somewhat deflationary budget, compensating for the earlier injection of inflation, will be far enough away from the next election to allow time to dispel the resulting unpopularity. The political business cycle can clearly be seen in recent British history. Britain is especially prone to it because British governments also have some control over the timing of the next election. Of course, democratic politicians make economic decisions on other grounds and manipulation of the economy can sometimes go badly wrong.

See also DISSOLUTION OF THE LEGISLATURE; ELECTIONS; VOTING BEHAVIOUR.

Reading

Goodhart C.A.E. and R.J. Bhansali. 1970. 'Political Economy'. In *Political Studies* XVIII.1, 43–106; Weatherford, M.S. 1988. 'Political Business Cycles and the Process of Economic Policymaking'. In *American Politics Quarterly* 16. January, 99–136.

political class   A term that became popular in the 1980s to describe all those people involved in political influence and POLITICAL POWER. Therefore it encompasses the leaderships of all political parties and pressure groups, senior bureaucrats and those among business leaders, church leaders, the military and academics that political leaders choose to consult.

See also ELITES; ESTABLISHMENT; RULING CLASS.

political communication   The political process depends upon a flow of information. For example, unless people know what the laws are they will be unable to obey them. Hence government needs to inform its subjects; but it can only do this, outside primitive societies where word of mouth may suffice, through an organized communication system. Until the advent of radio and television it disseminated information through the printed word where the population was literate. Since broadcasting began literacy has not been so necessary. Indeed, the spread of PROPAGANDA by totalitarian governments among illiterate peoples was greatly facilitated by the electronic MASS MEDIA. Communications affect all aspects of politics; but its two significant features in the contemporary world are communication between politicians and citizens, and between different states. Lack of communication can have serious consequences.

See also COMMUNICATIONS; MASS MEDIA; PROPAGANDA.

Reading

Deutsch, K.W. 1963. *The Nerves of Government*. New York: Free Press; Katz, E.

and P.L. Lazarsfeld. 1964. *Personal Influence: the Part Played by People in the Flow of Mass Communications*. New Haven: YUP; Nimmo, D. and K.R.F. Sanders. 1981. *Handbook of Political Communication*. Beverly Hills: Sage.

political community   *See* COMMUNITARIANISM.

political correctness   This is a term that only became common usage in the 1980s. Often referred to familiarly as 'PC' it is American in origin and part of the radical minority culture. Its intellectual provenance is the notion that use of language reflects IDEOLOGY. Thus it is not a concept fashioned by political scientists, but it has come to be accepted in academic discussion and has remained a subject for controversial debate. 'Correctness' in this context implies that certain terms are incorrect, offensive and only the mark of the ignorant and prejudiced. Such terms are, above all, those specific to gender, race, sexual orientation and physical condition. For example, the use of 'chairman' is wrong when applied to a meeting presided over by a woman. Hence 'chairperson' is the politically correct usage for people of either gender occupying the chair. Not only obvious racist terms like 'wop' and 'wog' are stigmatized; but also allusions to ethnicity such as 'fuzzy-haired', 'greasy' or 'yellow'. Indeed, a politically correct person would condemn all references to physical characteristics as discriminatory. This is the error of 'shapeism'. Thus 'blind' is corrected to 'visually challenged', 'bald' to 'follicularly challenged', 'disabled' to 'differently abled' and so on. Another error is that of 'ageism', the use of pejorative language about either the young or old (or middle-aged).

Inevitably the more extreme exponents of political correctness render it difficult to comment upon personal characteristics, political proclivities or socio-demographic origins. This not only imposes burdens upon social scientists who are intent on investigating such matters but also becomes a limitation of freedom of speech. Hence what began with claims to be liberal can become rather authoritarian. On the other hand, the more clamorous opponents of political correctness are often those who wish to make abusive and prejudiced assertions about race, gender and other people's political allegiances without refutation.

See also AGEISM; RACISM; SEXISM.

Reading
Beard, H. & C. Cerf. eds. 1992. *The Official Politically Correct Dictionary and Handbook.* London: Grafton; D'Souza, D. 1992. *Illiberal Education : the Politics of Race and Sex on Campus.* New York: Vintage; Morrice, D. 1993. 'Philosophic Errors of Political Correctness'. *Politics* 13. 2, 32–7.

political corruption   This term is difficult to define. To some all politics is corrupt because it involves the making of bargains and friendships benefiting all parties concerned. Some people perceive politicians' promises to bestow benefits on groups such as the old as corrupt because public money is being traded for votes that will help to keep the promisers in power. Corruption is best defined narrowly as a transaction between two parties in which one of them breaks the rules. The rules do not permit bribery. Even in terms of this 'thin' definition corruption seems to be widespread in contemporary politics. Although at one time it was known to be endemic in the developing countries, today it is clearly a feature of many democracies.

There are several explanations of corruption. One is that it is cultural. In a society where power is naturally seen as a path to wealth and it is common to give gifts, especially to the powerful, corruption is almost inescapable. Developing countries with simple power structures exhibit these features. Yet a highly complex power structure, such as exists in

planned socialist societies, may provide many opportunities for managerial and bureaucratic corruption. A somewhat similar situation obtains where governments set up all sorts of regulatory agencies and 'QUANGOS' bringing people out of the private profit-making sector into the public service. It is argued that corruption in democracies tends to be situational. Where one party or coalition has been in power a long time it becomes slack and lacks the discipline of competition for power. Those seeking favours concentrate on its members. Certainly it is easy to find examples like the Liberal Democrats in Japan, the PRL in Mexico and the Christian Democrat-led coalition in Italy. Less glaring instances are the Socialists in Spain, in power from 1982 to 1996 and the Conservatives in Britain from 1979 to 1997. Corruption is more serious for democracies because it weakens the culture of trust on which democracy is based.

See also CLIENTELISM; PATRONAGE.

Reading
Clarke, M. ed. 1983. *Corruption: Causes, Consequences and Control.* London: Pinter; Heywood, P. ed. 1997. *Political Corruption.* Special number of *Political Studies* 45. 3; Della Porta, D. and Y. Mény. 1995. *Démocratie et Corruption en Europe.* Paris: Editions La Découverte.

political culture   A term coined by Almond and Verba in their classic pioneering work, *The Civic Culture.* They defined it as the orientations a population possesses towards its political institutions, conventions and traditions. Such orientations are the result of cognition, affection and evaluation – knowing, feeling and judging. They examined five countries – Mexico, Britain, Germany, Italy and the USA – with a sophisticated questionnaire designed to distinguish the 'subject' and 'citizen' aspects of their political cultures. The former aspect was concerned with the degree of trust and LEGITIMACY people evinced towards their government; the latter with their dispositions towards political activity, especially their confidence that they could achieve anything by it. From their findings the authors drew up a typology of political cultures of which the CIVIC CULTURE, best exhibited in Britain and the USA, was the basis for stable DEMOCRACY.

The stimulus for the study of political culture came from the movement of political scientists into the study of the heterogeneous states of the world and especially the new developing countries. POLITICAL ANTHROPOLOGY and POLITICAL PSYCHOLOGY played their part in this quest, which was facilitated by survey methods. The aspiration was the discovery of 'laws' and theories of politics with universal validity. Such high ambition was bound to attract critics. Detractors have claimed that it was nothing more than 'national character' given a new name. It relates, however, only to the political part of national character, examined in much more detail than in classic authors like ARISTOTLE and Herder. Others have argued that people's actions are a response much more to immediate material needs than to cultural predispositions. Some have contended that class and institutional structures are far more important in fashioning national development. Perhaps all these factors react with each other. A good reason for thinking that culture is significant is the failure of Communist Russia, after 72 years of endoctrination, to inculcate a new socialist consciousness in most of its citizens.

See also CIVIC CULTURE; DEVELOPMENT; MARXISM; POLITICAL ANTHROPOLOGY; POLITICAL PSYCHOLOGY; SURVEY RESEARCH.

Reading
Almond, G.A. and S. Verba. 1963. *The Civic Culture*. Princeton: Princeton University Press; Almond, G.A. and S. Verba. 1980. *The Civic Culture Revisited*. Boston: Little, Brown; Pye, L. and S. Verba. eds. 1965. *Political Culture and Political Development*. Princeton: Princeton University Press; Wildavsky, A. 1979. *The Rational Peasant*. Berkeley: University of California Press.

political demography Population may affect the political life of states. High density of population could conceivably lead to conflict, though there is little evidence to support this notion. Governments' perceptions of their demographic situation often influences policies towards contraception and, as in India, sterilization. Conversely, incentives in the form of family and child benefits encourage a higher birth rate. Where there is cultural conflict a differential birth rate may affect attitudes. In Northern Ireland the perception of the Catholics that their higher birth rate will eventually give them a majority over the Protestants encourages their pressures towards a united Ireland. Conversely the same awareness strengthens Protestant resistance.

Reading
Berelson, B. ed. 1974. *Population Policy in Developed Countries*. New York: McGraw-Hill.

political development   *See* DEVELOPMENT; MODERNIZATION.

political ecology The influence of territorial environment upon political behaviour. For instance, electoral studies show that where a particular socio-demographic group is concentrated it will exhibit more common voting allegiance. Manual workers are more inclined to vote for left-wing parties in predominantly working-class suburbs than where they live among the middle classes. One must avoid the 'ecological fallacy'.
See also ELECTORAL GEOGRAPHY.

political economy This term dates from the seventeenth century, though it did not become popular until the eighteenth. Adam Smith, Professor of Moral Philosophy at Glasgow University, defined political economy in the *Wealth of Nations* (1776) as a study of the two purposes a ruler should possess – providing 'subsistence for the people' and for the state 'a revenue sufficient for the public service'. Smith's writings on how a prosperous economy should be achieved amounted to an attack on the prevailing MERCANTILISM which encouraged much state interference in commerce, especially trade between states. Yet mercantilism was an example of a relationship between the polity and the economy – a system of political economy – while the effect of Smith's ideas was very much to weaken this relationship and to free the economy from interference by the state. The Utilitarians, in their search for both good administration and good policies, both accepted free markets and carried the individualism of the classical economists like Smith and Ricardo into the political sphere. Bentham and John Stuart MILL (1806–73) supported REPRESENTATIVE DEMOCRACY. In his *Principles of Political Economy* (1848) the latter was concerned to depict a balanced society, not disturbed by class conflict. Yet Mill was much aware of the division of labour brought about by the logic of competitive production. Again there appears to be both an assertion of the laissez-faire principle and an acknowledgement of its inevitable impact on the polity.

Thus much confusion has always surrounded the concept of political economy. Karl MARX who perceived the polity and the economy inextricably linked under CAPITALISM foresaw a socialist society in which there would be no state and no politics. Social conflict would have been eliminated. This ambiguity has persisted to the present day. Most contemporary economists would prefer 'economics' or 'economic science', rather than political economy, as the title of their discipline. They perceive the subject as autonomous and self-contained and concern themselves with its internal logic, pursuing hypotheses with calculus and deductive reasoning. Yet there is another tradition concerned with the interaction between the economy, the polity and society. Practitioners in this field have examined public policy's impact on the economy, not only the pursuit of growth, but also policies designed to foster egalitarian and environmental objectives. In addition, there are international economists conscious of the implications of GLOBALIZATION. Political scientists have been active in these areas. The POLITICAL BUSINESS CYCLE is merely one instance of their increasing interest in political economy. GAME THEORY and PUBLIC CHOICE THEORY also impinge on such studies. Neo-Marxists like Claus Offe (1940–) explain the persistence of capitalism in terms of the ability of capitalists to exert their power in order to socialize their costs by compelling the state to provide numerous welfare benefits.

See also CAPITALISM; POLITICAL POWER; POLITICAL SOCIOLOGY; POLITICS; SOCIALISM.

Reading

Froman, C. 1984. *The Two American Political Systems: Society, Economics and Politics.* Englewood Cliffs: Prentice Hall; Hibbs, D.A. and H. Fassbender. eds. 1981. *Contemporary Political Economy.* Amsterdam: North Holland; Sen, A. 1990. *The Political Economy of Hunger.* Oxford: OUP.

political education   A term used in several senses. To MILL and BAGEHOT it was the learning process undergone by citizens who participated in democratic discussion. Michael OAKESHOTT in his famous inaugural lecture was concerned to make the point that politics is an activity in which success can never be the result of book learning or formal education, but comes from an understanding of the history of one's country and the values underlying its procedures and traditions. Bernard Crick perceives it as part of school and university education.

'Political literacy' is an essential component of the training of a democratic citizenry.

Reading
Crick, B. and A. Porter. 1968. *Political Education and Political Literacy*. London: Longman; Oakeshott, M. 1962. 'Political Education'. In *Rationalism in Politics* 111–36. London: Methuen. (First delivered as an inaugural lecture for the Chair of Government at the London School of Economics in 1950.)

political finance   The funding of political parties and their leaders and CANDIDATES has become increasingly important. Although money is needed to pay the salaries of workers in PARTY ORGANIZATION, the bulk of party finance is spent on election campaigns. The expenditure is on posters, SAMPLE SURVEYS, personalized mail, and television and broadcasting time, especially dear in North America. The decline of local organization and party memberships has resulted in much of this work being done centrally. In Britain this trend is accentuated by strict limitation of candidates' campaign spending. In the USA, where contenders for public office have to contest PRIMARIES to obtain NOMINATION before fighting a general election some weeks later, financing campaigns is a personal rather than a party problem. Presidential candidates who have to traverse the whole country spend enormous sums. One consequence is that it is difficult to be a Presidential candidate unless one is a very wealthy person; another is that one needs financial support from business corporations and/or trade unions, private millionaires and, in the USA, POLITICAL ACTION COMMITTEES. The revenue from party members' subscriptions has always been a small element for campaign purposes.

Large donors to party funds are likely to exert influence over policy. This has increasingly become a cause for complaint particularly where the benefactors are foreign. It was always known that the Soviet Communist Party gave money to Communist Parties in the West. More recently the American Central Intelligence Agency (CIA) donated funds to Italian parties. Hong Kong businessmen gave money to the British Conservative Party. The MULTINATIONALS, for obvious reasons, are keen to be on good terms with any party that is likely to govern. Scandals about party finance have become frequent in recent years. Consequently demands that parties should be funded from the public purse have become common. Yet where this has already happened, as in the USA since 1971, there is not much evidence to support the view that it has ended POLITICAL CORRUPTION.

See also CADRE PARTY; CAMPAIGNING; ELECTIONS; MASS PARTIES; POLITICAL CORRUPTION; PRIMARIES.

Reading
Alexander, H.E. ed. 1979. *Political Finance*. Beverly Hills: Sage; Pinto-Duschinsky, M. 1981. *British Political Finance 1830–1980*. Washington, D.C.: American Enterprise Institute.

political generations   Age cohorts of about 10 years in extent. Hence any nation may have about five such generations each of which may have been similarly influenced by events during their politically formative years, that is the years between 17 and the middle twenties. It is during this period that people vote for the first time, become part of the labour force, enter colleges and universities and undergo military service. All these experiences tend to shape views towards the outside world. When the period in question is marked by a worrying crisis such as economic depression or war, it tends to produce a feeling of solidarity among the generation involved. War is especially prone to have this impact. The World War II generation had experienced pre-war depression and were then called upon to make great sacrifices for the community, enduring hardship and danger. The result was a radical generation that did not measure worth in pecuniary terms. Later generations, without these experiences, could not be expected to have similar values. They were not radical to the same degree. See also POLITICAL SOCIALIZATION.

Reading
Mannheim, K. 1952. *Essays on the Sociology of Knowledge*. London: Routledge; Rintala, M. 1979. *The Constitution of Silence: Essays on Generational Themes*. London: Greenwood.

political geography   See ELECTORAL GEOGRAPHY; GEOPOLITICS.

political influence   See POLITICAL POWER.

political integration   Any attempt to bring political units into a closer relationship. The term is usually applied to the integration of separate territories or states into one state. Examples commonly cited are those of federal states such as Switzerland in 1848 and the USA in 1789. Unitary states also are often the result of an integration, like Britain – formed in 1707 from the union of Scotland and England. The effort to integrate European countries into the European Union is a popular theme with political scientists.
See also CENTRE–PERIPHERY RELATIONS.

Reading
Nicoll, W. and T.C. Salmon. 1997. *Building European Union*. Manchester: Manchester University Press.

political obligation   See CONSENT.

political participation   This can be of several kinds and at all levels of the POLITICAL SYSTEM. In authoritarian states it may be reserved for the ruling elite, though the masses may be mobilized and compelled to vote in elections in order to demonstrate the LEGITIMACY of the regime. Under DEMOCRACY, partici-

pation in politics is voluntary except in those few countries in which COMPULSORY VOTING is the law. There tends to be a feeling, however, among democratic citizens that they should vote. ROUSSEAU and MILL and, more recently, Pateman and Barber among others, have been enthusiasts for greater political participation. It is argued that taking part in the politics of one's country is good both for the moral and civic health of the individual and the political life of the nation. A public educated in the issues of the day will keep the politicians on their toes and ensure that only measures are adopted that are generally accepted. On the other side of the argument are those who fear too active a citizenry. SCHUMPETER (1883–1950) believed that 'the electoral mass is incapable of action other than a stampede' and considered that a DEMOCRACY was best in which people restricted participation to choosing between leaders at elections. Others argued that an apathetic public is necessary for good decision-making and the stability of the polity. It may also be a reflection of rationality: citizens refrain from interfering in the solution of problems they do not understand.

Studying participation is easiest at the level of ELECTIONS. One can easily calculate the turn-out. It is almost invariably lower in local elections, a disappointment for Millian liberals who believe this is the level at which the average citizen has most to contribute to the democratic process. Above the voting level political participation is slight. It has become common in research projects to study 'voters, ACTIVISTS and leaders'. This model of 'political stratification' can be refined by inserting party members between voters and activists, and 'stalwarts', those activists who regularly participate, between activists and leaders. One cannot do this without realizing how weak the desire for POLITICAL POWER is among the vast majority of democratic citizens. On the other hand, those who do not expect to exert power within the system or those who feel representative democracy and elections do not enable them to make a point, may turn to petitions, BOYCOTTS, strikes, demonstrations and POLITICAL VIOLENCE.

See also ACTIVISTS; PARTICIPATORY DEMOCRACY.

Reading
Barber, B. 1984. *Strong Democracy*. Berkeley: University of California Press; McLean, I. 1982. *Dealing in Votes*. Oxford: Martin Robertson; Milbrath, L.W. 1965. *Political Participation*. Chicago: Rand McNally; Morris-Jones, W.H. 1954. 'In Defence of Apathy'. In *Political Studies* 2, 25–37; Pateman, C. 1970. *Participation and Democratic Theory*. Cambridge: CUP; Schumpeter, J. 1943. *Capitalism. Socialism and Democracy*. London: Allen and Unwin; Verba, S., N.H. Nie and J.O. Kim. 1978. *Participation and Political Equality*. Cambridge: CUP.

political parties *See* AGGREGATIVE PARTIES; AGRARIAN PARTIES; CADRE PARTY; CENTRE PARTY; CHRISTIAN DEMOCRACY; CLASS PARTIES; ELECTORAL SYSTEMS; MASS PARTIES; PARTY ORGANIZATION; PARTY SYSTEMS; TOTALITARIANISM.

political philosophy *See* POLITICAL THEORY.

political power Power is the central concept in POLITICAL SCIENCE, yet it remains elusive. There is no unit of power so it cannot be quantified. We can speak of some having 'less power' or 'more power' but these are assessments, even guesses. Much wielding of power goes on 'behind the scenes'. It is often in the interests of power-holders not to allow how much power they possess to be discovered. Some may appear to hold power when they do not possess it: on the other hand, the perception that one has power may confer power on one. Studying power is therefore a problem. There is often great difficulty in identifying who is responsible for what has happened. Evaluating power is impossible where one cannot attribute responsibility for outcomes.

Probably the best known definition of power is that of Max WEBER (1864–1920) who described it as 'the chance of a man or number of men to realise their own will in a communal action against the resistance of others who are participating in the action'. This emphasizes will and opportunity, both important. 'Chance' may depend on circumstance but it will also involve the resources of power. These are many and various, including weapons, wealth, numbers of people, strategic location, information, political skills and reputation. Yet without the will to employ them power cannot be exercised.

Later commentators, like Bachrach and Baratz, pointed out that the decision to do nothing was a decision, although much more difficult to discern. Holders of power merely kept issues they disliked from appearing on political agendas. As many of these latter were 'hidden' the task of attributing power to someone, or some group, was far from easy. Lukes argued that real power was in the hands of hegemonies who fashioned people's perceptions and attitudes so that they indicated preferences that were not in their true interests. One implication is that DEMOCRACY is a delusion. Another is the presumption that it is possible to know others' true interests better than they do.

Styles of exercising power vary greatly. All STATES use coercion though some more brutally and arbitrarily than others. Power is exerted through sanctions of all kinds of which the most severe is the threat of death. It is an effective way of silencing one's political opponents. Another is imprisonment. But there are many milder sanctions such as fines. Manipulation is a form of control without sanctions or the threat of sanctions.

Manipulation of the masses can depend on the ability to control the sources and distribution of information. It may also depend on possession of oratorical skill and a capacity to understand people's prejudices. Influence is a style of power that is particularly undiscernable. It often is exerted in conversations between two people in back rooms. Formal power-holders such as ministers may seek the information and opinions of those held to be well-informed, wise and experienced. Such people are influential. The extent to which influence is important will depend on a country's POLITICAL CULTURE and the values of its politicians. Intellectuals are believed to be more influential in France than in Britain. (Like all statements about power this one is hard to verify.)

See also POLITICAL SCIENCE; POLITICS; SOCIAL CLASS; STATE.

Reading
Alford, R. and R. Friedland. 1985. *The Powers of Theory*. Cambridge: CUP; Bachrach, P. and M.S. Baratz. 1962. 'Two Faces of Power', *American Political Science Review* 56, 947–52; Dahl, R.A. 1963. *Modern Political Analysis*. Englewood Cliffs: Prentice Hall; Lukes, S. 1976. *Power: a Radical View*. London: Macmillan.

political psychology An infant social science which can be viewed in two main fields – the psychology of the masses and the psychology of political leaders. The political psychologist is concerned to investigate the behaviour and motivation of political actors and to relate it to factors of a personal nature. This is much easier to study in the case of political leaders as their memoirs and biographies are available. The outcome of the little research that has been conducted is that they are unusual people. It is not common to want power and those that desire might well be compensating for emotional deprivation in childhood. Much of the discussion about the psychology of those who do not want to lead has been in the field of social

psychology and related to the behaviour of crowds. It is very difficult to use the sophisticated questions psychologists want to ask in sample survey work. Most empirical work of a behavioural kind in this area has investigated the AUTHORI-TARIAN PERSONALITY.

See also AUTHORITARIAN PERSONALITY; POLITICAL ATTITUDES.

Reading
Barber, J.D. 1977. *The Presidential Character*. Englewood Cliffs; Prentice Hall; Knutson, J.M. ed. 1973. *Handbook of Political Psychology*. San Francisco: Jossey-Bass; Lasswell, H. 1949. *Power and Personality*. London: Chapman and Hall; Lasswell, H. 1930. *Psychopathology and Politics*. Reprinted 1952 in *The Political Writings of Harold D. Lasswell*. Glencoe: Free Press; Payne, J.L. and O. Woshinsky. 1984. *The Motivation of Politicians*. Chicago: Nelson-Hall.

political recruitment The term tends to overestimate the conscious efforts undertaken to introduce people to politics. Only in totalitarian states is there some policy of the selection of cadres from amongst ideologically reliable and administratively competent young people. In democracies the important part of the selection process is self-selection. Most people refuse to be recruited. They do not want to participate in politics. Political parties sometimes undertake membership drives and, in recent years, have given up door-to-door methods in favour of adver-tisements in newspapers asking joiners to give their credit card numbers. Such impersonal recruitment emphasizes that the party member is not expected to be an ACTIVIST, though a small proportion might end that way. From among activists willing CANDIDATES for local government might be chosen and a few of these might be recruits for candidatures for the LEGISLATURE. The result of these processes to date has been legislators who are an unrepresentative bunch. White, middle-class men predominate. Political scientists have tended to concentrate on elite recruitment and studies that see the process as a whole are needed.

See also ACTIVISTS; PARTY ORGANIZATION; REPRESENTATION.

Reading

Eulau, H. and M. Czudnowski. eds. 1976. *Elite Recruitment in Democratic Politics.* Beverly Hills: Sage.; Ranney, A. 1965. *Pathways to Parliament.* Madison, Wisc.: University of Wisconsin Press; Prewitt, K. 1970. *The Recruitment of Political Leaders.* New York: Bobbs-Merrill.

political science   The study of POLITICS at all levels of which the most basic is the study of conflict. Analysis of personal conflict may be a help to political scientists. Psychologists study aggressive instincts, or individual capacities to compromise, and these assist in understanding group conflict.

Collective conflict and its resolution is bound to be the main field of interest. Broadly speaking, study takes place at three levels: locally, nationally and internationally. Conflict between states is the core of the discipline INTERNATIONAL RELATIONS, sometimes taught as part of the syllabus of university departments of political science and sometimes taught in its own department. Conflict between local groups at the community level is also studied by political scientists. Groups may clash over the building of a new bypass or the closing of a footpath. In some countries local ethnic groups may resort to armed conflict.

A very large proportion of political science, however, is concerned with conflict and its resolution between nationally organized ASSOCIATIONS, of which there are two forms – PRESSURE GROUPS and political parties. Sometimes a case study might examine one of these in detail: frequently, however, comparative treatment yields greater comprehension of the political scene. This area of the subject is called COMPARATIVE POLITICS or political insti-

tutions. It involves some knowledge of CONSTITUTIONAL LAW, a good deal of the historical background to institutions and an understanding of a country's POLITICAL CULTURE which includes its value-system as it relates to politics.

Another wide field of political science is concerned with the implementation of political decisions. Modern STATES have large administrative apparatuses which need supervision and co-ordination. These themes come under the rubric of PUBLIC ADMINISTRATION, one of the early foundations on which academic study of POLITICS was built. Recently it has taken some stimulus from management studies and organizational theory. In addition it has extended into the study of policy-making because of the increasing influence of TECHNOCRACY.

A further sector of the discipline is devoted to studying reasons for the maintenance and breakdown of political systems. Rebellions and REVOLUTIONS are important watersheds in world history. The dramatic disintegration of the Soviet Union from 1989 to 1990 is a recent reminder of how an apparently stable regime may quickly collapse. Examination of revolutions leads to investigating CLEAVAGES within states, their depth and intensity and how to deal with them. This in turn has led to the exploration of environments of political systems, particularly where the POLITY overlaps with the economy and society. The two areas are known, respectively, as POLITICAL ECONOMY and POLITICAL SOCIOLOGY.

See also INTERNATIONAL RELATIONS; POLITICAL POWER; POLITICAL THEORY; POLITICS; PUBLIC ADMINISTRATION.

Reading

Ball, A.R. 1971. *Modern Politics and Government.* London: Macmillan; Bealey, F.W., R.A. Chapman and M. Sheehan. 1999. *Elements in Political Science.* Edinburgh: Edinburgh University Press; Dahl, R.A. 1963. *Modern Political Analysis.* New Haven: YUP; Duverger, M. 1968. *Sociologie Politique.* Paris:

Presses Universitaires de France; Laski, H.J.
1937. *An Introduction to Politics*. London: Allen
and Unwin; Laver, M. 1983. *Invitation to
Politics*. Oxford: Martin Robertson.

political socialization Socialization relates to the processes by which a person is
integrated into society. Hence it begins at
the age of infancy. Political socialization
is the process of adaptation and integration by which one becomes politically
aware. It is likely therefore to be at a later
stage of development, though precisely
when and to what extent socialization
affects the development of attitudes and
beliefs about politics are matters of
controversy. The family, the school and
the workplace are widely accepted as the
chief agents of political socialization,
though their relative influences are also
debated. Some argue that at a very early
age attitudes to parental authority determine later attitudes to political authority
and that children who are given an opportunity to share in family decisions become
confident and participatory citizens.
Another group is sceptical of the value of
questionnaires administered to children
and believes it is in contact with the wider
world, with authority and with peers at
school and in the workplace, that people
form their political opinions and allegiances. This latter group puts more
emphasis on experience and less on early
cultural influence. Only by using PANEL
samples could one investigate the relative
causal impacts of these factors. It is an
expensive method and likely to last for
two decades.
See also PANEL; POLITICAL GENERATIONS;
POLITICAL PSYCHOLOGY; POLITICAL SOCI-
OLOGY.

Reading
Dawson, R.E. and K. Prewitt. 1969. *Political
Socialization*. Boston: Little, Brown;
Greenstein, F. 1969. *Children and Politics*.
New Haven: YUP; Volgyes, L. 1975. *Political
Socialisation in Eastern Europe*. London:
Praeger.

political sociology A sub-discipline incorporating the concerns of both
sociologists and political scientists. Its
borders tend to be hard to determine.
Sociology has had more influence on
political science than the latter on sociology. WEBER and Durkheim, the two
'grand theorists' of sociology, influenced
political theorists, as did MARX. Weber
with his insistence on the importance of
the trinity of wealth, STATUS and power
was not widely known in the English-
speaking world until after 1945. Since
then, his concept of IDEAL TYPES and his
emphasis on the value-free nature of
social science speculation and research
have become part of the discourse.
His typology of AUTHORITY and his
characterization of BUREAUCRACY are
also widely accepted. Durkheim was
concerned with the sustainability of social
systems, especially as he saw society
becoming more specialized and interdependent. His study of *Suicide* (1897)
was the first to use empirical data to test
hypotheses systematically. Marx's perspective of politics was that of reaction or
revolution; but his theory of class and of
the relation between economy and polity
has influenced most state theorists since.

Political sociology was also the meeting
ground of disciplines through the work of
Talcott Parsons (1902–90). He was concerned with the problems of the
adaptability and survival of social systems. Individuals, he argued, are
socialized largely by cultural influence
into acceptance of the values of systems and so into acceptance of the
systems. Thus the system was maintained. It was easy to adapt this
structural-functional approach to POLITI-
CAL SYSTEMS as Easton demonstrated.
Political scientists, who in the 1960s
became interested in the survival or
collapse of new states and even, somewhat later, with the survival of
DEMOCRACY, often either consciously or
unconsciously used the Parsonian model.

Political sociology also became an area of political science through behaviouralism. Particularly for voting studies it was necessary to use a wide range of socio-demographic data. Class, generation, gender, religion and occupational grouping were related to political allegiance. Eric Allardt believes the term 'sociology of politics' is better used to cover this area; but most political scientists have not been so finely discriminatory. The result is that political sociology has become a wide field. When the sociologist, Seymour Lipset, invaded political science with his work *Political Man* (1960), he reflected all three approaches.

See also POLITICAL BEHAVIOUR; POLITICAL ECONOMY; POLITICAL PSYCHOLOGY; POLITICAL SCIENCE; STABILITY; SYSTEMS ANALYSIS.

Reading
Allardt, E. 1987. 'Political sociology'. In *Blackwell Encyclopaedia of Political Institutions*, 474–6. Ed. V. Bogdanor. Oxford: Blackwell Publishers.; Linz, J. and A. Stepan. eds. 1978. *The Breakdown of Democratic Regimes*. Baltimore: Johns Hopkins University Press; Pizzorno, A. ed. 1971. *Political Sociology*. Harmondsworth: Penguin.

political stratification   A division of a political system by the degree of participation different political actors evince. Thus a common stratification is that of leaders, activists and voters. A more complex one might include members of parties, politically committed voters, uncommitted voters and non-voters. It is common to relate the pyramid of participation which emerges from this exercise with SOCIAL STRATIFICATION.

See also SOCIAL STRATIFICATION.

Reading
Bealey, F.W., J. Blondel and W.P. McCann. 1965. *Constituency Politics*. London: Faber; Blondel, J. 1963. *Voters, Parties and Leaders*. Harmondsworth: Penguin.

political succession   The procedure by which one political leader succeeds another. It is usually applied to changes in governments and therefore is of the utmost importance in the life of a country. The differences between authoritarian and democratic states in this respect are great. In some totalitarian regimes, especially under Communism, leadership change takes place secretly after much conspiring in and outside committees. Often the details are only known long after the event and they do not appear to conform to any rules or conventions. In MILITARY REGIMES succession often takes place through COUPS D'ÉTAT. By contrast, in democracies leadership, often party leadership, gives way to alternative leadership according to well-established rules or conventions. The two most common are defeat of the government in the legislature or in elections, the holding of which will also be prescribed by rules. Another situation for relinquishment is where a leader's term of office is fixed by law. The willingness of defeated or terminated leaders to resign and give way to the successor designated by the rules is regarded as a crucial test of a country's democratic standing.

See also DEMOCRACY; MILITARY REGIMES; TOTALITARIANISM.

Reading
Rush, M. 1974. *How Communist States Change their Rulers*. Ithaca, NY: Cornell University Press.

political system   This term has developed two meanings. The traditional sense was about the interrelationship of executives, legislatures and judiciaries within a constitutional framework. ELECTORAL SYSTEMS and political parties and their parts in government formation and expression of political opinion would often be included. 'Regime' was then used, and still is, to describe a wider perspective, taking in methods of decision-making and values underlying the citizen-state relationship. One speaks of 'authoritarian regimes' and 'democratic regimes'. But 'political system', in its new meaning, has a still wider framework. Political science has borrowed the Parsonian concept of system and a political system is now a structural-functional model designed to explain and understand the situations of survival, maintenance, decay and collapse.

See also CONSTITUTIONS; MODEL; POLITICAL SCIENCE; POLITICAL SOCIOLOGY; SYSTEMS ANALYSIS.

Reading
Davies, M.R. and V.A. Lewis. 1971. *Models of Political Systems*. London: Macmillan; Easton, D. [1953] 1981. *The Political System*. Chicago: University of Chicago Press; Wheare, K.C. 1966. *Modern Constitutions*. Oxford: OUP.

political theory Sometimes this is a synonym for political philosophy; at other times a distinction is made. Political philosophy is taken to mean what philosophers like Plato and Hume said about POLITICS. This is sometimes called 'classical political theory' which tended to begin with statements about the nature of Man and his obligations to AUTHORITY. Teaching tended to concentrate on one political philosopher at a time and to be concerned with the internal logic of each. Political theory tended to spend some time on intellectual and cultural backgrounds and to attach importance to the history of concepts like the STATE. Yet these were only tendencies. The terms were often used interchangeably.

'Modern political theory' has been more a theory of politics than a philosophy of politics; but it has taken various forms. One group of writers has turned to the examination of age-old concepts such as JUSTICE, but has dealt with them more acutely. Another has analysed the behaviour of political actors in terms of models of rational choice like the Prisoner's Dilemma. A third, beginning

with Ernest BARKER, has sought to relate political ideas to political behaviour. After Barker POLITICAL SOCIOLOGY facilitated this enterprise. Finally there are the theorists of political science who examine the premises and METHODOLOGY of their own discipline.

See also GAME THEORY; JUSTICE; PUBLIC CHOICE THEORY; RATIONAL CHOICE; SYSTEMS ANALYSIS.

Reading
Barker, E. 1942. *Reflections on Government*. Oxford: OUP; Brown, A. 1986. *Modern Political Philosophy*. Harmondsworth: Penguin; Oppenheim, F. 1981. *Political Concepts*. Oxford: Blackwell; Ryan, A. 1970. *The Philosophy of the Social Sciences*. London: Macmillan.

political violence This can be an all-embracing term as violence is ubiquitous; but it is usual to use it only to mean domestic political violence and to exclude 'state violence', violence committed by the STATE against its citizens, and also repression without physical harm often called 'structural violence'. Hence political violence means rebellion, rioting, looting, sabotage, TERRORISM and physical conflicts between groups. This last includes communal violence, usually between different ethnic and/or religious groups which, at its worst, can descend into CIVIL WAR and massacres. Statistics show that the worst examples have been in Africa and Asia and coincide frequently with autocratic rule. Internal extremes of wealth and poverty are often associated with political violence, especially where economic difference is linked to ethnic difference. Violent groups also seem to emerge in countries which have lost wars so that a decline in national self-esteem may provoke political violence.

See also CIVIL WAR; GENOCIDE; GUERRILLA WARFARE; REVOLUTIONS; TERRORISM.

Reading
Gurr, T.R. ed. 1980. *Handbook of Political Conflict*. New York: Free Press; Hibbs, D.A.

1973. *Mass Political Violence*. New York: Wiley; Rule, J.B. 1988. *Theories of Civil Violence*. Berkeley: University of California Press.

politician Someone who practises politics. Usually the word describes national practitioners, but there are local and even part-time politicians. Some societies respect their politicians more than others, but in general it is not a greatly respected profession. Politicians are seen to be glib, dishonest, cunning and self-interested. Journalists and biographers may use the term 'statesman' to describe someone whom they believe to be better because less influenced by sectional interests. Statesmen, however, are often better endowed with the political arts of persuasiveness, deviousness and skill in bargaining strategies than mere politicians.

See also POLITICS.

politics The term has been used in at least four ways. To many citizens politics is a remote activity of a vaguely disreputable kind. It is indulged in by people they do not respect or trust, arguing about policies they do not understand. In authoritarian regimes it may be seen merely as the words and deeds of governments. In democracies, to the minority of politically interested people, politics is what is featured in the media concerning the 'affairs of state' – gladiatorial arguments between contentious politicians at home and relations between states abroad.

A political science definition might be that politics is activity that involves collective conflict and its resolution. Conflict is here used in a wide sense to mean contestation. All group interrelationships, whether between STATES, or between factions within states, will display some disagreements. There will be disputes about what objectives are to be reached and disputes about how to

reach them. A very large majority of human beings prefer peace and STABILITY to instability and WAR. Where this majority affects the outcomes of disagreements the skilful politician will be the one who is able to resolve disputes peacefully. Of course, this requires skill and the willingness to bargain on both sides of the contestation.

Much of the conflict within states is about the allocation of material resources. Markets cannot be entirely relied upon to do this without a framework of LAW AND ORDER. When people draw guns normal trading ceases. Social and economic relationships of all kinds are therefore dependent upon the regularization and institutionalization of processes of discussion, bargaining and compromise. Politics is necessary for the continuation of a decent existence.

See also POLITICAL POWER; POLITICAL SCIENCE; STATE.

Reading
Crick, B. 1982. *In Defence of Politics*. Harmondsworth: Penguin; Ferns, H.S. and K.W. Watkins. 1985. *What Politics is About*. London: Methuen.

polity Often used as a synonym for POLITICAL SYSTEM, the term is a translation of the Greek *polis* which in ARISTOTLE's typology of governments was an uncorrupted form in which the many ruled for the public good.

poll tax A poll is an old-fashioned term for a head. Hence elections, or 'polls', were about the counting of heads. A poll tax is a tax of equal amount on each adult individual. The term has an unsavoury connotation as it was used in some southern states of the USA to prevent blacks from voting and this use was outlawed in the 24th amendment to the Constitution (1964). In England a poll tax led to the Peasants' Rebellion in 1381. Officially called the Community Charge, its introduction in Scotland in 1989, and its extension to all the UK a year later, led to rioting and the downfall of Prime Minister Thatcher. New taxes are always unpopular.

See also FISCAL CRISIS; LOCAL GOVERNMENT; RATES; TAX REVOLTS.

polyarchy   A word introduced into the language of political scientists by DAHL and LINDBLOM in *Politics, Economics and Welfare* (1953). Literally meaning rule by the many, it describes a situation in which power is not centralized but divided among numerous interests and groups. Dahl illustrated this feature of DEMOCRACY in his study of New Haven. Later he emphasized that he had not implied that all groups had equal power: indeed, a few might have too much power.

See also DEMOCRACY; PLURALISM.

Reading
Dahl, R.A. 1971. *Polyarchy*. New Haven: YUP; Dahl, R.A. 1985. *A Preface to Economic Democracy*. Cambridge: Polity Press.

popular fronts   This expression is from the lexicon of left-wing movements, though it sometimes includes radical liberals of the left-centre. It is associated also with coalitions against Fascism in the 1930s, though in 1988 a Popular Front was formed in Estonia to campaign for independence from the USSR. The need for a front against Fascism first led the Third (Communist) International to call for a 'United Front' of the working-class; but this was broadened to a 'Popular Front' to unite all opponents of Fascist aggression after the USSR entered the League of Nations in 1934. In Britain where Communism was weak the Labour Party refused to support it; but Popular Fronts were formed as electoral alliances in Spain in 1936, where its victory sparked off the Civil War, and in France where the Popular Front government (1936–8) carried out a radical social programme. More generally throughout the democratic world popular fronts campaigned for aid for the Spanish Republican government.

See also SECOND BALLOT.

Reading
Cole, G.D.H. 1937. *The People's Front*. London: Gollancz.

popular sovereignty   See SOVEREIGNTY OF THE PEOPLE.

populism   This term has two connotations. It is used to describe political movements and to characterize a type of politician. Most populist movements have been agrarian. The earliest, in the 1870s, was in Russia. The People's Will, or *narodniki*, were intellectuals who identified themselves with the peasantry and went to live amongst them in the belief that true values and the ideal community could be found in the village. At first they were received with suspicion, but later their efforts resulted in the foundation of the Social Revolutionary Party, suppressed by Lenin in 1918. Peasant parties were much more successful in Poland, Bulgaria and Rumania. In the USA agrarian radicalism in the 1890s was preached by the Populist Party which was strong in the poorer farming states. In the 1896 election their candidate, William Jennings Bryan, was the nominee of the Democrats and came close to victory. Agrarian radicalism tends to be a protest against the control of farming products' prices by remote markets in which finance CAPITALISM is perceived as a hostile force. Populism also distrusts distant legislators and tends to believe in DIRECT DEMOCRACY.

Populist politicians can often be found leading populist movements. Elsewhere they are the sort of political leader whose gestures and use of symbols is meant to proclaim identification with the PEOPLE. Appeals to NATIONALISM and attacks on those regarded as unpatriotic may characterize their pronouncements. Hence they may be rather short on explanation of policy and more inclined to indulge in rhetoric. Intellectuals, the 'chattering classes' and foreign influences may be easy targets.

See also PEOPLE; POUJADISM.

Reading
Canovan, M. 1981. *Populism*. London: Function Books; Ionescu, G. and E. Gellner. eds. 1969. *Populism: its Meaning and National Characteristics*. London: Weidenfeld.

pork barrel Any money or promise of investment obtained by a US Representative for her/his Congressional District, or Senator for her/his state, is said to come out of the 'pork barrel'. Chairs of committees are especially good at procuring federal defence contracts for their constituencies.

See also BOSSES; PATRONAGE.

positional goods A term coined by Hirsch to describe goods which are valued for their position. Thus a remote beach will only have value as long as it remains undiscovered by the multitude.

Reading
Hirsch, F. 1977. *Social Limits to Growth*. London: Routledge.

positive discrimination A way of compensating for social inequalities by applying easier standards of selection to under-privileged groups. It has obvious political implications. Familiar examples are the privileged treatment in applications for places in higher education for the lowest castes in India and blacks and Hispanics in the USA.

positive law *See* LAW.

positivism First used by Comte (1798–1857) to denote a rational, 'scientific' methodology. Hence a positivistic approach tends to favour quantitative research and to exclude considerations of feelings, beliefs and values. It influenced philosophy and gave birth to logical positivism. Few social scientists today accept its crudest implications as some of the exponents of behaviouralism did in the 1950s. Political scientists are aware that people's values and beliefs influence their actions. Counting is no substitute for understanding.

post-colonial state A category of states which have gone through the process of DECOLONIZATION. They have many problems in common. Most of these are connected with their cultural backgrounds and their THIRD WORLD status. Their economic programmes are often unrealizable in the globalized economy and their judicial and police systems are unable to control the level of POLITICAL VIOLENCE which is often the result of tribal and ethnic conflict. Their governability and even, in some cases, their viability is at risk. Such scenarios, however, are not exhibited only by post-colonial states. Yugoslavia after 1989 had very similar difficulties. Partition may be one solution though BALKANIZATION has its own problems.

See also COLONIALISM; DEPENDENCY; NEO-COLONIALISM.

post-fordism An era which social and economic theorists believe is succeeding the Fordist phase of history. Post-fordism will be a new era of capitalist accumulation which will differ from the preceding era in that oligopolistic conflict will follow oligopolistic stagnation. It will be connected with GLOBALIZATION and the freeing of world trade. The MULTI-NATIONALS are being forced to adopt more flexible production methods and to indulge in product differentiation and competition. New technology will lead to increased unemployment.

See also CAPITALISM; FORDISM; GLOBAL-IZATION.

Reading
Aglietta, M. 1979. *A Theory of Capitalist Regulation*. London: New Left Books.; Amin, A. ed. 1994. *Post-Fordism: a Reader*. Oxford:

Blackwell; Boyer, R. and J-P. Durand. 1993. *L'Après-Fordisme*. Paris: Syros.

post-industrial society This term, which assumes that INDUSTRIAL SOCIETY has passed away, encourages prophecy. The difficulty is that many of the main features of modern industrial society – poor wages, low pay, urbanization, factory employment – are still with us. Indications of change are the expanded service sector of the economy and the new information technology exemplified by the Internet. Perhaps in time many more people will work at home and communicate with workmates by computer. This assumes a society in which quality of life is the main concern and a technological, scientific intelligentsia has replaced present economic and political hierarchies.
See also INDUSTRIAL SOCIETY; POST-MATERIALISM; TECHNOCRACY.

Reading
Bell, D. 1974. *The Coming of Post-Industrial Society*. London: Heinemann; Kumar, K. 1978. *Prophecy and Progress*. Harmondsworth: Penguin.

post-materialism The values of western society have been seen as materialistic – concerned with 'getting and spending' and technological advance. Post-materialist values, it is argued, are more oriented towards the quality of life, self-expression and rejection of technology where it is detrimental to these ideals. 'Post-materialists' also tend to believe more in sexual freedom and are opposed to NATIONALISM and RACISM. They are often members of environmental and human rights movements. Inglehart believed that the value-change was likely to be inter-generational: those born since 1945 would be more 'post-materialist'. He tested this hypothesis in 1970 in cross-national surveys and discovered great differences between young and old. Later surveys in 1985 showed that ageing did not lead to any decline in post-material values. Hence these values are becoming more established.

These findings must be qualified. Materialists still remain in the majority and support in the 1980s for Reaganism and THATCHERISM shows that materialism still has great appeal. Again, opposition to some technological advance, such as that with environmentally damaging implications, can coincide with enthusiastic adoption of other aspects of technology. Thus a generation living in trees or tunnels to impede the building of motorways and airports can still be one well-equipped with laptop computers.
See also ECOLOGICAL POLITICS; INDUSTRIAL SOCIETY; NEW SOCIAL MOVEMENTS; SINGLE ISSUE POLITICS.

Reading
Deth, J. van. 1983. 'The persistence of materialist and postmaterialist value orientations'. In *European Journal of Political Research* 11, 63–79; Inglehart, R. 1977. *The Silent Revolution*. Princeton: Princeton University Press; Inglehart, R. 1990. *Culture Shift in Advanced Industrial Society*. Princeton: Princeton University Press.

postmodernism The problem with this term is that one needs to define what 'modernism' was and when it ended. The postmodernists might define the beginning of the postmodern era in 1968. In the field of social and political thought (much of postmodernist argument is concerned with art and architecture) the ideas appear to have germinated in the Parisian student riots of 1968. The leading intellectuals – Foucault, Barthes, Lyotard and Derrida – are French. There is diversity in their thought; but it can be summarized as a reaction against universal explanations and grand theories. Hence 'meta-narratives', such as MARX's and HEGEL's accounts of history, are delusions and the belief that science and reason could ensure a steady progress to a better life for all disappeared with the Holocaust. Postmodernists also reject the notion that there is a general unity of mankind. Hence the Rights of Man and other declarations of human rights are regarded by them as erroneous outcomes of the ENLIGHTENMENT. Foucault (1926–84) argued that power is decentralized. Thus the implication is that political action should be localized and in support of small groups. NEW SOCIAL MOVEMENTS appear to reflect this contention. Lyotard advocates living in the present and giving up the struggle to understand. Hence Nietzsche (1844–1900) is his moral guide. Postmodernism is more an attitude to life and living than a system of ideas.

See also IDEALISM; MARXISM; POST-MATERIALISM.

Reading
Foucault, M. 1969. *The Archaeology of Knowledge*. London: Tavistock; Jameson, F. 1991. *Postmodernism, or the Cultural Logic of Late Capitalism*. Durham, NC: Duke University Press; Lyotard, J-F. 1984. *The Post-Modern Condition*. Minneapolis: Minnesota University Press.

poujadism   Pierre Poujade was the founder of the Union de Défense des Commerçants et Artisans in 1953. This was an organization of shopkeepers and small businessmen formed to protest against the rationalizing economic policies of post-war French governments. The taxation policies of Mendès-France, who became Prime Minister of the Fourth Republic in 1954, incensed the UDCA and they became a political party, winning 53 seats and gaining two and a half million votes (12 per cent of the total) at the 1956 election, thus contributing greatly to the instability of the Republic and its supercession by the Fifth Republic in 1958. Thereafter they collapsed, though much of their support went into the National Front. Poujadism as a term survived and passed into the vocabulary of political scientists. It connotes a mobilized lower-middle class movement, inspired by populist oratory,

with an anti-Semitic, racist vocabulary and condemning big business and trade-union movements alike. Poujadistes everywhere are contemptuous of democratic processes and institutions.

See also ANTI-SEMITISM; FASCISM; POPULISM; XENOPHOBIA.

Reading
Hoffman, S. 1956. *Le Mouvement Poujade*. Paris: Colin; Taguieff, P-A. 1989. *Le National Populisme*. Paris: La Découverte.

power   *See* POLITICAL POWER.

pragmatism   The art of the practical. A pragmatic politician is one who is good at assessing what can and what cannot be done. She/he is concerned less with ends than the more ideological politician, who believes one should be true to one's objectives even at the risk of incurring unpopularity and losing power. The term tends to be used in 'Ya boo!' politics with conservative politicians claiming possession of it in contrast with their doctrinally influenced left-wing opponents. But there is a more serious basis to this dichotomy. Whereas the left may claim its philosophic basis in the ENLIGHTENMENT with its belief in reason, the right remains sceptical of theories about improvement, putting its trust in INSTITUTIONS that have stood the test of time.

See also CONSERVATISM; LIBERALISM; RATIONALISM; SOCIALISM.

prefect   A government agent of great seniority appointed to be chief administrator of a local authority area. In France Napoleon created the Prefects in 1800 and stationed one in each of the *départements*, the 81 (now 96) local government units set up by the Revolution. Their function was to ensure the will of the central government was known and acceded to. Consequently they were often unpopular and were suspected of interfering in parliamentary elections. The smaller sub-units, the *communes*, were given sub-prefects. As France also had local elected governments the relationship with these central appointees was bound to be difficult. The prefects exercised the *tutelle*, tutelage over the councillors; on the other hand, because of their legal knowledge and central connections, they were often crucial in obtaining central government investment for their *départements*. After 1964 when 22 regions were created, a regional prefect was appointed in each one. The *loi Defferre* in 1982, however, transferred the chief executive power to chairmen of elected councils. After unification in 1870 Prefects were appointed in each Italian province. They never exercised the same control as the French prefects.

See also DECENTRALIZATION; FIELD SERVICE ADMINISTRATION.

Reading
Machin, H. 1977. *The Prefect in French Public Administration*. London: Croom Helm; Tarrow, S. 1977. *Between Centre and Periphery*. New Haven: YUP.

preferential voting *See* ELECTORAL SYSTEMS.

prerogative The executive right to exercise powers without check by the legislature. In nearly all democracies these have been progressively limited. In Britain what was once the 'Royal Prerogative' is in the hands of ministers. Compared with other English-speaking countries its extent is considerable consisting of the right to declare war, make peace, conduct foreign affairs, appoint to civil and military positions and dissolve Parliament. The judiciary has always been reluctant to interfere though it has done so more often in recent years.

In the USA the Presidential prerogative is much more restricted. The Constitution makes him commander-in-chief of the armed forces and in that role he appoints senior military and naval officers. It also gives him the right of pardon for federal crimes except in cases of impeachment. Governors of states exercise the right of pardon for murderers. In contrast, the President of the Fifth French Republic has a wide prerogative. He has the power to declare an emergency when he thinks the safety of France and the integrity of its institutions are imperilled. He has the power to nominate and dismiss PRIME MINISTERS and to chair the council of ministers. He is HEAD OF STATE and chief of the executive.

See also PARLIAMENTARY SYSTEMS; PRESIDENTIAL SYSTEMS.

Reading
Corwin, E.S. 1940. *The President: Office and Powers*. New York: New York University Press; Duverger, M. 1959. *La Cinquième République*. Paris: Presses Universitaires de France; Jennings, I. 1959. *Cabinet Government*. Cambridge: CUP.

presidential systems Political systems with executive presidents. Dignified presidents are usually found in PARLIAMENTARY SYSTEMS. A distinguishing feature of presidential systems is the separation of legislature and executive. A consequence of this is that the executive cannot participate in legislation and cannot be responsible to the legislature. The classic example is the USA. France under the Fifth Republic has a hybrid system which Duverger calls a 'semi-presidential system'. There is an executive with two heads. A popularly elected President with great powers and a Prime Minister with a cabinet which not only sits in the legislature but also, under Article 20 of the constitution, is 'responsible to Parliament'. Consequently a vote of censure leading to the government's defeat can be moved against it.

See also CONSTITUTIONS; PARLIAMENTARY SYSTEMS; PRESIDENTS.

Reading
Duverger, M. ed. 1986. *Les Régimes semi-presidentiels*. Paris: Presses Universitaires de France; Rose, R. and E.N. Suleiman. eds. 1980. *Presidents and Prime Ministers*. Washington, D.C.: American Enterprise

Institute; Wheare, K.C. 1966. *Modern Constitutions*. Oxford: OUP.

presidents Constitutionally presidents can be divided into two groups: dignified presidents and executive presidents. Dignified presidents have few powers but they are HEADS OF STATE. They receive ambassadors, bestow medals and perform at national ceremonies. Their position is similar to that of constitutional monarchs (whom they now greatly outnumber), except that they are elected for terms shorter than that of the length of reign of the average monarch. Their method of election varies. The Irish President is elected by popular vote for seven years; the Italian by the two parliamentary chambers for seven years; and the German for five years by an ELECTORAL COLLEGE half composed of the deputies in the Bundestag and half of delegates elected from the different Länder by Proportional Representation.

Executive presidents are both heads of state and chief executives of their countries. The American and the French presidents are the prominent ones in the democratic world. The US President is chosen for four years by an electoral college, consisting of a number of electors from each state allotted on a proportionate basis and chosen by popular vote. The French has a term of seven years and is elected popularly by the SECOND BALLOT method. The office is much more powerful in France because constitutional constraints on the Presidency are so much weaker. The American President is constantly checked by Congress and his domestic power is limited. Abroad he is much more powerful. As Commander-in-Chief of the armed forces he can deploy US forces around the world. Those Latin American countries that adopted US presidential government often became military DICTATORSHIPS because of this provision. In the USA Congressional control on military spending and the right of Congress alone to declare war, as well as Senate checks on treaty-making, prevents this outcome.

See also PARLIAMENTARY SYSTEMS; PRESIDENTIAL SYSTEMS.

Reading
Kellerman, B. 1984. *The Political Presidency*. New York: OUP; Neustadt, R. 1980. *Presidential Power*. New York: Wiley.

pressure groups Sometimes this term includes INTEREST GROUPS. A distinction can be made in that INTEREST GROUPS are not primarily concerned with exerting and organizing pressure publicly. Their *raison d'etre* precludes much open political action. On the other hand pressure groups exist for exerting pressure, usually on the STATE and frequently on other groups. Their activities are inevitable where democracy ensures FREEDOM OF ASSOCIATION.

Pressure groups have been categorized in various ways. The most common is the division between sectional groups concerned with the material interests of their members and promotional groups which publicize causes. The most familiar sectional groups are the SOCIAL PARTNERS, business and labour. Much of their energy is expended in bargaining with one another. They have some interests in common and others which conflict. Relative advantages will partly depend on the economic situation; but each is capable of pressing governments to introduce policies and legislation that favour one to the disadvantage of the other. Other important sectional groups are those that attempt to persuade the government to allocate the surplus so that they benefit. Old age pensioners' groups claim they most deserve a larger slice of the cake. Businesses argue for more favourable taxes. Farmers are among the most vociferous groups in pressing their case for agricultural subsidies. Sectional groups concerned with production and distribution may have power when governments need them; for example, when the nation is at war or when the government is undertaking management of the economy. This is the situation known as neo-corporatism.

Promotional groups are frequently representative of quite small sections of public opinion. Their strategy is to convert a majority of the public to support their cause which may be world disarmament, the legalization of cannabis, saving the whale, or the banning of fox-hunting. It may help if they can persuade a large political party to embody their objective within its programme. One tactic may be to permeate a party through converting the ACTIVISTS within the local branches. Most commonly, however, promotional groups seek attention from the media by staging dramatic incidents and holding demonstrations. Television has done much to assist these tactics. It is a necessarily gradual process. More violent extremist groups, such as those on the fringes of the Animal Rights and Pro-Life movement, will lose their causes much popularity.

The methods pressure groups adopt are affected by the institutional structures of the country in which they operate. The extent of their access to the legislative agenda is the key factor. In PARLIAMENTARY SYSTEMS, where executives have more power within the legislatures, pressure groups will find it difficult to obtain acceptance for their goals. On the other hand, in PRESIDENTIAL SYSTEMS where executive and legislature are separate their chances are greater. This is particularly the case in the USA where party discipline in Congress is weak and, in the House of Representatives, members have to be re-elected every two years. The paid lobbyists of the pressure groups try to buttonhole a majority of the membership (218) and secure support for the desired measure.

See also CORPORATISM; FREEDOM OF ASSOCIATION; INTEREST GROUPS; PLURALISM; SINGLE ISSUE POLITICS.

Reading
Finer, S.E. 1966. *Anonymous Empire*. 2nd edn. London: Pall Mall; Schlozman, K.L. and J.T. Tierney. 1986. *Organized Interests and American Democracy*. New York: Harper and Row; Truman, D. 1951. *The Governmental Process*. New York: Knopf; Wilson, F.L. 1987. *Interest Groups in France*. Cambridge: CUP.

pre-state political systems   Very early types of tribal organization with a chief or council of elders. Earlier primitive groups of hunters and food gatherers had no organization.
See also POLITICAL ANTHROPOLOGY.

primaries   The American method of candidate selection. Originally called 'direct primaries', the primaries were a method of excluding from the nominating process party organization which was involved with corruption. Primaries allow the voters for a party to select the party's candidate for the next election. Several aspirants for the NOMINATION may contest the primary: after the voting one candidate emerges as the party's champion. Primaries are used in nearly every state for local, state and Congressional elections. There are also 'Presidential primaries' but these are for selecting delegates to the party conventions held to nominate a candidate for the Presidency. Each state has its own rules.

The procedure evokes obvious questions. How is it ensured that only party voters vote in party primaries? The answer is that as ballots are secret it cannot be ensured. Voters have been required to swear oaths that they voted for the party at the last election; but this precaution does not satisfy everyone and, anyway, it is well known that many people forget who they voted for some two or more years earlier. States, who in most cases regulate primary elections by law, have adopted two main strategies. Either they require each party to draw up a register of its voters, so that to vote in a primary one has to put one's name on the party register. This produces the 'closed primary'. Or they merely allow the voter on polling day to vote in which primary she/he prefers. This is the 'open primary'. Another question is: How are people nominated for the primaries? There is great variety in state law in this respect. In a few states there are 'run-offs', preliminary polls to decide the two or three people who go on the primary ballot. In most states the system involves detailed legislation.

The primaries affect American politics in several ways. Each state has its own electoral law. The addition of primary laws adds to the complexities of getting elected. In the primaries different interests and personalities in the same party fight each other. This is bound to weaken party loyalties. Moreover, no primary contestants can count on the party organization and treasury to support their campaigns. They are forced to construct a personal machine and find their own money. Primaries are against parties, party discipline and PARTY ORGANIZATION. The formal party organizations become little more than instruments for nominating Presidential candidates. Parties are easily penetrable because the primary contests make ideological coherence an impossibility.

See also NOMINATION; PARTY ORGANIZATION; POLITICAL PARTIES.

Reading
Jewell, M.E. and D.M. Olson. 1982. *American State Political Parties and Elections*. Homewood, Ill.: Dorsey; Price, D.E. 1984. *Bringing Back the Parties*. Washington, D.C.: Congressional Quarterly Press.

primary party organization   *See* CELL.

prime ministerial government A term first used by Richard CROSSMAN to describe what he perceived as a new and centralizing trend in British politics. Journalists sometimes have gone as far as likening Prime Ministerial dominance to

'Presidential government'. There are some factors which have increased the PM's power in recent times. The most important is probably television and the way in which it has projected the image of the party leaders in election campaigns. Another is the proliferation of Cabinet committees and sub-committees, the memberships of which are all appointed by the PM. The Prime Minister's role as co-ordinator is enhanced by this growing complexity. One consequence has been the institution of prime ministerial policy units. Furthermore, the Cabinet Office has become more and more a tool of 10 Downing Street.

See also CABINET GOVERNMENT; PARLIAMENTARY SYSTEMS; PRESIDENTS.

Reading
Campbell, C. 1985. *Governments Under Stress*. Toronto: Toronto University Press; Crossman, R.H.S. 1972. *Inside View*. London: Cape; Hennessy, P. 1986. *Cabinet*. Oxford: Blackwell.

prime ministers Heads of governments and cabinets outside pure PRESIDENTIAL SYSTEMS. Sometimes the term 'premier' is used and in Germany 'Chancellor'. Their roles differ greatly dependent on the constitutional framework and, especially, the configuration of the PARTY SYSTEM. In federal states federal prime ministers will be constrained by the prime ministers of the territorial sub-governments. This is so in Australia and Canada and in Switzerland the post is little more than chairmanship of a committee of ministers from diverse parties. Where there is no majority party in the legislature the prime minister of a COALITION GOVERNMENT is likely to spend much time 'power-brokering', as in the Netherlands. It follows that prime ministers are likely to be most powerful in unitary states with MAJORITY PARTY GOVERNMENT. British prime ministers have the rights to appoint and dismiss ministers; to advise the monarch on the dissolution of the House of Commons;

and to speak for the government on any issue or policy.

See also COALITION GOVERNMENT; MAJORITY PARTY GOVERNMENT.

Reading
Jones, G.W. ed. 1991. *West European Prime Ministers*. London: Frank Cass.; King, A. ed. 1985. *The British Prime Minister*. London: Macmillan; Weller, P. 1985. *First Among Equals: Prime Ministers in Westminster Systems*. Sydney: Allen and Unwin.

primitive accumulation The process by which wealth is first concentrated. As described by MARX it begins with durable commodities, then precious metals and ends with finance capital, the basis of industrial capitalism and exploitation of people and resources for private profit.

See also CAPITALISM; COMMUNISM; MARXISM.

primitive communism In primitive societies, MARX and Engels argued, there was collective property and therefore no class domination. They acquired this notion from reading Lewis Morgan. Engels used it in his delineation of historical materialism.

See also DIALECTICAL MATERIALISM; MARXISM.

Reading
Engels, F. [1884] 1954. *The Origins of the Family, Private Property and the State*. Mosow: Foreign Languages Publishing House; Morgan, L.H. 1877. *Ancient Society*. London: Macmillan.

privatization A policy of returning publicly owned enterprise to the private sector. A key plank of British Conservative governments after 1979, it had an ideological slant in that it was designed to overturn the nationalizing policies of previous Labour governments. The contention is that private enterprise is more efficient and less bureaucratic. Governments are bad at running industries and services. Privatization can be achieved by selling to the highest bidder and/or sale to employees, or selling company shares through the stock market. Another reason for privatization may be the need to raise more revenue for the state treasury.

For the above reasons many countries indulged in privatization programmes from the 1980s onwards. New Zealand was a prominent example, but Chile, Nigeria, Malaysia, Singapore and France, among others, also privatized. The most noteworthy cases, however, were the post-Communist countries after 1989. Almost all enterprise including the farms were in the public sector and there was no apparatus, as in the other instances, for selling state-owned concerns. There were no private banks or stock exchanges. The main problem these states faced was that many of the buyers were the former managers, ex-Communist APPARATCHIKS who were frequently corrupt. Another problem, also applicable to the developing countries, was that domestic industry might be bought up and then asset-stripped by the MULTINATIONALS.

See also NATIONALIZATION; THATCHERISM.

pro-choice The position that a woman's right to have an abortion is based on her inalienable right to have control of her own body. The Supreme Court decision *Roe* v. *Wade*, 1973, ruled that a woman's constitutional right to privacy gave her the right to an abortion in the first three months of pregnancy.

See also FEMINISM; PRO-LIFE; REPRODUCTIVE POLITICS.

programme A listed statement of policy goals most commonly drawn up for electoral purposes. Political parties which promulgate programmes, with the serious expectation of achieving most of the policies, are known as 'programmatic parties'. Such an outcome is only possible where after elections there is likely to be a MAJORITY PARTY GOVERNMENT. Where ELECTORAL SYSTEMS

produce COALITION GOVERNMENT programmatic parties will not thrive.
See also MANDATE; MANIFESTOISM.

programming, planning, budgeting systems (PPBS) *See* BUDGET.

progressive taxation
A taxation system in which the amount one pays varies with what one can afford. Income tax is progressive because it increases as income increases. Moreover, wealthier people are often taxed at higher percentage rates.

progressives
A very general term intended to indicate a group of people with innovatory policies. The best-known Progressives were a movement rather than a political party which took shape in late nineteenth-century USA. They were a protest against politics being dominated by corrupt politicians linked with big business interests, especially the railway companies and the newly formed trusts. Reforming professional people led the Progressive movement which flourished in the years before 1914 and especially under the Presidency of Theodore Roosevelt (1901–9). In Britain the label has been used in local politics, frequently by groups opposed to local Labour administrations who did not wish to call themselves either Liberal or Conservative. Usually they were one or the other, or alliances of both.

proletariat *See* WORKING CLASS.

pro-life
A position opposed to abortion. In the USA 'pro-lifers' wish to reverse *Roe* v. *Wade*, 1973. It is in keeping with the official stand of the Roman Catholic church, though many fundamentalist Protestants now hold the same views. Some supporters of pro-life may have reservations about abortions for pregnant rape victims or mothers in labour whose life is in danger.

See also FEMINISM; PRO-CHOICE; REPRODUCTIVE POLITICS.

promotional groups *See* PRESSURE GROUPS.

pronunciamento
A Spanish term for a successful officers' revolt. Common in Central and South America, the most recent *pronunciamento* in Spain was General Franco's overthrow of the Spanish republic in 1936. A fine distinction, made by some officers, is that the word is only properly used when the action reflects the popular will; and any other military intervention is a COUP D'ÉTAT (in Spanish *golpe de estado*).
See also COUP D'ÉTAT.

propaganda
Systematically slanted information which is intended to affect the outlooks and attitudes of whole peoples. Originally a Vatican term concerned with the propagation of the faith, the word acquired a pejorative ring after World War I. Adolf Hitler (1889–1945) alleged that the collapse of the German Army in 1918 had been largely the result of clever manipulation of the news by Lord Northcliffe appointed by the British government for this purpose; and also of the effects of Bolshevik propaganda. He became convinced of the need for the 'big lie'. By the 1930s Fascist and Communist regimes were broadcasting propaganda internationally. In 1937 Yale University set up the Institute for the Study of Propaganda. Early research by social scientists concentrated on 'content analysis', the noting of repetitive phrases and symbolic terms. More recent work has been concerned with changes in attitudes as a result of media campaigns, especially during elections. It must be remembered that in democracies all propaganda has to face counter-propaganda, probably from several quarters. Totalitarian propaganda would lose much of its force (indeed Communist propaganda did so) if it were not

accompanied by an embargo on outside information.

See also DEMOCRACY; MASS MEDIA; POLITICAL COMMUNICATION; TOTALITARIANISM.

Reading
Chakotin, S. 1940. *The Rape of the Masses*. London: Routledge; Doob, L. 1948. *Public Opinion and Propaganda*. New York: Holt; Roetter, C. 1974. *The Art of Psychological Warfare*. New York: Stein and Day.

property A controversial concept. Proudhon (1809–65) said 'All property is theft'. He was advancing the anarchist view that private property is unnatural: in a properly ordered society property will be collective and will belong to no individual. To a lawyer that would mean there is no property because property must be legally defined. Indeed an ordered society is only possible when it becomes clear who owns and who does not own. Historically property in land was the first important problem and was solved by the invention of the trust deed. This gave landowners rights of use and disposal. As few people owned land inequality was marked. When entrepreneurs acquired land, built factories and organized productive enterprise they found their labour from among those without any property, who then sold their labour to the entrepreneur. Thus a new sort of inequality emerged with the capitalists owning the means of production and the exploited proletariat having nothing but their labour value in the market and even that was not always in demand. For the vast majority with little property political power through collective action became the compensatory strategy.

Property therefore lies at the intersection of legal, economic and political systems. It should be a crucial concern of political theorists. The LEGITIMACY of property is challenged by anarchists and communists. The rights of property owners in land, capital and financial assets can be and often are qualified by the actions of holders of political power. In democracies they may well be governments representing the demands of the comparatively poor. The distribution of property of all kinds has been central to the analysis of social inequality. Arguments about social justice and demands for the redistribution of property have been prominent in all political debates over the last century and a half.

See also ANARCHISM; CAPITALISM; COMMUNISM; JUSTICE; LAW; SOCIALISM; UTILITARIANISM.

Reading
Nozick, R. 1974. *Anarchy, State and Utopia*. New York: Basic Books; Rawls, J. 1971. *A Theory of Justice*. Cambridge, Mass.: HUP; Tawney, R.H. 1926. *Religion and the Rise of Capitalism*. London: John Murray.

proportional representation *See* ELECTORAL SYSTEMS.

protectionism *See* FREE TRADE.

provinces An ancient division of territories associated with monarchic rule. Thus the French revolutionaries abolished them and divided France into smaller *DÉPARTEMENTS*. Canada is divided into ten provinces, each with a provincial government and parliament.

psephology A term coined by F.R. Hardie and popularized by David Butler to describe the sub-discipline of electoral studies. It is derived from *psephos*, Greek for a pebble. Ancient Athenians voted by putting pebbles in urns.

Reading
Butler, D.E. and D. Kavanagh. 1997. *The British General Election of 1997*. London: Macmillan; Heath, A., R. Jowell and J. Curtice. 1985. *How Britain Votes*. Oxford: Pergamon.

public administration ADMINISTRATION in the public sector. A second meaning refers to a sub-discipline of political science This is concerned with describing and analysing administrative rules, practices, performances and personalities.

See also ADMINISTRATION; BUREAUCRACY; POLICY MAKING.

Reading
Chapman, R.A. 1988. *Ethics in the British Civil Service*. London: Routledge; Chapman, R.A. 1999. 'Public Administration'. In Bealey, F.W., R.A. Chapman and M. Sheehan. *Elements in Political Science*. Edinburgh: Edinburgh University Press; Greenwood, J. and D. Wilson. 1989. *Public Administration in Britain Today*. London: Unwin Hyman; Hood, C. 1990. *Beyond the Public Bureaucracy State: Public Administration in the 1990s*. London: LSE.

public choice theory The application of economic theory to politics. It is concerned with what choices political actors – voters, politicians, bureaucrats and PRESSURE GROUPS – make and how they interact with each other in making their choices. The initial premise is that, like economic actors, people in politics act rationally and selfishly in pursuit of their maximum satisfaction. Public choice theorists have found that democratic governments often behave unfairly and inefficiently. For example, they prefer invisible taxes and highly visible benefits without any consideration of costing. They also indulge in such manoeuvres as stimulating the POLITICAL BUSINESS CYCLE in spite of its damage to the economy. Directed at voters, public choice theory discovers that low participation in INTEREST GROUPS and even ELECTIONS is much influenced by individual opportunity costs. In themselves these findings are not remarkable. Politicians like power so much that it is better to please the voters than to observe strict financial rigour and sound economic advice. Ordinary democratic citizens say: 'There are enough people involved in political activity to keep it going. So let those who want to, do it and the rest of us can get on with what we like more'.

Other public choice theorists have concentrated on BUREAUCRACY and POLICY MAKING. Buchanan and the 'Virginia school' have looked for 'rent-seeking', the practice of benefiting from maximizing positional power. This is not uncommon in bureaucracies where inefficiency arises from administrators building 'empires' in order to improve their promotion prospects. Thus individual rational economic behaviour is irrational from the perspective of the PUBLIC INTEREST. In democratic policy formation the haggling in so-called 'policy communities' of self-seeking groups, politicians and bureaucrats over the distribution of the national surplus produces outcomes which are bad for everyone. One consequence of the work of the Virginia school has been to strengthen the feelings of right-wing politicians that bureaucracies are far too large and inefficient and should be pruned.

See also EXIT, LOYALTY, VOICE; GAME THEORY; RATIONAL CHOICE THEORY; SOCIAL CHOICE THEORY.

Reading
Buchanan, J.M. 1975. *The Limits of Liberty*. Chicago: University of Chicago Press.; Mueller, D.C. 1989. *Public Choice*. 2nd edn. Cambridge, Mass.: HUP; Olsen, M. 1965. *The Logic of Collective Action*. Cambridge, Mass.: HUP.

public corporation *See* CORPORATIONS.

public good A good which cannot be supplied to an individual without everyone obtaining it. It is not possible to exclude anyone from its consumption. Hence ordinary market forces will not provide it nor can it be produced by voluntary subscriptions. Clean air is a public good. So is national defence.

See also PUBLIC CHOICE THEORY.

Reading
Snidal, D. 1979. 'Public Goods, Property Rights and Political Organization'. *International Studies Quarterly* 23. December, 4, 532–66.

public interest A vague term which may refer to some highly technical, rational decision-making, perhaps in the area of the economy, which turns out to be very unpopular with the public. Hence the term may refer to the aggregate of individual interests, whatever that is. Like the 'common good' and the 'GENERAL WILL' it is easier to talk about it than to determine what it means.

public opinion Frequently used, this concept is far from rigorous. When the statements of journalists are examined, 'the public' they have consulted for opinions often turn out to be very limited. Politicians' impressions of public opinion are notoriously subjective. Hence it is best to take the electorate as the public. Then statistical samples of the electorate will provide a better indication of public opinion than anything else. When this is done it reveals that the public is much divided, both in its opinions about issues and in the intensity with which it holds them. Many people do not have very clear ideas or detailed information about ISSUES and so their opinions can scarcely be the result of rational consideration.

Consequently public opinion may be more of a limitation on democratic POLICY MAKING than a positive affirmation of preference.

See also CAMPAIGNS; ELECTIONS; IDEOLOGY; POLITICAL ATTITUDES; POLITICAL PSYCHOLOGY; SAMPLE SURVEYS.

Reading
Crotty, W.J. 1970. *Public Opinion and Politics.* New York: Holt; Lane, R.E. and D.O. Sears. 1964. *Public Opinion.* Englewood Cliffs: Prentice Hall; Wilson, F.G. 1962. *A Theory of Public Opinion.* Chicago: Regnery.

purge A political cleansing process carried out by authoritarian regimes. Sometimes it is done quickly as with the Nazi 'blood purge' when in June 1934 Ernst Roehm, his followers and other enemies of Hitler were gunned down by assassins. Communist purges tended to be longer processes. Beginning in 1922 they happened periodically and were at their severest in the late 1930s under Stalin's 'great cleansing' in all ranks of the party. Millions died in prisons camps as a result.

See also CONCENTRATION CAMPS; GULAG; TERROR.

Reading
Conquest, R. 1971. *The Great Terror.* Harmondsworth: Penguin.

putsch *See* COUP D'ÉTAT.

Q

quango An acronym for 'quasi-non-governmental organization'. Quangos are bodies inaugurated and funded by governments to undertake public services and duties. Governments appoint the directors and, not infrequently, all the members. Thus they operate so closely to government that they might be regarded as governmental organizations. This becomes more plausible when governments ensure their memberships are composed of political supporters. It is argued that their value is that they have more independence than a department of government; they are outside the direct control of legislatures and treasuries; they allow for the use of the expertise of people who would never want to stand for election or be public administrators; and they do not involve an expansion of public bureaucracies. Critics argue that they are a form of government by PATRONAGE; they are a device for increasing BUREAUCRACY while pretending to slash it; and, most importantly, that they are a threat to democracy because they avoid the ACCOUNTABILITY of both the electoral process and legislative monitoring and questioning.

See also ACCOUNTABILITY; PATRONAGE; THATCHERISM.

Reading
Barker, A. ed. 1982. *Quangos in Britain*. London: Macmillan; Jenkins, S. 1995. *Accountable to None: the Tory Nationalization of Britain*. London: Hamish Hamilton; *Parliamentary Affairs*. 1995. Special issue on Quangos. April. 48, 2.

quantitative methods Statistical data is usually available for political scientists in the areas of voting studies and legislative behaviour, from census returns and voting records respectively. The use of SAMPLE SURVEYS extends research into people's political behaviour and opinions. A much smaller field where enumeration is possible is that of content analysis. Finally, change can be studied by comparing quantitative data in time sequences. Studying opinions in this way necessitates using a PANEL.

Once that data is available different forms of statistical testing may be used to discover the validity, or otherwise, of relationships between important variables. The most common test is the 'chi-square', but others are regression analysis and correlation. In studies of VOTING BEHAVIOUR respondents' declared party support will be related to other variables such as SOCIAL CLASS, age and religion. The tests will show the statistical significance, or insignificance, of these associations; that is, the probability that the distribution in the statistical table is not a random one. If one declares that a relationship between two variables is 'statistically significant' to a degree of 0.1 per cent it means that the odds are very high that the hypothesis that a relationship exists is a valid one.

Quantification was popularized by the 'behaviourists', some of whom made exaggerated claims for it. It certainly gives much more precision to description of political phenomena and where it can be employed it should be. On the other hand, it may not always be much help with explanation and this is especially the case where rather unexpected results emerge from research. Then the student has to turn to documentation, interrogation and observation.

See also POLITICAL BEHAVIOUR; SAMPLE SURVEYS.

Reading
Davis, H.T. 1954. *Political Statistics*. Evanston, Ill.: Principia Press; Duverger, M. 1961. *Méthodes des Sciences Sociale*. Paris: Presses Universitaire de France; Williams, F. 1979. *Reasoning with Statistics: How to Read Quantitative Research*. New York: Holt.

quasi-judicial In British legal terminology a judicial decision was one where the law was applied. A quasi-judicial decision was where administrative policy, which probably involved rules and precedents, was used to resolve the dispute. American usage of the term tends to apply it to judicial decisions made by non-judicial bodies. In recent years the British position has changed and the courts have been inclined to impose on administrators and administrative bodies the procedural restrictions of natural justice.

See also JUDICIARY; LAW; NATURAL RIGHTS.

Reading
Wade, W. 1982. *Administrative Law*. Oxford: Clarendon.

queens There are two kinds of queen, those that are sovereigns in their own right and those that are queen consorts, the wives of male sovereigns.

questionnaires These are a systematic method of obtaining political information from people. There are two basic types. The structured questionnaire is used in surveys of samples of the population. At least 100 and possibly 1000 questionnaires are printed and the crucial feature is that every questionnaire is exactly the same. Interviews are likely to be much shorter than with unstructured questionnaires. These latter are more likely to be used with small elite groups where the information elicited is not easily quantified. There will be more 'open-ended' questions (where the optional answers are not just 'Yes', 'No' and 'Don't know') and also opportunities to ask supplementary questions that suggest themselves as the interview proceeds.

See also QUANTITATIVE METHODS; SAMPLE SURVEYS.

Reading
Moser, C.A. 1958. *Survey Methods in Social Investigation*. London: Heinemann.

quorum The minimum number of members who must be present in order to make a gathering valid. In the House of Commons this is 40 and in the House of Lords three.

quotas A device for restricting foreign imports. Instead of taxing them (as with TARIFFS), the home country limits the number permitted entrance.

quota sample *See* SAMPLE SURVEYS.

R

race   Usually defined in terms of physical characteristics of which pigmentation is the most important. More quasi-scientific factors might be the shape of noses or the appearance of a cross-section of hair looked at under a microscope. While these categories undoubtedly exist, most biologists and social scientists do not accept that race is a valid concept. Yet historically it has been important. Phrases like the 'British race', if now less common, are still used to mean the 'British nation'.

See also ETHNICITY; NATION; NATION-STATE; RACISM.

Reading
Banton, M. 1987. *Racial Theories*. Cambridge: CUP.

racism   Feeling against people who are seen to be of another 'race' may take various forms. At its least intense it may be a reaction against the strangeness of people who dress differently, profess another religion and speak a different language: at its worst it may descend into racial theory in which one's own 'race' is believed to be superior to all others. In between are those who feel threatened by economic competition from incomers. These different forms are expressive sometimes of different situations. There is racism, as in India, eastern Europe and the USA, where indigenous ethnic groups have lived side by side for generations. There is racial resentment against immigrants from former colonies, or 'guest-workers' from poorer countries, in west European democracies. Finally there is an intellectual expression of racism in racial philosophy which may originate in fear and insecurity as a result of supposed world threats such as the 'yellow peril' or an 'international Jewish conspiracy'.

Racism is an area where LIBERALISM and DEMOCRACY may be in conflict. Majorities sometimes have succeeded in forcing governments to bring in illiberal measures to restrict IMMIGRATION and even limit political asylum. 'Race riots' have occasionally occurred in Britain and the USA. These have been spontaneous outbursts, often ignited by a relatively trivial incident; but expressive of the feeling of being constantly under threat. In authoritarian countries attacks by mobs on ethnic minorities have sometimes been encouraged by governments. Political parties with racist programmes have been a common feature in the modern world. On the other hand, among intellectuals and the young hostility to racism is increasing. PRESSURE GROUPS supporting CIVIL LIBERTIES and more actively mobilizing movements such as the Anti-Nazi League in Britain and *SOS Racisme* in France have opposed the racist National Fronts in both countries.

See also ANTI-SEMITISM; NATIONAL SOCIALISM; XENOPHOBIA.

Reading
Benedict, R. 1942. *Race and Racism*. London: Routledge; Layton-Henry, Z. 1984. *The Politics of Race in Britain*. London: Allen and Unwin; Miles, R. 1982. *Racism and Migrant Labour*. London: Routledge; Omi, M. and H. Winant. 1986. *Racial Formation in the United States*. London: Routledge.

radicalism　The term is derived from the Latin for 'root', *radix,* and in the nineteenth century was used to describe a trend to drastic reform. British nineteenth-century Radicals wanted to extend the suffrage and reform the political system. European Radicals in the twentieth century have been parties of the centre left. In France and Italy Radical parties have been anti-clerical. Under the Third Republic (1870–1940) the Radicals were the most important French party with their social centre of gravity in the anti-clerical peasants and businessmen. By contemporary standards they were rather conservative.

raison d'état　See REALPOLITIK.

random sample　See SAMPLE SURVEYS.

ranking member　A statement about seniority. In the American Congress the term is applied in LEGISLATIVE COMMITTEES to one member in each party with longest continuous service. The one from the majority party by convention becomes chairperson.

rates　A local tax levied in Britain on occupiers of land or buildings. It amounted to about 60 per cent of the revenue of local authorities. Each property was given a valuation which, in conjunction with the rate fixed by the specific authority, determined the amount the occupier paid. It was thus a progressive tax, but the amount demanded varied considerably with the revenue needs of each authority. In the late 1980s the Thatcher government replaced it with the POLL TAX. The succeeding Major government replaced the latter with the council tax, very similar to the rates.

See also FISCAL CRISIS; LOCAL FINANCE; POLL TAX.

rational choice theory　The theorists start from the assumption that everyone is rational in selecting the most effective means to secure their goals. They employ the techniques of micro-economics. Rationality implies everyone wants as much as possible but with limited resources has to make sophisticated choices between commodities which compete. The outcomes of the theorists' deductions can be tested against the way political actors behave. An obvious objection is that rationality is only possible with complete information which no political actors possess. A riposte might be: 'Neither do economic actors'.

See also PUBLIC CHOICE THEORY; SOCIAL CHOICE THEORY.

Reading
Barry, B. and R. Hardin. eds. 1982. *Rational Man and Irrational Society*. Beverly Hills: Sage.

rationalization　A term with two meanings. One is applied to the process of putting organizations and/or procedures in better order. If the way they operate is deemed inefficient, it is argued that the application of reason or rationality will elevate them to the highest level of effectiveness. The other meaning is pejorative. A 'rationalization' is a claim to rationality as the explanation for some course of action, though the actual reason is something far less worthy.

See also DERIVATIONS.

rationalism　A very general intellectual attitude that bases its beliefs on the authority of reason. Its roots go back to Descartes (1596–1650) who made mathematical certitude his ideal. Rationalists are sceptical of established practices that cannot be justified by rationality or by technical expertise. Historically the important rationalist landmark was the ENLIGHTENMENT and the French Revolution which rejected such irrational constructs as revealed religion, aristocracy and hereditary monarchy. Hence agnosticism, EGALITARIANISM and LIBERALISM are rationalist in origin. Some Utopian rationalists have also claimed that rational techniques can produce ideal societies. Thus, large-scale planning of the type practised by the Soviet Union was an exercise in rationalism, demonstrating that some rationalists lack scepticism. It was rationalism gone mad. *See also* COMMUNISM; LIBERALISM; SOCIALISM.

Reading
Diesing, P. 1973. *Reason in Society.* Westport: Greenwood; Heath, A. 1976. *Rational Choice and Social Exchange.* Cambridge: CUP; Reagan, D.E. 1978. 'Rationality in Policy Making: Two Concepts Not One'. *Long Range Planning* 11. October, 85.

reactionary   A pejorative term to describe someone who is opposed to social and political change. Moderate conservatives adapt to change. Literally it could apply to anyone reacting against any course of action; but from the nineteenth century onwards it seems to have been applied to those attempting to halt 'the march of progress'. As a descriptive term today every instance of its use should be treated with scepticism.

realignment   A marked change in voters' political allegiances that results in a different prospect on the political scene. In recent years it has often been associated with new generations with different values connected with a variety of factors like affluence, changing class structures and the emergence of new ISSUES like gender, REPRODUCTIVE POLITICS and environmentalism. It is alleged to emerge at 'watershed elections'.
See also DEALIGNMENT; SINGLE ISSUE POLITICS.

Reading
Key, V.O. 1955. 'A Theory of Critical Elections'. *Journal of Politics* 17, 9–18; Sundquist, J. 1973. *Dynamics of the Party System.* Washington, D.C.: Brookings.

realism   In its everyday sense the term means looking at things as they are rather than as one would like them to be. Realist thinkers have seen human nature as acquisitive and aggressive. MACHIAVELLI and HOBBES were both concerned with the struggle for survival in a harsh world. Unlike the philosophers of IDEALISM they believed knowledge could only be gained by experience and their experiences told them that the STATE, far from being a metaphysical concept, was merely a necessary instrument to control disorderly behaviour.

The term is normally used today by students of INTERNATIONAL RELATIONS. The traditional approach has been to perceive the relations between states as a Hobbesian struggle in which, unlike the domestic situation, it is impossible to have a paramount, legitimate, coercive force. Thus the BALANCE OF POWER was the dominant model. It was the best realistically attainable situation for international peace. At its base it was largely a balance of military forces. Morality, therefore, was scarcely a consideration. In a nuclear world the balance of power became a 'balance of terror'. Realists are not impressed by the potentialities of the United Nations Organization, although its activities and statements are an element in the international imbroglio. Realists see power as the continuing motivation of states.
See also BALANCE OF POWER; COLLECTIVE SECURITY; DETERRENCE; IDEALISM; INTERNATIONAL LAW.

Reading
Carr, E.H. 1946. *The Twenty Years' Crisis, 1919–1939.* 2nd edn. London: Macmillan; Krasner, S.D. 1978. *Defending the National Interest.* Princeton: Princeton University Press.

realpolitik A German term familiarized by its use as a description of the policies of Bismarck, Chancellor of Prussia and Germany (1862–90), who unified the German Empire as a result of successful short wars against Austro-Hungary and France. He declared that the German problem could only be resolved by 'blood and iron'. An earlier exponent was MACHIAVELLI who is believed to be the originator of the phrase 'raison d'état' (reason of state), implying that the only justification of a policy is its success. It could be argued that practitioners of *realpolitik* are merely honest believers in REALISM. On the other hand, the crude assertion and unscrupulous use of military power are not common attributes of all international statesmen.

Reading
Meinecke, F. 1957. *Machiavellianism: the Doctrine of Raison d'État and its Place in Modern History.* London: Routledge.

rebellions *See* POLITICAL VIOLENCE.

recall The method by which elected representatives can be made to stand for re-election in the event of a number of their constituents finding them unsatisfactory. The exact number, usually a percentage of the electorate, is specified by law. In order to set the recall process in motion, they must sign a petition. The recall was advocated by MARX and embodied in the Soviet constitution, though its organization was entirely in the hands of the Communist Party. Its democratic use has been largely at the local level, especially in the western states of the USA, but the long and cumbersome process has discouraged any frequent employment. When used it has usually been unsuccessful.

See also DIRECT DEMOCRACY; INITIATIVE; REFERENDUM.

reciprocity The principle of making mutual concessions and according rights to those who accord the same rights to oneself. In INTERNATIONAL LAW it arises from the recognition of the sovereignty of states. If one claims sole jurisdiction over one's own territories as a principle, it is difficult not to accord it to other states. Consequently reciprocity is often part of interstate bargaining. Where international agreements comprise many states, as with the General Agreement on Tariffs and Trade, reciprocity will be widely diffused.

redistribution The reallocation per state of seats in Congress and the relocation of the boundaries of electoral districts in order to allow for population movements. In the USA, where the process is often called 'reapportionment', the variation in population between Congressional districts should be less than 1 per cent. Redistribution takes place every ten years. The number of seats for each state is calculated and it is the responsibility of states to draw the new boundaries. Most states hand the task to their legislatures.

In Britain and the Commonwealth the practice is to set up Boundary Commissions who report every ten to fifteen years. The British Boundary Commission is composed of the Speaker of the House of Commons in the chair, a High Court judge, the Surveyor-General and the Registrar-General, and two lawyers. They are supposed to ignore political considerations. Otherwise the principle of reallocation is equality, except that a few unusual constituencies, like Orkney and Shetland, with a good deal lower than average population are allowed a member.

See also APPORTIONMENT.

Reading
Butler, D.E. 1963. *The Electoral System in Britain Since 1918*. Oxford: Clarendon; Grofman, G., A. Lijphart, R. McKay and H. Scarrow. eds. 1981. *Representation and Redistricting Issues in the 1980s*. Lexington, Mass.: Lexington Books.

reference groups A category or group of people referred to by way of comparison. We may compare our own social and economic position with those in a similar trade or occupation to ourselves, our own 'peer group'. Groups may also refer their situation to those of other groups. It is an important concept in INDUSTRIAL RELATIONS. In a large, complex industry trade-union bargaining may proceed on reference-group lines. It is noticeable that workers relate their wage levels to those of adjacent groups. For example, unskilled workers are not concerned with the pay of white-collar staff or managers, but with comparing their own pay with that of semi-skilled workers. To them that is the important 'differential'. Relative welfare benefits are important politically for the same reason. Tenants of municipal housing are often highly sensitive to the rents paid by tenants on nearby estates. RELATIVE DEPRIVATION can breed a sense of injustice which may make itself felt electorally. *See also* INDUSTRIAL RELATIONS; RELATIVE DEPRIVATION.

Reading
Hyman, H.H. and E. Singer. eds. 1968. *Readings in Reference Group Theory and Research*. New York: Free Press.

referendum A device for referring votes on ISSUES to a total electorate rather than to a council or legislature. Referendums can be either consultative or mandatory. They can be used to make national or local decisions. Switzerland is the only country where referendums, both national and cantonal, play the predominant part in the nation's decision-making. In the USA there has never been a national referendum; but over 20 states use it for various purposes. In California, where it is supplemented by the INITIATIVE, the voters have shown a capacity to embarrass state administrations. In 1978, in passing Proposition 13, they limited local authorities' assessments of property taxes to 1 per cent, resulting in nearly a third of the state's teachers being under threat of dismissal. In Australia, which holds both federal and state referendums, majorities of voters have shown a strong inclination to vote 'No' to constitutional reforms. In Europe referendums have largely been used for national constitutional revisions and, more recently, for questions relating to the European Union.

There can be no doubt that in recent decades the democracies have shown an increased tendency to use referendums. This may be because of the emergence of new issues of national importance which are not clearly part of the programmes of major parties and on which the latter are divided. The belief of NEW SOCIAL MOVEMENTS that legislatures are poor instruments for implementing their projects and that a nation-wide vote would be the best facilitator has also probably contributed. Referendum campaigns certainly educate citizens on single issues; on the other hand, they are not suitable for drafting detailed technical policy, nor for criticizing administration, nor for holding governments to account. Hence LEGISLATURES and their committees are unlikely to lose their main functions. *See also* DIRECT DEMOCRACY; INITIATIVE; PLEBISCITE; RECALL.

Reading
Bealey, F.W. 1988. *Democracy in the Contemporary State*. Oxford: OUP.; Bogdanor, V. 1983. *The People and the Party System: the Referendum and Electoral Reform in British Politics*. Cambridge: CUP; Butler, D. and A. Ranney. eds. 1978. *Referendums*. Washington, D.C.: American Enterprise Institute; Magleby, D.B. 1984. *Direct Democracy: Voting*

on Ballot Propositions in the United States. Baltimore: Johns Hopkins Press.

reform A widely-used term to describe improvements or the abolition of malpractices and deficiencies. Whether 'reforms' actually improve matters is open to the assessments of historians. The answers, anyway, are bound to be subjective. It cannot be disputed, however, that at certain periods great changes take place. 'Reform programmes' are associated in Britain with the Liberal government before 1914 and the Labour government after 1945; and in the USA with the Presidencies of Franklin Roosevelt and Lyndon Johnson.

refugees People who take refuge in another country because of persecution in their own. They are frequently escaping imprisonment and/or death. The mass exodus of refugees has become quite common as a result of ethnic hatreds resulting in massacres. The first example of the problem being dealt with on an international scale was a conference at Evian in 1938 concerned with the Jewish refugees from Germany. In 1951 the United Nations recognized the world problem in a Convention Relating to the Status of Refugees and then set up a High Commission for Refugees (UNHCR). The present High Commissioner is Mary Robinson, former President of Ireland. There are now 20 million refugees in the world. A major difficulty is that most of them are from poor countries and they have fled to adjacent poor countries who cannot afford to feed and house them. Meanwhile the developed countries have introduced stricter rules to bar their entrance.
See also FUNDAMENTAL RIGHTS.

regime *See* POLITICAL SYSTEM.

regionalism The term has been used in two ways. One is the strength of feeling in part of a country based on geographical and cultural distinction. It may also have roots in the past and may, or may not, be expressed politically in demands for devolved authority. The other meaning is that of a political and administrative belief that a country is managed most efficiently by being divided into regions instead of into much smaller local government areas. Sometimes called 'regionalization' this is a technocratic concept. Of course, these two tendencies are not irreconcilable in all cases.

Regionalism as a 'grass roots' movement is often fuelled by ethnic feelings of being different. These feelings may be stronger where language is involved. Thus Brittany, Quebec, Catalonia and the Basque country are examples of regions where autonomy from central government, to a greater or lesser extent, is a reality. Regionalism as a technocratic notion is very much a feature of the second half of the twentieth century, and is associated with ideas of economic planning for growth through new capital investment. It is argued that large areas of sub-government are better for this purpose because local transport and new industrial development can be planned within them: it is not realistic to plan growth in a region through liaising with many small local authorities. In addition, a larger area will be able to support a group of expert planners who understand both economic and legal technicalities.

In France both strains have been evident. The old right, which never accepted the Revolution, on coming to power during the Vichy regime (1940–4), abolished *DÉPARTEMENTS* and replaced them with the traditional Royalist provinces. Within these a new breed of technocrats began to operate. After the liberation the provinces were abolished but unelected regional committees were set up to assist regional planning. In 1956 France was divided into 22 'programme regions' in which regional committees operated under the umbrella of the National Plan.

In 1961 there was further impetus from the European Community's decision to divide member states into regions. France was divided into nine. Finally in 1982 the new Socialist government gave all the regions representative government. Though their functions were still largely confined to economic management, the regional councils gave an opportunity for democratic expression to Bretons, Corsicans and others.

Where regionalization was imposed out of technocratic motives its life was likely to be as long as those notions remained part of governmental purpose. Scottish regions were instituted in 1975 without any appreciable regional demand. They were part of the dominant administrative ideology of the time. When Thatcher came to power in 1979 their days were numbered; and they were finally abolished in 1992. The general decline of national planning as a policy implies that, except where there are strong regionalist feelings, the notion of regionalization (outside the European Community) is in decline.

See also CENTRAL–LOCAL RELATIONS; CENTRE–PERIPHERY RELATIONS; DE-CENTRALIZATION; DEVOLUTION; LOCAL GOVERNMENT; PLANNING; SEPARATISM.

Reading
Gras, C. and G. Livet. eds. 1977. *Régions et Régionalisme en France de XVIIIe Siècle à nos Jours*. Paris: Presses Universitaires de France. Morgan, R. ed. 1986. *Regionalism in European Politics*. London: Policy Studies Institute; Schmidt, V. 1990. *Democratizing France*. Cambridge: CUP; Tarrow, S., P.J. Katzenstein and I. Graziano. eds. 1978. *Territorial Politics in Industrial Nations*. New York: Praeger.

registration   The act of compiling electoral rolls. Normally this is either delegated to local governments as in Britain, or a governmental unit is responsible for it. In the USA, where the Constitution makes the franchise a state matter, registration is left to the citizen. It is believed that only about two-thirds of those qualified to vote actually register. Where geographical mobility is great even the best registration system may be deficient.
See also TURNOUT.

regressive taxation   The opposite of PROGRESSIVE TAXATION. This type of tax takes a much higher proportion of a poor person's income. Taxing essential foods is regressive.

regulation   An imposed and promulgated rule. Although legislatures pass laws they may under such legislation allow an agency to issue regulations with the force of law. The European Commission passes regulations, called 'directives', which direct member governments to pass laws to accomplish some Community purpose.

The term, however, has come to have a specialized meaning. It refers to control of privately owned monopolies by regulators appointed by the government. It began in Britain with an act in 1844 regulating safety on the railways; but its recent application has arisen with the privately owned monopolies created by Conservative PRIVATIZATION of public monopolies. But regulatory agencies are a predominantly American institution. The best known are the Environmental Protection agency, the Federal Communications Commission, the Federal Trade Commission and the Securities and Exchange Commission. Appointed by the President, members are supposed to consider the PUBLIC INTEREST and give consideration to such matters as pricing policies and consumer safety.
See also NATIONALIZATION; PRIVATIZATION.

Reading
Derthick, M. and P.J. Quirk. 1985. *The Politics of Deregulation*. Washington, D.C.: Brookings Institution; McConnell, G. 1966. *Private Power and American Democracy*. New York: Knopf.

reification The tendency to confuse an abstract concept or MODEL with reality. The ideal becomes a 'thing', that is a concrete phenomenon. For social scientists who approach research with explanatory models reification is always a danger. They may find what they expected to find instead of what is there.

relative deprivation An idea first advanced by ARISTOTLE as an explanation of political discontent and revolt. Those who seek to disturb the stability of society, he argues, are not necessarily the poorest and most under-privileged. Any group or social category that feels it is not being given due reward for its status and merits may become discontented. It has an obvious implication for the contemporary world where middle-class people who feel they are over-taxed are capable of rebelling against the status quo. Reactions may be as different as COUPS D'ÉTAT and TAX REVOLTS. Groups tend to relate their own position to another group they can perceive. Thus unskilled industrial workers feel relatively deprived if the differential between them and semi-skilled industrial workers moves to their disadvantage. They do not compare their situation with workers in developing countries on much lower pay.
See also REFERENCE GROUPS; REVOLUTIONS.

Reading
Aristotle [c.335 BC] 1959. *Politics*. London: Dent; Runciman, W.G. 1966. *Relative Deprivation and Social Justice*. London: Routledge.

religious politics See CLERICALISM/ ANTI-CLERICALISM; CHRISTIAN DEMOCRACY; LIBERATION THEOLOGY.

rent-seeking The attempt to gain profit from becoming the sole producer and/or distributor of a good or service. If a government is prepared to grant a licence or franchise to provide a commodity in such circumstances, competition for it will be fierce and as the putative provider will reap monopoly profits it will be prepared to spend much money on lobbying activities. Hence it is undertaking political rather than economic activity to gain its profits. A rent is being acquired from the consumer.

representation There can be representation by LEGISLATURES and representation by individuals. In the former case one might say a parliament is representative if it has been elected by the electorate according to the rules. On the other hand, if one means 'representation' in its original sense of a likeness, most parliaments are unrepresentative. All the legislatures of the world under-represent women and manual workers: they are full of professional men with a preponderance of lawyers. Representation by individuals can also refer to the electoral process; but it may signify the willingness of the REPRESENTATIVE in question to put forward the views, or the requests and complaints, of the people she/he represents. This may present a problem as constituents will hold diverse views and put forward conflicting demands.

The methods of representation are numerous. At different times and in different places who is represented has varied. Until the twentieth century it was common for the voting right to be greatly restricted. Early PARLIAMENTS often contained only male landowners elected by male landowners. Today in democracies it is common for all adults over 18 to hold the FRANCHISE. It is usual for representatives to be returned from a territorial unit with boundaries; but FUNCTIONAL REPRESENTATION of occupational and professional organizations is used for the French Economic and Social Council. Finally ELECTORAL SYSTEMS vary in their mechanics and their outcomes. Other things being equal, Proportional Representation results in a somewhat fairer representation of the electorate than FIRST-PAST-THE-POST, but also in COALITION GOVERNMENT which may sometimes provide uncertain direction; while SECOND BALLOT produces outcomes that are broadly intermediate between these two systems. 'Things', however, are seldom 'equal' because a nation's CLEAVAGES, as represented by its political parties, are the main factor in determining its pattern of representation.

See also CLEAVAGES; ELECTORAL SYSTEMS; FRANCHISE; FUNCTIONAL REPRESENTATION; WOMEN'S SUFFRAGE.

Reading
Birch, A.H. 1971. *Representation*. London: Pall Mall; Pennock, J.R. ed. 1968. *Representation*. New York: Atherton; Pitkin, H.F. 1967. *The Concept of Representation*. Berkeley: University of California Press.

representative Someone who acts for someone else. A political representative is usually an elected person chosen under the varied circumstances of particular REPRESENTATION systems. There is much argument about the proper role of a representative. At the one extreme is the contention of BURKE who defended VIRTUAL REPRESENTATION and praised the role of the 'trustee'. At the other is the idea of the DELEGATE who obeys the demands of the majority of his constituents.

See also DELEGATE; VIRTUAL REPRESENTATION.

Reading
Bogdanor, V. ed. 1985. *Representatives of the People? Parliamentarians and Constituents in Western Democracies*. Aldershot: Gower.

representative democracy The alternative version of democracy to DIRECT DEMOCRACY. With representative democracy, which might be called 'indirect democracy', people elect a small number of other people to represent their views and interests in parliaments.

The advantages of this system are that it provides a gathering that is small enough to discuss policy at length and finally to produce a detailed policy draft. Furthermore, a legislature can rationalize and prioritize policies in a PROGRAMME. It can also examine petitions, suggestions and complaints transmitted from citizens. Above all, representative democracy provides what direct democracy never can – a nucleus of people from whom representative governments can be chosen. DEMOCRACY is not viable without government.

The disadvantages of representative democracy stem from the distance it creates between representatives and people. It is not only a geographical distance. Being a representative is a highly specialized role and inevitably it has become professionalized. People elected are socially distant from ordinary citizens in many ways. One is that they want to be near to power and to hold it and most people do not want power and the responsibility that goes with it. Professional politicians are often from the professional classes. There is thus both a psychological and social gap between representatives and their constituents. All these differences are accentuated by political parties. Mostly they select their candidates without reference to the voters. Their programmes may exclude issues citizens would like to discuss and their competition may descend into childish abuse which is a discredit to democracy. Hence direct democracy has a function in compensating for many of these weaknesses.

See also DIRECT DEMOCRACY; ELECTORAL SYSTEMS; POLITICAL PARTIES; POLITICIANS.

Reading
Bealey, F.W. 1988. *Democracy in the Contemporary State*. Oxford: OUP; Fishkin, J. ed. 1981. *Ethics*. Special Issue on Representation, 91; Mill, J.S. [1861] 1946. *Considerations on Representative Government*. Ed. R.B. McCallum. Oxford: Blackwell.

reproductive politics A term first used by women in the USA in the 1970s. In 1978 the Women's Global Network on

Reproductive Rights was founded to counter both the growing popularity of population control in some countries and the growing strength of the anti-abortion movement. It affirmed the right of women to choose whether they had children or not. The women's movement demanded effective contraception and abortion services; pre-natal and ante-natal care; and better instruction for women everywhere about these matters. Women had already had some success sponsoring resolutions at the UN and it had adopted a Convention on the Elimination of All Forms of Discrimination Against Women, Article 16 of which gave women equal rights with men over decisions about reproduction.

Although the UN decade for women, ending in 1985 with the successful Nairobi conference, was an important landmark in the struggle for reproductive rights, there have since been signs of reaction. The continuing debt crisis of the 1990s and outbreaks of ethnic violence in Europe, Asia and Africa have made the lot of poor women and children much worse, exposing them to risks of murder, kidnapping, enforced prostitution, rape and venereal disease. The growing strength of the PRO-LIFE movement has been given impetus by the collapse of the Communist regimes of eastern Europe which provided abortion almost on demand.

See also FEMINISM; PRO-CHOICE; PRO-LIFE.

Reading

Craig, B.H. and D.M. O'Brien. 1993. *Abortion and American Politics*. Chatham, NJ: Chatham House Publishers; Petchesky, R.P. 1984. *Abortion and Women's Choice: the State, Sexuality and Reproductive Freedom*. London: Longman.

republic Derived from the Latin, *res publica*, which originally meant public affairs. From this it came to mean the realm of politics and then the STATE. Today to say that a country is a republic means that it is not a monarchy: its HEAD OF STATE is a president and not a hereditary monarch. Those in monarchies who wish to make their countries republics are known as 'republicans'.

See also CONSTITUTIONAL MONARCHY.

reselection The renomination, usually by a local party organization, of an incumbent REPRESENTATIVE. It is common for incumbents to be reselected. Where they are not the term 'deselection' has been coined.

See also CANDIDATES; NOMINATION.

residues The term used by Vilfredo Poreto (1848–1923) for the residual or permanent elements forming the temperamental and psychological bases of human predispositions to act. He placed these in six classes, but Class 1 and Class 2 were much more important than the others. The Class 1 residue was the 'instinct for combinations' or the predisposition to combine. A society with a preponderance of this residue would be innovatory. The Class 2 residue was the 'persistence of aggregates', the instinct to preserve. Class 1 residue, therefore tended to liberalism, while Class 2 was conservative.

See also DERIVATIONS.

responsibility In its general moral and legal sense to be responsible is to be liable for one's own actions. One may be blamed or condemned, punished or rewarded, for what one has said and done. Responsibilities in ADMINISTRATION are those duties and obligations that one is told one has to observe and perform. Problems of responsibility may arise, especially in complex organizations, when duties and obligations have not been clearly specified. Hence they need to be put in writing. Frequently one may be responsible to senior people in an organization to whom one will have to account for one's actions and at the same time have junior people responsible to oneself. Chains of responsibility are not uncommon.

In British politics there is both ACCOUNTABILITY of governments to Parliament, which means they must both answer for their actions and risk dismissal by votes of censure; and there is individual ministerial responsibility of ministers for their departments. Contrary to popular belief this has not resulted in ministers resigning when their mistakes have been revealed. They have argued that the errors were committed by their underlings and Prime Ministers and other leaders of their party have been anxious for them not to resign because that would be a 'scalp' for the Opposition. Governments and ministers respond, in the sense of being responsive and sensitive to criticism, but the ultimate responsibility is to the electorate at election time.

Electors should also take their share of responsibility for electing and dismissing governments though they can easily evade direct censure because of the ballot being secret. If a show of hands was required it could be seen who among the citizenry voted for what parties and policies. As it is, the voters can claim that both the duplicity of the politicians and lack of information about policies absolves them from responsibility. As few voters want power for themselves they can take comfort in blaming those who have wanted it and been successful in its pursuit. Making assessments about the merit of new CANDIDATES for office is bound to be difficult. Voters are better at appraisals of past behaviour.

See also ACCOUNTABILITY; COLLECTIVE RESPONSIBILITY; GOVERNMENT; VOTING BEHAVIOUR.

Reading
Birch, A.H. 1964. *Representative and Responsible Government*. London: Allen and Unwin; Finer, S.E. 1956. 'The Individual Responsibility of Ministers'. *Public Administration* 34, 377–96; Key, V.O. 1968. *The Responsible Electorate*. New York: Random House.

responsible government *See* ACCOUNTABILITY; COLLECTIVE RESPONSIBILITY; PARLIAMENTARY SYSTEMS; RESPONSIBILITY.

revenue sharing The distribution of national revenue from a specific tax to different levels of government by a legal formula. It is especially common under FEDERAL GOVERNMENT and became important in the USA after 1972 when the second Nixon administration turned over $30 billion of federal revenue to be shared by state and local governments. Other examples can be found in Switzerland, Canada and India.

See also FEDERAL GOVERNMENT; INTERGOVERNMENTAL RELATIONS.

Reading
Break, G.F. 1980. *Financing Government in a Federal System*. Washington, D.C.: Brookings. Hunter, J.S.H. 1977. *Federalism and Fiscal Balance*. Canberra: Australian National University Press; Nice, D.C. 1987. *Federalism: the Politics of Intergovernmental Relations*. New York: St. Martin's Press.

revisionism A term now applied to any account or statement of opinion that revises a hitherto accepted interpretation. In the recent past it was part of the jargon of the left. For example, those members of the British Labour Party who wanted to expunge from the party's constitution the famous Clause IV, affirming the need for the common ownership of the means of production, distribution and exhange, were called 'revisionists'. But originally the term was given to Marxists who first began to question Marxist theory. Prominent among these was Edouard Bernstein (1850–1932), one of the parliamentary leaders of the German Social Democrats. Already in the 1890s he had concluded that CAPITALISM was both more endurable and more adaptable than MARX had argued and that socialist measures could be enacted by democratic methods without a proletarian REVOLUTION. His thesis was largely accepted by the Second International and most members of western European labour and socialist parties.

See also CAPITALISM; MARXISM; SOCIALISM.

Reading
Gay, P. 1962. *The Dilemma of Democratic Socialism.* New York: Collier.

revolutions The word is taken from astronomy and means a 'turning around'. It invariably signifies great change. Thus in British history there is the Scientific Revolution of the seventeenth century, the Agricultural Revolution of the eighteenth and the Industrial Revolution of the nineteenth. Political revolutions take their derivation from Renaissance Italy. *Revoluziones* described the almost cyclic changes in power in the Italian states as one faction overthrew another.

Contemporary usage is twofold. Great changes in society and the economy resulting in power shifts between classes, with perhaps the rise of new social classes, are sometimes regarded as the indications that a revolution is in progress. Yet insurrectionary movements, even on a small scale, which with some violence throw out the incumbent rulers and replace them with others, are also called 'revolutions'. The former are often described as 'social revolutions' and the latter COUPS D'ÉTAT. The revolutions that encompass both might be designated 'cataclysmic revolutions'. They shake much wider areas than the country concerned. This was clearly the case with the American (1776), French (1789), Mexican (1910), Russian (1917), Chinese (1949) and Iranian (1979) Revolutions. The European (so-called) Revolutions of 1848 failed and so hardly fit the definition; but the successful European Revolutions most resembling 1848, those overthrowing Communism in 1989, clearly do.

Historians and social scientists concerned with this grand theme have asked the question: 'In what circumstances do revolutions occur?' They have answered in various ways. MARX anticipated the future revolution of the proletariat against the bourgeois class and the capitalist state. No revolution has fulfilled his prophecy. Brinton found analogies between different phases of the English, American, French and Russian Revolutions and prophesied the latter would have its Thermidor. He concluded that a sign of revolution was an elite that was losing confidence and beginning to doubt the legitimating values on which its power was based. Gurr approaches revolution and other political violence from the psychological angle. Johnson believes a fierce clash of values and ideologies leads to the breakdown of order. Skocpol, in examining the French, Russian and Chinese Revolutions, concluded that the nature of the pre-revolutionary state in each country portended crisis and rebellion. Other analysts have cited as causal factors rapid population growth and its social and economic consequences, and wars and other international uncertainties. Easton's model of the political system would tell us that when pressures on it are greater than what its supports will withstand, it will collapse.

It seems that revolutions are all preceded by a period, perhaps a generation, of intellectual ferment. All revolutions, after spontaneous popular outbursts, are directed by intellectuals who are discontented with almost all aspects of the prevailing regime. Yet revolutionary ideas are not sufficient in isolation. At the same time economic unrest has been present in all revolutionary situations. Two scenarios have been advanced – the 'revolution of falling expectations', where people anticipate a bad future but it is even worse than expected; and the 'revolution of rising expectations', where improvement in the economy is not as great as predicted. Politicians may exacerbate such crises with inflated promises. The history of revolutions contains many instances of authority in trouble introducing 'reforms' which extend and deepen the crisis. Elite behaviour is clearly important and a ruling elite or class that is losing faith in the credibility of its prescriptions is likely to behave erratically when challenged. In developing countries rapid modernization, as in Iran, have accounted for much social and economic instability which inexperienced bureaucracies have found impossible to handle. *See also* MODERNIZATION; POLITICAL SYSTEM; POLITICAL VIOLENCE.

Reading
Brinton, C. 1965. *The Anatomy of Revolution.* rev. edn. New York: Vintage Books; Calvert, P. 1970. *Revolution.* London: Macmillan; Davies, J.C. 1962. 'Towards a Theory of Revolution'. *American Sociological Review* XXVII. January, 5–19; Dunn, J. 1989. *Modern Revolutions.* Cambridge, Mass.: HUP; Goldstone, J.A., T.R. Gurr and F. Moshiri. eds. 1991. *Revolutions of the Late Twentieth Century.* Boulder: University of Colorado Press; Johnson, C.A. 1964. *Revolution and the Social System.* Stanford: Stanford University Press; Skocpol, T. 1979. *States and Social Revolutions.* Cambridge: CUP; Tilly, C. 1978. *From Mobilization to Revolution.* Reading, Mass.: Addison-Wesley.

rhetoric   Originally a medieval term meaning persuasion by argument, it has been adopted by journalists to refer to the often unpersuasive oratorical flourishes of politicians.

rider   An addendum to a resolution, verdict or bill. In the USA it has the special meaning of an addendum attached to a Congressional bill which has no relevance to it. It is usually a tactic to provoke a Presidential veto, or to obtain the passage of some small unimportant measure that legislators, keen

to pass the major measure, will not bother to remove.
See also ITEM VETO.

ridings   Canadian electoral districts.

right   *See* LEFT AND RIGHT.

rights   *See* BILL OF RIGHTS; CIVIL LIBERTIES; FUNDAMENTAL RIGHTS; NATURAL RIGHTS.

rising expectations   *See* REVOLUTIONS.

risk   A concept of economists. Risk is important in market theories because with perfect competition it is borne by the producer and distributor and not by the consumer. Risk is an important factor in entrepreneurship. Although it is often combined with uncertainty it has been argued that risk can be calculated, while no precise calculations can be made in a state of uncertainty. Yet there is so much misinformation in the world that it appears difficult even to predict amount of risk. Politicians frequently miscalculate risks involved in certain policies.

roll calls   The term used in the US Congress to describe the procedure by which votes are recorded. Each member's name is called out from a roll. They have to answer 'Yea', 'Nay', or 'Present'. In 1973 the House of Representatives decided to adopt electronic voting. Although roll-call procedure is not used in every democratic legislature, they all print records of how members vote on measures. Political scientists analyse these to study legislative behaviour. Degrees of party cohesion can be compared.

romanticism   A vague term with at least two connotations. In the demotic sense it refers to the tendency to 'be romantic'. 'Romancing' is telling a story, probably with embellishments. In academic discourse the term refers to a cultural and artistic movement at its peak in the first half of the nineteenth century. It was a revolt against the emotional restraints and conventional structures of classicism. The Romantic artists stressed the need to show emotions and passions and to allow freedom of expression. The need to be natural was best expressed in English by the poet, William Wordsworth (1770–1850) who, in the Preface to the *Lyrical Ballads,* 1800, wrote of 'low and rustic life' as his inspiration because in it 'the essential passions of the heart . . . are less under restraint and speak a plainer and more emphatic language'. The influence of ROUSSEAU's 'noble savage' and the emotions of the French Revolution are unmistakeably linked to the Romantic movement.

The political impact of Romanticism is therefore emancipatory and liberal. It was bound to be associated with the nineteenth-century struggle for nationhood. Symbolically the Romantic poet, Byron (1785–1824), died leading the Greek rising against the Turkish empire. Throughout Europe liberal intellectuals, inspired by the Declaration of the Rights of Man, 1789, connected democratic institutions with national emancipation. In supporting national movements they looked back to heroes (sometimes mythical) in the national past, investing them with their own sentiments. This involved them in 'romanticization'. Nostalgia is often an emotion of conservatives. Consequently romanticism can be both liberal and conservative. Politicians of both left and right are capable of exploiting its resonances.
See also CONSERVATISM; LIBERALISM.

Reading
Butler, M. 1981. *Romantics, Rebels and Reactionaries.* Oxford: OUP; Cranston, M. 1994. *The Romantic Movement.* Oxford: Blackwell.

rotten boroughs   An eighteenth-century term, used in Britain to denote constituencies with few electors. They were abolished by the 1832 Reform Act, but the term is sometimes still wrongly used about a very safe seat.

royal prerogative   *See* CROWN.

royalty   People in a monarchy close to the crown either by relationship or marriage. In the British media they are often referred to as 'royals'. There is a general feeling that there are too many of them receiving public funding.

rule-making powers   *See* DELEGATED LEGISLATION.

rule of law   A term coined by DICEY, since developed by other commentators. Dicey described the concept as embodying the predominance of law over discretionary authority; equality before the law; and the law of the British constitution deriving from courts asserting individual rights. This last stipulation, implying that only Britain had the rule of law, has ceased to be acceptable to legal theorists. DUE PROCESS OF LAW and lack of arbitrary treatment are recognized and to this has been added the maintenance of order as necessary for law to prevail.

The United Nations declaration on Civil and Political Rights and the European Convention on Human Rights include the idea of 'due process' but more absolute statements of FUNDAMENTAL RIGHTS are not necessarily consistent with the rule of law. As Raz affirms, the rule of law is 'not to be confused with DEMOCRACY, JUSTICE, EQUALITY, . . . human rights of any kind or respect for persons or for the dignity of man'. It has no moral content. A state which decreed that the first born should be put to death would be in breach of the rule of law if this were not done. Yet in a democracy decisions made by processes agreed by everyone must be obeyed if democracy is not to break down. Hence the rule of law is not a *distinguishing* feature of democracy – undemocratic states may observe it – but it is a *necessary* feature.

See also DUE PROCESS OF LAW; FUNDAMENTAL RIGHTS; LAW.

Reading
Dicey, A.V. [1885] 1959. *Introduction to the Study of the Law of the Constitution.* 10th edn. London: Macmillan; Raz, J. 1979. *The Authority of Law.* Oxford: Clarendon; Unger, R.M. 1976. *Law in Modern Society.* New York: Free Press.

ruling class   A whole SOCIAL CLASS cannot 'rule' in the sense that political scientists understand ruling; that is exercising executive and administrative power. Hence the term can only make sense in two circumstances: (1) if 'class' is defined in quite different terms from the normal sociological definition (as in POLITICAL CLASS); (2) if it refers to a situation in which the rulers represent the interests and objectives of an economically and socially dominant class and are recruited from among them. The second instance is the Marxist position. The capitalist class controls the STATE because it controls the means of production. MILLS, who claimed not to be a Marxist, took a similar position. His 'power elite' includes people such as top corporation executives and generals, who are not POLITICIANS but have the same backgrounds. Hence the power elite is characterized by social and political cohesion. They are united by the need to oppose Communism and to defend the 'military-industrial complex'.

Two Italian theorists did much to shape the concept. Mosca (1858–1941) argued that domination by a ruling class had always existed and that even under democracy it would continue. Any ruling class needed a 'political formula' to legitimate their authority. This formula, or myth, might change with succeeding phases of history. Pareto (1848–1923) conceived that ruling elites circulated between two basic types: the 'lions' and the 'foxes' – the strong defenders of the status quo and the adaptable and cunning innovators. Both ideas contributed to Fascist doctrine.

See also ELITES; ELITISM; ESTABLISHMENT; GOVERNMENT; MARXISM; POLITICAL CLASS; SOCIAL CLASS.

Reading
Finer, S.E. ed. 1966. *Pareto: Sociological Writings.* London: Pall Mall; Mills, C.W. 1959. *The Power Elite.* New York: OUP; Mosca, G. [1896] 1939. *The Ruling Class.* New York: McGraw-Hill; Stanworth, P. and A. Giddens. eds. 1974. *Elites and Power in British Society.* Cambridge: CUP.

S

sample surveys The notion of this research technique is that a small proportion, a 'sample', of a large group or category can be taken as representative of the whole. There are different ways of determining a sample. The most 'scientific' is the random sample. One begins with a list of the whole population that needs to be surveyed. With voting surveys in most democracies electoral rolls provide this 'sampling frame' of the whole electorate. Each voter must then be numbered notionally. One then obtains a book of random numbers and continues drawing numbers from it until one has reached the agreed size of sample. Names and addresses of voters chosen are given to interviewers who then administer the questionnaire. The advantage of this type of sample is that it produces one which proportionately reflects the socio-demographic structure of the population. Furthermore, because the method is purely statistical – it is chosen in such a way that every member of the population has a equal chance of being selected – sampling error can be calculated.

This last point does not apply to quota samples. These depend on one's country taking its census in such a way that the results give a break-down of local units, for electoral studies preferably con-stituencies, in terms of categories known to be related to voting preference such as occupation, gender and age groups. With the proportions of such groups from the census one can prepare a quota sample of the population with the groups in the same proportion. Hence interviewers are required to find and interview (say) a certain number of professional women between the ages of 35 and 55. Thus quota sampling puts much onus on the interviewers who require even more experience and training than those who use random samples. Not unexpectedly, quota samples tend to be less accurate as reflections of the population. Respondents in every sub-group are likely to be the more active part, because interviewers without assignments specific to name and address are bound to make more contact with people in public places. Furthermore, no statistical error can be calculated. Yet, in spite of its weaknesses, quota sampling is used much more than random sampling. This is because it is much cheaper.

See also EXIT POLL; PUBLIC OPINION.

Reading
Conway, F. 1967. *Sampling*. London: Allen and Unwin; Kalton, G. 1984. *Introduction to Survey Sampling*. Beverly Hills: Sage; Moser, C.A. 1958. *Survey Methods in Social Investigation*. London: Heinemann.

sanctions A sanction is a method of enforcing a law by imposing a penalty on those who break it. The term has become familiar in political discussion since the League of Nations imposed sanctions on Italy when it invaded Ethiopia in 1935. It had the choice of using military or economic sanctions and opted for the latter. In consequence member states were not supposed to trade with Italy except for allowing it to import oil which was excluded from the embargo. Unsurprisingly the policy was a failure.

Sanctions are not necessarily collective: they can be applied by a single state against another. For example, the USA put an embargo on the export of grain to the USSR in 1980 in an unsuccessful attempt to get it to withdraw from Afghanistan. It was easy for the Russians to find alternative sellers. For obvious reasons the more countries exerting sanctions the better the chance of their success, which explains why their history has been largely an account of multinational action. With the League of Nations and the United Nations the hope has been that pressure from many nations would deter aggressors or punish them when sanctions were applied. The problem has been that military sanctions involve going to war to enforce international law. This is not popular in democracies where politicians fear the unpopularity of risking for a principle many young men's lives in a remote country with whom there is no quarrel. Hence economic sanctions are favoured, or bombing which involves few casualties. With a determined and armed aggressor neither of these options is likely to succeed.

See also AGGRESSION; COLLECTIVE SECURITY; CONTAINMENT.

Reading
Doxey, M.P. 1980. *Economic Sanctions and International Enforcement*. London: Macmillan; Hanlon, J. and R. Omond. 1987. *The Sanctions Handbook*. Harmondsworth: Penguin; Hufbauer, G. and J. Schott. 1985. *Economic Sanctions Reconsidered*. Washington, D.C.: Institute for International Economics.

scientific management See FORDISM; POST-FORDISM; TAYLORISM.

scientific revolution First used to refer to the 'Copernican revolution' which overthrew the Ptolemaic system with its erroneous belief that the earth was the centre of the universe. It raised theological and political implications. Other scientific and technological discoveries have made social and political impacts but the 'steam and rail', 'electronic' and 'computer/satellite' revolutions have not destroyed prevailing paradigms.

Reading
Kuhn, T.S. 1970. *The Structure of Scientific Revolutions*. Chicago: Chicago University Press.

secession When part of a state breaks away and declares it is an independent state, it has seceded. It is more common in federal states where sub-governments have more AUTONOMY and it is always possible to argue that the state's foundation was contractual. For example, the rebel states in the South of the USA, in declaring themselves in 1861 a Confederacy, claimed the right of secession had always existed, although no such right was in the American Constitution. Conversely, although the federal 'Stalin' Soviet constitution of 1936 for the USSR included a right of secession, Stalin made it clear that secession would not be granted to any of the republics. The 'Brezhnev' 1977 constitution, on the other hand, did not include the right yet no serious attempt was made to prevent the Baltic republics seceding in 1991. The most important factor is the determination, or otherwise, of the larger part of the state to assert unity. Thus the northern states of the USA fought a bitter civil war to prevent secession, so did

Nigeria a century later to stop the Biafran breakaway. Pakistan could not forestall the secession of Bangladesh, from which it was separated by India, who supported the secessionists. Czechoslovakia divided into two states quite peacefully because neither Czechs or Slovaks thought it was worth fighting about. A similar outcome would follow the secession of Scotland from the rest of Britain, or Quebec from Canada.

See also ETHNICITY; FEDERAL GOVERNMENT; NATIONALISM; SELF-DETERMINATION.

Reading
Bucheit, L.C. 1978. *Secession*. New Haven: YUP.

second ballot An electoral system with single member constituencies that prevents any candidate winning who does not gain the majority (50 per cent +1) of the total votes cast at a first ballot. A second ballot is then held a week or two later. At the second ballot the one with most votes is elected. In France where it has been used in all elections (except in 1986) for the National Assembly since 1958, first ballot candidates who do not get an eighth of the electorate to vote for them are disqualified. Furthermore, there is bargaining among candidates to secure withdrawals so that most commonly only two or three contenders present themselves at the second ballot. While it does not result in Proportional Representation, the second ballot encourages electoral alliances. In the past it was common before the election for the left-wing parties to agree that in any constituency at the second ballot only one candidate from amongst them, the one with most votes at first ballot, should go forward to the second. The same system is used for French, Austrian and Finnish presidential elections.

See also ELECTORAL SYSTEMS; POPULAR FRONTS.

second chambers Often referred to as 'upper houses' because their origin was in ESTATES, medieval representative chambers. In modern times their legitimacy and effectiveness has often been questioned, yet most states are still bicameral. Only ten democracies are unicameral.

See also BICAMERALISM; FIRST CHAMBERS; LEGISLATURES; UNICAMERALISM.

Reading
Marriott, J.A.R. 1927. *Second Chambers*. Oxford: OUP.

secret police Common in authoritarian systems the secret police use networks of agents, illegal methods of information-gathering, arbitrary arrest and torture, and a link with top authority to instill fear in opponents of the regime and ordinary citizens. They are usually the domestic arms of SECRET SERVICES. From the mid-nineteenth century, secret, plain-clothes police spied on students, intellectuals and any other group suspected of being critical of governments. Totalitarian regimes recruited much larger, more complex, secret police organizations, keeping records on card indexes and arresting hundreds of thousands of people. The German Gestapo and the Russian OGPU (later KGB) were salient examples, but there is no reason to think that the collapses of the Third Reich and the Soviet Union signalled the end of secret policing.

See also POLICE; SECRET SERVICES; TOTALITARIANISM.

Reading
Barron, J. 1974. *The KGB*. London: Hodder and Stoughton; Crankshaw, E. 1956. *The Gestapo*. New York: Viking; Mosse, G.L. ed. 1975. *Police Forces in History*. London: Sage.

secret services Probably all nations have secret services. In totalitarian countries espionage, both domestic and international, is likely to be the province of the SECRET POLICE. In the USA intelligence gathering and spying is carried out by the Central Intelligence Agency

(CIA), famous for its 'dirty tricks' department set up to counter the operations of the KGB. MI5 is responsible for British internal counter-espionage and MI6 for external spying. The Israeli secret service, Mossad, is often said to be the most efficient. All secret services use foreign agents. Since the end of the COLD WAR TERRORISM and drug trafficking have been the main intelligence operations. In the democracies there have been moves to make them more accountable.

See also SECRET POLICE.

Reading
Richardson, J.T. 1995. *A Century of Secret Services*. Oxford: OUP; Wright, P. 1987. *Spycatcher*. Richmond, Victoria: Heinemann Australia.

sect Originally a group which had broken away from a major religion in order to perform its own rituals which were frequently less formal. The Puritan sects had an important political influence in the English Revolution (1648–60). Today the word still has this politico-religious connotation. 'Sectarianism', Catholic-Protestant hostility, is still the main source of trouble in Northern Ireland or Glasgow politics; but it is sometimes used to describe rather rancorous ideological group conflict.

secularization The first usage was a reference to the expropriation of church property. The French Revolutionaries, however, not only confiscated the lands belonging to the Catholic church, but set up a system of public, non-religious education. The clergy were deprived of their high status, young priests could be conscripted for the army and civil marriage was introduced. This was the 'secular' or 'lay' state. RATIONALISM and rationality were its characteristics. Secularizing forces in the last four centuries have been science, technology, industrialization and urbanization. These have weakened the appeal of revealed religion.

It should be noted that secularization exists where the church is established, as in Britain or Scandinavia; while in the USA, where religion is much stronger, a secular state is ensured by the First Amendment to the Constitution declaring that 'Congress shall make no law . . . respecting an establishment of religion'.

Reaction against secularizing influences has been a feature of all the major religions. Among Christian sects it has led to both evangelical and monastic secessions, though largely without political implications. In Israel, however, the secular tendencies of the founders are increasingly threatened by the Orthodox rabbinate and its crucial support in the religious parties. In Muslim states there has been an especially powerful reaction against secularization and MODERN-IZATION. It has affected the politics of the Middle East, North Africa and Asia.

See also FUNDAMENTALISM; MODERN-IZATION; RATIONALISM; THEOCRACY.

Reading
Schlucter, W. 1981. *The Rise of Western Rationalism*. Berkeley: University of California Press.

security A concept used in discussions of foreign policy, but it is appropriate to the situations of individuals as well as those of states. It is bound to be partly a matter of perception and partly a matter of material circumstances. The feeling of insecurity which pervaded Thomas HOBBES seems partly the temperament of a tremulous bachelor and partly the troubles of his age. Born in the year of the Spanish Armada, his later years were disturbed by the English Civil War. He was fearful of a return to a state of nature in which life would be 'nasty, brutish and short' and concluded that coercive authority, Leviathan, was needed to ensure the security of humanity.

With states, their almost obsessive regard for external security stems from the absence of a Leviathan. There is an uncertain structure of INTERNATIONAL LAW, but no international police force. Hence the international 'state of nature' is semi-anarchic. States must rely on themselves to make a correct appraisal of their needs and resources. Their needs will depend much on their geographical and strategic situation and its relation to potential friends and enemies. An obvious resource is a military arsenal, but others are diplomatic skill, especially in forging alliances, and a strong engineering industry for arms manufacture. Trained manpower, an easily mobilizable army and good communications all bolster a state's perception of security. Finally, in the contemporary world, insecurity may arise from environmental threats like world pollution and 'global warming'.

See also ALLIANCE; BALANCE OF POWER; DETERRENCE; FORCE MAJEURE; INTERNATIONAL RELATIONS.

Reading
Buzan, B. 1983. *People, States and Fear.* Chapel Hill: University of North Carolina Press.

segregation A policy of deliberately separating people according to a certain distinction. Some segregation may happen without deliberation, as when housing estates are built charging standard prices or rents and, in consequence, people of approximately the same income find themselves living side by side. Sometimes segregation may not give offence as when boys and girls are educated separately. It is ethnic segregation which is politically sensitive and which has given rise to agitation in the American South and South Africa. In the former case, segregation between black and whites in the school system was ended by the Supreme Court verdict *Brown* v. *Board of Education* (Topeka, Georgia), 1954, and by Presidential action thereafter. In the latter, the vicious APARTHEID system was ended with the advent to power of Nelson Mandela in 1990.

See also APARTHEID; CIVIL LIBERTIES.

select committees Also known as 'specialist committees' because they concentrate on some particular area of policy. They are legislative committees, appointed to oversee government departments. Hence in Britain they differ from the normal committees of Parliament, the STANDING COMMITTEES, which concentrate on specific bills. Select committees investigate both past and present government activity and cross-examine ministers and senior civil servants about their actions and intentions. In the USA Congressional committees are all of this kind though the term 'select' is not used. They are much more powerful than British select committees because the American executive is relatively weak. In fact, almost everywhere one finds stronger legislative committees than exist in Britain. Attempts in the last two decades to give the House of Commons stronger select committees have been only partially successful.

See also LEGISLATURES; STANDING COMMITTEES.

Reading
Bradshaw, K. and D. Pring. 1981. *Parliament and Congress.* London: Quartet; Drewry, G. ed. 1989. *The New Select Committees.* Oxford: OUP.

self-determination The self-determination of peoples became a popular cry with the end of World War I in 1918, but it had first been proclaimed by the French Revolution and upheld by Mazzini and other romantic nationalists in the mid-nineteenth century. In 1918 President Woodrow WILSON saw it as a way of settling the problem of the succession states – the new states created by the collapse of the German, Russian and Austro-Hungarian empires. Where necessary a PLEBISCITE could be held to allow ethnic groups to determine where they belonged. Lenin perceived it as a weapon against the imperialist powers with their colonial possessions. In 1945 the principle was given legal status in the UN Charter. If applied consistently it might lead to the BALKANIZATION of the world.

The main question about its application is 'Who is the self to be determined?' For example, in a referendum held in the island of Ireland about whether Northern Ireland should be part of the United Kingdom or the Irish Republic, should the vote in Northern Ireland, or in the whole island, determine the province's fate?
See also BALKANIZATION; PLEBISCITE; SECESSION; SEPARATISM.

Reading
Cobban, A. 1945. *National States and National Self-Determination.* Oxford: OUP; Hannum, H. 1990. *Autonomy, Sovereignty and Self-Determination.* Philadelphia: University of Philadelphia Press; Ronen, D. 1978. *The Quest for Self-Determination.* New Haven: YUP.

self-government   *See* AUTONOMY.

senates   Derived from the Latin word meaning 'old', the original Senate was regarded as the council of elders of the Roman Republic. Numerous countries, including the USA, Italy, France and Australia, now give their SECOND CHAMBER this name.

seniority   It is common for length of continuous service to be the criterion for appointment to office in political institutions. In parties it prevents internecine conflict. It also ensures that someone is in charge who knows the background of the business to hand. In the US Congress seniority among the members of the majority party determined the chairmenships of legislative committees. One important result politically was that Senators and Representatives from safe seats were often chairmen. When the Democrats were the majority party many

of the chairmen were from the South and used their positions to block Democratic liberal measures. The seniority rule was relaxed somewhat in the 1970s, allowing party leaders to nominate chairmen.
See also LEGISLATIVE COMMITTEES.

separation of powers   A constitutional concept stated most clearly by Montesquieu (1689–1755) in *The Spirit of the Laws* (1748). He defined three functional divisions of government which are the 'powers' referred to in the term. Furthermore he maintained that good government required that these three powers – the legislative, the executive and the judicial – should be kept quite separate. If these powers were joined liberty would be in danger. Forty years later the American revolutionaries were impressed by this argument and adopted it for their Constitution, making it impossible for a member of the legislature to be a member of the executive and, vice versa, for a member of the excutive to sit in the legislature. The independence of the judiciary was taken for granted, possibly because it already existed as part of the colonial inheritance.

Indeed, it is an accepted feature of democratic practice that the judicial power must always be independent of the executive and legislative powers. So that when political scientists speak of the 'separation of powers' they are referring to the separation between legislature and government. The general effect of the US situation is to make for relatively weak executives and relatively strong legislatures. The separation of powers must not be confused with federalism, though FEDERAL GOVERNMENT also causes diffusion of power.
See also CHECKS AND BALANCES; MIXED GOVERNMENT; PRESIDENTIAL SYSTEMS.

Reading
Gwyn, W.B. 1965. *The Meaning of the Separation of Powers.* New Orleans: Tulane University Press; Vile, M.J.C. 1967.

Constitutionalism and the Separation of Powers.
Oxford: OUP.

separatism   Separatists are those who
wish to form an autonomous or semi-
autonomous government that is separate
from a larger jurisdiction. They may live
in provinces of a federal country and want
to break away. This is so with many
French Canadians in Quebec who desire
independence from Canada. Yet unitary
countries are not always free of separatism. For example, there are Basques
who wish to live in a state separate from
Spain. Frequently separatism has an
ethnic and cultural basis.
See also AUTONOMY; DECENTRALIZATION;
DEVOLUTION; ETHNICITY.

serfdom   An institution found in rural
societies where peasants hold their land
from which they live on terms of subjection to their landlords. The condition
of serfdom is a feature of FEUDALISM.
See also FEUDALISM; SLAVERY.

Reading
Bloch, M. 1975. *Slavery and Serfdom in the
Middle Ages*. Berkeley: University of California
Press.

sexism   A gender discrimination in
word or deed. At its worst it may be
discrimination against a woman in
employment. A much slighter sexist
transgression might be talking about
'mankind' instead of 'humankind'.
See also AGEISM; DISCRIMINATION; FEMI-
NISM; POLITICAL CORRECTNESS.

shadow cabinets   Alternative governments formed by opposition leaders to
challenge the incumbent government.
Each member of the shadow cabinet will
'shadow' her/his opposite number in the
government. Consequently, if and when
the opposition comes to power, it is often
convenient for the shadow minister to
take over the department she/he has
shadowed. Though this is by no means
assured it frequently occurs. Such a

probable outcome could only happen
under a TWO-PARTY SYSTEM where one
major party succeeds another sooner or
later. Where COALITION GOVERNMENT is
likely shadow cabinets are impracticable.

Left-wing shadow cabinets, such as
those of the Australian and British
Labour parties, elect most of their
members from their parliamentary
parties. In right-wing parties, like the
British Conservatives, it is usual for
the leader to appoint members.

Reading
Punnett, R.M. 1973. *Front-Bench Opposition*.
London: Heinemann; Turner, D.R. 1969. *The
Shadow Cabinet in British Politics*. London:
Routledge.

single issue politics   This style of politics is associated with NEW SOCIAL
MOVEMENTS and the emergence of the
values of POST-MATERIALISM. It is
argued that the old style of politics, based
on cleavages of religion and SOCIAL
CLASS, has gradually declined as SECU-
LARIZATION and consumerism have
slowly eroded it. DEALIGNMENT of strong
party allegiances and party organization
much weakened by television have
resulted in PRESSURE GROUPS becoming
more popular among the young. The
most popular groups are those with non-
economic and/or global themes such as
crime, drugs, ENVIRONMENTALISM,
human rights, PRO-LIFE, PRO-CHOICE
and FEMINISM. All these issues have
international implications, another
reason why the young, increasingly internationally oriented, support them.

The decline of the old ideologies and
the salience of these new ISSUES makes it
difficult for the old parties to aggregate
them for electoral appeals. Consequently
ELECTIONS are fought between leaders
on the national media. Parties try to
accommodate most of the single group
pressures without making too many
promises. Otherwise they claim they are

better at managing the economy than the other parties.

See also NEW SOCIAL MOVEMENTS; POST-MATERIALISM.

single transferable vote Known as STV, this electoral system is used in Ireland and Australia. It involves multi-member constituencies, commonly three to seven members are to be chosen. The voter is asked to put the candidates in order of preference by writing a number after their names. First preferences are counted and those candidates who have reached the DROOP QUOTA are declared elected. Their surplus votes, over and above the Droop quota, are then assigned to the candidates with the next highest support on their ballot papers. When no further CANDIDATES are returned by this method, if there are still some to be elected, the candidate with fewest first preferences is eliminated and her/his second preferences are distributed. This process continues until the required number of candidates have been returned.

See also DROOP QUOTA; ELECTORAL SYSTEMS.

slavery A condition in which people are owned and their life and freedoms completely controlled by their owner. It arises when local labour is unwilling to do the work and there is a reservoir of labour that can be enslaved and that costs little except scanty food and barracks to house it. ARISTOTLE excused slavery in Athens because slaves were mean-natured. The Nazis had a similar view. Communist Russia used millions of slaves with the excuse that they were criminals under re-education. Christians in the American South and South Africa used the strange justification that in Genesis God had decreed that Ham should be a servant of his brothers. It first became a moral issue in the late eighteenth century. The American Declaration of Independence 1776 proclaimed 'all men are created equal', but it needed a bloody CIVIL WAR

nearly ninety years later before blacks could approximate to equality. The French Declaration of the Rights of Man 1789, however, resulted in all the slaves in the French Empire being freed. The British Empire freed its slaves in 1833. In the twentieth century the growth of belief in human rights has led to slavery being discredited, but it still exists in Saudi Arabia and Burma.

See also SERFDOM.

Reading
Davis, D.B. 1984. *Slavery and Human Progress*. Oxford: OUP.

small group politics There are numerous kinds of small groups. Politics of a kind can exist in primary groups in families, offices and factories. AUTHORITY, leadership, disagreement and compromise can be found in all small groups. Other small groups larger than primary groups may function within large groups like political parties. Political communities, like wards or parishes, may have their own type of politics. The politics of all these groups will be different from those of large organizations like mass parties. For instance, in primary groups rules will not be promulgated. The general tendency will be to avoid painful face-to-face conflict. The more thrustful members will not want formal agendas and institutional structures. Decisions will be made by interpretation and not by majority voting. If and when this method of consensus-building breaks down there may be intense personality clashes of a kind that seldom characterizes large groups.

Reading
Bealey, F.W. 1987. 'Small Group Politics'. In *Blackwell Encyclopaedia of Political Institutions*, 567–8. Ed. V. Bogdanor. Oxford: Blackwell; Dahl, R.A. and E. Tufte. 1974. *Size and Democracy*. Oxford: OUP; Sprott, W.J.H. 1958. *Human Groups*. London: Penguin; Steiner, J. and R.H. Dorff. 1960. *A Theory of Political Decision Modes*. Chapel Hill: University of North Carolina Press.

social choice theory The relationship between the preferences of individuals and choices the whole society may have to make. It begins in 1785 with Condorcet (1743–94) who pointed out that if there were three people with three options X, Y and Z, it was possible that majorities would prefer X to Y, Y to Z and Z to X. Hence whichever option was chosen a majority might prefer another. 'Condorcet's paradox' makes the idea of a 'will of the people' meaningless. Obviously applicable to voting theory, it was forgotten until the 1950s, except by the mathematician Dodgson (Lewis Carroll). It was rediscovered by Kenneth Arrow and Duncan Black who appeared to have proved that methods of social choice that seemed to be quite rational were apparently capable of autocratic application. Most political scientists do not understand the mathematical ramifications of recent social choice theory, but its implications are that most voting procedures are unfair and incapable, in a society of complex opinions, of demonstrating what people really want.

See also ELECTORAL SYSTEMS.

Reading
Arrow, K.J. 1951. *Social Choice and Individual Values*. New York: Wiley; Black, D. 1958. *The Theory of Committees and Elections*. Cambridge: CUP; Dummett, M. 1984. *Voting Procedures*. Oxford: Clarendon; Riker, W.H. 1982. *Liberalism Against Populism*. San Francisco: Freeman.

social class Political scientists have used this concept in two connections. Theoretically they have been concerned to associate, or disassociate, class and the exercise of POLITICAL POWER. Empirically they have employed it in studying political behaviour.

Much of the discourse of social and political theorists has ranged around the ideas of MARX and WEBER. Marx explained class in terms of relationships within the productive process. Weber thought one's class was determined by one's life chances in the market. Both men distinguished class from STATUS. (They are different words in German.) Marx viewed status as a relic of FEUDALISM which lingered on. For example, in the *Revolution and Counter Revolution in Germany* (1852) he mentioned the following categories: feudal nobility, bourgeoisie, *petite bourgeoisie,* upper and middle peasantry, free lower peasantry, serfs, agricultural labourers and industrial workers. Only the last was a class. Weber perceived status ranking as a matter of according prestige and esteem and thus it was a matter of social values; but in capitalist society this might well depend on one's position in the workplace. Then the distinction between class and status would not be so important.

In analysing the link between class and politics the threefold division of power delineated by Alford and Friedland is useful. *Situational power,* the relationship between superordinates and subordinates, might explain how capitalists dominate the STATE and its political managers if it could be demonstrated that capitalists act as a class and directly instruct, or manipulate, political rulers in capitalist interests. Yet capitalists often compete and political rulers often act against the interests of capital. *Institutional power* implies that the state embodies class interests. There is a class bias in its operations distilling only those policies beneficial to capital. This is best illustrated by its revenue-raising activities. Social benefits help to maintain the health and reproductiveness of the work force. *Systemic power* is the capacity of the social system to ensure that capitalist interests are satisfied. Neo-conservatives and neo-Marxists can accept this form of power, though because of quite different assumptions about the relationship of democratic politics to the economy.

Empirical studies by political scientists have been concerned with the association between class and political activity, usually voting. Researchers have viewed class as an objective classification, though they have also asked people how they saw their own class position. (This latter is called 'self-assigned class' or 'subjective class'.) One easy method in Britain is to use the Registrar-General's Census categorization based on occupation, familiar as: A – Higher managerial or professional; B – Intermediate managerial or professional; C1 – Clerical and junior professional; C2 – skilled manual; D – semi-skilled manual; E – unskilled manual. Retired people are assigned to their former occupational group and housewives to their husband's. This is really a status categorization. A refinement, introducing an element of class, was to separate the business proprietors from all the Census categories and to aggregate the residues of A and B and C2, D and E. (See A.H. Birch. 1959. *Small Town Politics*. p. 106 and F.W. Bealey, J. Blondel and W.P. McCann. 1965. *Constituency Politics*. p. 149.) Later voting studies, such as Heath, Jowell and Curtice, have used a five-fold division of the electorate into Salariat, Routine Non-manual, Petty Bourgeoisie (including small businessmen and farmers), Foremen and Technicians, Manual Workers. Other studies have found type of housing to be important. In parts of Europe religion and ETHNICITY influence voting and class is relatively unimportant.

See also CLASS CONFLICT; CLASS CONSCIOUS-NESS; CLASS PARTIES; MARXISM; MIDDLE CLASS; POLITICAL POWER; RULING CLASS; STATUS; WORKING CLASS.

Reading
Alford, R. and R. Friedland. 1985. *The Powers of Theory*. Cambridge: CUP; Heath, A., R. Jowell and J. Curtice. 1985. *How Britain Votes*. Oxford: Pergamon; Therborn, G. 1978. *What Does the Ruling Class Do When it Rules?* London: Verso; Wright, E.O. 1993. 'Class and Politics'. In *Oxford Companion to Politics of the World*, 143–50. Ed. J. Krieger. Oxford: OUP.

social contract With the Reformation and the decline of the LEGITIMACY of kingship there was the need to explain the nature of government and people's obligations towards it. Hence the growth of a theory of contract. Philosophers intended that it should elucidate the process by which humanity made the transition from a state of nature, before there was society, into a society as they knew it in which AUTHORITY existed. Their scenarios were ahistorical, imaginative and in the nature of parables. Their conception of pre-society depended on their view of human nature.

HOBBES (1588–1679) perceived people as naturally selfish and violently aggressive. His 'state of nature', as Locke said, was a 'state of war'. Hence Hobbes's contract (he usually called it a 'compact' or 'covenant') was between men who decided to end ANARCHY by installing a ruler they must all obey. LOCKE (1632–1704) saw the state of nature quite differently. Most people behaved in an orderly fashion, but there were a few who threatened life, liberty and property. Consequently a system of law was needed and a government to enforce order. A contract was then drawn up between men and their rulers under which both sides had obligations. Unlike Hobbes's contract, Locke's made the citizens' obligation to obey dependent on the ruler's preservation of social order and their liberties. If he did not keep his side of the bargain they had the right of revolt. ROUSSEAU (1712–78) was influenced by the idea of the 'noble savage' and believed people lived happily in a state of nature until someone claimed the right of property. Institutions were then inaugurated to protect property. With Rousseau the contract is really 'social' – society is based upon a contract and the less political institutions intrude the better. No contract should involve people delegating their individual wills to a sovereign. The PEOPLE are sovereign. Consequently all decisions must be made by DIRECT DEMOCRACY. There is freedom in participation. When people disagree it is because many do not know the difference between real and apparent public interest. Those mistaken must be 'forced' to be free.

The contractarian approach to LIBERALISM was replaced by the utilitarian in the nineteenth century. Recently, however, it has been revived by the work of Rawls.

See also AUTHORITY; LIBERALISM; OBLIGATION.

Reading
Barker, E. ed. 1948. *Social Contract. Essays by Locke, Hume and Rousseau*. Oxford: OUP.; Hobbes, T. [1651] 1962. *Leviathan*. New York: Collier; Rawls, J. 1971. *A Theory of Justice*. Cambridge, Mass.: HUP.

social credit The remedy of C.H. Douglas (1879–1952) for defeating the inter-war depression. He argued that in peacetime the amount of money held by consumers is not enough to buy the goods on sale at their market prices. The sellers cannot afford to reduce their prices. Hence the answer is to give consumers spending money in the form of what Douglas called a 'national dividend'. Social Credit, a sort of crude Keynesianism, especially appealed to struggling farming communities. In Canada and New Zealand Social Credit parties were formed. In New Zealand it never achieved more than a fifth of the votes but in Canada it won control in Alberta in 1935 and provided the Premier until 1970. In British Columbia it remained in power, with a three-year gap, from 1952 until 1991.

See also KEYNESIANISM.

social democracy At one time 'social democratic' was a term used to describe most left-wing parties, including those that claimed to be Marxist. The German Social Democrats dropped the need to be revolutionary, influenced by the REVI-SIONISM of Bernstein. The Russian Marxist party originally called itself 'Social Democratic' but the Bolshevik faction became the Communist Party under the leadership of Lenin. In general, however, as working-class Socialist parties discovered they could, through parliamentary methods, secure many of the reforms advocated by MARX and Engels in the *Communist Manifesto* (such as a progressive income tax, the nationalization of transport, the abolition of child labour and free education for all), they became converted to democratic methods.

Social democracy has thus come to be used to describe a political and economic system. Social democratic parties support the WELFARE STATE, the nationalization of public services, a mixed economy, socialized medicine and full employment policies. They prefer taxing and spending to saving and tend to risk inflation rather than increase unemployment. They often favour public ownership of national banks. The archetypal social democracy is in Scandinavia, especially in Sweden, where the Social Democrats have been in power for most of the time since the 1930s. Elsewhere there has been much debate about the difference between social democrats and democratic socialists. In general the former have been more to the right. In Italy the divide was about the attitude to NATO. It was supported by the Social Democrats and opposed by the Socialists.

See also COMMUNISM; DEMOCRACY; MARXISM; SOCIALISM.

Reading
Barry, B. 1989. *Democracy, Power and Justice*. Oxford: OUP; Paterson, W. and A.H. Thomas. 1986. *The Future of Social Democracy*. Oxford: Clarendon; Przeworski, A. 1985. *Capitalism and Social Democracy*. Cambridge: CUP; Scase, R. 1977. *Social Democracy in Capitalist Society*. London: Croom Helm.

social engineering A term first used by Karl POPPER to describe the comprehensive social and economic planning of Communist regimes. He contrasted social engineering with what he called 'piecemeal engineering', a policy of judicious state intervention in appropriate places at appropriate times and not on a comprehensive scale. This was consistent with social democratic government.

See also PLANNING; SOCIALISM; TECHNOCRACY.

Reading
Popper, K.R. 1945. *The Open Society and its Enemies*. 2 vols. London: Routledge.

social justice   *See* JUSTICE.

social market economy   The prototype of the social market economy was the West German economy in the 30 years of the republic's inauguration after 1949. It was a complicated mixture of free market economics and a generous WELFARE STATE. Competition took place within certain limits. There was co-operation between the private and public sectors to which the government gave encouragement, though this never went as far as CORPORATISM. An important part of the strategy was management of the labour market largely achieved by great support for industrial training. Good industrial relations were achieved through *mittbestimmung*, the obligation for larger enterprises to set up councils to consult with elected representatives of employees.

See also CORPORATISM; INDUSTRIAL RELATIONS; POLITICAL ECONOMY.

Reading
Wunche, H.F. ed. 1982. *Standard Texts on the Social Market Economy*. Stuttgart: G. Fischer.

social mobility   Movement from one class or one status group to another. There is 'upward social mobility' and 'downward social mobility'. The former can be the result of hard work, winning a lottery, passing examinations and marriage. In general, degrees of mobility reflect opportunity and equality, or the lack of them, in society. While it is clear that modern trends are towards greater professionalism at one end of the social scale and the decrease in numbers of dirty degrading jobs at the other, it is by no means certain that hierarchies of status and power are in decline. It is possible that superordinates are fewer though more powerful than ever.

See also SOCIAL CLASS; SOCIAL STRATIFICATION.

Reading
Goldthorpe, J.H. 1980. *Social Mobility and Class Structure in Modern Britain*. Oxford: Clarendon; Heath, A. 1981. *Social Mobility*. London: Fontana.

social movements   *See* LABOUR MOVEMENTS; NEW SOCIAL MOVEMENTS.

social order   'Order' is a confusing term. In one sense it relates to a society in which there is control and an 'ordering' of things as in 'law and order'. In another it refers to a particular pattern or status quo that has remained intact. In yet a third it may have an ideological implication as in the term 'New Order' which involves both a controlled ordering and, historically, a determination to ensure permanency. For example, Hitler's New Order was the 'thousand year Reich'.

social partners   A term first used in Austria to describe a co-operative relationship between the state, business and labour, clearly one of the important relationships of the modern pluralist state. All governments, especially democratic governments, want industrial peace and prosperity; and, although to some extent the interests of business and labour conflict, they also have a common interest in high productivity and employment. The triangular relationship tends to become regularized when governments need to consult and bargain with the social partners. War is one such situation: another is a serious inflationary crisis.

This latter threat in the 1970s was responsible for the development of 'tri-partism', or 'neo-corporatism', as it was variously known.

See also CORPORATISM; INDUSTRIAL RELATIONS; TRADE UNIONS.

social stratification   A pattern of stratification depends on who stratifies by what criteria. Social stratification by STATUS is a matter of according more or less prestige to individuals, groups, housing estates and so on. An individual can carry out this exercise but a collective picture of status ranking can be done by SAMPLE SURVEY. It will be a subjective evaluation; but nevertheless revealing about people's perceptions and, therefore, possible sources of motivation. Stratification by SOCIAL CLASS is usually based on occupation and/or income.

See also POLITICAL STRATIFICATION; SOCIAL CLASS; STATUS.

socialism   A much used, and abused, term. It can be employed to refer to quite different social and political systems. In eastern Europe before 1989 the 'socialist states' referred to the Communist countries; while all other states, including those where SOCIAL DEMOCRACY prevailed, were known as 'capitalist countries'. In western Europe socialism was regarded by most observers as quite different from 'Communism', the Soviet political and economic system. This was because DEMOCRACY had come to be seen by them as an essential ingredient of socialism.

Socialism as a set of policies has two fundamental ingredients. One is a belief in public ownership as a fairer and better form of enterprise than private ownership. There is much debate among socialists about how much industry ought to be publicly owned. Communists claim almost all, while many socialists would go no further than public utilities such as gas and water. Again, Communists would nationalize most distribution while socialists tend to believe almost all retailing should remain privately owned. Thus the Communist state had a COMMAND ECONOMY, while Socialist countries to a great degree allowed MARKET FORCES to operate.

The second basic component of socialist policy is the WELFARE STATE. EGALITARIANISM is a socialist idea, though socialists may vary in their attachment to it. But there is general agreement in redistributive measures which take from the rich in taxation and allocate the surplus to children, the aged, the impoverished and the sick. The belief that no one should be allowed to sink below a certain living standard is encapsulated in the concept of a 'National Minimum'.

Socialism, both as a system of thought and as a movement, is best interpreted as a reaction against the Industrial Revolution and its consequences. Socialist thought in the early nineteenth century was Utopian and prescriptive. By the end of the century socialists like William Morris (1834–96), who were of this kind, were in reaction against the ugliness of industrialization and mass production. Their solution tended to be a unrealistic reversion to rural society. 'Scientific socialism', of which Karl MARX (1813–83) claimed to be a proponent, benefited from a much greater experience and understanding of what industrial CAPITALISM implied. Marx thought it was inevitable that it would be succeeded by a socialist society, though he was extremely vague about how a socialist economy would operate. The 'revisionist socialists', who have been in a majority among post-Marxist socialists, beginning with *Evaluating Socialism* (1899) by Edouard Bernstein (1850–1932), leader of the German Social Democrats, tended to discard strategies of revolutionary working-class action and turned to taming capitalism through democratic majorities and legislative action. SYNDICALISM, however, was still a creed supported by some socialists with trade-union links.

In the twentieth century the Russian Revolution in 1917 led to a division among socialists that was to last for at least 70 years. The Union of Soviet Socialist Republic, as Russia became, did not recognize the democratic socialist parties of Europe as 'socialist'. Much of the argument raged around the relationship of democracy to both capitalism and socialism and was complicated greatly by the COLD WAR. A more competitive world economy and the inability of Keynesian measures to deal with the inflationary crises of the 1970s led to a retreat by western socialist parties from their basic positions.

See also CAPITALISM; COMMAND ECONOMY; COMMUNISM; MARKET FORCES; MARX-ISM; REVISIONISM; SOCIAL DEMOCRACY; STATE CAPITALISM; STATE SOCIALISM; SYNDICALISM.

Reading
Bealey, F.W. 1999. 'Socialism'. In Bealey, F.W., R.A. Chapman and M. Sheehan. *Elements in Political Science.* Edinburgh: Edinburgh University Press; Crick, B. 1987. *Socialism.* Milton Keynes: Open University Press; Korpi, W. 1983. *The Democratic Class Struggle.* London: Routledge; Miliband, R. 1961. *Parliamentary Socialism.* London: Allen and Unwin.

socialist parties   See CLASS PARTIES; LABOUR MOVEMENTS; LABOUR PARTIES.

socialization   See POLITICAL SOCIAL-IZATION.

society   A term that can be used to mean 'club' or small cultural group. At one time it referred to 'high society', the social elite. Spelt with a capital 'S' it refers to the complex network of relationships within which most of humanity lives. (Hermits and 'dropouts' may be excepted.) All societies have this pattern of relationships, but modern industrial society's networks are far more elaborate and yet, at the same time, often more impersonal than those in agricultural societies. Tonnies (1855–1936) distinguished between *Gemeinschaft* forms of society where people are connected by custom and family ties and *Gesellschaft* forms where more distant but numerous relationships are controlled by law and contract. Political relationships are more evident in the latter form. They are different from other relationships because they are characterized by the exercise of POLITICAL POWER, usually originating in the STATE.

See also PLURALISM; STATE.

Reading
McIver, R.M. and C.H. Page. 1950. *Society.* London: Macmillan.

solidarity   In left-wing terminology the concept indicates the necessity for working-class cohesion in facing the demands of the capitalists. It is especially appropriate to the industrial struggle, from whence it derives, because in the confrontation over bargaining for better wages and conditions, any sign of lack of unity may be detrimental to a successful outcome. Facing the implacable Communist employer-state in 1980, it was natural that the Gdansk shipyard workers under Walesa should call their union Solidarity.

For social scientists the term will always be reminiscent of Durkheim (1858–1917) who distinguished between *mechanical solidarity* where there is consensus derived from common values and experiences, resulting in a relatively unspecialized society based on custom; and *organic solidarity,* a situation based on a highly differentiated division of labour, in which people have to develop a system of inter-dependencies in order to survive. These are IDEAL TYPES, but the former represents an older era and the latter modern society.

See also DIVISION OF LABOUR; TRADE UNIONS.

Reading
Durkheim, E. [1893] 1984. *The Division of Labour in Society*. London: Macmillan.

sovereignty A claim to authority, originally by sovereign monarchs, but by states since the Treaty of Westphalia in 1648. A state becomes sovereign when other states recognise it as such. The term cannot be a synonym for complete independence, though states may argue it is. No states in the world today are without dependence, in some form, on other states. Similarly the claim that some make that the British Parliament has 'parliamentary sovereignty' is without validity except in a strictly legal sense.
See also CONSTITUTIONAL LAW; KINGSHIP.

Reading
De Jouvenal, B. 1957. *Sovereignty*. Chicago: Chicago University Press; Hinsley, E.H. 1986. *Sovereignty*. Cambridge: CUP; Marshall, G. 1971. *Constitutional Theory*. Oxford: OUP.

sovereignty of the people The intellectual origins of popular sovereignty are derived from the French Declaration of the Rights of Man, 1789, Clause III: 'the nation is essentially the source of all sovereignty'. This was soon changed by the Revolution to 'the people . . . '. In view of the juristic and political conceptions of SOVEREIGNTY it can only have validity if emphasis is put on 'source'. Then it has a strong emotive appeal, though what sovereignty the PEOPLE want exercised in their name will always be a problem for politicians.
See also PEOPLE; SOVEREIGNTY.

soviets The Russian word for councils. In the twentieth century it refers to 'workers and soldiers' councils'. Soviets were first set up in the 1905 Revolution in Russia. Later, in the 1917 Revolution they were the main avenue by which the Bolsheviks came to power. Lenin, who had condemned them in the 1905 Revolution, realized on returning to Russia in April 1917 that they were ripe

for permeation. Hence they were incorporated in the constitutional structure of the Union of Soviet Socialist Republics (USSR), a country referred to in American COLD WAR jargon as 'the Soviets'.

spatial theory A sub-division of SOCIAL CHOICE THEORY relating to the 'policy space' in which voters and CANDIDATES locate themselves and each other. Downs used the economic theory of duopoly to argue that POLITICIANS who desired re-election would tend to position themselves and their policies as near as they could to what they perceived to be the position of the median voter. Successful politicians, therefore, tended to be close to one another's position. The assumption about voters is that they can calculate the ideological distances between themselves and the candidates and vote either for the one nearest to their own position or, tactically, for the one they expect to win nearest to their own position. The assumption is likely to be unwarranted in quite a few cases and where ISSUES are widely distributed in policy space it is difficult to discern a median.
See also MODEL; PUBLIC CHOICE THEORY; SOCIAL CHOICE THEORY.

Reading
Downs, A. 1957. *An Economic Theory of Democracy*. New York: Harper and Row; McLean, I. 1982. *Dealing in Votes*. Oxford: Martin Robertson.

speakers A term used for those who preside in legislatures. It originates with the British Speaker who, in spite of being an MP attached to one of the parties, remains impartial in calling on participators in debate, maintaining order and interpreting rules and conventions. Speakers do not vote except, by tradition, to vote 'Aye' when there is a tied vote. Canada appears to be the only other country practising this detachment. Australian and American Speakers are partisan. In the USA the office is a leading one in the majority party in the House of Representatives. The Senate is chaired by the Vice-President. In the French National Assembly 'Le President' is chairman of a committee, usually with a government majority, which draws up the parliamentary agenda. She/he tends to be aloof and rarely speaks in debates.

Reading
Laundy, P.A.C. 1964. *The Office of Speaker*. London: Cassell.

spin doctors   A term derived from baseball. Specialists in spin who coach pitchers are known as 'spin doctors'. As the expression 'spinning a yarn' is often taken to be the same as 'telling a tall story', 'putting a spin' on political PROGRAMMES and policies has become a well-known public relations exercise. Spin doctors in political terms are POLI-TICIANS who are good at dealing with the media and depicting their own party and its leaders in favourable terms. They have become active at all times, but are particularly prominent during election campaigns.

spoils system   *See* BOSSES; PATRON-AGE; PORK BARREL.

sponsorship of candidates   The British Labour Party's constitution stipulates that election expenses of parliamentary candidates should be paid by one of its affiliates. These include constituency parties; but the term 'sponsored candi-date' has only been applied to those sponsored by trade unions or the Co-operative Party. Today the practice is not as important as it once was when the unions, especially the miners, were more powerful. Sponsorship never allowed a union to control an MP's vote or be-haviour in Parliament.

Reading
Ellis, J. and R.W. Johnson. 1974. *Members from the Unions*. London: Fabian Society.

stability   A concept often used by political scientists as though the term has a moral connotation. In fact, whatever one's stance, one cannot make a moral assessment without asking: 'What par-ticular values and features are stabilized?' Stability is not a virtue in itself: a country might be stabilized in sloth, brutality and corruption.

The emphasis on stability as a virtue in itself was a characteristic of the writings of some social scientists in the 1950s. Two factors probably accounted for this attitude. The COLD WAR engendered an international atmosphere in which both SUPERPOWERS sought client states. The Soviet Union's policy of encouraging radical movements in developing countries led to the USA favouring regimes where social dissidence was not encouraged. Stability was also a feature of Parsonian models which stressed the importance of regime adaptability and survival. Electoral studies tended to support SCHUMPETER's conception of democracy as one where citizens only participated at election time when they chose between the leaders of different elites.

Yet democracies can never be stable in the sense of consensus about the values and goals of society. Democracy stimu-lates disagreement and challenges basic social attitudes. Only the procedures need to be stable: otherwise democracies exist in a climate of change. Rulers change and policies change. The most stable regimes are sleepy authoritarian states.

See also AUTHORITARIANISM; DEMOCRACY; MODEL.

Reading
Bealey, F.W. 1987. 'Stability and Crisis: Fears about Threats to Democracy'. *European Journal of Political Research* 15, 687–715; Dowding, K. and R. Kimber. 1983. 'The Meaning and Use of Political Stability'. *European Journal of Political Research* 11, 229–44; Rosenthal, U. 1978. *Political Order*. Alphen aan den Rijn: Sijthoff and Noordhoff.

standing committees A misnomer for the committees in the British House of Commons set up to examine the details of a BILL after it has passed its second reading. Once finished with the bill they disband. Other English-speaking chambers tend to use the term to mean continuing committees, what are called SELECT COMMITTEES in the UK.

See also LEGISLATIVE COMMITTEES; SELECT COMMITTEES.

Reading
Lees, J.D. and M. Shaw. eds. 1979. *Committees in Legislatures*. Oxford: Martin Robertson.

state A complex concept used in at least three contexts – philosophic, legal and political. These areas are inter-related, both historically and within the wider social framework.

The classic perception of the state was as an abstraction of the ideas of power and AUTHORITY. The main concern of early philosophers was the relationship between human beings and political authority. ARISTOTLE (384–322BC) spoke of the 'polis', meaning both the city state and a society. Cicero (106–43BC) wrote about *auctoritas* which stemmed from the Senate, the ruling body of the Roman Republic. Usually it is MACHIAVELLI (1469–1527) who is credited with the first use of the word 'state' in his work, *The Prince*, written as a text-book of statecraft. He was only concerned with the Italian statelets; but he employed the term in its modern meaning of a territory with defined borders and a central authority which had to be obeyed. Towards the end of the Middle Ages the notion of independent territories with governments holding supreme power within them and enforcing a single source of law became recognized. Bodin (1529–96) called this capacity SOVER-EIGNTY, the indispensible feature of a state.

Later political philosophers were much

exercised by the relationship between individuals and the state, the problem of POLITICAL OBLIGATION. Questions like 'Why should I obey the commands of the state? When can I disobey them, if ever?' were implied. The answer depended upon one's view of the nature of human-kind. HOBBES (1588–1679) believed in the essentially aggressive nature of men. In consequence they lived in fear of each other and so they had made a compact and set up the state to ensure that an ordered society was maintained through the exertion of power by unassailable authority. LOCKE (1632–1704) believed that people were, on the whole, good and the state existed to ensure that wrong-doers did not disrupt ordered society. Locke also asserted that individuals had basic rights which should be enshrined in a contract with the state. If the state broke its side of the contract, the right of revolt existed. ROUSSEAU (1712–78) was concerned with the problem of how to obtain a kind of society in which everyone was as free as in the state of nature and yet at the same time everyone's person and property were protected. His solution was the SOCIAL CONTRACT, an agreement between people by which they entered into a civil association, giving up their rights to find true freedom to laws prescribed by themselves. The old dynastic sovereigns would be overthrown to be replaced by the SOVEREIGNTY OF THE PEOPLE.

The American (1776) and French Revolutions (1789) cast the relationship between individuals and the state in new terms. The Industrial Revolution was the motivator for collective forces which made compelling demands upon political authority. Liberal economists like Adam Smith (1723–90) attacked the prevailing mercantilist theory that the state could control trade when it thought it necessary. Herbert Spencer (1820–1903) argued that the state should be no more than a 'night watchman'. It should limit itself to safeguarding LAW AND ORDER and the sanctity of business contracts. Ethnic groups demanding statehood threatened the multi-ethnic Russian, Austro-Hungarian and Turkish empires. A reaction against fragmentary forces came especially from HEGEL (1770–1831) who believed the state should further the quest for perfection in reason and morals, uphold SOLIDARITY and correct the lurches towards instability to which CIVIL SOCIETY was prone.

Another perception of the state is as an international actor with recognition under international law. Sovereignty as defined by Bodin implied complete independence in the international context. It meant the capacity of a state to maintain its integrity by ensuring that its frontiers and its nationals were respected by other states. A state only becomes one under INTERNATIONAL LAW when it it is recognized as such by other states and, today, by the United Nations. A state's sovereignty may be impaired when another state has military installations on its territory, or by another state dominating economic investment within its borders. Very small states can hardly feel sovereign when a multinational corporation employs a large part of its labour force. In practice, however, interdependency of states is so marked in the contemporary world that no state has 100 per cent sovereignty.

A third perception of the state is the most familiar. It is a bureaucratic apparatus of control, a conception associated with Max WEBER (1864–1920) who defined the state as the possessor of ultimate coercive power within defined borders. The modern state had both legality and LEGITIMACY and it controlled through a BUREAUCRACY with numerous functions. To the traditional functions of dispenser of law, upholder of order and guardian of property the modern democratic state, as a result of electoral pressures, has added all kinds of collectivist functions. The contem-

porary state provides education for all children, insurance for the sick and unemployed, charity for the impoverished and health care for the ill and aged. It is able to do this by redistributing income – taxing the better-off to help the worse-off, a policy that in the last two decades has met with electoral counter-pressures. The welfare and distributive functions, it has been truly said, are ways of 'allocating values'. Some sections of society are rewarded and others penalized. Since the late nineteenth century, politicians from a spectrum stretching from paternalistic conservatives to social democrats have, to a greater or lesser degree, supported such functions. They conceived the state as an instrument for promoting the policies they favoured.

Much modern theory of the state has assumed that its controlling power has dwindled, or is destined entirely to disappear. MARX argued that while under CAPITALISM the state was a tool of the capitalist class, but once the workers took power and set up socialism/communism there would be no further use for it. It would 'wither away'. Neo-Marxists have been at pains to explain why this has not happened. Gramsci (1891–1937) argued that the capitalist state had disseminated a dominant ideology that ensured consent to its activities. Habermas (1929–) saw this IDEOLOGY, which he located in the affluence resulting from science and technology, as losing its legitimacy. Poulantzas (1936–79) argued that capitalist democracy had survived because of its capacity for balancing various factions in society. As a result DEMOCRACY was in decline and a regime he called 'authoritarian statism' was displacing it. MARCUSE (1898–1979) wrote that the working-class had failed in its historical revolutionary role and the impetus had to be found elsewhere, among students, 'drop-outs' and the under-class. Offe (1940–) contended that the democratic state was excluded from making decisions about investment and that its policies were constrained by the need for capitalist accumulation. Welfare benefits were a way of socializing employers' labour costs.

Pluralists perceived the state as merely one wielder of power in a society where power had many sources. The early prescriptive pluralists, like LASKI and the Guild Socialists, foresaw a highly decentralized society with corporatist structures. Later pluralists after World War II were mainly political scientists who had discovered the power of PRESSURE GROUPS. They perceived the state as possessing limited power between various intermediate groups, such as business and labour, and performing the role of either referee or broker. Reaction against both the neo-Marxists and pluralists is to be found among those who want to 'bring the state back in', asserting that states are unique structures with their own histories. Foremost among these is Theda Skocpol who traced the history of the state apparatuses of France, Russia and China.

See also BUREAUCRACY; COLLECTIVISM; IDEALISM; LEGITIMACY; POLITICAL POWER; REALISM; SOVEREIGNTY.

Reading
Dahl, R.A. 1971. *Polyarchy*. New Haven: YUP; D'Entrèves, A.P. 1967. *The Notion of the State*. Oxford: Clarendon; Dunleavy, P. and B. O'Leary. 1987. *Theories of the State*. London: Macmillan; Dyson, K. 1980. *The State Tradition in Western Europe*. Oxford: Martin Robertson; Skocpol, T. 1979. *States and Social Revolutions*. Cambridge: CUP.

state capitalism A phrase used by Lenin to describe Bolshevik economic policy between 1918 and 1921. It implied that Russia could not be socialist until there was a certain amount of industrial development which the New Economic Policy after 1921 was designed to implement. The term was later used by Trotskyists as appropriate to the situation in the Soviet Union where the state as employer repressed the workers.

See also COMMUNISM; SOCIALISM; TROTSKYISM.

state of nature See SOCIAL CONTRACT.

statesman See POLITICIAN.

state socialism Public ownership of the means of production controlled by a highly centralized state. It is the opposite of other decentralized forms of public ownership such as ANARCHISM, communal socialism, co-operative ownership, GUILD SOCIALISM and municipal socialism. Both in the Soviet Union and Communist China there was argument about which was the best form.

See also NATIONALIZATION; SOCIALISM.

states' rights Under FEDERAL GOVERNMENT there is bound to be some conflict between central power and the autonomous powers of the sub-units – 'cantons' in Switzerland, 'provinces' in Canada and 'states' in Australia and the USA. In the USA there was a 'states' rights' party from the beginning and in 1791 the 10th Amendment was passed stating: 'The powers not delegated to the United States by the Constitution, nor prohibited by it to the States, are reserved to the States respectively, or to the people'. By the mid-nineteenth century the Southern states in their defence of slavery were arguing that they were sovereign bodies with the right of SECESSION. States' rights has remained an issue in American politics, though since the 1930s central government has increased its powers relative to the states. This has happened in other federal systems, except for the Canadian.

See also FEDERAL GOVERNMENT; SECESSION; SEPARATISM; UNITARY GOVERNMENT.

statism A translation of the French word *étatisme*, meaning a system in which the state intervenes purposively and frequently in the economy by directing investment, controlling wages and prices and supervising labour markets.

See also CORPORATISM; *DIRIGISME*; MERCANTILISM.

status A term used in at least two senses. Originally it meant a social position defined by law or custom. Thus 'lord', 'freeman' and 'serf' were statuses: medieval society was a 'status society'. Hence when Maine (1822–88) wrote about the movement from 'status' to 'contract' he was describing a historic trend from a society based on dependency to one based on agreement between people. In post-medieval society social position was no longer defined by law or custom.

MARX was aware of this connotation when, in commenting on the Luddite machine-smashers, he said they were 'seeking to recapture the vanished status of the medieval craftsmen'. He believed status distinctions belonged to a past age and were being replaced by class differences. WEBER also adapted the medieval dimension to his classic definition of status, the one now generally accepted by most social scientists. It was not now a legally defined stratification, but an order of ranking based on 'prestige', 'honour' or 'esteem'. (It depends on the translator.) Hence one's ranking depends on others' perceptions of one's reputation; how we assess one another will depend on values.

Consequently there are many varieties of status systems. In small face-to-face communities where people are more or less equal in economic terms and power is not exerted, high status might be attributed according to some valued accomplishment such as growing the best leeks or making the best cakes. In highly populated cities status rankings can only be achieved for a few prominent citizens whose reputations will only be second-hand. The status of housing estates and associations, however, will often be easily ascertained by questionaire methods. Nation-wide surveys reveal citizens have status rankings for professions, newspapers and national institutions. Similarly status will vary from age to age and country to country. In a highly theocratic society saintly priests without worldly wealth may have the highest status, while in a materialistic, capitalist society where wealth is greatly valued the highest status may be given to billionaires. In complex modern INDUSTRIAL SOCIETY there will be much disparity among status rankings, reflecting the different values possessed by different groups.

See also POLITICAL POWER; SOCIAL CLASS; SOCIAL STRATIFICATION; VALUE JUDGEMENTS.

Reading
Gerth, H.H. and C.W. Mills. 1948. *From Max Weber*. London: Routledge; Lee, J.M. 1963. *Social Leaders and Public Persons*. Oxford: Clarendon; Maine, H.S. [1861] 1931. *Ancient Law*. Oxford: OUP; Merton, R.K. 1968. *Social Theory and Social Structure*. New York: Free Press; Packard, V. 1961. *The Status Seekers*. Harmondsworth: Penguin; Williams, W.M. 1956. *The Sociology of an English Village*. London: Routledge.

statute law A body of laws or acts passed by a parliament in accordance with proper legislative procedures. Statutes are of various kinds. Some merely amend or repeal previous laws. Others may codify earlier legislation on a subject. Some statutes may be general and leave either DECREES or interpretations by the courts to fill in the details. This has been the practice in Europe. In Britain the tradition until the twentieth century was for statutes to be drafted in great detail. Much recent innovative social legislation, however, has necessitated recourse to DELEGATED LEGISLATION.

See also BILLS; DECREES; DELEGATED LEGISLATION; LAW.

Reading
Miers, D. and A. Page. 1983. *Legislation.* London: Sweet and Maxwell.

statutory instruments The main source of British DELEGATED LEGISLATION. The Statutory Instruments Act 1946 contains the rules controlling their issuance. They may be annulled within 40 days if the parent Act makes them subject to negative laying procedure. If subject to affirmative procedure they do not come into effect until approved by affirmative resolutions of both Houses. A Scrutiny Committee of both Houses of Parliament decides whether statutory instruments should be drawn to Parliament's attention on special grounds.

Reading
May, T.E. 1983. *Parliamentary Practice.* London: Butterworth.

sticks and carrots A metaphor in common use among political journalists. It envisages an entity – state, association or institution – as a donkey which must be induced to take some course either by penalties or by rewards: either by 'sticks' or 'carrots'.

strategic weapons In COLD WAR language these were inter-continental nuclear weapons with a range capable of reaching the USA when fired from the Soviet Union, and vice versa.

strategy A military term that denotes a long-term plan, to be distinguished from 'tactics' which relates to conduct of battles. 'Theatre strategy' refers to planning in a particular theatre of war, while 'grand strategy' is concerned with military logistics and continental or world war. A famous grand strategy was the von Schlieffen plan devised before 1914, by which German forces would hold Russia in the East while invading France through Belgium. NATO grand strategy in the COLD WAR was CONTAINMENT. In recent years the popularity of long-term economic policy has led to 'strategy' becoming a general political term and it is also widely used by large-scale business enterprises.

Reading
Channon, D.F. 1973. *The Strategy and Structure of British Enterprise.* London: Macmillan; Clausewitz, C. von. [c.1835] 1984. *On War.* Princeton: Princeton University Press; Earle, E.M. ed. 1971. *Makers of Modern Strategy.* Princeton: Princeton University Press.

stratification *See* POLITICAL STRATIFICATION; SOCIAL STRATIFICATION.

strikes *See* INDUSTRIAL RELATIONS.

strong mayor plan An American type of city government. It has especially been adopted in large cities. The 'plan' is to give the Mayor wide powers to appoint heads of departments, draw up annual budgets and act as general policy strategist. It is thus similar to the CITY MANAGER type of local government but Mayors are elected. They tend to be at the centre of all publicity and to be held accountable for everything. If they are chosen because they are celebrities, and are without relevant administrative experience, 'strong mayors' may prove to be weak and ineffective.
See also CITY MANAGER; WEAK MAYOR PLAN.

structural functionalism For political scientists the most familiar example of this methodology is the classical characterization of 'political systems' consisting of three structural features – legislatures, executives and judiciaries – with their three functions of making laws, implementing them and interpreting them. Later and more ambitious attempts to compare very diverse types of political regimes can be seen in structural-functional models popularized by Easton. Here 'structures' are, for the most part, not institutional entities, but

cultural and social supports. 'Functions' are related to adaptation and survival.
See also FUNCTIONALISM; POLITICAL SYSTEMS; STRUCTURALISM; SYSTEMS ANALYSIS.

Reading
Easton, D. 1965. *A Framework for Political Analysis*. Englewood Cliffs: Prentice Hall; Gouldner, A. 1970. *The Coming Crisis of Western Sociology*. New York: Avon.

structuralism At its vaguest this term means little more than the belief that explanation of societies and systems should be predominantly in terms of social mechanisms and not in terms of individual behaviour. Thus political scientists studying political systems should pay little attention to the personality and behaviour of political leaders. Structuralism is consistent with some of the realist theories in the social sciences, including MARXISM. It also has an application to INTERNATIONAL RELATIONS theory. In the field of international economics it lies at the base of DEPENDENCY theories and it is relevant to the study of world instability, WAR and peace.
See also DEPENDENCY; FUNCTIONALISM; STRUCTURAL FUNCTIONALISM.

Reading
Giddens, A. 1987. 'Structuralism, poststructuralism, and the production of culture'. In *Social Theory Today*. Eds. A. Giddens and J. Turner. Stanford: Stanford University Press; Waltz, K. 1979. *Theory of International Politics*. New York: McGraw-Hill.

student politics Students have traditionally been involved in radical and revolutionary politics since the nationalist movements culminating in the 1848 revolutions. They have more free time than others in their own age group and their education inclines them to IDEALISM and a questioning of authority and the status quo. The heyday of student RADICALISM was the 1960s and early 1970s when large numbers of American students were involved in the Civil Rights movement and, later, demonstrations against the war in Vietnam. The events of May 1968 in Paris, when student riots shook the Gaullist Presidency, was an incentive for students in Europe to campaign, not only against university authorities, but also against CAPITALISM and the STATE. In Italy and Germany a few students were involved in anarchist terror groups. MARCUSE in his writings encouraged students to think of their revolutionary potential. Less dramatically, students became important as a pressure group because of their vast expansion of numbers and the extension, almost everywhere, of the franchise to those between 18 and 21.
See also UNDERCLASS; YOUTH MOVEMENTS.

Reading
Cockburn, A. and R. Blackburn. eds. 1969. *Student Power*. Harmondsworth: Penguin.

subsidiarity An idea that goes back to Aquinas (1225–74) who argued that the responsibility for functions should be allocated, as far as practicable, to the lowest levels of society. The basis of this contention was the wish to place decision-making as far away from the STATE as possible and so defend the Catholic Church from its encroachments. It later emerges in Catholic corporatist theory, expressed in the PAPAL ENCYCLICALS, *De Rerum Novarum* (1891) and *Quadragesimo Anno* (1931). Among contemporary political scientists subsidiarity has become a concept supporting federalism and delegation to small units. The regionalists in the European Union use it to give LEGITIMACY to their vision of a Europe where the NATION-STATE is weak and regions and local governments have much AUTONOMY.
See also DECENTRALIZATION; FEDERAL GOVERNMENT.

Reading
Morgan, R. ed. 1986. *Regionalism in European Politics*. London: Policy Studies Institute.

subversion   The attempt by secret or surreptitious means to undermine a social and/or political structure. In Britain the earliest fears related to French revolutionary ideas being spread through pamphlets and by agents. Since 1917 it has been commonly linked in official minds with Communist infiltration and espionage. In the USA after 1945 'McCarthyism' was an almost hysterical reaction to these activities. More recently subversion has been seen, not only as an attempt to overthrow a government, but also as a form of conspiracy to emasculate a culture and demoralize a society.
See also ENTRYISM; REVOLUTIONS.

successive voting   This term is used in two ways. First, it can refer to a procedure by which legislative proposals are ranked in order according to some rational criterion (such as expense). Each is then related to the status quo and voted on until one is adopted, or the status quo stands. This device is used in the Norwegian parliament. Second, it can refer to a refinement of Proportional Representation by which CANDIDATES elected are ranked in preferential order; for example, to decide who holds committee chairmanships.

suffrage   *See* FRANCHISE.

superpower   A COLD WAR term referring to either the USSR or the USA.

supply-side economics   Among the 'new Conservatives' of the 1980s this was seen as an alternative, or additional, policy to MONETARISM. First propounded by the economist Arthur Laffer, it was taken up by President Reagan. Its attraction was that it appeared to be a justification for cutting taxation and public expenditure. The argument is that money released from taxation will be invested, thus increasing employment and productivity and leading to higher prosperity. It will also lower INFLATION.

The poorer part of the community will benefit from the 'trickle down' of greater spending and increased economic activity by the rich.

supranational government   Rule by the authority of an association of states, much looser than a federation because all members retain considerable sovereignty. Yet it is a form of government with more formal conditions than CONFEDERATIONS demand. A supranational organization makes rules binding on all the citizens of all the members. It has some financial independence and power to enforce its decisions. The European Union is an obvious example.
See also CONFEDERATION; FEDERAL GOVERNMENT.

Reading
Capotorti, F. 1983. 'Supranational Organisations'. In *Encyclopaedia of Public International Law*, Instalment 5, 262–8. Amsterdam: Elsevier; Schermers, H.G. 1980. *International Institutional Law*. Alphen aan den Rijn: Sijthoff and Noordhoff.

supreme courts   As a general term this is used to refer to the highest court in the land. For instance, in Britain the House of Lords in its judicial capacity (meaning only the Law Lords sitting) has been described as a 'supreme court'; although the Judicature Act of 1873 refers to the High Court and Court of Appeal in this way.

Normally, however, Supreme Courts are associated with FEDERAL GOVERNMENTS. This is because in federations there must be a written constitution defining the relationships of the federal government to the sub-governments. Inevitably there will be disputes about the powers of both as defined in the constitution and, consequently, it is necessary to have a judicial body to adjudicate on conflicting claims made about interpretations to the constitution. One result of the operation of higher constitutional courts is that there is a distinction between constitutional law and ordinary law. Another is to give more power to lawyers. The USA and Canada have Supreme Courts and in Australia a similar body is known as the High Court. Germany and Switzerland also have constitutional courts.

Yet UNITARY GOVERNMENTS can also have supreme courts. (All such systems except Britain and Israel have written constitutions.) France was given a Constitutional Council by the constitution of the Fifth Republic. It has the power to rule on the constitutionality of bills before Parliament, but not laws. Judicial review of executive action is the role of the Conseil d'État, at the summit of the system of administrative law. Confirmed in its powers by the law of 1872, it has become the champion of French citizens' rights and the rule of law in a country with a powerful and centralized administration.

See also ADMINSTRATIVE LAW; CONSTITUTIONAL COURTS; LAW; FEDERAL GOVERNMENT.

Reading
Hayward, J. 1973. *The One and Indivisible French Republic*. London: Weidenfeld; McCloskey, R.G. 1972. *The Modern Supreme Court*. Cambridge, Mass.: HUP.

surplus value The value of the amount of work the capitalist extracted from the worker and part of MARX's theory of exploitation. Suppose a labourer works ten hours a day for his employer. In the first six hours the value of the goods he produces will be enough to sustain himself and his family. Consequently in the last four hours the value of his production – the surplus – will go to his employer. This will be a clear profit 'appropriated' from the worker. The employer will try to increase his surplus in two ways: by lengthening the working day and by improving productivity while keeping the same working day. In the latter case he might do it by replacing workers with machinery.

See also CAPITALISM; MARXISM.

survey research Social surveys were pioneered by Charles Booth (1840–1916) in his nine-volume work, *Life and Labour of the People in London, 1891–97*. Over many years he conducted numerous interviews in his efforts to analyse the condition of the poor and the reasons for unemployment. Today the term would be taken to refer to SAMPLE SURVEYS which date from the 1930s.

See also SAMPLE SURVEYS.

swing The degree of change between one election and the next. It can be calculated by averaging the losing party's percentage loss of voters and the winning party's gain. While this is a good rule of thumb there is the obvious objection that it can only be used in a two-party situation. Other difficulties are that abstentions cannot be taken into account and that the electorate will have changed somewhat between the two elections.

See also ELECTIONS.

Reading
Butler, D.E. 1953. *The Electoral System in Britain 1918–1953*. Oxford: OUP.

syndicalism Derived from the French word for trade union (*syndicat*), the term denotes a form of trade-unionism that distrusts political methods and relies on DIRECT ACTION. Its peak period was in the years before 1914 when wages were low and unskilled workers were only beginning to be organized. In the USA its manifestation was the *Industrial Workers of the World*, a union of lumberjacks, dockers and mineworkers. Its most successful field of operation was in France, Italy and Spain where large-scale industrial development was late and union organization was at the local level. Local spontaneous strikes were common by workers in small-scale industries, forming the basis of anarcho-syndicalism. The movement as a whole was inspired by Georges Sorel's (1874–1922) *Reflections on Violence* which advocated class war through the General Strike in order to overthrow CAPITALISM. Syndicalist tendencies have always been stronger in those unions where workers feel they are in control of their work situations. This is often the case in transport. Syndicalism's failure came with the rise of workers' parties. Socialist and especially Communist parties were hostile to its indiscipline and Utopianism.

See also DIRECT ACTION; LABOUR MOVEMENTS; LABOUR PARTIES; TRADE UNIONS.

Reading

Geary, R.J. 1981. *European Labour Protest 1848–1939*. London: Croom Helm; Julliard, J. 1971. *Fernand Pelloutier et les Origines du Syndicalisme d'Action Directe*. Paris: Seuil; Sorel, G. [1908] 1961. *Reflections on Violence*. New York: Collier.

systems analysis Such analysis stems from the concept of a social system, an adaptation of an ecological system, developed by Talcott Parsons (1902–79) from the 1930s onwards. He saw social systems as adaptive, integrative, directed towards objectives and with latent resources. Maintenance and stability were consequently the primary purposes of such systems.

David Easton adapted the Parsonian scheme for his model of the political system. He characterized its concern as trying to answer the question: 'How does it happen that political systems come into being, survive, take certain forms, change and disappear?' In his own attempt he envisaged a political system as a box into which 'inputs' from the social environment flow. Within the box they are then converted into 'outputs' – policies which may affect the social environment from where 'feedbacks' may return as more inputs. The system may be maintained by 'supports' – socialized values and institutions – which, if they are sustained strongly enough, will prevent the outputs or 'demands' overloading and eventually destroying it.

See also FUNCTIONALISM; POLICY MAKING; STRUCTURAL FUNCTIONALISM; STRUCTURALISM.

Reading

Easton, D. 1965. *A Framework for Political Analysis*. Englewood Cliffs: Prentice Hall; Easton, D. 1967. *A Systems Analysis of Political Life*. New York: Wiley; Parsons, T. 1951. *The Social System*. New York: Free Press.

T

tactical voting The practice of voting, not for the candidate one most prefers, but against the candidate one most dislikes. This type of tactical voting is most common in single-member constituencies in FIRST-PAST-THE-POST systems where there are more than two candidates. The voter will have some idea of how the contest might go from the preceding election result. This will probably have been some years earlier. Recent OPINION POLLS, therefore, are a better indication. If the candidate most disliked is expected to win, tactical voters, preferring CANDIDATES expected to end in third or lower places, will switch to a less disliked candidate expected to be in second place. It has been demonstrated that in the 1997 British General Election voters 'exhibited a striking tendency to opt for whichever of the two opposition parties appeared best placed to defeat the Conservatives locally'.

See also ELECTORAL SYSTEMS; FIRST-PAST-THE-POST; VOTING.

Reading
Curtice, J. and M. Steed. 1997. 'The Results Analysed'. In Butler, D. and D. Kavanagh. *The British General Election of 1997*, 295–325. London: Macmillan.

tariffs *See* FREE TRADE.

taxation Without taxation there can be no STATE. Defence of the realm and policing, the two basic functions of a sovereign state, cannot be carried on without paying people to fight and police. Hence the early dynastic states, once they had established a currency, began to tax. The modern state with its multiple functions collects a high proportion of gross domestic product (GDP) in taxation. A peak of 54 per cent was reached in Sweden in 1990. Industrialized democracies raise most in taxation, especially if they have left-wing governments. Developing countries raise least, they have very small 'tax bases' (resources which can be taxed). Uganda takes only about 2 per cent of its GDP in tax.

Taxation is bound to be a contentious political issue. It has been argued that three revolutions – the English, the American and the French – began as the result of the introduction of new taxes. What kind of tax, how much to raise and how to raise it have been some of the most difficult problems governments have had to face. The kind of tax will depend on several factors. The developing countries rely heavily on tariffs, taxes on imports, because these are easy to collect. Developed countries are more likely to rely on corporation taxes which bring in revenue but offend only a few.

'Taxing the rich' tends to be popular with most voters. Sales, or consumption taxes, are also quite common, though they are very unpopular with shopkeepers. Items for which the demand is inelastic (price rises only slightly deter consumption), like tobacco and alchohol, are great revenue raisers. Such taxes are 'invisible'. Consumers are often unaware they are paying them. Visibility of taxation makes it harder to sustain. Property taxes are visible, unpopular and difficult to administer at the national level and are therefore often left to local governments to use.

Income tax remains the most constant and common form of taxation, amounting to 32 per cent of world revenue in 1990, though it may have declined somewhat since. It is regarded as just because, unlike other taxes, it is progressive and hits the rich more severely than the poor. (For this reason it was advocated by MARX and Engels in their *Communist Manifesto*.) Unfortunately, as the wealthy are few, only a small proportion of revenue can be raised from them. Hence income tax tends to fall heavily on the increasingly large number of people in the middle. Democratic politicians, faced with high public expenditure, have therefore tended in recent years to increase indirect and social security taxes. The globalization of the world economy, resulting in competition for investment, has tended towards the lowering of tax rates, putting pressure on REDISTRIBUTION and welfare payments.

See also POLITICAL ECONOMY; TAX REVOLTS; WELFARE STATE.

Reading
Musgrave, R. and P. Musgrave. 1980. *Public Finance in Theory and Practice*. New York: McGraw-Hill; Steinmo, S. 1993. 'Taxes and Taxation' in *The Oxford Companion to Politics of the World*, 900–1. Oxford: OUP.

tax revolts   New types of taxation often lead to revolt and political dismissal. Thus Premier Mendès-France's new sales tax in 1956 led to the rise of the Poujadistes, a new anti-tax party, and the downfall of his government. Similarly Prime Minister Thatcher's 'Poll Tax', adopted against the advice of her ministers, led to riots, refusals to pay and her resignation in 1990. Otherwise cumulative increase in taxation may ultimately lead to revolt. The classic case is that of Mogen Glistrup's newly formed anti-tax Progress Party in Denmark. At the 1973 election it won 16 per cent of the vote, coming second to the Social Democrats. The result of all these signals by the voters was the lowering of taxation somewhat in the last decades of the twentieth century.

taylorism   The term derives from F.W. Taylor (1856–1915) and the theme of his famous book, *Principles and Methods of Scientific Management* (1911). His scientific approach to the way workers operated on lathes laid the basis of 'time and motion study', a phrase which he much disliked. Because of opposition from craft unions in particular, the science of industrial management became a political issue. It also led to the study of industrial psychology.

See also FORDISM; POST-FORDISM.

Reading
Taylor, F.W. 1911. *Principles and Methods of Scientific Management*. New York: HarperCollins; Urwick, L. and E.F.L. Brech. 1949. *The Making of Scientific Management*. London: Management Publications Trust.

technocracy   The application of science and social science to government. Technocrats are administrators with specialized expertise. They have many of the features of bureaucrats such as anonymity and impersonality and they are used to operating within hierarchical organization. Where they differ is that technocrats are involved with policy-making on a scale that the classical Weberian-type bureaucrat with his role of policy-implementer could not have envisaged. Bureaucrats are involved with precedents and rule-books: they are in the past, while technocrats are concerned with the future. Hence the main problem with technocrats is that, in drafting policy, they are usurping the role of the elected representative. An important contemporary issue is the relationship between technocracy and DEMOCRACY. See also BUREAUCRACY; POLICY MAKING.

Reading
Meynaud, J. 1968. *Technocracy*. New York: Free Press.

television and politics *See* COMMUNI-CATIONS; MASS MEDIA; POLITICAL COMMUNICATION; PROPAGANDA.

territorial politics The relations be-tween the central state and the regions. Thus it includes CENTRE–PERIPHERY RELATIONS, but adds relations between the centre and areas which are not peripheral. It not only refers to formal institutional relationships between government and sub-governments, but also to the impact of regional interest groups on the national scene.
See also CENTRAL–LOCAL RELATIONS; CENTRE–PERIPHERY RELATIONS; FEDERAL GOVERNMENT; LOCAL GOVERNMENT; RE-GIONALISM.

Reading
Bulpitt, J. 1983. *Territory and Power in the United Kingdom*. Manchester: Manchester University Press; Tarrow, S., P.J. Katzenstein and L. Graziano. eds. 1978. *Territorial Politics in Industrial Nations*. London: Praeger.

terror A conscious policy used by governments in order to maintain power by securing the easy compliance of their frightened subjects. Mass terror directed against some large segment of the popu-lation is likely to pre-empt opposition. In addition it has often been a weapon of revolutionary movements with intentions of re-shaping society. The Jacobin 'reign of terror' during the French Revolution was of this nature. Lenin, who was not a cruel man, was aware of the value of terror: Stalin, who was, used it on a vast

scale to carry out policies of COL-LECTIVIZATION and industrialization and to stifle any possibility of dissent. In this short-term respect, terror served the Russian revolutionaries well, but in the long run its result was a passive popu-lation lacking in initiative.
See also GENOCIDE; REVOLUTIONS; TOTALI-TARIANISM.

Reading
Conquest, R. 1971. *The Great Terror*. Harmondsworth: Penguin.

terrorism Terrorism is the violence of desperate men. (Very few women are involved.) The term is commonly used to describe small groups of armed assassins and saboteurs who operate in democratic societies. Unable to achieve their aims through persuasion and the ballot box, they resort to bombs, arson and hijacking aircraft. In consequence they often maim and kill innocent people. Resorting to explosives gives terrorism an arbitrary quality, though some anarchist terrorists are directing their violence against society as a whole. Although they may be very few in numbers, terrorists have the capacity to spread fear and insecurity everywhere. The response in democracies has been the application of measures indicating a determination not to give way. Hence terrorism has the opposite effect to what the terrorists hoped and intended. It makes LAW AND ORDER a highly popular policy.

Terrorism against authoritarian regimes may have a larger backing. Economic and/or ethnic groups may be-come guerrilla organizations, as did peasants and Indians in Central America, and fight what amount to small-scale wars. The state may mount campaigns of what has been called 'state terrorism' against them in which villages are burnt, their inhabitants massacred and known opponents of the regime 'disappear' to torture chambers and unmarked graves. The official view of such activity is that it is 'counter-terrorist'. The insurgents claim they are not terrorists but resistance fighters. The line is not always easy to draw.

See also CIVIL WAR; GUERRILLA WARFARE; POLITICAL VIOLENCE.

Reading
Laqueur, W. 1988. *Terrorism*. London: Weidenfeld; Wilkinson, P. 1977. *Terrorism and the Liberal State*. London: Macmillan.

thatcherism The term, based on the long British premiership of Margaret Thatcher (1979–90), has been used to describe both a style of leadership and a set of policies founded on certain simple ideas. It is now used to describe similar leaderships and programmes elsewhere. The Thatcher style was especially admired among foreign electorates who had no way of assessing the impact of her policies. Expressed with complete conviction and considerable force – she never seemed to doubt the infallibility of her opinions – it was based on the view that Britain took the wrong turning at the 1945 General Election. Conservative governments had made the mistake of accepting the achievements of the post-war Labour government. In fact, as far as it is an IDEOLOGY (and there are certainly ideological strains in its pedigree) Thatcherism could be described as an anti-ideology. SOCIALISM and CORPORATISM were its targets.

The policies she pursued were directed to eradicating these impurities. PRIVATIZATION of most of the public sector reversed the NATIONALIZATION of the Labour governments. The WELFARE STATE was pruned and municipal housing was made available for purchasing by occupiers. Legislation restricted the trade unions and weakened their power: close relations between government and INTEREST GROUPS were discouraged. Unemployment was no longer regarded as an evil and Keynesian precepts gave way to MONETARISM, the belief that INFLATION could be prevented by controlling the money supply. As a result of these measures public expenditure was somewhat trimmed. Revenue was boosted by the sale of the nationalized industries and the export of North Sea oil which came 'on stream' in the 1980s. Consequently TAXATION could be lowered, an electorally popular measure.

Thatcherism has some clear effects and some that are not yet clear. Obviously it reverses a long egalitarian twentieth-century trend. The gap between the poorest and wealthiest increases. There is more visible affluence and the reappearance of beggars on the streets. Individualism is encouraged and people are made to feel less responsible for one another. They also become more likely to put a price on their services: the commercial instinct emerges in the public sector as a compensation for cuts in government funding. Flexibility in the labour market brings an insecurity to the middle classes they have not experienced in their lifetimes. The social and psychological effects of Thatcherite policies are more difficult to evaluate than the economic effects.

See also CONSERVATISM; MONETARISM; NATIONALIZATION; PRIVATIZATION; SOCIALISM; WELFARE STATE.

Reading
Jenkins, P. 1987. *Mrs. Thatcher's Revolution*. London: Jonathan Cape; Kavanagh, D. 1989. *Thatcherism and British Politics*. Oxford: Clarendon; Thatcher, M. 1995. *The Path to Power*. London: HarperCollins; Thatcher, M. 1993. *The Downing Street Years*. London: HarperCollins; Young, H. and A. Sloman. 1986. *The Thatcher Phenomenon*. London: BBC.

theocracy Literally rule by God, it has come to mean a state dominated by priests and religious rules and observances. Historic examples are ancient Israel and Geneva under Calvin. In the twentieth century, Tibet, under the Dalai Lama, the incarnation of the Buddha, remained a theocracy until the Chinese annexation. Yet the most salient example of theocratic influence can be found in the Islamic nations, all to a greater or lesser extent penetrated by Islamic fundamentalist ideas. The concept of an Islamic state founded on Islamic law, the *sharia*, the word of God, inevitably implies great power to the clergy. Countries affected include Iran, Afghanistan, Saudi Arabia and the Muslim republics of Central Asia.

Reading
Goldstein, M.C. 1989. *A History of Modern Tibet, 1913–1951: the Demise of the Lamaist State*. Berkeley: University of California Press; Keddie, N.R. ed. 1972. *Scholars, Saints and Sufis: Moslem Religious Institutions since 1500*. Berkeley: University of California Press; Mitchell, R. 1969. *The Society of Muslim Brothers*. Oxford: OUP.

think tanks Originally applied to scientific research institutes in the USA, since the 1960s the term has been used to describe research bodies engaged in the analysis of economic and social problems and the drafting of policy to deal with them. Some think tanks have been independent bodies, though willing to undertake contract work for anyone, including governments. Others have been part of government or a political party. The earliest was the American Brookings Institute, dating from 1916. Another famous US think tank, the Rand Corporation, was set up in 1946 by the US Air Force, but became independent in 1946. Contemporary think tanks are frequently multi-disciplinary and staffed by experts drawn from the university and the public service. In Britain the Heath government formed the Central Policy Review Staff in 1971 to perform a think-tank function. It was shut down by Mrs. Thatcher in 1983. Other British think tanks are the Policy Studies Institute, the

Adam Smith Institute, Demos and the Centre for Policy Studies.

Reading
Dror, Y. 1984. 'Required Break-throughs in Think Tanks'. *Policy Sciences* 16, 199–225; Plowden, W. ed. 1987. *Advising Governments*. Oxford: Blackwell.

third world A term coined during the COLD WAR to indicate those countries belonging neither to the western or Soviet bloc. Consequently it referred broadly to the countries of Africa, Asia and Latin America and by association it was linked with poverty and under-development. Yet not all the states in these geographical areas were poor and, anyway, the term seemed to suggest low status. A commission under Willy Brandt, former German chancellor, in 1980 recomended that the distinction should be between a developed 'North' and a less developed 'South' and these terms are now often used. 'Third World' has become 'politically incorrect' and the states concerned prefer to be known as 'the developing countries'.
See also FIRST WORLD.

Reading
Mittelman, J.H. and M.K. Pasha. 1997. *Out from Underdevelopment Revisited*. Basingstoke: Macmillan.

threat assessment Part of strategic thinking, the term is from the vocabulary of INTERNATIONAL RELATIONS and refers to a necessary part of defence and foreign policy. Questions a state's policymakers must ask are: 'From where will threats arise? What will be the nature of the threat? What will be its scope? What can we do to counter it?' It will be impossible to make these assessments without bringing the military planners into the policy making and they will need military intelligence. The problem for the civilian foreign-policy experts is that the military will be inclined to over-estimate external threats as a way of increasing their own importance and supporting their claim for greater military expenditure.

See also ARMS RACE; DETERRENCE; STRATEGIC WEAPONS.

ticket-splitting The opposite of 'straight ticket' voting. In virtually all American elections the voter is required to vote for CANDIDATES for numerous offices on the same day. Very often they are all on the same ballot paper and the 'ticket splitter' chooses candidates irrespective of their party affiliation. She may vote for the Republican candidate for state Governor and the Democratic candidate for mayor of her city. Ticket-splitting is very common and signifies what little allegiance US voters have towards party.

Reading
De Vries, W. and V.L. Tarrance. 1972. *The Ticket Splitter*. Grand Rapids, Mich.: Eeerdmans.

toleration The practice of not interfering with beliefs and actions that one does not like. There may be various degrees of abstention. One can ignore uncongenial opinions and acts, or one can express one's dislike and attempt to refute unpalatable opinions. Tolerance is clearly a basic value of democratic theory. Freedom of speech and a free press imply tolerance of political OPPOSITION. People who want to stop the free expression of opinions they do not like are clearly undemocratic. The question arises: To what extent do we allow the intolerant freedom? The answer is that a democratic state allows FREEDOM OF EXPRESSION even to those who are inimical to DEMOCRACY; but it does not tolerate actions beyond a certain point. 'Saying' and 'doing' are necessarily distinguished.

Reading
Locke, J. [1690] 1950. 'Essay on Tolerance'. In Gough, J.W. *John Locke's Political Philosophy*. Oxford: Blackwell; Mendus, S. and D. Edwards. eds. 1987. *On Toleration*. Oxford: OUP.

totalitarianism First popularized by the Italian dictator, Benito Mussolini, this term is derived from the Italian *totalitarismo*. It indicates a totality of control by the STATE. This implies a relationship in which the state through its instruments dominates society. Hence in the totalitarian state all political, economic, social, cultural and intellectual activities should be directed towards fulfilling the aims of the state. There is no PLURALISM.

Nor is there DEMOCRACY. Totalitarian ideas are a reaction against democracy occasioned by cynicism about its supporters' intentions or disillusion with its outcomes. Totalitarianism is a modern form of AUTHORITARIANISM. Old-fashioned ABSOLUTISM existed before democracy emerged and it lacked modern instruments of control. Totalitarian leaders use repressive methods stifling expression of opinions contrary to their own, while they disseminate their own ideologies through the media. Population indexing and internal passport systems allow them to control and to exercise surveillance over people's movements.

The two main forms of totalitarianism, FASCISM and COMMUNISM, though quite different in philosophic origins, possessed ideologies with similar features. Each put forward a set of propositions, both normative and empirical, intended to explain the human condition. Both claimed universality for their precepts and each achieved the status of a secular religion. Each was concerned with interpreting the historical process and prophesying its final phase as a glorious future. Thus they proclaimed that salvation from the corruption of the present could be found in the realization of a new moral order for the world, replacing the old order in which discredited and deviant goups dominated. These latter were variously depicted as capitalists, socialists, liberals, imperialists and people of lesser breeds of humanity including Jews. They must be eradicated and overthrown. Consequently totalitarian movements emphasize the need for revolutionary action.

Other varieties of totalitarianism can be found of which the principal is the Chinese form of Communism, Maoism, named after its leader. Such forms are often attractive to the leaders of developing countries who see one-party domination and repression of dissent as a short cut to the prosperity of the developed world through rapid industrialization and technological advance. This can only be achieved by mobilizing the population. Such a strategy will prevent the fragmentation of national will, the natural result of democracy which allows tribal and/or ethnic groups to assert their minority interests.

All totalitarian regimes, either of the left or right, exhibit the following features: an official IDEOLOGY propounded to the exclusion of all other statements about what to believe and what to do either individually or collectively; the dissemination of this ideology through the media and through the officially recognized single political party which has a selected membership of men and women dedicated to the ideology and to the policies of the party leadership, and is hierarchically organized and centralized, with a main function of supervising the population and mobilizing them towards the attainment of official goals; a charismatic leader at the top of the party with a personality and presence prominently displayed; all aspects of communication controlled both internally and externally and travel, especially abroad, made difficult; and finally an apparatus of TERROR, controlled by the party, ensuring compliance and earning the label of 'POLICE STATE'.

See also AUTHORITARIANISM; DEMOCRACY; PLURALISM; SECRET POLICE.

Reading
Arendt, H. 1973. *The Origins of Totalitarianism.* New York: Harcourt; Duverger, M. 1961. *De la Dictature.* Paris: Julliard; Friedrich, C.J. and Z.K. Brzezinski. 1964. *Totalitarian Dictatorship and Autocracy.* New York: Praeger; Langer, A.L. 1974. *The Totalitarian Party.* Cambridge: CUP; Menze, E.A. ed. 1981. *Totalitarianism Reconsidered.* Port Washington: Kennikat; Revel, J-F. 1976. *The Totalitarian Temptation.* London: Secker & Warburg.

town meetings A feature of local democracy in New England townships with less than 5000 inhabitants. The whole population is entitled to attend the town meeting and, by a show of hands, elect their administrative officers and fix their municipal taxes. This form of DIRECT DEMOCRACY existed before the Union and is rivalled only by one or two of the smallest Swiss cantons.
See also DIRECT DEMOCRACY.

Reading
Sly, J.F. 1930. *Town Government in Massachusetts 1620–1930.* Cambridge, Mass.: HUP.

trade unions Collective organizations of employees, formed to safeguard the terms and working conditions of their members. They have sought to do this in several well-known ways.

Their primary relationship is with their employer or, in most cases, the organization of employers for which their members work. In order to guarantee regular meetings with employers to put their members' grievances and requests, an early objective must be union recognition. If employers are reluctant to grant recognition then trade-union activity will be hampered. If the unions are strong they may successfully undertake industrial action which usually means strikes. Contrary to a common notion, neither union leaders nor their members like strikes. Members lose their wages and so bring pressure on themselves and their families as well as employers.

Once recognition is achieved the main activity of unions will be collective bargaining. In many instances collective bargaining about both wages and employment conditions goes on almost continually. Sometimes the one may be bargained against the other. For example, higher wage rates may be acceded to as long as the workers give up their demand for another week's holiday. Sometimes conditions in the actual workplace, safety arrangements, sanitation and ventilation have all featured in bargaining. If collective bargaining is carried out on a nation-wide scale between union leaders and employers' representatives, any agreement setting up national wage rates is equivalent to a regulation of wages and conditions in the industry. The general aim of trade-union movements is not to destroy CAPITALISM, but to regulate and control it. They pursue collective profits.

When unions are frustrated in their attempts to achieve the above objectives they may turn to political action. Historically trade unions have behaved in this way when the law courts have delivered verdicts prejudicial to their activities. The American courts did this for several decades. In Britain the Taff Vale judgement of 1901, by which the House of Lords ruled that unions were liable for damages committed by their members during strikes, did much to solidify union support for the Labour Representation Committee, set up by the unions in 1900 to secure the election of trade unionists to Parliament. In 1906 this became the Labour Party with which the unions have ever since been associated.

Political action, however, may take the form of pressure by the unions on governments. American unions have never launched a political party: they have relied on their lobby in Congress. Once trade unions acquire a certain size and status they begin to use their power to sponsor legislation, not only to legalize their own activities, but also to introduce industrial legislation about safety at work, an 'eight-hour day' and a minimum wage. In the developed industrialized states this began in the late nineteenth century. There followed support for social policies such as sickness and unemployment insurance and old age pensions. In industrialized countries the trade-union movement was likely to be the PRESSURE GROUP with the largest membership.

The study of trade unions has become part of the academic discipline of Industrial Relations, closely associated with Economics and Political Science. The classical categorization of trade unions was between 'craft', 'industrial' and 'general' unions. Craft unions organize skilled trades: in practice this means those with an apprenticeship system. They were the earliest unions. Their members could read and write and have been called a LABOUR ARISTOCRACY. Industrial unions organize one industry and accept members from every level of skill and type of occupation. They tend to be more militant than craft unions. Familiar instances are miners, railwaymen and dockers. General unions recruit people in almost any trade, though they tend to be organizations of unskilled workers. A fourth category might be 'employment unions', unions in industries with only one firm. Unions in the public services tend to have only one employer in contrast with the other types who have numerous employers to deal with.

All these categories are IDEAL TYPES for numerous reasons. Technological advance changes the nature of occupations. Ancient skills may no longer be needed. In Britain the engineers were formerly a craft union but by the mid-twentieth century the engineering industry had become so heterogeneous that the huge union organizing its workers really best fitted the 'general' category. General unions with their capacity for accepting anyone had organized skilled workers in the motor industry and many of indeterminate skill in newer industries such as plastics. FORDISM inevitably produced a new sort of unionism. Mass production industry depended heavily on a semi-skilled adaptable work force, employed in large-scale enterprise. Militancy characterized its unionism which often depended on the CLOSED SHOP.

Economic and political climates also affect trade-union attitudes. Militancy may be of little use in a slump when workers are competing for jobs and the demand for labour is slack. In times of prosperity when unemployment is low and demand for labour rises, trade unions are most likely to profit. But the political situation may affect the demand for labour. It is greatest during wars when the labour market is depleted by mobilization for the armed forces and there is an urgent need for labour in the armament industries. In democracies wars always enhance the strength of trade unionism.

The configuration of national trade-union movements is also affected by social and intellectual attitudes to capitalism. Where the Catholic/clerical cleavage has been important, mainly in southern Europe, trade-union movements have tended to divide roughly between Catholic and Communist unions. In northern Europe the unions have been oriented towards SOCIAL DEMOCRACY and, except in Britain, have not been unwilling to be involved in corporatist relations with the STATE. In the USA 'business unionism' and low levels of trade-union organization have prevailed. Where DEMOCRACY and PLURALISM do not exist, as in the former USSR, there were bodies called 'trade unions' but they were only trade unions in name.

See also CLOSED SHOP; CORPORATISM; LABOUR; LABOUR MOVEMENTS.

Reading
Banks, J.A. 1974. *Trade Unionism*. London: Collier-Macmillan; Flanders, A. 1952. *Trade Unions*. London: Hutchinson; McCarthy, W.E.J. ed. 1985. *Trade Unions*. Harmondsworth: Penguin; Perlman, M. 1958. *Labour Union Theories in America*. Row: Peterson; Webb, S. and B. 1894. *Industrial Democracy*. London: Longman.

traditionalism The attitudes, values and customs that one generation hands down to another constitute a tradition. Tradition is therefore usually a matter of culture. This culture in the contemporary world is most likely to be challenged by the forces of MODERNIZATION, usually in the form of technological advance and bureaucratization. Some may accept such innovation, but traditionalists will oppose it. Thus in Britain the Campaign for Real Ale is a protest against the standardizing of the product of the increasingly oligopolistic and rationalized brewing industry.

Traditionalism in politics is opposition to modernizing tendencies which may challenge the culture of society and/or POLITICAL CULTURE. Eastern societies, whose culture may be closely linked to their religion, may accept new technology but attempt to reject all other trends. Thus Islamic fundamentalists welcome the most up-to-date arms and computers, but institute near-theocracies, retaining Islamic law and its ordinances about the role of women. Whether such structures can withstand the expansion of a professional and managerial class with rational expertise is questionable. In Europe it led to the ENLIGHTENMENT and the French Revolution, introducing an entirely different political system. In Russia it destroyed the Soviet Union. Yet this latter event led to the revival of the nineteenth-century Slavophils supporting the restoration of the Tsar. Political traditionalism with its nostalgia for ROYALTY and ARISTOCRACY is likely to be with us for a long time.

See also ANCIEN REGIME; CLERICALISM/ANTI-CLERICALISM; MODERNIZATION.

Reading
Friedrich, C.J. 1972. *Tradition and Authority.* London: Pall Mall; Oakeshott, M. 1962. *Rationalism in Politics.* London: Methuen.

trans-nationals *See* MULTI-NATIONALS.

treaties   A treaty is a written agreement between states by which they contract to observe certain rights and duties. The parties are supposed to consider it binding. Today a treaty should be registered with the United Nations. There are over 30,000 on the register. The three main occasions for concluding a treaty are at the end of a war, when an alliance has been formed, and in order to set up an international organization. Treaties at the end of a war may mark a watershed in world history. Such were the Treaty of Westphalia, 1648, by which Protestant states were accepted and the Vatican ceased to exercise much temporal power; and the Treaty of Versailles, 1918, bringing to an end the long struggle of many European nations to achieve statehood. The North Atlantic Treaty was formed to resist Soviet expansion in 1949. Its meetings were formalized in an Organization (NATO) which had 16 members by 1982. International organizations which have been inaugurated by treaty include the United Nations and the European Economic Community (now the European Community), founded by the Treaty of Rome in 1957.

Joining the European Community involved changes in the domestic law of all members. All treaties are subject to international law. Obligations should be fulfilled, though treaties can be interpreted in terms of the intentions of the signatories. The Vienna Convention on the Law of Treaties, 1969, has codified such principles. Applicable to all ratifying parties since 1980, it acknowledges that a basic change of circumstances may make a treaty out of date.
See also DIPLOMACY; INTERNATIONAL LAW.

Reading
McDougal, M.S., H.D. Lasswell and J.C. Miller. 1967. *The Interpretation of Agreements and World Public Order.* New Haven: YUP.

tribalism   Used in two ways the anthropological meaning of the term refers to the type of society which preceded the primitive state. Groups of hunter-gatherers or pastoralists, probably linked by kinship, formed regular organizations in which chieftainship would later develop. These might be called clans or tribes.

The term is also used to describe a sort of political system in which nepotism and CLIENTILISM predominate. Hereditary political families are prominent, while programmatic and ideological conflict is still not intense. Policies tend to be implemented by trading favours.

trotskyism   A world-wide movement of small Marxist organizations federated in the Fourth International. For many of them their only common feature is that they claim Leon Trotsky (1879–1940) as their ideological inspiration. He had participated in the 1905 Revolution and was prominent in the 1917 Bolshevik Revolution, organizing the Red Army to win the Civil War. Regarded as natural heir of Lenin, after the latter's death Trotsky was out-manoeuvred by Stalin and driven into exile in 1928. The clash with Stalin was not only personal, but also doctrinal. Trotsky had opposed Stalin's autocratic methods of running the party and the policy of 'socialism in one country'. He had always been more in favour of mass participation and the foremost champion, as the chief founder of the Communist Third International, of international working-class revolution. In *The Revolution Betrayed* (1936) he argued that the Soviet Union was ruled by a bureaucracy which had set up a system of 'STATE CAPITALISM'. He condemned the type of Communist party organization which had developed with its strong central control of lower levels. International proletarian action was needed to bring about SOCIALISM quickly. He called this strategy 'PERMANENT REVOLUTION'.

Trotskyism has appealed to Marxist groups who dislike the strict discipline of the Communist Party. It has had little appeal to the WORKING CLASS. The Fourth International remains a unimpressive federation of disparate groups. It combines entryist organizations of European students and parties of landless Latin American and Asian peasants. Denounced as 'wreckers and saboteurs' by official Communist parties, Trotskyists have taken refuge in sporadic acts of subversion and revolt.

See also COMMUNISM; ENTRYISM; MARXISM; PERMANENT REVOLUTION.

Reading
Trotsky, L. 1962. *The Permanent Revolution and Results and Prospects*. New York: Pioneer; Wistrich, R. 1979. *Trotsky*. London: Robson.

trusteeship The United Nations trusteeships were the successors of the League of Nations mandates. Developed nations, mostly the old colonial powers, were made trustees of developing countries with the obligation to govern them in the interests of their inhabitants. The main departure from the mandate system was that they were regularly visited by United Nations inspectors. The trusteeship territories were expected to advance towards self-government and in general they did, swept on by the prevailing current of anti-colonialism after 1945.

See also COLONIALISM; IMPERIALISM; MANDATES.

Reading
Hall, H.D. 1948. *Mandates, Dependencies and Trusteeship*. London: Stevens.

turnout The proportion of registered voters who 'turn out' to vote at ELECTIONS. It is much higher, almost everywhere, in national than in local elections. In national elections it also varies. It is highest, above 90 per cent, in countries with COMPULSORY VOTING. Otherwise 70–75 per cent is the average. Different factors may affect turnout. Weather on polling day may be one. The marginality of the seat may apply where there are single-member constituencies. The higher the number of CANDIDATES, the higher the turnout is another observed phenomenon. National proportions are more likely to be matters of POLITICAL CULTURE. Where political parties have close links with cultural and social organizations the latter may help in mobilization. If the parties are perceived by the voters to have distinct supporting groups, ideologies and policies, voters may be more likely to go to the poll. Where the reverse, as in Switzerland and the USA, the low turnout can be explained by the feeling that an election is unlikely to bring a change.

See also ABSTENTION; COMPULSORY VOTING; ELECTIONS; ELECTORAL SYSTEMS; POLITICAL CULTURE.

Reading
Crewe, I. 1981. 'Electoral Participation'. In *Democracy at the Polls*. Eds. D. Butler, H.R. Penniman and A. Ranney. Washington, D.C.: American Enterprise Institute; Verba, S., N.H. Nie and J. Kim. 1978. *Participation and Political Equality*. Cambridge: CUP.

tutellage A system of legal and administrative supervision of public authorities found in western Europe. Stemming from Roman law, its best known expression has been in France where it was extended and elaborated by Napoleon in the control by prefects of local government activities, known as the *tutelle*. The supervision was not always effective, but it naturally invoked much opposition from the locally elected representatives and was always a symbol of central power. Decentralization, with the institution of regions in Spain and Italy, led to its destruction in the 1970s and a decade later the *tutelle* was ended by the *loi Defferre* in France.

See also ADMINISTRATIVE LAW; CENTRAL–LOCAL RELATIONS; PREFECT.

Reading
Ridley, F. and J. Blondel. 1964. *Public Administration in France*. London: Routledge.

two-party systems   Political systems in which two parties dominate the electoral process and the LEGISLATURE: *not* political systems in which there are only two parties. Britain and the USA are usually cited as countries with two-party systems; but both have many parties. In Britain over a dozen parties contested the 1997 General Election and ten secured representation in the House of Commons; but the Conservative and Labour Parties combined won more than seven-eighths of the seats. In the USA there were three main contenders for the Presidency at the 1992 Presidential election. Ross Perot as an Independent won a higher proportion of the vote than any third candidate since Theodore Roosevelt in 1912. There are always other minor party candidates but they secure very little representation, if any, in Congress which is dominated by the Democratic and Republican parties.

See also PARTY SYSTEMS; POLITICAL PARTIES.

Reading
Drucker, H.M. ed. 1979. *Multiparty Britain*. London: Macmillan; Finer, S.E. ed. 1975. *Adversary Politics and Electoral Reform*. London: Anthony Wigram; Le Blanc, H.L. 1982. *American Political Parties*. New York: St. Martin's Press.

typology   A list of categories that is used for classification. Political scientists have drawn up typologies of constitutions, political parties, pressure groups, political cultures and states. They are of assistance for comparative method. Some instances may fit more easily into a category than others and some may overlap. This does not imply typologies are useless but rather that they must be used with caution.

See also IDEAL TYPE.

tyranny   See KINGSHIP.

tyranny of the majority   A phrase taken from John Stuart MILL's essay *On Liberty*. It introduces an important debate among democratic theorists. Mill said the tyranny of the majority might be no better than the tyranny of the magistrate. 'There is a limit to the legitimate interference of collective opinion with individual independence: and to find that limit, and maintain it against encroachment, is as indispensible to a good condition of human affairs, as protection against political despotism'. Yet democratic decision-making cannot proceed without majority voting and democratic states' decisions restrict 'individual independence' all the time. The problem lies with deciding where the 'limit' lies. Ultimately this will be decided by a majority and it may vary in time and place. Theorists, however, advance different views. At one end of the spectrum it is argued that even heavy TAXATION exceeds the limit, at the other that a democratically elected government has the right to nationalize industry.

See also BILL OF RIGHTS; DEMOCRACY; LIBERALISM.

Reading
Bassett, R. 1935. *The Essentials of Parliamentary Democracy*. London: Macmillan; Bealey, F.W. 1988. *Democracy in the Contemporary State*. Oxford: OUP; Fishkin, J.W. 1979. *Tyranny and Legitimacy*. Baltimore: John Hopkins Press; Svensson, P. 1993. *Theories of Democracy*. Aarhus: Institut for Statskundskab.

U

ultra vires A legal term meaning 'outside the powers'. It can apply to those taking decisions, or to the procedures by which decisions were made. It gives the courts considerable powers. It can apply to government departments, local governments, corporations and companies. Thus it is a check on the abuse of governmental power and a way in which the rules of natural justice are asserted. A contract ruled *ultra vires* has no standing in law. Procedures ruled *ultra vires* cannot be used effectively again.
See also JUDICIAL REVIEW.

underclass A class 'below' the WORK-ING CLASS in the sense that they have less wealth. The underclass consists of the unemployed, tramps, beggars and the homeless in the streets. With any increase in unemployment the underclass will obviously become larger. Another factor which will probably swell the ranks of an underclass is the breakdown of family life and a consequent increase in juvenile delinquency. The underclass will consist for the most part of those deprived of equality of opportunity which has become increasingly attainable for most of the working class. MARCUSE, who had become increasingly disillusioned with the working class as a revolutionary agent, believing that relative affluence and the mass media had made them pris-

oners of an IDEOLOGY of technology, pinned his hopes for revolution on an underclass of the unemployed, 'drop-outs', students and blacks. Underclass could be a synonym for MARX's term for the least privileged of the workers. He called them the 'lumpenproletariat', but he had little faith in them because they had supported Louis Napoleon (1808–73) in the Eighteenth Brumaire.
See also NEW LEFT.

Reading
Marcuse, H. 1969. *An Essay on Liberation.* Harmondsworth: Penguin.

unicameralism The belief in, or the situation of, possession of a LEGISLA-TURE with only one chamber. This is uncommon: it is usually considered that, for various reasons, two chambers are necessary. Only small countries are uni-cameral. Israel, Denmark, Finland, Greece, Norway, Sweden and New Zealand have one chamber. The two latter have abolished their second chambers since 1945. Nebraska is the only American state with one chamber: a legacy of the Populist movement of which Nebraska was the centre. It can be argued that SECOND CHAMBERS are undemo-cratic because the sovereign people can only be represented once and FIRST CHAMBERS, usually elected on a more popular franchise, are the appropriate place for that. Federal states, however, are bound to be bi-cameral.

See also BICAMERALISM; FIRST CHAMBERS; LEGISLATURES; SECOND CHAMBERS.

unilateralism The renunciation by one side of an advantage, usually a military resource, in an international confrontation. More specifically, in the 1950s the term was applied to the abandonment of the nuclear option. The British Campaign for Nuclear Disarmament (CND) was founded in 1958: there were similar organizations in other western countries. Pacifists, who favour all DIS-ARMAMENT, naturally joined, but there were others who believed in conventional arms who favoured giving up nuclear weapons. In Britain some CND members believed the country could not afford it and could rely on the American nuclear warheads; others argued that, like Denmark and Norway, Britain should not allow their stationing on its soil because it made their installations the first target of Soviet attack; other non-pacifists advocated British withdrawal from the North Atlantic Treaty Organization. Although these policies may not have been completely pacifist, they would have tended to weaken the principle of COLLECTIVE SECURITY on which the alliance was based. The Partial Test Ban Treaty 1963 weakened support for unilateralism, but it revived during the 'second cold war' in the 1980s, only to decline again with the fall of Soviet Communism after 1989.

See also COLD WAR; COLLECTIVE SECURITY; DISARMAMENT; PACIFICISM; PACIFISM.

Reading
Byrne, P. and J. Lovenduski. 1983. 'Two New Protest Groups: the Peace and Women's Movements'. In *Developments in British Politics*. Eds. H. Drucker, P. Dunleavy, A. Gamble and G. Peele. London: Macmillan; Ryle, M.H. 1981. *The Politics of Nuclear Disarmament*. London: Pluto; Taylor, R. and C.

Pritchard. 1980. *The Protest Makers*. London: Pergamon.

unitary government The constitutional type that is the opposite of FEDERAL GOVERNMENT. Most countries have unitary government: that is, they do not have sub-units of government with autonomous powers. Other features of federal government such as a written constitution and a higher or constitutional court may be part of unitary constitutions.

See also CONSTITUTIONS; FEDERAL GOVERN-MENT.

Reading
Wheare, K.C. 1966. *Modern Constitutions*. Oxford: OUP.

united fronts The United Front was tactic for all Communist Parties, adopted on Lenin's recommendation at a meeting of the executive of the Third (Communist) International in 1921. The intention was that Communist Parties in the colonial EMPIRES in particular should join forces with other radical groups aspiring to independence. In the process the Communists would absorb the other movements. The tactic was a failure. The Second (Socialist) International rebuffed their approaches. So did the Congress Party in India. The United Front did not stop Chiang Kai-Shek repressing the Chinese Communists nor Indonesian Communists being massacred.

See also COMMUNISM; POPULAR FRONTS.

Reading
Braunthal, J. 1980. *History of the International*. London: Nelson; McKenzie, K.E. 1964. *The Comintern and World Revolution*. New York: Columbia University Press.

upper class A vague term which can have several meanings. As often used in Britain it separates the 'U' from the 'non-U'; that is, it is a distinction based on background, speech, dress, deportment and general behaviour, though these features do not necessarily coincide. They relate to STATUS rather than class. The ARISTOCRACY and gentry are a tiny proportion of society. On the other hand their accents and behaviour can be learnt in public schools and at the older universities. The groups who possess these characteristics today are likely to be a mixture of wealth and MERITOCRACY.

American usage is more likely to refer to wealth which is very unevenly distributed. It has been calculated that about the richest tenth of the population own two-thirds of the wealth. Almost everywhere it is commonly assumed that the wealthy have political power and in Marxist terms that they constitute a RULING CLASS. Yet in democracies it is difficult to argue that those in power always favour people either of high status or great wealth. The POLITICAL CLASS are by no means people of this kind.

For social scientists anxious to find a satisfactory definition of 'upper class' there might thus appear to be a choice between either a rather unsatisfactory objective categorization based on measurable wealth (though measurement may not be as easy as it sounds); or observation of social characteristics in an anthropological manner.

See also ARISTOCRACY; ELITES; ESTABLISHMENT; SOCIAL CLASS; STATUS.

Reading
Bendix, R. and S.M. Lipset. eds. 1953. *Class, Status and Power*. Glencoe: Free Press; Bottomore, T.B. 1965. *Classes in Modern Society*. London: Allen and Unwin; Giddens, A. 1973. *The Class Structure of the Advanced Societies*. London: Hutchinson; Ossowski, S. 1963. *Class Structure in the Social Consciousness*. London: Routledge.

upper houses   *See* SECOND CHAMBERS.

urbanization   The growth of large cities is part of the process of MODERNIZATION. It is clearly also linked with industrialization: indeed, the Industrial Revolution created the cities. Large

labour forces were required to man the new factories and the recruits came from the countryside, especially landless peasants. The development is often associated with CAPITALISM; but the experience of the Soviet Union, when it decided to industrialize massively with the Five Year Plan, was very similar. Industrial cities everywhere have produced a different sort of person in a different kind of culture from rural counterparts. Urban life throughout the world has been characterized by overcrowding, housing problems, poverty and crime. ALIENATION has been a common theme of writings about city populations. Responses to this have been drunkenness, evangelical – even millennarial – religion, and radical or revolutionary politics. While these were only features of European and North American experience at one time, in the late twentieth century the same phenomena can be found in South America and Africa.

See also ALIENATION; CAPITALISM; MODERNIZATION; URBAN POLITICS.

Reading
Harvey, D. 1985. *Consciousness and the Urban Experience*. Oxford: Blackwell; Mumford, L. 1966. *The City in History*. Harmondsworth: Penguin; Thompson, E.P. 1963. *The Making of the English Working Class*. London: Gollancz; Wirth, L. 1938. 'Urbanism as a Way of Life'. *American Journal of Sociology* 44, 1–24.

urban politics   In the 1950s the study of COMMUNITY POWER turned from small towns to large cities with Hunter's work on Atlanta and DAHL's book on New Haven. Their conflicting analyses of the nature of power inspired numerous other studies. The general conclusion was that the pattern of power and the way power was exercised varied from place to place. There was also an increasing tendency for local decisions to be influenced by decisions elsewhere, especially at the headquarters of large corporations and in national capitals by central governments. This emphasized the importance of CENTRAL–LOCAL RELATIONS.

It also stimulated urban analysis in other fields. The Marxist political economists led by Castells argued that the important function of city governments was the control of goods provided by central government – services such as housing, transport, education and health care. These played an important part in the national economy. The cities therefore had become the arenas of CLASS CONFLICT in which new urban social movements arose to challenge the dominant capitalist class. Meanwhile urban geographers and spatial planners were concerned with problems of new industrial location, public transportation and environmental impact. Political scientists became involved with the FISCAL CRISIS and its effect on cities and with comparative studies of municipal decision-making.

See also COMMUNITARIANISM; COMMUNITY POWER.

Reading

Banfield, E.C. 1965. *Big City Politics*. New York: Random House; Castells, M. 1977. *The Urban Question*. London: Arnold; Friedland, R. 1982. *Power and Crisis in the City*. London: Macmillan; Lupo, A., F. Colcord and E.P. Fowler. 1971. *Rites of Way: the Politics of Transportation in Boston and the US City*. Boston: Little, Brown; Newton, K. 1976. *Second City Politics*. Oxford: Clarendon; Yates, D. 1978. *The Ungovernable City*. Cambridge, Mass.: MIT Press.

utilitarianism   A theory of morals and politics first developed by Jeremy Bentham (1748–1832) and James Mill (1773–1836). Bentham began with the assumption that British government and laws were archaic. He wanted good government and, accepting the views of the classical economists, came to the conclusion that it could only be achieved by the maximization of pleasure and the minimization of pain. This was encapsulated in the catch-phrase, 'the greatest good for the greatest number'. If this maxim was applied government would be at its best.

It involved, however, moving from the individual good to the PUBLIC GOOD. This must mean the aggregation of individual pains and pleasures to discover what the population preferred. Bentham's concept discounted any difference between people. It was essentially egalitarian and, therefore, implied universal adult suffrage and free self-expression. It was also unmoral. There was no implication that one pleasure was better than another. 'Pushpin was as good as poetry', Bentham famously declared. All that was needed was to work out what he called the 'felicific calculus' which could only be done by ELECTIONS. Hence he presented in the *Constitutional Code* a system for annual elections, a prime minister elected by the LEGISLATURE for a four-year term and thirteen heads of DEPARTMENTS. He was very concerned to develop a system of governmental RESPONSIBILITY with the RECALL for ministers.

John Stuart MILL, the son of James, has been said to have 'spiritualized Bentham'. He argued that all pleasures could not be treated equally. There were 'refined' pleasures and 'gross' pleasures. 'A pig satisfied' was not better than 'Socrates dissatisfied'. Above all the greatest pleasure was liberty. Thus he believed in universal suffrage, but it rather alarmed him as he believed the majority had little understanding of the finer points of policy which would be best left to the professional classes. Ordinary citizens, he argued in *On Representative Institutions*, would be better occupied with LOCAL POLITICS.

Utilitarianism is nearer than any other philosophy to a scheme of how democratic governments actually make their decisions. Welfare economics, for example, is basically utilitarian. It is a form of practical LIBERALISM. But the modern approach of Rawls and others tends to be

a return to contractarian philosophy. This involves value judgements and therefore belongs to a different stream of thought.
See also SOCIAL CONTRACT; UTILITY.

Reading
Bentham, J. [1789] 1970. *An Introduction to the Principles of Morals and Legislation*. Ed. J.H. Burns and H.L.A. Hart. London: Athlone; Bentham, J. [1824] 1983. *Constitutional Code*. Ed. F. Rosen and J.H. Burns. Oxford: Clarendon Press; Halevy, E. [1928] 1972. *The Growth of Philosophic Radicalism*. London: Faber; Mill, J.S. [1863] *Utilitarianism*; [1859] *On Liberty*; [1861] 1960. *On Representative Government*. 4th edn. Ed. A.D. Lindsay. London: Dent.

utility   In its simplest sense the word means usefulness and was first advanced as a principle by Hume (1711–76). For economists utility is one of the factors determining price – the other is the cost of production. Yet price is no gauge of utility. Air is usually unpriced and yet its use is life-preserving. It is scarce goods that are priced. The theory of the rational consumer in the market can be illustrated by the housewife trying to get as much utility as possible from her weekly expenditure. The assortment of goods she chooses is the one that gives her greatest utility. The concept becomes more elaborate with the Law of Diminishing Utility which states that the utility of a commodity diminishes with the amount possessed.

The concept of utility is thus associated with the idea of the rational individual making choices rationally. Its importance for political scientists springs from the acceptance of the economics of Adam Smith (1723–90) by the Utilitarians. They were concerned with relating the principle to government and governmental policies.
See also UTILITARIANISM.

utopianism   A disposition to believe in a form of ideal society. The word is derived from Sir Thomas More's work, *Utopia*, published in 1516. More (1478–1535) did not think a perfect society was possible; but other writers, such as Plato in his *Republic*, seemed to believe that in certain circumstances good rule and social justice would prevail. Campanella (1568–1639) and Bacon (1561–1626) in the *City of the Sun* (1602) and *New Atlantis* (1627) respectively were early precursors of the belief in social perfectability through the advance of knowledge and science. In the twentieth century the portrayal of 'dystopia', authoritarian societies controlled by technology, became common. Utopianism had already been denounced by MARX who argued that early 'Utopian socialists', such as Fourier (1772–1839) and St. Simon (1760–1825), had overlooked the harsh realities of industrial conflict as a result of not understanding the historical process. To them he opposed his own analysis, 'scientific socialism'.

Reading
Manuel, F.E. and F.P. Manuel. 1979. *Utopian Thought in the Western World*. Oxford: Blackwell.

V

value judgements A value is demonstrated when someone expresses a liking or approval, or dislike or disapproval, of something in relation to something else. Value judgements are forms of ranking abstractions, activities, institutions, experiences, societies, political systems and people. When one says 'I prefer A to B', one is making a value judgement. Parsons argued that a society can only sustain itself with a certain degree of CONSENSUS about values. In any modern society there are bound to be conflicts of values, though some will be more widely held than others. Democratic governments, usually reflecting majority values, will attempt to prioritize them in terms of its policies. As Easton says, governments are concerned with the allocation of values.

The concept of 'value freedom', regarded by WEBER as the ideal position for social scientists, requires them to collect data and make assessments of it in a completely impartial manner. This does not necessarily imply that social scientists do not make value judgements. It can be an assertion that one must understand what 'is' before one says what 'ought' to be: that one is clear about objective reality does not mean that one accepts it. Of course, it may be difficult, or even impossible, for any researcher to free her/himself completely from cultural socialization, or the intellectual and ideological context in which the study is conducted.

See also POLITICAL ATTITUDES.

Reading
Rokeach, M. ed. 1979. *Understanding Human Values: Individual and Societal.* New York: Free Press.

vanguard of the proletariat MARX, Engels and later Lenin had described the first phase when CAPITALISM was overthrown as the DICTATORSHIP OF THE PROLETARIAT. The working class would be in power. This REVOLUTION could only be accomplished when the proletariat had become conscious of its exploitation, of its need to organize as a class and of its role in history. These were difficult concepts and only likely to be known to someone who was familiar with, and schooled in, the works of Marx. Lenin had laid down in 1903 his theory of a small revolutionary group as opposed to the Menshevik view of a mass party. After the Revolution it became apparent that SOCIALISM was going to take a long time to accomplish. The industrial proletariat was only about 5 per cent of the Russian nation and hardly conscious in the Marxist sense. Those who were Marxist-conscious were the intellectuals of the Bolshevik leadership. Of necessity an elite was needed to stimulate consciousness and endoctrinate the masses. Hence this had to be a 'vanguard', a phrase first attributed to Lenin. They were conscious of the 'class-consciousness' doctrine of Marx.

See also CELL; COMMUNISM; DICTATORSHIP OF THE PROLETARIAT.

vetoes A blocking vote by a minority or even one individual. For example, by Art. 1, section 7 of the US Constitution the President can veto a bill passed by Congress. For it to become law Congress must then pass it over his veto by a two-thirds majority. Any of the five permanent members of the United Nations Security Council – Britain, France, China, Russia and the United States – can veto a resolution, thus preventing action.

See also ITEM VETO.

Reading
Copeland, G.W. 1983. 'When Congress and the President Collide: Why Presidents Veto Legislation'. *Journal of Politics* 3. 45, 696–710.

virtual representation A term coined in eighteenth-century Britain to justify the disfranchisement of almost all the population. Opponents argued in debates over Parliamentary Reform that it was not needed because everyone was 'virtually represented' by someone of like mind who was a Member of Parliament. It overlooked Parliament's unaccountability to the mass of the people.

See also REPRESENTATION; REPRESENTATIVE DEMOCRACY.

Reading
Brock, M. 1973. *The Great Reform Act*. London: Hutchinson.

voice *See* EXIT, LOYALTY, VOICE.

voluntary associations Associations are groupings or organizations of people. Few are involuntary though the family is one obvious example and the STATE is almost one because one is born into it and it is difficult to give up membership of it (though not quite as hard as it used to be). People may join and leave voluntary associations freely. They have been categorized in various ways and can be recreational/cultural, religious, socio-economic and political. Socio-economic associations include business CORPORATIONS and TRADE UNIONS. Political associations can be divided into PRESSURE GROUPS and political parties. Most of them will have rules and memberships able to participate in rule-making and determining policies. Their purposes can be general or highly specific, their scope national or local and their duration ephemeral or more or less permanent.

As FREEDOM OF ASSOCIATION is a civic liberty the existence of voluntary associations is one indication of DEMOCRACY. Moreover, the experience of participating outside the family and within an organization can be regarded as a form of democratic education. Weighty evidence from surveys confirms that citizens who belong to voluntary associations are better informed about politics and more politically active than those who are not members. Social activity is conducive to political opinion-forming.

See also ASSOCIATION; PLURALISM.

Reading
Gordon, C.W. and N. Babchuk. 1959. 'A Typology of Voluntary Associations'. *American Sociological Review* 24, 22–9; Sprott, W.J.H. 1958. *Human Groups*. Harmondsworth: Penguin.

voting To vote is to express support for a policy or person. Usually it involves choice; but in the Communist states one could only vote for or against the party's candidate and it was dangerous to vote against. Voting can be by a show of hands, electronic devices or filing into different lobbies, as in the House of Commons. Most commonly, however, it is done by placing a cross against a candidate and/or party on a ballot paper and then placing it in a box. The procedure is not new: it was done in ancient Athens, some Swiss cantons from the fifteenth century onwards and the Venetian Republic. The Cardinals elected Popes and the Polish aristocracy their kings. Elected assemblies existed long before universal suffrage. Only a limited few voted for them. In consequence elections were characterized by rioting, bribery and corruption of all kinds. Charles Dickens in *Pickwick Papers* describes such an election in the fictional town of Eatanswill. With the advent of mass electorates in the twentieth century the voting act became a symbol of CITIZENSHIP. Even so in most democracies ABSTENTION amounted to about a quarter of the voters at most elections, though the rest saw voting as at least a civic obligation.

voting behaviour Voting behaviour is studied by political scientists at two levels. The votes of legislators have received a good deal of attention. These are published in most legislative records. They enable their constituents to check whether or not they keep their promises and enable researchers to trace a pattern of their policy preferences. These may be enlightening in a legislature like the US Congress where party discipline is weak; but even where it is strong, as in the British House of Commons, the identification of dissidence is very interesting.

Most attention has been given, however, to the behaviour of the mass electorates. This has been made possible through the use of SAMPLE SURVEYS. In the six decades since these surveys began to be used voting behaviour has inevitably changed; but the main broad tendencies still persist. The UPPER and MIDDLE CLASSES tend to vote for right and right of centre parties, while the WORKING CLASS tend to vote for left and left of centre parties. Rural voters are more to the right and urban voters more to the left. Women are more conservative, or less radical, than men. Younger voters are less politically conscious than others and less likely to vote; but those that do tend to be more on the left. Religious affiliation seems to have little relevance and there is a noteworthy tendency for the relationship to differ from place to place. French Catholics are more conservative than other French voters; but British Catholics disproportionately vote for the Labour Party. (The vast majority of them are descendants of poor Irish immigrants.)

None of these connections are so strong that one can make a prediction about how anyone will vote based on their socio-demographic status and cultural characteristics. It is all in the realm of probability. Nevertheless political scientists will always be studying voting behaviour in every DEMOCRACY, plotting its changes from election to election.

See also ABSTENTION; ELECTIONS; SAMPLE SURVEYS.

Reading
Alford, R.R. 1963. *Party and Society: Anglo-American Democracies*. Chicago: Rand McNally; Campbell, A., P.E. Converse, W.E. Miller and D.E. Stokes. 1964. *The American Voter*. New York: Wiley; Finer, S.E., H.B. Berrington and D.J. Bartholomew. 1961. *Backbench Opinion in the House of Commons 1955–59*. Oxford: Pergamon; Heath, A., R. Jowell and J. Curtice. 1985. *How Britain Votes*. Oxford: Pergamon; Lipset, S.M. and S. Rokkan. eds. 1967. *Party Systems and Voter Alignments*. New York: Free Press.

W

war Armed conflict between organized groups with objectives they deem to be irreconcilable. Definition is difficult because war can be waged that is not formally war. Even between states armed conflict may occur without either side declaring war. Thus the USA fought a long war in Vietnam; but constitutionally it was not at war because Congress had not declared war under Art. 1, section 8, clause 11 of the Constitution. At other times war may be declared but little fighting ensue, a so-called 'phoney war'. The intensity of fighting and losses on both sides may be severest when war is between factions inside states. CIVIL WARS are notoriously brutal and may leave memories and psychological wounds that wars with external forces do not. The nature of the terrain and the state of military technology also will obviously affect the type of warfare experienced. GUERRILLA WARFARE is almost a study on its own. Naval and aerial warfare are different from the war soldiers fight.

These highly varied aspects of war have made the drawing up of 'rules of war' very difficult. Much of INTERNATIONAL LAW concerning the behaviour of belligerent parties is encapsulated in international codes of which the two most pre-eminent are the Hague Conventions, 1907, and the Geneva conventions, 1949. The latter specified acts against the sick, civilians and prisoners of war as grave breaches of its terms. The Additional Protocol of 1977 defined these as 'war crimes', though of course the term had long usage and had been widely used at the Nuremberg Tribunal in 1945.

See also CIVIL WAR; COLD WAR; GUERRILLA WARFARE.

Reading
Aron, R. 1962. *Peace and War Among Nations*. London: Weidenfeld and Nicolson; Buchan, A. 1966. *War in Modern Society*. London: Fontana; Starr, H. 1972. *War Coalitions*. Lexington: D.C. Heath; Thompson, W. 1988. *On Global War*. Columbia, SC: University of South Carolina Press; Waltz, K. 1959. *Man, the State and War*. New York: Columbia University Press; Wright, Q. 1964. *A Study of War*. 2nd edn. Chicago: Chicago University Press.

wards An electoral unit of a local government area and parliamentary constituency. They vary greatly in area: urban wards tend to be small and compact, while rural wards can be extensive. Large cities can have forty or fifty wards while small boroughs may have as few as ten. Wards also provide the substructure for party organization because the ward party tends to be its smallest and lowest unit. In some American cities wards are sub-divided further into precincts, while in some American towns there are no wards, elections are 'at large' with each voter possessing a number of votes equal to the number of the total council. This system has often been deliberately adopted in order to prevent town politics developing on lines of social cleavage.

See also CONSTITUENCY.

Reading
Adrian, C.R. June 1959. 'A Typology for Non-Partisan Elections'. *Western Political Quarterly* 12, 449–58; Bealey, F., J. Blondel and W.P. McCann. 1965. *Constituency Politics.* London: Faber.

warlords   A warlord is a general in command of a considerable body of troops owing little or no allegiance to any civil power. He probably obtains his arms from foreign suppliers and his supplies by brigandage and protection rackets directed against the local peasantry. Frequently warlords, as in parts of South-East Asia and Latin America, are involved in drug-trafficking. Large non-industrialized countries with physical features such as mountains and wide rivers, obstacles to centralized government, are prone to 'warlordism'.

The classic case is China between 1916 and 1925. The end of the Empire and the short-lived Republic that followed in 1916 brought about internal confusion. Administration collapsed and the bureaucracy disappeared. In this anarchy the only power was in the different provincial armies and their commanders who were soon sporadically fighting. They received some arms and encouragement from Japan, a state which in 1915 had presented China with twenty-one demands amounting to a virtual claim to suzerainty over Chinese territory. The period is sometimes called 'China under the warlords'.

See also GUERRILLA WARFARE.

Reading
Fitzgerald, C.P. 1964. *The Birth of Communist China.* Harmondsworth: Penguin.

weak mayor plan   As the USA largely inherited the English local government system the country originally had elected councils which chose their mayors. Finding this unsatisfactory, and perhaps taking their cue from presidential government, beginning in the 1820s American towns began to experiment with electing mayors by popular vote. Thus the weak mayor plan, few examples of which survive today, gave way to the STRONG MAYOR PLAN. Ironically this is now being advocated for British local government.

See also STRONG MAYOR PLAN.

Reading
Kotter, J.P. and P.R. Lawrence. 1974. *Mayors in Action.* New York: Wiley.

welfare state   A situation in which the STATE is largely responsible for providing cash benefits for the old, sick, unemployed and mothers of small children. Frequently free education and health care, and sometimes subsidized public housing, are assumed to be within the term. 'Welfarism', as the underlying philosophy of the welfare state is entitled, is based on values and policies associated with EGALITARIANISM. Benefits to the less fortunate must be paid for largely by the redistribution of income, that is direct PROGRESSIVE TAXATION, though some can be paid in the form of contributory insurance. (The latter is common with sickness and unemployment benefits.) Hence the penalized are the healthy, the employed, the young and the childless. The assumption is that they will pay willingly, either from charitable motives, or because they see a more egalitarian society as a happier one, or because they expect or fear one day to be sick, old, married with children and unemployed themselves. Hence 'transfer payments' are mainly from one generation to another and, it is argued, they are a social benefit even to those who pay them because they ensure a more pleasant society and one in which one can live with a good conscience.

The welfare state owed its origin to late nineteenth-century cyclic unemployment, leading to the discarding of the view, formerly held, that people could not find work because they were not trying. At the same time the extension of the suffrage enfranchised many men close to the poverty line and politicians discovered that egalitarian policies gained votes. In the twentieth century most democracies have become welfare states. Sweden was the first and foremost example under the long rule of the Social Democrats (1933–76); but even the USA introduced unemployment benefit under President Roosevelt's New Deal in the 1930s. World War II accentuated the trend. In Britain wartime camaraderie and sacrifice produced an intellectual climate in which a welfare state was readily acceptable. The Beveridge Plan, adopted by the post-war Labour Government, was said to provide a safety-net for the insecure 'from the cradle to the grave', but it was predicated on 'full employment' (by which was meant no more than 3 per cent unemployment). The view that people were not generally responsible for their misfortunes had become commonly accepted.

From the 1960s onwards welfare states have everywhere, even in Scandinavia, been under pressure. Several factors have been held reponsible for this trend of which the least disputable is the weakening competitive situation of the industrialized democracies as a result of the globalization of the world economy and the rise of 'tiger' economies in Asia based on low-cost labour. Pressure on industrial costs and on the wage packets of manual workers has led to successful calls for the lowering of direct taxation.

Consequently democratic governments have been forced by electoral pressures to cut their public expenditure at the expense of welfare benefits. On the other hand, increasing unemployment and ageing populations leads to demands for more expenditure. In this dilemma 'welfarism' has become a pejorative term in some quarters. 'Neo-conservatives' maintain that the welfare state has engendered a culture of dependence and that high public expenditures weaken national economies. Individuals, they argue, should be held responsible for their poverty and they should insure against misfortune. Even so, welfare remains popular with a large enough segment of the voters for no democratic government yet (1998) to dismantle it entirely.

See also CONSERVATISM; EGALITARIANISM; SOCIALISM; THATCHERISM.

Reading

De Swann, A. 1988. *In Care of the State: Health Care, Education and Welfare in Europe and the USA in the Modern Era*. Cambridge: CUP; Esping-Anderson, G. 1990. *The Three Worlds of Welfare Capitalism*. Cambridge: CUP; Flora, P. and A.J. Heidenheimer. eds. 1981. *The Development of Welfare States in Europe and America*. New Brunswick, NJ: Transaction Books; Myrdal, G. 1960. *Beyond the Welfare State*. London: Methuen; Titmuss, R.M. 1958. *Essays on the Welfare State*. London: Allen and Unwin; Wilensky, H.L. 1973. *The Welfare State and Equality*. Berkeley: California University Press.

weltanschauung A German term for 'world outlook' first used by HEGEL. It became popular in academic discourse through the work of Karl MANNHEIM with whom it referred to what might be called a collective 'mind-set'– the beliefs, attitudes and values of a group of people or a historic era. Hence it is a form of IDEOLOGY, though with Mannheim, as with Marx, ideology connotes error. Mannheim, therefore, saw people and groups as biased by their socio-cultural backgrounds and personal interests. Their *weltanschauungs* were irrational. From Pareto, he took the idea of DERIVATIONS. POLITICIANS in their desire for power were not concerned with rational argument and sought the argument most likely to convince people. From Freud (1856–1939), Mannheim drew the notion of the human unconscious. The masses were prone to irrationality, as were the intellectuals who became so convinced of the strength of their revolutionary ideas that they would consider no arguments against them.

The *weltanschauungs* of modern intellectuals were the concern of Shils who ascribed three traditions as their bases. *Scientism*, a world governed by rationality; *Romanticism* with its emphasis on creativity and spontaneity; and *Bohemianism*, repudiating sophistication. They all, in different ways, repudiate the past and depict a vision of the future.
See also IDEOLOGY.

Reading
Mannheim, K. [1931] 1960. *Ideology and Utopia*. London: Routledge; Shils, E. 1969. 'Ideology and Civility: On the Politics of the Intellectual'. In *Ideology, Politics and Political Theory*. Ed. R.H. Cox. Belmont: Wadsworth.

whigs   Originally the term denoted that faction of the British ARISTOCRACY that opposed royal privilege and believed in the supremacy of Parliament. The Whigs supported the 'Glorious Revolution' of 1689, which put paid to a Catholic monarchy and which also guaranteed religious toleration, an independent judiciary and a free press. It was a Whig government which secured the passage of the First Reform Act in 1832. Whigs then became part of the Liberal Party but between 1886 and 1910 many of them deserted to the Conservatives. The name was also adopted between 1834 and 1856 in America by a coalition which opposed the new active role of the Presidency adopted first by Andrew Jackson. They were a party standing like their British namesakes for legislative supremacy.

The 'Whig theory of history' was a version of British history which interpreted it as a slow but gradual triumph of freedom, attained by precedent broadening down into precedent. Thomas Babington Macaulay (1809–59) was its most famous exponent.

Reading
Southgate, D.G. 1963. *The Passing of the Whigs 1832–86*. London: Macmillan.

whips   Legislators nominated by party leaders to communicate between them and other legislators, to secure as large a turn-out in the chamber as possible and to ensure that all are there to vote. The term originated in Britain and stems from fox-hunting. It is believed that Walpole, Prime Minister (1721–42), who was a master of fox-hounds, first invented it. On the government side the whips are the managers of parliamentary business. They also wield power as they report to the Prime Minister on such matters as breaches of discipline and they may make recommendations about appointments to junior ministerial posts. They also communicate with opposition whips and arrange procedural compromises 'through the usual channels behind the Speaker's chair'. Confusingly, the term is also used for the paper sent to each of the party's representatives issuing directions about how to vote. The importance of the issue is indicated by the number of underlinings. A three-line whip is the most emphatic.

Other legislatures have similar figures though their efficacy will depend on the degree of party discipline that can be maintained. In the US Congress their disciplinary function does not extend much beyond the voting in the CAUCUS at the beginning of the session. After that they may exercise a communicating role.
See also CAUCUS; PARLIAMENTARY BUSINESS.

Reading

Norton, P. 1979. 'The Organization of Parliamentary Parties'. In Walkland, S.A. *The House of Commons in the Twentieth Century.* Oxford: OUP; Ripley, R.B. 1971. 'The Party Whip Organization in the United States House of Representatives'. In *Congressional Behaviour.* Ed. N. Polsby. New York: Random House.

white collar   *See* BLUE COLLAR.

white primary
A device used in Democratic Party primaries in the American South to prevent blacks from participating in the choice of a Democratic candidate. Texas was one of its last strongholds and it was in judgement of a case from there, *Smith* v. *Allwright*, 1944, that the Supreme Court declared the practice unconstitutional.

See also PRIMARIES.

Reading

Key, V.O. 1949. *Southern Politics.* New York: Random House.

withering away of the state

Referred to by MARX, the idea of the eventual disappearance of the state was developed by Engels who wrote that 'the society that will organize on the basis of a free and equal association of the producers will put the whole machinery of state where it will then belong: into the Museum of Antiquities, by the side of the spinning wheel and the bronze axe'. The notion quite logically followed from Marx's theory that coercive power, exerted through the state, belonged to those that owned the means of production. When no-one owned them, when they were administered by everyone, the coercive power of the state would not be needed.

See also COMMUNISM; DICTATORSHIP OF THE PROLETARIAT; MARXISM.

Reading

Engels, F. [1884] 1954. *The Origin of the Family, Private Property and the State.* Moscow: Foreign Languages Publishing House.

women's liberation
A movement dating from the 1960s and drawing its inspiration from the left-wing radicalism of the period. With its general objective the improvement of the position of women world-wide, its policies and activities took many forms. Those affecting fewer women, like 'bra-burning', or the rights of lesbian couples, inevitably attracted most attention in the tabloid press. Those with most impact were concerned with equal opportunity in education and the workplace; and more consideration for women's concerns in matters such as contraception, abortion, child-minding and male violence within marriage and without. The movement was also involved with POLITICAL CORRECTNESS and had some success in changing usages like 'chairman' to 'chairperson'. With women constituting slightly more than half of most democratic electorates the arousing of feminine consciousness by the movement was bound ultimately to bear fruit.

See also GENDER GAP; FEMINISM; REPRODUCTIVE POLITICS.

Reading

Millett, K. 1977. *Sexual Politics.* London: Virago; Rowbotham, S. 1972. *Women's Liberation and Revolution.* London: Falling Wall Press; Stacey, M. and M. Price. 1981. *Women, Power and Politics.* London: Tavistock Publications.

women's suffrage
The demand for women to have the vote began towards the end of the nineteenth century and was a natural consequence of the male struggle for the suffrage. It took place across the world. In the USA Wyoming gave women the vote in 1869; but they only secured the suffrage in federal elections by the 19th Amendment in 1919. New Zealand was the first country to enfranchise women in 1893; and Australia followed suit between 1893

and 1909. In Europe Finland led the way in 1906 (while it was still part of the Russian Empire) and Switzerland lagged behind everyone, not granting female suffrage until 1971. Women's assistance in World War I was recognized in Germany and Britain by the grant of the suffrage in 1918, though in Britain it was only for women over 30. Women over 21 had to wait until 1928. In France the lower house of parliament voted for it in 1919, but the more conservative upper house rejected it and it was not until 1945 that De Gaulle secured French women the vote.

In Asia the picture has been very varied. In Sri Lanka women had the vote while it was still a British colony. In India women have had the vote since independence in 1947 and have played an important part in Indian politics. In Muslim countries, where women achieve salvation through their husbands, there has been greater resistance to enfranchising women; but Pakistani women have the vote and at the 1997 presidential election in Iran, a fundamentalist Islamic regime in the minds of some, women appear to have voted heavily for the liberalizing candidate.

See also FEMINISM; WOMEN'S LIBERATION.

Reading
Epstein, C.F. and R.I. Coser. 1980. *Access to Power: Cross-National Studies of Women and Elites*. London: Allen and Unwin; Pankhurst, S. 1977. *The Suffragette Movement*. London: Virago.

workers' control Although 'control' is a strong word, this term is often used to describe a variety of positions in which 'workers' have more or less power in the enterprise or industry in which they work. It may imply participation and representation on committees concerned with amenities such as sports clubs, canteens and lavatories; or, as with German *mittbestimmung*, now part of the Social Chapter of the Maastricht Treaty, it may involve considerable worker involvement in the decision-making of nearly all enterprises. Finally, it may mean complete control: the workers own and manage the factories. In former Yugoslavia the factories were managed by committees of workers; but they were owned by the socialist state which laid down a framework of production schedules for them to operate in.

One problem is who should represent the workers. It is common for trade-union leaders, who speak for their members in collective bargaining at a national level, to resent local arrangements for workers' representation at a local level. They are opposed to shop-floor bargaining and even when it is not concerned with wages they tend to think local representatives in discussions with employers should be chosen by the union and not elected by the enterprise's workforce. Trade-union leaders have an industry-wide and not an enterprise-wide perspective. Some would see workers' control as trade-union control. This would be SYNDICALISM.

See also SYNDICALISM.

Reading
Coates, K. and A. Topham. 1968. *Industrial Democracy in Great Britain*. London: MacGibbon and Kee; Emery, F.E. and E. Thorsrud. 1969. *Form and Content in Industrial Democracy*. London: Tavistock Publications; Nichols, T. and P. Armstrong. 1976. *Workers Divided*. London: Fontana.

working class Still a fairly common term in Europe. Americans may prefer BLUE COLLAR workers. Social scientists generally prefer the designation 'manual workers'. The British Census categorizes manual occupations thus: E – unskilled manual workers; D – semi-skilled manual workers; and C2 – skilled manual workers. These categories are sometimes used by polling organizations and related to voting intention. The avoidance of the word 'class' may be because of its subjective connotations. People may identify with the class of their parents or their cultural background and belong to none of the above categories.

Yet the term still has some force and those with generations of manual occupations behind them will readily identify with the 'working class'. A common LIFE-STYLE and what WEBER called 'the same LIFE CHANCES in the market' (meaning the labour market) distinguish them. The wearing of certain clothes, weekly instead of monthly pay and the precise imperative of the assembly belt mark them apart from the MIDDLE CLASS. Increasing SOCIAL MOBILITY and educational opportunity has led to a decline in their proportion of the population in all the old industrialized countries. They are smaller than the proletariat of MARX which included, to use the Bolsheviks' phrase, 'workers by hand *and by brain*'.

See also BLUE COLLAR; SOCIAL CLASS.

Reading
Haraszti, M. 1977. *A Worker in a Worker's State*. Harmondsworth: Penguin; Thompson, E.P. 1963. *The Making of the English Working Class*. London: Gollancz; Winter, J. 1983. *The Working Class in Modern British History*. Cambridge: CUP.

world government   Usually regarded as a mirage by most political scientists, though there has been at least one attempt to draft a constitution for the world. A world state was suggested by Dante (1265–1320), Penn (1644–1718), ROUSSEAU and Kant (1724–1804) among others but until the twentieth century it had received little consideration by statesmen. Those who drew up the League of Nations Covenant in 1919 may have had a momentary vision, but it was quickly dispelled by the troubles of the 1930s. Briefly advocates of world government can be divided into three camps. The empiricists believe that international co-operation in numerous organizations to which sovereign states relinquish a little power will persuade them in the end that the NATION-STATE is out-dated. Realists argue that coercive force must be organized internationally to uphold INTERNATIONAL LAW: the first thing to do is by contract to construct a sort of international Leviathan. Idealists in such journals as the *World Federalist* attempt to convert world citizenry to the idea of world government.

Reading
Clark, G. and L.B. Sohn. 1966. *World Peace Through World Law: Two Alternative Plans*. Cambridge, Mass.: HUP; Resnick, P. 1997. *Twenty-First Century Democracy*. Montreal and Kingston: McGill-Queen's University Press.

X

xenophobia   A fear and hatred of foreigners, often reflected in harrassment of minority ethnic groups. It may begin as a dislike of people with strange dress and behaviour and develop into specific phobias about Jews or Pakistanis, for example. Xenophobia may be particularly rife where a community or nation feels threatened.

See also ANTI-SEMITISM; NATIONAL SOCIALISM; RACISM.

Reading
Rex, J. and D. Mason. eds. 1986.*Theories of Race and Ethnic Relations*. Cambridge: CUP.

Y

youth movements The conflicting tendencies towards politics among the young seem to be towards either great enthusiasm or apathy. They are often characterized by IDEALISM and/or rebellion against AUTHORITY, and this may be manifested in spontaneous demonstrations and even riots. Especially among students, the best educated part of their generation, the urge to overthrow a super-ordinate hierarchy, even a regime, may lead to sudden explosions of anger. One example is the 'events of May 1968' in Paris; but the best is undoubtedly the part played by students in the Czechoslovak revolution of 1989 which overthrew the Communist government. Frequently after such incursions into politics, young people lapse into quiescence and become cynical about the results of their activity.

One type of youth movement may be spontaneous, ephemeral and youth-led: the other is organized by adults. Many churches set up youth groups in the hope of retaining the allegiance of their worshippers' children. Other bodies, such as the Boy Scouts, may vaguely socialize their membership in civic values such as tolerance, obeying the law, helping others and public service. Democratic political parties usually have youth movements, to a greater or lesser degree guided by their elders, but with an embarrassing history of internal revolts, sponsoring outrageous resolutions at CONFERENCES and eventual suppression. Totalitarian parties organize the young from an early age with the purposes of endoctrinating and supervising them, and selecting leadership cadres from amongst them. *See also* STUDENT POLITICS.

Reading
Eisenstadt, S.N. 1956. *From Generation to Generation*. New York: Free Press; Marsland, D. 1978. *Sociological Explorations in the Service of Youth*. London: National Youth Bureau.

yuppies An acronym for 'young, upwardly-mobile, professional people'. It probably originates in the period when social scientists were noting the emergence of a new greatly expanded professional class with a different style of life and political allegiance. Other less well known acronyms are 'ouppies' (old . . .) and 'dinkies' (double-income, no kids).

Z

zero-sum game *See* GAME THEORY.

zionism   A belief that a Jewish national home should be set up in Palestine with its capital at Jerusalem, the ancient city of Zion. It dates from the Diaspora, the dispersal of Jews by the Romans after they defeated revolts in AD66 and AD132. From 1897, when Theodor Herzl (1860–1904) convened the first World Zionist Congress at Basle, it became a movement. Already there had been a trickle of Jewish immigration into Palestine during the late nineteenth century and this became an appreciable flow after the declaration in 1917 by Arthur Balfour, the British Foreign Secretary, that it should be a Jewish national home. After the collapse of the Turkish Empire and the granting to Britain of a mandate over Palestine by the League of Nations the KIBBUTZ movement was much encouraged. The extermination of six million Jews in the gas chambers in World War II made the Zionist issue much more pressing. In 1948 after much more Jewish immigration the state of Israel was inaugurated. The Zionist dream, however, remains not totally fufilled because Israel is surrounded by Arab enemies, peace with the Palestinians is not yet attained and Jerusalem is still not wholly Jewish. *See also* ANTI-SEMITISM.

Reading
Avineri, S. 1982. *The Making of Modern Zionism*. London: Weidenfeld and Nicolson; Hertzberg, A. 1969. *The Zionist Idea*. New York: Schocken.

zoning   A procedure by which local authorities restrict land-use. They create zones which can only be used for some function such as agriculture or house-building. National planning laws can assist this policy. The creation of national parks and wild-life reserves are further examples. The famous 'Green Belt' round London restricted building and the growth of suburban sprawl along the periphery of the capital. Zoning also has a long history in the USA and has been characterized by much litigation between individuals, public authorities and PRESSURE GROUPS representing environmentalist bodies.

Biographical Sketches: A Selected Political Science Who's Who

The people mentioned below have been important figures who have played a large part in the development of the discipline. Most are no longer living; but a few contemporary political scientists, whose names will be encountered by most readers of academic works in the subject, have been included. In addition, a few political theorists of past centuries, whose work is often cited in the above entries, are given a place.

Althusser, Louis (1918–90) The philosopher of French Stalinist Marxism who emphasized the scientific rather than the humanistic side of Marx. He elaborated the theory of economic determinism and the historical dialectic and developed a new epistemology in which knowledge was not concerned with externality but as a way of shaping concepts. He also argued that IDEOLOGY was an important weapon of CAPITALISM. His death was as controversial as his life. Works include: *For Marx* (1966) and *Reading Capital* (1970).

Arendt, Hannah (1906–75) Born in Hanover, she received her doctorate from Heidelberg where she studied under Karl Jaspers (1883–1969). (Later she edited two volumes of his work.) In 1933, a German Jew, she was forced to take refuge in France where for six years she arranged the immigration of Jewish children to Palestine. In 1941 she fled to the USA and later became an American citizen. In *The Origins of Totalitarianism* (1951) she described what it was like to be a persecuted citizen in a totalitarian state. Other important works were *The Human Condition* (1958); *On Revolution* (1963); and *Crisis in the Republic* (1973). Her work is assessed by M. Canovan in *The Political Thought of Hannah Arendt* (1974).

Aristotle (c.384–c.322BC) A student of Plato (c.427–c.347BC), Aristotle was at one time tutor to young Alexander the Great. He became leader of a school known as the 'Peripatetics' and sent his students around Greece collecting the constitutions of the Greek city-states. Much of his study of *Politics* is contained in a book of that name, believed to be a posthumous collection of his essays and lectures. It justifies the claim that he is the first political scientist. It includes the first TYPOLOGY of political regimes and the first attempt to link social status with POLITICAL BEHAVIOUR. He also examines the reasons for the instability of states, among which he identifies REL-ATIVE DEPRIVATION. Other works were *Ethics* and the *Athenian Constitution*.

Aron, Raymond   (1905–83) A twenti-eth-century sage, more esteemed in Britain and America than in his home country, France, where he was the chief opponent of Sartre (1905–80). Both a prolific journalist of high quality and a leading figure in academic circles, his range extended across philosophy, soci-ology and international relations. He rejected Marxism, contending that in 'modern industrial society', a concept he elaborated, it was the political nature of the regime that was significant. His analysis of POLITICAL SYSTEMS was comprehensive and antagonistic to the behaviouralists. Bureaucracies, social groups, political cultures, as well as rep-resentative institutions, must be studied in order to provide a proper explanation. His works include *Introduction to the Philosophy of History* (1938); *The Century of Total War* (1954); *Democracy and Totalitarianism* (1958); and *Progress and Disillusion* (1968).

Ashford, Douglas   (1928–93) A truly international scholar who was a visiting professor at British, French and German universities. From 1982 he was Professor of Political Science at Pittsburgh. His interests were wide-ranging. His first book was *Perspectives of a Moroccan Nationalist* (1964). Later works were con-cerned with European politics. These include: *Politics and Policy in Britain: the Limits of Consensus* (1981); *British Dog-matism and French Pragmatism* (1982); and *The Emergence of the Welfare States* (1988).

Bagehot, Walter   (1826–77) After brief spells in law and business, and standing unsuccessfully as a Liberal candidate for Parliament, Bagehot became editor of the *Economist* in 1860, a post he held until his death. In *Physics and Politics* (1860) he attempted to apply the principle of natural selection to politics. He is best remembered for *The English Constitution* (1867) in which he rejected MIXED GOVERNMENT, or the idea of balance between different institutions, and argued that the House of Commons was the real power in the land. The monarchy and the House of Lords provided the 'theatrical' or 'dignified' element. At the time he wrote British governments could easily be dismissed by votes of the Commons.

Barker, Ernest, Sir   (1874–1960) Prin-cipal of Kings College, London (1920–7) and Professor of Political Science at Cambridge (1928–39), Barker's early writings were historical and philosoph-ical; but he gradually turned to writing more and more about politics under the influence of the events of the 1930s and 1940s. Probably no one up to his time succeeded in relating POLITICAL THEORY and ideological doctrine to the nature of political regimes as well as he did. He wrote before POLITICAL SOCIOLOGY pro-vided more enlightenment. His many works include *Greek Political Theory* (1918); *Reflections on Government* (1942); *Essays on Government* (1945); and *Prin-ciples of Social and Political Theory* (1951).

Bassett, Reginald   (1901–62) At 25 he went from being a solicitor's clerk to studying at Ruskin College and from there to Balliol. After graduating, he spent 15 years as a Tutor for the Oxford Delegacy of Extra-Mural Studies in Sussex. He was an active member of the Independent Labour Party and keen to be adopted as a Labour candidate; but the 1931 Labour government crisis, which split the Labour Party, left him on the wrong side (as far as advancement in the party was concerned) as a MacDonaldite. This influenced his life and work. His first book *The Essentials of Parliamentary Democracy* (1935) argues that DEMOCRACY is a matter of seeking compromise and avoiding extremism. The immoderate demagogues of the early 1930s are castigated. In later works he sought to dispel the largely left-wing myths of the same period. *Democracy and Foreign Policy* (1952) is a detailed examination of public opinion during the Manchurian crisis. *1931: Political Crisis* (1958) similarly analysed events almost day-by-day. By this time he had in 1945 become a lecturer in Trades Union Studies at the LSE. In 1961 he was made Professor of Government. He was the first secretary of the Political Studies Association. A very conscientious teacher, he viewed politics in an old-fashioned light as the activities and interactivities of political leaders.

Beard, Charles (1874–1948) Beard was Professor of Politics at Columbia (1907–17) and Director of the Training School for Public Service in New York City (1917–22). He was both active in administration and in publishing. His works, translated into many languages, sold over ten million copies. During his postgraduate research in Britain he helped to found Ruskin College, Oxford. In his time in New York he played an important part in the drive against waste and inefficiency. Yet it is as a controversialist that Beard is most famous. He was convinced of the important part industrial and commercial groups played in politics. Although never a Marxist, his work gave great offence to more traditional interpreters of US history and politics. His works include *The Economic Basis of Politics* (1912); *An Interpretation of the Constitution of the United States* (1913); and *Economic Origins of Jeffersonian Democracy* (1915).

Becker, Carl (1873–1945) A Professor of History at Cornell from 1917 until his death, his numerous seminal works were largely concerned with American politics. They include: *Our Experiment in Democracy* (1924); *The Heavenly City of the Eighteenth Century Philosophers* (1932); *Progress and Power* (1936); *Modern Democracy* (1941); and *New Liberties for Old* (1942).

Beer, Samuel (1911–) An American political scientist who is a leading authority on British politics. This dates from his time at Oxford as a Rhodes scholar between 1932 and 1935. In 1952 he became Professor of Political Science at Harvard until his retirement. His classic work is *Modern British Politics* (1965), an analysis of different phases of development of the parties and their ideas since the eighteenth century. A more detailed work was *Treasury Control: the Co-ordination of Economic and Financial Policy in Great Britain* (1975). Another important work with A.B. Ulam was *Patterns of Government: the Major Political Systems of Europe* (1962). A later important book about Britain was *Britain Against Itself* (1982). Finally, *To Make a Nation: the Rediscovery of American Federalism* (1993), demonstrated he was equally conversant with US politics. Most of his numerous articles have been seminal. Within the subject he has been a major figure.

Bentley, Arthur F. (1870–1957) He was only briefly an academic and spent most of his life managing a farm. His most well-known work, *The Process of Government*, was written in 1908. It remained neglected until re-discovered by David Truman. Bentley argued that POLITICAL BEHAVIOUR was best studied by investigating the interactional behaviour of groups. Although his style is turgid and the discussion remains at an abstract level, somewhat removed from political life, he is claimed as the founder of the behaviouralist school and as the father of PLURALISM.

Berlin, Isaiah, Sir (1909–97) Born in Riga, his family emigrated to Britain after the Revolution. After graduating, he became a Philosophy don at New College and a Fellow of All Souls in 1932. After World War II, when he served in the embassies at Washington and Moscow, he returned to Oxford where he was Chichele Professor of Social and Political Theory from 1957 until 1967. His inaugural lecture, *Two Concepts of Liberty*, remains his best-known work. With its distinction between 'negative' FREEDOM and 'positive' freedom, it has become a starting-point for numerous students of modern POLITICAL PHILOSOPHY. Another famous work, the *Hedgehog and the Fox* (1953), was a study of Tolstoy's idea of history. Other books include a very perceptive survey of *Karl Marx* (1939) and *Vico and Herder* (1976). His written work, however, does not account for his immense influence as a teacher and as the leading British liberal intellectual of his time.

Brogan, Dennis W., Sir (1900–74) Professor of Political Science at Cambridge (1939–68) where the subject was scarcely taught. He was a popular lecturer and broadcaster and wrote two books which, though now out of date, introduced many students to the POLITICAL SYSTEMS of the USA and France. These were *The American Political System* (1933) which provided many lecturers with humorous anecdotes; and *The Development of Modern France 1870–1940*, still a readable history of the Third Republic. Other useful works include *The Free State* (1945); *The Price of Revolution* (1951); and *Roosevelt and the New Deal* (1952).

Bryce, James (1838–1922) Educated at Glasgow and Oxford, Bryce became Professor of Civil Law at Oxford in 1870. In 1880 he was elected MP and held office in Liberal governments. A friend of DICEY, he published *Studies in History and Jurisprudence* (1901). Meanwhile he had visited the USA on several occasions and been enthralled by it. In 1888 he published *The American Commonwealth* which discussed American politics at all levels and contained a detailed analysis of the political parties. It became a classic and still remains a model of how a political scientist should describe the government and politics of one country. He became a friend of LOWELL whose work is similar. In consequence of his American interests the Liberal Government appointed him Ambassador in Washington (1907–13). Later in 1921 he published *Modern Democracies*, a pioneering work of comparative government. It is no exaggeration to call him the founding father of British political science.

Bull, Hedley (1932–87) An Australian who taught International Relations at the London School of Economics from 1955 to 1967, except for a year as Rockefeller Fellow at Harvard. In 1967 he began a decade as Professor of International Relations at Canberra, returning to become a Fellow of Balliol and Professor at Oxford. Bull is regarded as a major figure in the theory of relations between states. He agreed with GROTIUS that international order was the norm and could be perceived in the way states behaved; it was not just a matter of theory. He believed an international society was emerging even among states without shared values because they had common interests in peace and security. The growth of international organizations was evidence for this development. He set out these ideas in *Control of the Arms Race* (1961) and especially in *The Anarchical Society* (1977).

Burke, Edmund (1729–97) While being an eighteenth-century Whig Member of Parliament, Burke published *Thoughts on the Cause of the Present Discontents* (1770), a criticism of George III's subversion of the power of the legislature with his government by cabals. He defended the autonomy of the individual MP in his *Speech to the Electors of Bristol* (1774). Today Burke is seen as a conservative political theorist who defended LAW AND ORDER and traditional citizen rights. Hence he supported the American colonists and their revolution in numerous speeches and letters (collected in *Speeches and Letters on American Affairs 1774–1781*); but he condemned the French revolutionaries in *Reflections on the Revolution in France* (1790).

Chester, Norman, Sir (1907–86) Educated at Manchester University, where he was a Lecturer in Public Administration (1936–45), his qualities as an administrator became evident when he was seconded to the Economic Section of the War Cabinet Secretariat in 1940. After the war he was successively Fellow of the newly established Nuffield College and then Warden (1954–78). In the latter position he was strategically placed to influence the social sciences in Britain for a quarter of a century. He wrote *The Nationalised Industries* (1951) and *Questions in Parliament* (with N. Bowring, 1962); and was editor of *The Organisation of British Central Government* (written by F.M.G. Willson, 1957). He was Chairman of the Committee on Association Football (1966–8).

Cole, Gordon D.H. (1889–1959) A left-wing polymath who covered many disciplines – history, economics and political science – and appropriately became Chichele Professor of Social and Political Theory at Oxford. Among his many activities was his work as a research assis-tant in the engineers' trade union. In the early 1920s he devised a scheme for the British trade-union movement to be reorganized with one union for each industry. He was a prolific historian of the labour movement, an interpreter of MARX and other socialist theorists and a leading proponent of the idea of WORKERS' CONTROL, a theme he had ingested from the SYNDICALISM he had encountered during his connection with the engineers. This developed into Cole's model for a decentralized socialist society in which TRADE UNIONS were organized in local guilds and representation was functional. He expounded this idea in several books, notably *Self-Government in Industry* (1917); *Social Theory* (1920); and *Guild Socialism Restated* (1920). GUILD SOCIALISM was a form of prescriptive PLURALISM, partly a revolt against the centralization of the wartime economy and partly a protest against the labour movement's growing attachment to the nationalization of industry on a large scale.

Crosland, Tony (1918–77) He would probably have been a don of Political Science if World War II, in which he served with distinction, had not intervened. In consequence after 1945 he became involved with Labour Party politics and was elected to Parliament in 1950. Having written *Britain's Economic Problem* (1953), he was made Minister of State for Economic Affairs (1964–5) and then promoted to be Minister of Education and Science (1965–7). In the later Wilson Government he was in charge of local government matters as Minister for the Environment (1974–6). While in opposition he wrote two well-known books: *The Future of Socialism* (1956), in which he set out the the best statement of British SOCIAL DEMOCRACY since 1945; and *The Conservative Enemy* (1962), an attempt to divert the left from attacking the party leadership and, instead, to turn its guns on the Conservatives.

Crossman, Richard (1907–74) Both a prominent politician and political scientist who managed to practise both at once. As a Fellow of New College, Oxford (1930–7) he wrote *Plato Today* (1937) and *Government and the Governed* (1939). During the war he was a civil servant, finishing as Assistant Chief of the Psychological Warfare Division. In 1945 he was elected as a Labour MP and soon became a leader of the Keep Left group, focusing criticism largely on foreign policy. After 1964 he gained office under Harold Wilson, entering the Cabinet as Minister for Local Government (1964–6) and becoming Secretary of State for the Social Services (1968–70). As a result of office he produced *Diaries of A Cabinet Minister* in three volumes (1975, 1976, 1977) covering the years 1964–70. They are essential material for any scholar of British cabinet government. He published three lectures on 'PRIME MINIS-TERIAL GOVERNMENT', a term he may have invented, as *Inside View* (1972).

Dahl, Robert (1915–) Perhaps the most influential of post-1945 political scientists. Numerous works attest to his great energy. Dahl is best known for his development of the concept of PLURAL-ISM. In his *Preface to Democratic Theory* (1956) he expounded the idea of POLY-ARCHY, later elaborated in *Polyarchy, Participation and Opposition* (1971). He had confirmed the notion that power in democracies is diffused as the result of CONFLICT and compromise between numerous groups in his empirical study of power in Newhaven, *Who Governs?* (1964). Later works such as *Dilemmas of Pluralist Democracy* (1982) and *Preface to Economic Democracy* (1985) were concerned with the inequalities of group power, especially that of the big corporations. Interested in the link between

economic and POLITICAL POWER, an early collaboration was with LINDBLOM in *Politics, Economics and Welfare. Planning and Politico-Economic Systems Resolved into Basic Social Processes* (1953). A discourse on the problems of exercising power was *After the Revolution? Authority in a Good Society* (1970). Another seminal work was with Edward Tufte – *Size and Democracy* (1973). In the same year he edited *Regimes and Oppositions*. A summary of responses to elitists and Marxists is contained in *Democracy and its Critics* (1989).

Deutsch, Karl (1912–92) Born in Prague he took refuge in the USA in 1938. He held three chairs at Yale, MIT and Harvard and was President of International Political Science Association 1976–9. Deutsch is best known as the inventor of the field of political cybernetics. His best known book is *The Nerves of Government* (1963). Others on a similar theme include *Nationalism and Social Communication* (1953); and *Political Community at the International Level* (1954). He also wrote textbooks: *Analysis of International Politics* (1968); and *Politics and Government* (1970).

Dicey, Albert V. (1835–1922) Probably the most important British jurist of his day and since. His book *The Law of the Constitution* (1885) became a classic text and is still required reading for undergraduate students of the British Constitution. In it he defined and developed PARLIAMENTARY SOVEREIGNTY, declaring that Parliament had the 'right to make or unmake any law whatever'. There could be no limitations to its legislative power. Dicey also defined the RULE OF LAW. It existed where LAW AND ORDER prevailed, everyone was equal before the law and there was no arbitrary or discretionary power exercised. Officials were as subject to the law and the courts as other citizens. Finally Dicey defined the CONVENTIONS OF THE CONSTITUTION as rules not enforceable by the courts. He went so far as asserting that only an unwritten constitution like the British could have conventions; though in later editions of the work he admitted that they could be part of any constitution. His later work, *Law and Public Opinion in England During the Nineteenth Century* (1905), is both a legal and a legislative history. Notably, he divided the century into three periods: old Toryism or legislative quiescence (1800–30); Benthamism or Individualism (1825–70); and Collectivism (1865–1900). This typology has stood the test of time.

Duverger, Maurice (1917–) The most distinguished French political scientist of his era. He was a professor in Law Faculties successively at the universities of Poitiers, Bordeaux and Paris (1955–71), where he founded and was first Director of a research body for the study of European Institutions and Cultures. He was awarded numerous honorary doctorates and the Legion of Honour. Duverger introduced a new dimension into the comparative study of politics with his first book, *Les Partis Politiques* (1951). He systematically examined the relationship of ELECTORAL SYSTEMS to political parties; and categorized the latter in terms of IDEAL TYPES. In *Les Régimes Politiques* (1961) he wrote a succinct introduction to a typology of the subject. In *Introduction to the Social Sciences* (1961) he set out an unrivalled schematic framework for empirical research. A more general work was *Sociologie Politique* (1968). *De la Dictature* (1961) is an admirable review of dictatorships of all kinds. Yet he did not neglect his native country. *La Cinquième République* (1959); *La Monarchie Républicaine* (1974); *La République des Citoyens* (1982) are only some of his

books on France. In the 1990s he has turned to Europe with *Europe des Hommes* (1994) and *Europe dans Tous ses États* (1995).

Ehrmann, Henry (1908–94) Born in Germany, he studied at the French Lycée in Berlin. Imprisoned and tortured by the Gestapo, he escaped to France. Arriving in North America in 1940, he taught in Canada at McGill and in the universities of Colorado and Dartmouth. His earlier work was about French politics, including *French Labour from Popular Front to Liberation* (1947); *Organized Business in France* (1958); and *Politics in France* (1960). Two later books of a comparative nature were *Interest Groups on Four Continents* (1964) and *Comparative Legal Cultures* (1976).

Einaudi, Mario (1904–94) A graduate of Turin he went to the USA when he was 23 and later became Professor of Politics at Cornell. He was an enemy of specialization in Political Science, demonstrated by the diverse nature of his works. The best known are *The Roosevelt Revolution* (1959) and *The Early Rousseau* (1967).

Fenton, Jack (1920–92) Wounded at the storming of Manila, he returned to take a Ph.D. at Harvard under V.O. KEY. The influence of Key is reflected in Fenton's *Politics in the Border States* (1957), *The Catholic Vote* (1960) and *Midwest Politics* (1966). His wide-ranging knowledge of US parties and voter-orientations are illustrated in *People and Parties in Politics* (1966). As a result of the student troubles he wrote with Gail Gleason *Student Power at the University of Massachusetts* (1969). He was a committed teacher as Professor of Political Science at the University of Massachusetts until he retired. He was also a visiting Professor at Aberdeen and California universities.

Finer, Herman (1898–1969) Professor of Political Science at Chicago (1945–68), Finer had taught at the London School of Economics from 1920. He was a Fabian socialist and, influenced by the WEBBS and LASKI, took an interest in PLURALISM, leading to his first work, *Representative Government and a Parliament of Industry* (1923), a study of the German Federal Economic Council. His sympathy with the Weimar Republic evoked a hatred of its Fascist destroyers. In *Mussolini's Italy* (1935) he exposed the hollowness of the regime. Remaining a socialist he wrote a riposte to HAYEK, *The Road to Reaction* (1945). For most political scientists, however, his major contribution will be *The Theory and Practice of Modern Government*. This was published in 1932 as a study of mainly four democracies, Britain, France, the USA and the Weimar Republic. Revised in 1949, much of the detail in the book is out of date; but it still remains a model of the comparative approach across institutions rather than by dealing with one country after another.

Finer, Samuel E. (1915–93) Younger brother of Herman and one of the few British political scientists since World War II with an international reputation. Successively he was a Fellow of Balliol College, Oxford, Professor of Political Institutions at Keele, Professor of Government at Manchester and Professor of Government and Public Administration at Oxford. He was a colourful figure and a lively, not to say assertive, conversationalist. He spoke French and Italian and also read Spanish. He had wide-ranging interests and besides producing some useful texts published four path-blazing works. In his *Life of Edwin Chadwick* (1952) he illuminated the administrative history of the nineteenth century. In *Anonymous Empire* (1958) he wrote the first study of British PRESSURE GROUPS. *Backbench Opinion in the House of Commons* (with H.B. Berrington and D.J. Bartholomew, 1961) was a pioneering venture both in method and content. *The Man on Horseback* (1965) was the first British study of MILITARY REGIMES. It revealed his familiarity with works on POLITICAL SOCIOLOGY and POLITICAL CULTURE. Tireless, in his last days he was working on *The History of Government*, published posthumously in three volumes in 1997.

Frankel, Joseph (1913–89) Educated at the University of Lwów in Poland, he left to farm in Australia from 1938 until 1947, when he became a postgraduate at the London School of Economics. He was a Lecturer in Politics at Aberdeen (1951–62) and Professor of Politics at Southampton (1962–73). All his work, which was highly regarded, was in the field of INTERNATIONAL RELATIONS. Publications include: *The Making of Foreign Policy* (1962); *International Relations* (1963); *International Politics* (1969); and *British Foreign Policy 1945–1973* (1975).

Gellner, Ernst (1925–95) Born in Prague, he took refuge in Britain from the Nazis, becoming a soldier in the Czech Army at the end of World War II. An important intellectual influence, his works overlapped the borders of philosophy, anthropology and political science. He was Professor of Philosophy at the London School of Economics (1962–84) and Professor of Social Anthropology at Cambridge (1984–93). In 1980 he helped to found the journal *Government and Opposition*. Publications include: *Thought and Change* (1964); *Cause and Meaning in the Social Sciences* (1973); *Legitimation of Belief* (1975); *Nations and Nationalism* (1983); *Culture, Identity and Politics* (1987); *Postmodernism, Reason and Religion* (1992); and *Anthropology and Politics* (1995).

Gosnell, Harold F. (1896–1997) A member of the 'Chicago school' who took his Ph.D. under MERRIAM and in 1924 published with him *Non-Voting*, a study of political indifference and inertia. In the same year his thesis appeared as *Boss Platt and His New York Machine*. He was a pioneer of the study of 'grass roots politics'. To write *Getting Out the Vote* (1927) he interviewed 6000 voters in 12 different Chicago neighbourhoods. He also distributed notices urging citizens to register and found that it increased the TURN-OUT among the least educated. Later works included *Why Europe Votes* (1930); *Negro Politics* (1935); and *Machine Politics: Chicago Model* (1937). He was Professor of Political Science at Harvard from 1962 until 1970.

Griffith, Ernest S. (1897–1997) Professor of Political Science at the American University from 1935 to 1958. In 1954 he published *The American System of Government*, which became a standard textbook, ran to several editions and was translated into 25 languages. In 1957 he helped to found the School of International Service and a year later became its first director, serving until 1968.

Grotius, Hugo (1583–1645) A Dutch lawyer who spent much of his life in exile in France, he is regarded as the founder of INTERNATIONAL LAW. The basic notions in his famous work *De Iure Belli ac Pacis* (1625) (concerning the law of war and peace), are that human beings have fundamental instincts that dispose them to act peacefully. Hence there is a natural law irrespective of whether there is a divine law or not. Consequently rational leaders should perceive the advantages of the peaceful settlement of disputes even when there is no supra-state authority to control relations between states. He maintained that a basic premise was that promises must be kept. Only defensive wars were justified.

This is known as the 'Grotian world system'.

Hallowell, John (1915–92) His several decades as Professor of Political Science at Duke University were distinguished by his success in persuading the university to integrate the Faculty and by his editorship of the Lilly Foundation Research Program in Christianity and Politics. A devout Anglican, his teaching and writing asserted opposition to moral relativism. DEMOCRACY, he insisted, must be based on moral values. He wrote *The Decline of Liberalism as an Ideology* (1946); *Main Currents in Modern Political Thought* (1950); and *The Moral Foundations of Democracy* (1954).

Hayek, Frederick von (1899–1992) Born and educated in Vienna, he arrived in Britain in the 1930s and became a British citizen in 1936. Soon after this he became Professor of Economics at the London School of Economics but spent his last years as a Professor at Chicago. He was a great protagonist of the market and an early advocate of MONETARISM. Hence he was bitterly opposed to the prevailing KEYNESIANISM of his day. Indeed, he had very little time for most academics. Other economists he regarded with near contempt. Historians had misrepresented the rise of a powerful STATE as a cultural achievement. Politicians and planners were beyond the pale. Only commerce could spread culture and civilization. Thus, though he was an economist, he was much involved with the political debate. In 1944 he published *The Road to Serfdom* in which he argued that the socialist ingredient in Nazism had been largely ignored. If Britain elected a Labour Government it would be 'on the road to serfdom'. Later, in *The Constitution of Liberty* (1961), he set out the framework of institutions and law in which a free market would guarantee FREEDOM generally. In his last days he was much admired by Thatcher and Reagan as a prophet of the 'New Right'.

Heckscher, Gunnar   (1909–88) A political scientist who, unusually, managed to combine being a politician with research activity. A graduate and doctor of Uppsala, he went on to teach at Stockholm University where he was a Professor of Political Science between 1941 and 1948. In the latter year he was elected to the Riksdag where he remained until 1965. He was then appointed ambassador to India (1965–70), and Japan (1970–5). None of this activity stopped him publishing and becoming one of the leading figures in Scandinavian political science. His works include *Staten och Organisationerna* (1951); *The Study of Comparative Government and Politics* (1957), a pioneering work about the methodology of approach to comparative work; and *Asiatiskt Maktspel* (1977).

Hegel, Georg Wilhelm Friedrich
(1770–1831) A philosopher of IDEALISM who influenced both POLITICAL THEORY and politics itself. His work has not been popular in the English-speaking world, probably because of its turgidity and obscurity. Yet his impact on European thought has been considerable. He depicted the advance of a rationalist spirit through different phases of history, ending in its ultimate realization in the final, German phase. History would proceed through the 'historical dialectic' – a pattern of 'thesis' and 'antithesis' resulting in a 'synthesis' which will break down under its internal contradictions. This cycle will continue until final 'synthesis' is achieved. These ideas were borrowed and adapted by MARX. Hegel put great emphasis on the STATE and the necessity of laws to uphold it. Law was an expression of RATIONALISM, a theme often encountered in WEBER. His most important works were *Philosophy of Right*

(1821) and *Philosophy of World History* (1857).

Hobbes, Thomas   (1588–1679) A very sophisticated political theorist who tried to construct a model of a POLITICAL SYSTEM from his initial premise about the nature of Man (women hardly appear in his writings). Men are both aggressive and, therefore, fearful of being attacked. In a state of nature this will produce a situation of 'war of everyone against everyone' in which 'the life of man is solitary, poor, nasty, brutish and short' and in which 'there is no place for industry . . . no arts, no letters, no society'. The solution is to imbue AUTHORITY with unassailable POLITICAL POWER. Ideally this should be a single ruler. Men are sufficiently rational to make a contract between themselves in order to install such a ruler – *Leviathan*, as Hobbes calls him in his book of that name published in 1651. Law thus emanates from the monarch and not from any divine source. Only MACHIAVELLI preceded Hobbes in this view of the conflictual nature of man and political activity which is a repudiation of the idea, accepted largely until that time, that mens' natures predispose them to live in harmony. It also rejected GROTIUS's perception of international order. 'Covenants, without the sword, are but words', Hobbes insisted.

Hobhouse, Leonard   (1864–1929) He had an unusual career, resigning his Fellowship at Merton in 1897 to become a journalist on the *Manchester Guardian*. His interests were in both the condition of the working classes and in philosophy. In 1889 he had taken up the cause of New Unionism, the larger organizations of unskilled workers, and in 1893 he published *The Labour Movement*. While a journalist he published *Mind in Evolution* (1901) and *Democracy and Reaction* (1902). In 1907 he returned to academic life as the first Professor of Sociology at London University. His two most important works in this period were *The Metaphysical Theory of the State* (1918) and *Elements of Social Justice* (1922). The latter is often said to be an attempt to reconcile UTILITARIANISM and IDEALISM.

Hobson, John   (1858–1940) His only academic activity was teaching economics for the Oxford and London Extra-Mural Delegacies. Yet as a freelance journalist he wrote several works which were highly influential on the thought of his day. *The Evolution of Modern Capitalism* (1894, revised edns 1907 and 1917) was the first scholarly attempt to examine the structure of organized large-scale CAPITALISM. His opposition to the Boer War inspired *The Psychology of Jingoism* (1901) and *Imperialism* (1902) from which Lenin drew much of his material for a booklet of the same name. Some of his articles and *Work and Wealth* (1914) contained explanations of the business cycle and unemployment from which Keynes drew his theories. In his memoirs, *Confessions of an Economic Heretic* (1938), he repeated his main ideas.

Jennings, W. Ivor, Sir   (1903–65)   A constitutional lawyer who became one of the founding fathers of British political science. Among his numerous books were three which generations of students were told to read. In *The Law and the Constitution* (1933), which ran to five editions, he rejected some of DICEY's ideas, especially what the latter said about CONVENTIONS OF THE CONSTITUTION. *Cabinet Government* (1936) and *Parliament* (1939) are still authoritative texts. *The Approach to Self-Government* (1956) was the result of his association with Ceylon (now Sri Lanka) where he helped to set up the University of Ceylon, becoming its first Vice-Chancellor

(1942–55). In a very distinguished career at Cambridge he was Master of Trinity Hall from 1954; Downing Professor of the Laws of England from 1962; and Vice-Chancellor of the University (1961–3).

Kelsen, Hans   (1881–1973)   Born in Prague, he held Chairs of Law at Vienna (1911–29) and Cologne (1929–33). From 1933 until 1940 he was Professor of International Law at Geneva. Leaving for the USA, where he became a citizen in 1945, he was Professor of Political Science at Berkeley (1942–52). Besides drafting the Austrian Constitution in 1919, Kelsen originated what is known as 'the pure theory of law', an advanced statement of legal positivism. His works included: *Society and Nature* (1943); *General Theory of Law and State* (1945); *Principles of Industrial Law* (1952); and *Communist Theory of Law* (1955).

Key, V.O.   (1908–63) One of the outstanding political scientists of his time. With his work the discipline reached maturity. In *Politics, Parties and Pressure Groups* (1942), he not only produced a detailed map of American politics but also indicated a model for others to use in describing the politics of their own countries. The work ran to five editions before his early death and has remained a classic. *Southern Politics* (1949) was a study of one-party politics in the eleven Southern states. Not only did it provide a sketch of the politics of each state, it was also a comparative work and included much aggregate data. In his two later works, *Public Opinion and American Democracy* (1961) and *The Responsible Electorate* (1966) he examined the relationship between the American voters and their leaders. Were the leaders accountable and did they try to maintain a trust in democracy? His answers are a qualified affirmative, though he was aware of shortcomings. Key held chairs at

Johns Hopkins, Yale and Harvard and influenced several generations of students as well as enlightening much of the political science world.

Lane, Robert E.   (1917–) An innovative political scientist who pioneered the study of the area where economics, psychology and political science overlap. Educated at Harvard, in 1962 he became a Professor of Political Science at Yale where he stayed until his retirement. His earliest work was *The Regulation of Businessmen* (1954). In *Political Life* (1959) he produced a textbook surveying most levels of American political activity. An interest in political attitudes led to *Public Opinion* (1964) with D.O. Sears. This followed his best known book, *Political Ideology* (1962), a study of in-depth interviews of the opinions of workingmen in Westport, Conn. *Political Thinking and Consciousness* (1969) and *The Market Experience* (1991) further pursued these themes.

Laski, Harold J.   (1893–1950) Professor of Political Science at the London School of Economics from 1926 until his early death, Laski had taken a history degree at Oxford before going on to teach at McGill and Harvard. In America he had been impressed by Wilsonian liberalism and the constitutional diffusion of power. His lifelong interest in American politics was demonstrated in his book *The American Presidency* (1940). US experience also influenced his prescriptive PLURALISM. In *Studies in the Problem of Sovereignty* (1917) and *The Foundations of Sovereignty* (1921) he attacked the concept of the SOVEREIGNTY of the STATE as both undesirable and remote from reality. This theme was continued in *A Grammar of Politics* (1925) which was used as a textbook in much of the English-speaking world. After the collapse of the two Labour Governments and the onset of the slump in the 1930s he became influenced by MARXISM. Convinced of the class nature of the state he wrote *Democracy in Crisis* (1933) and *The State in Theory and Practice* (1935). He was Chairman of the Labour Party when it came to power with a large majority in 1945. Laski was a stimulating teacher who had an especial influence on Indian students. He had wide interests in the subject and was one of the founders of the British Political Studies Association.

Lasswell, Harold   (1902–78) A student of the pioneer behaviouralist, Charles MERRIAM, he was greatly influenced by Freud and Reich and became convinced that psychoanalysis was the proper scientific basis for understanding politics. He was Professor of Political Science at Chicago (1922–38) and Professor of Law and Political Science at Yale (1946–71). His thesis was published as *Propaganda Technique in the World War* (1927). In *Psychopathology and Politics* (1930) and *World Politics and Insecurity* (1935) he interpreted politics in terms of the psyches of world leaders, arguing that their quest for power was the result of their efforts to compensate for low self-esteem. His work tended to be ignored until the 1950s when there was a renewed interest in POLITICAL PSYCHOLOGY.

Lazarsfeld, Paul F.   (1901–76) An Austrian immigrant to the USA who founded the first university survey centre, the Bureau of Applied Research at Columbia. He wrote books on METHODOLOGY such as *Mathematical Thinking in the Social Sciences* (1954); but to political scientists he is best known for his work on mass communications and especially VOTING BEHAVIOUR. *The People's Choice: How the Voter Makes up his Mind in a Presidential Campaign* (1944) was the first survey-based study of a national election. It was a seminal work, much copied in other countries.

Le Bon, Gustave (1841–1931) An early French psychologist who began by studying Arab civilization. He was clearly a social psychologist by 1894 when he published *Les Lois Psychologiques de l'Évolution des Peuples*. He became famous with his next book, *The Psychology of Crowds* (1895), which influenced sociologists and political scientists. The book was an early attempt to examine crowd behaviour with implications for the study of MASS SOCIETY and revolutionary activity.

Lindblom, C. Ed (1917–) A graduate of Stanford with a Ph.D. from Chicago, he was Professor of Political Science at Yale from 1961 until retirement. Lindblom could be said to have renovated the study of POLITICAL ECONOMY. This began with his book with Dahl, *Politics, Economics and Welfare* (1953) and continued with *The Intelligence of Democracy* (1965); *Politics and Markets* (1977); and *Democracy and the Market System* (1988). The burden of his discussion was that large-scale PLANNING and DEMOCRACY are incompatible; open pluralistic bargaining as practised in the USA makes democracy more accountable; and the large CORPORATION does not fit into the democratic framework. A more recent work, *Inquiry and Change: the Troubled Attempt to Understand and Shape Society* (1990), discusses the problems of applying social science methods to public policy formation.

Lindsay, Alexander (1879–1952) A Glasgow graduate in Philosophy, he went on to become a Fellow of Balliol (1906–22) and, eventually, Master of Balliol (1924–49). 'Sandy' Lindsay, as he was known, was an educationalist, a Christian moralist, a liberal internationalist, a crusader for DEMOCRACY and a moral and political philosopher. All these activities seemed to complement one another. He had grown up in the Free Church of Scotland and this led him – in

The Essentials of Democracy (1929) and *The Modern Democratic State* (1943) – to trace the origins of British democracy back to the seventeenth-century Puritans and their belief in rule by congregations. In *Christianity and Economics* (1933) he put forward an ethical view of how governments should manage MARKET FORCES. Closely associated with the labour movement, he achieved national fame when at a by-election at Oxford in February 1939 he stood as an independent anti-appeasement candidate. (Although a friend of Gandhi he was no pacifist, having fought in World War I.) The post-war Labour Government ennobled him as Lord Lindsay of Birker. Even in retirement he founded what became the University of Keele and was its first Principal (1949–52).

Locke, John (1632–1704) As a political philosopher his work sometimes lacks internal logic but his influence on politics was enormous. In his works, *Two Treatises of Government* (1689) and *Essay Concerning Human Understanding* (1690), he sought to justify the 'Glorious Revolution' of 1688, a crucial assertion of parliamentary over monarchical power. His ideas were seized by the American revolutionaries and echoes of his phrases can be found in the Declaration of Independence, 1776. Locke was concerned to defend the rights of property against the abuse of power. Most men were rational and orderly in his state of nature, but the STATE was needed to defend rights against those who were not. It was formed as the result of a SOCIAL CONTRACT between men and those in AUTHORITY by which the latter promised to uphold natural individual rights. If rulers broke this promise the right of rebellion existed. Hence Locke was the theorist of responsible GOVERNMENT and also government with restricted powers: the core of CONSTITUTIONALISM. To secure this, Locke said, executive power must be separated from legislative power. This notion, later repeated by Montesquieu (1689–1755), was the basis of the American constitution.

Lowell, Abbott L. (1856–1943) One of the founders of American political science. At Harvard he was Professor of Political Science (1900–9) and President (1909–33). His massive two-volume country-by-country work *Governments and Parties in Continental Europe* (1896) inspired students of politics all over the world and was a stimulus to his friend BRYCE. His detailed study of British politics, *The Government of England* (1908), though now out of date, has never been surpassed for its meticulous detail. In *Public Opinion and Popular Government* (1914) he compared the advantages of REPRESENTATIVE and DIRECT DEMOCRACY and followed this with *Public Opinion in War and Peace* (1923), much influenced by wartime and post-war moods. Without the advantage of survey data, Lowell was asking the right questions.

Machiavelli, Niccolo (1469–1527) A leading politician in Florence during the wars of the Medici, Machiavelli used his experiences of torture, imprisonment and dismissal to write his guide for rulers, *The Prince* (1513), a work characterized by moral indifference in which politics is assumed to be an end in itself. Those in power are concerned only with maintaining their position and their tactics should be adapted to this end. Success was the important value. This has become known as 'Machiavellianism'. To what degree it is a disapproving summing-up of politics as he found it, and to what degree it represents his real values is difficult to determine. In *Discourses on the First Ten Books of Titus Livius* (1513) he expresses somewhat similar views, though he does show some liking for popular government. Both books appear to demonstrate a belief that good government depends on force and cunning, shockingly subversive in the intellectual climate of his time. For political scientists Machiavelli is an innovator: the first writer after the Middle Ages to describe politics as it was. He first used the term 'the STATE'.

Mackenzie, William (1909–96) In many ways the institutional architect of British political science. A classicist by training, though also with an Edinburgh law degree, he became an Oxford Classics don; but in 1936 he began to teach Politics as well. In 1948 he became the first Professor of Politics at Manchester and soon expanded the department until it was the largest in Britain. He was much concerned with the appointment of chairs for other departments and with the newly founded Political Studies Association. From 1952 to 1960 he advised the Colonial Office on African constitutions. Later he represented political science on a UNESCO panel reporting on the state of the social sciences. Because of his training he had a wide coverage and his works include *Free Elections* (1958); *Politics and Social Science* (1967); and *Power, Violence and Decision* (1975).

Mannheim, Karl (1893–1947) A Hungarian sociologist who escaped to Britain in 1933 and taught at the London School of Economics. His classic work, *Ideology and Utopia* (1931), is important for political scientists because of its development of the concept of *weltanschauung* or 'world overview'. HEGEL first used the term to mean an image of the world. With Mannheim it refers to the beliefs, attitudes and values of a group of people or of an era. As with MARX, ideology connoted error for Mannheim. Any social group's experience must be limited and its ideas therefore could not be objective. Yet whereas Marx believed that proletarian consciousness could discover the truth, Mannheim believed the WORKING CLASS was as prone to error as any other. From Pareto (1848–1923) he derived a belief in the irrationality of politicians' attempts to rationalize and from Freud the idea of 'unconscious interests'. Utopia was the ideology of insurgent groups. Only a 'free intelligentsia' might think and act objectively.

Marcuse, Herbert (1898–1979) A German political philosopher who fled from the Nazis in 1934 and settled at the University of California. His early work was on HEGEL and Marx's *grundrisse*. From MARX he took the idea of ALIENATION and struggle, but he rejected economic determinism. In the 1960s he became 'the father of the New Left' and the guru of student radicalism. In *One Dimensional Man* (1964) he argued that faith in technology was the IDEOLOGY of modern society. It promised the WORKING CLASS unlimited consumer goods, so promoting a false consciousness that would abort their historic revolutionary role. In *Repressive Tolerance* (1965) he attacked the liberalism of the democratic state which prevented any violent change. Yet it was a form of violence. Consequently REVOLUTION would not come from the working class and the burden of revolt must be taken up by an UNDERCLASS composed of blacks, 'drop-outs', students and opponents of the consumerist, technological MASS SOCIETY.

Marx, Karl (1818–83) For a summary of Marx's ideas and development of them by later commentators who claim to be in his tradition, see the entry 'MARXISM' above. For its adaptation by politicians and political parties, see 'COMMUNISM'. The Marxist scriptures are so vast that it is not difficult to find inconsistencies in them. It must also be remembered that he wrote as a journalist, as well as a rather polemical theorist. Major works are: *The*

Eighteenth Brumaire of Louis Napoleon (1852); *Revolution and Counter Revolution: Germany in 1848* (1851–2); *A Contribution to the Critique of Political Economy* (1859); *Capital.* 3 vols (1867, 1885, 1894). With Friedrich Engels he wrote *The German Ideology* (1845); and *The Communist Manifesto* (1848). *Writings of the Young Marx on Philosophy and Society* (1967) were translated and edited by L.D. Easton and K. Guddat.

McKenzie, R.T. (1917–82) A Canadian who first appeared at the London School of Economics in the uniform of the Vancouver Rifles. He became Professor of Political Sociology there in 1964. He was a familiar figure on election nights on television with his 'swingometer'; so much so that after his death even Mrs. Thatcher said 'an election would not be the same without him'. With Allan Silver he published *Angels in Marble* (1968), a study of Conservative working-class voters, but the work for which he is most famous is *British Political Parties* (1955). Essentially this was a comparative study of the party leaderships. It perhaps over-estimated the power of Labour leaders because it was written in a period of Labour success when the troublesome activists were relatively quiescent. On the other hand, for many its revelation of the harrowing experiences of Conservative leaders was its major importance. This has since been illustrated by the ruthless way the parliamentary party dispatched Margaret Thatcher in 1990.

Merriam, Charles (1874–1953) He held Chairs of Political Science at Princeton (1946–51) and Yale from 1951 until his death. One of the most distinguished social scientists of his generation, his works, which progressed from the empirical to the conceptual, include *Primary Elections* (1908); *Non-Voting* (with H.F. Gosnell, 1924); *Political Power*

(1934); and *Public and Private Government* (1944). He also served with distinction in the public service as a member of the Hoover Commission on Recent Social Trends and as one of 'three wise men' in the Roosevelt Committee on the Administrative Management of the Presidency.

Michels, Robert   (1876–1936) Born in the Rhineland, Michels was educated in Germany, France and Italy. As a young man he was a militant, syndicalist-leaning member of the German Social Democratic Party. In consequence he was 'blacklisted' for an academic post in his native land in spite of WEBER supporting his case. In 1907 he went to teach at the University of Turin where he was influenced by the ELITISM of Gaetano Mosca (1858–1941). In 1911 he published his best known work, *Political Parties*, which displays a complete disillusion with DEMOCRACY. The argument is based on his detailed knowledge of European socialist parties. His disappointment with them was the result of their inability to give power to what he calls 'the masses', by which he meant the party members. He cites numerous examples of socialist party leaders being treated obsequiously by the party rank-and-file or riding roughshod over their wishes. From this he concluded that if socialist parties did not have internal democracy, DEMOCRACY was impossible. After Mussolini came to power, Michels joined the Fascist party. He is best known for his IRON LAW OF OLIGARCHY – the inevitability that a few would always hold power in any organization. Yet he did not understand that it is electors, not party members, that democratic party leaders are responsible to, and he wrote before any European socialist party had held power. His most perceptive analysis is of the nature of party leadership. Political leaders become remote from their followers for 'technical' reasons – geographical distance, inaccessability of legislatures and the specialized nature of their work – and for 'psychological' reasons – power places them on a pedestal and sycophancy makes them lose touch with proletarian reality.

Miliband, Ralph   (1924–94) A refugee with his father from Belgium in 1940, he proceeded through further education to the London School of Economics where he fell under the spell of LASKI. After service as an Able Seaman in the Royal Navy, and later in the Belgian Navy, he returned to the LSE after the war. His thesis was about SOCIALISM in the French Revolution. From 1949 to 1972 he was a lecturer at the LSE, and was known as a conscientious teacher. He proceeded to the chair of Political Science at Leeds in 1972. Six years later he retired and thereafter occupied several visiting chairs. Although a Marxist, he was an unusual one and had never had any connection with the Communist Party. His works include *Parliamentary Socialism* (1961); *The State in Capitalist Society* (1969); *Marxism and Politics* (1977); *Capitalist Democracy in Britain* (1982); and posthumously *Socialism for a Sceptical Age* (1994).

Mill, John Stuart   (1806–73) A philosopher of UTILITARIANISM, much influenced by the school's founder, Jeremy Bentham (1748–1832), and by his father, James Mill (1773–1836). He gave it a new direction: it is said he 'spiritualized Bentham'. He was much more aware than the earlier Utilitarians of the problems of the principle of 'the greatest happiness for the greatest number'. After reading DE TOCQUEVILLE on America, he expressed his concern about the TYRANNY OF THE MAJORITY in his best known work, *On Liberty* (1859). The book is a defence of personal and intellectual freedom and the right of self-expression which Mill could see might be endangered by decisions made through democratic processes. As a professional man and an intellectual he feared the 'uninstructed' might want 'class legislation' which would neglect practical and technical considerations. In *Considerations on Representative Government* (1861) he advocates local representative institutions as a place where ordinary citizens would learn to operate democracy. In *Utilitarianism* (1863) he stated the roots of his liberal philosophy. It was an abandonment of sheer egoism and a belief in individual development by education. His statement: 'it is better to be Socrates dissatisfied than a fool satisfied' sums up his liberal ethic. Other works include *System of Logic* (1843); *Principles of Political Economy* (1848); and *The Subjection of Women* (1869).

Mills, Wright   (1916–62)   A radical American sociologist with a world-wide reputation who was often wrongly thought to be a Marxist because his work was critical of American society and its social inequalities. In fact, he was distrustful of HISTORICISM and his books are distinguished by their wealth of empirical data. His study of ELITISM made him important to political scientists. In *Power Elite* (1956) he traced the common social backgrounds of the USA's military, big business and political leaders and inspired numerous other similar projects. Other publications include *America's Labor Leaders* (1948); *White Collar* (1951); *The Sociological Imagination* (1959); and *Listen Yankee: the Revolution in Cuba* (1960). He became Professor of Sociology at Columbia at 30, but died at an early age.

Mosher, Frederick   (1913–90) An outstanding scholar in the field of Public Administration. For some years after graduation he worked in the public service. First for the Tennessee Valley Authority and, after he was called up, in the Pentagon. When the war ended he was employed for two years by UNNRA and then went to the State Department. His academic career began in 1949 when he became Professor of Political Science at Syracuse University. From 1952 until 1957 he edited *Public Administration Review*. His works include: *Program Budgeting: Theory and Practice* (1954); *Democracy and the Public Service* (1968); *The Quest for Accountability in American Government* (1979); and *A Tale of Two Agencies: the General Accounting Office and the Office of Management and the Budget* (1984).

Nove, Alec   (1915–94) Born in Leningrad, he was brought to Britain after the Revolution and educated at the London School of Economics where he eventually became a lecturer. In 1958 he was appointed Director of the Institute of Soviet Studies at Glasgow and Professor of Economics from 1963 until his retirement in 1982. He was an international authority on the Russian economy, writing among other works, *Was Stalin Really Necessary?* (1965); *The Economic History of the USSR* (1969); *Stalinism and After* (1976); and *Glasnost in Action* (1989).

Oakeshott, Michael   (1901–90) A political philosopher who was Professor of Political Science at the London School of Economics from 1950 to 1969. He remained sceptical of much political science and in his best known work, *Rationalism in Politics* (1947), he described learning about constitutions as 'a curriculum of study of unimaginable dreariness'. He much preferred history. The historian he wrote, 'loves it as a mistress of whom he never tires and whom he never expects to talk sense'. To Oakeshott CONSERVATISM was a disposition to think and behave in certain ways. Governments were to keep subjects at peace with one another, not to make people good. Hence his aversion to rationalists with their plans and general ideas for the world. He condemned the infection of conservatism by rationalism, singling out HAYEK especially for attack. Influential for a generation, his philosophy was really a return to BURKE. His earliest philosophic work, *Experience and its Modes* (1933), was in the tradition of English IDEALISM.

Olson, Mancur (1932–98) Although he was an economist by training, he made his greatest impact on political science. A Rhodes Scholar at Oxford, he went to Harvard where his doctorate, *The Logic of Collective Action*, was published in 1965. It popularized the term FREE RIDER which describes a typical consumer who expends neither time nor money to support any collective organization to bring down prices, expecting or hoping that all the other numerous consumers will do it. This explains why producers are so much more powerful and why we have producers' strikes, but hardly any consumers' strikes. Producers have fewer free riders because their gains from organization are so much greater. In *The Rise and Decline of Nations* (1982) he argued that stable democracies were inefficient because their pressure-group systems had led to a form of economic inertia. Posthumous work when published is likely to demonstrate further scepticism about conventional social science wisdom. Olson spent the last 20 years as Professor of Economics at the University of Maryland.

Ostrogorski, Moisei (1854–1919) One of the founders of modern political science, he was born and died in Russia, but was partly educated in France. His research in both Britain and the USA resulted in the famous two-volume work, *Democracy and the Organisation of Political Parties* (1902). The book is a criticism of the power of organization in politics, then

quite recent, which he saw as manipulative. It was responsible for the success of demagogic leaders and the debasement of rational political argument. Consequently, what was wanted was the abolition of parties and the choice of representatives on the basis of their integrity and ability.

Pennock, J.R. (1906–95) Professor of Political Science at Swarthmore, he was a strong believer in the integrality of Political Theory to Political Science. He demonstrated this with his attention to concepts like the RULE OF LAW and CONSTITUTIONALISM and with his works on DEMOCRACY. He wrote *Liberal Democracy: its Merits and Prospects* (1950); *Democratic Political Theory* (1979); and, with Davis G. Smith, *Political Science: an Introduction* (1964).

Popper, Karl (1902–94) An Austrian social scientist and philosopher who emigrated to Britain and became Professor of Scientific Method at the London School of Economics. The work that made him famous was *The Open Society and its Enemies* (1945) which was an attack on HISTORICISM. It was also a rejection of TOTALITARIANISM, including COMMUNISM with its rationalist planning of society. Popper called it 'social engineering', a comprehensive attempt to shape human activity. He was not averse to 'piecemeal engineering' of the kind social democratic governments might practice. Among social scientists Popper is renowned for his theory of falsifiability. This was developed in *The Logic of Scientific Discovery* (1934) and *Conjectures and Refutations* (1963). Scientific method is not capable of proving things to be true, but it is capable of disproving many hypotheses.

Prebisch, Raul (1901–86) An Argentinian economist and diplomat whose ideas and achievements had a world-wide political impact. The nucleus of his thought was in *The Economic Development of Latin America and its Principal Problems* (1949). In consequence, in 1950 he was made director of the Economic Commission for Latin America (ECLA). His main contention was that technical progress and the increase in world income resulted in the under-developed 'peripheral' countries wanting more industrial goods, while the 'central' developed countries needed fewer primary goods as a proportion of their total incomes. This explained structural unemployment, the increasing gap between rich and poor and deteriorating terms of trade in the under-developed countries; their only way out of this vicious spiral was by industrialization. In *Towards a Dynamic Development Policy for Latin America* (1963), he argued for agricultural reform and redistributive policies internally. He thus became the leader of the DEPENDENCY school of thought, and in 1964 the founder-director of the United Nations Conference on Trade and Development (UNCTAD). Finally, in *Peripheral Capitalism* (1981), he contended that all these features prevented the proper development of CAPITALISM in peripheral countries.

Riker, William (1921–93) An American political scientist best known for *The Theory of Political Coalitions* (1962). Other areas in which he pioneered were RATIONAL CHOICE THEORY and 'structure-induced equilibrium'. The latter idea stems from his assumption that complex societies must be inherently unstable. Majority rule can never be permanent: there is no set of policies that could not lose in a contest with another set. Because politicians out of power will constantly be searching for such a winning combination, and sometimes finding it, history will proceed in 'cycles'. In *Liberalism against Populism* (1982) he traced American history in these terms.

Only institutions had maintained the balance of the USA.

Robson, William A. (1893–1980) Professor of Public Administration at the London School of Economics (1947–62). In World War I he flew with the Royal Flying Corps and wrote his thesis afterwards on air transport. His interests were wide. He was a Fabian who helped to found the *Political Quarterly* in 1930. His concern with local government remained throughout his life. With Clement Attlee he published *The Town Councillor* (1925). Later works included *The Development of Local Government* (1931); *The Government and Misgovernment of London* (1938); and *Local Government in Crisis* (1966). He was an authority on legal theory and an admirer of French administrative law, writing *Justice and Administrative Law* (1928) and *Modern Theories of Law* (1938). During World War II he worked as a temporary civil servant in four government departments. After the election of the Labour Government in 1945 he became interested in the constitutional implications of public ownership and wrote *Problems of the Nationalised Industries* (1952).

Rokkan, Stein (1921–79) Born on the periphery of Norway in Lofoten, he was at Oslo University when the Germans invaded. After the war he was involved in a UNESCO study of DEMOCRACY and spent some time in the USA and Britain. A period at the Institute of Social Research in Oslo in the 1950s was followed by a post at the University of Bergen where he was Professor of Comparative Sociology and Politics from 1966 until his death. Rokkan was one of the great figures in international political science in the post-war period. He was chairman of the International Political Science Association (1971–3) and one of the founders of the European Consortium for Political Research.

His early research was in Norwegian electoral studies. As a result he became aware of how important cultural and historical factors were in shaping POLITICAL ATTITUDES. The form which early mobilization of voters had taken was affected by, for instance, the timing of franchise extension. From this he became interested in social CLEAVAGES, not only in Norway, but also in the whole of Europe. He realized the significance of tensions between the centre and the peripheries in the process of nation-building. All this involved much research in archives looking for data and also co-operation with many collaborators. With R. McKeon, Rokkan edited *Democracy in a World of Tensions* (1951); with Lipset, *Party Systems and Voter Alignments* (1967); with Allardt, *Mass Politics* (1970); and with Derek Urwin, *The Politics of Territorial Identity* (1982, posthumously). *Economy, Territory, Identity: the Politics of West European Peripheries* (1983), written by Rokkan and Urwin, was published after his death by the latter.

Ross, Alf (1899–1979) The leading Danish political scientist of his day, he graduated as a lawyer in 1922 and until 1926 studied in Austria (under KELSEN), France and England. In 1929 he took his doctorate in Uppsala and soon became well-known for his analytic powers. In 1938 he was appointed a Professor in the Law Faculty at Copenhagen University. His earliest work was on Danish law; for example, a textbook on common law published in 1942. Interests widened with *The Constitution of the United Nations* (1950) and, in 1963, *The United Nations*, demonstrating his grasp of international law. His international reputation was especially enhanced by *Why Democracy?* (1946), in which he linked constitutional development with political ideas and expressed a strong rejection of dictatorship. From 1959 to 1971 he was a judge in the European Court of Justice on Human Rights.

Rousseau, Jean-Jacques (1712–78) The most influential eighteenth-century political thinker. Philosophers may point out his lack of internal logic but there can be little doubt that his thought inspired the nineteenth-century movements for popular sovereignty and PARTICIPATORY DEMOCRACY. He played a large part in the demolition of the structures of the ANCIEN REGIME. In the *Origin of Inequality among Men* (1755) he attacked contemporary institutions. In a state of nature the 'noble savage' had no property of his own. Society had been corrupted by selfish group interests attempting to defend their property rights. In *Émile* (1762) he attacked conventional education and emphasized the need for the full development of the human personality which had been prevented by traditional institutions and culture. In the *Social Contract* (1762) he argued that true DEMOCRACY was only possible in a small community where, like his native Geneva, decisions were made by REFERENDUMS. He had little time for REPRESENTATIVE DEMOCRACY: the British were only free, he said, at election time. Freedom consisted in obeying the General Will, to be arrived at by everyone thinking and voting, not selfishly, but in the PUBLIC INTEREST. Those that did not obey had to be 'forced to be free', a strange concept giving rise to the view that Rousseau was the prophet of 'totalitarian democracy'.

Rustow, Dankwart (1925–96) Professor of Politics and Sociology at the City University, New York, for many years, he was prominent in comparative and international politics. He was the founder and editor-in-chief of *Comparative Politics*. Among his works were *The Politics of Compromise: Parties and Cabinet Government in Sweden* (1955); *A World of*

Nations: Problems of Political Modernization (1967); and *Middle Eastern Political Systems* (1971). With Robert E. Ward he wrote *Political Modernization in Japan and Turkey* (1964).

Schapiro, Leonard (1908–83) Professor of Political Science with reference to Russian Studies at the London School of Economics (1963–75). His well-known works on the USSR included *The Origins of the Communist Autocracy* (1955); *The Communist Party of the Soviet Union* (1960); and *The Soviet Worker* (1981).

Schmitt, Carl (1888–1985) A leading German jurisprudentialist in the interwar years who helped the transition of German *staatsrecht* into political science. He perceived political relationships as being between either friends or enemies. Hence action should characterize political leadership, a view he advanced in *Political Romanticism* (1919) and *The Concept of the Political* (1932). He strongly supported President Hindenburg's use of emergency powers under Article 48 of the Weimar Constitution; but in *Legality and Legitimacy* (1932) he opposed giving the Nazis and Communists the same rights of electoral competition as other parties. In 1933, however, he joined the Nazi Party after Hitler came to power and defended the 'Night of the Long Knives' in 1934.

Schumpeter, Joseph A. (1883–1950) An Austrian economist, born in Vienna, where he became a professor at the University of Graz, in the same year publishing *The Theory of Economic Development* (1911). This was an unusual book for an economist, as much of it was a study of the personality and style of the entrepreneur, a subject neglected by the classical economists. In the much smaller Austrian Republic after World War I he was briefly minister of finance in 1919 and then from 1920 to 1924 presi-

dent of a bank. But in 1925 he left Austria for a chair at Bonn and in 1932 moved to his last one at Harvard.

Although he was trained as an economist, much of Schumpeter's work has an importance for political science. For example, in a technical work he developed the idea of the 'tax state', which was an early warning of the problems democracies were to suffer as they allocated so much of their gross national product to public expenditure. A good deal of his writing was sociological. His monograph on *Imperialism* (1919) was a refutation of Marx and Lenin, while that on *Social Classes* (1927) emphasized the fact of SOCIAL MOBILITY. Yet undoubtedly his most important work for political scientists is *Capitalism, Socialism and Democracy* (1942), in which he showed the influence of WEBER in his contention that CAPITALISM and SOCIALISM were likely to converge because both were becoming increasingly bureaucratic. His perception of the democratic process, a competition for power in which the leaders of organized parties contended for votes (an implied analogy with oligopoly), made a great impact, especially on American political science and voting studies in the 1950s.

Siegfried, André (1875–1959) One of the architects of contemporary political science. He is best known as a pioneer of ELECTORAL GEOGRAPHY. The first of these, *Tableau Politique de la France de l'Ouest sous la Troisième République* (1913), illuminated the politics of that part of his native France he knew best. In *Tableau des Partis Politiques en France* (1930), he extended the study to the whole country. His method was to use all available data on ELECTIONS and to relate these to the speeches and behaviour of the local POLITICIANS, the ecology and social and cultural characteristics of the constituency and its religious affiliations. He collated and mapped this data from the 1880s onwards in order to examine the changes. (He had no computers.) His conclusion was that the human geography and social features of a CONSTITUENCY could help greatly to explain its politics and that over time political loyalties remained fairly stable. From this he concluded that national character and tradition were important.

As a Protestant he was interested in the Anglo-Saxon political systems. Visits to Canada and New Zealand produced books about them and a trip to the USA resulted in the enlightening *America Comes of Age* (1927). He was especially interested in Britain and in *La Crise Britannique au XX Siècle* (1931) identified some of the problems the country had to face. His work was seminal and prolific, inspiring many students at the *École des Sciences Politiques* and elsewhere in the world.

Stokes, Donald (1927–97) He laid much of the foundation of American electoral studies in *The American Voter* (1960) with A. Campbell, P. Converse and W. Miller. The book found the voters were much influenced by family allegiances and, later, by the state of the economy and images transmitted by the media. Two important articles he wrote were 'Spatial Models of Party Competition' and (with W. Miller) 'Constituency Influence in Congress'. He contributed to British election studies, writing with David Butler, *Electoral Change in Britain* (1969). From 1974 to 1992 he was a distinguished dean of the Woodrow Wilson School at Princeton.

Tawney, Ralph H. (1880–1962) A British Christian Socialist who was both a political thinker and an economic historian, as well as being active in the labour movement. He was one of the majority of the Sankey Commission which recommended NATIONALIZATION

of the mines (1919), rejected by Lloyd George, and he played a large part in the writing of the 1928 Labour Party programme, *Labour and the Nation*. His SOCIALISM was egalitarian. He believed in redistribution in favour of the less fortunate and the obligation of the educated professional classes to help and educate the WORKING CLASS. Thus he was an active member of the Workers' Educational Association. During World War I he served as an infantry sergeant and was wounded on the first morning of the Somme. His books *The Acquisitive Society* (1921) and *Equality* (1931) reflect his experiences, his religion and his repudiation of the more material kinds of socialism, including MARXISM. In his best known historical work, *Religion and the Rise of Capitalism* (1926), he rejected MARX's view that CAPITALISM was a factor in the emergence of Protestantism and was close to WEBER's analysis which perceived Protestantism as a cause of capitalism.

Tingsten, Herbert (1896–1973) After obtaining his doctorate at Uppsala in 1923, he began a career as a political scientist and was appointed to a chair in that subject at the Stockholm High school in 1935, leaving to become editor of the Stockholm daily, *Dagens Nyheter*, in 1946. A major intellectual figure in Sweden, his numerous published works include *Americansk Demokrati* (1929); *De Konservatina Idéerna* (1939); *Demokratiens Problem* (1945); and *Argument* (1948).

Tocqueville, Alexis de (1805–59) An early political scientist and sociologist whose theoretical views are implicit and not explicit. In the nineteenth century he greatly influenced J.S. MILL and in the twentieth, DAHL. He spent much time observing political life and making shrewd judgements about it. His best known work is *Democracy in America*, written as the result of a long visit there, and published in two volumes in 1835 and 1840. He was impressed with the richness of associational life in the USA and with the vitality of LOCAL GOVERNMENT as witnessed in the New England townships. Although an aristocrat, he warmed to the prevailing value of EQUALITY which he connected with DEMOCRACY. (Indeed, like so many others since he tended to confuse the terms.) At the same time he wondered whether EGALITARIANISM might not be detrimental to respect for AUTHORITY; and although an admirer of American DECENTRALIZATION he feared that in the end it might lead to the dissolution of the state. Returning to France he was briefly a deputy and foreign minister under Louis Napoleon. His second great book *The Ancien Régime and the French Revolution* was published in 1856. His detached analysis attributed the Revolution to corrupt nobility, incompetent BUREAUCRACY and the crazy rationalism and egalitarianism of the regime's opponents. Even greater CENTRALIZATION had resulted from the latter's reforms. The value of de Tocqueville's comparative study of two young regimes is that he looked under institutional structures in order to analyse values and political cultures.

Toinet, Marie France (1942–95) Director of Research at the *Centre d'Études et Recherches Internationales* of the *Fondation Nationale des Sciences Politiques*. She studied at numerous American universities, received her doctorate in 1969 from the Sorbonne, and became the leading French authority on American politics. She wrote *Le Congrès des États-Unis* (1972); *Le Système Politique des États-Unis* (1987); and *Les Chemins de l'Abstention: une Comparaison Franco-Americaine* (1993).

Wallas, Graham (1858–1932) A contributor to *Fabian Essays in Socialism* (1889), though he resigned from the society in 1904. Wallas was an Oxford graduate who became Professor of Political Science at the London School of Economics. His most famous contribution to the discipline is *Human Nature in Politics* (1908) in which he drew attention to the irrationality of both political leaders and followers. This was intended as a warning and six years later in *The Great Society* he emphasized that rational thought should be used to attain egalitarian social objectives.

Webb, Beatrice (1858–1943) Born Beatrice Potter, the daughter of a railway magnate, she was a formidable intellectual with a social conscience who was prepared to move among the industrial workers as part of her research. As a young woman she suffered from her unrequited love for Joseph Chamberlain (1836–1914). These years are described in *My Apprenticeship* (1926). Attracted to both politics and politicians, she married SIDNEY WEBB in 1892, having become a socialist after reading Fabian Essays. In London she ran a political salon to which the younger progressive politicians were invited, with the intention of using the Fabian tactic of 'permeation' on them. One example of this was the way in which Winston Churchill, when Home Secretary (1910–11), was persuaded to introduce and pass the 'anti-sweating' laws. In 1905 she was appointed to the Royal Commission on the Poor Laws and was one of a minority producing a report recommending their abolition and the payment of social benefits instead.

Her work with Sidney is described in *Our Partnership* (1948). She tended to conceive of the ideas and the frameworks while Sidney provided the empirical detail and organized the presentation. They produced a series of authoritative histories of British society and institutions, beginning with a lengthy (2 vols) *History of Trade Unionism* (1894 and 1897), followed by *Industrial Democracy* (1902), 10 volumes on local government (1898–1929) and another large volume on co-operatives (1921). In their *Methods of Social Study* (1932) they explained their techniques. These were found lacking in their study, *Soviet Communism: A New Civilisation?* (1935), because they could not speak or read Russian and were too prone to believe in the rational, institutional solutions that Stalin's policies appeared to be on paper. They could be naive when they were out of familiar contexts. This was after the defeat of two Labour governments in 1924 and 1931 convinced Beatrice that there was a dearth of intellectual ability among Labour leaders.

Webb, Sidney (1859–1947) Sidney was secretary of the Fabian Society when Beatrice met him. He had written one of the Fabian essays. He coined the phrase 'the inevitability of gradualism', characterizing the gentle determinism of the Fabians. He also believed there could be no separation between theoretical SOCIALISM and putting it into practice. In 1892 he was elected to the London County Council as a member of the Progressive Party and until 1910 was a leading figure on its Education Committee. In 1895 he helped found the London School of Economics, intending that it should be a centre of training for the social and political administrative cadres needed to govern a socialist Britain. He was a member of the Royal Commission on Trade Union Law (1903–6) and also sat with Beatrice on the Poor Law Commission. With Arthur Henderson he rewrote the Labour Party's constitution in 1918 and also contributed to its programme, *Labour and the New Social Order*. He was President of the

Board of Trade in the 1924 Labour Government and Secretary for the Colonies, 1929–31. Thus he was much more involved in politics than Beatrice. Yet he was an indispensable collaborator in all her work except her two autobiographical volumes. Their pioneering work remains a model for historians of social policy and institutions.

Weber, Max (1864–1920) One of the three or four most important social scientists. Both in sociology and political science his work was seminal and still remains the source of much controversy. He held chairs at Freiburg, Heidelberg, Vienna and Munich and published work which sought to answer numerous questions about the nature of the modern world. In *The Protestant Ethic and the Spirit of Capitalism* (1904) he argued that most of the entrepreneurs who founded early industrial enterprises were Calvinists. Religion was another of his fields. He published books in 1915 and 1916 on the respective religions of China and India. *Ancient Judaism* followed in 1917 and it was all summed up and conceptualized in *The Sociology of Religion* (1921).

Much of Weber's work was published after his death. Some of it was unedited and there were also his writings in the *Archive for Social Science and Politics*. Hence his three great works – *Economy and Society* (1921), *General Economic History* (1923) and *The Theory of Social and Economic Organization* (1914) – are variously collated, edited and re-edited. In them the major socio-political problems of our time are presented. For example: Why is modern industrial civilization so different from other world-forms? His answer was that it is characterized by rationality which is a legacy of the SCIENTIFIC REVOLUTION, its detached critical form of investigation and its reliance on quantitative method. Secularism and materialism are results of the decline of irrationality. LAW with its documentation, lack of arbitrariness and appeal to reason is another factor. In consequence the organization of society will become more rational and BUREAU-CRACY will be the administrative form the apparatus of control will take.

For political scientists Weber's analysis of forms of AUTHORITY and power are important. This is connected with his concept of LEGITIMACY. Where rule is accepted as right and proper by those at whom it is directed it is legitimate. The exercise of power which is not accepted is not legitimate. Hence rulers can attempt to make their rule legitimate but the real gauge of legitimacy is whether the ruled concur. Obedience is not enough: the ruled may obey because they are frightened of crude power. Authority is legitimized power.

Weber had a three-fold typology of authority which is an example of his notion of the IDEAL TYPE. (An ideal type is an 'identikit' of a concept, a list of features which an ideal instance would possess.) Traditional authority is exemplified by the dynastic state and often will have religious associations. Rational/legal or procedural authority is legitimized by rules and constitutional procedures and is exemplified by democracy. The third type of authority is legitimized by CHARISMA, the qualities and character of an individual. Weber saw this as transitional. He obviously had revolutionary leaders in mind. Charismatic rule will either revert to traditional rule, or it will become 'routinized' and change into legal/rational authority. But an important point is that in the real world Weber expected regimes to be mixtures of these types. There was also an implicit theory of DEVELOPMENT here: Weber expected the world to move towards greater rationality.

Yet he was no historicist, unlike MARX. Moreover, while Weber accepted that the nature of politics is conflict he did not entirely perceive it in terms of CLASS CONFLICT. His approach was through the trinity of class, STATUS and party. Class was a matter of one's 'life chances in the market': it was more than a matter of income – one's chances of promotion and advancement were crucial. Status was determined by the amount of esteem other people ascribed to someone, or some institution. 'Status groups' were composed of people with similar life chances and lifestyles. Like classes they could be organized in political parties. He portended the rise of a larger administrative and technological status group as qualifications and bureaucracy were extended. Status and class allegiance might conflict. In contrast to Marx, Weber saw society becoming more complex.

Although he expected bureaucracy to increase, he became increasingly critical of it. At first a German nationalist and a supporter of the *Kaiserreich*, in his later days he transferred his loyalty to the Weimar Republic, though he was uncertain about its constitutional arrangements. At first in favour of parliamentarianism, the difficulties of decision-making in the multiparty Reichstag persuaded him that a more presidential system was needed. He remained too much of a conservative to put his faith in popular sovereignty.

Wheare, Kenneth C., Sir (1907–79) A modest Australian constitutional lawyer who wrote several definitive works and was a Fellow of University College, Oxford (1939–44) before becoming a Fellow of All Souls (1944–57) at the same time as he was a Fellow of Nuffield and Professor of Government and Public Administration (1944–57). Later he was Rector of Exeter College (1956–72) and Vice-Chancellor of the university (1964–6). His publications include *The*

Statute of Westminster and Dominion Status (1938); *Federal Government* (1946); *Modern Constitutions* (1951); *Government by Committee* (1955); and *Legislatures* (1963).

Wildavsky, Aaron   (1938–93)   A scholar of international reputation who was Professor of Political Science at Berkeley. He had prodigious energy and published or co-authored 39 books, several of which were highly influential. Among his works are: with D. Carpoch, *Studies in Australian Politics* (1958); *The Politics of the Budgetary Process* (1964); and *Budgeting* (1986), a comparative study. His book written with H. Heclo, *The Private Government of Public Money* (1981) is regarded as one of the great works on British administration. He never stopped writing and *Accounting for the Environment* was published posthumously in 1994.

Wildenman, Rudolf   (1922–93)   Professor of Political Science at Mannheim from 1964 until retirement, he played a major part in the modernizing of German political science. He used to say that being taken to Canada as a prisoner-of-war was the best thing that happened to him. An enthusiast for quantitative methods, he made a detailed statistical study of the 1961 General Election. He also founded at Mannheim, ZUMA, a unique research institute. After graduating at Heidelberg he published *Partei und Fraktion: ein Beitrag zur Analyse der politischen Willensbildung und des Parteiensystems in der Bundesrepublik* (1954). His interests extended far beyond Germany and he was one of the founders of the European Consortium of Political Research.

Williams, Philip   (1920–84)   Between 1950 and his death he was a Fellow at both Jesus and Nuffield Colleges. He was distinguished as an authority on both French and British politics; but he made his mark with a very scholarly study of the French Fourth Republic, *Politics in Postwar France* (1954). On the Fifth Republic he wrote *The French Parliament 1958–1967* and *Politics and Society in De Gaulle's Republic* (1971). He also wrote a biography, *Hugh Gaitskell* (1979).

Wilson, Thomas Woodrow   (1856–1924) Professor of Jurisprudence and Political Economy at Princeton (1890–1902), he then became President of the University. In 1912 he was elected President of the USA and re-elected in 1916. He defined the difference between ADMINISTRATION and POLITICS and wrote a 5-volume *History of the American People* (1902); but his best known work is *Congressional Government* (1885) in which he contrasted the American system unfavourably with British parliamentary government and concluded that leadership in the USA must be asserted by either President or Congress. He argued that improved party government would help. When he became President he tried to assert Presidential leadership in which attempt he was assisted by the circumstances of a European war. In 1917 Congress declared war on the Central Powers and Wilson emerged as leader of the democratic world and the movement for an international institution to maintain peace and to guarantee that the world had been made safe for DEMOCRACY. After peace came in 1918 he completely failed in this effort because Congress blocked his foreign policy. The USA refused both to sign the Treaty of Versailles and to join the League of Nations.

Zimmern, Alfred Sir   (1879–1957) One of the Founding Fathers of the study of British International Relations. Appropriately, he was the first occupant of the Woodrow Wilson chair of International Relations at Aberystwyth.

Dedicated to the idea of the League of Nations he was deputy director of its Institute of Intellectual Co-operation (1926–30). From 1930 to 1944 he was Professor of International Relations at Oxford. His numerous works include *Nationality and Government* (1918); *Europe in Convalescence* (1922); *The Prospects of Democracy* (1929); and *Spiritual Values and World Affairs* (1939).

Index